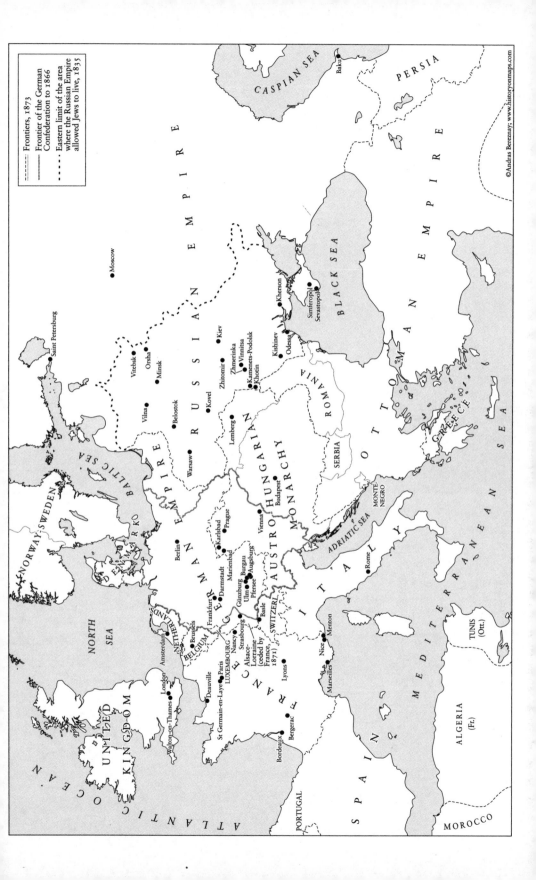

CASPIAN SEA

PERSIA

Baku

RUSSIAN EMPIRE

BLACK SEA

OTTOMAN EMPIRE

Moscow

Saint Petersburg

Kherson
Simferopol
Sevastopol

Vitebsk
Orsha
Minsk

Kiev
Zhitomir
Zhmerinka
Vinnitsa
Kamenets-Podolsk
Khotin
Kishinev
Odessa

ROMANIA

Kovel

Vilna
Belostok

Warsaw

Lemberg

SERBIA

GREECE

AUSTRO-HUNGARIAN MONARCHY

BALTIC SEA

NORWAY/SWEDEN

DENMARK

Vienna
Budapest

Prague
Karlsbad
Marienbad

Berlin

MONTE-NEGRO

ADRIATIC SEA

ITALY

Rome

NORTH SEA

NETHERLANDS

Amsterdam

Brussels

BELGIUM

LUXEMBOURG

Frankfurt

Darmstadt
Günzburg Burgau
Ulm Augsburg
Pfersee
Basle

SWITZERL.

Günzburg

MEDITERRANEAN SEA

UNITED KINGDOM

London
Walton-on-Thames

Strasbourg
Nancy
Alsace-
Lorraine
(ceded by
France,
1871)

FRANCE

Deauville
Paris
St Germain-en-Laye

Lyons

Nice
Menton
Marseilles

TUNIS
(Ott.)

Bergerac

Bordeaux

ALGERIA
(Fr.)

SPAIN

PORTUGAL

MOROCCO

ATLANTIC OCEAN

©Andras Bereznay; www.historyonmaps.com

THE GUNZBURGS
A Family Biography

Also by Lorraine de Meaux

Saint-Pétersbourg. Histoire, promenades, anthologie, dictionnaire (ed.)
Paris, Robert Laffont, coll. "Bouquins", 2003.

La Russie et la tentation de l'Orient
Paris, Fayard, 2010.

*Intelligentsia. Entre France et la Russie, archives inédites du xxe siècle
(ed. with Véronique Jobert)*
Paris, Beaux Arts éditions, 2012.

Les couples illustres de l'histoire de France (ed. with Patrice Gueniffey)
Paris, Perrin, 2017.

THE GUNZBURGS

A Family Biography

Lorraine de Meaux

Translated from the French by
Steven Rendall

HALBAN
LONDON

First published in Great Britain by
Halban Publishers Ltd.
2019

www.halbanpublishers.com

A CIP catalogue record for this book is available
from the British Library.

ISBN 978-1-905559-99-2

Originally published in French under the title
Une Grande Famille Russe:
Les Gunzburg
Paris/Saint-Pétersbourg xixe-xxe siècle

Typeset by AB, Cambridgeshire

Printed in Great Britain by
CPI Group (UK) Ltd, Croydon CR0 4YY

THE GUNZBURGS
A Family Biography

Contents

Part III
Horace: Banker, Patron of the Arts and Philanthropist

Part IV
Heralds of Jewish Culture

Part V
The Dark Years

Part VI
From One Exile to Another

Author's note

In this book Russian names are given in a standard transliteration that reproduces, more or less, Russian pronunciation. The spelling of the name "Gunzburg" differs depending on the country, period and branch of the family, some French descendants having chosen "Gunzbourg", others "Guentsburg", "Guenzburg" or "Ginzburg". The use of the particle "de", indicating nobility, was adopted following the ennoblement of Joseph Evzel Gunzburg in 1874, but does not exist in Russian. Numerous people bear the same name, but this book concerns exclusively Joseph Evzel de Gunzburg, his ancestors and direct descendants.

The founder of the dynasty of the Barons Gunzburg is designated by the double, redundant forename Joseph Evzel. That is the name he himself gave to the bank created in St Petersburg in 1859 – "I. E. [for Iosif Evzel] Gintsburg" – and its French branch – "J. E. [for Joseph Evzel] Gunzburg". In this way he emphasised the dual dimension, Hebrew and Yiddish, of his forename. He did not adopt the Russian use of the patronymic which sometimes appears in writings about him: Evzel [or Iosif] Gavrilovich Gintsburg.

The dual dating of some cited documents corresponds to the difference between the Julian ("old style") calendar used in Russia until 1918 and the Gregorian ("new style") calendar adopted in most European countries, e.g. 2/14 September 1866. From 1800 to 1900 the difference between them amounted to twelve days.

Some unpublished manuscripts are unpaginated, and references to them therefore do not mention page numbers.

Part I

Dream World: Joseph Evzel in Paris

> At our home on Rue de Tilsitt we lived in style. Each of our families had its own horses. The carriages had an elegance that has long since disappeared. There was a Dorsay coupé with eight springs, a four-seater calèche, and Grandfather had a little omnibus in which he took us to the park.
>
> Alexandre de Gunzburg[1]

1

The Hôtel des Trois-Empereurs

AUTUMN, 1857: AFTER a stay at the Marienbad spa in Bohemia, Joseph Evzel Gunzburg decided to continue his journey on to Paris, resolutely turning his back on his Russian homeland.[1] Every move involved a major logistical effort, especially for a large family. As well as his wife Rosa and their five children (two of whom were already married), Joseph travelled with a full entourage, including his business staff and an indispensable domestic retinue: personal assistant, secretaries, tutors, wet-nurses and nannies, coachmen, ladies' companions, valets and maids, and even a *shochet* who was responsible for slaughtering animals and ensuring that *kashrut*[2] was duly respected. After a journey lasting several days, the Gunzburg family and entourage moved into the Hôtel des Trois-Empereurs on Rue de Rivoli. This showcase luxury hotel, whose construction had been sought by Napoleon III, boasted rare comforts: lifts, a bus service, bureau de change, and interpreters.[3] The Gunzburgs' arrival aroused a definite curiosity that the French press picked up on, noting that this "most opulent Russian family" was staying in "a succession of suites that form three sides of the little island, with some twenty windows looking out onto Rue Saint-Honoré, the whole facade of Place du Palais Royal, and Rue de Rivoli". However, it was made clear that the Gunzburgs had "not settled permanently in Paris; they are just trying it out."[4] Obviously well-off, they were well received. Paris during the Second Empire was in fact favourably disposed to rich foreigners, including Jews – anti-Semitism was not widespread, and the initial commentaries on their presence in Paris did not mention that they were Jewish, at least not explicitly. Spending freely, Joseph Evzel was seen as a "nabob", as the expression went. His occupation, merits, and source of wealth were of little importance: he was one "millionaire" among others in a city where money was abundant.

But money was not everything. Charm counted too. Unable to rely on his wife, the daughter of a postmaster who was poorly educated and spoke mainly in Yiddish, Joseph was fortunate to be accompanied by his daughter-in-law Anna, his son Horace's wife, whose qualities were universally admired. Anna was only just twenty, but was well educated and spoke excellent French. Her manner was both simple and elegant and won her general approval: *Le Monde illustré* described her as "a young and lovely person". As much at ease on the banks of the Seine as in her native Podolia,[5] she was her father-in-law's ideal partner for the family's integration into Parisian society. Contacts were rapidly made, most of them among the Jewish bourgeoisie to whom the Gunzburgs were introduced by the Heines, a family of bankers (which included the poet Heinrich Heine) who had originally come from Lower Saxony and been resident in France since the beginning of the nineteenth century. Madame Heine, who presided over a glittering salon, was a highly effective intermediary. In short order the Gunzburgs were being invited around the city, and themselves had guests, especially for musical soirées. In May 1858, a few months after they arrived in Paris, they gave their first ball, at very great expense. The evening was successful enough to make it the subject of a gently mocking review by Henri de Pène in *Le Figaro*:

Two days before *Le Figaro* disported itself at the Hôtel du Louvre, there was a Thorn ball at the Hôtel des Trois-Empereurs in the apartments of M. and Mme Gunzburg, nabobs from Russia, millionaires thirty, forty, even fifty times over, whom no one knew yesterday, and whom everyone is talking about today.

People have such short memories in our good city that I wager the above expression, "Thorn ball", requires an explanation.

M. Thorn was an American who was introduced to Parisians in 1840 by his wealth. He wanted the flower of the Faubourg Saint-Germain at his table, and he had it, by dint of magnificence. This mischievous Yankee took great pleasure in subjecting the smartest people, the most famous names and noblest families, to his slightest whim. It was, for example, decreed that no one would be admitted to his apartments after ten p.m. If you arrived at five minutes past ten, whether you were a duchess, a banker or a tenor, the door would be unceremoniously shut in your face.

Viscount de Launay said that if M. Thorn wrote on his invitations that "Guests will be admitted only if wearing nightcaps," Parisian high society would come running in its nightcaps. M. Gunzburg does not treat us so haughtily. He is related to M. Thorn by his millions, by the splendour of his parties, by the ambition of his hospitality, and by his lack of roots in society, but not by his hospitality itself. His last ball cost 80,000 francs and was almost worth that much.

His guests were no more diverse than they usually are on such occasions, but they were much more brilliant. It was a kind of charity ball. Everyone greeted the patroness, from whom he received a ticket, before going to greet the masters of the household. It was a charity ball from another point of view too. M. and Mme Gunzburg had had the clever idea of presenting their compliments to the Faubourg Saint-Germain and, holding out the golden bough of charity, had sent a thousand francs to this noble lady seeking donations, a thousand écus to another; these ladies, in return, attended the ball with their escorts.

The most assorted names: Mme the Duchess of Riario-Sforza, M. Ricord [physician], Mme Mélanie Waldor [novelist], Mme Labédoyère, Prince Montléar, Albéric Second [playwright], Countess Bathyany, M. Hugues de Cosal, son-in-law of M. d'Audiffret, former man of letters and presumed author of the *Mémoires de Lola-Montès*, etc. etc.

The Marquise de Boissy who was at home on the same evening ended up at the Gunzburgs', having brought her guests with her.

A notable advance! No more the eternal second lieutenant in uniform ripping lace gowns with his spurs and pouncing on the trays of food like a wolf: that scourge, that inevitable scourge of the salons that we have noticed recently. He may be invited once, never twice.[6]

This last jibe aimed at the "second lieutenant in uniform" aroused the ire of a group of officers who had attended the ball in mufti: the unfortunate Henri de Pène received fifty challenges to a duel. At his second encounter de Pène suffered a perforated lung; the affair was widely talked about, which may not have displeased Joseph Evzel, who one senses had a taste for drawing attention to himself. The account of the ball in *Le Monde illustré* makes it sound like a working-class girl's dream: "Sixteen reception rooms lit *a giorno*, profusely bedecked with flowers, sumptuously decorated, two orchestras, two buffets… Around 2 a.m. a magnificent supper was served in two of the *salons*, whose menu was one of those gastronomic landmarks which remain etched on the gourmet's memory. They say there were a hundred pheasants served, five hundred bottles of the choicest wines etc etc." The Hôtel des Trois-Empereurs had been specially redecorated: "Several of the reception rooms had been draped with silk for the party. Elsewhere walls had been demolished and partitions torn down. They say a steward had been handing out money to the poor since the morning!" Last but not least, the thousand guests were welcomed "with tireless grace" by Anna, assisted "by several members of Parisian high society". Everyone who was anyone in Paris was there: "the Faubourg Saint-Germain and the Chaussée d'Antin – two classes separated, as everyone knows, by more than the Seine – government officials and distinguished foreigners, had hastened to accept invitations sponsored by three or four families, including two ducal households." With a single jarring note that is not without interest: "It was rumoured that their compatriots held back from accepting M. and Mme Gunzburg's invitation. We do not know on what evidence this claim and the insinuation it implies are based; but we can clearly state, *de visu et auditu*, that in the ball's numerous rooms we came across many important names ending in *-ky* and in *-ov* [i.e. Russian family names]."

For anyone familiar with Russian realities, the insinuation was clear: Russian aristocracy was snubbing the Gunzburgs, whom it regarded as Jewish parvenus who had only just emerged from their province… In spite of everything the ball had nevertheless been "a complete success; people talked about it everywhere, and in different ways, for a week before it happened and a week after it was over."[7] Joseph Evzel had the satisfaction of being "the man no one had heard of yesterday and whom everyone is talking about today." The Gunzburgs had entered the society pages and never left them again.

From 1858, the year of the ball, we have a fine portrait of the "nabob" from Russia, painted by Edouard Dubufe: with a high forehead, soft brown hair, intense bluish-grey eyes, generous lips, and a short, carefully trimmed moustache and beard, Joseph Evzel is a good-looking man who has everything he needs to be at his ease in Paris society. A ring on his right index finger, a handsome pocket watch, and pale leather gloves in his left hand add a dashing impression.[8] Was the portrait accurate? Théophile Gautier generally wrote off Dubufe and his society portraits:

"If other artists accuse him of flattery and mannerism, his models certainly don't complain about him; he is fresh, silky, transparent. His brush erases all wrinkles and fatigue: he paints a pretty picture."[9] A later photograph contradicts the famous writer's words: Joseph Evzel's imposing presence was real. He had chosen well. "Portrait painting is dominated equally by Edouard Dubufe and Winterhalter, both men of talent," the critic Etienne-Jean Delécluze wrote at the time, adding: "Edouard Dubufe is in fashion and deserves to be."[10] He had already painted a famous portrait of the Empress Eugénie and he had no lack of imperial commissions. The same year Horace, Joseph Evzel's son, also sat for Dubufe in his studio at 15 Rue d'Aumale: the commission is confirmed by the artist's notebooks, even though the painting itself has now disappeared. Well-known Parisians were flocking to the painter's studio to sit for him, and the Gunzburgs met artists, writers, politicians, financiers and ladies belonging to the *monde* or even the *demi-monde*, at Rue d'Aumale.[11]

Although newspapers tell us the effect the Gunzburgs were having on Parisian society, few sources provide much information about the family's impressions of the city. The facts speak for themselves: the return to Russia was frequently postponed, until finally the decision was made to settle in Paris. With its social life and its natural splendour enhanced by Baron Haussmann's projects, with its innumerable industries and workshops, Paris was the economic and cultural leader of a Europe in which industrialisation was in full swing. In the France of the Second Empire, where business fever reigned and where new men found ways of employing themselves usefully, the Gunzburgs were in their element. For his business affairs, Joseph Evzel, accompanied by his son, travelled regularly to Russia and in 1859 founded in St Petersburg the "J. E. Gunzburg Bank", one of the first private financial institutions in the tsar's empire. In Paris Joseph Evzel did not confine himself to spending; he observed astutely. Banking was being transformed into the lifeblood of industrial development. The following year the new banker left the Hôtel des Trois-Empereurs and rented part of the Dassier mansion – named after a Genevan banker – at 8 Rue de Presbourg, still called Rue Circulaire, near L'Etoile. No doubt he had it luxuriously remodelled: gossips claimed he had a solid-gold bed in the drawing room.[12] Three generations of Gunzburgs lived together in this comfortable residence. Joseph Evzel's two eldest children, Alexandre and Horace, had two young sons each; the third, Ury, was a young adult, old enough to marry; the two youngest,

Mathilde and Salomon, were twelve and eight years old respectively when they arrived in France. Anna, Horace's wife, kept a mother's watchful eye on the younger generation, her own children (her youngest had been born in the Hôtel des Trois-Empereurs), her nephews, her younger sister (whom she had brought from Podolia), and her cousins, including Salomon and Mathilde Gunzburg: she was also their sister-in-law, since her husband Horace was their brother. The practice of marrying within their social milieu, as was customary at the time, safeguarded the family's interests: Anna was the daughter of Elka, Joseph Evzel's beloved sister, and Horace was thus her first cousin and her father-in-law her uncle.

Particular care was given to education, religious and secular, for boys as well as for girls. Joseph Evzel was proud of his daughter Mathilde, who was ardently pursuing her studies in her new Parisian environment: in addition to learning French, English and Italian, she continued to improve her Russian and German; she also played the piano.[13] She probably also knew the rudiments of Hebrew, since her father's librarian took the trouble to draw up, for her fifteenth birthday, a charming tribute in verse, *Le-Yom Huledet*, whose dedication ran "To Mademoiselle Gunzburg on the occasion of her birthday, 5 August 1859, from her very devoted Senior Sachs". When it was time for her to make her debut in society, a partner was quickly found for her. On 11 March 1862, shortly before her eighteenth birthday, Mathilde Gunzburg was married to Paul Fould. A photograph shows the young fiancée in the crinoline and gathered ribbons typical of the period: slight, smiling, with bright eyes and a short, upturned nose, she is pleasant-looking without being pretty, taking after her mother more than her father. The picture was taken by Adam Salomon, a fashionable artist (only the best for the Gunzburgs). Mathilde, then, was the first of the family to become French, by marriage. But that was not the real point. Joseph Evzel was not seeking a new country for his family. Proud of being Russian, he was concerned to transmit his original culture to his children and grandchildren. On the other hand this marriage furthered the family's ascent. Five years after they first started living in France, it marked the official entry of the Gunzburgs into the Parisian Jewish *haute bourgeoisie*, a milieu still in the process of establishing itself, because Paul Fould was the nephew of Napoleon III's finance minister, Achille Fould.

2

Mathilde's Marriage

FEW DETAILS HAVE come down to us about the feelings and circumstances that furthered Mathilde Gunzburg's marriage to Paul Fould. "They met, fell in love, and married," as their eldest daughter summed it up in an account written many years afterwards. "This elite creature, with her fortune and the social position acquired by her family, was truly what is called a great catch. My father was, too."[1] They undeniably represented an excellent match. He was twenty-five years old, she was seventeen. The marriage, quickly and efficiently arranged, was one with which both families could be satisfied. The social and economic importance is clear: Paul belonged to a new milieu, established over two generations, that was an engine in the modernisation of French economic life. The history of the Fould family was emblematic of that of Jews in France and of a new dynamic from which they had benefited since the end of the eighteenth century. For this modest family from Metz, settling in Paris had been the point of departure for an impressive success.[2] Under Louis XVI in the mid-eighteenth century, the capital had been opened up to Jews after several centuries of prohibition. Since 1394 a royal edict had closed France to all Jews, an exclusion that was confirmed in 1613; but thanks to territorial annexations, some Jewish groups had nonetheless been tolerated, so that at the end of the *ancien régime* in 1789, 40,000 Jews were living confined to strictly delimited regions: Lorraine, Alsace, the Bordeaux area and the Comtat Venaissin surrounding Avignon. There were about 3,500 Jews in Metz, confined to a ghetto and burdened with taxes and fees, without a future. In 1787, Berr Léon Fould chose to flee this life of poverty and obtained permission to live in Paris. Shortly afterwards the country's political evolution considerably improved conditions for Jews: on 27 September 1791, under the newly established constitutional monarchy, civil rights were extended to all Jews living on French territory. Paris became the centre of French Judaism: in 1789 there were 500 Jews in Paris; in 1861 there were 11,164. At the time of Paul's marriage the Foulds already represented an old, established family in this recent community.

By sheer energy, Berr Léon Fould had developed a banking business. After an initial bankruptcy, he created a new enterprise by associating himself with the Frankfurt banker Oppenheim. At the end of the July Monarchy in 1848, when Louis Philippe abdicated and the Second Republic was established, Fould could be proud of this institution, whose solidity was based on the reliability of its founder and the family's solidarity. When he died in 1855, the Fould-Oppenheim bank came under the control of the Heine family, who had also come from Frankfurt. The connection between the Foulds and the Gunzburgs was probably favoured by Paul's elder brother Benoît's wife, née Oppenheim, who was close to the Heines. Mathilde's fiancé was a descendant of Berr Léon's younger brother, Abraham, who had also come to Paris to seek his fortune a few years afterwards, in the first third of the nineteenth century. One of his eight children, Emile (1803–1884), Paul's father, had opened a notary's office in 1832: he was thus the first Jew to practise this very regulated profession. The Fould firm soon established itself as one of the most important in Paris, handling not only most of the documents concerning the Fould and Fould-Oppenheim bank, but also most of the business of the capital's Jewish community.[3] Emile Fould had thus built up a large fortune, as shown by his credit balance at the Bank of France: 5.8 million francs in 1852, 8.2 million in 1861, 4 million in 1869.[4] Called upon to succeed his father, Paul was a "handsome, intelligent, distinguished young man, an auditor at the Council of State".[5] His younger brother, Alphonse (1850–1913), was no less brilliant: he studied at the Ecole Polytechnique, married Fortunée Léonie Dupont, and, like his father-in-law, embarked upon a career in iron manufacturing at Pompey, in Lorraine. The three daughters of the notary Fould also made advantageous marriages: Juliette was then already married to Eugène Pereire, the son of Isaac, the creator of French railways; Berthe wed Charles Weisweiller, a banker, and Gabrielle wed Henri Raba, the scion of a well-known Bordeaux family.

The Foulds acquired particular fame after the establishment of the Second Empire in 1852 and the accession to power of Louis-Napoleon

Bonaparte, whose powerful finance minister was Achille Fould, Paul's uncle. After the coup d'état of 2 December 1852, which completed the transformation of the Republic into the Second Empire, and when the prince-president became Emperor Napoleon III, Achille became even more indispensable: a minister of state and of the emperor's household, he was the organiser of the new regime. He served as Civil Registrar for the emperor's marriage with Eugénie de Montijo.[6] After an interruption of a few months in 1860–61, he returned to the Tuileries in 1862, again as finance minister, and remained there until his death in 1867. Since his youth, Achille had successfully devoted himself to politics, whereas his elder brother Benoît pursued their father's work in the sphere of banking. The two brothers rose together: having become a minister, Achille supported the interests of France and those of finance, thus in part those of his friends and family. The famous story of Crédit Mobilier, a financial institution of a new kind that functioned in a somewhat ambiguous way, illustrates this collaboration: Benoît headed the organisation, and the Pereire brothers were his principal partners; ties with the imperial regime were close. The third member of the siblings, Emile, was not forgotten: his notarial firm handled Crédit Mobilier's documents from its inception in November 1852.[7] Achille Fould incarnated the spirit of the Second Empire, a period of great public works, vast financial operations, and stock-market euphoria. An incontestable symbol of success, he was, however, an unpopular figure, detested by many of his contemporaries and by Napoleon III's immediate entourage. Mathilde nevertheless entered a family on the rise, with a bright future.

The marriage, uniting the two families, marked a twofold ascent, formally sealed before a notary through a contract: the "Marriage contract between Monsieur Paul Fould and Mademoiselle Gunzburg signed before M. Delaporte, notary in Paris, on 9 March 1862" is a model of its kind.[8] In his short novel *Le Contrat de mariage* Balzac describes the calculations and deceptions that were often hidden behind the "happy union" of two young people. In this case, neither of the parties had reason to regret the commitments that had been made. Particular care was given to the form as well as to the content: there was a lot at stake. This contract now constitutes the sole concrete testimony to the efforts, discussions and hopes that accompanied the union of these two families that had previously been foreign to each other.

Bound in luxurious leather decorated with delicate gilding, the contract comprises about twenty pages on which titles and capital letters are illuminated in red and gold. The content is no less impressive: taking up in turn the matrimonial regime, provisions for the dowry, a cooling-off period, and use and reuse of funds, its articles and paragraphs proceed with great technical detail. But then the fiancé was a specialist in this area: for his diploma from the University of Paris's law school, three years earlier, on 24 March 1859, Paul Fould had defended a thesis entitled *De jure dotum, "Du contrat de mariage"*. In his introduction to this learned work he pointed out that "The marriage contract is the convention through which two persons who are to be united in marriage settle their relationships and their pecuniary interests. Marriage, on the contrary, is the union of the spouses itself, consecrated in law and determining their respective rights and duties."[9] It was no doubt he who decided the regime that was to regulate his "relationships and pecuniary interests" with his wife-to-be: "The future spouses declare that they have adopted as the basis of the union the dowry regime as it is established by the Napoleonic Code, save for the exceptions resulting from the following articles: all goods, moveable and immoveable, present and future, shall depend on the dowry arrangement [...]. There shall be, between the future spouses, a commonality of acquisitions whose effects will be regulated by articles 1498 and 1499 of the Napoleonic Code."[10] In the dowry settlement, the wife's goods were transferred to the husband, who managed them. This commonality of acquisitions gave the marriage a "communal" character that reinforced the conjugality of the union. It was generally constituted by "acquisitions made by the spouses together or separately during the marriage and proceeding from both common industry and savings made by each of them from the fruits and earnings of and from their goods." Thus there existed a common mass of assets that would be managed by the husband. This commonality of acquisitions allowed the wife to benefit from the "profits" made by her husband, to which she contributed often indirectly. Mathilde's dowry provided major assets that would constitute an essential part of the future household's financial ease. And when the time came, at her father's death, she could count on her husband to protect her interests against those of her brothers.

The dowry was the heart of the marriage contract: Joseph Evzel's provision in his daughter's favour was commensurate with his reputation as a multimillionaire. He gave her, in anticipation of her future inheritance,

"1,110 bonds issued by the [Russian] Imperial Railway Company in the nominal amount of two thousand francs, each producing four and a half per cent interest guaranteed by the Russian government." At the death of her father, the young woman was thus to receive 2,220,000 francs, or a sum equivalent to 8,080,522 euros.[11] The historian Cyril Grange has studied the size of the dowries provided for young women in Parisian high society: consider the case of Louise Le Hon, the illegitimate daughter of the Duke of Morny, who married Prince Poniatowski in 1856 and received a dowry of twelve dresses from the Worth fashion house valued at 1 million francs, plus a mansion on the Champs-Elysées. Twenty years later Rachel Poliakov, the daughter of the Russian railway magnate, brought 1,150,000 francs to her marriage with Georges Saint-Paul.[12] Dowries greater than 2 million francs were rare: Mathilde appears to have been one of the best endowed brides of her time. As the dowry consisted of the wife's share of her father's legacy, during Joseph Evzel's lifetime the husband received only the interest on the sum, providing an annual income of 100,000 francs. This income was the basis of the new household's establishment: it ensured the couple would be able to lead a suitable way of life, in this case a very comfortable one. "By express agreement of the present [signatories], the future spouses may not dispose of the aforesaid bonds during Monsieur Gunzburg *père*'s lifetime without his consent, and shall have only the right to receive the interest when it falls due. The bonds must remain in the hands of M. Gunzburg who will have the right to dispose of them if he considers it appropriate to do so, on condition that he replace them with other securities, also foreign, providing an equivalent income of a hundred thousand francs per annum. Monsieur Gunzburg shall receive the interest on these bonds or securities when it is due, and will, as he promises, pay or remit them personally to the future spouses if he is in Paris, or, in the event of his absence, by means of a note on his banker in Paris, each quarter starting on the day of the marriage, in their entirety and in advance."[13] This arrangement made it possible to avoid immobilising his capital, a major concern for the banker. The young Fould's financial position was the subject of a separate clause: "Monsieur and Madame Fould give to the future husband, their son, who accepts as an advance on their future legacies [...] the sum of two hundred thousand francs which they agree and are jointly liable to pay to the future spouses the day before the marriage, the celebration of which shall constitute a full discharge of the donors' obligation." To this sum the notarial office was to be added: "M. Fould *père* agrees to cede to M. Fould his son, the future spouse, who accepts [...] the notarial office and firm in Paris [...]. The price of this office and its accessories, not including the receivables and guarantee, may not exceed 500,000 francs, which will be payable only upon the death of M. Fould *père* if he should die during his son's exercise [of the office]."[14] What is unusual here is that the bride's dowry is greater than the groom's; and so, through the marriage of his only daughter, Joseph Evzel secured his place in the Parisian financial milieu only five years after the Gunzburgs' departure from Kamenets-Podolsk, the modest city in the then Russian province of Podolia where the young bride had been born. The timing was perfect for him to join this new elite, based on substantial international connections and united by financial and matrimonial interests, which was then consolidating its power and influence.

Far from being a private act carried out hastily in the secrecy of a notarial office, the signature of the marriage contract was accompanied by a formal social occasion. The Gunzburgs received the relatives and friends of both families at their home in Rue de Presbourg. The notary began by reading the contract. Its last words, "such are the agreements of the parties in the presence of...", are followed by the signatures, first of the fiancés, their mothers and fathers, then of the relatives and friends; in addition to those of their respective families, Mathilde and Paul's contract bears the signatures of 109 people. A decade later, Béatrice de Rothschild and Maurice Ephrussi would collect 500 signatures, but Mathilde and Paul's contract was still exceptional. It provides above all a very early reflection – we are in 1862 – of what this Jewish *haute bourgeoisie* was like as it took its first steps. Most of the witnesses to the Fould–Gunzburg marriage left a lasting mark on the history of finance; representatives of almost all the Jewish families were there: Furtado, Oppenheimer, Koenigswarter, Stern, Halphen, Hollander, Weisweiller, Rodrigues Henriquès, Goldsmith, Ellisen, Beer, Sarchi, Pereire. Also of note are the names of Ferdinand de Lesseps; members of the diplomatic corps such as His Excellency Hassan Ali Khan, minister of Persia; M. Nazar Aga, first secretary of the Persian embassy; and M. de Meismes, the Russian vice-consul; Sadi Carnot, then a young student at the Ecole Polytechnique, also signed the contract, as did a handful of senators and other members of the old nobility (Baron Reiset, Viscountess Rancher). The absence of the Rothschilds is easily explained: the Foulds belonged to the imperial circles of Napoleon III, whereas James de Rothschild and his descendants, who had been particularly active during the July Monarchy of Louis Philippe I, still showed their Orléanist sympathies. But the two families eventually became related: one of Paul and Mathilde's granddaughters married Edouard de Rothschild in 1905. Other notable absentees were the Ephrussi and Camondo families, which is not surprising since neither was in Paris at the time. Arriving from Istanbul, the Camondos settled in France in 1869 and also moved to Rue de Presbourg. The Ephrussis, compatriots of the Gunzburgs who came from Odessa and had founded a bank in Venice, arrived in Paris in 1871.

The Gunzburgs had joined the upper crust of Second Empire society. Although they were not members of the Emperor's immediate entourage, they were received at the Tuileries.[15] Yet history does not record whether uncle Achille Fould honoured the young couple with his presence at their marriage on 9 March 1862. The signature of the contract was followed by a civil marriage on 11 March, at the *mairie* of the 2nd arrondissement, then by a religious ceremony, no doubt at the Gunzburgs' home. Paris still did not have a synagogue of sufficient status. The Rue de la Victoire synagogue was inaugurated only in 1874.

Was this perfect match a happy union? Mathilde had done quite well for in-laws: her father-in-law was "an excellent man, simple, liked by everyone, hospitable, easy-going",[16] and her mother-in-law, née Palmyre Oulman, though authoritarian, was an intelligent woman. The future should have smiled on the young couple. But according to Louise, their eldest daughter, Mathilde's health started to decline with her first pregnancy in 1862, and although she gave birth to two more daughters, she never knew the joys of happy motherhood. "One treatment followed another, and her misfortunes isolated her, keeping her away from the normal society life for which she had been destined. I always saw her weary, lying down, often in bed; we used to go to spas in the south, which was sad for us. My father ended up going out by himself, which left her miserable and lonely, but he liked society, conversation and ladies, who liked him, too! Despite my youthful naivety, I understood how hurt my mother was, and I truly felt for her, even though she was always serene, kind and friendly to everyone. People are not sufficiently aware of the perspicacity of children, who judge by instinct."[17] Mathilde found consolation and support in her pious, kind mother, Rosa, who was always ready to care for her and comfort her with a devotion that characterised her: she was herself very isolated in this Parisian world, most of whose manners she found objectionable. And although Mathilde had left her father's house, contact with her brothers, her sisters-in-law and her nephews and nieces remained frequent, if not without friction. "All these good people, who were distinguished and blessed with the best feelings of solidarity and mutual devotion, lived on more or less bad terms, and I did not understand the terrible complications that led to their frequent quarrels alternating with lyrical effusions," Louise Fould recalled.[18] Religious holidays and family events were always an occasion to meet, all the more because, having become the owner of a mansion, Joseph Evzel henceforth spent most of his time in France and liked to gather all his close family and friends around him.

3

7 Rue de Tilsitt

ON 28 MAY 1867 Joseph Evzel signed a contract for the purchase of two building sites: the larger of the two, 1693.04 square metres, was located between the Arc de Triomphe, Avenue Wagram and Avenue du Prince (now Avenue Mac-Mahon); the second, 831.65 square metres, was across from the first, on the other side of Rue de Tilsitt.[1] The public works firm of Lescanne-Perdoux and Co., "acting on behalf of the city of Paris," sold him both properties for the sum of 366,228 francs and 75 centimes. "Of this price, Monsieur Gunzburg presently paid in cash and gold and silver coin and Bank of France notes, counted and delivered before notaries [...] the sum of 272,227 francs and 75 centimes." The rest – principal and interest – was to be paid within a period of seven years. A receipt dated 20 May 1876 attests to the payment of the total balance remaining. The purchase contract for these lots counted as a commitment to construct a "mansion on Place de l'Etoile" before 1 May 1868, "construction, roof, and the installation of gates included". Construction began immediately. To keep an eye on the work, Joseph Evzel had only to walk the short distance from Rue de Presbourg, where he was renting part of the Dassier mansion, to the other side of Place de l'Etoile. The whole quarter was then being renovated. The transformation of Paris was in full swing: 20,000 buildings were to be razed and 43,000 built.[2] Dust, rubble composed of old and new building stones, piles of lumber and beams: the city was living to the rhythm of construction companies, most of them from the Creuse in the heart of France, which completed one project after another with exceptional skill. By building a house on Rue de Tilsitt, the

Gunzburgs had acquired one of the most prominent addresses in the capital.

The Champs-Elysées had been the object of much speculation since Fanny Le Hon, the Duke of Morny's mistress, had had a luxurious mansion built at number 13. From this vantage point she kept an interested eye on the intersection of roads known as L'Etoile. As soon as she discovered that the Emperor was signing contracts to install a gas supply in that area, she purchased there, with Morny, immense tracts of land that she quickly resold to the city of Paris. L'Etoile, which at that time seemed too far from the city centre ever to be divided into plots, became an attractive neighbourhood. The law of 26 June and the decree of 13 August 1854 provided for the complete redevelopment of Place de l'Etoile and the area around it. The goal was to give the Arc de Triomphe, which was surrounded by tumbledown buildings from another age, a more suitable environment. The specifications were strict: the plans called for the construction of prestigious private town houses, and nothing else. Paris was beginning its elegant conquest of the west side of the city: the Bois de Boulogne, reorganised and enlarged, partly on the model of Hyde Park, was to become a Mecca for high society; the new neighbourhoods were intended for wealthy residents. Seconded by the prefect of the Seine, Baron Haussmann, and encouraged by Achille Fould, Napoleon III wanted to make Paris the capital of the civilised world, in accordance with the new canons of comfort, hygiene, air and light. The streets were designed for the passage of vehicles, and pavements were to be wide enough for crinolines. In the space of a few years Parisians found themselves living in a new city, described by Théophile Gautier: "Sometimes, looking at these broad streets, these great boulevards, these vast squares, these endless rows of monumental homes, these splendid quarters that have replaced the fields of market gardens, we wonder whether this is really the city where we spent our childhood."[3]

The Gunzburgs were making a leap into modernity: what a contrast with the little towns of southern Russia, where there were no pavements, and snow, mud and waste water made everything filthy! All around L'Etoile the great urban project was astonishing: "pavements, stone-laying, roads surfaced with asphalt, [...] construction of sewers under the new streets along with galleries necessary to locate and connect new sewers to those that may exist under neighbouring streets, and water conduits in the galleries", a water system, gas lighting, the planting of trees and shrubs with "protective fences", and "public urinals of a type to be chosen by the administration". Only the "costs of pavements and asphalting" were to be borne by the property owners, "these pavements to be made with granite paving stones or asphalt with granite borders". For the mansions surrounding the Arc de Triomphe the design was drawn up in advance by the architect Jacques Ignace Hithorff: facades "of dressed stone with pilasters, balusters, projecting mouldings, cornices and other ornaments of the same kind" and "gable roofs made of zinc, connected by a cast-iron gallery, and with mansards projecting from the lower part of the roof [...] The grounds between the fences and the buildings shall be cultivated in ornamental beds and may not under any pretext become places for public gatherings." The Gunzburg mansion still exists: it is a modern urban palace, impressive in its dimensions. Joseph Evzel hired the architect Charles Rohaut de Fleury as the project supervisor; the sculptor Frédéric-Louis-Désiré Bogino created the external decoration and the painters Charles Chaplin, Alexandre Deruelle and Alexis-Joseph Mazerolle were in charge of the ceilings and the wood panelling. Mazerolle was a prominent artist accustomed to painting large mural compositions: his *Amour and Psyche* adorning the ceiling of the main reception room on the *piano nobile* can still be seen today, an impassive witness to a past time.[4] Nymphs, *putti*, garlands of flowers and blue skies decorated the walls.

In 1869 the Gunzburg mansion was finally ready to receive this family that was "as numerous as it was opulent".[5] According to Sasha, Horace's fifth child, who was celebrating his sixth birthday when they were moving in, everyone had their own floor:

It was the biggest house on Place de l'Etoile between Avenue de Wagram and Avenue Mac-Mahon. A double staircase provided access to the three floors. On the ground floor on the left was Uncle Salomon's apartment, in the centre was the billiard room and the smoking room, both in the Arabic style; on the right was the library, where Senior Sachs, the famous connoisseur of Hebrew and Arab poetry, worked. On the first floor were my grandfather's rooms and all the reception rooms, including the *domovaya kontora* (business office) and another smoking room right at the end of the corridor. The dining room was unusual in that it was decorated with modern tapestries from the Braquenié company representing Renaissance hunting scenes in which members of the family were portrayed as the main hunters. The second and third [floors] were divided in the middle; on the left was Grandmother's apartment and above it lived Aunt Rosalie, Uncle Alexander's wife; around 1875 she left the house to take up residence on Avenue Foch (then Avenue de l'Impératrice), and Uncle Ury occupied her apartment, to which a few rooms on the second floor were added. We occupied the second [and third] floor on the right, on the second floor were our parents [Horace and Anna] and the reception room, and on the third floor all the children.[6]

The amenities were sufficiently exceptional to warrant mention: running water on all floors and even hot water in the kitchen and the pantry; a bathroom for each apartment, "but it was the famous water-carriers, all from Savoie, who brought on command their copper bathtubs and hot water contained in barrels of the same metal";[7] and one toilet per bedroom. Joseph Evzel spent a fortune on the whole house: more than two million francs. At least that was the value the fortunate owner set on his property when he drew up his French will a few years later, and he imagined leaving Mathilde the town house to replace the famous bonds he had promised as part of her dowry.

The Gunzburgs' Parisian kingdom came to fascinate their contemporaries. "Marvellous works of art decorate this magnificent residence. There is in particular one of the finest collections of Meissen porcelain in existence, and pieces of malachite of extraordinary value. Beyond the ballroom comes a loggia ornamented with superb Gobelin tapestries."[8] Anna was the true mistress of the house: the home was imbued with her charm and taste. Her portrait by Edouard Dubufe hung on the wall alongside those of her father-in-law and husband. It shows an elegant young woman, with a faintly exotic style: brunette, and with a pale complexion, she wears a long black lace veil attached to her hair and partly covering her generous breasts. Her respect for the Jewish custom of hiding her hair gives her an almost Spanish air, in tune with the fashion since Napoleon III's marriage to Eugénie de Montijo. Three strings of pearls, a lovely bracelet with medallions, and the sparkle of an earring reveal her femininity without making her coquettish. The painter has particularly emphasised her bluish-green eyes, full of good will and intelligence. Surrounded by craftsmen and painters, Anna devoted herself with enthusiasm to the decoration of the interior of the house on Rue de Tilsitt. Her husband's bedroom and smoking room were in the

Renaissance style, an eclectic mixture of Gothic, Henry II and Louis XIII. "The smoking room, a tiny version of the great hall in the Palace of Fontainebleau, was in ebony and the ceiling consisted of oak beams against a blue background. The walls were covered with Cordovan leather silvered and then dyed blue."[9] Coming across a shipment of Cordovan leather, Anna had used it as the basis for her design of the room. While the craftsmen struggled to find the corresponding colour for the ceiling, the painter Gustave Ricard "advised her to scrape a corner of the Cordovan leather to see on what colour the blue had been painted, and to proceed in this way to obtain the colour for the ceiling. It turned out that the leather was covered with a layer of silver under the arabesques."[10] Mauve fabrics woven in Lyons completed the ensemble. For her bedroom, en suite toilet room and boudoir, Anna chose a Louis XVI decor described by her son: "The ceiling of the toilet room had been commissioned from [Voillemot] and represented angels. He was a very fashionable painter during the Second Empire. For the boudoir, Maman had found chairs that came from the Trianon and bore on their undersides, burned on with a hot iron, the three fleurs-de-lys of the House of France."[11] For the small dining room, Anna chose a Pompeian style, having craftsmen make a chandelier based on old models and seeing to every last detail: "The crockery and linens all had a Greek decoration."[12]

Although each couple lived separately in their apartment, Joseph Evzel insisted on everyone being present for the Sabbath dinner on Friday evening. "The table was set for at least twenty-five persons. A family dinner is always considered a boring duty, and each family hurried to return to its apartment. But as children we enjoyed ourselves immensely. The low end of the table was our territory. Once Marc [Horace's third child] was sitting between Lisa Merpert (later Schwarz) and Monsieur Bonbernard, Ury's [...] Swiss teacher. Marc was flirting with Lisa, and, since he was greedy, he had set aside on his plate the truffles from his portion of *poularde aux truffes*. Bonbernard, taking advantage of Marc's concentration on Lisa, stole the truffles from his plate."[13]

Across Rue de Tilsitt from the town house a building held the stables and the coachmen's lodgings; with a "Dorsay coupé with eight springs" and "a small omnibus", the Gunzburgs were amply equipped. A ride through the Bois de Boulogne was a special moment Joseph Evzel shared with his grandchildren. "Grandfather took a carriage ride every day and one of the grandchildren regularly accompanied him. I recall that he reproached me for not improving fast enough in Russian," Sasha wrote. "Once the horse took fright and the carriage jumped onto the pavement. The shock caused our cousin Jacques to fall from the seat, where he had been sitting next to the coachman, and he broke his front teeth."[14] Like a proper patriarch, Joseph Evzel watched over the family's cohesion. He was all the more concerned about the younger generation because some of his sons did not always take their responsibilities seriously. Out of the four boys he had with Rosa, only Horace (1832–1909) completely fulfilled his hopes: reliable and hard-working, he was his father's true collaborator. Alexandre (1831–1878) and Ury (1840–1914) were rakes and gamblers who led their young brother Salomon (1848–1905) to join in their excesses. In reality, Joseph Evzel was no less inclined towards amusements, but he knew the price to be paid. "Grandfather liked to gamble, but his son Alexandre surpassed him by far and was recognised as one of the biggest gamblers in Petersburg. One evening, in a reception room, some ladies were teasing Grandfather, saying to him: 'How is it that you gamble so modestly, whereas your son Alexandre takes such great risks?' 'It's very simple,' he replied. 'Unlike him, I don't have a father wealthy enough to pay my debts.'"[15]

From the balcony of the town house, the children observed the events of Paris and learned the *Marseillaise*: "It was from up there that we saw passing by, shortly before the [Franco-Prussian] war [of 1870–71], the funeral procession of Victor Noir [the very young editor-in-chief of the *Pilori*, who had been killed by Pierre Bonaparte, the son of Lucien and thus a relative of Emperor Napoleon III, as a result of a duel connected with a quarrel between Pierre Bonaparte and the journalist Henri Rochefort, for whom Victor Noir was one of the seconds]. The street was covered with people, the crowd leaving the Champs-Elysées and plunging into Avenue de la Grande Armée, the hearse very simple, a single carriage, Rochefort's they said. He was currently waging war on the Empire in his pamphlet *La Lanterne*. Everyone was singing the *Marseillaise*, which was prohibited at that time, and from our third-storey perch we bellowed out these revolutionary strains."[16] The wind was changing: the government, increasingly unpopular, was overwhelmed by opposition. War with Germany was to complete Napoleon III's fall. When the conflict broke out on 19 July 1870, it caught the Gunzburgs by surprise on holiday in

Normandy. "When war was declared, we were in Veules, a very small place on the cliff near St-Valéry-en-Caux. Mama had rented the little villas belonging to Madame Bornibus, whose name you still see on the signs of their mustard factory," Sasha recalled. No one could imagine that France would be defeated. "Very soon after the beginning of the hostilities, the mayor of St-Valéry arrived in an open carriage, waving in his hand a dispatch announcing a great victory, and in the evening lamps were lit and there were fireworks at our place. It was the Battle of Forbach, if I remember correctly, and the next day we learned that the battle had turned into a terrible defeat."[17] French patriotism was such that Anna, worried about her young sister Théophile, who was married to Siegmund Warburg in Hamburg, even telegraphed her to tell her to join them. When the Emperor was taken prisoner at Sedan, there was widespread panic. Anna and her children took refuge in Switzerland. As a foreigner, Joseph Evzel's movements were not restricted, so he was able to evacuate his Fould granddaughters from Boulogne to Menton, passing through Germany![18] The rest of the family settled at Ouchy in Switzerland. At the Beau Rivage Hotel they met Adolphe Thiers, to become the first president of the Third Republic in 1871, who was going to meet with European sovereigns to urge them to act as intermediaries between the belligerents. "That was where we saw him, accompanied by his wife and Mme Dosne. They greatly admired Berza's nurse, or perhaps just her Russian clothing."[19] Anna had just given birth to her eighth child, Dimitri, nicknamed Berza. The Gunzburg children showed their patriotism: "We were deeply francophile in the family, and after the armistice, when our train was blocked at Augsburg by German troops returning from the front, we sang the *Marseillaise*. The German officers did not draw their sabres, but they shook their fingers at us, not without smiling. Mama promptly put an end to this demonstration."[20]

Joseph Evzel was not immune to the ordeal France was suffering: he transformed the house on Rue de Tilsitt into a military hospital and made his son-in-law Paul its director. With the Russian Embassy's agreement he flew the Russian flag (at that time yellow, white and black) alongside the French tricolour.[21] The project inspired enthusiastic praise:

[This] magnificent hospital [is] comprised of thirty beds. It is no longer mere comfort, but princely luxury. The meals are provided by a restaurateur, and M. Gunzburg treats his wounded men like great lords.

The surgeons are named Hénocoque and Monot, and the physician Barthez. One day the director of the hospital, though a Jew, desired to attend, without being seen, the prayer service that was held every morning and evening. He listened and fell into profound meditation. When the nurses came to re-join the director after the last sign of the cross was made, they found him with his eyes full of tears. He told them, "This prayer, said with such simplicity and sincere piety by these brave soldiers, moved me more than I can say." All expenses are paid by M. Gunzburg, who has each wounded or sick man given a certain sum of money when he leaves the hospital after he has been cured.[22]

When the Germans entered Paris, a Prussian general moved into the house with his staff. "He did not steal the clocks and left his visiting card when he left," Sasha remembered.[23] When peace returned in 1871, the Gunzburgs came back to Paris, now the capital of a republican France. The man who was called "the richest of the Russian bankers" was at the head of a flourishing enterprise to which his son Horace dedicated himself unsparingly. In particular, Horace had made close ties with members of the House of Hesse, who were customers of the J. E. Gunzburg Bank. In recognition of services rendered, Horace was named Hesse's consul-general in St Petersburg and became the first Jew to be honoured with such an office in the tsars' capital. In 1870 the Prince of Hesse granted him the title of baron, which he accepted only on condition that the title also be given to his father, and thus by heredity to his brothers. Four years later, that was what happened: on 2 August 1874, Ludwig III, Grand Duke of Hesse and the Rhine, created Joseph, a merchant of the Russian Empire, Baron Gunzburg, "Freiherr von Günzburg". The document of ennoblement was illuminated and bound in elegant red leather.[24] In 1879, Emperor Alexander II authorised the Gunzburgs to use the title of baron in Russia, though without incorporating them into the Russian nobility.[25] The Gunzburgs thus entered the restricted circle of ennobled Jewish families and added a nobiliary particle to their name. The baronial crown decorated their carriages, silverware, stationery, crockery and linen in Rue de Tilsitt. A coat of arms was adopted: quartered in argent and gules, it is ornamented with an arm in armour and a beehive surmounted by three bees; a stag and a lion serve as supports. As a motto the Gunzburgs chose *Laboremus* ("Let us work!"), a reference to the last word of Septimius Severus, an emperor devoted to his task.

4

The J. E. Gunzburg Bank

THE PAGES HAVE not yellowed, and the inscription is very readable: J. E. Gunzburg (or Günzburg, depending on the case), 1 Rue Saint-Georges. Letterhead, paying-in and withdrawal slips, receipt books, all the usual stationery testifying to the bank's activity.[1] These few relics come from files relating to the records consulted: since we do not have the archives of the Gunzburg bank itself, we have to look for references to it in the Fould-Heine papers preserved in the National Archives of the World of Work in Roubaix or in the Rothschild Archives, which are in Roubaix as well, and also in London, in the imposing New Court building.[2] Discretion being a constitutive element of the practice of banking, it is not surprising that we have only scattered sources. The Gunzburgs' twofold Franco-Russian ties might also have muddied the water and might explain certain silences in the historical record: Nicolas Stoskopf's comprehensive work on Parisian bankers and financiers under the Second Empire does not mention the Gunzburgs.[3] Knowledge of nineteenth-century banking is generally patchy. The period was prosperous, however, especially for banks in Paris, which orchestrated not only France's economic and financial development but also that of much of Europe.

In Second Empire Paris, the opening of a bank was not an exceptional event. In financing his radical programme for the urban transformation of Paris, Baron Haussmann clashed with traditional financiers, in particular with the great Orléanist bank run by the Rothschilds, and thus favoured the appearance of new banks such as Crédit Mobilier, established by the Pereire brothers, and Crédit Foncier, which was created by merging several mortgage banks. A whole banking system came into being. Conditions meant that setting up a new business could not have been simpler: all that was needed was an office, some seed money and a licence. The circulation of money and stock-market speculation were encouraged: "Between 1851 and 1870, fiduciary issue is said to have tripled. The Paris stock market underwent a rapid expansion, establishing itself as the main market for large government loans. In 1851 it listed 118 securities worth 11 billion francs. By 1869, 307 securities were listed, totalling 35 billion francs. Louis-Napoleon was convinced that money should no longer be seen as shameful but rather as a tool for economic development."[4]

An astute observer of economic activity in Paris, Joseph Evzel wagered that an equivalent phenomenon would occur in Russia: hadn't the architecture of the stock market building in St Petersburg, at the tip of Vasilyevsky Island, been inspired by that of the Paris stock market? A market for securities trading was just emerging in the tsars' capital, and the Gunzburgs were counting on playing an essential role in it.

In the *Annuaire-Almanach du commerce et de l'industrie*, the "Gunzburg (J. E.)" firm is listed with the annotation "Banking operations, chiefly with Russia".[5] It is not ranked among the prestigious group of the Rothschild brothers' "Great Bank" (*Haute Banque*), Fould-Oppenheim, Hottinguer & Co. and other firms with old, established reputations. The J. E. Gunzburg Bank was founded in St Petersburg on 15 November 1859, and boosted by the addition of a French branch eight years later, in October 1867.[6] By means of a document signed before a notary, Horace was recognised as a partner on 2/14 September 1866:[7] he was put in charge of daily operations in Russia, while his father supervised from afar, having chosen to remain in France most of the year. The Paris office, which was more modest, was entrusted to Salomon, who was then about twenty years old. After a few years, the two firms merged and Joseph Evzel handed over his shares and the management to his sons, in proportion to their respective merits: he gave 60 per cent to Horace, 30 per cent to Salomon, and reserved 10 per cent for himself. Dated 13 September 1875, a "partnership agreement" was clearly spelt out: "For the proper conduct of business" each partner would contribute a proportional part to the capital of 2 million roubles: Horace 1,200,000, Salomon 600,000 and their father 200,000.[8] According to the exchange rate between franc and rouble in the 1870s (1 rouble equalling 2.70 francs), the bank's capital thus amounted to 5,400,000 francs.[9] Preserved in a descendant's archive, this agreement offers an interesting explanation of how the institution functioned:

> Business is conducted paternally by duly organised offices. The general management of each house is in the hands of the resident for everything that enters into the nature of the banking business, with immediate communication to the partners. *Nota bene*: the authorised agents of the respective firms correspond from St Petersburg with Baron Horace de Gunzburg, those in Paris with Baron Salomon de Gunzburg. [...] On 31 December each year, an inventory taxing each account is drawn up. Securities are accepted at the price of the last quotation of the year. After the deduction of interest on the working capital at the rate of 5 per cent per annum, after the deduction of losses, after setting aside the exchange value of doubtful assets, the yearly profit is calculated, and after deducting the percentages for the managers and others, the balance is shared among: Baron Joseph de Gunzburg 10 per cent, Baron Horace de Gunzburg 60 per cent, Baron Salomon de Gunzburg 30 per cent. As dividend, each of these can withdraw from his share in the business: Baron Horace de Gunzburg 100,000 roubles, Baron Salomon de Gunzburg 50,000 roubles. And the costs of representation in St Petersburg will be allocated from the 10 per cent share of the net profits [owed to Joseph Evzel de Gunzburg]. [...] By my own free will, I, Baron Joseph de Gunzburg, hand over the management of business to my two sons Horace and Salomon de Gunzburg on the basis of the present accord, assuming that they are still in agreement. In the event of litigation, after having listened to both sides, my vote, added to one of the others, will be decisive.[10]

Joseph Evzel definitively excluded from the banking business his two other sons, Alexandre and Ury, as a punishment for their dissolute behaviour: *Laboremus*, the family motto, reveals the patriarch's state of mind. Agents represented the Gunzburgs: in Paris, Adolphe Grube established himself as an efficient collaborator and ended up as a partner in the St Petersburg bank. According to one anecdote, during the war of 1870, "manager Grube was evacuated in Michel Ephrussi's four-in-hand carriage, along with the lady friend of the latter, who was a great horse lover. This created a sensation in the German outposts!"[11] In St Petersburg,

Hermann Bertheson, Clément Podmenner and F. Höhne also provided valuable help.

Although the economic climate was favourable for banking, the international situation seems not, at first glance, to have been propitious for the establishment of a Russian firm in France: Joseph Evzel arrived in Paris when the cannons of the Crimean War were still smoking. From 1853 to 1856, three years of fierce battles had been fought between the French (and their allies, the Ottomans, British and Piedmontese) and the Russians. The whole European diplomatic apparatus set up by Napoleon III was based on hostility to the tsars' empire, Austria and Prussia announcing an "armed" neutrality. Nonetheless, the atmosphere in which the Treaty of Paris was signed in 1856 was not overtly hostile to Russia. Alexander II's accession to the throne in 1855 had made it possible not only to bring the conflict to an end but to initiate a rapprochement between the two enemies. Behind the scenes, and meticulously briefed, the Duke of Morny had been entrusted with an unofficial mission of seduction.[12] In late 1855, he made secret contact with Prince Gorchakov, who was the tsar's ambassador to Austria and soon to be his foreign minister. He was aided in his transactions by Baron Sina, a Viennese banker competing with the Rothschilds who had close ties with the Pereire brothers' Crédit Mobilier. On 13 February 1856, Morny arranged to meet the tsar's envoys, Count Orlov and Baron Brunnow, in Paris, at the home of Madame de Lieven. Orlov was soon to become Alexander II's ambassador to France, and his path often crossed that of the Gunzburgs. The peace negotiations in which all the belligerents participated took place from 25 February to 30 March. During that time, Paris saw nothing but balls and receptions; the treaty saved the sultan's tottering throne but did not include any clause that was humiliating to the tsar. Subsequently appointed ambassador to Russia, Morny renewed his attempts to bring about a rapprochement, and he launched business partnerships, paying little heed to the ethics of his office. He put the Pereire brothers in contact with a group of Moscow bankers to develop the embryonic Russian railway system. He arranged for French experts to go to the tsars' old capital, and a draft treaty provided for the construction of several networks with shares underwritten by French and Russian capital. The famous *Grande Société des chemins de fer russes* thus came into being: on the French side, it was established through collaboration between the

Pereires and the Hottinguers, with an enormous capitalisation of 300 million francs.[13] As we know, Joseph Evzel Gunzburg was able to purchase 1,110 bonds (which formed Mathilde's dowry a few years later). When he returned to France in the summer of 1857, Morny brought with him a young wife, Princess Sofya Trubetskaya (who was said to be an illegitimate daughter of the late tsar, Nicholas I). In Paris, the Princess, who was used to the Russian court, found the entourage of the French imperial couple *prostoy*: "vulgar". We have no way of knowing whether the Gunzburgs' social life crossed with that of the beautiful exile. It is likely, however, that business brought Joseph Evzel into contact with Morny, who sat on the Imperial Council with Achille Fould.

Through the bank, the Gunzburgs were now associated with the great European Jewish families: the Warburgs in Hamburg, the Mendelssohns and Bleichröders in Berlin, the Hoskiers, Camondos and Ephrussis in Paris, the Habers and Hirsches in Frankfurt-am-Main, and the Rothschilds in London. Unlike Joseph Evzel, most of these families belonged to banking dynasties that had been active for several decades. When in 1869 Abraham (1829–1889) and Nissim (1830–1889) Camondo arrived in Paris, they were following a pattern of familial dispersion driven by economics. The Isaac Camondo Bank had been founded in Constantinople in 1802 by their great-uncle Isaac. The move to Paris was spurred by the conviction that it was now easier to negotiate loans contracted by the Ottoman Empire from a great European capital. But Paris's charm was not solely economic, as is attested by a letter from Nissim to his brother: "Since I do not detest Paris, or the life that is led there, certainly I shall settle there as well, though from time to time I shall spend the summer on the Bosphorus."[14] Residing at 6 and 7 Rue de Presbourg, the Camondos were Joseph Evzel's neighbours until the town house on Rue de Tilsitt was ready. Among the banks active in Paris, the Hoskier (formerly Dutfoy) and Ephrussi firms, which were older than the Gunzburg bank, also specialised in the Russian market. A Frenchman, Armand Dutfoy (1814–1885) had lived for a few years in Moscow, where his father manufactured artists' canvases. Married to a Russian, in 1840 he founded a trading house in Paris "to engage in banking business, acting as an intermediary for all sorts of merchandise and for commissions". One year later, he entered into partnership with William Kinen (1819–1882), a Frankfurt banker who was originally from Moscow. In June 1861, the bank of A. Dutfoy, Kinen & Co. served as intermediary for an exchange of precious metals valued at 31 million francs between the Bank of France and the Russian State Bank, which wanted to mint silver coins. Separating from Kinen in 1863, Dutfoy became a partner of Henri Lefèvre before becoming once again, in December 1865, the sole head of A. Dutfoy & Co., which had a capitalisation of 3 million francs, including 1.8 million contributed by four shareholders – significantly less than the 5,400,000 franc capital of the J. E. Gunzburg Bank, held in the Gunzburgs' own right. Dutfoy then began working with his nephew by marriage, Emile Hoskier, to whom he passed on his bank.[15] Grain merchants and bankers from Odessa, the Ephrussis divided their time between Austria and France.[16] Whereas the elder brother, Ignace, had settled in Vienna in 1856, his brother Léon took charge of the Paris firm in 1871, helped by his son Jules. Their cousins Michel and Maurice also ran a bank in Paris. Business ties and friendship soon drew the Ephrussis and Gunzburgs together. The Gunzburgs also had ties to four European banking firms, because all the sisters of Horace's wife Anna, eldest of seven children including five daughters, had married bankers: Théophile had married Siegmund Warburg of Hamburg, Rosa had married Joseph von Hirsch Gereuth of Würzburg, Rosalie had married Siegmund Herzfelder of Budapest, and Louise had married Eugène Ashkenasy of Odessa. In 1873, at the time of the crash of the Vienna stock market, the Gunzburgs were induced by Anna to come to the aid of the Herzfelder firm. "[The Herzfelder Bank] applied to our firm for help, but we found that it was, as it were, impossible," Sasha reported. "Then Mama declared that she would sell her jewels if her brother-in-law was driven into bankruptcy. Your grandfather [Horace] had to give way, and the liquidation proceeded in a suitable way."[17]

Everything depends on a banker's reputation: the value of his signature and the degree to which he can be trusted to respect his commitments are paramount. In St Petersburg, the Gunzburg firm had informally taken over the Stieglitz bank; the customers and partners it inherited from this renowned financial institution included the Rothschild bank.[18] Between 1860 and 1869, regular exchanges of promissory notes, coupons and drafts between the Rothschild bank and the Gunzburg bank give us an overview of activity at the time: in October 1861 the Gunzburg bank supplied various clients, including members of the Gunzburg family, with 200,000 francs' worth of capital drawn on the Rothschild bank;[19] in December of the same year it supplied 100,000 francs to their "friend" Benedikt

Goldschmidt [the banker], which Joseph Evzel asked him to "kindly receive".[20] As well as Goldschmidt, who was often involved, the operations mention the bankers Robert Warschauer of Berlin and L. Behrens and son; in December 1862 Joseph Evzel took advantage of his role as intermediary in a transaction between the Royal Bank of Würtemberg and the Rothschild bank to obtain, to his benefit, a contribution of 20,000 pounds sterling to a Russian loan of 1862. Designated by the Russian government to issue its bonds, the Rothschild bank controlled the sale of the securities. Joseph Evzel wrote:

> I have the pleasure of sending you the present message regarding a transaction I have made with the Royal Bank of Würtemberg in Stuttgart [...].
>
> The Royal Bank having informed me that it has given you all the details of this transaction, I am taking the liberty of asking you if you might wish to sell me, on the same terms, 20,000 pounds sterling of the Loan, on which I would pay you the exchange value between now and 1/13 July at the latest, while reserving the right to liquidate the matter before that date.[21]

The Gunzburg firm sometimes provided opportunities for the Rothschild bank's customers to participate in Russian transactions. On 23 July 1870, "at the request and on behalf of M. Henry Schilling of Moscow", Joseph Evzel sent "herein enclosed, by rail, a packet containing: 300 Nicholas [Russian Railway] bonds [and] 1,867 May 1870 entitlement warrants".[22]

For large financial enterprises the French branch was particularly useful. Two examples may be given: on 3 March 1870 Joseph Evzel was one of the forty-one subscribers to the capital of 25 million francs raised by Raphaël Bischoffsheim to found the Franco-Egyptian Bank in agreement with the Turkish viceroy in Cairo, initially with the goal of renegotiating Egypt's debt, but also of placing the Ottoman loans;[23] and in the spring of 1877, Joseph Evzel was involved in the very lucrative business of a new Russian loan. Whether they were traded openly on the stock market or behind the scenes (for unofficial listings), state loans drew on foreign capital raised very discreetly for a group of initiates. The extant part of the correspondence provides a good illustration of how these bank contributions functioned. To meet the colossal cost of the new war against Turkey, Emperor Alexander II launched an "external loan at 5 per cent" of 374 million francs. On 26 May/7 June 1877, 750,000 bonds of 500 francs each were issued by imperial ukase.[24] Everything had already been arranged in advance: Reutern, the finance minister, had signed an agreement with the Mendelssohn Bank of Berlin, which undertook to advance the money to the Russian government until the banking consortium could raise the funds on the financial market.[25] To collect this sum, the German bank worked with Dutch and French bankers: MM. Lippman, Rosenthal & Co. in Amsterdam and the Comptoir d'Escompte in Paris (CEP). The latter, a rival of the Rothschilds, took advantage of the tensions between Russia and Britain to dislodge the famous Anglo-French firm, which was accustomed to place Russian loans in Paris and London. In turn, the Comptoir d'Escompte put together a "bankers' syndicate" in Paris. For an advance of 75 million German marks, the commission was set at 0.5 per cent per annum – it was to be 1 per cent higher than the rate of advances on securities agreed by the Bank of Prussia. The syndicate consisted of Armand and Michel Heine (who had taken over Fould & Co.), Henri Bamberger (Bank of Paris and the Netherlands), A. Dutfoy & Co. (for Crédit Lyonnais) and Vernes & Co. Each of the participants was entrusted with a subscription of 6 million francs: to belong to the syndicate, one had to be well informed and well respected, and belong to the group of usual partners. On Thursday 3 May, Joseph Evzel declared himself a candidate at the Heine bank:

> Dear Sir,
> Baron Haber has just now told us that you are so kind as to wish us to participate in the new Russian deal. We agree, with many thanks, to make a contribution of one million francs.
> Please inform me if I should visit you tomorrow morning, and be assured of our discretion.
> Best regards,
> J. Gunzburg[26]

The son of the banker to the court of the Grand Duchy of Baden, Samuel de Haber was a friend of Joseph Evzel's.[27] Like the Gunzburgs, the Habers maintained business relationships with the grand dukes of Hesse: Maurice, Samuel's brother, was the co-founder of the Darmstadt Bank of Commerce. At first, Heine was not sure he could invest Joseph Evzel's million francs: "Baron Haber must have told you that it is not we who are handling the Russian deal; that we were asked to participate on the condition that we make a decision today before 4 p.m. I am therefore very sorry that the Baron has not seen you and that we did not know your wishes earlier, since I may no longer give anything, but I will see tomorrow morning if there is still some way to involve you, delighted as I would be, this time as always, to be able to oblige you."[28] The following day, Joseph Evzel wrote again: "Many thanks for the content of your letter of yesterday evening, please do not forget us this morning. Thank you in advance for what you are able to do for us."[29] The matter was satisfactorily resolved on 5 May: the Heines obtained an additional 1,200,000 francs worth of securities to be placed, which the Comptoir d'Escompte de Paris ceded back to them,[30] and Joseph Evzel was one of the nine partners chosen by the Heines. The latter subscribed for 2,050,000 francs, Haber and Gunzburg for 1 million each, and then Maurice Ephrussi and José Luis de Abaroa for 500,000, Cahen d'Anvers for 250,000, Beer and Salz for 200,000, A. Lapia for 200,000, Huilier for 150,000, and Eugène Denfert-Rochereau for 150,000. The assistant manager of the Comptoir d'Escompte de Paris, the latter preferred to act on a personal basis, dealing with a firm other than his own. On 1 June, Joseph Evzel made an initial payment of 400,000 francs by means of a bank draft on the Bank of France, followed by a second payment of 600,000 francs on 5 July. When the profits were distributed by the bankers' syndicate, the Heines received 8 per cent of the sums invested on 21 January 1878, 3 per cent on 8 February, and 2.98 per cent on 26 February, or "838,000 francs as profit on the first six million". Their advance – 3 million – was reimbursed between 26/27 November and 17 December 1877, giving them a profit of exactly 1,061,686.20 francs from tying up their capital for five months. Thus this brief period alone must have generated a profit of 13.98 per cent and an annual return, for 1877, of the order of 33 per cent. Such a profitable investment is not an everyday occurrence. On 28 November Joseph Evzel began to receive interest on the loan made to the Russian state. The final payment of 26 February 1878 must have found the Gunzburg house in mourning, because Joseph Evzel had died in January. In total, he received 1,313,861.70 francs, a profit of 313,861.70 francs. With its day-to-day transactions and one-off investments, the St Petersburg bank of J. E. Gunzburg, with its branch in Paris, was thus well integrated into European financial operations: in one generation, the Gunzburgs had become bankers, a family tradition that was to be perpetuated.

5

High Society and the Demi-Monde

ONCE THE SHOCK of the defeat by Prussia and the French government's brutal crushing of the Paris Commune in 1871 had passed, Paris more or less recovered its spirits and the Gunzburgs moved back into their home in Rue de Tilsitt. The Tuileries palace had been burned, and Napoleon III's court was no more, but social life resumed: "Last night there was a splendid party at the home of the richest of the Russian bankers, that of M. Gunzburg," *Le Gaulois* reported in its 24 January 1875 issue, under the heading "Echoes of Paris". Managed by the eccentric Arthur Meyer, this newspaper carried an eagerly read society column: "[Emile] Waldteufel conducted an orchestra of thirty musicians, joined by twenty singers. A Rabelaisian supper with all the first fruits of spring in winter. Dazzling gowns, diamond necklaces, flowers, oceans of jewels, nothing was lacking in this party's splendour. The dances, which began at 10 p.m., were still going on at dawn, which comes late at this time of year."[1] At the head of his musicians, Waldteufel directed mazurkas, polkas and waltzes (including the famous *Amour et printemps*). Among the guests were the financiers of Jewish origin who constituted the inner circle: among others, "Baron Reinach, M. and Mme Bamberger, Baron Max Koenigswarter, M. and Mme Louis Koenigswarter, Baron Camondo, M. and Mme Ephrussi, J. Stern, Raphaël Bischoffsheim, Armand and Michel Heine". Prominent Russians passing through Paris, such as General Count Muravyov, the famous conqueror of the Far East, are mentioned;[2] the aristocracy were not forgotten: for example, Count and Countess Lagrange, Count and Countess La Rochefoucauld, Montgomery, Count and Countess

Louvancourt, Marquis Saint-Georges and Count Langsdorf, the new president MacMahon's aide-de-camp; and lastly, the gauge of a highly successful party, a few famous names from politics, the arts and journalism: Symphorien Boittelle, the former prefect of the Paris police and the former head of Napoleon III's national police, the painter Henri Thomas de Barbarin, the jeweller Bapst, and the music critic Marie Escudier.

Seen by the Gunzburg children, these balls at the town house on Rue de Tilsitt were things of wonder: "[It] was fashionable to illuminate the house when one gave an evening party, and our house had a garland of gas lights on the roof for that purpose. Once or twice, choirs from the conservatory were hired to accompany the dances. I remember how when we were children we got up early on the day after the balls to see the last couples leave and we ran into the reception rooms to pick up the debris from the cotillion, which sometimes included bows, swords and shields, all made of cardboard."[3] In their refinement, such parties were not common, as is stressed *a posteriori* by Gustave Schlumberger in an assessment in which anti-Semitism breaks through: "This Jewish society before the Dreyfus affair without doubt outshone anything I had seen in terms of luxury and splendour. Except for a few of my very wealthy women friends, who lived in a world that was ultimately very shut-off, I saw nothing that came close to it. The Faubourg Saint-Germain, even the non-Jewish financiers, seemed poor in comparison. It was what might be called 'the period of plovers' eggs'. At the time, that was the most expensive dish. No great Jewish lady would have considered giving a dinner without offering her guests plovers' eggs."[4]

The tone was set by the aristocracy, whose customs were adopted by the new elite: in the Gunzburgs' home, though Rosa officially received on Saturdays, in reality it was her daughter-in-law Anna who received guests.[5] Joseph Evzel relied on Anna to make the family known in Paris society. The role of mistress of the house was not to be taken lightly: with her lady's companion, Anna drew up the guest lists, prepared the invitations and handled the logistics.[6] The Gunzburgs also invited guests for morning visits, to amuse the younger children: "Fashionable performers sang and declaimed on a stage. Berthelier, who made a name for himself at the Palais Royal, sang for us. Samary, who was still a student at the Conservatory, and was later famous at the Théâtre Français for his laugh, declaimed.

Mischievous little boys, we noticed right from the start that his costume, which was very modest, had split under the arm. Charton (was that his name?), the magician dressed as a chef, opened an immense pastry from which he produced gifts for everyone. Once there were *tableaux vivants*, in which the children of the house took part. The final scene, in Russian costumes, was a great success."[7] The Gunzburg house was famous for the variety and splendour of its receptions. Its owners now belonged to "high society", which was defined not only by its financial power but also by the adoption of a certain number of codes.

Subscribing to the Opéra was obligatory for members of Paris's high society. In the building the architect Charles Garnier had just finished, the masquerade ball given on Shrove Tuesday, 9 February 1875, aroused the crowd's curiosity: "To the usual Sunday attendance was added the extraordinary attendance of idle onlookers. At 11 a.m., people wearing black masks and clothes of all kinds emerged from the famed restaurants along the boulevard. From all the streets between the Faubourg Montmartre and La Madeleine emerged carriages that passed and re-passed one another as best they could. At the intersection with the Chaussée d'Antin, the traffic became almost impossible. Only when one reached the corner of Place de l'Opéra could one breathe again."[8] The Opéra had been transformed: a temporary wooden floor covered the orchestra to provide a space for dancing; the foyer had become an enchanted garden with banks of flowers and greenery; on the buffets, iced fizzy drinks and champagne were served. "The boxes were full, crowded with people." The Gunzburgs were not only among the eight thousand dancers present but were also counted among the celebrities: "It was a real Opéra event; all the subscribers were there, and we will not name them all," recorded *Le Gaulois*. "We spotted the Count of Paris, whose box was adjacent to that of Viscount d'Harcourt; then M. Agùado, MM. Schickler, De Clercq and Prince Sagan, who must have been happy to see his plan succeed with such good fortune and energy, the Rothschild family, the principal private secretaries of several ministers, etc. On the other side of the room, on the second floor, Count Laferrière, MM. Binder and Chennevières, whose boxes are next to one another, and M. Dreyfus; Doctor Mand, in whose box we believe we saw Théo, blond Théo, and some journalists, whom the doctor always welcomes; next to Doctor Mand's box, the box of the Cercle des Champs-Elysées, that of M. Gunzburg, Duke Fitz-James, M. H. Delamarre, the Sporting Club, the

Cercle de la Rue Royale, the Russian embassy, M. André, M. de Bastard, Count Saint-Sauveur, Princess Trubetskaya, M. Garnier and his family."[9] Armed with his orchestra director's baton, Strauss "made the temporary floor tremble"[10], for a memorable evening, to the beat of his famous waltz.

Like the nobles who divided their time between Paris and their original estates, the new financial elite needed a country house to uphold their rank: Simon de Haber bought the Château de Courance; Louis Cahen d'Anvers bought Champs-sur-Marne; Moïse de Camondo bought the Château d'Aumont; the Rothschilds were at Ferrières; Joseph Evzel thought about acquiring the Château de Maisons, Mansart's masterpiece, but in the end chose a more modern residence: the former officers' mess of the Imperial Guard in Saint-Germain-en-Laye. In the shadow of the Château de Saint-Germain, the house at 1 Rue Lemierre had been bought new by Napoleon III's guard in 1857. Joseph Evzel became its owner shortly after the war of 1870.[11] On the ground floor were the dining, reading and games rooms, while the mess's former smoking rooms were easily converted for the family's use. A service area in the basement was fully equipped with ovens, laundry and washtub.[12] An enormous cast-iron cooker, today covered with dust, remains as mute witness to tremendous feasts. On the first floor were apartments and bedrooms for family members, and on the second floor the servants' rooms. The garden was not large, but the surroundings were rural: at the end of the street, the gates of the chateau opened on to the royal park. Outings on horseback or in carriages made it possible to enjoy this superb countryside on the banks of the Seine. The young went riding, an elegant, virile sport, at their own risk, as Sasha reports: "I remember how in Saint-Germain we took my elder brothers home after the horses had run away and thrown them. Mama didn't turn a hair."[13]

Among the factors of social integration, hunting occupied a prominent place. In the Gunzburg family Ury and Salomon were crack shots. Salomon rented, with Michel Ephrussi, the emperor's former hunting grounds at Fontainebleau: both of them were described as "elite hunters" in the columns of *Le Gaulois*. On foot or on horseback, hunting put the new elite in contact with crowned heads, even if they had been deposed: Salomon was seen at the home of Monsieur and Madame Fabry, at the Château de Fromont, "in the company of LL. AA. [Leurs Altesses, Their Highnesses] Prince and Princess Joachim Murat, Prince and Princess Louis Murat."[14] Ury bided his time, organising a splendid hunt in honour of

Grand Duke Nicholas Nikolayevich, Tsar Alexander II's brother, at his Château de Chambaudoin, at Erceville near Orléans, in the autumn of 1879.[15] In this elegant residence recently purchased from the Marquis of Saint-Mars, the second son of Joseph Evzel lived nobly, combining French taste and Russian extravagance. A spectacular picture by Dmitriev-Orenburgsky, a renowned painter, immortalised the event:[16] pheasants, woodcock and other birds lie on the ground, while the hunters converse, gathered in a circle, holding their broken guns over their arms. They are fine looking, wearing tweeds, bowler hats and impeccable gaiters. One can almost hear the yapping of the dogs and the calls of the old huntsmen and young beaters. The centre of the scene is dominated by the imposing figure of the grand duke, a genuine colossus who impressed viewers at the Paris Salon of 1880 as much as his Cossacks, of whom he was a much-liked leader. On the right, Ury, with his long beard *à la* Tolstoy and his bulging belly, is a jovial host. In contrast, slimmer and more unassuming, Salomon looks very much the Parisian dandy. On the left, recognisable by his handsome squarish face and his white beard, is the writer Ivan Turgenev, a friend of the Gunzburgs. For the grand duke, hunting at Ury's home became a habit. Another regular guest, the painter Bogolyubov, sent Horace his memory of a similar day:

> I returned only yesterday from Chambaudoin, where your charming brother Ury Osipovich[17] marvellously received and served the grand duke Nicholas and his entourage – two aides-de-camp, Vonlyarovsky and Evreinov, and his physician, Shershevsky, as well as Dmitriev [the painter]. On your brother's side, the guests included Salomon Osipovich (but he was not well and did not come), myself and Popov, whom his Majesty calls "the governor". This is how it went: Friday morning at 8 a.m. we went to Chambaudoin by train, in a special coach fitted out with a lounge, arriving at 11 a.m. for a luncheon at noon. The weather was grey but nonetheless pleasant and in fact favourable, because there was a great deal of game that we flushed out, and the grand duke bagged fourteen roe deer. We got to the house at dusk, rested a bit and then had a superb meal and played billiards. At 10.30 p.m. we went to bed. We resumed the hunt at 10.30 a.m. It was a beautiful, perfect spring day.[18]

With 184 kills shown in the picture (hares, foxes and roe deer), the hunt was a success. Ury was a peerless host: "The grand duke was clearly satisfied and thanked your brother very warmly. The whole organisation was royal, as was the food and the excellent wines. There was an enormous number of attentive servants. Ury Osipovich acted as though he had nothing to do with it, and that was the most agreeable part of all. Ury had also set up a stable of trotters at Chambaudoin – at great expense, moreover, as with everything he did."[19] The management was entrusted to Mikhail Popov (who was present at the hunt), a former horse breeder from Russia who had left his fortune there, just as Ury was to leave his in his sumptuous amusements. "The pearl of this stable was a certain trotter, 'Polkanchik', which had won great prizes in Moscow" and performed brilliantly at the races at Vincennes.[20]

Another aristocratic tradition adopted by the Gunzburgs was the family portrait. In Paris or in Saint-Germain-en-Laye, representations of family members adorned the mantels. Commissioned from fashionable artists, some of these works have now disappeared, but others have been preserved by descendants or in museums.[21] Edouard Dubufe's portraits of Josef Evzel, Horace (missing) and Anna have already been mentioned; that of Salomon, which may also be by Dubufe, was stolen by the Nazis and has never been found. Portrait painter Léon Bonnat's relationship with the Gunzburgs began in 1874, as revealed in a letter dated 10 September sent to Anna:

Madame,

I have just received the letter you did me the honour of sending to me. I hasten to reply. I have not forgotten the promise I made you and I am very grateful to you for having been so kind as to remind me of it. Unfortunately, I still have not finished the work that I undertook for the Palais de Justice, and will not be able to put myself at your disposal before the beginning of the winter. Would that time be disagreeable for you?

As for the price of the three portraits, it would be twenty-five thousand francs, the dimensions being for me a matter of complete · indifference.

I assure you, Madame, that I regret that I am not able to put my time at your disposal sooner, and beg you to accept my deepest respects.

L. Bonnat[22]

Of the three portraits mentioned by the painter, only two have been listed: those of Anna and Henriette de Gunzburg, Salomon's young wife. Painted in 1882, the latter portrait has disappeared, but there is an engraved reproduction of it in the family archives. The correspondence between Bonnat and the Gunzburgs testifies to their cordial relationship, even if the letters often remain factual in character: a visit to the studio ("I shall be at home tomorrow and the day after tomorrow in the afternoon, between three and six o'clock, and I should be very happy to have the honour of your visit"[23]), news about the work in progress ("However, though I have written little to you, I have not forgotten you, and I have worked on the portrait as much as I have been able"[24]), regret at not seeing one another ("I found here, in Paris, the letter from Monsieur Marc [the son of Horace and Anna, who wanted to be a painter]. I also learned that the missive had been sent to St-Jean-de-Luz. During that time I was at the home of Madame de Montalivet. I regret that I was not in my country while you were there."[25] And when Anna died prematurely, Bonnat was deeply moved. He agreed to paint a posthumous portrait of her, which he completed in 1878, very successfully: in a traditional Russian costume of green silk (matching the colour of her eyes), richly embroidered with gold and fur, Anna looks entirely the distinguished aristocrat, to the extent, in fact, that the picture was mistakenly identified as being that of Countess Potocka and is now in the collections of the Counts Potocki in the castle of Łańcut.[26] With her hair dressed in a severe chignon partly covered by a black satin veil, she wears only one jewel, a beautiful golden pendant with an original motif: the beehive from the Gunzburgs' coat of arms. Bonnat also expressed friendly compassion at the time of Joseph Evzel's death in January 1878: "I share, dear Monsieur Horâce [*sic*], in all the sorrows that torment you. But it is said that to be truly a man, one has to have undergone them all."[27]

A friend of Bonnat's, Auguste Ricard had become close to the Gunzburgs. He painted a charming portrait of Anna. Inspired by the old masters whose manner he tried to replicate, Ricard devoted many hours to this work, but the result was deemed so disappointing that the Gunzburgs asked that the picture be destroyed: fortunately, the painter did not comply. On his death, the painting was bought by Bonnat, who exhibited it for a long time in his studio in Rue de Bassano, in memory of his twofold attachment to Ricard and to Anna de Gunzburg, and later bequeathed it, along with the rest of his collections, to the Bayonne museum.[28] In 1870 Ricard also depicted Rosa, Joseph Evzel's wife, making ribbons: this work has unfortunately been lost;[29] his portrait of Horace, which was considered a failure, no longer exists either. Other fashionable painters worked for the family: Alexandre Cabanel painted a good portrait of Ida, Ury's wife, a stubborn woman-child with a milky complexion, in a deep red Empire gown, against a background of Chinese motifs; Ury had himself painted by Ernest Meissonier, a sought-after artist who was particularly expensive (the work cost 15,000 francs[30]): this lost portrait was also among the spoliations of the Second World War.[31] And lastly, the famous sculptor Adam Salomon made a bust of Joseph Evzel that ornamented, before the Bolshevik revolution, the sacristy of the St Petersburg synagogue; it was later lost, probably in the storerooms of the Museum of the History of Religion and of Atheism created during the Soviet period.

Horace and Anna's numerous children often posed. Auguste Ricard's portraits of Babita at the age of three ("in a white dress, teasing a Scotch terrier with a bit of pastry, like the Strozzi child in Titian's picture"[32]) and Sasha at the age of six have disappeared. To keep the children quiet, the painter gave them eclairs. Mihály Zichy's portrait of Vladimir, recently put on public sale, shows a three-year-old tot with long blond curls wearing a satin suit, full breeches, lacy collars and precious slippers with pompons.[33] The atmosphere in the house on Rue de Tilsitt is discernible: the child has just picked up a doll and thrown his top on a Savonnerie carpet; in the shadows the gilded brilliance of a Louis XV armchair glows discreetly. The whole emphasises the refinement of the Gunzburg children's clothing: Anna "was always very elegant for her children, and we were very amused in the house when Louise or Babita told us that some ladies they knew, meeting them while they were on a walk, had lifted up their skirts to examine their undergarments."[34] There is another, less evocative portrait by the same painter, showing Louise at the age of fourteen. Hungarian in origin, Zichy was considered one of the Russian court's official painters: he had begun by illustrating the palace menus before keeping albums of the tsar's travels and hunts. He lived by turns in Vienna, Paris and St Petersburg. His bubbling wit made him an entertaining guest.[35] The Gunzburgs had commissioned him to create a series of illustrations for *Faust* and owned a few of his erotic sketches, a genre that had made his reputation.

Hence the Parisian elite's social codes were soon absorbed. Membership of high society also involved mastering good manners, and for young people that meant lessons in music, dance and drawing. It was an opportunity for the family to be in regular contact with interesting artists. Hugues Merle and Victor Chavet were responsible for painting, Camille Saint-Saëns and Jules Massenet for music. Massenet had been recommended by Madame Emile Oulman, Paul Fould's aunt and a great friend of Anna's. Sasha writes:

> At that time, Jules Massenet was beginning his career, giving piano lessons for twenty francs, and he took Marc, Louise and me (aged eleven) on as pupils. I can no longer say whether Mama also worked with him, but she probably did, because she played the piano and was always trying to improve herself in every way. For example, during this period she took part in the drawing lessons we had at home. [...] He [Massenet] was not content just to give his lesson; he tried also to make us understand the technique and meaning of the music. Our notebooks were full of emphases, exclamation points and marginal annotations [...]. Massenet gave us a course on the history of music. This took place in the evening with him seated at the piano, telling us the story and playing characteristic excerpts from the compositions he was analysing.[36]

Although he was very young, Massenet was very clever, which came through in his teaching. "One example among many: he analysed Verdi's *Aïda*, and when he came to the famous march played on the stage with a fanfare sounded by trumpets at least a metre long, he played it solemnly. All at once, a flurry of false notes – that, he said with a straight face, was the procession turning on the stage, which was always too small, so that the musicians never succeeded in keeping their trumpets pointed in the desired direction."[37] Like Zichy and other teachers, Massenet gladly took part in family dinners: he was so funny that he provoked irrepressible fits of laughter. Sasha remembered that "one evening at dinner, when he had made everyone burst out laughing, our valet Adrien, who was serving dessert, could not control himself, and, setting the fruit bowl on the table, cried: 'Ah, what a joker!'"[38]

Dancing was taught by Mademoiselle Michelet: she lived in an annexe and gave lessons to Louise, Anna and Horace's eldest daughter, her cousins and all their friends, "that is, to all the Jewish bankers' families in Paris".[39] Among the girls, one dancer in particular attracted everyone's attention: Henriette Goldschmidt, a girl of fifteen who was as beautiful as she was rich. The boys watched for her arrival, hoping she would look at them. Her portrait by Auguste Ricard is a faithful one: wearing a red ribbon in her clouds of hair, with her gracious neck and deep eyes, she is simply ravishing. The dancing lessons prepared young women for their debut in society, which was soon followed by marriage: Henriette quickly became the fiancée of Salomon, the youngest of Joseph Evzel's children and the last to leave the nest.

Men had their own social lives in which pleasure and business were astutely combined. They met in restaurants and cafés; the nineteenth century had fashioned a growing "masculinisation" of work and spaces that replaced the mixed court society of the *ancien régime*.[40] Thus they were led to frequent the "demi-monde", a neologism coined by Alexandre Dumas to designate this social group that was defined by the presence of courtesans and that also brought together financiers, artists and men of letters, great names and politicians. Paris was the capital of those famous "sophisticated parties" that literature faithfully described. From Dumas's *La Dame aux camélias* to Zola's *Nana*, by way of Maupassant's *Boule de suif* or *La Maison Tellier*, the courtesans or "great horizontals" were the queens of a society oriented towards pleasure.[41] They held salons, like one of the most famous, the Marquise of Païva, who received Paris's literary and social elite at her town house on the Champs-Elysées (the present-day Travellers Club). A Jew of Polish origin who had settled in Moscow, born Thérèse Lachman, she had no doubt met the Gunzburgs before she was suspected of engaging in espionage and forced into exile in 1877. Around the courtesans there formed, against a background of socialising, a network of interests and influences: a society of pleasure-seekers that included Duke Charles de Morny as well as Prince Trubetskoy and the bankers Charles Lafitte and Raphaël Bischoffsheim. Gilded youth and respectable elderly men thus frequented these women of easy virtue, not without attracting publicity. The financial milieu was particularly well represented: it is said that Berr Léon Fould was the inspiration for Balzac's Baron de Nucingen and that Raphaël Bischoffsheim was the inspiration for Zola's Steiner. While Zola the moraliser saw in the frequenting of loose women nothing but licentiousness and hypocrisy, there were clear professional benefits too. Courtesans and gambling, but also cafés, restaurants that opened late into the night, and clubs were a part of financiers' daily life.[42] The lifestyle offered to a mistress was a display of wealth intended to prove a man's credit and financial capabilities. The gifts were intended to be seen, and, better yet, be mentioned in the press. At a time when the Paris stock market functioned with a limited network of brokers, businessmen and bankers, "personal success was considered the best guarantee of their business acumen and the health of their investments."[43]

The Gunzburgs were no exception: both father and son appeared in the files of the vice squad, which recorded events in the demi-monde with a particularly well-developed taste for detail. At the age of eighteen, Salomon "committed such follies for Mlle Gervais [an actress at the Bouffes-Parisiens] that his father sent him off to Russia."[44] Joseph Evzel was aware of the danger: a few years earlier, Gustave Fould, the son of the minister, very infatuated with Mademoiselle Valérie of the Théâtre-Français, had fled to England before marrying her. But Salomon was able to reassure his father: on his return from Russia, the latter "gave him an annuity of fifty thousand francs a year. After making the acquaintance of Pépita Sanchez, he sought out his father and told him that, wanting to remain a respectable man, he could not make such a sum stretch to meet his needs, given that he had a mistress whom he adored, and to whom he wanted to give everything she might desire. His father was pleased by his frankness and doubled his annuity. This liaison lasted until the end of the Commune."[45] The message was clear: Salomon did not want to dip "dishonestly" into the bank's reserves, of which he was a signatory, to maintain Pépita. A courtesan whose fame had faded, she was a Spanish beauty "about 36 years old". The police kept track of her lovers, among whom were Henri Meilhac, Offenbach's famous librettist, Admiral Bouët-Willaumez, the explorer of the Senegal River, and the banker Ernest Fould, the minister's second son. But "for the past year, she had been kept by the youngest of the Gunzburgs' sons, a stockbroker, with whom she lives as if they were husband and wife." Salomon was a generous lover: he set his mistress up in "a magnificent eight-room apartment on Boulevard Haussmann" that "included an antechamber, kitchen, two reception rooms, a dining room, four bedrooms, and toilets for a rent of 7,500 francs"; she had five servants and had at her disposal five horses and two or three carriages"; in the summer, he lived with her in Chatou, in "a chalet costing around eight thousand francs. They gave dinners for thirty, and among the guests, who stayed several days, Caroline Assé, who lived in Rue d'Albe, was specially mentioned." The whole affair smacked of *La Traviata*, when the courtesan decided to live in the country with her true love. But unlike in Verdi's opera, household expenses were paid by Salomon. He showed his attachment in truly extraordinary gifts: "Recently, the young man had a magnificent horse sent from St Petersburg, a very valuable animal that he also gave to his mistress."[46]

Women who belonged to the demi-monde led roller-coaster lives: one minute clandestine prostitutes, the next high-flying courtesans. Before meeting Salomon, Pépita Sanchez had "for many years [...] been unhappy, and lived in a furnished apartment in Chaussée d'Antin". After opulence, poverty often returned: Blanche d'Antigny, the model for *Nana*, died destitute at the age of thirty-four. A police record recounts her burial in Père-Lachaise on 29 June 1874, and notes the presence of a Gunzburg: "Blanche [...] died yesterday evening from typhoid fever. She was buried the next day, and in her funeral procession were noted Laure Eymann, Berthe Legrand, Lucie Lévy, Louise Manvoye, Alice Régnault, Marguerite de Bosredon, Hortense Schneider, Lucie Verneuil, Pauline Nozières and Barté de Vaudeville. We also saw MM. Dolfus, stockbroker, Guntzbourg [*sic*], Alequier [*sic*], banker, the son of the Count of Cambridge [perhaps George FitzGeorge], and the actors Train and Dupuis."[47] It is difficult to say which Gunzburg came to honour the memory of the deceased actress: like his brothers Ury and Alexandre, who were notorious rakes, and like their father Joseph Evzel, Salomon frequented the demi-monde. In 1873, Joseph Evzel set up a young woman named Aria at 6 Rue du Bel-Respiro, currently Rue Arsène-Houssaye, not far from the Champs-Elysées: "It is said that she was raised with the aid of Monsieur Guntzbourg Sr, who subsequently sent her to boarding school where she acquired a certain education. Today Monsieur Guntzbourg is supposed to have made her his mistress, to the great dismay of his children. He keeps her in a very luxurious style, and not long ago he is said to have given her horses and carriages."[48] As for Alexandre, he was the lover of Sylvia Asportas, whom he had met at Pépita's apartment. According to the police reports, Sylvia was "a very pretty girl" who possessed "a great deal of wit" (the record notes), "aged 28, born of Spanish parents, but in France. For a time she performed at the Palais-Royal."[49] The informer added that Alexandre, who was married, lived separately from his wife (who resided, of course, in the house on Rue de Tilsitt). But Sylvia proved to be an unfaithful courtesan, and Alexandre a jealous lover:

> After living for several months with Mr de Ligondès, who kept her in luxury, Sylvia took up with Mr Gunsbourg [*sic*], who didn't let her lack for anything. He gave her enormous sums, rented her a carriage by the month, with which she went to the Bois in the most eccentric and gaudiest get-ups, and gave her address to the gentlemen who asked her for it and received them at her home during the absence of her lover. She frequented procurers and made assignations there. Finally Mr Gunsbourg, her lover, who was very jealous, demanded that she give him a second key to her apartment. She flatly refused; from that resulted a quarrel between them, and Mr Gunsbourg, learning that he had been deceived, ceased all relations with Sylvia. Before long she fell into poverty, her interior decorator had taken over her rent, her creditors descended en masse and seized everything she had, right down to her clothes and precious jewels.

For his part, in 1875 Ury was frequenting Stella Galineti, "a tall, beautiful blonde woman who had just arrived in Paris"; she was King Victor-Emmanuel II's former mistress...[50]

Although courtesans promoted, in their way, the family's integration into professional circles, marriages ensured the consolidation of the social network: thus for foreigners a twofold integration through women took place. Salomon's marriage was dictated by this high-society logic: the contract for his marriage to Henriette Goldschmidt was signed on 6 August 1877. She was the daughter of Benedict Hayum Goldschmidt and niece of Raphaël Bischoffsheim, both of whom were associated with the bank of Bischoffsheim, Goldschmidt & Co.[51] Like Mathilde and Paul Fould, they married in accord with the dowry system, with acquisitions as common property. To the marriage Salomon brought as his own property "furniture, clothing, linens, fabrics, jewels, horses, carriages and other objects for his personal use, the whole being worth 150,000 francs",[52] as well as a "sum of five hundred thousand roubles, nominal value, which he possesses in cash and as the value of his share capital and working capital in companies in Paris and in St Petersburg owned by him, his father and M. Horace Gunzburg for the purpose of banking and ·

financial business." Since "the current exchange rate for the rouble is declared to be 2 francs seventy centimes," his personal contribution thus amounted to 1,350,000 francs. In addition, his parents granted him a dowry of 1 million francs. In all, Salomon could thus count on 2,350,000 francs, or a sum almost identical to that granted his sister Mathilde fifteen years earlier. Henriette's contribution was smaller: "dresses, linens, fabrics, jewels, laces and other objects [...] worth 70,000 francs" and a "dowry of 400,000 francs" to be paid on her wedding day. In accordance with the custom, the contract was read and signed by friends and witnesses who had come to the Goldschmidts' home on Rue de Milan to celebrate the new union: we find the signatures of the Foulds, the Sterns, the Bischoffsheims, the Beers, the Hirsches, the Cahen d'Anvers, the Pereires, the Kanns and the Montefiores. We must note the presence of almost all the Ephrussis (Michel, Ignace, Charles), who were great friends of Salomon's, as well as that of Prince Orlov, the Russian ambassador, and the faithful Mathias Mapu, Joseph Evzel's secretary. The religious ceremony took place in the new synagogue on Rue de la Victoire.

When they moved into the house on Rue de Tilsitt, Henriette and Salomon made a handsome couple. Considered one of the most elegant women in Paris, the young wife was nicknamed "the pretty little baroness" in the columns of *Le Gaulois*. She indulged her tastes at the shop of Madame Virot, a fashionable milliner: "Baroness Gunzburg varies her pleasures between a Psyche bonnet in Chantilly lace which is a pretext for an outbreak of roses, and a lovely toque in pheasant-coloured velvet, bordered with feathers, with two large gold rings in the satin pompom on the side. The pretty little baroness, all pink and white, looks equally delightful in her little baby bonnet of pleated red grosgrain silk with its velvet ruffles and posy of daisies peeking out from the large bow at the front."[53] At the races, at balls, in Deauville, in Dieppe, her outfits often aroused admiration: "a pink dress in satin and tulle, with a necklace of diamonds and rubies", "green velvet trimmed with otter fur", "an embroidered sea-green dress, and hat with feathers and black pearls", "a brown dress with a jabot of cream-coloured lace, and a straw hat with a bow formed of yellow and red ribbons". Henriette was so popular that Salomon, to remove her from the assiduous courtship of the Duke of Morny's son, did not hesitate to take her to spend a few months in St Petersburg.

6

The Patriarch

"FOR MY BIRTHDAY, Grandfather gave me a travel clock with an alarm," Marc wrote to his father.[1] Sasha also remembered that among the gifts he received as a child, "the best naturally came from Grandfather, like the locomotive mounted on a tricycle, on which we made trips from one end of the apartment to the other."[2] In the house on Rue de Tilsitt, the children were kings, and Joseph Evzel proved to be an attentive patriarch. Just one of the letters he sent to one of his grandchildren has come down to us: "My dear David, your kind letter of 2 September gave us – your grandmother and me – inexpressible pleasure, informing us as it did that, first, the operation was a success, thank God, and second, that you at once began to regain your health."[3]

David had just had an operation on his eyes, and his grandfather recommended that he not tire himself with too much reading, the young man's favourite pastime. Although the young Gunzburgs were pampered, they were also properly educated. Descended from a long line of rabbis, Joseph Evzel had inherited an observant Judaism that set great store by the study of the sacred texts. He took care to raise his descendants as practising Jews: in his will, he even went so far as to disinherit anyone who abandoned their Judaism or their Russian nationality.[4] In his case, and this is worthy of emphasis, integration did not mean assimilation, on the contrary. The family was exclusively Jewish: as we have seen, in the Gunzburg household marriages were governed by a strict social code that only allowed for Jewish spouses, and the spouses were all Jewish, whether born in Russia or elsewhere. The matrimonial arrangements Joseph Evzel sought for his children would be rigorously followed by most of the next generation of his descendants. The Gunzburgs' circle of friends had the same priority: the Habers, Ephrussis, and Camondos were regular visitors to their home.[5] But between tradition and adaptation, the everyday life of an immigrant Jewish family in the Paris of the Second Empire involved making some compromises, or at least striking a new balance.

The Gunzburg town house lived according to daily orthodox religious practice that no one violated. Prayers were said morning and evening, during which the usual separation of men and women was respected:[6] "We prayed in the billiard room reserved for women and in the smoking room reserved for men. In this [room, decorated in the Moorish style] there was a statue representing an oriental slave woman who was almost naked, so it was covered with a carpet on Saturdays and holidays. The *hazan* was a young man with a very fine voice who sang *Hallel* ['Praise'] and the psalms to airs taken from Italian opera."[7] The form mattered little; Joseph Evzel urged his family to respect what was essential. There was no question of being late for this morning rendezvous: "We had figured out a way of taking off our shirts along with our waistcoats and jackets so we could put them on together the following morning. Uncle Jacques Rosenberg [who was the same age as his nephews] went even further: he put on his tefillin in the evening so that he would not be rushed in the morning.[8] Having arrived in a French capital that still lacked prestigious places for Jewish religious services, the Gunzburgs had got accustomed to worshipping at home, even on the Sabbath and holidays. "It was in this improvised synagogue that we received, one Yom Kippur, a surprise visit from a valet who had come to ask what we would like. It was the moment of the *moussaf* ['additional prayer'] and he was sent away, but he came back, saying that the bell wouldn't stop ringing. We thought the bell was broken, but it turned out that Madame Levine [Rosa de Gunzburg's lady's companion] had fallen asleep and her back was pressing on the button."[9]

Religion served to bind the family together; each week it joined Joseph Evzel and Rosa for the Friday evening meal, which the children's nurses and teachers also attended. With about thirty guests, the meals were rather lively: Miss Sheppard [the Rosenberg girls' governess since the 1830s] left the table if people decided to speak Russian in her presence![10] Thanks to the *shochet*, Monsieur Goldstein, "whom the [non-Jewish] servants called 'the sacrificer'," the food obeyed the rules of *kashrut*.[11] The cook,

Charlemagne, nonetheless prepared the best French cuisine (such as the *poularde aux truffes* already mentioned), but Rosa also liked to cook traditional dishes. The writer Octave Mirbeau (who later became famous as a valiant defender of Dreyfus), having witnessed a dinner at Rue de Tilsitt, noted the presence of Jewish customs at the heart of high-society Paris: "To be sure, the Israelites mix with the rest of society, getting along very amiably with the Christians; look at their salons, however, even the most elegant ones, even those most liberally open to everything that matters from a social point of view: they remain marked in a very characteristic way by the stamp of the race of the master of the house. I can still hear Mme Hirsch speaking Hebrew to her son the baron amid a great reception at the town house on Rue de l'Elysée; I see the dowager Baroness de Gunzburg having served at table, during a great dinner one evening, a cake she had made herself, in the Israelite manner."[12]

As a "dowager baroness" Rosa occupied a marginal place in the family's life. The move to Paris had been a trial for her; less well educated than her husband, she could not claim to have equivalent social skills. She also had to put up with the banker's amorous indiscretions. When, exasperated, she threatened to leave, Joseph Evzel had as his only resort his sister Elka Rosenberg, who was a wise counsellor: he "sent a telegram to [the latter] in Kiev, asking her to take the train to Paris immediately. Crises were so frequent that [she] always had her trunk packed."[13] But in the transmission of religious principles, Rosa's role was not negligible. Her grandson Sasha described her as "a very simple person, very pious, and very good-hearted. She spent her time praying, accompanied by her housekeeper, who often gave us candy and packages of nuts, and by a few other women. She [...] made by herself, with the help of her women, the great 24-hour candles of brown wax for Yom Kippur and the little ones for Fridays."[14] A few minutes before sunset, Rosa lit the Sabbath candles at Rue de Tilsitt. Louise Fould also remembered this maternal grandmother who "remained strictly faithful to her Russian habits, without wishing to adapt to her new French environment, even though the customs of a small Jewish village in Podolia could never be in harmony with Parisian life." If, privately, the Gunzburgs practised orthodox Judaism, social life required numerous deviations, which Rosa judged severely, as one of her granddaughters revealed: "She ate her meals in her apartment, and since she could not walk to synagogue on Saturdays and holidays, she spent part of them in prayer. At least that is what I saw when I went to see her. She was kind, charitable, received me lovingly, and stuffed me with cakes made from special flour and jam for which a different sugar was required. I've often thought that this touching loyalty to her religious duties made my grandmother morally superior to those of us who have sacrificed some of the same duties to social requirements."[15] For the young Gunzburgs raised in Paris, Rosa was the link with the original Judaism from which the family had emerged. The sole extant photograph of her shows an aged woman with heavy, ungraceful features, a caricature of an old woman who has grown rich. She was above all a devoted mother; for example, she cared for her daughter Mathilde, whose health was fragile, until the latter's death; she showered affection on her grandchildren, whom she provided with smoked tongue and cakes she had made for their long trips; she was especially attentive to the well-being of her granddaughters, to whom she bequeathed her goods; she also fully supported her husband in his charitable activities within the Paris Jewish community, practising *tsedakah*, giving donations to the most impoverished, with exceptional devotion.

For his part, Joseph Evzel was a great promoter of Jewish learning and culture in his Paris house. The heir to a distinguished intellectual tradition, he spoke impeccable Hebrew, an elegant mixture of the liturgical language and modern literary expressions, which he used in his correspondence, notably with his father. This fact is sufficiently rare to merit notice: Hebrew, replaced in everyday usage by Yiddish, was on the way to becoming a sclerotic scholarly language. Starting in the 1830s and 1840s, the emergence of a literary trend promoted the shaping of a renewed language. But among the Gunzburgs, the use of Hebrew seems never to have been abandoned. To avoid breaking with this family tradition, Joseph Evzel recruited in Paris expert teachers of Hebrew: a Talmudic scholar specialising in the Karaites and Hebrew and Arab antiquities, Adolf Neubauer worked for a few years at Rue de Tilsitt. His teaching even led to David, Horace's son, developing a scholarly vocation and becoming a respected orientalist in turn. Though a highly intellectual teacher, Neubauer was unfortunately a brutal tutor: having beaten Marc, the least scholarly of all the children, with his belt, he was dismissed by Anna, who would not tolerate corporal punishment. He had been Renan's collaborator for his *Histoire du peuple d'Israël*, writing the last volume, which was on Hebrew literature.[16] He then became librarian of the

Hebrew section of Oxford's Bodleian Library, and from there he remained in contact with the Gunzburgs.[17] Dr Kisch, the future chief rabbi of Prague, succeeded Neubauer as the Gunzburgs' Hebrew teacher. To prepare Sasha for his bar mitzvah, in 1876, Joseph Evzel recruited the first *hazan* of the Rue de la Victoire synagogue, Monsieur Naumbourg.[18] The chief rabbi, Zadoc Kahn, also occasionally came to teach the children religion.

Thus Joseph Evzel surrounded himself with men of letters who made the town house on Rue de Tilsitt a living site of enlightened Judaism. In addition to the Hebrew teachers, who were not only language teachers but expert Talmudic scholars with whom the master of the house liked to converse, he hired learned men from the Jewish provinces of Russia. Since 1857, Senior Sachs (or Shneur Zaks, 1816–1892) had been his official librarian. Located on the ground floor of the town house, the library was the heart of the house. Its nucleus was the original collection of books that Joseph Evzel had inherited from his father and brought from Podolia, which was continually being added to. Although the library was not composed exclusively of works on Judaica, such books constituted an essential and original part of it. In Paris, Ury was in charge of new acquisitions, and he was helped by Sachs, who drew up the annotated catalogue.[19] Manuscripts and incunabula of great value were thus carefully collected. A specialist in medieval Hebrew literature, Sachs was an attractive personality, devoted exclusively to his studies and to the Gunzburg family: he dedicated his edition of Ibn Gabirol's poetry to Horace and Anna on the occasion of the bar mitzvah of Gabriel, their eldest son, in 1868.[20] Before he was recruited by Joseph Evzel, Sachs had experienced difficult *Wanderjahre*, typical of those faced by young Jewish intellectuals in Russia, who were the victims of a twofold oppression, by the tsarist government and by Jewish communities who were resisting secularisation. Born in Zagare, Lithuania, he had been trained in Talmudic studies by his father before he discovered the works of Isaac Erter, who had been excommunicated for his interest in non-religious disciplines. Having joined the latter in Brody, in Austrian Galicia, where Erter was practising medicine, Sachs was forced by his parents, who were demanding his return, to break off his studies. Arrested during his journey, which was made without a passport, he was imprisoned for five months in Kremenets and freed thanks to the efforts of Isaac Baer Levinson, a central figure in the Jewish enlightenment movement. He then had the opportunity to study at the University of Berlin with the Romantic philosopher Friedrich Schelling. In addition to Hebrew and Russian, Sachs spoke German and Syrian. In Paris, he was in contact with the philosopher Salomon Munk, a professor at the Collège de France who was also a frequent visitor to the house on Rue de Tilsitt. Mathias Mapu, another figure typical of Jewish culture of this period, also shared the Gunzburgs' life: he had entered the family as Anna's French teacher at the time when the family was still living in Kamenets-Podolsk, in Podolia,[21] before becoming the private secretary of Joseph Evzel, for whom he served as amanuensis and intimate counsellor at the time when the family was establishing itself in Paris (1857) and in St Petersburg (1859).[22] He was the brother of Abraham Mapu, who is considered the founder of the modern Hebrew novel.[23] Living hand to mouth in the Russian provinces, Abraham Mapu envied the resources available to Mathias and Senior Sachs, as is shown by a letter of 1859, written in awkward French: "Since you introduced into your boss's house the unattractive S. S. [Senior Sachs], who tries to diminish everyone's merit in order to shine all alone, couldn't I be in his place? But you lack the energy and I live in obscurity and below what I deserve."[24] Originally from a suburb of Kovno, in Lithuania, the Mapu brothers were the sons of a poor *melamed* (teacher). In 1837, in Rossieny, where he in turn had become a teacher, Abraham had made the acquaintance of Senior Sachs. While his brother entered the Gunzburgs' service in Kamenets, he worked as a tutor for the Otapovs, a rich family in Vilna (Polish, Wilno; Yiddish, Vilne), where he was badly treated. Finally, in 1861, he also had the satisfaction of staying at the Gunzburgs' home in St Petersburg; and in 1867, when he was ill, his brother suggested that he join him in Paris, but Abraham unfortunately died en route, in Koenigsberg. Mathias worked all his life for the Gunzburgs, first for Joseph Evzel and then for Horace, and his son Max joined the family bank in St Petersburg: "On the one hand, the fidelity of old Mapu, and on the other the gratitude of our family, knew no limits. Just as old Mapu lived very near us his whole life, so his tomb in the Montparnasse cemetery is adjacent to ours."[25] At the heart of Parisian luxury, among Gobelin tapestries and malachite collections, a small, almost secret Jewish and Russian literary coterie existed.

In this highly intellectual atmosphere the Gunzburg children were also encouraged to receive a Western-style education: access to instruction, officially limited for Jews in Russia, was one of the reasons for the decision to reside permanently in France. Before the 1870 war, the eldest of the boys had been enrolled at the Lycée Condorcet, which was then called the Lycée Bonaparte; later on, no doubt out of distrust of republican schools, instruction took place exclusively at home. In the room designated for that purpose, a series of teachers visited every day except Saturday: Jules Labbé, an alumnus of the Ecole Normale, taught French, history and classical languages; Robert Rohmann, an engineer by profession and a native of Odessa, was the head tutor; he supervised everyone's work, gave Russian lessons, and did not hesitate to programme visits to factories to awaken a taste for technology. Having fallen in love with Louise, the eldest of Horace's daughters, he had to leave his position;[26] the young poet Nikolay Minsky (his pseudonym was Vilenkin) took his place for Russian lessons; Madame Delaporte, of the Théâtre français, was in charge of elocution;[27] the painter Pokhitonov also gave lessons on Russian and, curiously, mathematics. Instruction was thus organised as they thought best, and included inevitable moments of pandemonium: "In the classroom there were always at least four of us, and we had figured out how to make spitballs and throw them at the ceiling. They stuck perfectly, and it was a very appealing sport. Soon Mark had the idea of cutting out little paper figures and attaching them to strings. [...] The ceiling became populated by puppets that fluttered agreeably when the teachers opened the door to come give their lessons. They did not think of looking up at the ceiling, and we had the satisfaction of having a visible secret toy, so to speak."[28] The balance struck by Joseph Evzel between traditional Jewish culture, Western education and an attachment to Russia instilled an unusual spirit in the family, giving his descendants shared core values that time would not erase.

The dream had become a reality. At the heart of the most beautiful city in the world, the Russian-Jewish immigrant had given his name to a magnificent private town house and from his office windows he could contemplate the Arc de Triomphe, where his grandchildren took pleasure in seeing their name engraved in stone: the inscription "Guntsbourg" adorns the eastern pillar of the famous monument, among the names of the 158 glorious battles of the Napoleonic armies.[29] This was a simple geographical coincidence: Joseph Evzel's ancestors had taken the name of the city in Swabia from which they came. But just when everything was going so well, a cruel blow struck the family: while giving birth to her eleventh child, Anna died. After her death, nothing at Rue de Tilsitt was ever the same again. Even as a child, she had been the pride and joy of her parents, Elka and Heshel Rosenberg: once, on a journey across Russia, families and servants travelling in three carts, the little girl had been forgotten when they stopped at an inn. By the time they had noticed and returned to the inn, the child had been taken away by a Baltic baron who, the innkeeper told them, finding her so charming, had decided to adopt her. He had left his address so that her parents could reclaim her, should they return. The whole family went to Riga to get Anna back.[30] When she was seven, "her toys were taken away from her so that she could care for her brothers and sisters, being the eldest."[31] When she reached marriageable age, her mother was so concerned to find the right man for her that she opted for a close relation about whom she felt sure: her first cousin Horace, Joseph Evzel's third son, had thus been the happy choice. Many years later, a letter from Anna to Horace shows the tender intimacy shared by husband and wife:

> My dear Horace, I am adding a few lines to the letter that David wrote yesterday. I wrote at length to your father, and, since I was tired today, and for good reason, I spent much of the day in bed, so that I have little time left to chat with you if I want the letter to be sent today. [...] I don't plan to go out again tomorrow, so I shall have to fill pages, [and] if it is to you that they are addressed, I have only to let my heart talk freely and they will become countless. Yet I need not say anything to you. You must know everything I know, everything I am, everything I feel. So when I am near you I do not need to speak and often remain silent. Your Anna.[32]

For her children, Anna was a loving mother, by turns accomplice, nurse, and educator. Shortly after their arrival in Paris, Horace had received an invitation to dine with Emperor Napoleon III. For the occasion, a gown had been ordered from the House of Worth; a few hours before the dinner, a dresser had delivered the gown, which had to be laced to fit perfectly. Once she was ready, "Anna came downstairs to keep her children company as they ate their meal. One of them exclaimed: 'You're so pretty, I'd like you to stay with us.'" Deeming it more important to honour her children than the court at the Tuileries, Anna succeeded in convincing Horace to go to the imperial dinner alone.[33] While they were still very little, she took the children to the Opéra, and spent Saturday mornings with them in her bed.[34] When her eldest daughter, Louise, had measles, she offered her own face and hands for Louise to scratch. She was equally devoted to all those she loved: in 1872, when her mother Elka had pneumonia in Kiev, Anna, taking with her two of her children, who were still nursing, left the same evening, the day before Rosh Hashanah. She was not a high society lady but in Paris she played to perfection her role as mistress of the house, not hesitating to stand up to her father-in-law, of whose loose morals she disapproved. One day when Joseph Evzel was urging her to leave Menton for Paris on the occasion of a ball, she learned that her father-in-law's lover, Madame Benardaki, was to be there, and she refused to play hostess; and when Madame Benardaki was given an equipage with the same livery as hers, she stayed away from the capital for three years, until Joseph Evzel put an end to this relationship.[35] Menton was her favourite holiday resort: a photograph from 1867 shows her surrounded by her husband, her children, one of her sisters and her mother in front of the villa rented by the Gunzburgs. The composition is vividly true to life: a smiling baby on her lap, three children on one side, three on the other, with Horace behind her, Anna is clearly a mother and a satisfied woman. Every spring, she met her close friends Alice and Mathilde Oulman in Menton. Failing that, she spent her time with a few ladies who, like her, came from Russia: Mesdames Varshavskaya and Lyubov Kanshina. Her charm attracted general affection. But she thought the finest compliment she ever received was the one paid to her by a little Parisian boy at the time of the Hôtel des Trois-Empereurs: "She was running errands under the Arcades on Rue de Rivoli when there suddenly appeared in front of her a little boy playing with a hoop, who stopped dead, crying: 'Oh, what a pretty lady!'"[36] Talented people liked her: remember the esteem the painters Bonnat and Ricard had had for her. A similar sentiment was expressed by the composer Modest Mussorgsky in a letter addressed to his friend, the art critic Vladimir Stasov, about his Hebrew chorus *Josué Navine*: "If your memory is good, you will remember that during one of the artistic soirées that were held at your place the marvellous Baroness Anna Hinzbourg [*sic*] recognised it as authentic."[37] The young woman's death left a void that was difficult to fill.

"One Saturday morning, 9 December [1876], Monsieur Rohmann (*sic*) came into our bedroom earlier than usual, had us hastily dressed, and took us to Mama's room. Stretched out on her bed with a blue ribbon around her neck, Mama seemed to be sleeping. Papa was sitting at the foot of the bed. She was dead."[38] In accordance with popular custom, their grandmother Rosa attached a napkin to the deathbed and put a bowl filled with water on the floor. "That was, she explained to the children, for the angel of death, so as not to irritate him if he came during the night and might conclude that no one had thought about him." The newborn child was given her mother's name, but was called only by her diminutive, Aniouta. She was an easy baby who brought a certain comfort to her father, who often spoke of her in his letters: "We believe that Aniouta will [soon] have a tooth, not against the people around her, but to bite and to eat, she is becoming very interesting and is in marvellous health."[39] The portrait of Anna by Bonnat was also a cause for satisfaction. "Bonnat is going to paint a very beautiful portrait of our deceased," Horace wrote. "It looks like her and when he returns in September he will have only to touch up a few places and everything will be done."[40] But behind the attempt to put on a brave face, the family remained inconsolable and an era had come to an end. Horace and his children were soon to leave France and go back to Russia.

The "marvellous" Anna was thus the first to find her place in the Gunzburgs' mausoleum in the Montparnasse cemetery. Fitted with a massive bronze door whose "Florentine patina" remains impressive, the "575th perpetual concession of 1872" stacked six tombs vertiginously on top of each other, each with twelve berths, making seventy-four [*sic*] places in all. With its elegant, pyramidal roof, two solid columns in pink marble, and decoration of flowers, garlands and crowns, it is an admirable monument of funerary art: the inscription "Gunzburg Family" appears in both Hebrew and French. In financing this vast mausoleum, which is still today the largest in the cemetery, Joseph Evzel asserted his dynastic ambition. Despite his attachment to Russia, it seemed to him wiser to gather his family's dead on the banks of the Seine: history has proved him right.

Part II

The Time of Battles: In Tsarist Russia

> But glory to the just man who is the son of the just! He wears a double crown on his head and God has said in his immortal Decalogue: "I reward parents in their children down to the thousandth generation."
>
> Lazare Isidor, chief rabbi of the Jewish Consistory of France, "Remarks made at the tomb of Baron Joseph de Gunzburg"[1]

7

Rabbis in Swabia and Lithuania

JOSEPH EVZEL MAY never have set foot in the small town of Günzburg, in Bavaria, from which his family came. The very idea of a pilgrimage in search of his ancestors would probably never have occurred to him. Resolutely of his own time, he looked towards the future. He adopted the manners of those who, having started from the bottom, proudly took possession of the place they had conquered, acknowledging that they were "newcomers" or, as they were then called, "parvenus". But although he embodied a new phenomenon, he was nonetheless descended from a distinguished family line. To be sure, in Parisian salons it might not have been opportune to boast about a genealogy of famous Talmudic scholars going back fifteen generations. Joseph Evzel took care not to make any allusion to them. But within the family or the community he was not averse to references to these prestigious ancestors, as is shown by the posthumous homage paid to him by the chief rabbi, Lazare Isidor:

And where did he find those great thoughts, those ideas of devotion and sacrifice, that holy ardour for his faith and for his worship? He found them in his heart, in his intelligence, in his sacred knowledge, and he found them especially in his family's traditions. He came from one of the most honourable, most esteemed families; his ancestors included the most illustrious rabbis, and above all Loeb, the chief rabbi of Prague, whose name had become legendary and whose memory is surrounded by a halo of holiness even today! Gunzburg was proud of this origin, this title of nobility![1]

Down to and including Joseph Evzel's father, all the Gunzburgs bore the title of rabbi. Joseph Evzel himself engaged in many efforts to encourage Jewish studies and faith. And although the genealogical connection with Rabbi Loeb of Prague, also known as the Maharal,[2] who lived in the mid-sixteenth century, cannot be proven with certainty, it repeatedly fed the family's self-image. Sasha, Joseph Evzel's grandson, remembered going with his mother to meditate at the rabbi's red sandstone tomb in the old Jewish cemetery in Prague. Rabbi Jehuda Loeb is a landmark figure in Judaism. He embodies religious erudition par excellence: his ability to approach divine omniscience won him a reputation as a miraculous master. Legend reports that he had fashioned from clay a living creature, the Golem, who breathed and moved but lacked intelligence and soul, which are divine attributes. He served the rabbi but could not control his movements: a pitcher had to be taken from his hands before he literally threw it on the table! Mentioned in Talmudic literature, the golem, a prefiguration of the robot, subsequently inspired Jewish folklore and even fantastic culture (down to his avatar, the Terminator).[3] It is also said that Rabbi Loeb lived to a ripe old age (almost one hundred) because the angel of death could not take him when he was studying sacred texts, and the Maharal never stopped working.

Generally speaking, Joseph Evzel's ancestors won fame by their intellectual qualities, though some were also astute businessmen, and most married into prestigious families. These three attributes sufficed to distinguish them from other people and to ensure that some ancient biographical information regarding them has been preserved. The chief rabbi of France was not exaggerating when he said that the Gunzburgs were truly "the most illustrious rabbis" in Swabia and Lithuania. From this family past, which is difficult to reconstitute precisely because of a lack of documentation, emerges the atmosphere peculiar to the Jewish communities of eastern Europe in the modern era, which were shaped by Talmudic culture at a time when printing was renewing this ancestral knowledge: in 1523, in Venice, Daniel Bomberg published a monumental edition of the *Babylonian Talmud*, the product of several centuries of study.[4] Each city that had a large Jewish community also had its yeshiva, where the teachers taught the Talmud and Torah and their commentaries and delivered their own interpretations. The rabbis' abilities and authority were defined by their knowledge. Talmudic knowledge is the product of constant study and interpretation of sacred Jewish texts. Joseph Evzel could pride himself on an ancestry of learned men, in the strongest sense of the term.

Rabbi Simon Gunzburg has been identified as the first bearer of the name.[5] Born in 1506, he died in 1585, at the age of eighty, "rich in years", according to the expression used by the genealogist David Maggid, who in 1899 published a work on the Gunzburgs.[6] Although it was probably financed by the family, Maggid's work is not a commissioned genealogy fabricated to please the "barons de Gunzburg"; the scholar produced a meticulous compilation of sources found in the archives of synagogues and Jewish communities: *pinkas* (registers), the records of rabbinical tribunals, funerary inscriptions, chronicles – materials that today have often disappeared. From Bavaria to Russia, Maggid tracked down the Gunzburgs: as they changed their place of residence according to political and economic circumstances, they moved in an environment that was at times German-speaking and at times Polish-speaking. On the map of central and eastern Europe their itineraries zigzagged and circled, a reminder that Jewish destinies are woven from instability. The Gunzburgs were descended from the medieval Jewish community of Germany known as Ashkenazi, formerly made up of Jewish migrations within the limits of the Roman Empire. Their cradle was in Swabia, a region attached to the Duchy of Bavaria, which was ruled by members of the House of Wittelsbach.

Simon thus spent most of his life in Günzburg, his native city, ranging out over a vast territory to conduct his private business and his public role in the Jewish community. The use of the family name Gunzburg indicates his social status: only people of honourable standing, mentioned in chronicles and official documents, were endowed with a family name, an unusual phenomenon in Judaism, which normally used patronymics, and where he is known as Simon ben-Eliezer, "the son of Eliezer". Hence the use of a family name is a mark of having joined the non-Jewish elite. The Gunzburgs are one of the oldest Jewish families known by their family name, even though the latter was subject to a few variations: sometimes it became Gunzburg-Ulmo or Ulmo-Gunzburg, and sometimes it even disappeared for a generation in favour of another name. Simon was not only one of the wealthiest businessmen in Swabia, an opulent Bavarian province, but also the Jews' elected representative to the Bavarian authorities for almost forty years, from 1543 to his death in 1585, on 8 Shevat 5345, according to the *Memorbuch* of the Jewish community of Pfersee, in which his name is mentioned in capital letters (as was the custom for rabbis), immediately after the usual list of the twelve martyrs of the First Crusade in 1096. Although Günzburg was then the seat of the central rabbinate, Simon also had a representative and an agency in the town of Pfersee, near Augsburg, the duchy's capital, which was forbidden to Jews. "In his time, there was no German Jew more influential than he was," wrote his contemporary David Gans in his chronicle *Zemach David*, published in Prague in 1592. Before him, his father Eliezer had acquired a certain renown: he was a native of Ulm, from which Jews were excluded in 1499, which explains why the family settled in Günzburg. Versed in medicine, he is mentioned as the physician of King Ferdinand's daughter in Innsbruck in 1534, and at the imperial court in Vienna in 1545, where his feats made him indispensable despite the opposition of some of his colleagues.[7] Eliezer had obtained a pass for himself and his sons from King Ferdinand, who was at that time the archduke of Tyrol and the brother of Emperor Charles V.

Within the Bavarian Jewish community, Simon worked not only for freedom and security for Jews but also for the consolidation of their culture. In particular, he contributed 8,000 florins to pay for the edition of the Talmud undertaken by the Basle printer Probus in 1578–81. This edition appeared after Pope Pius IV authorised the publication of the Talmud again (it had been prohibited by Julius III), on the condition that "passages offensive to Christianity be omitted from it".[8] Overseen by the censors, the Basle edition thus offered a "mutilated" Talmud that had been deprived of certain expressions. But in 1592 Pope Clement II banned the Talmud again. Although he was a Talmudic scholar, Simon was equally engaged in the study of secular subjects, such as mathematics and astronomy. In the course of his journeys he was in contact with the learned men of his time. In this tense context of Judeo-Christian relations, Simon sought to uphold his religion and his traditions. In the 1560s, he had the first Jewish cemetery in Swabia established at Burgau, on the Mindel River, not far from Günzburg, where he was later buried, along with his wife and some of his children, and where one of his sons was to finance the construction of a synagogue.[9]

Simon's immense fortune probably had its source in the river trade between Bavaria, Austria and Bohemia, that is, in the basin of the Danube and its tributaries. "His enormous fortune aroused envy and his success won him many enemies."[10] Various documents testify to his opulence, such as the loan granted to Cardinal Otto of Augsburg[11] for the construction of his episcopal see in Dilligen. The subsequent lawsuit between Simon and Otto's successor, who refused to honour the debt, attests to this loan. Simon was involved in another famous dispute: from 1564 to 1571 he had to sue his former representative, Nathan Châtin, arousing a fierce polemic between the rabbis of Frankfurt and those of Swabia, and requiring the intervention of the famous rabbi of Worms and even the duchy's non-Jewish authorities. Nathan had left the agency in Oberhausen to go to Frankfurt, depriving Simon of his share, which amounted to three-quarters of the profits and assets.

Simon married Hendele, who died in Günzburg in 1594 and was also buried in Burgau. She was a daughter of Rabbi Isaac ben Eljakim Linz, a renowned teacher at the Frankfurt yeshiva. His mother was Schönle, the daughter of Asher of Ulm. The given names Isaac Eitsik and Asher were subsequently often used by their descendants. The Gunzburg and Ulmo families were connected as early as the beginning of the sixteenth century. Simon and Hendele had many children, of whom eight boys and seven girls have been identified. Those who settled in Pfersee are famous for having owned the most complete manuscript of the Babylonian Talmud, which dates from the fourteenth century and is today the property of the Bavarian state library in Munich.[12] Not all of Simon's children enjoyed happy marriages: the records of the rabbinical tribunal of Günzburg testify to the conjugal quarrels that Simon had to resolve. Two of his children, a son and a daughter, had to cope with divorces that were all the more complicated because their in-laws were well known and respected.

There were apparently no such matrimonial difficulties for Joseph Evzel's ancestor Asher Aaron Ulmo-Gunzburg (1535–1603), a man about whom we know little except that he was noted for "his loyalty, his intelligence, his generosity and his knowledge".[13] A respected rabbi from Swabia, he succeeded his brothers Moses and Eliezer at the paternal trading agency in Pfersee.[14] His son Jacob Gunzburg-Ulmo was a widely esteemed teacher who married his first cousin; she was the offspring of the prestigious marriage of Jacob's paternal uncle Eliezer, Simon's eldest son, with the daughter of the extraordinary rabbi Moshe Isserles (1522–1572) known by the acronym Rema. This marriage showed that Simon and his descendants belonged to the Ashkenazi elite. Rema's father, who was banker to King Sigismund II Augustus, had commissioned the construction of a synagogue in Cracow, named "Rema" in honour of his son, which is still visible today. Jacob is recognised as one of the "definitive" codifiers of Jewish practice: in his work *ha-Mapah* (*The Tablecloth*), he composed crucial additions to the *Shulkhan Arukh* (*The Set Table*) written by his teacher Rabbi Yossef Karo (1488–1575). This work on Hebrew law, presented with Rabbi Isserles's commentaries, still serves as a guide in the domains of religious life, food prescriptions, family law and financial practices.[15] And in the lawsuit that set one of Simon Gunzburg's daughters against her in-laws, it was this very same Rabbi Moshe Isserles who proved the validity of the divorce contested by the former husband even though the young woman had already remarried.[16] The Isserles and Gunzburg families were thus closely related in several ways. Jacob proved himself worthy of such a connection: as a rabbi in Friedberg in Bavaria and in Friedland in Bohemia, his interpretations of the Law were much sought after. He received the honorific title of *gaon* in recognition of his wisdom and moral authority. Among the many students at his yeshiva, some became important commentators, such as Yom-Tov Lipman Heller, the author of *Tossefot Yom-Tov* (a commentary on the Mishna).[17]

A rare, richly embroidered cloth made in honour of the circumcision of one of Simon's grandsons, bearing the boy's name, that of his parents and the usual good wishes, also dates from this period.[18] The silky fabric in bronze tones depicts a partly figurative scene: alongside the child and the *Mohel* the parents are shown in the rich attire of the period. The father wears a greatcoat and a plumed beret; his wife wears a fine gown with puff sleeves. The presence of a synagogue also attests to the family's involvement in community life. Various ornaments (a bestiary, stars, greenery) complete the whole. This embroidered fabric provides, in a moving way, the Gunzburgs' first "family portrait" and at the same time constitutes an interesting testimony to Jewish life in Swabia in the early seventeenth century.[19]

Simon, Jacob's son, also known as Simon Schatles, an eminent community authority and also a *gaon*, settled in Frankfurt. In the complex web of the German Holy Roman Empire, Frankfurt was at the time one of the most important cultural centres in Europe. There, Simon held the prestigious offices of head of the beth din (rabbinical court), administrator of the community, "school leader" and a member of the yeshiva. For his daughters Simon chose husbands from the best society: one of them married Nathan Grünhaut, the treasurer of the Jewish community of Frankfurt, to whom she bore a son, David, the author of *Tob Roi*, a work that proudly mentions grandfather Simon; a second daughter, who married Rabbi Abraham, also gave birth to a future scholar, the *gaon* David Oppenheim (1664–1737), who settled in Brisk, Lithuania, and was one of the great men of letters of his time. His library is now preserved in Oxford. Among Simon's sons, only Joseph Evzel's ancestor is known to us: in 1610, Isaac Eitsik gave rabbinical advice in Pfersee; he studied for a time at the yeshiva in Worms, a small city in the Palatinate, before being driven out in 1615 by the edict expelling Jews; he died in Rödelsee, where he served as a rabbi.[20] The situation of Jews in western Germany was increasingly uncomfortable: they were the targets of popular violence that grew with the unstable climate of the Thirty Years' War, which broke out in 1618 and divided Germany into two camps. Encouraged by the papacy, an anti-Jewish campaign at the court of the Habsburgs prompted many departures to Poland. The Union of Lublin (1569) merged Poland and Lithuania into a single kingdom.

In the kingdom of Poland-Lithuania, the rights and privileges conferred on Jews by King Sigismund III were ratified in 1632 by his son, Ladislas IV, and honoured by his successors. Between 1670, the year when Isaac Eitsik's son Aaron settled in Vilna,[21] and the birth in 1793 of Gabriel Yakov, Joseph Evzel's father, the capital of the grand duchy of Lithuania took in several generations of Gunzburgs.[22] In 1676, 40,000 Jews were living in the grand duchy as a whole, including about 3,000 in Vilna, or a quarter of the city's population.[23] In the Polish-Lithuanian sphere, several administrative tiers organised the Jewish communities as a whole: nationally, these communities were brought together from the sixteenth century onwards in the Council of the Province of Lithuania (*Vaad medinat Lita*), and then in the Council of the Four Provinces (*Vaad arba aratsot*), which enjoyed multiple juridical, economic and religious prerogatives. For example, the council was entrusted with collecting the taxes Jews had to pay to the royal treasury.[24] At a local level, the communities governed themselves under the supervision of a council, the *kahal*, that consisted of local officials, including rabbis and administrators (*gabaim* and *parnassim*), as well as notables (*gevirim, roshei hair*).

At the confluence of the Neris and Vilnia Rivers, the present-day city of Vilnius spreads harmoniously over hills surrounded by immense, leafy forests. Once one has passed through the Dawn Gate (a suspended chapel with its famous icon of the Virgin of Mercy), a series of streets leads down a gentle slope towards the city centre: first the main street, where Jews did not have the right to do business, and then, a few dozen metres further on, at the junction of the current Jew Street, Glassmakers' Street and Gaon Street, there is a small square that used to be the site of the Tolkuchka market, the economic heart of the old city. The streets are narrow and attractively paved with river stones. The brick houses, which are sometimes stuccoed, have a very provincial simplicity. A wooden balcony reached by an external stairway runs along the whole length of the facades to provide access to apartments. According to the "List of Houses in Vilna",[25] which was drawn up annually from 1715 onwards, at the beginning of the eighteenth century Aaron's descendants did not own such a residence; they probably rented from a *pan* (lord) or a religious community, the nobility and the Church being the masters of the city. The facades are interrupted by passages leading to inner courtyards that are now deserted. All of life was organised in these courtyards, which sometimes contained minuscule shops – a butcher, barber, grocer, baker, tinsmith, blacksmith, tanner – and also a *heder*, the primary school where children learned to read the Torah.[26] In the heart of the old Jewish quarter, Syrvido Square looks strangely empty: large trees, weeds, a basketball court and a kindergarten constructed during the Soviet period have taken the place of the great synagogue, which was damaged during the Nazi occupation and then destroyed by the Soviets. Completed in 1633, harmoniously constructed on five levels and richly decorated, it had been one of the biggest and most beautiful synagogues in Europe. The houses and streets that surrounded it have also been razed. Next to the kindergarten, a small archaeological excavation has uncovered the foundations of the *mikva*, a ritual bath used separately by the women and men of the family for regular purification, and especially on the day before Yom Kippur. The *shul*, synagogues and places of prayer, which were often associated with guilds, have also almost completely disappeared, as has Piramont, the Jewish cemetery along the river, which the Soviets transformed into a park and "sports centre" after the Second World War, allowing only a few tombs to be transferred to new locations. Constructed in 1971, the present concrete complex is now unused, while the park is neglected and its future a subject of controversy: property development is opposed by those who strive to keep the memory of Piramont alive. No tomb reminds the visitor of the presence of the Gunzburgs in the Lithuanian capital.

A commercial city and the administrative capital of the grand duchy, Vilna was also an intellectual city: the Jesuits had founded there one of the first universities in Europe and the monogram IHS (the Company of Jesus's symbol based on the first three letters of "Jesus" in Greek) still adorns this venerable institution. Its centre for oriental studies, which taught Hebrew, was particularly dynamic, and was intended to fuel Catholic theologians' debates and polemics with Jewish scholars. At this time, in the seventeenth century, the latter were so numerous in Vilna that the city was called "the Lithuanian Jerusalem". Aaron belonged to this intellectual caste: referred to as "Aaron, Vilna's political representative", he is mentioned in the region's records as an *ikorim* (delegate).[27] He was one of the three hundred Talmudic scholars who represented the city to the council of the four provinces, *Vaad arba Aratsot*.[28] The representatives were the intermediaries between the culturally closed world of the Jewish inhabitants and the rest of the country: they were competent in the two languages – Hebrew and Polish – and in the two cultures. A representative had to be capable of resolving not only religious questions but also economic disputes. Thus he had extensive knowledge of the exemptions granted: in addition to the confirmation of earlier rights, Ladislas IV (who reigned from 1632 to 1648) authorised Jews to engage in commerce in money, jewellery, goldwork, wood, meat and food products.

Among Aaron's children, Asher, also known as "Asher son of Rabbi Kalman of Vilna", was also a delegate to the Vaad from 1673 to 1687, but in his case, it was the *Vaad Medinat Lita*, which represented only Lithuania within the Polish kingdom. The period remained a dark one: a Cossack insurrection against the government, a war between Russia and Poland, and a Swedish invasion had been among the dramatic external circumstances that destabilised the life of the community. The Lithuanian Council of State collected per capita taxes for the Crown, but also all the community's internal taxes. It organised economic life, protecting trade and existing businesses, and intruded on all other domains: morality, education and *tsedaka* (charity). The political turbulence that was buffeting the kingdom directly affected the Jewish population: the military frequently targeted Jews and massacred tens of thousands of them. The Vaad, which was responsible for organising help and support, was also weakened. The grand duchy's anti-Jewish atmosphere, encouraged by the Jesuits and the guilds of local craftsmen, grew ever worse. In 1681, Jewish property and houses in Vilna were destroyed; in 1695, two Jews were executed after being accused of ritual crimes. External conflicts also weighed on Poland's future: at the beginning of the eighteenth century, the city was occupied by the Swedes and then by the Russians. Its economic prosperity collapsed. Jews had difficulty paying the taxes they owed to private property owners and to the Church. The community's life continued under very difficult circumstances. Asher's son, Isaac Eitsik, the administrator of the Jewish community in Vilna, was married to the daughter of Rabbi Moses Goldès of Pinsk: their son, Kalominos Kalman (c. 1690–c. 1758), married the daughter of a wealthy property owner, Simon, from Bialy, and had a son named Asher after his paternal grandfather. Perhaps in order to flee difficulties, they settled in Pinsk, where Kalominos Kalman presided over the community.

Asher returned to live in Vilna. An influential public figure, he was born around 1710 and died, "rich in years", in 1791. According to the genealogist Maggid, "he was one of the most famous wealthy men of this city and was renowned for his charity, his piety, his love of study, and the help he accorded all those who devoted themselves to it." He was a witness and an actor in a century full of upsets at a time when the Jewish community in Vilna was shot through with virulent religious and social antagonism. A contemporary of Elijah ben Shlomo Zalman, the famous "*gaon* of Vilna" (1720–1797), he witnessed both the most brilliant expression of Lithuanian Jewish culture and the slow decline of the kingdom of Poland-Lithuania until it was partitioned among the three neighbouring powers, Prussia, Austria-Hungary and Russia. From 1764 onwards, the Polish throne was occupied by Stanislas Augustus Poniatowski. His reign was initially supported by Empress Catherine II, but she ended up annexing Lithuania to her empire in 1795. Although he was well disposed toward Jews, Poniatowski could not prevent the disappearance of the council of the four provinces, which had been weakened by internal dissension. Deprived of an official champion, the Jewish population was a regular target for popular violence. Vilna had become a large agglomeration of more than 50,000 inhabitants. Among the 3,500 individuals listed in the *Review of the Jewish Population* in 1765,

Asher, son of Kalman, and his family are mentioned: "Asher Kalmanowicz Klaczko, formerly a member of the *kahal*, his wife Yuta and their three sons, Leib, Simon and Wulf."[29] The document adds that they live in the "Kalowey" house, on Yatkovaya Street (present-day Mèsini gatve), at the heart of what was to be, under Nazi occupation, the great ghetto, and where the Jewish Information Centre is now located. Asher was known by the family name of his father-in-law, the *gaon* Abram Aba Klaczko, out of deference to this eminent family, which included Rabbi Loeb of Prague among its ancestors, whence the Gunzburgs' connection with the latter. Other documents mention Asher: in 1761 a rental contract signed with the Carmelites mentions his fabric shop, which was located in a house on Schlachthof Street, which looked out over the market. Asher paid an annual rent of two thalers and undertook to cover maintenance costs. In this luxury trade profits were large: in 1779 he sold Lord Mikush 28,585 florins' worth of fabric to make clothes for the marriage of his daughter. In 1784 the whole Asher family seems to have been living over the shop, the building then housing thirty-three Jews, including employees and servants. Asher had two other houses or apartments on Glassen Street (currently Gaon Street) and Ashkenazi Street. The extent of his wealth is indicated by the size of the debt owed him by the community in Vilna: at 91,000 florins (with interest), it made him the biggest creditor, after the Friedländer Bank in Berlin.

His brother-in-law Perec Klaczko, described as "extremely rich",[30] is mentioned in the *kahal*'s account books for taxes paid in the silk trade.[31] Asher's marriage to Yuta proves once again that the Gunzburgs belonged to the grand duchy's economic elite. It also reveals a family tendency, rarely deviated from subsequently, to pursue successful matrimonial alliances. Like his brother-in-law, Asher was a member of the *kahal*, of which he was a *starshiy* (elder), no less, and more precisely the "treasurer-administrator".[32] In 1750, "although young" (about forty), he had already been consulted regarding the election of the new president of the rabbinical tribunal: the nomination document bears his signature.[33]

From the 1760s, Asher and his sons seem to have been the leaders in a battle waged by some of the community's notables and theologians against Rabbi Shlomo ben Avigdor. The latter had obtained his office as a rabbi after his father-in-law donated a large sum of money to the *kahal*, to which he later sought to name his relatives, provoking the anger of other members of the council. The supporters of the *kahal* and those of the rabbi engaged in a ruthless conflict that lasted more than thirty years and was recounted by the writer Samuel Joseph Fuenn:

> And the sons-in-law, relatives by marriage, those close to him and the friends of the rav among the major figures in the city rose up in anger and traded invective. The war took over the city, which was divided into two camps, one half in favour of the rabbi and the other half in favour of the *kahal*. Families fought with families, men quarrelled with one another, women quarrelled with one another, and people argued in the synagogues and the houses of study, in the markets and in the streets. They confronted one another in debates, exchanging words laden with hostility and threatening with fists full of malice.[34]

The magnitude of the quarrel is explained by religious divergences and rivalries over power, even though the political crisis in the grand duchy was general. Shlomo ben Avigdor did not hesitate to appeal to the voivode Razzivil, who brought a lawsuit against the *kahal* over the question of taxes. As the treasurer, Asher was at the forefront.[35]

Avigdor's supporters, mainly minor craftsmen and merchants, were, moreover, hostile to the *gaon* Elijah ben Shlomo Zalman, also known by the acronym HaGRA (*HaGaon Rabbenou Eliyahu* – Our Master Eliah the Genius) or by the nickname "*gaon* of Vilna". The Gunzburgs were related to him, and he was in general close to members of the *kahal*, not only for intellectual reasons: Asher's daughter, Malka, had married the *gaon*'s nephew, Yissakhar ber Klatzki.

With its numerous Hebraic print shops and its *yeshivot*, the "European Jerusalem" rivalled Amsterdam and the cities of northern Italy for intellectual activity. At that time, the Jewish world was shot through with antagonistic currents: the *gaon* of Vilna was the chief instigator of the *mitnagdim*, the declared "opponents" of Hassidism, a spiritual trend that was gathering more and more supporters in eastern Europe at the time.[36] Claiming an alliance of faith and reason, the *mitnagdim* were rationalists, rigorous, excellent exegetes in the Talmudic and rabbinical tradition, and open – with due caution – to secular culture, insofar as it enabled them to deepen their study of the Bible. They fought intellectually and, when necessary, physically, against the *hassidim*, "these mystics who are like leprosy on the body of Israel", as the *gaon* put it. More mystical, the *hassidim* relied on the inspiration that certain rabbis received from

Heaven, constituting a kind of intermediary authority between mortals and God, handed down from father to son. The intensity of the quarrels that rocked the Jewish community in Vilna in the middle of the eighteenth century left an enduring mark on the family memory. Joseph Evzel told how, in the fury of a religious dispute, his great-grandfather Leib, Asher's son, seized an axe so that he could strike the first *hassid* who crossed the threshold of his house![37] The Gunzburgs remained faithful to this religious spirit that derived directly from the *mitnagdim*, which was based on a good knowledge of Hebrew, study and reason. This religious concept led them in due course, as they progressively accomplished their own integration into the economic reality of the Russian empire, to become supporters of the *Haskalah*, the Jewish Enlightenment movement, which advocated opening up Judaism to non-Jewish secular culture.

Leib and his wife Hayé, the daughter of a rabbi from Sokolov, had four sons, one of whom was Naftali Herz, who became head of the Jewish community in Vilna, despite his extreme youth, and who died prematurely in 1797, leaving behind him a single son, Gabriel Yakov, born in 1793. To remind us of Naftali Herz, there remains a finely sculpted holy Ark bearing the legend, in German: "To Rabbi Naftali Herz Gunzburg [from] the community of the Sons of Israel of the city of Vilna."[38] According to Maggid, of Leib's children only Naftali Herz retained the name Gunzburg, his brothers taking the name Klaczko. They all embraced a career in commerce. So at the dawn of the nineteenth century the Gunzburgs belonged to the Jewish cultural tradition known today as *litvak*. As Jews of Lithuania, they are distinguished from *Galizianer* (Jews of Galicia), *Pollaks* (Jews of Poland) and *Roumeyners* (Jews of Romania).[39] The Jews of Vilna thought of themselves as the ultimate in Judaism, heirs to a great body of thought. Joseph Evzel's tranquil self-assurance in religious matters can be understood as the product of a familial and cultural heritage. His mastery of literary Hebrew is one of the ostensible marks of this. But his Swabian origin should not be forgotten, either: in addition to the use of German, which he and his descendants continued to speak until the beginning of the twentieth century, the intellectual heritage of the Bavarian rabbis influenced the family's values. In a universe subjected to new political realities, the family networks established in earlier times within the German Holy Roman Empire could still be effective. Drawing on this twofold origin, Swabia and Lithuania, Joseph

Evzel was aware that he belonged to the elite of the Ashkenazi world. Out of fidelity to this page in the family history, he continued to contribute funds to the Talmud Tora of Vilna, where his father, Gabriel Yakov, son of Naftali Herz, had received the title of rabbi while still a young man.[40]

8

Gabriel Yakov, *kupets* (merchant)

BORN IN 1793, Gabriel Yakov hardly knew his father, who died when his son was only four years old. We know nothing about his mother, Tebel Safra. Although an orphan, Gabriel benefited from a stable environment in the Lithuanian capital, all the more because the terrible quarrels in the community had finally subsided. In his grandfather Leib Gunzburg he found the support necessary for his education. His title of rabbi shows that he acquired a good knowledge of the Torah and the Talmud, but for all that he was not destined to become an ordained rabbi. His training allowed him to be considered a learned man, capable of providing interpretations useful for coping with family life, social relations, or occupational hazards, and, if the occasion arose, for joining the community's leading authorities. He grew up in contact with his paternal uncles, who were all members of the *kahal* (Jewish community) and energetic merchants: Mordecai Klatzki, "considered wealthy", owned a business that dealt in porcelain and rugs, which was to become a bank. Mordecai married his only daughter to the "extremely rich" Moses Halevi Rosenthal: years later, their son Lev Rosenthal, who had become a famed economist in St Petersburg, was to be one of Joseph Evzel's closest friends; Mordecai's brother, Josel Klatzki, was related through his wife Shana to the powerful family of the Katzenelenbogen.[1] When his grandfather Loeb died in 1808, Gabriel Yakov was a young man of fifteen ready to assume the role of head of the family. His *shidduch* (matrimonial arrangement) was a successful operation: in 1812 he married Léa, the daughter of Joseph Josel, a *nagid* (wealthy merchant) who lived in Vitebsk. He thereupon left

Vilna for good and moved to that little town on the Polish-Russian border, in what is now Belarus.

Only one image of Gabriel Yakov has survived, an impersonal, old-fashioned photograph, probably taken around 1850: bald, with a broad forehead and big eyes, a fleshy mouth, a flourishing moustache and a short beard, Gabriel Yakov is wearing a Western suit with a starched collar and an elegant tie that reveal that he is a member of the Europeanised Jewish bourgeoisie. A sepia daguerreotype of his wife Léa is more evocative: the harmonious plumpness of her face, sly smile, laughing eyes and beautiful, wavy hair worn up in a chignon all suggest a charm that we find again in their son Joseph Evzel. There was also an oil portrait of Gabriel Yakov, which has unfortunately disappeared. The mere mention of this portrait in an inventory made after his death shows that this merchant in Vitebsk had been successful enough to adopt the custom of the family portrait, an unusual practice among Jews in provincial Russia during the 1820s.

At that time, Vitebsk was a small, industrious town with a large Jewish community: about 3,000 individuals in 1808, or a quarter of the population, most of them craftsmen or merchants. The atmosphere was significantly less intellectual than Vilna's. The production and sale of linen, tobacco and timber, shipped down the Dvina River to Riga, spurred a great deal of trade. Little shops offered everyday consumer goods – clothing, fabric, hosiery, footwear and food – especially from Germany. The Jewish population also included numerous butchers, dyers, tailors, carpenters, bookbinders and goldsmiths who worked both copper and gold. In addition to these trades, there was also a Jewish printshop and a textile factory that produced in particular *tallits* or prayer shawls. Like the rest of the former kingdom of Poland-Lithuania, since the sixteenth century the community in Vitebsk had benefited from statutes of autonomy before being annexed to Russia in 1772, at the time of the first partition of Poland. At first, the status of Jews did not change, and the *kahal* continued to function as a local, autonomous governmental authority. But Catherine II (reigned 1762–96) soon had to introduce legislation: in the course of the annexations of Polish territory (after 1772, 1793 and 1795), she came to reign over the largest Jewish population in Europe (around 2.5 million people). She thereupon established the principle of the "Pale of Settlement", forbidding Jews to live outside the regions where they had already settled: parts of modern-day Poland, Lithuania, Ukraine, Belarus and Moldavia, to which must be added

Crimea, a vassal principality of the Ottomans that was conquered in 1792. In this multi-ethnic empire, the status of individuals was defined by which ethnic and social group they belonged to. The empress decided to include Jews in the newly created category of the "petite bourgeoisie" (*meshchanstvo*, from *mestechko*, village, or shtetl in Yiddish), or, in the case of the wealthiest, that of "merchants" (*kupechestvo*). The status of *kupets* (merchant) implied that one was on the registers of the First, Second or Third Guilds and paid an annual tax proportional to one's capital.[2] In addition to these two categories of "petits bourgeois" and "merchants", the empress's subjects were divided into the nobility, the clergy and the peasants, many of the latter being serfs bound to private or state land. The imperial decision regarding Jews did not take into account the fact that most of them were then living in the countryside, in villages or small towns.

Without challenging Catherine II's decision, Tsar Alexander (reigned 1801–25) tried to clarify the "Jewish question" and had the various legal provisions concerning Jews compiled. The result was a special jurisdiction subject to numerous rewritings. In 1803 the emperor approved a new statute providing for the expulsion of Jews from rural areas, in conformity with their theoretical status as "bourgeois"; depending on the inclinations of the local police, Jews were either tolerated or driven out of villages. The tsar, who had become a mystic, also had the idea of giving Jews – converted to Russian Orthodoxy if possible, but not necessarily – land in the New Territories of the South (around Odessa and Crimea) so that they could engage in agriculture there. Between expulsion and conversion, these various measures created a climate of instability for the Jewish population. Paradoxically, the conflict with Napoleonic France was to interrupt these expulsions, even as part of the Pale of Settlement was being transformed into a battlefield.

Although the war disturbed Gabriel Yakov's life at the beginning of his marriage, no personal document tells us how he felt about these events. We have to be content with his contemporaries' testimonies. Did he witness the entry of French troops into Vitebsk on 28 July 1812? When the First Russian Army, under the command of Barclay de Tolly, retreated as the French approached, the locals were seized by a general panic. Christians loaded their possessions into carts and fled; the Jews, who had nowhere to go, remained in town and witnessed Vitebsk's pillaging: "The shops and wine cellars were emptied, doors broken down, the panes and frames of windows smashed. During the three months of [the] presence [of French troops] in Vitebsk, neither bells nor roosters were heard: the former were outlawed and the latter eaten."[3] Contrary to received ideas, Jews did not like Napoleon, who they felt was too atheistic, and were loyal to their new homeland. The Jews were a minority in a particularly uncomfortable position. The rabbis made ringing appeals to defend Russia.[4] In making military arrangements, Jews proved to be a useful intermediary for informing and supplying the army, using their economic and community networks as well as their excellent knowledge of the terrain.[5] When the Russians retook Vitebsk on 26 October 1812, Jews naturally participated in its liberation: out of twenty-eight residents decorated for "loyalty", five were Jews. Thus it was in a recently pacified town that Gabriel Yakov's young wife gave birth to her first-born son, probably in her parents' house, on 4 January 1813. The child was named after his maternal grandfather, Josef Josel, which Russification turned into Iosif Evzel, later Gallicised as Joseph Evzel. A few years later, on 8 December 1819, still in Vitebsk, Joseph Evzel's beloved sister Eleone, called Elka, was born. A second daughter, Bella, soon followed, but we know neither the date nor the place of her birth. The siblings remained together, even with the marriages of the three children and their successive moves: Joseph Evzel married Rosa Dynin, from Orsha, in 1830, Elka married Heshel Rosenberg, from Zhytomyr, in 1837, and Bella married Zeev, the son of Nathan Merpert, from Chernigov, in 1840. Members of the Dynin, Rosenberg and Merpert families were always welcome at the Gunzburgs' home on Rue de Tilsitt in Paris. Regarding the childhood of Joseph Evzel, Elka and Bella in Vitebsk, we know only that in their father's house they received "an excellent upbringing", the most tangible proof of which is that they subsequently used it as a model for their own children.[6] Another concrete detail proves that the Gunzburgs belonged to the enlightened circle in Vitebsk: Gabriel Yakov had a library, notably including ancient Hebrew manuscripts that were to form the initial core of Joseph Evzel's future library, to which we have already referred.[7]

Initially associated with his father-in-law's shop, Gabriel Yakov gradually developed his own business that obliged him to travel frequently. His field of activity was broad: it probably included wood, wheat, sugar and alcoholic beverages. Was he involved in the large-scale public works projects the state entrusted to Jewish entrepreneurs in the 1820s, with the construction of the so-called "magisterial" roads from Vitebsk to Smolensk, Vitebsk to Orsha, and Vitebsk to Nebel? In the absence of precise information, only his success is certain: in 1849, he joined the First Guild of merchants and received the title of "honorary citizen". All his male descendants were also listed in the registers of the "merchants of the First Guild", including those who lived in France. Since his childhood in Vilna, Gabriel Yakov had had to show an exceptional ability to adapt. He was faced with a juridical-administrative apparatus much less favourable than the one his father and grandfather had had to cope with in Lithuania. Thus in 1823, Jews in the governorates of Vitebsk and Mogilev were forbidden to travel around the governorate's territory with their merchandise and to go to villages and rural areas to engage in trade.[8] In 1824, they were forbidden to own or even to rent a cabaret, bar, inn or post house. Gabriel Yakov had to obtain special permits: his education, which was both traditional and open to Western culture, allowed him to deal directly with the imperial administration. He was probably one of the small minority of Jews who had learned Russian and belonged to the restricted group of "emancipated" Jews who had adopted Western clothes and manners. He was therefore active in the first generation of "Russian Jews": contemporaries of Pushkin, these young Jews experienced their emancipation from traditional Jewish culture at the very time when Russian culture was undergoing its own emancipation from Western culture. In this particular context, they learned to love Russia. Long afterwards, Joseph Evzel's deep attachment to his country can be understood as loyalty to his father, who was in his own way the pioneer of a new way of being Jewish.

Around 1830, Gabriel Yakov left Vitebsk and went to Kamenets-Podolsk, in Podolia, in southwestern Ukraine: from there, he travelled around a large part of the Pale of Settlement, where he had established branch offices more or less everywhere, and also sometimes went to St Petersburg. Joseph Evzel was already initiated into the world of business: working with figures, stocktaking, contact with customers. Father and son worked together, as is shown by two letters dating from 1832, a rare testimony for that period.[9] A young man of nineteen, Joseph Evzel is writing to his father about their activities: he shows great deference and expresses himself in meticulous Hebrew. The content remains opaque for noninitiates; it refers to deliveries, future or completed, in different localities, and mentions employees and official documents. We can infer a relatively large-scale activity, with numerous intermediaries and points where goods are stocked or sold. The letters end with the habitual wishes for good health: "Until I see you again, be in peace. I hope to receive from you good news and news of things that are going well." The correspondence also reveals that Gabriel Yakov had left the house in Kamenets-Podolsk: he now lived in Simferopol, in Crimea, having apparently taken another wife, a woman named Shifrah Blüme, to whom the letters are also addressed. His wife Léa remained with her son in Kamenets-Podolsk.

At the end of a very full life, Gabriel Yakov died in Simferopol, at the age of sixty, in 1853. He was a public figure respected for his success and his good deeds, sung after his death in an elegy by the poet Adam Hacohen.[10] "Having amassed a great fortune, he gave considerable sums to charities. These liberalities, to which his co-religionists were not accustomed, had the effect of creating for him a reputation for generosity that continued to grow among the Jews of the period."[11] Among his good works, we must cite the financing of the Talmud Torah of Vilna, the Vitebsk orphanage, of which Joseph Evzel remained the administrator until his death, and a hospital in Simferopol.[12] Above all, Gabriel Yakov left behind him children capable of being even more successful than he had been: Joseph Evzel also joined the class of "merchant of the First Guild", but in 1833, at the age of twenty, fifteen years earlier than his father! An important detail: only merchants of the First Guild were allowed to leave the Pale of Settlement, temporarily and for their business affairs. At the death of his father, Joseph Evzel thus already occupied a position that was exceptional in several regards.

9

Kamenets-Podolsk and the Gunzburg Trading Agency

A CITY WITH character, Kamenets-Podolsk was described by Nicolas de Fer, one of Louis XIV's cartographers, as a "fortified town of the states of Poland and Upper Podolia with the Title of Bishopric and Palatinate, located on the summit of a mountain surrounded by the Smotrich River and enveloped by rocky cliffs". The site is exceptional: perched on a high plateau, the city dominates the river, which winds around it in an almost perfect circle. A spectacular Turkish rampart stands a few hundred metres in front of the old town. Abrupt cliffs look down on sandy banks. Constructed on the surrounding plateau or below it, the suburbs are connected to the upper city by a series of bridges. De Fer notes that "the fortress was taken from the Poles by the Turks on 29 August 1672". The cathedral of Saints Peter and Paul, to which a minaret was added, was "transformed into the main mosque" and the Jacobins' convent of St Michel served as "lodging for the janissaries [the Ottoman sultan's elite infantry troops]". The Frenchman does not mention the great synagogue, though it had already been built. Since the sixteenth century Kamenets-Podolsk had had a Jewish population which, unusually, was half Sephardi and half Ashkenazi. After a brief period under Ottoman control, the city became Polish again in 1699, before being annexed to Russia in 1793. It then became the administrative capital of the governorate of Podolia. The Gunzburgs made Kamenets-Podolsk the centre of their business activity and their main place of residence from the early 1830s to between 1857 and 1859, when they left for Paris and St Petersburg.

In 1840, out of 14,700 residents, 4,629 were Jewish, a common proportion in the Pale of Settlement. The old seventeenth-century synagogue, which had been burned down during a pogrom, had just been replaced by the Gros Alter Shul on Dovga Street, in the heart of Jewish spiritual life, also the location of the Beth Midrash (Talmudic school), the great Tailors' synagogue, and other smaller ones.[1] Many different religious trends enlivened the city, which notably experienced the influence of Jacob Frank (1726–1791), the founder of a sect inspired by both Christianity and Judaism, who finally converted to Catholicism. In the nineteenth century supporters of the *Haskalah* mixed in this sect together with renowned *hasidim*. The intellectual movement of the *Haskalah*, from the Hebrew word meaning "wisdom" or "erudition", advocated a modernisation of Jewish life. The Gunzburgs belonged to the intellectual and economic elite of the city, which at that time had about sixty merchants of the First and Second Guilds (a combination of Jews and Christians), including Joseph Evzel and his father.[2] Among the Jews, the other merchants were small shopkeepers, whose places of business surrounded the Polish Market at the heart of the city. Christians, who were in the majority, constituted a complex society that reflected the turbulent history of these Polish-Russian borderlands: it included Polish nobility, the Russian administrative elite, humble Ukrainian-speaking people, along with numerous representatives of the clergy – priests, monks and nuns, who were further divided into Catholic and Orthodox Christians (Poles and Russians, respectively).

The apparent tranquillity of the little city in Podolia was deceptive: in 1833, the municipal government limited Jews' right to build new houses and shops, a restriction that was renewed in 1859. Generally speaking, the reign of Nicholas I (1825–55) accentuated Jews' distrust of the imperial administration. In 1827 the tsar promulgated the decree instituting the system of Jewish "cantonists", which forced each *kahal* to provide a specified number of boys between the ages of twelve and eighteen for twenty-five years of military service; the institution of certified rabbis and state Jewish schools was also perceived as an attack on traditional culture; and finally, in 1825, the "Regulation Regarding Jews" confirmed the principle of the Pale of Settlement but authorised Jews to live in villages again and to acquire land within the limits of the Pale. But Nicholas I's reign was particularly favourable for the development of Joseph Evzel's business activities. His success must not mask the obstacles he had to overcome, however, even if there are no documents testifying to his efforts and difficulties.

*

The Gunzburg trading agency occupied a large block of buildings on Trinity Street, near the monastery and church of the same name: the offices and warehouses belonging to Joseph Evzel and his father were so large that for a time the street was renamed *Kontornaya ulitsa*, Trading Agency Street.[3] The imposing building in the classical style classified its owners among the well-off. Josef Evzel lived there with his family: in 1830, at the age of seventeen, he had married Rassia (later called Rosa), the daughter of David Sizkind Dynin, whose beauty made up for her lack of education. According to one of their descendants, "the Dynin family did not have much *ishus*" – the Yiddish term *yichus* (pedigree), which was uncommon, insinuating that the "alliance" was not very honourable as the Dynins did not belong to the Ashkenazi elite.[4] But Rosa's father was the postmaster in Orsha: "In this capacity, he played a certain role in the city, because the Orsha post office at the junction of the roads from Petersburg to Kiev and from Moscow to Warsaw was very important."[5] Another family version, romanticised, offers an account of the two young people's meeting:

> Especially in the winter, [Joseph Evzel] travelled immense distances in a sleigh, covered with furs, often stopping at an inn. The innkeeper was Jewish, and had a hotel and a small restaurant where people warmed up and changed horses. And it is certain that this innkeeper was extremely flattered, honoured and delighted when he received a person who had, on the one hand, a certain elegance, and, on the other, a considerable social standing, who was accepted by the Russians and was a Jew, which could obviously only enhance his reputation with this postmaster. This postmaster, Dynin, had a daughter. She was pretty, it seems, and sixteen years old. She probably caused this impressive man to spend pleasant evenings. On one occasion, he expressed the desire to take her with him, which was arranged, and he married her.[6]

Their first child, Alexandre Sizkind, was born in Orsha, probably in the post office, on 15 April 1831. The inn was a prosperous establishment: like all inns, it had its own equipment for producing alcoholic beverages, an activity that was at that time mainly carried on by Jews, in particular because of the use of wine for the *kiddush*, a blessing over wine on the Sabbath and all Jewish holidays.[7] Jews' production of alcoholic beverages (wine, vodka, beer and mead) was traditional in the Pale of Settlement: in 1811, the Senate had restored to Jews the right to hold a concession for the production of alcoholic beverages in localities belonging to the Crown, but only within the limits of the Pale of Settlement.[8] To show the importance of her parents' establishment, Rosa liked to tell her children and grandchildren about the visits of Emperor Alexander I, who was fond, she said, of her mother's Jewish cooking: the emperor's aides-de-camp reached the inn on planks thrown over the muddy streets to collect the dishes made for the sovereign.[9] The choice of the given name Alexandre for the eldest of the Gunzburg children can thus be understood as a posthumous homage to the emperor. Joseph Evzel and Rosa were soon blessed with more children: Naftali Herz, called Horace, was born on 25 December 1832[10] in Zvenigorodka, and Ury was born in Khotin, on 22 September 1840. The two youngest children, Khaya-Matla (who became Mathilde) and Salomon David, were born in Kamenets-Podolsk on 21 July 1844 and 11 September 1848, respectively.[11] The diversity of their birthplaces shows that Joseph Evzel's business activity required him to move about a great deal: at that time, he was working in the *otkup* sector,[12] that is, he had a "concession for the production of alcoholic beverages", which over the course of thirty years made him one of the wealthiest men in Russia.

During Nicholas I's reign the production and sale of alcoholic beverages was a state monopoly that the government farmed out to private entrepreneurs. In exchange for the payment of pre-established sums determined by the quantity of alcoholic beverages sold, these entrepreneurs contractually obtained this lucrative trade in a specific geographical zone. Access to the status of *otkupshchik*, or "alcoholic beverage concessionaire", was not granted to just anyone: one had not only to master the whole process but also have pecuniary resources sufficient to deposit large sums in the hands of the Treasury as a guarantee; moreover, the allocation of a concession to a Jew was rare. Joseph Evzel's case was therefore very exceptional. In partnership with his father, Joseph Evzel advanced from one stage to another: as a young man he worked as a supervisor for a Polish nobleman who owned breweries; from 1835 to 1839 he was employed by the *otkupshchik* Alexander Borozdin, who came from the old Russian nobility, and whose alcoholic beverage concession in Kamenets-Poldolsk he managed. At that time Joseph Evzel received an annual salary of 20,000 roubles, a significant sum that served as the basis for the capital for his own business.[13] His organisational and management skills justified the confidence that Borozdin had in him. Their collaboration provides an example of a fruitful partnership between Christian and Jewish entrepreneurs. From 1839 Joseph Evzel worked for himself: in association with his father, he obtained the *otkup* for retail sales in the city of Khotin, where he took up residence with his family, since that is where his third son, Ury, was born. Buoyed by this initial collaboration with the state, in the 1840s and 1850s the Gunzburgs signed concessions for numerous cities and rural areas in Podolia, Bessarabia, Poltava, Volhynia and the regions of Kiev, Vitebsk, Minsk and Taurida – that is, across much of the Pale of Settlement. Their success resulted from a commercial strategy that paid off: they chose to sell more beer and mead, which were less expensive than vodka, and thus were likely to be bought in larger quantities. Giving priority to small profits on a large scale, they ended up with a very high turnover.[14] In one decade, Joseph Evzel became one of the biggest alcoholic beverage concessionaires in the Russian Empire. This made him an essential partner for the state, which drew from such concessions a major part of its budget (40 per cent of state revenues in 1860). Joseph Evzel also became one of the biggest employers in the Pale of Settlement.

According to the high official Pyotr Brok, Joseph Evzel received the title of "honorary citizen" in 1849 in recognition of "the contribution made to the Treasury through the concession for alcoholic beverages". At the end of 1850, his contribution amounted to 3.5 million roubles. If the state's profits were large, those of the concessionaires were very significant. According to official statistics, in 1856 trade in alcoholic beverages brought in 151 million roubles, comprising 82 million for the Treasury and 69 million for the concessionaires, a figure that has been contested as much too low. Of the 216 concessionaires in 1859–63, the wealthiest was Dmitry Benardaki, a member of a Greek family that had emigrated to Russia and that *otkup* had enriched to the tune of 20 million roubles (in Paris, Benardaki's daughter became Joseph Evzel's mistress, as already noted, a situation that understandably led to some tension within the family). For his part, Joseph Evzel had profited by 8 million roubles. The alcoholic beverage concessionaires formed a separate caste, which provided the basis for the Gunzburgs' social life. The Mamontov brothers (the father and uncle of Savva, a famous art collector) were part of this caste; other Jewish concessionaires, such as the Gorotsky, Brodsky, Utin,

Varshavsky, Friedland and Kronenburg families, became close friends. Since the *otkup* business was carried on directly in St Petersburg, Joseph Evzel was in regular contact with the imperial administration,[15] and ended up forming a friendship with Fyodor Vronchenko, Nicholas I's finance minister from 1844 to 1852, as his grandson Sasha reports: "Grandfather regularly travelled from Kamenets to Petersburg to take part in the adjudication of concessions for eau de vie. Since these concerned whole provinces, they often had to deal with the finance minister in person. Minister Vronchenko liked to converse with our grandfather and did not limit himself solely to technical questions about the concessions. One day when they were talking about officials' probity, Nicholas I's minister said to the Jew: "Here, the *vzyatka* (bribe) is the equivalent of the British *habeas corpus*."[16] The whole *otkup* sector was in fact corrupt, a situation that cast opprobrium on those who benefited from it: officials, concessionaires and their employees.

The *otkup*, however, was also based on an activity whose energy created a virtuous circle. The writer Nikolay Leskov, who worked in this domain, emphasises that the alcoholic beverages concessions drained off talented and dynamic people. A whole economy depended on it, from production to sales, including storage, transportation and tax collection. "This trade required a large organisation with a group of paid employees: negotiations had to be conducted with officials, the lords who had breweries and the merchants to whom the lessors entrusted sales, to ensure that none of them sold the alcohol secretly or obtained it as contraband smuggled in from abroad."[17] Joseph Evzel sold his supplies only to Jews, so that out of the 8,000 Jewish *aktsizniks* (resellers) listed in the statistics of the period, the majority worked for him. Thus the Kamenets-Podolsk trading agency was the heart of a large enterprise based on an immense network of collaborators, including guards and inspectors. Joseph Evzel was known for treating his employees well. The most minor reseller received 500 roubles a year from him.[18] As Avraam Paperna notes, "Such a salary was considered a great fortune, because professors, synagogue employees and small shopkeepers, who at that time lived on 150–200 roubles a year, had reason to envy it." The *otkup* was attractive to young men in the Pale of Settlement, and since it involved contact with the authorities and the ability to keep accounts, candidates had to know Russian and mathematics. "It was therefore not surprising that manuals of grammar

and mathematics were so popular among young Jews [at that time],"
Paperna observes, pointing out that "better than any other means, reselling
led Jews to acquire a general education."[19] This remark allows us to
conclude that Joseph Evzel's interest in his co-religionists' general
education, which he later made his hobbyhorse, was based on his
experience as a businessman: access to various kinds of employment, and
thus to honourable ways of earning a living, was the main goal.
Nevertheless, trading in alcoholic beverages was held in contempt, and
participating in the arrangements set up by the government resulted in a
number of problems for Jews, particularly anti-Jewish attacks based on
the accusation that Jews were responsible for alcoholism among peasants.
This claim was obviously unfounded, because the consumption of alcohol
in the Pale of Settlement, where Jews kept the inns, was no higher than
in the rest of the Empire.

In Kamenets-Podolsk, Joseph Evzel moved in with his sister Elka, whose
husband, Heshel Rosenberg, worked as a lawyer and agent for the
Gunzburg firm. Heshel later became a notable trader. He settled in Kiev,
where he played an important role in the sugar industry, while his wife
established herself as an authoritative figure in the Jewish community.
Elka and Heshel posed for a portrait together: seen from a three-quarters
angle, sitting on a couch, turned towards one another, they give a
reassuring impression of provincial opulence. Elka's thick, dark hair is
pulled up in a bun and impeccably parted. Her way of dressing is a
compromise between Western elegance and the traditional costume; a
white lace veil covers the lower part of her hair and falls over her
shoulders. In his dark suit and immaculate white shirt front, Heshel is
elegant. His beard, long and well groomed, and his large eyes with finely
drawn eyebrows remind us of a Persian miniature. Elka, older than her
sister-in-law Rosa, is depicted as a woman of character. A photograph of
their children offers another visual testimony to the Kamenets-Podolsk
period: three little girls posed leaning on a classic balustrade. They have
dark brown hair and their clothes display a certain opulence: the two
eldest girls wear dolmans with blouses, and pretty, worked leather boots
with heels. The youngest girl wears a velvet dress with a lace collar. They
are probably the sisters of Anna, Joseph Evzel's future daughter-in-law,
who is not in the picture. Given the Parisian way of life that the
Gunzburgs led in 1857, we can infer that life in the Russian provinces

was already quite luxurious. The girls had an English nanny, Miss Sheppard, who was "of an exemplary severity".[20] Family memoirs have preserved only a few details regarding this period, all of them anecdotal: "The two families [Rosenberg and Gunzburg] lived together. A fire broke out. Everyone tried to save what they could. Grandmother Gunzburg ran into Grandmother Rosenberg in the hallway: 'What are you carrying in your apron?' 'A loaf of bread.' 'What are you going to do with that?' 'I completely lost my head, I meant to take the baby.' Fire was a recurrent problem in the towns of the empire: when it struck a house, it usually meant complete ruin.[21] For the Gunzburgs, the situation was entirely different. They not only lacked nothing but were even able to help the unfortunate: Rosa took in "cantonists", as Sasha inaccurately called the young men fleeing the conscription imposed by Nicholas I. One of them, Moses Ackermann, remained in the service of the family, which he accompanied when they moved to Paris. As Joseph Evzel's major domo, he left the Gunzburgs only after the town house on Rue de Tilsitt was sold in 1887. According to family accounts, "in the Kamenets house there were for a time as many as twenty, not to say thirty [conscripts] ranging from eight to sixteen years of age. They were housed in the cellars and fed until they could be spirited away. During the cholera epidemic of 1832 (or 1836) the illness crept into the cellars, which made the situation rather dangerous."[22] In addition, while the governor or the chief of police was being received in the parlour, terrified children were hiding in the pantry. "Some of them believed that the governor knew what was going on but pretended not to."[23] In fact Joseph Evzel enjoyed the governor's confidence, the latter no doubt benefiting from the famous "sweeteners": he authorised without hesitation the dispensation for the marriage of Anna, who married Horace before she turned sixteen, a limit set by law. Another event illustrates the nature of relations between the Gunzburgs and representatives of the government: during the Crimean War, Joseph Evzel learned of the signing of the armistice by means of the "Jewish grapevine", which circulated information more efficiently than the official postal service; at that time, the latter was still using the old technology of semaphores. He went to inform the governor and told him that he planned to illuminate his house that same evening: the governor asked him to wait until the following day, after the official announcement had reached him.[24]

*

Within the family, Joseph Evzel maintained the practice of study, respecting his father's rigorous Judaism while at the same time making his house a centre of the *Haskalah* that was open to the *maskilim*, intellectuals who were often banned from Jewish communities because of their alleged irreverent attitude with regard to tradition. As in the time of Gabriel Yakov in Vilna, learning Hebrew was a priority, not always appreciated by children: "At the age of seven or eight, [the elder son] Alexandre did not like the Talmud lessons that a *melamed* with a long beard gave him at home. These lessons bored him all the more because the learned man sometimes fell asleep as his pupil was reciting his text by heart. One day, he found a way of taking revenge on the fellow, whom he considered his torturer. The latter had fallen asleep, resting his chin on the table where his beard was spread out like a fan, and Alexandre used sealing wax to attach the beard to the table. At that time, children were punished by whipping."[25] Although Alexandre paid for his insolence, the tutor was soon replaced. Thus Horace received lessons from Markus Sukhostaver (1790–1880), to whom he showed great deference for the rest of his life. A *maskil* who came from Galicia, Sukhostaver was a disciple of the philosopher Nakhman Krokhmal, a Jewish theologian trained in Kantian philosophy and the author of a commentary on Maimonides' *Guide for the Perplexed*. Sukhostaver, who was learned in the thought of medieval Jewish theologians, gave the young man an exemplary education that permanently influenced his character. Horace was a gifted student who memorised many passages from the *Nevi'im* (*Books of the Prophets*). Through his tutor, the boy became friends with the poet Yakov Eichenbaum (1796–1861), who had translated into Hebrew Euclid's *Elements* and the works of the French mathematician Louis-Benjamin Francoeur. Sukhostaver was close to Joseph Evzel, serving as his secretary for many years.[26] He left the Gunzburgs only to become a professor at the "State Rabbinical Seminary" in Zhytomyr, an institution established by Sergey Uvarov, the education minister, with a view to reforming it.[27] The choice of enlightened teachers must be emphasised: at that time, very few Jewish families had the courage and the ability to free themselves from Orthodoxy. In Podolia, the *tzadiks* condemned any openness toward Russian Christian culture, rejecting wholesale a mixed secular and religious education. But for Joseph Evzel, whose grandfather had been close to the *gaon* of Vilna, faith and reason were in no way opposed. Mathias Mapu, to whom we have already alluded with regard to the

Gunzburgs' intellectual entourage in Paris, is another example of the *maskil*. Having entered the Kamenets household as a French teacher, he became Joseph Evzel's right-hand man, his amanuensis and adviser. In 1851, two talented writers were in Kamenets, where they were teaching in Jewish schools that received financial support from the *maskilim*: the poet and translator Avrom Ber Gotlober and Mendele Moykher Sforim, who was the first author to write in Yiddish and who produced *Fishke der Krumer* (*Fishke the Lame*). Joseph Evzel's employees included other intellectuals. In the Simferopol branch, there was Veniamin Mandelstam (1805–1885), who played an important role in enlightened circles; in the 1840s he wrote a notable memorandum on the internal causes of the Jews' poor situation in Russia.[28] In this text sent to Moses Montefiore, the British Jewish businessman and philanthropist who defended many Jewish causes, he criticised his co-religionists' ignorance of Russian, their attachment to traditional clothing and their disdain for the sciences, craftsmanship and agriculture. The Gunzburg papers also contain a no less interesting document, a handwritten essay composed in Russian, probably in Kamenets-Podolsk, dated 1850 and entitled *On the Note "Regarding the Situation of the Jewish People in Russia"*.[29] Although neither the author of this work nor the person who commissioned it can be determined, it is clear that Joseph Evzel had something to do with it. Alongside his business activities, he was in fact beginning to reflect generally on the living conditions of the Jews under the tsars' rule. Contrary to Mandelstam's memorandum, the difficulties underlined in this note are linked to causes that are external to the community and connected particularly with the administrative context. The text asks the following question: "How can young [Jews] be encouraged to leave their everyday torments behind and pursue education?" By referring to the "diseases" from which the Jewish population suffers, the author indicts a "long habit of putting up with humiliations" that prevents Jews from fighting for their "equal rights". He outlines a programme to be carried out over the next five years, if possible in the official framework of a deputation to the tsar. Five proposals for change are presented: 1) the establishment of a residence permit outside the Pale of Settlement for all workers (merchants of the three guilds, craftsmen, coachmen), with the authorisation to make business deals; for young people from fourteen to thirty years of age, the authorisation to move about, either to work as an apprentice to a craftsman or to pursue education in a school; 2) authorisation for Jews to keep inns in all cities and villages, including in Belarus; 3) acceleration of the introduction of agriculture among Jews by establishing colonies – without, however, exempting from military service those who have signed up to become farmers but have not yet been allocated lands; 4) suppression of the prohibition on Jews residing in a band fifty versts wide along the border with Austria and Prussia, because of alleged smuggling, and the communities' commitment to put any smugglers on trial; 5) through all these measures the suppression of "idleness" or inactivity among Jews who can find jobs. The ideas contained in this note were subsequently at the heart of the battles the Gunzburgs waged for the rights of their co-religionists.

As in all families, joys followed troubles: in 1848, Joseph Evzel lost his mother, who succumbed to a cholera epidemic, but had the pleasure of having a fifth and final child, Salomon; the older children were already of marrying age, and Joseph Evzel was soon a grandfather. On 13 January 1851, Alexandre and his wife Rosalie Ettinger had a first son, Michel. Then, on 15 December 1853, they had a second, Jacques, who was to become Joseph Evzel's favourite grandson. Many years later Jacques became a brilliant trader on the Paris stock market, conducting his business with an audacity and talent that were reminiscent of his ancestor's. Horace and Anna, who married on 7 July 1853, soon had two sons; Gabriel was born in Zhytomyr in 1855, and David was born in Kamenets in 1857; they were the eldest of what were to become very many siblings. A few scraps of memories suggest the ambiance of family life at the heart of provincial Russia, where character was formed by contact with a harsh nature: "One winter great-grandfather [Joseph Evzel] was travelling in a *troika* with grandfather [Horace], Gabriel and Jacques. As they were crossing the bridge over the Dnieper, the horses bolted and the carriage overturned, throwing great-grandfather into the river. He was saved thanks to his *shinel*, a sort of fur-lined greatcoat people use in Russia. It spread out on the water, and because the fur made it waterproof, it gave people on the riverbank time to launch a boat and come to his aid."[30] Photographs of Joseph Evzel taken at that time show a man with piercing eyes that betray an iron will. The trip from Kamenets to Paris was to be for him no more adventurous than the roads of Ukraine.

Would the Gunzburgs ever have left Podolia without the Crimean War (1853–56)? That conflict allowed Joseph Evzel to gain not only wealth but also fame. Since the military operations took place within his *otkup* territory, he was charged with supplying the Russian armies with alcoholic beverages. And even though the tsar's soldiers lacked everything else – food, clothing and equipment – they enjoyed ample supplies of vodka and beer. According to the testimonies, Joseph Evzel "acted marvellously" during the blockade of Sebastopol: "He was one of the last persons remaining in the southern part [of the city] with his trading agency, along with the commander of the garrison."[31] The commander-in-chief of operations in Crimea, General Alexander von Lüders, also recalled the "marvellous concessionaire" who was able to supply the soldiers "despite the general rise in prices and the lack of means of transportation". According to Lüders, "Gunzburg showed unfailing zeal in regularly supplying alcoholic beverage rations to the regiments, building up major stocks at designated depots and in general being able to satisfy all the regiments' demands at their various billeting sites, moving from one zone to another and selling alcohol at a price that was not only no higher than in peacetime but even discounted."[32] At the same time that he was providing supplies, Joseph Evzel was also involved in alleviating the famine that was affecting Podolia and in financing the reconstruction of cities and villages that had been damaged by the fighting.

The war is said to have brought Joseph Evzel 900,000 roubles... and, above all, a name. The new finance minister, Pyotr Brok, proposed that he be recognised by the emperor, and Alexander II, the new tsar who had just taken power, awarded Joseph Evzel a medal "for zeal", along with the ribbon of the Order of Saint Andrew. He had already been awarded, "for zeal", the less prestigious Order of Saint Vladimir two years before that. Gunzburg was thus a noted personality in the reign that was just beginning. Moreover, the tsar chose to maintain the expression of his gratitude despite the publicity given to an anonymous denunciation criticising the "greed" of the alcohol concessionaires, who were said to have drained, over a period of ten years, "nearly all Russia's wealth", notably the "Gunzburgs [who] made a profit of 8 million roubles [...] [and] could live nowhere but in Count Uvarov's dacha." The letter accused the late finance minister, Vronchenko, of having drawn aristocrats and high officials into wheeling and dealing and commercialism. Although Alexander II ordered that this accusation "not be pursued", he took care to forward it to the finance minister so that it might be added to the files on current business for the year 1856.[33] But the tsar had no intention of immediately challenging the system of concessionaires or their extraordinary increase in wealth, on the contrary: the cash produced by trade in alcohol could provide the investments necessary for Russia's nascent industrialisation. While Joseph Evzel was becoming increasingly active in economic and social life, St Petersburg was establishing itself as a new horizon.

10

Joseph Evzel,
Head of the St Petersburg Jewish Community

[JOSEPH] EVZEL GUNZBURG was one of the first to move to St Petersburg and to found a bank at a time when private banks had just begun to appear. The bank immediately took on a European appearance, no longer resembling at all the organisation of the *otkup*. At this time, other young concessionaires (Gorovits, Varshavsky) and entrepreneurs from the North (the Friedlands and the Malkiels) were also establishing themselves in St Petersburg. Those who came from the Pale of Settlement underwent a complete metamorphosis: the concessionaire was transformed into a banker, the entrepreneur into a high-flying businessman, and their employees into dandys in the capital. The stock market, where speculation in securities was just beginning, led to prodigality.[1]

As described by this anonymous witness, the Gunzburgs' arrival was part of a general development. But even more than a symbolic reflection of Joseph Evzel's individual success, their settlement in the Russian capital in 1859 (two years after their sojourn in Paris) represents a historical landmark: that of the official creation of a Jewish community in St Petersburg. Off limits to Jews since the reign of Elizabeth, the daughter of Peter the Great, the "Venice of the North" had under Catherine II remained forbidden to Jews with the exception of former conscripts: thus there was a handful of old Jewish soldiers who had retired to the banks of the Neva and whom the city authorities allowed to practise their religion discreetly in modest places of prayer. A visitor today finds an elegant synagogue, fittingly situated next to the opera and perfectly integrated into the urban landscape with its Byzantine-Moorish style, but cannot suspect the void on which this Jewish community, which was to have such a bright future, was built. The proportion of Jews in the city's total population never exceeded 2 per cent. But through their economic, artistic and intellectual dynamism the capital's Jews were more influential than their numbers would suggest. In the early twentieth century, the poet Osip Mandelstam described St Petersburg's Jews as if they had always been there: "There is a Jewish quarter in St Petersburg: it begins right behind the Marie theatre, where the ticket scalpers freeze, behind the corner of the Lithuania prison that burned during the revolution [of 1905]. There, in the commercial streets, one sees Jewish signs with a steer and a cow, women wearing wigs that peek out of their headscarves, and old men full of experience and love for children, trotting along with their overcoats reaching to their heels. The synagogue, with its pointed turrets and onion domes like a sumptuous foreign fig tree, is lost amid humble buildings."[2] And during a solemn religious service the poet notes "two gentlemen in top hats, magnificently dressed, shimmering with wealth, moving elegantly, like men of the world, [who] touch the heavy book, emerge from the circle and, for everyone and witnessed by all, carry out an honourable mission, the main mission. Who is this one? Baron Gunzburg. And that one? Varshavsky."[3] We could find no better evidence for the exceptional status of the Gunzburgs than Mandelstam's childhood memory. Without giving specifics, he describes the ceremony inaugurating the St Petersburg synagogue on 20 September 1893. Community leaders used a silver key to open the central door before carrying the scrolls of the Torah into the hall. Joseph Evzel had died more than twenty years earlier, but Horace was present; he was the first to enter the sacred building, carrying the first scroll, followed by Mark Varshavsky and Lazar Polyakov carrying lit candles. Joseph Evzel had very largely financed its construction, from its launch in 1869 – although construction only began fourteen years later – through to its completion in 1893. In 1863 St Petersburg's Jews had set up their own community council, whose first president was Joseph Evzel.[4]

The right won by Joseph Evzel in 1859 was the result of an initiative undertaken a few years earlier. In July 1856, at the head of a group of eighteen Jewish merchants, he asked the tsar to authorise various categories of the Jewish population to settle in Russia's interior: the merchants of the First and Second Guilds: graduates of the university and of technical schools, soldiers who had performed twenty-five years of service, and the best craftsmen.[5] The tsar then established an official committee assigned to examine the reforms envisaged for "organising Jews". The finance minister, Pyotr Brok, who maintained cordial relations with Joseph Evzel, was entrusted with reviewing the order restricting Jews to rights involving commerce. He relied on the proposal of the governor-general of Kiev, Podolia and Volhynia, Prince Illarion Vasilchikov, who thought it "useful to give honourable citizens and merchants of the First Guild the right to engage in commerce and industry and to found banking agencies in the internal governments", that is, outside the Pale of Settlement. In referring to future "banking agencies", was Vasilchikov ahead of Joseph Evzel, or, having been contacted in advance, was he supporting the latter? In the course of his seventeen years of activity in the Pale of Settlement, from 1855 to 1872, Vasilchikov provided constant support for the Jewish population. He justified his position to the imperial administration by emphasising the patriotism of the Jews, in contrast to the Polish population, which was then involved in a bitter struggle against the Russian authorities. Prince Vasilchikov improved the fate of Jews in Kiev, which fell under his direct jurisdiction, at the time when Elka and Heshel Rosenberg, who had also decided to leave Kamenets-Podolsk, settled there. In August 1858, the Minister of the Interior, Alexander Knyazhevich, finally presented a bill to the Council of State that was more restrictive than Joseph Evzel had wanted, since it permitted only Jewish merchants who had been members of the First Guild for ten years to live and work outside the Pale of Settlement. Examination of the bill showed that only 108 individuals met this twofold requirement, including the Gunzburgs; the authorisation was then broadened to include those who had been members of the First Guild for two years before the decree and for five years after it. On 15 March 1859, Tsar Alexander II promulgated the ukase or decree that gave certain Jewish merchants of the First Guild the same rights as "Russian" merchants. Thus it took three years for Joseph Evzel's request to bear fruit, long enough for him to get used to Paris, where no one forbade him to live.

The precious ukase had hardly been promulgated before Joseph Evzel made arrangements to settle his family and employees in St Petersburg: "I recall very well that grandfather had received authorisation to keep with him up to ten persons, who without that would not have had the right to reside there," Sasha writes.[6] Joseph Evzel chose a home in the aristocratic quarter of the Admiralty, the historic centre of the city, near the Neva: the air was full of sea spray and the horizon was vast.[7] Quays, avenues, the river, canals, bridges – everything was grand, solid and broad. Petersburg does not resemble any other capital city: produced by Peter the Great's imagination, constructed on swamps, it was built over decades thanks to the talents of architects and craftsmen who had come from all over Europe to create a city on the same scale as the largest empire in the world. Joseph Evzel could admire Vasilyevsky Island and the grandiose buildings of the university and the Academy of Fine Arts, not to mention the stock exchange, a symbol of a new era.[8] A city of government officials and military men, St Petersburg had the reputation of being formal and cold. With Tsar Alexander II, who was more liberal, the capital lost part of its traditional rigidity. Joseph Evzel was already familiar with how the city functioned: for twenty years he had frequented governmental circles, especially the Ministries of Finance and the Interior, both for *otkup* negotiations and to participate from time to time in committees dealing with the Jewish question. A few hundred metres from his home he founded, on 15 November 1859, the J. E. Gunzburg Bank at 22 Galernaya Street (4 Zamyatin Lane), which could boast of a certain experience in the money market: he used his sojourn in Paris to invest some of his profits from the *otkup* on the European gold exchange market. Living in a palace, at the head of a bank with a very visible sign, the Gunzburgs soon adopted St Petersburg manners: opera, theatres, balls, holidays spent on the islands or in Tsarskoye Selo, sleigh rides...

At that time, the Russian financial context was very different from that in Paris, but the difficulties and delays manifest in the Russian economy were no less favourable to the creation of a bank: in fact, the disastrous financial situation after the Crimean War had led to the dissolution of the state's monopoly on banking. The creation of the Gunzburg bank thus came at a moment of transition and provided a way of filling a gap in the Russian financial system: established in the capital, the bank was close to the decision-making centre; with its French branch, it enabled its customers to manage their commercial activities outside Russia; and above all, it benefited from the professional network that had been built up during the *otkup*. Some of Joseph Evzel's former employees created private banks in various provincial cities, with which the Gunzburg bank was naturally associated. With the help of his son Horace, Joseph Evzel was thus at the start of the development of a large part of the Russian banking network; in 1868, the Gunzburgs provided part of the capital for the "Private Commercial Bank" in Kiev and the St Petersburg Discount and Loan Bank; in 1871, the "Russian Bank of External Commerce" operated with a capital of 7.5 million roubles divided into 30,000 shares of 250 roubles each held by ten shareholders, including Joseph Evzel, his distant cousin Lev Rosenthal, his friends the Ephrussis and the Eliseev brothers, Stepan and Grigory, members of the famous merchant dynasty.[9] The Siberian Commercial Bank, with a capital of 4 million roubles, was founded in 1872; the Gunzburgs were among the seven shareholders, along with Count Pavel Shivalik, Dmitry Baradari and again Lev Rosenthal. In 1879, the Discount Bank of Odessa was founded.[10]

The Gunzburg bank rapidly acquired a solid reputation. Thanks to the marriages made in the milieu of Parisian finance by Mathilde and Salomon – the former to Paul Fould and the latter to Henriette Goldschmidt – and those made by the Rosenberg daughters, Joseph Evzel's nieces, to German, Hungarian and Russian bankers,[11] customers understood that they were dealing with a reliable establishment. The bank was among the country's principal financial institutions that delivered promissory notes, even for transfers to foreign countries. Since Baron Stieglitz, an eminent predecessor, had just liquidated his business, his clientele naturally moved over to Joseph Evzel.[12] The new bank also enjoyed special trust among groups close to the Court, and especially to the Grand Duke of Hesse, the tsar's brother-in-law. At the imperial level too, the bank was very active: it provided credit to entrepreneurs and merchants who had not obtained help from the state banking network. It also served as an intermediary in financing railway companies by promoting the distribution of bonds on western European markets. In the promising sector of railways, although the Gunzburgs provided the credit necessary for many transactions (the purchase of concessions, the provision of materials), they were on the other hand not in a position to invest directly: neither Joseph Evzel nor Horace was able to establish a lasting connection with the ministers concerned.[13] This failure led them to move into other sectors: gold and platinum mines, shipping companies, insurance companies, metallurgy, etc. Their ability to diversify their activities was based on an aptitude for risk-taking: Horace fully shared the entrepreneurial spirit embraced by his father. But alongside their involvement in innovative sectors, neither of them shied away from investment in a more classical domain: land.

In 1861, Joseph Evzel bought 50,368 desyatinas (about 55,000 hectares, or 212 square miles) in Bessarabia, a territory annexed by Russia after the Treaty of Bucharest (1812), in the region of Bender. The domain of Shmelnik was sold to him by Count Nikolay and Count Vladimir Levashov, and Joseph Evzel's brother-in-law Alexander Dynin served as its manager.[14] Joseph Evzel became the owner not only of forest and agricultural lands (and not poor ones, since this was rich "black earth" or *chernozem*), but also of villages and serfs.[15] In the course of the following years, the abolition of serfdom and the critical situation of the nobility, which was often in debt and forced to sell, provided new opportunities for purchasing: in the 1870s, the Gunzburgs owned 126,000 desyatinas (192,682 hectares or 744 square miles), a colossal accumulation that remained in the family until the revolution. To the domains in Bessarabia were added domains in Podolia (beet production and sugar refineries) and in Crimea (including 50,000 hectares of land and salt pans). Investment in land was a secure asset, whereas the stock market in St Petersburg suffered from instability; moreover, with inflation growing, land allowed Joseph Evzel to maintain his capital and in the long run to develop it, since the value of land was also going to grow. It served, in a way, as a guarantee for other enterprises that took longer to turn a profit, as in the gold mining and insurance sectors, where major investments were necessary. The social value of such an investment was not negligible, either; landed property was a sign of membership of the Russian social elite.[16]

To manage his numerous enterprises, Joseph Evzel surrounded himself with capable men, all involved in Russian economic modernisation. Accountants and lawyers by training, they were symbols of the new Russia. Thus he recruited the Zak brothers: Abram, the J. E. Gunzburg Bank's accountant, was "ceded" to the Discount Bank when it was founded and became its director; Isaak remained in Joseph Evzel's service as the manager of his personal assets, and as such he took responsibility for handling his estate when the time came. Adolphe Grube, an employee in the Paris branch, joined the offices in St Petersburg in 1870 and became an associate in 1884; Clément Podmenner worked there at first as an accountant, then as an authorised agent, and when the Gunzburg bank closed down in 1893, he became the director of the Bank of Commerce and Industry. Alexey Stolpakov came up with the idea of agrarian banks, of which the Gunzburg house was the instigator and which were among the Gunzburg bank's best clients. Isaak Krasnoselsky, the cousin of the composer Anton Rubinstein, managed the gold mines; Jules Averbakh successfully directed the shipping company on the Sheksna River; Alexander Dynin (Rosa's brother, and thus Joseph Evzel's brother-in-law) efficiently managed the properties in Bessarabia; Veniamin Mandelstam, Lev Lvov and later Konstantin Reshko managed the properties in Crimea;[17] and Aaron Gordon worked for twenty years on the domain of Mogilno before emigrating to Israel and founding the first *kibbutzim* there.[18] As his father had done for him, Joseph Evzel naturally involved his sons in his work. While Horace served as his right-hand man in St Petersburg, Alexandre represented him on the ground in the provinces. The family chronicle happily records his numerous adventures in the Russian provinces, which testify to the general atmosphere and to the strong personality of the eldest of Joseph Evzel's children.

> Having arrived at a station, [Alexandre] had tea served while the *troika* was being fetched. Two young officers arrived after him and asked for horses. The postmaster apologised, saying that he had only one *troika* left and that it was being hitched to this gentleman's carriage. "That doesn't matter, this gentleman will wait and the horses will be hitched to our *tarantas*." [Alexandre], impassive, continued to sip his tea. His air of calm flummoxed them. "You heard that we're going to take your horses. What are you going to do?" "I'm going to knock your block off," he replied, without raising his voice. Since uncle [Alexandre] was a magnificent man and the officers were small, the roles were reversed and they became very quiet as the *troika* was assigned to our uncle.[19]

In the face of presumptuousness from an official, a show of resistance was rare, and still more so when one was Jewish. Among the Gunzburgs, family tradition, along with imposing presence and wealth, inspired a certain self-assurance. Alexandre also shared with his father a taste for women and elegant dinners: since in that regard St Petersburg offered fewer possibilities than Paris did, it happened that three generations of Gunzburgs dined at the same time in the private rooms of the Café

Anglais, a famous restaurant on the Nevsky Prospect. When the waiters brought the bill, Michel sent it to his father, Alexandre, who passed it, along with his own, on to his father, Joseph Evzel..."[20]

As in Paris, though with less freedom, the group of financiers enlivened St Petersburg life in a new way. Often descended from the concessionaires, banking and entrepreneurial families made up the Gunzburgs' inner circle of friends. This milieu has been little studied by Russian historians, and remains generally unknown, especially in the period 1860–70. The description of it given by one of Joseph Evzel's descendants is all the more valuable:

> As soon as he settled in Petersburg my grandfather had become friends with the *otkupshchiki*, his colleagues, the Kanshins, the Benardakis, the Utins, the Feigins and the Kharitovs. All these families had left offshoots in St Petersburg society. For a long time the Kanshins kept an open house where all of society liked to gather. The soul of the family was Madame Camille Kanshina, who was a great friend of my mother [Anna]. Old man Benardaki had won fame by giving a battery of cannons to the new Greek government towards the middle of the last century. The Utins' offspring made their names as merchants, lawyers and engineers. The youngest of them, Nikolay, was an engineer who had been sentenced to death [in absentia] for the student rebellions of 1863. That did not prevent him from taking part in 1876, with Polyakov, in the construction of the strategic Bender–Galatz line; but that line, which was supposed to ensure transportation of supplies for the Russian army, was on Romanian territory. Afterwards he was pardoned and continued to work in Russia. One of the Utin daughters, Lyubov, who was one of the first women to take examinations at the university, became Madame Stasyulevich. A Mademoiselle Feigin married the historian Bilbasov.[21]

Connections were thus made between business circles and the St Petersburg intellectual milieu. Among the Gunzburgs' close friends we must add Vladimir Ratkov-Rozhnov, the mayor of St Petersburg, Leopold Kronenberg, the founder of the Discount Bank, the three Polyakov brothers (Samuel, Yakov, and Lazar), famous railway magnates who bought the former Stroganov palace on the English Embankment,[22] Edward Meyer (whose bank was the second largest after that of the

Gunzburgs[23]), Hipolit Vavelberg, who had returned from Warsaw in 1869, the Ephrussis and the Varshavskys, with whom the Gunzburgs associated in both St Petersburg and Paris. All of them made up a society that was sometimes condemned: in *Ballet*, written in 1866, Nikolay Nekrasov refers to the theatre boxes where the "bankers' wives" scintillated, "hundreds of thousands of roubles on their breasts", exhibiting their "gilded bodies" and their husbands, "Jewish, young, strong, full of assets".[24] Among the newcomers, many were indeed Jews, but not all of them remained Jews. Utin "converted rather early, so that his youngest children, including Madame Stasyulevich, were actually born into the Orthodox religion", and "his eldest son, who was a magistrate who later became the head of the Discount Bank, particularly distinguished himself by the size of the signs of the Cross that he made in public when the occasion arose."[25] In the imperial capital, the officially accepted values of "autocracy, orthodoxy and Russian nationality" decreed under the reign of Nicholas I imbued ministries and salons. The traditional St Petersburg elite proved hostile to Jews: the episode of the first ball given by the Gunzburgs at the Hôtel des Trois-Empereurs in Paris, which the Russian aristocracy declined to attend, is revealing in this regard. But Joseph Evzel was not pessimistic: the progress made since leaving Kamenets-Podolsk confirmed his hopes for integration. Moreover, in 1874, at the request of the new finance minister, Mikhail Reutern, the tsar granted Joseph Evzel the prestigious title of "commercial counsellor". Before reaching that high office, Reutern had been one of the instigators of the project of the Grand Russian Railway Company and the reform of the banking system. His career and that of Joseph Evzel were thus closely connected. This honorific reward officially recognised the banker's contribution to Russian development, as the minister's remarks show:

> Gunzburg leads banking operations involving significant sums. His firm is famous in Europe, he has offices in Petersburg and Paris and relations with major commercial houses throughout Europe. [...] [He] has contributed to the establishment in Petersburg and other cities in Russia of dozens of banks through stocks and two insurance companies for which he assembled the capital, and helped strengthen many companies in the sugar business. [...] He personally owns two sugar refineries in the governorates of Podolia and Kiev, with revenues of 2 million roubles per annum, and he is a shareholder in three gold-

mining companies in eastern Siberia and also in the steam shipping company on the Sheksna.[26]

When Moses Montefiore came to St Petersburg in 1872, he was favourably struck by the contrast with his earlier stay there in 1846: "I was happy to see in this city a significant number of our co-religionists wearing imperial decorations of various kinds. I talked with Jewish merchants, men of letters, publishers of Russian periodicals, craftsmen and military veterans, and all of them described their current situation with great satisfaction. [...] Now the Jews here dress in the manner of the *gentlemen* of England, France and Germany."[27] The bankers even inspired young novelists: in *Ispoved deltsa* (*Confession of a Businessman*) Lev Levanda (1835–1888), the first Jewish author to write in Russian, describes the epic adventure of Mordecai Shmalts, who has become a millionaire in St Petersburg thanks to his stock-market speculations.[28] The owner of a palace in a fashionable quarter, the hero lives like an aristocrat. The Gunzburgs might have served as an inspiration for this fiction, since Levanda benefited from the generosity of Joseph Evzel, with whom he shared the same vision of Jewish emancipation. Thus St Petersburg was established as a new kind of Jewish cultural centre: within a single decade, an educated Jewish society had appeared in the wake of the successful businessmen, who brought with them lawyers, journalists, physicians and other representatives of the liberal professions. At the heart of this brilliant society, the men who became the Gunzburg barons were *primi inter pares*: the richest, the most famous and also the most "Jewish", in the sense that they saw to it that their religious affiliation had a recognised place in the capital.

In 1860, 1,500 Jews were officially residing in St Petersburg; eight years later, there were 2,612, or in reality more than 6,000 individuals living at the heart of western Russia, very far from their native shtetl and their traditions.[29] Unlike the Pale of Settlement, where autonomous customs and institutions provided a collective framework from the cradle to the grave, St Petersburg had no Jewish community framework. To remedy this situation, in 1863 Joseph Evzel created a "council". Fifteen delegates were named, including Joseph Evzel and Horace. The Gunzburgs recruited a rabbi trained in Germany: Abraham Neuman (1803–1875), a religious reformer who came from the twofold culture of the yeshiva and the university. He presided over the first meeting in Hebrew and in German, languages with which the Gunzburgs were familiar. To organise this numerically insignificant community, the traditional system of the *Korobka*, a tax on kosher meat, could not function as a source of community revenue. It was therefore decided that community life would be financed by voluntary contributions made by a small number of wealthy families, including the Gunzburgs, and also the Polyakov brothers and Abram Varshavsky. In 1869, Joseph Evzel was named president of the Jewish community of St Petersburg. Because of his frequent absences, since he now spent most of his time in France, Horace often replaced him in this important office.

Everything had to be created: a synagogue, schools, orphanages, charitable institutions... Even before it was possible to launch the construction of a large synagogue,[30] a place of worship had to be found: first in the house on the English Embankment, and then in a house bought by the Gunzburgs, near the Egyptian Bridge, close to the Fontanka canal, which Sasha remembered:

> In 1872 there took place in the Fontanka synagogue a solemn service, I no longer know on what occasion, perhaps the hall's inauguration. My father [Horace] did not miss the opportunity to interest the official world in the development of the community, and I remember the entrance of Prince Suvorov, who was to become the governor of the province, and General Trepov, the famous chief of police, both in dress uniforms. It was certainly the first time that Suvorov had entered a synagogue, because Trepov had great difficulty in making him keep his cap on his head; that clearly did not correspond to his ideas about the holiness of the place.[31]

Horace was the chairman of the Economic Council of the temporary synagogue, which could hold three hundred people. He maintained a cantor and a chorus of six adult singers and two children: the musical qualities of this Jewish ensemble left its mark on contemporaries, including the composer Modest Mussorgsky. An orphanage was set up above the synagogue, which Rosa and Anna took a particular interest in, with the help of "old Seberling".[32] Later on, the council founded, at Anna's instigation, a larger orphanage that received more than a hundred children between the ages of four and eleven or twelve, at 37 Tenth Line on

Vasilyevsky Island. This institution functioned until the revolution, and the building still exists. After Anna's death, her sons' wives took great care of the orphanage. Anna was also involved in creating, within Princess Helen of Saxe-Altenburg's Society for the Defence of Women, a "Jewish section that could take advantage of all the mother society's prerogatives". The usual charitable bodies were organised: *Bikur kholim* (Visiting the Sick), *Tsdoko gdeïlo* (Great Kindness), and the *Moès khitim* (Money for Wheat) committee which provided the most indigent with *matsa* for Passover.[33] The question of burials also had to be resolved: in 1874, the Jewish cemetery finally found its site near the Preobrazhensky church, six versts from the capital. Another area that was of the utmost importance to the Gunzburgs was education: in 1865, the Lazar and Anna Berman schools for girls and boys sought "to educate children in the spirit of the law of Moses, preparing those who desire it for entrance into the third class in secondary school". In 1868, in the official report on the operation of the school, it appears that "1,560 roubles were given by Monsieur Gunzburg, and 1,740 roubles by the Jewish community of St Petersburg, thanks to the tax on Jewish candles, and 1,000 roubles from enrolment fees." Joseph Evzel supported several scholarship students. With 135 students in 1869, the Berman school was in his view the ideal Jewish school, both a local Talmud Torah and a place of general education.[34]

The community that bloomed on the shores of the Baltic was naturally an outgrowth of the *Haskalah*. From 1872, the poet Yehuda Leib Gordon (1831–1892) was employed as the community's secretary. His work is a call to break Jews' cultural isolation. An imperative that issued from *Hakitsah 'ami* ("Awake, my people!"), "Be a man in the street and a Jew at home," became the slogan of the Russian *Haskalah*. His poem "Kotso shel yod" ("The Hook of the Yod" or "The Dot on the i") is a vibrant plea for the improvement of the condition of women in the Jewish community. Gordon's position frequently led him to work with the Gunzburgs, whose modernising conception of Jewishness he shared. Violently attacked by the traditional authorities in the Pale of Settlement, Gordon found in St Petersburg a haven of creativity that conformed to his own ideas. When he was imprisoned and sentenced to exile in 1879, Horace and other members of the community exercised pressure to arrange for his rapid return.[35] His arrest had been motivated by a false accusation of engaging in "activities that undermine the foundations of the government". It was actually an act of revenge on the part of Jewish religious orthodoxy, against which Gordon had been fighting for many years in the pages of Jewish periodicals.[36]

Far from being on the margins of the rest of the Jewish population confined within the Pale of Settlement, St Petersburg was now the centre of struggles for the rights of Jews that were being waged throughout the Empire. Joseph Evzel's influence and that of his family were likewise felt far beyond Peter the Great's capital city.

11

The Struggle for Civil Equality:
Military Service

JOSEPH EVZEL GRADUALLY assumed the role of *shtadlan* – intercessor between Jews and the official authorities – which was later played by his son Horace and his grandson David. By naturally taking on this function, he was continuing the family tradition begun by Simon, a Swabian rabbi and the elected representative of Bavarian Jews. Having begun in the Middle Ages, the tradition of *shtadlanut* grew stronger at the time of the absolute monarchies in central and eastern Europe because of the centralisation of power. In the case of Russia, the practice became institutionalised when a Jewish community was established in St Petersburg. But even in Kamenets-Podolsk Joseph Evzel had used his direct access to the government to criticise the poor situation of the Jews. During the reign of Nicholas I, however, he had quickly understood that any attempt at improvement was doomed to fail. Even Moses Montefiore, who had come recommended by Queen Victoria, had not been able to do anything. With the new tsar, liberally inclined at the start of his reign, the time had come to fight for the harmonisation of the rights of Jews with the Empire's general legislation. Spontaneously Joseph Evzel organised an Office of Jewish Affairs that also functioned as a charitable fund. Everything was connected: on the one hand the day-to-day sufferings of the Jewish people had to be relieved by providing concrete help, and on the other a legal battle had to be waged for their rights. He hired as his right-hand man a figure who always remained in the background: Emmanuil Levin (1820–1913), author of most of the reports, memoranda and projects signed by Joseph Evzel.

Before entering the Gunzburgs' service, Levin had been a teacher at the Talmud Torah in Minsk, and then at the public school in Proskurov and the rabbinical school in Zhytomyr. With his short beard, delicate round glasses and receding hairline, he looked like a *maskil*, an enlightened intellectual of the 1860s. His great ability to summarise, his legal skills and his linguistic mastery were undeniable assets: "He had a marvellous knowledge of the Russian language and knew how to set forth artfully all the considerations expressed in his countless memoranda written for the government. Levin was a living encyclopaedia of the Jewish problem in Russia. Baron Gunzburg entrusted him with the task of writing up a collection of all the laws on Jews contained in the fifteen volumes of the Empire's vast legal codes. In this collection, all the articles of the law are followed by commentaries by the Senate and the ministerial circulars connected with them. It makes a large volume and presents a long martyrology of the Jews in Russia."[1] This legal compilation facilitated knowledge of laws regarding Jews, but unfortunately was also useful for ill-intentioned administrators looking for restrictions that had fallen into disuse.

After Joseph Evzel's death, Levin worked with Horace. The famed historian Simon Dubnov was unjust when he ironically presented the operation of the "Gunzburg office": "In dealing with the Russian government, Horace de Gunzburg was the *shtadlan* of all the Jews. When some *gzeyre* ["disastrous decree" in Yiddish] or new repression threatened us, he assembled a few Jewish notables in his office and held a meeting with them; then his secretary Emmanuil Levin wrote a note addressed to this or that minister, in which he showed which new restrictions on rights regarding Jews would not fail to result from the decree."[2] Although it was often disappointing, the battle waged on a legal level was always based on a well-considered logic of loyalty to and confidence in the imperial regime, attitudes that made sound sense in the context of the 1860s and 1870s, when it was permissible to hope for an improvement.

Astonishing archives testify to the indefatigable tenacity of the "Petersburg group", also known as the "Gunzburg circle", in the fight for the rights of Jews.[3] In fact, before he died Levin gave his notes to the historian Elias Tcherikower, who later deposited them at YIVO, a Yiddish institute established in Vilna in 1925. Following the Nazi and Soviet occupations during and after the Second World War, part of YIVO's collection of documents was taken to New York, where Levin's notes can now be found filed under "Gunzburg Papers".[4] Running to hundreds of pages of petitions and reports, they let us hear the voice of Joseph Evzel, who, from the late 1850s to his death in 1878, submitted in his own name numerous messages to the tsar and his ministers. His activism sought to change the way the government saw the Jews. A memorandum of 1862 explains the necessity of promoting agricultural work among Jews and authorising craftsmen to live in the interior of Russia. This memorandum led to an exchange of views between the central government and the local authorities, who gave a favourable response accompanied by vast documentation. This documentation, along with the opinions expressed by the governor-generals, suggested that the project of Count Bludov, the former chairman of the Committee on Jewish Affairs during the change of reign in 1856, which called for gradually giving Jews rights equal to those of the rest of the population, was going to be realised in the near future. Moreover, in August 1862 Modest Korf, the director of the Second Department of the imperial chancellery, invited Joseph Evzel to join a new Jewish committee that was reflecting on "the suppression of certain existing restrictions in the legislation concerning Jews". Because of this generally open atmosphere, Joseph Evzel was convinced that the government would bring about the equality of civil rights "by stages".[5] In 1862, all those engaged in professional activities (meaning midwives, pharmacists and dentists) received the right to live outside the Pale of Settlement; in 1865, it was the turn of craftsmen, and in 1867 that of veterans who had completed their fifteen years of military service. The requests sent by the Gunzburg office were not fruitless. Joseph Evzel then took up another major battle: the military question.

Back in Kamenets-Podolsk, the Gunzburgs had helped child soldiers fleeing enlistment. In St Petersburg they followed attentively the cases of Jewish soldiers who were still interned in military fortresses for various disciplinary reasons, even though Tsar Alexander II had done away with the cantonist system.[6] But that did not mean that Jews were exempt from "military recruitment". In January 1855, Joseph Evzel had raised with the finance minister, Pyotr Brok, the thorny subject of Jewish tax debts connected with conscription: "With ten other merchants from various governorates", he asked that "the Emperor consider a request for the equalisation of Jews with other population groups in the Empire in the domain of military service."[7] The question was complex: in his approach to the Jewish population, Tsar Nicholas I had drawn a distinction between "productive elements and non-productive elements" (ukase of 23 November 1851), which had been applied to conscription for military service, introducing recruitment among the "non-productive" elements (ukase of 4 August 1852). At that time, these were to be "temporary rules" that were supposed to be quickly cancelled. But nothing had changed and the Crimean War distracted the government's attention. Recruitment had been organised as an obligation, physical or financial, to be assumed by communities: instead of delivering men, Jewish communities could pay a tax. Because of the shared responsibility of the wealthiest members in levying taxes within the community, Joseph Evzel and the other petitioners feared they would have to bear the weight of this so-called "recruitment" tax. The sum due having risen to eight million roubles, the merchants protested that it had become impossible to honour it: "Under the existing conditions, Jews will not be able to obey the demands made by the Treasury and by conscription."[8] They referred to the distress in which Jewish communities found themselves and emphasised that the situation was incompatible with the fact that at the present time "each son of the homeland is ready to take his share [of the responsibility] for himself and his children."[9] The problem was not only financial: normalised participation of Jews in military service was supposed to allow them to emerge from their cultural isolation and seemed to be the first condition for the recognition of their rights.

A few years later, the tsar launched a major reform of military service. Joseph Evzel took advantage of this to promote his ideas within the governmental committee, but also with his co-religionists, in a letter dated 15 May 1873 and published in the Jewish press.[10] In it, he demonstrated that "the honour" of the "nation of the sons of Israel" was at stake:

The first day of the month of Sivan in the year 5633,[11]
    Respectable and venerated Rabbis,
    Each of you knows that last year His Majesty the Tsar convoked a special committee to modify the rules of military service in our country of Russia. In accordance with the preliminary report, the committee has deliberated and decided on a different treatment between our brothers the sons of Israel and others, in order to reduce

their rights in certain details, the most important of which are the following: a) the sons of Israel will be obliged to be involved in the army up to the age of thirty (for the others, up to twenty-one and no more) b) the sons of Israel who are soldiers will not have the right to rise in rank and become officers.

The motive that led the members of the committee to make an exception for the sons of Israel is that the latter are seen by the government as people who evade military service by using tricks, and unfortunately we have again recently received information concerning numerous cities in the Empire where many Jews have managed to change their age in the registers. [...] To confound these children of Israel, the members of the committee want to create a special system for the sons of Israel, and who now does not realise the great problem that confronts the whole of our nation if the majority approves the committee's proposal?

It matters little, we can have hope because the majority may endorse the minister's mercy with respect to us and the decision which I support, to establish the same service for us, and the minister is prepared not to make a distinction between Jews and non-Jews living within the limits of the Empire. [...]

This hope was accompanied by a guarantee that equitable rights would be granted later. [...]

For that reason we are very worried and concerned, because we know that now and in the future Jews' lives and their success depend on this question.

If the children of Israel accept and hearken to the voice of the government and perform their service in the army honestly so that everyone sees, they will gain only benefits from it and we will be able to survive and hope that our people will receive the other rights of which we are currently deprived, and it will be our hope that we will be able to succeed and make improvements in the future. [...]

For that reason I have felt obliged to turn to the chief rabbi and the leaders of the community to draw your attention to this question and ask in the name of our holy people that you intervene personally to ensure that Jews young and old do not continue to do bad things and change their age in the registers. And if someone is caught doing that, he shall be treated without pity and will not be protected. [...]

I ask my distinguished colleagues, when they receive this letter, to use their influence in the cities and to commit themselves to try to act and do things in favour of this important question and not to let themselves be distracted from all this, because it is important for the honour of our nation, and the present and the future depend on it.

The welfare of our people is in your hands. Good-bye.

The one who honours you and carries you in his heart,

Joseph [Iosif] Gunzburg

Through his ideas and the strength of his conviction, Joseph Evzel established himself as a charismatic *shtadlan* who was not afraid to contradict the opinion of some of his co-religionists. In 1861, Tsar Alexander II had commanded his new Minister of War, Dmitry Milyutin, to reorganise the army, whose defects had been convincingly demonstrated by the Crimean War. After ten years of work, the reform of universal obligatory military service without class distinction was imminent. The preliminary version suggested proposing an exemption for Jews under certain conditions: for the Gunzburgs, that was a sign that Jews would never be able to obtain equal rights. Joseph Evzel and Horace manoeuvred to be heard by the special committee chaired by Grand Duke Konstantin Nikolayevich, who presided over the Imperial Council and was known for his liberal ideas. Horace succeeded in convincing Milyutin, the Minister of War and vice-chairman of the committee, as well as the head of the military tribunal, Vladimir Filosofov. For his part, Joseph Evzel promised, in the name of his co-religionists, that Jews would no longer seek to escape military obligations. On 1 January 1874, obligatory military service was decreed without any special clause or mention of Jews in the text of the decree: for the first time, Russian imperial law included Jews in the population as a whole.

In 1876, an ukase authorised Jews who had performed their military service to live outside the Pale of Settlement, reassuring Joseph Evzel that his initiative was going in the right direction. He could not foresee that this law was ultimately going to be applied in a restrictive sense, solely for those who had performed their service under the old rules. Helped by Levin, Horace exerted pressure and continued his father's battle: from 1875 to 1884, he established and had published annual statistics proving that Jews were not evading military service, or in any case no more than other population groups in the Empire, contrary to the perfidious claims made by the anti-Jewish press.[12]

Joseph Evzel believed that his family had to show exemplary patriotism. With two exceptions on health grounds, all his grandsons performed their military service. In 1874, as soon as the law was promulgated, he even encouraged one of them to anticipate the call, as Sasha reported: "My grandfather was determined to set an example of obedience to the new law, and he insisted that his grandson Jacques, who was also his favourite, enter military service."[13] Born in Kamenets-Podolsk on 20 November 1853, Jacques had been brought up in France, where he had been awarded a Bachelor of Science degree at the University of Poitiers. His return to Russia at the age of twenty-one was not a sinecure: "The law did not abolish certain prejudices, and Jacques was not admitted to the Guard as a volunteer. He joined the hussars of Narva in Vilna [a regiment commanded by General Pushkin, the poet's son]. As inspector general of the cavalry, Grand Duke Nicholas the elder [the tsar's brother] noticed the volunteer and took an interest in him. He tried to get him accepted in a regiment of the Guard but failed."[14] Jacques' equestrian talents ended up gaining him a certain notoriety:

At the end of his [service], Jacques took part in the *razvod*, an inspection of candidates for officer rank carried out by the emperor. This review usually took place at the Michel stable and was considered a strictly military celebration from which the general public was excluded. Jacques told us that at that time a friend from France was visiting him, and to make it possible for him to attend the ceremony he put a suitcase in his hand and passed him off as his valet. This friend told Jacques that he had never seen such an imposing spectacle of this kind and that he had been moved to the point of tears. Emperor Alexander II picked Jacques out from among the other horsemen and thanked him, which was at that time a distinction.[15]

Jacques was not made an officer on that occasion, however. The young soldier had to wait for another review of the troops conducted by the emperor in Odessa, shortly before their departure for the battlefield in Turkey, before he was finally promoted. He was one of the first unconverted Jews to become an officer in the Russian imperial army.[16] Wounded, awarded "the order of St Stanislas with sword" for "personal bravery in fighting the enemy",[17] he was an exemplary soldier. Like him, thousands of Jews took part in the battles against Turkey in 1877–78, representing one quarter of the troops of General Skobelev's 16th division and of the 13th division formed in the governorates of Minsk and Mogilev. Thus during the assault of 30 August 1877, a group of Jewish soldiers under the command of an NCO named Faynerman rushed forward shouting "Shema, Ysrael [Hear, O Israel]!" Counting his years of service and active duty, Jacques spent ten years as a soldier in the hussars. Unfortunately, his promotion to the rank of officer remained an exception, as his cousin points out:

> For one decade, Jews could be promoted without restrictions, three members of our family were officers, and in all there were about twelve or fifteen until anti-Semitism began to influence the government's acts under Alexander III [1881–96]. General [Pyotr] Vannovsky, Minister of War [from 1881 to 1898], added a marginal note concerning [my brother] Alfred's promotion, and prohibiting henceforth the nomination of Jewish candidates. [Alfred was then serving at Zambrovo in the 17th regiment of dragoons.] Some even say the note was written by the emperor himself. It must be emphasised that this decision was made only as a result of their anti-Semitism, because no complaint had been lodged against these fifteen Jews regarding their loyalty or their proper performance of their duty. Jacques retired with the rank of second captain; another Jew named Perlman, if memory serves, reached the rank of captain. In general, they even stopped naming Jews as NCOs and admitting them in special units.[18]

At the time that he was involved in this battle, on which he thought the present and future "success" of Jews in Russia depended, Joseph Evzel could not have imagined that the expectations of the "sons of Israel" would be so cruelly disappointed.

Joseph Evzel de Gunzburg newly arrived in Paris from Podolia, by Edouard Dubufe, 1858.

Elka, Joseph Evzel's beloved sister, and her husband, Hefsel Rosenberg, around 1840.

The Gunzburg town house finished in 1869 at 7 Rue de Tilsitt, overlooking the Place de l'Etoile.

The Gunzburg coat of arms.

Horace de Gunzburg, by Alexey Kharlamov, 1880, after the portrait by Ivan Kramskoy (later lost).

His wife Anna, by Edouard Dubufe in 1858.

Horace and Anna (on the right) with their first seven children, and Elka Rosenberg, Horace's aunt and Anna's mother, with her daughter Rosa, her son-in-law Joseph de Hirsch and their son Gabriel, in Menton, 1867.

A hunt hosted by the Gunzburgs on Ury's estate at Chambaudoin (Loiret) in honour of Grand Duke Nicholas Nikolayevich (centre), with Ury and Salomon on each side of him and on the far left, with a white beard, the writer Ivan Turgenev. By Nikolay Dmitriev-Orenburgsky, 1880.

The sculptor Mark Antokolsky, the Gunzburgs' protégé, in his studio on Rue Bayen in Paris.

Marc de Gunzburg (right), the artist in the family. The only one of his works that has survived is the portrait of his brother Pierre (below), painted in 1876. The young painter died of tuberculosis in Madeira, in 1878.

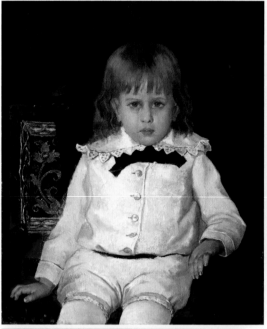

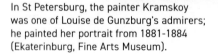

In St Petersburg, the painter Kramskoy was one of Louise de Gunzburg's admirers; he painted her portrait from 1881-1884 (Ekaterinburg, Fine Arts Museum).

Dimitri de Gunzburg, called Berza, during his military service in Russia, 1897. Close to Diaghilev, he was the administrator of the Ballets Russes. Having volunteered for service in the "Savage Division" during the First World War, he disappeared in the Caucasus during the revolution.

12

Hevra Mefitsei Haskalah:
Society for the Promotion of Culture

"WHAT IS INTERESTING to note is that in the family people were eager to associate themselves with the intellectual movement known as the *Haskalah* – the [Jewish] Enlightenment of the eighteenth century – and this movement reached its highpoint with my grandfather Joseph's foundation of the 'Society for the Promotion of Culture among the Jews of Russia',"[1] his grandson Alexandre observed. Created in St Petersburg in 1863, *Hevra Mefitsei Haskalah* was the first Jewish organisation authorised by the imperial government, which it outlived, surviving until 1929.[2] Its longevity testifies to its success. Even more than military service, the question of education was a central concern for Joseph Evzel. He saw himself "as someone who takes on the role of an intercessor, so to speak, between the government and the Jewish population in the domain of education."[3] His professional experience had long since convinced him of the value of developing a Western-type education within a Jewish population that was almost entirely cut off from European knowledge. In addition, the government made it very clear that the acquisition of rights was linked to the development of education. Lev Rosenthal, who co-founded the Society for the Promotion of Culture with Joseph Evzel, described this political context *a posteriori*:

We were convinced that the government did not wish us ill, that it was ready to expand our rights and valued the abilities that we could put in its service [...]. High-ranking personages with whom we clashed and to whom we addressed our requests and our memoranda on the improvement of our co-religionists' fate constantly complained to us that Jews were wallowing in obscurantism and fanaticism, and remained foreign to everything Russian by engaging in harmful and ridiculous activities. Officials who were well disposed towards us asked us: "How can you hope that we will open up the country to Jews in the current state? Why don't you do something to help your people to emerge from its low moral situation? Why don't you organise its liberation from your obscurantists?" Every time we spoke of civil rights for Jews, officials demanded that we present tangible proof that Jews were improving and deserved these rights. [...] So a few of us decided that we had finally to step forward and publicly inform our people that the time has come to take ourselves in hand and rid ourselves of our worldly shame. With the creation of the Society for the Promotion of Culture, we can hope that the goal – civil equality, which is impossible to obtain without knowing the language of the country and without general culture – will be achieved.[4]

Count Bludov's report to the tsar in 1856 put things no less clearly: "We can give Jews equal rights with the Russian population only slowly, in accordance with the fact that education will have to be broadened among them and that they will [have to] change their way of life and have productive jobs." Alexander II noted on the report: "Absolutely right."[5] The Society could thus provide the government with a guarantee that changes were under way.

On the education front, the battle was waged step by step, and many actions had been attempted before the foundation of the Society for the Promotion of Culture: in September 1858 Joseph Evzel, heading a group of merchants, sent to the education minister, Evgraf Kovalevsky, a memo in which he proposed to make enrolment in state schools obligatory for children of Jewish merchants of the First Guild and of honorary citizens, whether these schools were general or Jewish.[6] At the same time, the minister received from Jewish merchants in different regions of the Pale of Settlement a commitment to send their children to the state schools. Joseph Evzel took care to raise his co-religionists' consciousness in a didactic letter: "When the government sees our indifference in the area of education, it considers us to be opposing its will, and then the acquisition of rights for our people is in danger."[7] The goal was in fact twofold: on the one hand, to transform the ways non-religious education was seen within the Jewish community, including among the most well-off, and on the other hand to obtain from the government guarantees to promote this education. Joseph Evzel also proposed to the minister that four fifths of Jewish schools be changed into ordinary schools, and that the costs of instruction in religion in Jewish schools be reduced by half, since the family had to take responsibility for this domain; in addition, he envisaged the foundation of private Jewish schools for girls; and finally, he explained the importance of establishing scholarships for students in secondary school and higher education: a hundred scholarships and four hundred half-scholarships, for a total of 60,000 roubles a year, financed by the tax on sabbath candles.[8] This petition led to a fruitful dialogue with the administration: the law of 4 May 1859 introduced obligatory school attendance for the children of Jewish merchants belonging to the guilds and honorary citizens. The head of the Kiev school district, Nikolay Pirogov, then consulted Joseph Evzel to resolve the problems of applying the new law: "[In the law] it is not explained how to put this decree into practice. Finding myself on the point of turning to the higher administration regarding this matter, [...] I ask you for your opinion on the subject."[9] In September 1859, Joseph Evzel sent another letter to the minister to draw his attention to the existing obstacles: many merchants lived in cities where there were no Jewish state schools and could not easily find well-trained *melameds* to provide education at home. Aware that his interlocutors in St Petersburg knew little about the situation of the Jews, on this occasion he pointed out that "the Talmud Torahs are not secular schools but homes for poor children and orphans."[10]

In June 1861, Joseph Evzel turned once again to Alexander II with the goal of obtaining for graduates of institutions of higher education the right to live outside the Pale of Settlement.[11] His letter refers to the imperial decree dividing "useful" Jews into four categories: "1) those who have completed courses of study in science in specialised institutions of higher education 2) merchants 3) craftsmen 4) retired soldiers." He expressed the hope that these four categories themselves testified to "three important civil qualities that the government wants to see in Jews: education, productive ability and union with the general Christian mass of the population." Behind the term "union" (*sliyanie*), which was then fashionable, we must not see the idea of assimilation but rather a desire to effect a cultural rapprochement with the Christian population. The tools necessary for that integration are clearly defined by Joseph Evzel: only access to general education would make it possible to understand the language and culture of the country to which the Jews belonged. Joseph Evzel emphasises the fate of graduates of secondary schools and higher education: "Given Jews' legal situation, wherein all sectors except for medicine are closed [to them], all our young people who desire a better situation go into medical science," even though "in general, our students in medicine [have been left] under the restrictive regulations." The ukase of 27 November 1861 gave Jews holding advanced degrees the right to reside outside the Pale. An identical scenario was repeated again and again: the request was taken into account, but only partially. Although limited, these successes encouraged Jews to keep fighting. Joseph Evzel sent petitions to the tsar, the ministers and governmental leaders. On 6 July 1862, the request for permission to found the Society for the Promotion of Culture among the Jews of Russia was sent to the education minister;[12] on 10 November 1862, the minister gave his consent, but its official creation had to wait until the Minister of the Interior validated it on 2 October 1863.

The Society was a response to a strong expectation that found an echo in the journal *Rassvet* (*Dawn*), a weekly Russian-language Jewish newspaper, which in 1860 published a letter from a government official, Nikolay Pigorov, directly targeting Joseph Evzel: "I am astonished by the fact that the defenders of education among the Jews scattered around in various places cannot find the means to unite and act together to fight obscurantism. The latter has already grown considerably stronger in recent years. If there are active people among the lovers of darkness, active and benevolent people have to be found in the domain of education."[13]

Regarding the lack of educational institutions for Jews, a man named Rabinovich expressed his indignation in the same periodical: "What would it cost our millionaires to let go of a few thousand?"[14] The necessity of an organisation that would centralise Jews' efforts in this area was not in doubt: "We have heard that the idea of such a foundation has already been mooted by some of our co-religionists in Petersburg, and we hope that it will be quickly transformed into action. And it is in the capital, which attracts the best of our young people, that the Society must have its headquarters, but it must grow, like a majestic oak, and spread its branches into all the governorates. Such branches might be found in different places, for example, in Vilna, Minsk, Berdychiv, Poltava and Odessa." He concludes: "Whose heart does not beat faster at the very idea of the possibility of such a happy event?"[15]

In response to these diverse expectations, Joseph Evzel appealed to his usual group of friends. He produced the final version of the Society's statutes in collaboration with his son Horace, Emmanuil Levin, Abram Brodsky, Abram Varshavsky, Rabbi Neuman and Lev Rosenthal: "The Society's goal is to propagate education among Jews living in Russia, to encourage literature, and to provide young people with the means to pursue an education. To this end, it plans to propagate the study of the Russian language among Jews, to publish and to support the publication of useful books, translations and periodicals in both Russian and Hebrew, in order to propagate education among Jews and by these means to encourage young people to devote themselves to knowledge."[16] The Minister of the Interior, Count Valuyev, welcomed this initiative, which recognised "the necessity of moving beyond the narrow sphere of the study of the Talmud",[17] but added an important restriction to the statutes: the Society could not have the right to publish books. At that time, the whole publishing industry in Russia was governed by strict rules of censorship.

The founding members of the Society were all rich entrepreneurs.[18] At the first meeting, held at the Gunzburgs' home on 17 December 1863, Joseph Evzel was elected president, Abram Brodsky a "distinguished member", Lev Rosenthal treasurer, Horace first deputy, Rabbi Neuman second deputy, and Emmanuil Levin secretary. Joseph Evzel agreed to pay one half of the Society's operating expenses during his lifetime.[19] Lev Rosenthal was recognised as the second most important contributor, and Abram Brodsky saw to the foundation of a major branch in Odessa, a city that was then becoming a flourishing centre of Jewish intellectual life. A member of the brotherhood of sugar magnates, Brodsky was the only person on the executive committee who did not live in St Petersburg.[20] Sasha de Gunzburg notes that he was "the husband of the ravishing Rosa Brodsky, who was a great friend of my mother's... and had a son with Uncle Alexander (the son was also named Alexander)."[21] The Brodskys were later connected with the Gunzburgs in a more conventional fashion, since one of Horace's sons married a niece of Abram's. After working in the *otkup* with Joseph Evzel, Lev Rosenthal, a cousin of the Gunzburgs, became his associate in many banking enterprises. Like Joseph Evzel, he was a fervent defender of Hebrew. In 1865, the Society had 227 members, among them many rabbis and writers, representatives of the nascent Jewish intelligentsia. Among the latter, Levanda, Gordon, Garkavi and Mapu must be mentioned. The Society promoted contact between individuals with different perspectives on the Jewish cause. Intellectuals and businessmen had little occasion to see each other and economic modernisation had made the Jewish world more compartmentalised than before. Thus Leib Gordon was very surprised that Horace could read Hebrew. But Horace had read Gordon's novels *Ahavit David* and *Michal*. Christians belonged to the Society, such as the celebrated journalist Andrey Krayevsky, the editor of the popular *Golos* (*The Voice*) and *Otechestvennye zapiski* (*Annals of the Fatherland*), and A. Skachkov, the editor of the review *Birzhevye Vedomosti* (*Stockmarket News*); converted Jews also worked with Joseph Evzel, such as Professors Daniil Khvolson, Boris Utin and Vladimir Fyodorov (real name Grinbaum). The latter worked for the government of Kiev as a censor of books in Hebrew. Having become a recognised organisation, the Society responded to requests of all kinds coming from the Pale of Settlement: a call to encourage the creation of a new Hebrew typography, a protest against a local decree closing secondary schools for boys in the governorate of Vilna, a condemnation of anti-Jewish actions by the director of the secondary school in Mogilev, etc.

For Joseph Evzel, "the primary activities of the Society should be principally to organise support for young people seeking a secular education and the propagation of knowledge generally useful among the people."[22] But the question of schools led to lawsuits and ran into practical problems: should the state Jewish schools created in the 1830s, which were too few in number and disliked by the Jewish population, be developed and improved? Wouldn't it be better to encourage Jews to go back to the general curriculum by putting pressure on the government and developing a system of scholarships? How could the traditional *melameds* be transformed into enlightened teachers? As Rosenthal judiciously emphasised, "We are fighting on two fronts: on the one hand against the culture of obscurantism and of the *hassidim* internally, and on the other against our external enemies, the detractors of the Jewish people."[23] The traditionalists did not see why it was necessary to change the traditional system; they did not want anything to do with the system of state Jewish schools; and they were indifferent to the secularised knowledge the Society was promoting. Against this opposing force, the Society chose to participate in the reorganisation of the educational system: after the closure of the state Jewish schools in 1873, it encouraged in 1874 the development of primary schools that were intended to teach Russian and sometimes included religious instruction. It favoured evening courses or "Saturday schools". Another dilemma was what the language of instruction should be. Hebrew, Russian or Yiddish? The Society united Russian intellectuals studying and writing in Hebrew, who would in two or three decades renew the language of the Torah in the form of a literary Hebrew adapted to the contemporary world; and it provided financial support for publications in Hebrew, such as *Ha-Melitz* (*The Advocate* or *The Fine Talker*, depending on the translation), the first Jewish weekly newspaper, founded in 1860 by Alexander Tsederbaum in Odessa;[24] but learning Russian was a priority. Levin proposed a translation of the Torah into Russian in order to break down the linguistic barrier. Joseph Evzel pinned his hopes on the creation of a Russian-language newspaper, as is shown by a letter he sent from Paris to Emmanuil Levin:

> Since its creation, the Society for the Promotion of Culture has had as its goal to have its own journalistic mouthpiece, but that has not worked, because the desired editor has not been found and we do not have the money required to set up an organ of the press. I have recently received a letter from Monsieur Zederbaum in which he informs me that he has decided to settle in St Petersburg in order to publish his authorised newspaper *Posrednik*; he is asking for material assistance from jurists and proposes to take on as a collaborator Dr Kulisher or someone like him.[25]

The Society henceforth supported *Vestnik russkikh evreyev* (*The Courier of Russian Jews* was the name finally settled upon), edited by Tsederbaum for a short time, from 1871 to 1873, but also *Evreyskaya Biblioteka* [*The Jewish Library*] and *Voskhod* [*Sunrise*]. Commonly called "jargon", Yiddish was universally opposed by most of the Society's members, who represented the first generation of the *Haskalah*. The Society favoured the emergence of a Judeo-Russian intelligentsia that reached its apogee in the 1860s and 1870s: around its initiatives gravitated a group of journalists and poets who had come to the capital in search of the positive effects of its intellectual dynamism. Lev Levanda was the first Jewish writer in the Russian language; born in Minsk and educated at the state rabbinical school in Vilna, he lived in St Petersburg, where he worked for various Jewish reviews published in Russian.

Despite the enthusiasm and talent, the Society encountered insurmountable barriers. Changing outlooks within the rigid framework of an autocratic empire was a Sisyphean task. Thus in 1867 the preparation of a two-volume work in Russian, *A Collection of Articles on Jewish History and Literature*, turned into a fiasco. In the context of official Russification, this project seemed realistic. But it encountered immense difficulties: whereas these volumes were intended to be a way of propagating Jewish scholarship that was compatible with secular culture, the censor saw in it nothing more than propaganda for Jewish religion! Salomon Munk's article, "A historical survey of Jewish philosophy", was accused of being too free-thinking; Mikhail Morgulis's "The right of succession in Mosaic-Talmudic jurisprudence" committed, according to the censor, the blunder of elevating the Talmud into law, whereas only the law of the Gospels was valid in the Orthodox Empire; the reference to the story of Solomon in Yehuda Leib Gordon's "An essay on the history of stories among the Jews" was criticised as blasphemous, and so on. Delayed and abridged, the published work did not achieve the desired goal. Joseph Evzel and Horace, who had contributed financially to this project, got nothing for their investment. Confronted by increasingly frequent public attacks on Jews, which were reported and fuelled by the press, the Society for the Promotion of Culture was able to put up only a weak resistance.

In 1873, Horace wrote a "plan for disarming the press hostile to Jews", which he sent to Levin. In a telegraphic style, he drew up a list of priorities: "to found a newspaper in the form of a private company of three or four members", "every financial aspect not depending on the editors", "to find an editor", "costing about 30 per cent less than other dailies", "the editorial stance of the journal must be assiduously liberal [...] and defend *Russia's just interests and welfare*. It must not serve as an organ for any political party or category"; in any case the editor-in-chief and his collaborators must not be Jewish. In addition, during the first year of its existence the newspaper must not engage in any *special polemic* relating to the Jewish question."[26] Such a strategy could never work.

The principal task of the Society for the Promotion of Culture was to support students: the number of Jewish students in secondary schools was constantly growing: 159 in 1853, 552 in 1863, 2,045 in 1870, 2,362 in 1872. The children of *melameds*, craftsmen or small shopkeepers, they needed financial help throughout their studies. Joseph Evzel persuaded the government to allocate 24,000 roubles for scholarships for Jewish students in primary and secondary schools, financed by the tax on candles.[27] Through the Society or within its office personnel, he granted numerous supplementary scholarships. The students knew that there was a "Mr Gunzburg educational agency".[28] Thus, in 1864, the sculptor Mark Antokolsky, who had just been accepted at St Petersburg's Academy of Fine Arts and was the only Jew in his graduating class, became one of Joseph Evzel's scholarship students.

For these men of good will, the hardest trial was building relationships of trust with the central or local authorities: every achievement was fragile. At the end of his life, after twenty years of constant combat, Joseph Evzel was forced to recognise that the hopes raised at the beginning of Alexander II's reign had been dashed. Even within the government, hostility towards Jews was expressed more and more openly. One of the people responsible for this deterioration was a certain Yakov Brafman, a converted Jew who became very famous during the reign of Alexander II. Born in Minsk and a teacher at the rabbinical school, he claimed to be an expert on Judaism but in reality he was the propagator of an insidious anti-Judaism: in 1869, in *The Jewish Brotherhood, Local and International*,[29] he accused the members of the Society for the Promotion of Culture of being "the Jesuits of Judaism", active agents of the "Jewish conspiracy".[30] His *Book of the Kahal*, which was successful enough to be reprinted several times, is a violent criticism of Jewish elites: it is clear that the author was settling accounts with a society against which he nourished a deep resentment. For members of the imperial bureaucracy, these two essays commonly served as an introduction to Jewish life. They soon developed an irrational distrust of the society created by Joseph Evzel and his friends: the latter did not receive authorisation to open new branches or to send rabbis abroad to complete their training, and allocations for university students were ended. It happened that the Gunzburgs had earlier been in contact with Brafman: in the 1840s, Joseph Evzel had successfully organised the defence of a Jew accused of ritual murder in Saratov. The trial had resulted not only in the accused man's acquittal but also in Emperor Nicholas II's decision to prohibit putting people on trial for ritual murder.[31] At that time Brafman wrote an essay that claimed to be learned in which he assumed the existence of blood sacrifice among Jews and tried to make use of it to blackmail Joseph Evzel. His grandson Sasha reports:

> He brought his work to my grandfather and demanded a sum of money for not publishing and delivering the manuscript. Grandfather found this so ridiculous that he flatly refused, and sent Brafman away. The book appeared and was very successful in certain groups, and to the end of his days Grandfather regretted not having paid him off.

At the time, Joseph Evzel had adopted a different strategy: financing a scholarly book by Professor Daniil Khvolson, another convert, to refute the existence of such a tradition. When *The Book of the Kahal* was published, Joseph Evzel bought as many copies as he could and had them destroyed. But in a Russia that was becoming steadily more anti-Jewish, the battle was taking on insurmountable dimensions.

Despite difficulties and certain setbacks, Joseph Evzel had become a popular figure: he was the model for the character of HaSar Emmanuel, "Minister Emmanuel", in Abraham Mapu's novel *Ayit Tsavua*. As a *shtadlan* and philanthropist, he inspired hope and admiration among the Jewish population that had been so sorely tested. A letter sent by students in Kharkov shows what his name meant to young Jews in Russia:

> The rights that have recently been granted to us Jews in accordance with the law of 27 November 1861 have aroused in us a great desire to move away from the past where the education and progress of our people are concerned... The number of tireless labourers among us has gradually increased year by year. [...] [But] we find no support, either moral or material, among our co-religionists. [...] At this moment you are the only person to have acquired a colossal spiritual influence over Russian Jews. Your name will occupy an eminent place in the history of our people's civilisation: you are our Novikov [...]. There is no more time to lose, and we are asking all representatives of our people to throw off the age-old dust of isolation characteristic of humans and to emerge from the selfish, narrow circle in which they have imprisoned themselves... They must consider that their indifference towards us, we who are thirsty for education for the good

of our people, will not prevent us from reaching our goal. Consequently, they must understand that they may find in us offended and bitter sons. The shadow of such justified bitterness is unfortunately already looming. In the wake of those few examples who have been able, despite that bitterness, to extricate themselves, we cannot get far: we can only remember a few remarkable individuals of our time, for whom the same fate as the Levinsohns and Eichenbaums inevitably awaited.[32]

Comparing Joseph Evzel with Novikov, the students reveal their profound esteem for the president of the Society for the Promotion of Culture: in Catherine II's time, the journalist Nikolay Novikov (1744–1818) had been the greatest defender of the Enlightenment in Russia, encouraging the development of education within the Russian people. Even though Joseph Evzel took on the responsibility of being a latter-day Novikov for the Jews of Russia, and even though he supplied himself with the means to do so by working ceaselessly and having effective allies, he too found himself helpless when confronted by the magnitude of the problems.

13

Last Wishes

IN THE AUTUMN of 1875, Joseph Evzel began to show the first signs of ill health. At his side in the house in Saint-Germain-en-Laye, Horace informed his son David, who was then studying philology at the University of St Petersburg: "My son, my journey depends on many things. Grandfather was indisposed, but his indisposition continued and has now been going on for the past five weeks. That is no joke at his age."[1] Two years later, on 12 January 1878 Baron Gunzburg died at his home in Paris. He had just celebrated his sixty-fifth birthday, an honourable age. The words spoken by the chief rabbi of France, Lazare Isidore, at the time of his burial in the Montparnasse Cemetery sketch a faithful portrait of the battles he fought:

> Ah! Gentlemen, had this good man's funeral taken place in St Petersburg, the whole city, without distinction of religions, would have walked in the procession! Abundant tears would have flowed from every eye, and in all the temples prayers for the repose of his soul would have rung out! Twenty years ago, gentlemen, St Petersburg did not exist for Jews; there was in that city neither rabbi nor synagogue, nor school; it was a city closed to our brothers, and to live there one had to renounce one's faith. Today it is a splendid community, and Gunzburg played a large part in that work of rehabilitation; today there are schools, orphanages, institutions of every kind.[2]

Through the rabbi's speech, the charisma of "the indefatigable champion of the Jewish cause" is clear. "And how many friends, how many relatives, who hoped to be able to take shelter for a long time yet in the shade of that powerful tree!" Rabbi Isidore emphasised Joseph Evzel's constant concern for the Jews of Russia:

> You live in France, he often said to me; you're free, you have the same rights, the same privileges, and every door is open to you. But over there, in the country where I was born, I left brothers who are suffering, who are groaning in poverty, who live in ignorance and sometimes in persecution, who are deprived of their rights, and who are rejected because they are Jews. I was raised among them, it is there that my ancestors are buried; it is to that population that I owe everything I am, and I want everything that God has given me in strength and intelligence, in fortune and consideration, to serve its emancipation; I want to strike off their chains everywhere I can, and, where I cannot, I want at least to make them lighter.[3]

In St Petersburg Jewish craftsmen and military veterans showed their gratitude by having a gold medal made bearing his image.[4] A delegation of students listened to the funeral elegy given in his honour in the Russian capital.[5] Many years later, when the great synagogue of St Petersburg had finally been built, the bust made by the French sculptor Adam Salomon came to decorate the entrance hall, where it remained until the Bolshevik Revolution.[6] In France his death was less commented upon than the balls he had given a few years earlier. A brief notice in *Le Figaro* announced a "discreet" funeral service, in accordance with the family's wishes; in *Le Gaulois*, a fanciful obituary referred to his "Jewish origins", gave erroneous information according to which "he began by being an orange-seller," and made his fortune the result of "risky speculations", concluding banally, "Recently, he had a splendid town house built for himself on Rue de Tilsitt, where he ended up attracting the world of finance. It is said that this house holds works of art of the greatest value."[7]

Joseph Evzel had taken care to write down his last wishes in the form of a long will that he dictated in Paris on "20 July/1 August 1876" to his loyal friend Mathias Mapu, who also translated it into French. In addition to practical arrangements, it formulates, by way of a conclusion, a precise moral legacy urging his descendants to remain faithful to Judaism and to Russia:

Thus ending all questions concerning the distribution of my property, I bequeath to all my heirs the belief in a single God, the religion of our fathers, and attachment to the Emperor and to the homeland. That is why if one of my heirs or descendants should have defamed during my lifetime the honour of my name by taking part in a state crime or in another [crime] connected with the deprivation of rights, or if he has emigrated from the homeland and not returned to it when requested by the government, I withdraw from him in advance any right to the heritage that may remain after me, and the share assigned to him by this will I give to his legitimate heirs, who will be authorised to replace him in the order of succession.[8]

The general tone of the document shows great intellectual rigour, a sound business sense, and a concern, not without severity, for his descendants.

"Providing for the well-being of [his] dear family", he divides his property in accord with the respective merits of his heirs: he begins by reserving for his wife "Rassia" (Rosa) an annual pension of 30,000 roubles and full ownership of all the movable goods without exception (precious objects, ornaments, jewellery, finery, paintings, household ornaments, furniture, horses and carriages, and "wine of every kind"), as well as the house in Saint-Germain-en-Laye "with all its furnishings and outbuildings"; for the rest of his "whole fortune" in Russia and abroad, made up of "buildings, lands, fees, concessions, businesses, houses, bills of various credit institutions, stocks, bonds and other papers of value, in debts on persons and places", he names his "three sons Herz [Horace], Ury and Salomon David" as his heirs, while favouring Horace: "The remaining inheritance is to be shared among them in such a way that Herz, because of the good morals, filial love and attachment to his family that distinguish his character, has as his share 50 per cent and the two others each have 25 per cent." In contrast, the eldest of his children, Alexandre, was formally disinherited, and Joseph Evzel gave this justification:

I tried in every way to set up my eldest son [Alexandre] Susskind so that he would be able to have his own independent capital, and with my help ensure his ability to support himself and the future of his family. To this end I allocated to him a portion of the profits of a few of my old, advantageous businesses that, combined with a more than adequate allowance from me, could have allowed him to make a very fine fortune. But despite my fatherly exhortations, through his careless living he not only dissipated everything I allotted to him but even reduced my capital by about 300,000 roubles. Such careless behaviour constantly worries me, and since I myself acquired my whole fortune, I exercise the right that the law grants me to credit the aforementioned 300,000 roubles to the account of my son Salomon from the legacy that will remain after me and as a result of the division already made I deprive my son Susskind of his right to inherit, even should he claim the inheritance or some parts of it that are located outside the Russian Empire according to laws foreign to our homeland.[9]

However, as a severe but just patriarch, Joseph Evzel took steps to ensure that his granddaughter Rosalie and his grandsons Michel and Jacques would have decent incomes. For his "daughter Mathilde (Khaya-Matla)" Joseph Evzel notes that he left a "special supplementary will written in French", in which he gave her "[his] house in Paris at Rue de Tilsitt no. 7, along with the associated quarters at no. 18 on the same street", a "capital of one million francs for the education and establishment of her children", and "a life annuity of 50 thousand francs per annum". The will also mentions his heirs' continuation of his charitable activities "in favour of the Jewish community's charitable institutions in St Petersburg" and "the offering of seventy thousand roubles" for the construction of a synagogue. Moreover, he wished to assign the revenues from "fifty thousand desyatinas of land located in the governorate of Tauris", in Crimea, for a Jewish agricultural colony, "as he had already begun to take the official steps but of whose success he cannot be sure". The agricultural institution was to bear the name "Rassia-Anna" in twofold homage to his wife and to his beloved late granddaughter. Despite the efforts of Horace and his legal advisers, the "Rassia-Anna" agricultural colony was never to see the light of day.

This will can also be read as an interesting testimony to Joseph Evzel's talents as a manager. He provided that "in the course of the first three years from the day of [his] death, all [his] affairs were to be continued in common by [his] three inheriting sons mentioned above, just as [his] banking house in St Petersburg and his agency in Paris had to exist as they had previously." Following their father's recommendations, Horace, Ury and Salomon set up an "Office of Baron J. E. Gunzburg's heirs" that worked for three years managing the property in common before dividing it up. In 1882, Isaak Zak, their faithful accountant, drafted a fair copy of the "division of the inheritance" among "Messieurs the Barons Horace, Ury, and Salomon". In the end, the assets, including an estimate of the properties (lands, securities, contributions) amounted to significant sums: Horace received 1,604,704.72 roubles, and each of the other two sons received 802,352.36, in accordance with the shares of 50 per cent and 25 per cent stipulated by Joseph Evzel. Taking the lowest exchange rate for the French franc during that period, that comes to a total of 7,702,582.66 francs.

In another astonishing sign of modernity, Joseph Evzel mentions the possibility of appointing mediators in the event of litigation among his heirs:

> I shall die caressing until the last moment the sweet feeling that in the mutual relations of my heirs and in general of all the members of my family an inviolable peace and perfect harmony will reign, so that they will never give each other cause for trouble. However, if – God forbid – misunderstandings and discontents should arise among them regarding either the interpretation or the execution of this will, then to avoid inconveniences and the prejudice that can result from a lawsuit, I urge them to settle their disputes by arbitration, choosing as arbitrators: 1. The private counsellor Evgeny Ivanovich Lamansky, 2. The current private counsellor Alexandre Antonovich Abaza', and 3. The commercial counsellor Ivan Egorovich Kondoyaki, who, I allow myself to hope, will not refuse to acquiesce to my last wish and will carry it out in good conscience.

The document concludes by mentioning the witnesses who could attest that Joseph Evzel was in fact "of sound mind and body", among them Mathias Mapu and Mayak Israel, son of Isaak Zak. In the absence of a quarrel, the heirs had no need to resort to the arbitration proposed.

In fact, the three designated heirs hastened to correct the part of the will concerning their brother Alexandre. With the agreement of Ury and Salomon, Horace immediately went to Turin, where Alexandre, who was currently living in Naples, came to meet him. To soften the severe arrangements made by their father, they signed "a family pact on their respective honours and good faith".[10] The three heirs promised to pay each of their nephews, Michel and Jacques, 150,000 roubles, thus doubling the sum provided by the will, payable six months after the death of their father Alexandre. In the meantime, interest at the rate of 5 per cent per annum would be paid to Alexandre in the form of a living allowance of 6,000 francs per month. The capital Joseph Evzel bequeathed would be paid without waiting for their uncles' deaths, at the time of their marriage "if the latter occurs with the consent of the family Council" or when they reached the age of thirty-two. The "family Council" was, moreover; formally designated: it comprised their grandmother, father, mother and uncles. Horace, Ury and Salomon promised to pay Alexandre's debts, amounting to 300,000 roubles, and to pay him a sum of 500,000 francs. They forgave the debt of 60,000 roubles owed by their sister-in-law Rosalie, who was living separately from her husband, on condition that she promised to ensure all her property was in bare ownership, in other words so that she did not have the right to enjoy and use it, "in particular the town house situated in Paris on Avenue Bugeaud, no. 10" to her sons Michel and Jacques. Finally, "as a commitment on honour", Horace renounced his rights to his future inheritance from his mother in favour of Alexandre. In correcting their father's severity, the three brothers showed that they felt no hostility towards Alexandre, whose main fault was to have lived carelessly and expensively. They were also sensitive to the fate of their nephews, one of whom was admired by all: at the time of Joseph Evzel's death, Jacques was valiantly fighting on the Turkish front. No doubt they were glad they had acted in this way when in December of the same year Alexandre died suddenly at the age of forty-seven.

In Paris, the reading of the French will did not please Mathilde. As the "assisted and authorised wife of Monsieur Paul Fould, the counsel of the Council of State, a Chevalier de la Légion d'Honneur, with whom she lives in Paris, Avenue des Champs-Élysées no. 138", she informed her brothers of her discontent via her lawyer.[11] At thirty-two, as the mother of three charming daughters, she set her conditions: there was no question of exchanging the "eleven hundred and ten Russian Railway Company bonds at four and a half per cent", provided as a dowry by her marriage contract, for the town house on Rue de Tilsitt, or being content with the one million francs accompanied by the life annuity of 50,000 francs stipulated by her father. She "intended to exercise [her rights] regarding her father's legacy both in Russia and in France by virtue of the law of 14 July 1819 and of the international convention of 1 April 1874." The transaction document of 24 February 1878 presents the compromise reached, not without friction, between the young woman and her two brothers:[12] in addition to the 2 million francs, a further 1 million francs was to be paid in 1881 (by part-mortgaging the lands in Bessarabia); the life annuity of 50,000 francs was to be paid to her at her home in Paris, every three months; Horace, Ury and Salomon promised to pay Mathilde's heirs 811,000 francs after her death; and she agreed to sell her brothers the rights and shares that she owned in the saltworks at Chongar (now Chonhar) in Crimea for 1 million francs. Moreover, she ceded the securities held in her account at the Gunzburg bank, with the exception of her shares in the shipping company on the Sheksna. Mathilde thus inherited from her father approximately 5 million francs. Joseph Evzel had left his heirs a veritable empire: until the 1917 revolution, his descendants worked to exploit this patrimony, from which they drew most of their resources. "Because of the good morals, filial love and attachment to his family that distinguish his character",[13] Horace was singled out to play a special role in continuing his father's work, a role that he performed conscientiously until his own death.

Part III

Horace: Banker, Patron of the Arts and Philanthropist

This was a man whom no one ever disparaged.

Nicholas II, Emperor of Russia,
speaking of Horace de Gunzburg (1909)

14

A New Head of the Family

SURROUNDED BY HIS eleven children, eight sons and three daughters aged from two to twenty-three, Horace (Herz in Hebrew) naturally assumed the role of head of the family upon the death of his father. Without having the latter's audacity, he was intelligent and a hard worker. Physically, he resembled his father to the point that in some photographs the two men could be confused with one another: dark beard and moustache, a broad forehead and sparkling eyes. One photograph shows him wearing a mink hat: the shimmering brilliance of the fur draws attention to the regular features of his face. But in addition to looking like a worthy heir, Horace reflects a wiser image. His qualities compelled admiration:

> He was the very embodiment of an aristocrat in the most elevated sense of the word. A big man of imposing stature, elegant, distinguished, with soft eyes, a kind smile on his lips, he breathed good will. Everything about him was attractive: his way of speaking (he expressed himself more easily in French than in Russian), his gestures that were so full of dignity and his comments that were never curt, even in cases where the subject provoked his indignation. He seemed to be addressing the heart of his interlocutor, whom he persuaded not so much by argument as by the emotion with which he himself was overwhelmed and which he made his interlocutor share. This cordiality was the basis of his influence and of the charm that emanated from his person.[1]

With his innate tact and thoughtfulness, Horace acted prudently. His numerous letters to family members, written mainly in French, reveal a kind, engaging person.[2] After the death of his beloved wife Anna in 1876, his mood darkened. However, he tried to keep moving forwards. The year 1878, which began so sadly with the death of Joseph Evzel, unfortunately brought more trials: in December, Horace lost not only his brother Alexandre but also his son Marc (1859–1878), the third-born and the artist in the family.

Marc was photographed at the age of seven wearing a suit and sitting on a low stool with a thick sketchbook on his lap. He holds a pencil in his hand, as if ready to begin drawing. His dark hair, cut short, shows off his large, anxious eyes. The pose is sufficiently unusual to suggest that in his case a taste for drawing was a precocious passion. Although Horace often reproached Marc for not studying hard enough, he admired his son's talent as a "budding painter": "Your laziness must be very pleasant," he wrote, "but since you are not alone in this world you mustn't become too addicted to it. It is said that all the knowledge in the world would give no pleasure if it could not be communicated to others. Although laziness has its charms, they cannot be enjoyed if one is too indolent to talk about them and to paint – I mean, to describe – their delights. I forget that I am talking to a budding painter."[3] Horace maintained a relation with Marc that was simultaneously demanding and loving, as is shown by this other letter:

Nice, 25 February 1876

Dear Marc,

    Tomorrow it will be seventeen years since a third son was born to us. A new child is a new worry. What will he be like? How will he do? [...] When he is young, worries are small, in adolescence they grow rapidly – but ultimately, what joy when one sees a good point, a ray of light! The good is so sweet and so beneficial that no sooner does one feel it than all the ill one has suffered is forgotten. If you only knew how much we rejoice at each little step forward that you take, what enthusiasm the slightest good thing coming from you excites. Being sentimental and cordial, you would do good every day, and your mother and I bless you for each noble idea that your letters bring us. [...] Your father, Horace.[4]

During the winter of 1878 Marc contracted pneumonia, but this did not arouse great concern. To speed his recovery, Horace sent his family to Menton, with which the Gunzburgs were already familiar, while he went to St Petersburg to deal with problems raised by their inheritance. He left David, then twenty-one years old, to watch over his brother and keep him informed. The first news was reassuring: "What is really pleasant and admirable is the whole group's good humour and cheerfulness," David wrote. "Grandmother [Rosa Gunzburg] has never been so content. She seems very happy to be at the head of our little regiment. Marc continues to cough, but less frequently than in Paris [...]. The doctor has just left. He says that one of Marc's lungs was hardened by his pneumonia and that it is still making noise."[5] The medical treatment prescribed was typical of the period, and of doubtful efficacy: fresh air, donkey milk, cod liver oil, walks in the sun with a parasol, etc. The arrival of spring did not bring the hoped-for improvement. Marc began coughing blood. In Berlin, tormented by worry, Horace sought advice from a renowned physician and tried to reassure his family:

Dear mother and my beloved children,

You can imagine the state your telegrams put me in. I have already twice consulted Freriche, a man competent in every respect. Here is what he said: "Sputum containing blood and even haemorrhaging are not serious in someone who has had pneumonia. The lesion at a site opens and bleeds. There is no reason to panic, bleeding is not the worst thing. Every physician knows how to stop it." [...] Since no one in our family has suffered from lung disease, there is no danger that this might take an unfortunate turn.

[...] Above all, don't lose your head and don't scare Marc. He needs all his health and all his strength to attenuate and overcome the disease. You give me news without saying whether the congestion is increasing, and which side it is affecting. Does he have pain elsewhere? Is he sweating too much? What about his temperature and his appetite? Freriche is against too much medication. Good food, calm, speaking little and not staying in bed, but rather walking slowly, and never along the seaside. Do you need another recommendation? Get well, my child. Love and kisses. Horace.[6]

Feeling guilty for not having given Marc the necessary care at the beginning of his illness, whose first symptoms had appeared at the time of Joseph Evzel's death, Horace tried to send him comfort and affection from afar:

> Marc, my son,
>
> It is my fault and that of the sad circumstances that you remained in Paris longer than you should have. I am obliged to go and set straight what your grandfather left, on the moral as well as the material side. Everything being urgent, I shall not continue my journey if I don't receive today or tomorrow reassuring news about you. Each time you coughed I felt it in my chest [...] Take care of yourself. Courage and perseverance!
>
> [...] Ah! I am a very sad sire when I have to leave you and go so far away from you. May God protect you, my children, and may he give me an opportunity to be with you. Hug Louise and all the others for me, your father who loves you as one can love only a child as sweet as you are. Horace.
>
> Your two paintings will be in Petersburg. *Le Vieillard* went directly, and *Graziella* is with me, along with a few of your drawings.[7]

By taking to St Petersburg the works the ill young man had painted in France, Horace hoped to get them included in the corpus of paintings presented by Russia at the Paris Universal Exhibition: "Your *Graziella* was well-received and when you can, write a few words to Bogolyubov to thank him for his help."[8] (The painter Alexey Bogolyubov had added a few finishing touches.) Marc's work was rewarded by a silver medal from the Academy of Fine Arts, an honour that delighted the whole family.[9] Asked for their opinion, the painters Ivan Kramskoy and Pavel Bryullov (the nephew of the famous Karl Bryullov) were encouraging: "If the doctor allows it, think about doing some painting, cultivate your art. You have such aptitude as a colourist, but to become what your sketches promise there is a lot to be done. [...] May God grant you health and self-fulfilment."[10] For his part, Horace took advantage of his stay in St Petersburg to see the works of the "Wanderers". Set up as an *Artel* (cooperative) around Kramskoy, these artists chose to paint close to the working people, not hesitating to travel through the Russian provinces, whence their name. Since the foundation of the movement in 1859, their work had acquired a certain fame. In 1879, they exhibited in the capital for the sixth time. Perspicaciously, Horace described for his son the works he admired:

> There are several beautiful things at the *peredvizhnaya* [Wanderer] exhibit. Kramskoy has a northern night, Kuindzhi a pine forest at sunset that produces a warm and very magical effect, Shishkin a wheat field with scattered trees – very beautiful! A magnificent pencil portrait – I forget the artist. Lutans [not identified] a machinist brightly lit by the hearth and the machine. In general, this exhibit contains many more beautiful things than the collection of paintings intended for the Universal Exhibition.[11]

Witnessing the birth of the new "Russian" art, Horace showed sound judgement. For example, Ivan Shishkin's famous painting of a wheat field (known under the title *A Rye Field*), which was bought at the time by Pyotr Tretyakov, is now a jewel in the gallery that bears his name. Rejecting the academicism that produced only a pale imitation of the West, the "Wanderers" were inspired by "Russian" subjects drawn from everyday life, religion, landscapes and so on. In mentioning the paintings, Horace wanted to make Marc aware of an innovative movement from which his Parisian upbringing had distanced him.[12]

Being far away allowed Horace to transmit experiences and reflections, and not only in the arts. In a letter, he draws up a list of his activities in Russia, taking care to share with his children news about the family business, their country and Judaism, three subjects close to his heart:

> My dear Marc,
>
> I should reply to David, who wrote me three letters, but I know he wants [me] to write to you, so he will not hold it against me if I write to you in response to his letters.
>
> I am sending you the map of the former European Turkey as outlined by the preliminary treaty. You will see that there remains nothing more than a single mouthful of it, and even then we are not talking about a German mouthful, which would happily swallow up the Sea of Marmara along with the British battleships.
>
> An excellent intellectual trend has appeared among Jewish students

of medicine. In the old days they used to turn their backs on Jewish people. Now that the animosity has become stronger, they have realised that Judaism is worth something and they ask us for books dealing with this subject. I am very happy about this, and I will have the Society [for the Promotion of Culture] send them as many books as possible.

Confidential.

For you two and for Louise; you can talk about this to grandmother, but on the condition that it not be written to Paris. Here it is: the annual statement for the bank here is very large [expression in Hebrew]. It is not a million that it shows in profits, but 1,670,000 roubles. We have never had such years. Be discreet and demand the same of others. Now, with all the payments made, the legacies, we three brothers together have the same capital as your late grandfather had alone. Grube did an outstanding job.

I embrace you, my dear children. David and Marc, may you always be as good friends as you are now.

Horace.[13]

On 3 March 1878, the victorious Russia had just imposed on the Ottoman empire the Treaty of San Stefano, which recognised the independence of Bulgaria and strengthened the tsar's influence in the Balkans. Russia's optimism was to be short-lived, because the Western powers quickly convoked an international congress in Berlin to come to an agreement regarding the Eastern question and to impede the tsar's imperialism. Privately, Horace could rejoice in the bank's solidity, three months after Joseph Evzel's death, but he could also congratulate himself on the usefulness of his commitment to the Jewish community. In the early spring of that year, he therefore allowed himself to spend a few weeks in France with his children:

God only knows how much I am unable to tear myself away from business and from other occupations, but I do not want to leave you alone for such a long time. I need to immerse myself again and get away a bit from the avalanche of business that is falling on me. I am no longer capable of doing this work [alone] and I expect and hope soon to have the help of my children. Praise God that there is room for all and that each of you will have your task, provided that you remain well and in good health.[14]

Unfortunately, Marc's illness had now been diagnosed as tuberculosis, and his health steadily declined. In July, Horace set him up in a tranquil villa in Fontainebleau. When Horace returned to Russia, he had his son sent two tickets to the Paris Universal Exhibition.[15]

From May to October 1878, the French capital hosted, for the third time, a Universal Exhibition (or World Fair): it provided an opportunity for the MacMahon government to show the whole world the new, republican France. On the Champ-de-Mars, a palace of 400,000 square metres paid homage to the products and new technologies of many countries. The Russians created a sensation by presenting Pavel Yablochkov's first electric light bulb: the general public realised that electricity could produce light. The Gunzburgs were involved in this at several levels: as a member of the Russian organising committee, Salomon, Horace's brother, was invested with the official title of "delegate of the Ministry of Estates". As the owner of gold mines in Beryozovsky (in the Perm region), he displayed at the exhibition "gold-bearing sands, lead and copper ore, and rocks";[16] the family also presented raw sugar from the refinery in Mogilno, in Podolia, noting that it provided "an annual production of between 8,000 and 11,000 quintals, thanks to seven generators with the power of 300 horses and 400 workers"; and finally the Fine Arts section showed, as planned, two paintings by Marc, which were Italian in inspiration: *Un patricien* (called *Le Vieillard* in the correspondence) and *Graziella*. Contrary to what Horace feared, the Wanderers were also present, Kramskoy with his *Christ au désert*, Repin with *Haleurs de la Volga*, and Shishkin with several forest landscapes. Horace lent a sculpture from his collections: the Parisians were able to admire a marble bust of Peter the Great made by Mark Antokolsky, of whom Horace was then the principal patron. For his whole body of work Antokolsky was awarded a gold medal in recognition of his powerful and original achievement. In painting, the French artists Cabanel, Meissonier and Jérôme also received the highest award, while Kramskoy was among a handful of Russian artists given more modest distinctions.

August 1878: Marc's situation was unchanged. While part of the family made its annual visit to the spas, he remained in Fontainebleau along with the youngest children and his Warburg aunt. His grandmother Rosa had biscuits sent to him from the spa town of Kreuznach:

My dear grandson,

You gave me great pleasure by the few lines that you added in your hand to Mlle Ickauer's letter. I was very charmed by them and I wanted to show you my satisfaction by sending you some "Kreuznacher [Bretzeln]". I hope they have reached you in good condition and that you will find them to your taste. [...] I embrace you lovingly and ask you to say hello to your dear brothers and sisters as well as to Mme Warburg and Mlle Ickauer, whose regularity in sending me her reports I greatly appreciate.

Your loving grandmother

R. Gunzburg.[17]

Following the doctors' recommendations, the decision was soon made to send Marc to Madeira, in the company of his brother David and their aunt Rosalie Herzfelder. The idea was not a good one: humid, as it often is in the Mediterranean in late autumn, the climate of the island was to be fatal to the young man suffering from tuberculosis. Before his departure, Horace had a few things prepared for him that constitute a moving *vade mecum*: "1) St Marc de Gérard [perhaps a reproduction of a painting?] 2) Aug[ustin] Thierry [historian] 3) A[ndré] Chénier [poet] 4) Le C[onte] de Lisle [poet] 5) maxims and proverbs from the Talmud and midras [*sic*] 6) a box of sweets 7) Beiglech [in Yiddish, a bagel] made by grandmother 8) your red fez 9) the frame for a portrait of Mama 10) photographs of the children. And maybe the travel clock."[18] Rosa, Marc's paternal grandmother, adds "a smoked tongue", accompanied by instructions: "Put it in water [...] and then cook until well done and afterwards eat [...] with the doctor's permission."[19] The tutor, Monsieur Rohmann, also went along. Horace took advantage of their trip to order Madeira wine, which he planned to give to the prince of Hesse, thanks to whom the Gunzburgs had received their title: "I request that M. Rohmann go in person to Mr Blaudy to ask whether his old *sercial* [one of the four types of Madeira wine] is sufficiently exceptional that I can give it as a present to the Prince of Hesse and to Prince Orlov [the Russian ambassador to France]. From Paris I will inform you by telegram how many should be ordered and sent directly to: His Highness the Grand Duke Monseigneur the Prince of Hesse, Darmstadt, Germany. You know the address of the Prince O."[20] For his part, Horace settled in for the autumn at the house on Rue de Tilsitt, from where he kept Marc informed regarding the return of his paintings after the closure of the Universal Exhibition:

My dear Marc,

[...] Your paintings have been returned to me. I've had the Louis XIII drawing room put back in order and have made a few changes in order to be able to arrange the courtyard the way Mama wanted it to be. I put the Gothic piece between the door of the other room and the door of the L. XIII drawing room, and then the piece that was there in the place of the wooden chest. The latter in the middle of the drawing room towards the second window. [Your] portrait of Pierrot in the place of the Gothic piece. *Graziella* in its old place and across from it, above the couch, *Le Vieillard*. They are my favourite paintings, each one has its own wealth of reminiscences, and their place will always be amid all the other objects dear to me.

I have just bought from M. Bogolyubov a study of Moscow, very pretty, I am having a frame made by Souty and I will hang the painting in my office between the chimney and the outside wall. Just imagine that B. charged me only 2,000 francs for his study-painting. Antokolsky is working on Spinoza for me. That will cost a lot more. [...] The artists' club has been sanctioned by the chief of police and we have everything in order. We meet there frequently, and interesting persons [wish] to sign up, the list of members is growing and we have 140, I believe. [...][21]

The "artists' club" that Horace mentions is the Society of Russian Artists in Paris (la Société des artistes russes de Paris), of which he was the treasurer. He was actively engaged in art patronage, out of personal taste, out of fidelity to his late wife, who had enjoyed the company of painters, and out of empathy with his son's passion. He also kept Marc up to date on family news, with its highs and lows. "Uncle Alexandre returned to Naples, where he fell ill," while at the home of Salomon and "the pretty little baroness" (to use the *Gaulois*'s expression), who had been married for a year, the mood was joyful, with the arrival of a first child at Rue de Tilsitt, Robert, born on 18 October: "Henriette is well. Bogolyubov saw her and told me that he was completely dazzled by her beauty, which has changed from Venus de Medici to Venus de Milo, plus her arms. The baby came to visit yesterday! Henriette and the infant go out when the weather permits. Not always; it is raining and the temperature is more than 15 degrees." Before his death, Marc received two more letters from his father: in the first, Horace promised his son reproductions of paintings: "I am going to ask whether there are photographs of Kramskoy. But which painting do you want to have? I will have photographs of your old man and the portrait of Pierrot made. But don't be impatient. Now, at the end of the year, photographers are very, very busy and God knows when they will take the order."[22] In the last letter, he expresses concern about Marc's health, while driving rain continued to immerse Madeira in a harmful humidity, and informs him that "in the [*Journal*] *Officiel* a pompous attestation has been given to Antokolsky,"[23] who received the Légion d'Honneur.

Marc died in Madeira on 22 December 1878, far from his father and cared for by his brother David. The family were devastated. The "budding painter" joined his grandfather, mother and uncle Alexandre in the family mausoleum in the Montparnasse cemetery. (Fate was to deal a further blow to David, who had to endure a similar trial several years later, when in 1891 he lost his son, also named Marc and also ill with tuberculosis, as he cared for him in Menton.) To adorn Marc's funerary plaque, Horace commissioned Mark Antokolsky to make a portrait of the young man. Fleeing the anti-Jewish atmosphere of the St Petersburg Academy of Fine Arts, the sculptor had just moved to Paris. He, too, had lost a son, and sublimated his pain in *La Perte irrévocable*, a delicate work in which the infant, lying on a pillow, seems to be asleep.[24] In memory of Marc, he created *Le Dernier Printemps*, a moving bas-relief in marble: wasted by his disease, Marc looks angular and distinguished, with a luminous intelligence. Antokolsky knew Marc, whom he genuinely liked and whom he expected to become a great artist. Horace also established the "Marc de Gunzburg" fund at the Academy of Fine Arts. The grant was intended for Jewish students, but was unfortunately seldom awarded because the Académie was increasingly closed to Jewish artists.[25] The family cellars held more than two hundred bottles of *sercial* from Madeira that were drunk a few decades later by members of the family who had fled the Bolshevik revolution. *Graziella* and *Le Vieillard*, along with the rest of Marc's paintings and drawings, are now lost, with the exception of the "portrait of Pierrot", which has been preserved at the home of a descendant in London. It is a moving and lively work that might be thought to have been commissioned from a venerable master, and in which we in fact see the "considerable aptitude as a colourist" emphasised by Horace. The four-year-old Pierre (called Pierrot) looks at his brother with intense blue eyes whose anxiousness contrasts with his adorable white silk suit adorned with a black satin bow and mother-of-pearl buttons.

15

Turgenev and the Society of Russian Artists in Paris

DEAR HORACE OSIPOVICH,

Having learned of the further misfortune that has struck you, the committee of the Russian Artists' Mutual Aid Society of Paris wishes to express its most sincere and deep sympathy.

All the members of the committee – and of the Society – are particularly stricken by the loss of your son – a young man with so much   promise and talent – because his natural tendencies, his favourite occupations, were precisely connected with what concerns most of us, that to which we devote ourselves.

In him you have lost an exemplary son and Russian art [has lost] one of its most promising young artists. Such wounds heal only with time. We do not seek to offer you inappropriate words of consolation, but we hope that you will not decline to receive from us, at this moment that is so sad for you, the repeated expression of our sincere respect, of our almost familial feeling, which you have been able to awaken in each of us and which only increases and grows stronger in view of the undeserved blows that have struck your wounded heart.

Paris
26 December 1878
The members of the Committee
I. Turgenev
A. Bogolyubov
A. Kharlamov

Baron Lev Frederiks

Mark Antokolsky.[1]

Such condolences reveal the friendship and esteem that bound Horace to the authors of this letter, including Ivan Turgenev. The two men had grown particularly close during their visits to Paris, even though they had also long had the opportunity to meet one another in St Petersburg at the homes of common friends, the Stasyulevichs. In 1859, when Turgenev created a "literary fund" in the Russian capital to provide aid to writers, Joseph Evzel and Horace had responded generously to his request for donations.[2] Founded on 10 December 1877, the Society of Russian Artists in Paris brought the two men together in support of an unusual philanthropic cause. The project's twofold ambition was to bring both financial aid and visibility to Russian artists living in Paris. Eugène Melchior de Vogüé had not yet published his famous essay on Russian culture. On this occasion, Rue de Tilsitt became a unique place where artists could meet and exhibit their work. Marc was being treated in Madeira, and Horace made his studio available to artists: to thank him for this act, which showed "his steadfast love for art and [his] well-known support for painters", the Society "considers it unnecessary to add that [the] studio will be returned to him whenever he wishes."[3] After Marc's death, the studio remained open to artists. The Society of Russian Artists was born of the friendship between Ivan Turgenev and Alexey Bogolyubov, two men who had much in common: with their bushy beards and long white hair, they were charismatic figures of "Old Russia"; recognised and accomplished artists, they were also moved by the same kindness and the same capacity for enthusiasm about young talent.

Initially a customer of the Gunzburg bank, Turgenev had become a friend, as is shown by the few letters that have come down to us.[4] The writer had found in Horace a helpful adviser on the management of his rather tangled financial affairs and liked to recommend the Gunzburg bank to his friends: "[The Gunzburgs] have handled many business affairs for me and have always dealt with me very fairly,"[5] he wrote from St Petersburg to a friend. On the occasion of the sale of his Tapki estate (between Oryol and Kursk), he showed the sales agreement to Horace and asked his advice. Horace suggested a judicious correction: "Dear Ivan Sergeevich, With figures one can prove anything (when one wants to). Your tranquillity, claims to be avoided, etc. are well worth a few million roubles."[6] Demonstrating by means of professional analysis that the commissions taken at various stages had caused Turgenev to lose 10,000 roubles, he concluded: "Excuse me for entering into such detail; although I am very busy, one of my most pleasant occupations is being useful to you. Very sincerely yours, H. Gunzburg."[7] The writer and the banker maintained a steady relationship, punctuated by the meetings of the Society of Russian Artists, high society musical and literary events, and the simple friendly meetings typical of the small Russian colony in Paris in the 1870s. Turgenev sought to draw Horace's attention to some of his protégés: "You know that most of the poor Russians turn to me when they are in need. They ask for work, a position, but almost always it ends in the gift of a little money. Among the Russians, there is one who attracted my attention. His name is Ivan Yakovlevich Pavlovsky, he is twenty-four years old. Like many others he was driven out of Russia for political reasons and went to America, where he spent two years doing hard work. He worked on a farm [...], rode horses, etc. He has learned English, which he speaks very fluently. [...] He will come to see you tomorrow at 11 a.m."[8] For the Gunzburg children, this relationship was a source of pride: "The first time I saw him," Sasha writes, "was at a morning charity event given by Mme Pauline Viardot in her house on Rue de Douai, around 1878. Everyone was old. Mme Viardot sang, in a (rather) cracked voice, a ballad, *Si la mort est le but.*" Turgenev read Pushkin's *The Gypsies*: "At first, his recital was too influenced by the rhythm of the verse, but later he warmed up and made the hall shiver when he delivered Aleko's apostrophe."[9] Another memory, this time of St Petersburg, regarding Turgenev: "I see him sitting on a bench in the villa where we were staying on the Kamenny Ostrov [an island near St Petersburg], with Aniouta on his lap, reciting Russian nursery rhymes to her, which, moreover, Stasyulevich had taught him."[10]

The Society of Russian Artists would never have come into being without Alexey Bogolyubov, a naval officer and painter who had been living in Paris since 1874. The grandson of Alexander Radishchev (a famous dissident writer of Catherine II's time), Bogolyubov was nonetheless on good terms with the imperial family, and notably with Grand Duke Alexander Alexandrovich, the future Tsar Alexander III. The artists in the Society were all his friends and most of them came to be close to Horace: Alexey Kharlamov, who had painted a portrait of Turgenev in 1875, made copies of the portraits of Horace by Kramskoy and of Anna by Bonnat, which are today in the collection of the Alliance Israélite Universelle in Paris; a former student at the Ecole des Beaux-Arts (School of Fine Arts) in Paris, Pantaleon Szyndler; was Marc's teacher for a short time and made copies of Rembrandt for Horace; Ivan Pokhitonov gave the Gunzburg children lessons in Russian and mathematics; Nikolay Sachs, a landscape painter, acted as the Society's secretary; Yury Leman, who was then just beginning his career, was to join the Wanderers in 1881; and as for Mark Antokolsky, he had just finished his bust of Turgenev. The Society also included wealthy amateurs such as Baron Lev Frederiks (1839–1912), a staff officer, and Pavel Zhukovsky (1845–1912), the poet's son.

This little circle functioned like a club: the members met at least once a week, recreating a little bit of Russia on Rue de Tilsitt. "We met in the evening, on Saturdays," one of them writes, "for tea without either sandwiches or zakuski. In these simply furnished rooms, there was enough room for people who liked to play cards or chess [...]. There was an abundance of pencils, sheets of paper, boxes of watercolours, brushes, water-pots – in short, everything necessary for drawing or painting."[11] According to Antokolsky, "[their artistic] interests were not Parisian but Russian." Moreover, most of the artists were close to the Wanderers. Work sessions were organised in the studio, where models and material were provided; artists could leave their works on deposit; a library and a billiard room added to the place's charm: on the occasion of literary soirées, Turgenev read his works or those of talented young writers, sometimes Jews, which he knew would please his host, as is shown by a letter addressed to Horace: "In addition, I want to read in our society a very interesting little narrative by a young writer, a Russian Jew, that gave me great pleasure."[12] With the Society, Horace combined the useful and the pleasant. The posthumous inventory of his possessions revealed that he bought works from many different artists: *Arabes sur un divan* by Szyndler, *Nature morte* by Kharlamov, *Marine* by de Pokhitonov, *Vue de Saint-Pétersbourg* and various studies by Bogolyubov, not to mention numerous sculptures by Antokolsky. In an article on Russian art published in the *Revue des Deux Mondes* in November 1882, Eugène Melchior de Vogüé referred to "this little group of artists, naturalised Parisians": Bogolyubov and "his delicate seascapes, his pretty bird's-eye views of cities" or Pokhitonov, "the creator of these minuscule views of Ukraine, so true, so curiously coloured, which have already won for this very promising painter the nickname of the Meissonier of the landscape."[13]

Once a year, a major exhibition showcased the work of the members. In 1879, Bogolyubov took advantage of the visit of the tsar's son, Grand Duke Alexander Alexandrovich, to France to arrange for the princely couple to come to Rue de Tilsitt. Sasha describes this memorable day:

> As fate would have it, during the visit of the grand duke and heir to the throne [...], the opening of the Russian salon was to take place one Sunday morning after the mass on Rue Daru. Precisely at the time when the imperial family was emerging from church, Bogolyubov made a sign to the secretary of the Society, Sachs, who was also wearing a beard and a wide-brimmed bolivar hat, urging him to take a cab to Rue de Tilsitt to announce that the grand duke would be arriving shortly. A member of the Russian secret police who was following all the grand duke's movements approached Count Olsufyev, the grand duke's aide-de-camp, and drew his attention to the words exchanged between the two painters, telling him that the grand duke had to be prevented from leaving, since the elderly gentleman was telling the young man where His Majesty was going. "Don't worry," the count told him, "that gentleman is a close friend of the grand duke."[14]

The visit went smoothly: "My brothers Pierre and Vladimir, who were seven and six years old, were charged with giving flowers to the grand duchess. Pierre was completely at ease and led the grand duchess off to see certain paintings that belonged to my father. The grand duchess went up to Vladimir and asked him, 'Why are you so quiet, my child?' 'I was told not to speak,' he replied."[15] The guests also admired the Gunzburgs' collections, including Dmitriev-Orenburgsky's spectacular painting, *La chasse offerte à S[on] A[ltesse] le grand-duc Nicolas aîné par le baron Ury de Gunzburg à Chambaudoin*, in which Turgenev's very familiar silhouette could be recognised. Horace was warmly thanked for having financed this exhibition.

At that time, Russians in Paris were living under intense surveillance: the Society was threatened with prohibition on several occasions because of the Russian police's suspicions regarding some of its members. In

Russia, terrorist revolutionary groups represented a constant danger to the imperial family's life. In February 1880, the tsar escaped a further assassination attempt: "Here, at noon, a solemn *Te Deum* was sung in the church on Rue Daru to thank Providence for having saved Emperor Alexander a fourth time."[16] Among the faithful, the press mentioned not only Baron Gunzburg but also the painter Bogolyubov. The Society of Russian Artists had another occasion to arouse the suspicions of the Russian secret police: "[Turgenev] was not interested in politics, and that was why one evening he brought along his friend [Pyotr] Lavrov, the famous revolutionary who [...] had been sentenced to death in his country. On this occasion there were again great difficulties with the Russian police."[17] Another incident was directly connected with the Gunzburgs: the young writer Nikolay Minsky (known as Vilenkin) began his career as a teacher of Russian to children. "Once, at a charitable event held at the Russian embassy, he was invited as a protégé of Turgenev who, as a great man, did not think to scrutinise artists' political opinions. Minsky read [his] play [*Tri Uspenski, The Three Sleepers*]. The very next day the Russian secret police sounded the alarm and demanded that the group of Russian artists be dissolved from Petersburg." Thanks to Bogolyubov's intercession with Grand Duke Vladimir, the president of the Academy of Fine Arts, the Society was saved... After Bogolyubov's death, Kharlamov became president of the Academy of Fine Arts, which survived until the revolution.

Horace and Turgenev's friendship was strengthened by the writer's benevolent attitude towards Jews, even if in that regard the banker had to endure a final disappointment: in 1882, Turgenev refused to support a public protest against pogroms, even though he had been the first to give 100 roubles to the subscription fund launched by Horace in aid of the victims. He thought that only a severe condemnation on the part of the tsar would be effective. Nevertheless, in 1858, he had signed a letter defending Jewish journalists.[18] On an everyday level, he disavowed his compatriots' anti-Judaism: having taken Ambassador Orlov to Mark Antokolsky's studio, he was outraged by the plenipotentiary's reaction to his sculpture of Christ. "How dare a Jew represent our God?" Orlov had protested. Turgenev pointed out that Jesus himself was a Jew. "I had the impression that he understood my words as blasphemy."[19] At the end of his life, Turgenev could count on the help of the Gunzburgs, to whom he sold his estate of Spasskoye-Lutovinovo in order to leave enough for his daughter and his grandchildren to live on.[20] When he died on 3 September 1883, the Society of Russian Artists established a grant in Turgenev's name. From Dinard, Horace sent to his son David the arrangements for the burial: "It is absolutely necessary that a deputation from our *obshch. Prosve.* [Society for the Promotion of Culture] be present at the burial. Perhaps even our *obshchina* [Jewish community] should be represented there as well, but that is debatable, and I leave it for the community to decide."[21]

16

Confronting the Pogroms

IN 1881, HORACE decided to gather all his children around him in St Petersburg, keeping the house on Rue de Tilsitt as an occasional pied-à-terre. Despite their recent trials, they formed a happy family, living sumptuously in a grand residence that he had just bought at 17 Konnogvardeysky [Horse Guard] Boulevard, a few dozen yards from St Isaac's Cathedral. On the day they moved in, Aniouta, the youngest daughter, gave her father *khleb i sol*, bread and salt, in accordance with the tradition.[1] In an old postcard showing the "Gunzburg home" the threshold is protected by an elaborate canopy that no longer exists. One now enters the building through a security door installed by Gazprom, which has established its St Petersburg office there. Otherwise, nothing has changed. Plump *putti* joyously frolic on the facade, which is stuccoed in reddish ochre, while muscular Atlases support the main balcony, and allegories of fertility and abundance crown the whole. Probably purchased by Horace after his father's death, the building was constructed in 1858 by the architect Roman Kuzmin (who later designed the Russian Orthodox church on Rue Daru in Paris), with ornaments and sculptures by David Jensen, a pupil of the renowned Danish sculptor Thorvaldsen, in the neo-baroque style then in fashion. As is often the case in St Petersburg, the building is part of a group of several buildings connected by interior courtyards. The bank's offices occupied part of the building, accessible by the bordering arteries, at 20 Galernaya Street and 4 Zamyatin Lane. The "Boulevard" – the expression used in the family – was the kingdom of Meyer, the steward and major-domo, who was always ready to receive visitors, friends and supplicants. He was a former cantonist, a veteran of the Crimean War[2] who had entered the Gunzburgs' service rather late. According to Sasha, "everyone in Petersburg knew him, including the members of the Hesse family, for whom he organised trips and ran errands in the city. By the time he died, he had become a knight of several orders, both Russian and Hessian."[3]

The house was vast, opulent and comfortable; the walls and mantels were ornamented with stucco decorations, either white or gilt, depending on the room; the richly sculpted, coffered ceiling can still be seen in the former dining room.[4] Horace chose Louis XVI furniture, adorned by the usual oriental carpets, porcelains, bronzes, wall clocks, mirrors and chandeliers.[5] The artworks are mostly signed by painters who were friends of the family: oils and watercolours by Mihály Zichy, family portraits by Ivan Kramskoy, and numerous canvases by members of the Society of Russian Artists. Through the large, sturdy windows, double-glazed to combat the cold and the humidity, there was a view of two rows of young poplars. Konnogvardeysky Boulevard was built over the Admiralty Canal, which is now underground. In St Petersburg, running water and stoves provided the comfort that the Gunzburgs were already familiar with from Paris.

A place for both living and working, the Gunzburg house was open to the outside: community meetings, assemblies of the Society for the Promotion of Culture, an office for grants, musical evenings, balls and so on. As in Paris, religious life gave the week its rhythm. Horace was a pious man who often referred to the Talmud, as his correspondence shows.[6] In particular he corresponded with Rabbi Yitzakh Elkhanan Spektor of Kovno, a prominent intellectual who encouraged Horace's involvement in the community.[7] For the *shabbat*, he gathered children and friends around him:

> His observance of the sabbath not only did not shock the representatives of other religions but even won him respect. No state minister would have summoned him for an audience on a Saturday, because they all knew that the baron could not use a carriage on Saturdays, and getting to a meeting on foot was difficult. On Saturdays, he signed nothing. The employees of his bank knew that and they all prepared the documents to be signed on Friday. He did not open a letter or telegram. They were brought to him already opened.[8]

Like his father, Horace felt himself to be Jewish and Russian. "This patriotism was shot through with a deep loyalty to the government and the dynasty. He knew the regime's imperfections, but he never fought against the existing order, following the Talmudic precept that says that the laws of the state are laws that require moral subordination. Any revolutionary movement made him sick."[9] In 1880, he even commissioned his friend Antokolsky to make a bust of Alexander II; he intended it for the great St Petersburg synagogue whose construction had just begun, but in the end he gave it to the Academy of Painting, where it was destroyed in 1917. At the "Boulevard", therefore, life seemed to offer only happy promises. But history decided otherwise: the assassination of the tsar triggered a disastrous chain of events.

On that fateful day of 1/13 March 1881, the whole family was busy organising the "Bazaar of the Jewish Children's Home" to benefit the orphanage created by Anna, as Sasha recounts:

> I recall very well how Valuyev [the former Minister of the Interior], who had begun a literary career at the end of his political one, asked our father to introduce him to [the publisher] Stasyulevich so that he could entrust the publication of his novel *Lorine* to him. The charity sale, the bazaar of the Jewish Children's Home, had been announced for 1 March. Louise [Horace's eldest daughter] had, as usual, been in charge of the book sale, and her counter always had lots of customers thanks to Stasyulevich and Wolf. Valuyev had promised her that on this occasion he would allow her to sell the first copies of his novel. Unfortunately, between noon and one o'clock, we heard a terrible explosion [the bazaar was held in an apartment of the Great Konyushennaya which the owner had made available to the orphanage]. The emperor had just been assassinated and the bazaar was closed.[10]

The consequences of this assassination were to be particularly grave for the empire's Jewish population. Even before this tragic event, dialogue between the Jewish community and institutions had been tense. For Horace, a respected *shtadlan* affectionately nicknamed *papasha*, it was already no longer a matter of broadening Jews' rights but of preserving those that had been gained earlier. Laws which, in the first part of Alexander II's reign, had liberalised the framework of Jewish legalisation, depended for their implementation on the attitude of the governor and his local agents, along with periodic sweeteners to the police to get them to close their eyes to the illegal residence of a Jewish family. From St Petersburg Horace organised the legal defence against the local administration's persecutions by appealing to the Senate. Success in many cases stemmed from the fact that in the Senate, at the head of the First Department, which dealt with Jewish affairs, was Viktor Artsimovich. Liberally inclined, he had been an actor in the reform of serfdom undertaken in 1861. He had subsequently become a friend of Horace, who had commissioned Antokolsky to make a bust of Artsimovich, not for official use but to put in his drawing room at the "Boulevard",[11] as a token of his gratitude for Artsimovich's support in the Kutaisi affair. This was an iniquitous lawsuit that had taken place in March 1879: near this small town in Georgia, in the province of Imereti, nine Jews had been accused of the "ritual murder" of a Christian girl. Alerted, Horace hired the famous attorney Pyotr Alexandrov and commissioned a brochure on the alleged ritual murders to be written by Daniil Khvolson, a professor of oriental languages at the university, with the title *Do Jews use Christian Blood?* A friend of the Gunzburgs, in 1861 Khvolson had already written a complete study of this subject, at Joseph Evzel's request. Alexandrov's defence in Kutaisi was resoundingly successful. In the wake of this case, the priest Ippolit Lyutostansky, a notorious anti-Semite, wrote a mendacious essay on Jews' use of Christian blood that was challenged by the journalist Alexander Tsederbaum in his newspaper, *Russkiy Evrey* (*Russian Jew*). Lyutostansky sued Tsederbaum for defamation: the trial took place in St Petersburg, attracting a certain amount of public attention. In September 1880, the judge, Trofimov, a friend of Artsimovich, ruled against Lyutostansky. This victory for justice offered only small comfort: anti-Semitism was expressed with increasing vigour in both words and deeds, and usually left unpunished.

Alexander III's accession to the imperial crown (reigned 1881–96) occurred in the tragic context of the regicide: before taking up his role he had witnessed the agony of his father, torn apart by the bomb thrown by young anarchists belonging to the little group *Narodnaya Volya* (*The Will of the People*).[12] The new tsar drew from this crucial event a complete determination to meet the challenge of autocracy, which he saw as an unshakeable rock. He was a *samoderzhets* or "autocratic" tsar, the holder of personal power that no one could share or limit. He commanded his former tutor, Konstantin Pobedonostsev, the Holy Synod's chief magistrate, to write his political *credo*, which was made public in his manifesto of 28 April 1881: "The voice of God orders us to put ourselves confidently at the head of absolute power. Trusting in divine Providence and Its supreme wisdom, full of hope in the justice and strength of the autocratic regime we are called upon to affirm, we will serenely preside over the empire's destinies, which will henceforth be discussed only between God and us."[13] In matters of domestic politics, the tsar reaffirmed his mystical bond with the Russian people. Although the assassination did not trigger the revolutionary chaos the terrorists had hoped for, it was followed by anti-Jewish violence in the Pale of Settlement on the occasion of the Russian Orthodox Easter, on the pretext that one of the eight conspirators of 1 March – Gesya Gelfman – was Jewish. The violence continued endemically for two years, in the course of which 250 pogroms were recorded. The term "pogrom", a neologism forged from the Russian verb *gromit'*, "to pillage", appeared for the first time in the press, even though official documents preferred to use the word *besporyadki* ("disorders").[14] The material, human and political damage was immense: the violence affected possessions far more than it did persons; it was estimated that the material losses amounted to several million roubles and the number of victims to around fifty, half of whom were *pogromshchiki* (looters) killed by troops who had opened fire to suppress the riots; but these figures do not take into account the wounds, rapes, trauma and helplessness experienced by thousands of Jews faced with the destruction of their homes, their tools and their merchandise. To organise aid, a committee to help Jews suffering from pogroms[15] was created in St Petersburg. Horace served as president. Local committees were formed in the cities concerned. In six months the committee raised 220,000 roubles, of which 38 per cent was donated directly by Horace, 33 per cent came from sources outside Russia, and 29 per cent from within the Russian empire.

The first pogrom had taken place in Elizavetgrad, in the province of Kherson, in Crimea, in the course of Easter week, on 15/27 April 1881. In the following days, Horace obtained the permission of the governor-general, Alexander Dondukov-Korsakov, to send 5,000 roubles to the victims through the mediation of the local administration: the money was delivered by the municipal council to the leaders of the local Jewish community. Shortly afterwards, a pogrom took place in Kiev: "For two consecutive days, 26 and 27 April/8 and 9 May, a mob with savage, wild instincts abused, robbed and sacked Jews living in the territory of southwestern Russia, Kiev and its surroundings, and left thousands of families in a desperate condition which they cannot escape."[16] On 1 October, the St Petersburg Committee had already distributed more than 150,000 roubles, two thirds of which went to the Jews of Kiev:[17]

> [With twelve thousand roubles] we have been able to feed about seven thousand men, women and children who, being without bread and without shelter, had camped in tents and even in the open near our fortresses and military hospitals. This kind of aid continued for twelve days until a large number of these unfortunate people could be evacuated, either by procuring for them the pecuniary means, clothing and railway maps to enable them to return to their native places, or by taking them back to their homes, even though they were still in ruins.[18]

The violence spread to the surrounding villages and to other provinces. In the Pale of Settlement, "the atmosphere was thickening": the towns were full of rumours; the Jews were waiting their turn.[19] On Christmas Day 1881, Warsaw was hit. The following spring, the territories of present-day Ukraine were struck again by a wave of pogroms, the most murderous of which was the one in Balta, 29 and 30 March 1882. Abroad, feelings ran high. In France, "The Anti-Semitic Movement in Russia" was the headline in *La République illustrée*; in Paris, Victor Hugo presided over the Aid Committee for the Jews of Russia, created in 1882, whose members included Prime Minister Léon Gambetta, the diplomat Ferdinand de Lesseps, the philosopher and historian of religion Ernest Renan, and the archbishop of Paris, Mgr Joseph Hippolyte Guibert, among others.

Although the priority was to provide aid to the victims, denouncing the violence and punishing it were no less essential. Horace was embarking on a new battle more difficult and thankless than the one he and his father had waged up to that point. Faced with this new phenomenon, against the particular background of a new monarch, Horace and those close to him tried to understand how these pogroms were perceived at the highest levels of the state in order to obtain a firm condemnation. The government's attitude seems in fact to have been a masquerade: officially, it blamed the rioters, and even punished the troublemakers, the arsonists and the looters, but the ambiguity was real: "When the rioters were asked why they were attacking the Jews, they replied: 'People say our little father the tsar wants it so.'"[20] It seemed essential to convince the tsar in person. But the emperor who a year earlier had visited in an almost friendly way the Russian exhibition on Rue de Tilsitt had become inaccessible, surrounded by heavy security, a recluse in his Gatchina palace. On 4 May 1881, Horace obtained a meeting with Grand Duke Vladimir Alexandrovich, the tsar's brother, who facilitated an official audience with the emperor. On 11 May 1881, Alexander III received a delegation composed of Horace, Abram Zak, the director of the Discount Bank, the lawyer Alexandre Passover and the businessmen E. B. Bank and M. I. Berlin.[21] Incomplete and second-hand, the available testimonies about the interview allow only a partial reconstruction. Faced with the emperor, Horace began by tactfully expressing his regret to see "loyal subjects of the tsar" unjustly mistreated, to which Alexander III replied that he considered "all his subjects to be equal irrespective of their origins or religious denomination." According to some newspapers, he even added: "Jews merely serve as a pretext, and it is the result of the anarchists' work."[22] The rest of his remarks were not reported in the press, but can be found in certain memoirs of the time: "There are certainly a few economic reasons that have contributed to it," the monarch is supposed to have added, "such as the Jews' exploitation of the peasants."[23] Far from accepting this suspicion, the banker Zak replied: "Jews are industrious but, finding no opportunities to work as craftsmen because of the peasants' poverty, they are forced to keep taverns as a way of surviving." Even as he acquiesced, the tsar added that Jews evaded military service, thereby helping to attract the peasants' hatred. Zak recognised that there was a tendency to flee military obligations, but explained that the duty to serve was scrupulously honoured by the merchant group. In conclusion, the delegation was invited to submit a memorandum to the Minister of the Interior, Nikolay Ignatyev.[24] For Horace and the representatives of the Jewish community, the task was hard: between anarchistic tensions and the alleged economic exploitation, they had to find arguments to convince a tsar who was obviously prejudiced against Jews.

The difficulty was aggravated by the personality of the new minister,

Ignatyev, who was as dangerous as he was incompetent, and who engaged Horace in a duel to see who had more influence. After the audience at the Gatchina palace, hope was still possible: the Odessa journalist Mikhail Morgulis wrote a 44-page report demonstrating that the economic constraints weighing on Jews were the source of the ill-feeling directed at them, and that only the suppression of the Zone of Settlement could resolve this situation of conflict. Contrary to what had been agreed, Ignatyev never passed this report on to the tsar. At the same time, Horace had Emmanuil Levin prepare a short memorandum intended to be circulated in official circles to counter the increasingly offensive anti-Semitic opinions in the tsar's entourage.[25] The tsar's former tutor, the councillor Konstantin Pobedonostsev, hoped to see the Jewish population diminish, in accordance with his sinister prediction: "One third will convert, another third will emigrate, and the rest will die of hunger."[26] With still greater malice, Ignatyev hounded Jews with a relentless hatred: his attitude introduced a profound rupture with recent decades during which Russian officials had shown themselves willing to improve the Jews' legal status, provided they made an effort to integrate. Ignatyev rejected the possibility of a fusion (*sliyanie*) between Jews and the empire's Christian population. Even as he created so-called objective inquiries and investigative committees he sought to isolate and exclude Jews from the empire's economic life. His public support for Jewish emigration was only another expression of this objective. The "Gunzburg group" waged a sophisticated battle against the Minister of the Interior, identifying those who could represent their ideas within official authoritative bodies, collecting and publishing information and statistics favoured by the Russian bureaucracy, mounting campaigns to inform public opinion in Russia and abroad, and coordinating the efforts and actions of Jewish members of the Ignatyev Committee. When the latter entrusted Count Kutaysov, an experienced man with a good reputation, to lead the inquiry, the Gunzburg group ensured that he would have a chance to meet rabbis, merchants and professors who spoke perfect Russian and were allies. All of them provided evidence showing that the pogroms were an anti-Jewish movement whose social and economic causes could be fought.

Horace had to wage a parallel battle within the Jewish community against the supporters of a new policy: convinced that the integration of the Jewish community was impossible, young journalists were challenging his role as *shtadlan* and advocating emigration. For example, three journalists at *Rassvet* pressed for the organisation of a great assembly of Jewish representatives.[27] At the same time, a delegation from Kiev, supported by its governor, Alexander Donduko-Korsakov, was fighting to provide a legal basis for people who wanted to emigrate. In late July 1881, the government informed Horace that he had to do everything he could to keep people from leaving, because the exodus encouraged a very negative image of the Russian government abroad. Thousands of refugees had in fact gathered at the border with Austrian Galicia. Horace obtained the government's authorisation to organise in St Petersburg, from 31 August to 7 September 1881, an initial meeting of representatives of Jewish communities, to be followed by a second meeting in April 1882. Horace's offices were involved in both these events, providing documentation and financial aid to the delegates. Levin provided secretarial services. Seconded by Samuel Polyakov, Horace tried to focus the discussions on help for the victims of the pogroms, avoiding the contentious question of emigration.[28] On 22 March 1882, a few days before the meeting of the second assembly, he succeeded in submitting to the emperor a brief statement of proposals for preventing future pogroms.[29] Horace explained that the disorders resulted from "dark forces" that mobilised a gang of vagrants against Jews and predicted that in the future this tactic might be used against the "non-Jewish population". Jews served as a target because they were perceived as foreigners to whom fundamental human rights could be denied. As a result of the authorities' failure to act, these disorders had become endemic. In conclusion, Horace asked an essential question: how did the state think it could ensure the security of towns in the Pale of Settlement while doing nothing to stop the growth of an "indigent Jewish proletariat"? Having been unable to prohibit the circulation of Horace's note, Ignatyev wrote a point-by-point critique of it. He took advantage of the opportunity to present Horace as the "hidden" representative in St Petersburg of the Alliance Israélite Universelle, an international Jewish organisation that was banned in Russia and suspected of defending the interests of the Western powers. Horace had in fact been an early supporter of the Alliance at the time of its creation, but after it had been prohibited in Russia, he had made absolute secrecy the condition of his involvement in it.[30] That allowed Ignatyev, the police and the press to make sinister use of this information: repeating Yakov Brafman's slanderous arguments, Ignatyev warned the tsar against the activities of "the international *kahal*".

It was in this deleterious context that the second assembly of the representatives of the Jewish communities took place in April 1882: the supporters of the new policy announced in the press that great attention would be given to emigration. But the conference expressed its opposition. Ignatyev had just declared: "The eastern frontier is open to Jews. They have already taken advantage of this right. Their emigration will not be hindered in any case." And to add to the general confusion, Polyakov was maladroit enough to propose that the government finance the creation of a Jewish colony in the areas of Central Asia that had recently been conquered. During the representatives' assembly, Mark Mandelstam, an eminent ophthalmologist, expressed his indignation: "We don't even have the rights granted to any animal, and now we are being permitted to go to Tashkent in order to get rid of us there forever." Horace was explicitly criticised for his anti-emigration position by the journalist David Gordon:

> It is impossible to understand why rich Russian Jews, with Baron Gunzburg at their head, should seek to prevent any general emigration, the only immediate remedy for the general destruction that is affecting our poor fellow Jews. These individuals, who are themselves doing nothing, are paralysing other people's efforts to aid oppressed Jews, on the pretext that equal rights and privileges are expected to be granted to all Russian Jews. But in truth they do not themselves believe in this expectation. Their attitude can only be dictated by their hard-hearted indifference, which is all the more shameful on the part of those individuals sitting calmly alongside their money, while their brothers in faith are exposed to the most terrible suffering.[31]

The same resentful desire for vengeance is expressed by the socialist journalist Ben Ami: "Even from those villains, from those devourers of the blood of the Jewish people, one had not expected that. But that's how it is: Ephrussi, Polyakov and Gunzburg have found refuge in this vile lie."[32] The historian Simon Dubnov, who was in St Petersburg in the 1880s, also helped to spread a negative picture of Horace and his collaborators, whom he described as "Baron Gunzburg's official circle".[33] It is interesting to note that for a long time these contemporary criticisms alleging indifference and inaction were not challenged by historians. But a thorough examination of the sources, recently carried out in particular by John Klier in the framework of his work on the pogroms, shows that Horace and his collaborators worked tirelessly behind closed doors in the chancelleries, with discretion, and thus without publicity. And if we judge by the results, the fiery articles written by young journalists were no more successful at preventing pogroms or the decline of the living conditions of Jews in Russia. However, as Klier ironically notes, supporters of the new policy benefited from a benevolent posterity: "There are streets in Jerusalem that bear the names of Moshe Leib Lilienblum and Lev Pinsker, but no Gunzburg Boulevard or Polyakov Avenue."[34]

After the second assembly of the representatives, in May 1882, the laws prepared by Ignatyev were promulgated. They were known as the "villainous laws" or the "anti-Jewish laws", and seemed to encourage violence, as is stressed in an article that appeared in the magazine *Novoye Vremya* (*The New Times*):

> Among all peoples there is a law that punishes inciting people to hate and scorn each other; in our country, a power higher than the laws has unleashed hateful passions and taken the persecutors under its protection. In all the provinces inhabited by Jews, committees have been named to seek the measures to be taken for the purpose of safeguarding the interests of the Christian populations against the encroachments of Jews. [...] The strangest proposals have been voted for with a marvellous unanimity. In one province the wish has been expressed that Jews be expelled from the cities, in another that they be expelled from villages; elsewhere people limited themselves to demanding that Jews be prohibited from living on the main streets.[35]

The "provisional Ignatyev solution" was based on the fact that the local populations maintained unfriendly relations with Jews and forbade them to live outside cities and towns in the Pale of Settlement. Inspired by a last hope, Horace tried to move the tsar by means of a *Memorandum* written in May/June 1882, 250 handwritten pages composed by Levin.[36] Proposing a Russian-style "Jewish emancipation", the text returned to the idea of the action of "dark forces",[37] demonstrating that Horace was convinced that the enemy could not be identified. All that counted were the steps to be taken to combat the multiple threats weighing on the

Jewish population. Horace knew that he could count on a few allies within the government itself.

The anti-Jewish policy was accompanied by financial complications for the Russian government: the finance minister, Nikolay Bunge, openly criticised the Ignatyev solution. In a report on the issuing of new gold bonds, he pointed out that Russia's foreign credit had been weakened by "the unsatisfactory condition of the Jewish question, which encouraged criticism of Russia among the principal and most influential foreign capitalists". After the pogroms of spring 1881, the Rothschilds had in fact drawn their partners' attention to the reprisals to be envisaged against Russia. In April 1882, Bunge added: "It is known that Rothschild has recently said to anyone who would listen that he would not buy Russian government bonds; Rothschild's words are very influential in the whole European stock market and the result has been an unusual decline in the value of our bond issues and of the stock market in general."[38] Apparently acting at Bunge's request, Count Pyotr Shuvalov approached the Rothschilds in Paris to explore the possibility of lifting their ban on Russian financial operations. On the subject of these negotiations, which lasted several months, Alphonse de Rothschild wrote to his cousins in London in February 1882: "In Paris there is a rumour that the [Russian] government had taken out a loan with us, because M. Gunzburg [*sic*] was seen with us. We talked about the unfortunate situation of Jews in Russia."[39] In reality, Horace had come to confirm that the bank could serve as a means of putting pressure on the government to bring about an improvement in the condition of the Jews.[40] Thus Alphonse let the Russian emissary know that the Rothschilds would have liked to have responded favourably to the government's proposal, but "unfortunately, it has made that impossible for us because of the persecutions of which our poor fellow Jews are the victims in Russia."[41]

17

A Season at the Spas

THE LONG MONTHS of fighting had been hard on Horace. The season to take the waters had come, and he left St Petersburg, leaving his son David in charge of both the bank and the management of community affairs. Eight children accompanied him: Louise, Sasha, Alfred (always known in the family as Mimi), Mathilde (known as Babita), Pierre (Pierrot), Vladimir and Aniouta. Their correspondence allows us to trace their movements during the summer of 1882. In July Horace took the waters at Marienbad and then at Franzensbad, another spa in Bohemia. In August he went to Frankfurt for a few days and then on to Paris, before spending the rest of the summer in Dinard, "the most aristocratic of the Breton beaches", according to *Le Gaulois*, which listed Horace among the bathers. His itinerary afforded an opportunity to see the whole family in the course of the trip: the Warburgs in Marienbad, Grandmother Gunzburg and Aunt Ida (Ury's wife) in Kreuzbad, Salomon and Henriette in Hamburg, Aunt Louise Ashkenasy in Karlsbad, and the Rosenberg grandparents in Franzensbad, a resort that Jacques, Alexandre's son, also regularly visited. The young people went to the theatre, concerts and balls, taking advantage of the amusements offered by the spa towns, especially Marienbad, which they regretted leaving to "go to that hole called Franzensbad".[1]

Distance transformed David into the family's epistolary confidant. Collected in a thick volume in the Russian National Library, the letters he received from his father, brothers and sisters weave an intimate account of the summer of 1882. Each correspondent reveals his areas of interest, questions, joys, hopes or disappointments. The boys took advantage of this to get closer to their cousins, as Sasha wrote: "Now that the situation is a bit more settled, surely you can get away for a while and enjoy the company of our aunts and cousins too? We have seen Aunt Rosalie and Aunt Louise, with whom Mimi and I were in Vienna. Esther is only here till tomorrow. Ernestine leaves next week... It's a pity Papa is so tired, we would have been able to have fun with so many charming people." But he adds, "Can you believe that something has happened that I never thought possible? I'm homesick. Is it because we are doing nothing at all here and this winter I got used to working, more or less? Is it my aversion to change? I don't know, but what's certain is that I'd already like to come back home, hoping to see you again too."[2] Thus Horace had succeeded in acclimatising his children to Russia... Louise also worried about David: "I'd like to know what you're doing up there all by yourself in Petersburg. I'm well aware that you're working, but I would[n't] want you to tire yourself out too much, because you are fond of pushing things a little too far."[3] Babita described for him their excursion to the theatre to see "a very good actor from Vienna, Schweighofer, whose plays *Stucker krieg/le Kaporal/der Krieger im friden* [sic]", which focused on the relations between Jews and Christians, were typical of Austrian cultural life in the 1880s: "The plays are all excessively silly. *Semit und antisemit*. He plays all the roles himself and he even sometimes plays the orchestra."[4] Babita also urges her brother to maintain contact with a certain Konstantin Dmitrievich: "P-s If you see K. D. give him very best wishes from me, please." Horace also handled with care the mysterious suitor (who would not end up as Babita's husband): "May he long play the leading man! Please give him my very friendly greetings."[5] The question of studies was another preoccupation: confronted by an official climate that was hostile to Jews, Horace feared that his sons would have difficulty enrolling in universities. Sasha expressed his concern about this to David: "So far as my examination is concerned, Papa does not want me to hurry (to put it off until next May). That's too bad because the influence of Count Tolstoy [recently appointed Minister of the Interior] will probably make itself felt on public education as well, and with my knowledge of ancient languages I will be more likely to fail next year than now."[6] Mimi wondered whether he should go to university or not: "Finally, advise me about next year. I don't believe that Papa will permit it, because he is very scared by Sasha's examination, but who knows? Maybe it will go well all the same, especially since for the last year or two I've thought only of going into business once university is finished, and considered the idea of starting this autumn only to get it over with faster."[7] There was no question of higher education for the girls. In a moving confession, Louise, who had been devoted to her brothers and sister since the death of their mother, revealed her hesitations as a girl who had "a thirst for knowledge":

21 July 1882, Franzensbad. It is so hot today that my hand trembles and it's difficult to guide my pen. But I am well aware that you don't mind if my writing makes zigzags so long as I come to bore you a little. [...] I don't know how I manage it, but here I don't have time to do anything. Above all, I lack time for serious reading. I have hardly an hour in the morning, or two hours on days when I don't bathe, when I can remain undisturbed. [...] I have so many instructive things to read, and I would like to read them in the course of the summer, because I have a thirst for knowledge, I would so much like to know things! When I'm alone I always read serious books. I am reading for a moment Duruy's history, people say it's dry but I don't find it dry at all. Yes, I see that you all, and especially you, think that I'm not capable of serious occupations, don't believe that, because my heart bleeds every time I see on your lips a smile of disdain, because, believe me, another girl in my position who had lived as I have for the past six years might not have learned even what I myself know. So I set to work, but I still have the best part of my life before me, and I still hope to be able to make up the time lost (except for my studies) because during that time I have learned a mother's duties. For truly I do not believe that a mother can feel more acutely than I do everything that is related to children, I am proud when I see them, but it breaks my heart to see in them just any little child.

I really don't know why I have said so many silly things, but I suppose that you won't hold it against me?

Grandfather [Rosenberg] has not been well, but it was nothing and he is rapidly recovering. [...] Last evening we went to the theatre to see Blasch, a comedian from Vienna who made us laugh a lot, even though the play was terribly silly.

Farewell, I embrace you with all my heart. Your sister who loves you tenderly, Louise.[8]

For Horace, visiting spa towns allowed him to attend certain business meetings: "Papa went on a walk to meet someone he hadn't previously met. The whole Polyakov family from Taganrog is here."⁹ A social life that combined healthcare, leisure and work reigned: the Gunzburgs were received by the Bleichröder, Oppenheim, Frerichs and Schwabacher families, who all belonged to the world of finance.¹⁰ Horace also took pleasure in the society of prominent figures in the Jewish world: letters mention the historian Heinrich Graetz and Dr Loewenstein, chief rabbi of Lemberg and a great connoisseur of Hebrew literature. The situation of Jews remained at the heart of his concerns, while in Russia people were debating the fate of the perpetrators of the pogroms. He told David how worried he was:

I was displeased when I read the Sunday *Golos* [*The Voice*] yesterday. It quoted the reply of *Russkiy Evrey*, which said that Jews have done everything to deserve *ravnopravie* [equal rights]; a little less haughtiness and more modesty: we need that to get into the saddle, impertinence will get us nowhere. [...] [But we must not hold back from creating] a certain amount of attention in order to obtain pardons for those sentenced to hang. Jews don't need slaughters, hard labour will suffice, and a scaffold will reawaken animosity. It would be politically good if Jews intervened. [...] A member of the Vienna committee [of the Alliance Israélite] asked what I thought should be done with the refugees who are not going to America, whether it would be a good idea to repatriate them, giving each of them 40 to 50 roubles or 200 roubles per family? That is the only way to repair the damage you have done them, was my reply. In America every technician, technologist or engineer who is not afraid of work will find a wide range of opportunities.¹¹

Although business, politics, philanthropy and community life were closely interwoven, Horace exhorted David to be prudent: "Be very careful with the Serb [unidentified]. [To begin with] never give him *papers* coming directly from my firm. Ign[atyev] has tried to place him in my firm as *his man*, naturally to spy and inform on me."¹² Dismissed from his post as Minister of the Interior on 30 May 1882, Ignatyev remained a member of the Holy Brotherhood (an organisation responsible for protecting the tsar against the threat of revolution) and the Council of State. At the age of twenty-five, David, Horace's designated successor, had neither his father's experience nor his skill. In the summer of 1882, he assumed for the first time the role of *shtadlan*. Horace showered him with advice from afar: "The only way to get anywhere is to speak frankly when one expresses one's opinion, if one is capable of defending it. One mustn't be afraid of one's opinion. There are so many wrong ones that our own is the least bad because it is honest. I am speaking about you and a little about myself. To look a minister in the eyes and try to divine his way of seeing things is to waste too much precious time, and the limited time of an audience."[13] In addition, David had to contend with the hostility of certain members of the community, including Nikolay Bakst (1842–1904), who took advantage of Horace's absence to assert his own views. A physiologist specialising in the nervous system, a professor at the Women's School of Medicine, an adviser at the Ministry of Education, and a columnist for the newspaper *Golos* [*The Voice*], Bakst had suddenly discovered the Jewish cause. From Dinard, Horace sent a clear-sighted reflection on the difficulties of the recent months and his own role:

> Yes, my son, there are times in life when everything seems to get away from you. People exaggerate my merits. Last year I did what any decent man must do. Three million souls had been abandoned, and I thought I had to remain and attend to them. Unfortunately, I merely served as a guard at the door, and was unable to save people from ruin.
>
> I am busy and working, maybe I will try to obtain vast sums to establish professional and agricultural schools. As for the idea of making a charitable contribution on the occasion of the coronation using the money set aside to celebrate the twenty-fifth anniversary of Alexander the martyr's reign, that should not be considered and from here I shout my veto, and along with me so do all the 23,000 or 26,000 subscribers. If it proves necessary, cast a [firm] veto in my name.
>
> If M. Bakst is truly concerned about the Jewish question, he must avoid upsetting absolutely anyone at all. You are on the side of the holy cause by your blood, and you must remain there from love. The manners adopted by these gentlemen mirror my own charity, and who could they put in my place who would have the trust of the unfortunate?
>
> Tell Bakst & Co. that they should think about that and not forget that morality is not so quickly acquired.[14]

Here Horace shows his strength of character: not only does he refuse to allow himself to be drawn into selfish quarrels, but he also reminds David that commitment to their fellow Jews is not a factual option: "You are on the side of the holy cause by your blood, and you must remain there from love." Horace gave David a final bit of advice: "I embrace you and wish and desire that you consult your simple heart and act without pretension."[15]

18

Encouraging Crafts and Agricultural Work (ORT)

As he wrote to David during the summer of 1882, Horace wanted to devote himself to a new project: "Maybe I will try to obtain vast sums to establish professional and agricultural schools."[1] Access to technical knowledge was to make it possible to procure worthwhile vocations for the young Jews in the Pale of Settlement who were becoming increasingly numerous and increasingly stigmatised in this time of growing anti-Semitism: in addition to the traditional accusations that they were "exploiters of the Christian people" or "fanatical obscurantists", they were now accused of being "revolutionaries".[2] Prey to galloping population growth and unfavourable economic conditions, Russia's Jewish population was growing steadily poorer: at that point, a quarter of it was living on the charity of the communities. The idea of a vocational education movement had been put forward as early as 1880, on the occasion of the preparation for the twenty-fifth anniversary of Alexander II's coronation, before the tsar's assassination: in order to associate himself usefully with the jubilee, Professor Bakst persuaded the industrialist Polyakov to create a "fund to aid the needy Jewish population in honour of the twenty-fifth anniversary of the tsar's advent".[3] Because of his experience in philanthropy, his knowledge of government circles, and the fact that it was impossible to envisage carrying on a large-scale action without him, Horace was naturally associated with the project. Polyakov was not involved in the Jewish community; for this same jubilee, he had even agreed to finance a home for students at the University of St Petersburg, which was closed to Jews. He had long been involved in technical education, however, having created specialised schools for the personnel of his railways. Bakst was already a member of the Society for the Promotion of Culture and was trying to found a Jewish theological academy to train "modern" rabbis. Although they were very different in temperament, Bakst and Gunzburg shared the same approach: critical with regard to emigration, they were seeking new solutions to the crisis of "Russian Judaism".

Any philanthropic initiative depended on the good will of the authorities: thanks to the official authorisation, granted on 22 March 1880, for the creation of the fund, it was possible to start raising money. In addition to the three men already mentioned, the signatories of the appeal to Jewish communities distributed on 10 April were all financiers close to Horace: Abram Zak,[4] Lev Rosenthal and Meer Friedland. The jubilee fund set itself a specific objective: helping existing Jewish schools of commerce, opening new schools, facilitating the mobility of craftsmen, aiding Jewish agricultural colonies and establishing new ones, and creating model farms and agricultural schools. On 30 September 1880, the Minister of the Interior, Loris-Melikov, approved the creation of a "provisional committee for the establishment of a society for artisanal and agricultural work among the Jews of Russia", which was to put the fund to use. Ten thousand letters were sent out: during a six-month campaign, reported on by the newspapers *Rassvet* and *Russkiy Evrey*, 12,457 individuals living in 407 localities contributed 204,000 roubles, to which must be added 25,000 roubles given by Polyakov and 25,000 roubles given by Horace, who also promised to contribute 1,500 roubles annually.[5] After a few preparatory meetings, the signatories of the appeal, joined by various public figures, named on 12 November 1880 the persons in charge of the "craft industry" (*Remeslenny Fond*): Polyakov served as president, Horace was a "principal member", Zak was the treasurer and Bakst the coordinator. Members of the committee responsible for the fund were associates of Nikolay Bakst or of Horace: Emmanuil Bank, Rabbi Avraam Drabkin, the lawyer Jacob Halpern, Arkady Kaufman, the mathematician Grigory Rabinovich, Yakov Rosenfeld, the businessmen Abram Varshavsky, Meer Friedland and Hipolit Vavelberg.[6] The owner of the Vavelberg Bank of Warsaw, the latter was a patron of Polish literature and Polish students in St Petersburg; he liked to participate in the Gunzburgs' charitable works. According to the journalist Mordecai Ben-Hillel Hakohen: "The Fund [...] reflected the dominant climate of that period. The government was less and less inclined to give equal rights to all Jews; at least the privileges granted to Jewish craftsmen could be extended to the largest possible number of persons. Consequently, progressive Jewish groups enthusiastically welcomed the idea of encouraging a class of skilled craftsmen. At this time, the hope that it would also be possible to develop agriculture among Jews was very real."[7]

The creation of the "Craft Industry Fund" marked the birth of what was to become ORT, Obshchestvo Remeslennovo i zemledelcheskovo Truda (Society for Agricultural and Artisanal Labour), an organisation that is still active through an international network of schools, mainly secondary and professional schools. After the Bolshevik revolution, ORT moved its headquarters to Berlin, then to Geneva and finally to London. Thanks to the fall of the Soviet Union in May 1995, a school was able to open its doors in St Petersburg under the name ORT-Gunzburg, providing high-level training in the new technologies and paying moving homage to Horace, almost a hundred years after his death.[8] At the time of its official foundation ORT had relied on the original capital of the craft industry fund, which had remained intact: in accordance with banking practice, the founders had stipulated as a rule of operation that expenditure should be backed up by revenue. Thus the money collected for the jubilee in 1880 could be transferred in its entirety to the Society for Agricultural and Artisanal Labour among the Jews of Russia, whose statutes were accepted in 1906: the only one of the three founders still alive, Horace served as president until his death in 1909.

Between 1880 and 1906, the fund and its allocations met with many obstacles. The first statute provided for financing training programmes in existing Jewish primary schools in crafts and agriculture, and for advancing, in the form of loans, the cost of travel (50 to 100 roubles) and settling in (200 roubles) to craftsmen who wanted to live outside the Pale of Settlement, as in theory they had the right to do. As regards agriculture, the statute envisaged the purchase of small parcels of land, ten hectares each, for families who wanted to establish themselves as farmers. The assassination of the tsar shattered all these plans. A product of the relatively liberal reign of Alexander II, ORT was doomed to develop in the hostile context of the persecutions and smothering restrictions of Alexander III's reign: although ORT's status was officially approved, the government blocked the purchase of agricultural parcels, and ORT's achievements were constantly hindered. The reports of the committee's activities regularly mention planned grants that were never made because of the government's pettifoggery. Thus for the first two years of its operation, ORT was unable to expend the totality of its budget of 26,000 roubles.[9] However, it was possible to found a vocational school in Dvinsk and to subsidise craftsmen who lived outside the Pale of Settlement by providing them with tools, particularly sewing machines; in the 1880s, 223 craftsmen received help to establish themselves outside the Pale of Settlement – a ludicrous figure compared to the hundreds of thousands of families in need. One-off grants were made to cope with unforeseen problems, such as fires or a lack of equipment. Primary schools were helped in Dombrova, Dubno, Elizavetgrad, Zhytomyr, Kishinev, Minsk, Mir, Odessa, Orsha, Ostrog, Starodub, Taganrog and Kherson; about a dozen students received scholarships to attend technical schools. But it was not until after the 1905 revolution that ORT's educational initiatives were able to affect a larger population: numerous school-workshops were opened at that time to train glassblowers, dressmakers, gardeners, mechanics, cabinetmakers, carpenters, cobblers, chauffeurs, etc.[10] During this whole period, Horace remained loyal to his father's last wishes, devoting himself in particular to the defence of the Jewish agricultural colonies, to which ORT supplied the occasional income necessary for the colonists to survive.[11] Created under Nicholas I (1825–1855), Jewish agricultural colonies were located chiefly in the regions of Kherson in Crimea (31 colonies), and Ekaterinoslav, the present-day Dnepropetrovsk, in southern Ukraine (17 colonies). With a typically bureaucratic lack of forethought, the lands allotted were in the steppes, far from any village. Moreover, since the first colonists had no experience of working the land, their life was extremely precarious. The initiative's main result was to create a "class of Jewish farmers" on the administrative level and to nourish the persistent dream of a Jewish peasantry: these colonists served as an inspiration for the *kibbutzim*, at the intersection of Tolstoyan, Zionist and socialist ways of thought. But forty years after their foundation, the Jewish colonies were in a critical situation. In addition, in 1887 the Minister of State Domains assigned an official to study their situation with the intention of doing away with them. A writer and journalist, Konstantin Sluchevsky, wrote an indictment based on information provided by Count Kankrin, the governor of Ekaterinoslav, who told him that the majority of the settlers had abandoned their land in order to settle in neighbouring towns. Horace turned to another expert, Lev Binshtok, who was assigned to carry out a genuine investigation. A former rabbi in Zhytomyr, Binshtok was not a specialist in agricultural matters either: he was simply to record the responses to a questionnaire prepared in advance. He returned to St Petersburg with a detailed description of the colonies: a census of the families, an inventory of their tools, the extent of the lands and area cultivated, the nature of the seeds and an evaluation of the harvest. Horace communicated the results to the Minister of the Domains and saw to it that they were published.[12] He also invited the representatives of the various colonies to come to St Petersburg, where they were received by ministers and high officials. The colonies were thus saved. However, drought and a series of poor harvests made their economic equilibrium fragile: through ORT, Horace provided a stream of grants that later passed through the Jewish Colonisation Association.

Under the reign of Alexander III, the role of the *shtadlan* became uncomfortable. Even though Nikolay Ignatyev, disavowed by the tsar, had been succeeded by Dmitry Tolstoy at the Ministry of the Interior, the damage was done. The lawyer Heinrich Sliozberg,[13] who worked closely with Horace, wrote concerning this dark period:

> For ten years, Horace de Gunzburg had to struggle against the disastrous effects of the Regulations of 3 May 1882 [known as the "May laws"], in other words, against the constant expulsions of Jews from the villages where they lived. The economic situation of the Jewish population of the cities and towns was becoming increasingly desperate. All of Gunzburg's efforts were unable to produce measures of a general kind, and were limited to providing legal aid to the victims of an illegal application of the restrictive laws. In each particular case, he showed his good heart by trying to defend the interests of those who found themselves threatened with expulsion.[14]

Described as "the great panic of the little guys" by the writer Sholem Aleichem, the expulsions deprived thousands of families of their meagre land, which they had to leave in haste: "They rented everything they could find, carts, horses, oxen, and set out *in extremis*, in haste, almost as abruptly as we left Egypt."[15] Those who could not "prove" that they were residents were subject to expulsion. From their formulation to their promulgation and application, the Ignatyev regulations were "illegal", or at least "abnormal" "from the legal point of view": they had been decreed in an uncustomary way, by the "decision of the Committee of ministers approved by the sovereign", whereas they should have passed through "the legislative channel of the Imperial Council", which was unfavourable to Ignatyev.[16] As a result, the complaints of thousands of expelled Jews were piling up in the Senate's chancellery. The government was forced to designate a new investigative and deliberative body, called the High Commission (or the Pahlen Commission, after the name of its chairman), to review existing laws concerning Jews; it carried out its work from 1883 to 1888. Horace and Abram Zak volunteered to provide the necessary statistics and information, a colossal and thankless task that proved rather sterile: this "further bureaucratisation of the Jewish question", imposed by the government on the *shtadlan*, did not in fact lead to a real improvement of Jews' living conditions.[17] In May 1887, Horace asked to be heard by the Commission, along with Nikolay Bakst, Abram Varshavsky, Abram Zak, Jacob Halpern and Mikhail Morgulis, all of them members of the craft industry fund. They submitted their conclusions in the form of twenty-five points: they demanded not the abolition of the Pale but the granting of authorisations for university graduates, veterans, merchants and craftsmen. They also took up questions regarding the rabbinate and Jewish agricultural colonies. The Pahlen Commission was divided between a liberal majority and a combative group of conservatives: by a vote of seven to six, it refused to authorise veterans and Jewish merchants of the Second Guild to live outside the Pale of Settlement. Thirty years after the first of Joseph Evzel's petitions, the battle for the Jews was at a standstill. The commission submitted its report to the tsar before ceasing its activities.

After the dissolution of the Pahlen Commission, the questions connected with the legislation concerning Jews were transmitted to a special council formed within the Ministry of the Interior and presided over by Vyacheslav von Plehve, who was then undersecretary of state. According to Sliozberg, Plehve was "not only an anti-Semite but also – for incomprehensible reasons – a bitter enemy of the Jewish people, an enemy all the more redoubtable because his hostility proceeded not from an innate feeling but from a cold, cerebral calculation that corresponded to his malicious nature. This man would have been capable of stepping over thousands of bodies in order to pursue his career. He was well aware of the antipathy – due to ignorance – that Emperor Alexander III had toward Jews, and persevered in following that line, not scorning any means [to his end]."[18] Far from seeking to soften the application of the provisional regulations by following the Pahlen Commission's recommendations, Plehve was determined to consolidate them: the cruelty of his directives turned Jews' lives upside down in an intolerable way. "Any absence, no matter how short, necessarily led to a prohibition on returning to the village and the expulsion of the whole family. Married daughters, as well as sons who had not reached the age of adulthood, had to be separated from their parents and expelled from the village. The right of Jews to leave the Pale of Settlement temporarily had to be limited to the same extent.[19] The law of 1865 authorising Jewish craftsmen to live outside the Pale of Settlement was abrogated: they were expelled. Any infraction was subject to prosecution followed by imprisonment. Since these bills had to be submitted to the Imperial Council for promulgation, Horace tried to advance the best-justified ideas: "He had frequent conversations on this subject with the finance minister, Vyshnegradsky, a great statesman who understood the disastrous consequences for Russia that would result from a medieval persecution of Jews and the impression that it would make throughout the civilised world."[20] Thanks to Vyshnegradsky's support for Horace's view, Plehve's plan partly failed.

Horace was a prominent public figure in St Petersburg: he had the rank of state councillor and was a member of various institutions such as the council of commerce and manufacturing, the stock market council and the municipal council. His philanthropic activities were broader than just the Jewish sphere. He endowed the Stock Market Hospital with a famous surgical department; within the municipal council he took an active part in the work of the educational committee presided over by his friend Mikhail Stasyulevich; and when in the 1880s Prince Alexander of Oldenburg founded in St Petersburg the Institute of Experimental Medicine, modelled on Paris's Institut Pasteur, Horace was one of the largest donors. He also founded a Society for Low-cost Housing, primarily intended for female students attending university-level courses – known as Bestuzhev courses – and women studying medicine. In all his contributions he set only one condition for his participation: a guarantee that the grants would be distributed without regard to the grantee's religion or nationality. But what did such a guarantee mean in the Russia of the 1890s? In 1892 Horace himself was to lose the right to sit on St Petersburg's municipal council because he was a Jew. Discouraged by so many trials, Horace resolved to address himself directly to the tsar, an omnipotent autocrat in whom he saw the ultimate recourse:

> Your Imperial Majesty, August Monarch, Most Benevolent Lord!
>
> Not for my personal interest but for deliverance from the hopeless situation of the whole people to which I belong, I turn toward the sacred feet of Your Imperial Majesty, piously expecting justice and kindness for a few million of Your Majesty's faithful subjects. In the Russian empire, the autocratic monarchy, the sole source of the laws that determine the life of peoples and of individuals, is the supreme power.[21]

In this long letter addressed to Alexander III on 6 May 1890, Horace asserts that Jews find themselves deprived of the protection of the laws as a result of functional problems – "without Your Imperial Majesty's approval", he adds. He draws up a general balance sheet that includes all the controversial questions: economic constraints, education, military service, revolutionary movements, emigration. Backing up his arguments with statistics, he refutes the accusations, point by point. He wants to convince the emperor once again that it is necessary not only to put a stop to the unjust repression of Jews but also to give them the rights to which they aspire "wholly legitimately". Preserved in the emperor's personal papers and recently exhumed, this document bears annotations in the emperor's hand. Reading them now proves chilling. When Horace regrets that the "highest ranks of military and civil service" are "closed" to Jews, the tsar writes in the margin: "God forbid, may it be forever so!" When the good *shtadlan* deplores the fact that the Jew is "humiliated and offended [...] not because he has committed some crime, but for the sole reason that he was born a Jew," Alexander III comments: "It's not really that. They forget the terrible words of their ancestors. Let His blood be upon us and upon our children! That's the source of their condemnation and the curse of Heaven!" Citing this extract from the Gospel of St Matthew (27:25), Alexander shows that he does not know the theological texts that condemn persecutions of the Jews as contrary to Christian ethics. In response to the reference to the "fusion" (*sliyanie*) of Jews with the rest of the population, the autocrat comments: "Where would we be if fusion were realised?" Apropos of the efforts made to encourage Jews to attend Russian schools, he writes: "They are cruelly mistaken!" And when Horace deplores the massive departures for Palestine and America, the tsar expresses his joy: "Thank God, may they continue!" Was Horace naive in believing he could touch the sovereign's heart, or at least his reason? Or was he simply misled, even tricked, by the tsar's hypocritical behaviour towards him? The "August Monarch" did after all share the trivial anti-Semitism of his most mediocre officials.

19

Louise, a Charming Girl

LOST IN HER reading, a girl sits in a comfortable chair: with large dark eyes underlined by faint rings and thick chestnut hair drawn back in a bun, her face bends over a book whose title cannot be made out. Her dress of white lace contrasts with a colourful cashmere shawl carelessly thrown over her shoulders. A somewhat low neckline and a high lace collar draw attention to her bosom. The three-quarter sleeves reveal charming forearms, while the hands holding the book are delicate. This *Portrait d'une inconnue, peut-être la baronne Léa H. Gunzburg* is now in the Museum of Fine Arts in Ekaterinburg. Dated 1881,[1] it is signed by Ivan Kramskoy, whose talent as a portraitist it well illustrates. Almost certainly, the adorable person absorbed in her reading is indeed Louise, who was also sometimes called by her biblical first name, Léa. The daughter of Horace and Anna de Gunzburg, she was born in Paris in 1862. Kramskoy makes her an ideal representation of a young girl: natural, pretty and serious. The charm of the picture reflects the painter's affection for his subject: although it was of course a commissioned work, the founder of the Wanderers was able to appreciate the qualities of the banker's daughter.[2] Louise was described by her brother Sasha as "correctness personified". "When she was six, Mama once said to her in English: 'Darling, why do you not say good morning to this gentleman?' and Louise replied: 'This gentleman has not been introduced to me.'"[3] The fourth child after three boys (Gabriel, David and Marc), Louise naturally assumed the role of substitute mother after Anna's death in 1876, at the expense of her education. At nineteen she wanted to make up for lost time, as is shown by the letter sent to

David already cited: "I have so many instructive things to read, and I would like to read them in the course of the summer, because I have a thirst for knowledge, I would so much like to know things!"[4] Regular visitors to the "Boulevard" were fond of her: the historian Konstantin Kavelin – a first-rate legislator who had implemented the reform of serfdom – wrote about her, when she was still living in France:

> How charming she is, our common friend Léa Horacevna! Her father wrongly thinks that in making her acquaintance one might be disappointed by her. All that she lacks is to live in Russia, the only place where, in my opinion, there is an authentic feminine type, as strange as that may seem. It appears to me that now the time has come for Léa Horacevna to live in Petersburg. Later, forgive me, it will be too late, for she will have already become like French women, sweet, gracious and attractive, but without that virile simplicity, that noble and incomparable boldness that is the charm and attraction of our girls and young women in Petersburg, and that exists nowhere else. It would really be a pity if a person as likeable as Léa Gunzburg received her finishing touches – if we can put it that way – in Paris and not in Petersburg.[5]

Kavelin's wishes were granted: in 1881, Louise went to live in the Russian capital, where Kramskoy made his portrait of a "charming" and "likeable" girl.

At the "Boulevard" the children led an ideal life under Horace's demanding but benevolent gaze: "There was something biblical, patriarchal, in the relations between father and children, who, being different in age, nature and situation, were all full of affection for and devotion to their father."[6] The gathering for the Friday evening meal was governed by an immutable ritual: "An atmosphere of holiness seemed to surround the family table."[7] Many prominent people visited them: young people old enough to be admitted to the society of adults thus mixed with writers, musicians, artists, statesmen, scientists, government ministers and businessmen. Whether it is simple chance or something more revealing, in the documents that have survived Louise is often the centre of attention. The famous author of *Oblomov*, Ivan Goncharov, thanked Horace "for his kind invitation which [I] shall certainly accept: how could one not be at Mademoiselle Louise's party?" Not without a sense of humour, he adds in a trembly hand: "The little old man excuses himself for writing in such an ugly way" and offers his "homage and sincere and affectionate congratulations to Mademoiselle Léa and to Monsieur le Baron de Gunzburg".[8] Discreet, sixty years old, the writer led a modest life "with a very simple wife, perhaps a cook, just like Oblomov". Sasha describes him as a witty man who liked to recount scenes from his voyage on the frigate *Pallas* when he was the secretary of Admiral Putyatin, with whom he sailed the Pacific from 1852 to 1855.[9] An undated visiting card, in French, mentions Louise again: "*Monsieur le baron* is begged to return the enclosed books to Mademoiselle Léa de Gunzburg, his gracious daughter, with distinguished compliments from Gontscharof [*sic*]." The works in question may have been intended for the stand at the charity bazaar for the Jewish orphanage. We recall that Minister Valuyev gave Louise the first copy of his novel *Larine* in 1881. Goncharov was an assiduous guest: declining an invitation to lunch on the pretext that he was already expected "at the Marble palace", he nonetheless suggested to Horace that he might "stop by to smoke a cigar."[10] Ivan Kramskoy also admired the girl's "internal qualities".[11] Two letters from the painter to Louise explicitly mention sittings: "If you could come tomorrow for a sitting, you would then be kind enough to wear that open dress (that is, the most open one)."[12] On another occasion, he sets a rendezvous for "the next day at his place, around 2 to 3 o'clock", "in that same dress, if it is available".[13] He also gave her painting lessons. "I profoundly beg you to excuse me for not being able to come today for your lesson (I'll go to your home tomorrow)."[14] Horace noted proudly: "Kramskoy is very happy with the progress in drawing that Louise is making under his guidance."[15] Generally speaking, the girl made a good impression, even in the tsar's entourage: "Louise has had great success here at the Court. She has twice caused the very charming tsarina to turn her head, and the young people who were passing by made their comments in a loud voice, which amused Louise very much."[16]

Attentive to the good organisation of his household and the well-being of his children, Horace launched into improvements whose realisation he entrusted to his son David:

> I want to make a change in my residence. I would like to put the girls

on the top floor, and completely separate the boys, putting the three of them and their tutor in Sasha's, Mimi's and Berza's rooms. Maybe install a partition to separate the drawing room, which is already separated by the arcades.

At any rate, I ask that you do the same with the upstairs kitchen as was done for you downstairs, that is, make it a bath with a toilet, etc. There will just have to be a hallway for the maids who are lodged above. This bath is indispensable [...] because for the time being the governesses and others are going to take over the bath on the boys' side.

Sasha and Mimi will have to be moved downstairs, and my bedroom made into my office. That will free up the other rooms. When the bath and toilet are installed in the kitchen, there must be a permanent, double washbasin, the way my bathroom in Paris is arranged, two taps for each basin. Hot and cold water. The water will be heated by the stove that will be there. But above all the boiler must be made to fill by itself to avoid burning out the heater.[17]

To improve the furnishing of the drawing rooms, Horace left an order for a sale by auction: "It would be a pity if the chairs, couches and stools covered in yellow silk got away from me."[18] At the "Boulevard" the Gunzburgs gave sumptuous balls that were described by Sasha:

People were invited to come at ten o'clock, but they never came before eleven. Opochinin (an admiral who was part of the conservatoire group) had to come at ten. Grandfather [Horace] and the sisters were beginning to dress for the occasion. David and I received him; he was offered tea, and then we began walking through the drawing rooms, where the lamps were being lit; at eleven o'clock the good admiral said good night, his bedtime having come.[19]

The orchestra was that of the horse guard regiment. One evening, "our ball took place on the same day as that of the palace," Sasha recounts. "Since at the palace people were sent home around midnight, the officers came from there to our place in their red Court uniforms, which considerably increased the splendour of the party. It was almost always officers of the horse guard who led the cotillion with my sister Louise. The best of these leaders was Pistohlkors, the first husband of the future [princess] Paley. She too once came to dance at our house; she was the daughter [of the doctor] Karnovich, and her beauty was dazzling."[20] Louise and her brothers were at ease amid all these elegant young people. Excellent dancers, they had been taught by Felix Kshesinsky, of the Imperial Ballet, who gave his lessons accompanied by his two daughters, who played the ladies' roles. Having become the star of the Imperial Ballet, Matilda Kshesinskaya was the future Nicholas II's first love: "People said that it was she who had been entrusted with the task of depriving the Grand Duke and heir to the throne of his innocence."[21]

St Petersburg high society met at the balls held at the "Boulevard": officers such as Colonel Telyakovsky, Count Vorontsov-Dashkov and Count Frederiks, who then commanded the Horse Guards regiment, and Bezobrazov, a captain in the same regiment. In addition to the artists and writers already mentioned, the first circle consisted of Jewish families that had been involved in the *otkup*: the Utins, Friedlands, Varshavskys et al. Apropos of these receptions, Sasha relates a telling anecdote about the behaviour of the imperial elite: a group of provincial governors invited to dinner by Horace were criticising the ethnic groups for which they were responsible. "Bobrikov complained about the Finns, who possessed both income equality and no illiteracy, Uxhühl criticised the Poles, Semyakin (the governor of Podolia) complained about Jews who spoke Russian too well but got in his way when he passed them on the pavement. I couldn't resist telling them: 'I see that you are all interested in the development of the Jews, Finns and Poles, but is there anyone in the government who is concerned with the Russian peasant, who is rotting away in ignorance and filth?' When the [governor-]generals had left I received a sharp reprimand from my father."[22]

Being well acquainted with prominent musicians, Baron Gunzburg offered his guests high-quality musical evenings at which one could hear the celebrated pianist and composer Anton Rubinstein, Karl Davydov, the "tsar of cellists" (to borrow Pyotr Tchaikovsky's expression), who played a Stradivarius,[23] or the violinist Leopold Auer, whose pupils Misha Elman, Jascha Heifetz and Efrem Zimbalist were long to enchant music-lovers all over the world. In St Petersburg, music was a passion. The 1880s were a golden age of creation and interpretation. At the age of fifteen Babita provides an overview of this musical frenzy:

A few days after my party, Papa gave a musical evening at which

Brassin, Davydov and Auer performed. Those who came as audiences [*sic*] would not interest you, except Mlles Mulher and Fleisen, who honoured the evening with their presence [...] Then we went to a musical evening at the Botkins, where Balakirev performed along with others whose names I do not know. Sarasate was and will be here, and he gave three concerts that we attended. Then he also played at a concert directed by Rubinstein, to which we also went. Then Louise heard him on Sunday evening at the Auers', where there was a musical evening at which Rubinstein was also present. Louise came home after 1 a.m., but the party lasted until 5 a.m. Since he gives concerts in several cities in Russia, Sarasate has arranged to pass through St Petersburg and to stay here a fortnight each time.[24]

Anton Rubinstein, the director and founder of the Petersburg conservatoire, was a prominent figure: "His exuberance, well reflected in his physique, was like that of a torrent."[25] Horace provided financial aid to students at the conservatoire, as he did for Jewish students in general. In return, Rubinstein, who was of Jewish origin, supported Gunzburg's protégés, and, thanks to him, at the conservatoire there was no *numerus clausus* applicable to Jewish pupils. Thus Moritz Goldenblum, one of Horace's scholarship students, was able to take courses at the conservatoire while at the same time working for the Jewish community as a composer and choirmaster.[26] Horace commissioned Kramskoy to paint a portrait of Rubinstein at his piano during a concert in the Assembly Hall of the Nobility. In the audience, the painter depicted Horace and his daughter Babita.[27]

In 1883, the Gunzburgs went to the parties given in Moscow to celebrate the coronation of Alexander III, which had been delayed because of the prolonged period of mourning after the regicide. Writing from Paris, their cousin Mathilde, Ury's daughter, was eager for details: "You must be in the middle of your preparations for the trip to Moscow. I would love to see Babita in her dress with a train and Sasha and Mimi, are they also going or are they obliged to remain in Petersburg because of their examination?"[28] The Parisians in the family were no less fond of balls and musical evenings. Mathilde reported on French social life for her cousin and fiancé David: "We were supposed to go to the Pasdeloup concert yesterday to hear M. Bresmer [...]. Olga was very excited. [But the police told people not to go out] because there was a riot in Paris. This morning we learned that there were four thousand people at the concert and there had been no riots at all."[29] In Paris as in St Petersburg, there was one ball after another. "Last week there were parties at the homes of Madame Constant Halphen and Madame Marchesi, where we had a lot of fun; we missed a party at the home of Madame Lazard because Mama was ill. I now take everywhere the fan you gave me, and it is much admired."[30] Religious holidays still brought the family together, as they had in the time of Joseph Evzel: "The day before Passover we dined at Grandmother's house with Henriette and Salomon. It was Gabriel [Horace's eldest son] who read the prayer during the two evenings. [...] And this evening we are invited to the grand opera by the marquise [Marchesi]. *La Juive* will be performed."[31] The girls pursued their educations: "We are still working on Italian and harmony, and I am playing the piano as much as possible, while Thérèse has gone back to serious study of drawing."[32] But the great question was their future marriages. Thérèse, the eldest of Ury's seven daughters, had been born in 1863, and was about to celebrate her twentieth birthday. For her it was imperative to receive guests. In Paris, the house on Rue de Tilsitt rediscovered the splendour of Joseph Evzel's era:

> We've finally made up our minds to give a very small party on 7 April; we've been so tormented from all sides that we feel obliged to do it. It will be small. The dancing will be on the upper floor, in our quarters, and we will invite only the people to whom we owe that courtesy. We are making some of the party favours at home, and in the evening the smoking room looks exactly like a workshop. I'm the secretary and I wrote all the invitations. We have no idea how well all this will turn out, never having given a party before.[33]

According to *Le Gaulois* for 9 April 1883, the reception was a success: "Saturday, a very elegant ball at the home of Baroness Ury de Gunzburg in her home on Rue de Tilsitt. Among the most attractively dressed were the Baroness de Vaufreland, Mme Villeroy, the Marquise de Saint-Mars, Mme Halphen, the charming Mme S[alomon] de Gunzburg, dressed very simply in white tulle, and without jewellery, no doubt to contrast with the party on Thursday at the Opera, Mme Beer, Mme Léon Fould and Mme Seligmann. A very gay cotillion, very animated and very briskly led by M. Joe del Valle, the cotillion is decidedly in fashion this winter." On the other hand, for the young woman in whose honour the reception was given the party ended with a cruel disappointment. Thérèse's suitor, the young Calmann Lévy, showed himself to be less than assiduous: "Our party was rather nice and I think everyone had a good time. You ask whether a certain person was there, it's Calmann Lévy you mean, isn't it? Well, we invited him as a dancer along with several other young people. To our astonishment he arrived on time and left half an hour later without having danced." But among the acquaintances, the season of engagements promised to be fruitful: "I have three engagements to tell you about," Mathilde wrote to David: "that of Louise Fould [their cousin, the daughter of Mathilde de Gunzburg] to Emile Halphen, son of Georges Halphen, that of Mlle Kulpe to Gaston Dreyfus (the brother of Ferdinand Dreyfus, who married Adèle Porges), and finally that of Mlle Alphonse de Rothschild to Maurice Ephrussi. It's only in our household that things are not going well. This Calmann Lévy fellow acted exactly as if he wanted to back out."[34] In Ury's family, morale was at its low point. "Next Sunday is Thérèse's birthday. It won't be very gay because everyone is so sad here at home: Papa, Mama and Thérèse, who worries because of this Calmann Lévy, who doesn't want things to go ahead. We will probably see him this evening at the ball at the Gubbays'. But what good will that do? He hardly dances with her any more, and yet everybody thinks that Thérèse is engaged to him."[35]

Driving the point home, in the spring of 1883 the press diagnosed "a dearth of suitors" for girls from the Jewish upper bourgeoisie:

People have been talking about it *sotto voce* for some time in high society, but it would have been indiscreet to echo those parlour remarks; only now is it permissible to announce the marriage of Mlle Béatrice de Rothschild to M. Maurice Ephrussi. The two families are accepting the congratulations of their friends. Mlle Béatrice de Rothschild, one of the most charming young ladies in Paris, is nineteen years old. She is the second daughter of the Baron Alphonse de Rothschild and his wife. Her beauty recalls that of her mother. [...] M. Maurice Ephrussi is thirty years old. He is a handsome gentleman who knows how to lead a cotillion as well as a racehorse. On the turf his colours are held in high regard, navy blue with yellow dots. The Ephrussis are almost as well known in Paris as the Rothschilds themselves, and they too are acclimatised in every way among us and accredited in the best Parisian society. Originally from Odessa, they made, through the major grain trading deals that are the specialty of their country of origin, an undeniable fortune, as did the Rafalovich family and a few others very rightly esteemed throughout the world. [...] The Ephrussi family includes, also among us, M. Ignace Ephrussi, a fine shot, M. E. Ephrussi, an eminent collector, and two sisters, one of whom married a Fould. Apropos of the Foulds, I open a parenthesis. Did you know that Mlle Fould, the daughter of M. Paul Fould and Mlle de Gunzburg, is going to marry the son of M. Georges Halphen and Mlle Stern? [...] This whole large family is thus extremely well connected in the Jewish world, and the marriage that will effect the entry of one of its members into the house of Rothschild is a perfect match. People are very right to say that extremes meet in this case: a Rothschild is as difficult to marry as a girl without a dowry [...]. Socially, the Jewish world, which commands the respect of all because of its very fine familial virtues, is circumscribed. In addition, for heiresses from this society, it may happen, as we saw earlier, that whatever their charms, virtues or fortunes, there is a dearth of suitors.[36]

For Thérèse, the difficulty was twofold: in addition to the limited milieu there was also a modest dowry, because Ury's fortune had diminished. He had squandered his inheritance on a chateau, hunting, artworks, racehorses and women, neglecting his business affairs. By May people were no longer talking about a marriage, because the household on Rue de Tilsitt was in mourning again after the death of Thérèse and Mathilde's sister Sophie: "A calamity that has just struck the Gunzburg family, all of whose members are so matriarchically united. The town house on Rue de Tilsitt is in mourning, and we respectfully associate ourselves with this despair. Mlle de Gunzburg, the daughter of Baron Ury de Gunzburg, has just been carried off by death at the age of eighteen. She was a young person endowed with every grace and merit, and her death will leave among her friends and family the most profound void."[37] However, the year 1883 ended with the marriage of Mathilde and her cousin David, on 20 December: "Yesterday, at two o'clock, in the temple on Rue de la Victoire, the marriage of Mademoiselle Mathilde de Gunzburg, daughter of Baron Ury, with her cousin David de Gunzburg, the son of Baron Horace. The whole Jewish aristocracy was there."[38]

In St Petersburg, between 1884 and 1900, Horace, unlike his brother Ury, successfully married off most of his children into the Jewish high society of Russia (Ashkenasy and Brodsky), Great Britain (Sassoon), Austria (Gutmann), Germany (Warburg) and France (Deutsch de la Meurthe). Through these connections, the Gunzburg dynasty strengthened its European scope. Unsurprisingly, the first to wed was Louise: in 1884, Joseph (called Joe) Sassoon travelled from Great Britain to St Petersburg to ask for her hand. He had lost his father, was twenty-two years old, and bore the name of an important Jewish family in the British empire that had originally come from the Baghdadi community in India. His mother Flora had made the decision for him: young, rich, beautiful, and a practising Jew, Louise was an ideal partner. The joyful dancer in cotillions was thus the first to leave the nest of the "Boulevard" for the residence of Ashley Park, in Walton-on-Thames in Surrey. On the occasion of her marriage, her various friends expressed their affection for her. Kramskoy congratulated her on this "happy event",[39] and Goncharov programmed a farewell visit:

> May I be so bold as to hope that you, Madame, and Monsieur the baron your father, will excuse me if I ask your permission to postpone my visit to you until another day when I can pay my respects to you and shake the hand of Madame Sassoon in all freedom and without hindrance. Insofar as the theatre is concerned, it would be a great pleasure for me to accept a small place in your box, but unfortunately I have had to give up plays because I understand almost nothing of what is said on the stage. Awaiting the pleasure of presenting myself at your home, I beg you, Madame, to accept my distinguished and affectionate homage,
>
> I. Goncharov.[40]

A year later, he sent her a letter at Ashley Park congratulating her on the birth of her first child and wishing her "much happiness".

Despite the distance, family ties were never broken. Brothers and sisters, father and cousins made frequent visits to England: "Ashley seems to me first rate," Sasha wrote. "I felt very comfortable the few days I spent there [...] Louise lives very simply. Her apartment is without pretensions, so we will be able to give her presents that will be of use to her."[41] Horace visited her every year, generally during the autumn holidays: "Thanks to

Louise, we spent Yom Kippur in a very charming fashion."[42] Among the youngest children, Pierre contracted a lifelong mania for all things English. The ties with the Sassoons were pleasant, even if Joe was a jealous husband with narrow interests. "He loved only two things: his children and golf."[43] In this bucolic environment, surrounded by her seven children, Louise could devote herself to her beloved books, as is shown by a photograph of her sitting on the steps leading to the estate's grounds, absorbed in a book and protected by a parasol, still just as pretty and faithful to the image set down by Kramskoy in his portrait of the ideal Russian girl.

In 1888, Babita married Ludwig von Gutmann, the son of the Austrian railway baron, entering one of the most prominent Jewish families in Austria. A businessman as competent as he was modest, Ludwig formed a happy alliance with Babita. They divided their time between the Gutmann palace in Vienna and their house in Baden, which Horace also frequented with pleasure. When their first child was born, David congratulated the happy grandfather, hoping "that the little boy who is going to enter our family is worthy of the great Jewish name and will give great joy to you, as well as to his parents. I also express my wishes for Babita's recovery; her strong constitution has no doubt made this trying time less dangerous than usual."[44] Babita was in fact big and strong, and she brought nine children into the world, including a little boy who died as an infant. Kind and cheerful, she was incapable of raising her two boys and six daughters strictly, and many of them led lives that were, if not dissolute, at least turbulent.

During this time, their unfortunate cousin Thérèse was still looking for a fiancé. The town house on Rue de Tilsitt having been sold in July 1886,[45] Ury and his family were doomed to wander across Europe. In January 1888, in Berlin, Ida told her daughter Mathilde: "There is a young Morpurgo here who pays a great deal of attention to Thérèse, but it seems that he has no money and is looking for a rich fiancée."[46] For the young woman's mother, the last hope lay in family solidarity:

> Thérèse goes out often and is very popular, but nothing comes of any of it and we will leave Berlin as we came.
>
> As for Benvenisti, he can't be counted on. [...] We were [aware] in Berlin that Thérèse does not have a large dowry and that is what does her the most harm, because except for that she has had a great deal of success. You can imagine how unhappy I am about that.

[...] How will all this end? In two months Thérèse will be 25 years old. If we could at least have a tempting dowry for her and she managed to marry, afterwards it would be easier with Olga [Thérèse's younger sister] because everyone finds her so pretty, but where can we get that dowry? Couldn't your father-in-law [Horace] persuade grandmother to give more?[47]

Writing to Mathilde in his shaky French, Ury criticised his wife's strategy: "One must never show that one wants to marry off one's daughters. I'm sure that having Olga with you, a sister, makes things less awkward and success is much more likely and easier. It's natural to have the mother decide, but it's disagreeable to be observed, and men don't like that."[48] Finally, a solution was found. Thérèse married Victor Mendel, the principal shipowner on the Danube, who lived in Brăila, in Romania, where she led a happy life until she fell ill with tuberculosis. She died prematurely in 1899, but not without having given birth to Vladimir (1890) and Nadia (1892).[49] Her sister Olga married the widower, to whom she gave another child. The situation had been resolved, to Ury's great satisfaction: "I had very good news from Olga, she seems to take pleasure in her new situation. She tells me that she feels she has been married for centuries."[50]

After Louise and Babita were wed, Horace's children continued to marry at a steady pace: in 1890, Sasha went to Menton to ask his aunt Théophile Warburg, his mother's sister, for his cousin Rosa's hand. The young people had fallen in love with one another the preceding year, while Sasha was doing an internship at the Warburg bank. For the marriage in Hamburg, Elka Rosenberg, their common grandmother, gave a grand "gypsy" party.[51] The newlyweds first set up house in Paris, then travelled to Karlsruhe and Florence before finally settling in St Petersburg. Rosa's dowry was used to buy a palace on Millionnaya Street, a stone's throw from the Winter Palace. Mimi (Alfred) married his cousin Sonia Ashkenasy on 17 March 1896: the gathering of the whole family in St Petersburg for this occasion resulted in a fine group photograph. As the head of the family, Horace is surrounded by his ten children and numerous grandchildren, his parents-in-law and his nephews and nieces. Fedia, Sasha's son and Horace's favourite grandson, sits regally on his lap; Aniouta, a slender young woman of twenty, poses next to the man who was to become her husband, Siegfried Ashkenasy, the bride's brother; Louise, still beautiful after twelve years of marriage, is accompanied by her easily offended husband Joe Sassoon.[52] *Le Gaulois* did not forget the Gunzburgs:

> The celebrations of the marriage of M. A. de Gunzburg and Mlle Aschkenasy [sic] were another occasion for the triumph of Parisian fashions in elegant St Petersburg society. Above all, the exquisite and rich laces of the East India Company, *points d'Alençon*, and appliquéd laces from England, Valenciennes and Chantilly that were the most graceful embellishment of all, elicited wholly justified and sincere admiration.[53]

Two years later, Aniouta married her cousin Siegfried Ashkenasy. At twenty-two, the little baby sister had become a ravishing young woman, merry and svelte. Siegfried was the grandson of Moses, the founder of the Ashkenasy bank, and the son of Evgeny, the sole heir, who had died when Siegfried was sixteen years old. Among the presents given her on the occasion of her engagement, Aniouta found a prayer book (bound by Grund in Paris), lace and jewellery: the stones (diamonds, emeralds, rubies and sapphires) had been bought in Kiev before being mounted by Cartier in Paris. Aniouta gave her fiancé a woollen *tallit*, in accord with the custom.[54] A mediocre banker, Siegfried was a famous womaniser, known for his collection of erotic books, which was said to be the most extensive in Russia. The "Wanderer" painter Nikolay Kuznetsov did a delightful portrait of Aniouta: in her house in Odessa, wearing a dress of shimmering moiré and lilac-coloured muslin, attractively décolletée and slender, she raises towards the spectator eyes whose intense blue recalls that of her brother Pierrot, a child immortalised by Marc, the family's painter.[55]

20

The *Vestnik Evropy* Group

BALLS AND SOCIETY life were necessary to maintain one's rank in St Petersburg and ensure one's children's future, but Horace was above all a serious man who liked the company of intellectuals. He was close to the group gathered around *Vestnik Evropy* (*The Messenger of Europe*), a monthly review with "westernising" ideas. Since the 1840s the world of Russian letters had been divided into two antagonistic currents: on the one hand the "westerners" defending the anchorage in Europe desired by Peter the Great as the best possible avenue of development; on the other hand, the "Slavophiles", who made Orthodoxy and Slavic identity a founding tenet of Russian identity. Although they were in the minority, the Slavophiles became influential in Alexander III's entourage. As a Jew and a businessman, Horace could only be a "westerner": for him, the Russian melting pot offered Jews an opening towards Western culture. His friendship with Mikhail Stasyulevich, the editor-in-chief of *Vestnik Evropy*, was also based on old ties with the Utin family, to which Stasyulevich was related. The son of a physician and a rigorous, almost rigid intellectual, Stasyulevich had married Lyubov Utina, the daughter of an alcoholic beverages agent who was close to Joseph Evzel. Boris Utin, the young woman's brother and a professor at the university, had arranged this marriage. A historian specialising in ancient Greece and the Middle Ages, Stasyulevich was Grand Duke Nicholas Alexandrovich's history tutor from 1860 to 1862. "During the student rebellion of 1862,[1] a group of very prominent professors including Kavelin, Pypin and Stasyulevich left the university and Stasyulevich's work at the Court came to an end."[2]

Starting in 1866, Stasyulevich tried to revive the review created in 1802 by the illustrious Karamzin. Its publication had been interrupted for several decades. Lyubov Utina-Stasyulevich played an active role in the Gunzburg family: after the death of Anna, who had been one of her dearest friends, she watched over the children's upbringing. Her presence was favoured by geographical proximity: the Utins and the Gunzburgs were neighbours on Horse Guards Boulevard.[3] Regularly mentioned in the family's correspondence, "Madame Stasyulevich" participated in family trips (to Dinard, to Ashley Park), evenings at the theatre, and sometimes meals. She managed Horace's household, to the point that some considered her his concubine.

The Stasyulevich home was a centre of the capital's literary and intellectual life. They received guests once a week for the "classic glass of tea". Children and young people were welcome: for the younger ones, the professor liked to wind up a magnificent music box that played birdsong. The tea was taken in his study, which was piled high with books and issues of the review bound in red, in the simple, natural atmosphere that Sasha describes: "In private, Stasyulevich was basically fun-loving, and played with the children as he did with little dogs. He was very fond of my sister Aniouta and sang Russian nursery rhymes to her. Moreover, among the habitués of the house on Galernaya Street there was a basic gaiety that was surprising in this austere, one might almost say Puritan, milieu."[4] The *Vestnik Evropy* group was characterised by a great openness of mind: in the time of Alexander III, it acted as a force opposing the obtuse absolutism of official circles and the conservative tendencies of the Muscovite Slavophile movement represented by *Les Annales de Moscou* and the *Messager de Moscou*, run by Mikhail Katkov, who was close to Alexander III. This battle waged in the press was made difficult by censorship, and even if the *Messenger of Europe* was not subjected to prior censorship, Stasyulevich showed prudence in the magazine's columns. The review served as a rallying point, but the influence of its contributors was broader: "The action of this group was not limited to the written word: the personal influence of most of its members was considerable."[5]

Stasyulevich thus introduced the Gunzburgs to all that Russia had in the way of "liberals", in whom Horace found precious support for the battles he had to fight on the Jewish front. Many jurists were useful interlocutors; for example, the law professor Spasovich, the jurist

Konstantin Kavelin, a professor at the academy of military law, and Anatoly Koni, the head of the court for the district of St Petersburg. A prosecutor during the trial of the Marxist revolutionary Vera Zasulich in 1875, at one point he saw the accused pale, and asked that she be given a glass of water. In reactionary circles, this gesture was criticised as showing favour for the enemies of public order.[6] Writers and artists also met at the Stasyulevich home: Ivan Turgenev, Ivan Goncharov, the historian Pypin, who specialised in Europe,[7] the painter Bryullov, who was married to Kavelin's daughter, and the painter and amateur Mikhail Botkin (the uncle of the physician), whose collection of Italian Renaissance art objects has remained one of the most famous of its kind.[8]

Also to be found at the Stasyulevich home, the philosopher Vladimir Solovyov (1853–1900) became bound to Horace by a lasting friendship founded on a common conception "in the domain of religion". Solovyov, who adhered to the Russian Orthodox church, undertook to learn Hebrew under Rabbi Goetz, and gradually moved closer to Catholicism and Judaism. He was particularly interested in the *Kabbalah*, hoping to find in it interpretive keys. Subsequently, he started studying the Talmud, and rapidly became a good connoisseur of Jewish thought. A mystic, a luminous mind, he found in Horace a valuable interlocutor for Jewish questions. He attended the *seder* at the Gunzburgs' home and gladly shared in the religious life of the family, all of whose members he liked. Sasha recalls:

> He spent hours talking about the Talmud with Papa and David. [...] Like almost all tolerant people, Solovyov was basically fun-loving; he liked witticisms and allowed himself to make some. [...] Everyone recognises him instantly, with his big beard, tousled hair and smile stretching from ear to ear. [...] He was very fond of Papa and thus of all his children. Naturally, he held David in high esteem because of his knowledge, and in his letters we see that he had time to tease our sister Babita, whom he called in one letter "baron's severe daughter".[9]

Solovyov was naturally associated with the Society for the Promotion of Culture among Jews in Russia and with various battles being waged by Horace. He often defended Jews in articles and lectures. His involvement flowed from his conception of history, his conviction that there was a fraternal continuity between Judaism and Christianity. Today, he is considered an authority on theology, and his thought helped influence the Catholic church's new doctrine regarding its relations with Judaism. He also provided constant support for David in his scholarly ambitions: he wrote a preface for David's article "The Kabbalah: the Mystic Philosophy of the Jews" and had it published in a prestigious review. With Horace and David at its core, the "Boulevard" became an influential site of Jewish culture, another facet of the battle waged by the Gunzburgs in the tsars' empire.

Part IV

Heralds of Jewish Culture

We Jews have suffered too much from
pretensions of infallibility for us to have any
desire to pretend to it in our turn, but isn't it
permissible for a Jew to speak up loudly when
it is a matter of his language, the last remainder
of a glorious past?

David de Gunzburg,
Monsieur Bickell et la métrique hébraïque, 1881

21

David, Bibliophile and Orientalist

ONLY ONE PHOTOGRAPH, probably taken between 1900 and 1905, shows David de Gunzburg in his library. He is in his fifties, leaning against the bookshelves and holding an open manuscript in his hands as he looks sullenly at the camera lens. Corpulent, bald, with a salt-and-pepper beard and moustache, he has his father's dark eyes. Behind him we can make out a series of rooms filled with books from floor to ceiling. Manuscripts are irregularly piled on small tables, waiting to be classified or consulted. A priceless treasure, this library, thought to number 35,000 volumes, was a lifelong passion.[1] Every volume bears an *ex libris*: in a cartouche, the Gunzburgs' coat of arms, surrounded by the inscription in Hebrew "Every part of you is fair, my darling, / There is no blemish in you," taken from the Song of Songs, 4:7, and surmounted by the notation "The books of MGD". This abbreviation, which has puzzled most experts, is simply a short form of Mathilde Gunzburg David, a touching amorous symbolism. David's library is an homage to Mathilde, his beloved wife, "the star that guided [him] throughout [his] life towards the ideal".[2] According to one of his relatives, "David was the only one of [Horace's] eight children who was not very handsome. But he married the prettiest girl in St Petersburg."[3] Mathilde had a mass of auburn hair and regular, distinguished features. Each book in the library bears the number of the bookcase, the shelf and the inventory. Some are marked with the name of Joseph Evzel or Horace; the family library that David inherited already contained 10,000 volumes, a small number of which came from the original collection of Gabriel Yakov. Aided by Senior Sachs and Ury, Joseph Evzel had made it one of the jewels of the house on Rue de Tilsitt. Horace enriched it with the prestigious collections of Pushkin's close friend Prince Pyotr Vyazemsky and Count Mikhail Vorontsov (another Pushkin connection: the poet had a hectic affair with Vorontsov's beautiful wife Elizaveta). With David, the Gunzburg library was transformed into a monument to Jewish culture.

In 1898, David left the "Boulevard" to take up residence with his family and his books on the other side of the Neva, on Vasilyevsky Island, line 1, no. 4. In this commonplace house that looked out on dull barracks, the library occupied a whole floor and David had it arranged in special ways that pleased him: "Petrovsky came to work for the first time; I explained my views concerning the way in which I wanted my library arranged: he is intelligent and set to work immediately; he will do a good job. The apartment is not yet ready, far from it; but I have my study, far from any noise."[4] Twice a year, Aaron Fliderbaum, a former orderly who had become David's secretary, cleaned all the books. The writer and translator David Frischmann (1864–1922) reports what David told him regarding his collection:

> It's my soul, the whole content of my life. I just dread the time when strangers will come and take one of these books in their crude hands, at random, pay a few roubles for it, and thus rip out part of my soul. They will dismember this living organism in which each book is dear to my heart. When I die, these books will go back on the market.[5]

But after 1917, when David had already been dead for seven years and his widow began negotiations with the Jewish Theological Seminary of America[6] for the sale of the library, the latter was nationalised and divided between Moscow and St Petersburg.[7] In Moscow, the Rumyantsev Museum, renamed the "Leninka" during the Soviet period, took most of the "Jewish" collection, which is still found there today.[8] David, who was a skilled Talmudic scholar and an orientalist, used his books in his work, and they bear his annotations in the margins.

The Gunzburg library is famous throughout the world for its exceptional collection of Judaica – 7,225 volumes, including religious books (Bibles, Talmuds, commentaries, volumes of Kabbalistic texts, prayer books) – and also secular poetry and works on ethics, psychology, lexicology, medicine, history, ethnography, etc. The whole offers a unique immersion in Jewish culture at the same time that it sketches an intellectual portrait of its owner. The collection of these texts in Hebrew, Syriac, Coptic, Aramaic, Arabic, Persian, Greek, Latin and Yemeni is the outcome of a patient quest among booksellers all over Europe. David deciphered, consulted and loved his books. He spoke about twenty languages, including seven Semitic languages.[9] According to his daughter Sonia, he "learned a new language every year."[10] Shortly before his death, he began studying Mahratta, a dialect of southern India. His immense learning allowed him to bring together items of exceptional quality. Thus among the twenty-two incunabula (works printed in Europe before 1500), two are unique: the first edition of the *Yossipon* (a history of the Jewish people during the Second Temple), printed in Mantua in 1475, and Levi ben Gershom's commentary on the Book of Job, printed in Ferrara in 1477. One of the first incunabula in Hebrew, Shlomo ibn Aderet's *She'elot u-Teshuvot* (*Questions and Replies*), is another rarity: it was printed in Rome in 1469–72. There are also many versions of the Torah, showing David's interest in the various forms of Hebrew, such as the dialects of the Jews of Bukhara, Crimea and Bombay, but we also find a polyglot Bible printed in Nuremberg in 1599, in Hebrew, with translations into ten languages. Dating from the fifteenth to the nineteenth centuries, the commentaries make up the largest part of the collection. The *Haggadah shel Pesach*, the account of the Exodus out of Egypt read every Passover, dates from 1725 and is now known as the "Gunzburg Haggadah".[11] David owned another curiosity on the same theme: the *Zaav seïva* (*Golden Old Age*) by the Ottoman rabbi Shlomo Al'gazi, an early opponent of the false messiah Shabbetai Zvi. It is one of the rare copies of his interpretation of the Haggadah printed in Constantinople in 1688, almost all of which were transported to Izmir, where they disappeared in an earthquake. Just as exceptional is the *Toledot Yaakov-Yosef* by Jacob Joseph of Polonne (1780), the first Hassidic book printed; most of the copies were destroyed on the orders of the *gaon* of Vilna. Among the Talmuds, David was proud to own a copy of the first edition printed by Bomberg in Venice in 1523. Some volumes show his interest in the Kabbalah, which he shared with his father: the library contains the first edition of Isaac Arama's *Hazut Kashah* (*A Difficult Vision*), printed in Sabbioneta in 1552, a work engaging in controversy with the Christians, and also a second edition of *Sefer ha-roheeh*, printed in Cremona in 1557 by Eleazar of Worms, a Talmudic scholar and Kabbalist. To this incomplete list we must add numerous *mahzors*, prayer books for religious holidays (Spanish, Italian, Provençal and African), bits of the Talmud saved from the flames of autos-da-fé, Yemeni manuscripts, the "divans" of the most important poets of the Spanish period, and the copy of the writings of St Cyril of Jerusalem that had belonged to Isaac Abravanel (or Abarbanel), an eminent fifteenth-century theologian and treasurer of the Spanish crown.

Even as a child, David devoted himself to his studies with the diligence that characterised his rabbinic ancestors. Born in 1857 in Kamenets-Podolsk, he was raised mainly in Paris. His intellectual aptitude earned him his father's favour: Horace held learning in great esteem and did not conceal his disdain for frivolity, as is revealed by his frequent criticisms of David's brothers Alexandre and Ury or of his elder son Gabriel.

Assigned early on the role of moral heir to his father, David showed that he was aware of the challenge that awaited him: "Since I am now entering my religious majority, I shall try as much as possible not to get angry any more and to cease to deserve the verse [...] that you often quote to me. I thank you very much for the confidence you have in me, and I hope to prove worthy of it."[12] David's scholarly vocation was encouraged by his contact with exceptional teachers such as Adolf Neubauer (1831–1907). "It was no doubt to him that my brother David owed in part his love of Hebrew language and literature," Sasha says.[13] Neubauer, who was born in Hungary, had been posted to the Austrian consulate in Jerusalem in 1850; he went to Paris in 1857 to pursue his research on Judaism, and then served as a Hebrew teacher at the house on Rue de Tilsitt. In 1864, probably thanks to the Gunzburgs' recommendation, he was called to St Petersburg to study the Imperial Library's Karaite manuscripts. He subsequently took a position at Oxford's Bodleian Library, where he established a catalogue of 2,500 Hebrew manuscripts. Senior Sachs, their well-read librarian, introduced David more specifically to poetry, both in Arabic and Hebrew. But the young man was determined to plan his own education. From Saint-Valéry, in Normandy, he wrote to his father: "I drew up a plan for Hebrew. In Russian, I am translating Pushkin (*Parussa*) [*sic*][14] and studying Suvorov's fables[15] [...]; in English, Wolfe's *The Burial of Sir John Moore*." For lack of a tutor, "I work alone," he adds. His father enjoyed their exchange of letters and told him: "You have only to let your pen go, you'll have no lack of ideas and your letters are really well written and very interesting."[16] In 1875 at the age of eighteen David started studying at the University of St Petersburg's school of oriental languages under the famous Baron Viktor Rosen, a young teacher of classical Arabic[17] (galvanised by Russian conquests in the east, the tsars' capital was asserting itself as a centre of oriental studies to rival London, Berlin and Paris). In a telegram sent after he had completed his course of study, David proudly notified his father of his good marks in the examinations: "Hebrew five Hebrew literature five Syriac five Arabic five Arab literature five Russian literature Tuesday love David."[18] In the Russian system, five was the best score. After an interruption to do his military service (in the regiment of lancers stationed in Łomża, Poland), he continued his studies in Paris with Stanislas Guyard, an Arabist and specialist on the Muslim world, and in Greifswald, a Hanseatic university city in Pomerania, with Wilhelm Ahlwardt, a great connoisseur of Arab poetry.

At an age when his siblings and cousins were frittering away their time in more or less futile amusements, David was starting down the austere path of a scholarly career, to Horace's great satisfaction. "My David, I await with impatience the work you have promised; even if it is beyond the range of my knowledge, I will understand what my son has written. Would it be good, after all, to print it here [in St Petersburg] rather than in Paris? [...] I told you that you shouldn't work to the point of exhaustion."[19] And again: "David, my dear, your achievements make my heart sing. Courage and perseverance. May it be God's will that the work you told me about be completed."[20] On 18 July 1883, Horace sent the young scholar a moving letter on the occasion of his twenty-sixth birthday. David was then in the midst of an emotional crisis that plunged him into great disarray. He had been in love with his cousin Mathilde since childhood, and had always thought that she would be his wife, but the young woman, then twenty-eight years old, was suddenly reluctant to take this step; her father Ury was encouraging her to marry outside the family. Horace suggested a solution for David's romantic predicament: "Human justice has not yet abandoned this humble world, I am going to try to get Mathilde to be allowed to go with us to Dinard, and after three to five weeks with us her fate will no longer frighten her." He also expressed his admiration for David, at the same time reminding him of his duties:

My son,

Today, 26 years [ago], a little being was born who cried very loudly, to the point of making himself hoarse for six weeks. This little fellow grew, made a racket, began his studies, all in a tearing hurry; ignoring and denigrating anything that lay outside the direct path that led him to his goal, a noble and generous goal: making something of himself, being useful to his family and friends, and holding high Judaism's banner. You have succeeded in taking an enviable place among your peers. You are called to continue the good work that my father and I have done.

You are discerning enough to know that to have influence on someone, on a group of people, you have to win their hearts, their trust – the moral side, which is the strongest. We can call upon the strength of our morality only by exercising it at any cost and not being afraid of every obstacle. [...]

May God bless you today on your path – no weakness and no hesitation. Your ardent love is too strong to be unable to overcome the greatest obstacles to your happiness, which constitutes a large part of your father's life. Horace[21]

In the summer of 1883, David therefore used this period of indecision as an opportunity to make a study trip to the eastern frontiers of the empire, in accordance with the tradition of the Russian school, spending six months in the Caucasus to learn Armenian and Georgian. In France, Horace's power of persuasion had happy effects on his young niece: on 18 December 1883, the wedding of David and Mathilde was finally celebrated in the Rue de la Victoire synagogue in Paris. In reality, they were not a very well-matched couple; their differences in character were accentuated by the opposite ways in which they had been brought up. A point of dispute appeared in the first days of their life together. The train taking them to Russia reached the border on Friday evening. "Since my father refused to travel on the Sabbath, my mother spent the night on a hard bench in the waiting room,"[22] their daughter Sonia remembers, adding:

Endowed with youth, beauty and charm, my mother was well received in St Petersburg. My father adored her. He composed poems for her every day, thought only of her, spoke only of her. [...] She respected his judgment, his generosity, his talents and his courage. She was grateful for his abundant love. But my father flew into sudden fits of rage, which blew over just as quickly. Even though they were never directed against her, she was very upset by them. In addition, Horace's children had been raised in a religious, traditional way, whereas my mother's family did not follow the commandments. [...] After she married my father, having to observe the dietary rules and the obligation to dine at her father-in-law's home on the day before the Sabbath was a burden for her.[23]

If David was subject to "fits of anger", his wife lacked a certain intellectual curiosity: she turned out to be incapable of sharing her husband's central interests. Moreover, no doubt because of their consanguinity (David and Mathilde were first cousins and so were their parents), of their five children, three suffered from physical or nervous problems. Moving from treatment at spas to consultations with physicians, their everyday life was sadly clouded, and David's innate dissatisfaction grew accordingly: his practice of erudition often disappointed him, either because he did not receive the recognition of his peers or because he deplored his lack of time; business and other obligations connected with the various family enterprises required much of his attention every day. His father frequently urged him to combat his demons. "Both bad and good must be accepted calmly," he reminded his son. "You go immediately to extremes, an unfailing friend, the bitterest enemy, and so on. Consider man in the fullness of his nature."[24] Or again: "No extremes of either pessimism or optimism, stay in the middle of the road but keep your eyes and ears open [...]. You are thirty-five years old and working. You have everything to be truly happy; don't spoil anything by becoming grumpy."[25] In 1890, at the age of thirty-three, David wrote a melancholy poetic confession:

> My blond hair is already going grey;
> Maturity's bells are tolling,
> Ringing out resonantly.
> Following the winding lane
> That leads to the temple of death,
> Sadly I contemplate my fate.
> I've been unable to make the use
> Of my knowledge that in childhood,
> Sure of myself and full of hope,
> I dreamed of under my bedside lamp.[26]

Déjà mes cheveux blonds grisonnent;
Les cloches de l'âge mûr sonnent,
Carillonnant à toute volée.
Suivant la sinueuse allée
Qui mène au temple de la mort,
Tristement je songe à mon sort.
Je n'ai pas su de ma science
Faire l'emploi qu'en mon enfance
Sûr de moi-même et plein d'espoir,
Je rêvais sous ma lampe au soir.

Quick to pour out his heart, David judges himself too severely. To be sure, he was not an exceptional poet. Nor did he claim to be. His many verses are addressed to only one person, Mathilde: "To celebrate your beauty would require genius; alas, for me poetry is only an obsession."[27] On the other hand, as an Arabist and a Hebrew scholar, he produced studies worthy of interest that were published in specialised journals in French, German and Russian. We may cite in particular his work *Le Divan d'Ibn Guzman, texte, traduction, commentaire.* But he was above all an original thinker regarding Judaism. Unfinished, in part unpublished, his own work, dealing with linguistics, theology and art history, is difficult to grasp. His name is attached in particular to one of the most ambitious Jewish intellectual projects of his time: in association with Rabbi Lev Katsnelson, David initiated and financed the *Evreyskaya entsiklopediya* (*The Jewish Encyclopaedia*) and took part in editing it. Published by Brockhaus and Efron in St Petersburg between 1908 and 1913, it consists of sixteen volumes on Jewish history, religion and culture in all periods and all countries, and remains a precious source of information today.

Involvement in Jewish studies was an ongoing battle. As a 23-year-old orientalist, David valiantly carried on a learned polemic during the winter of 1880–81: for the young philologist it was as much a question of enriching the Jewish patrimony as it was of defending his culture. He published in the *Revue critique* a refutation of the theses of the scholar Gustav Bickell (1838–1906) regarding biblical metrics,[28] accusing Bickell of misunderstanding the grammar, vocalisation, accentuation and intonation of Hebrew. An expert on the Fathers of the Church and a Catholic priest, Bickell was a professor of Christian archaeology and

Semitic languages at the University of Innsbruck. David's refutation provoked a virulent counter-attack by Edmond Bouvy (1847–1950), a priest and a member of the Augustinians of the Assumption who specialised in Byzantine studies. David replied in turn, writing not in the name of Russian scholarship but as a Jewish scholar:

> We Jews have suffered too much from pretensions of infallibility for us to have any desire to pretend to it in our turn, but isn't it permissible for a Jew to speak up loudly when it is a matter of his language, the last remainder of a glorious past? I am reproached for having attributed to it an antiquity of six thousand years: well! Good God, go and estimate in that case how long it has existed, and when you've completed a very exact calculation, come and show it to me, and I will adopt your opinion.[29]

The young man defended his conception of Hebrew and linguistics with convincing historical arguments:

> People like to ridicule us for insisting on Hebrew vocalisation. [...] *Pace* R. P. Bouvy, the language of a people is nourished by everything that constitutes it; if pronunciation were of so little value, why would the Académie française and the Comédie française be so rigorous about it? I intend to show, therefore, that although the doctors of Judaism invented vowel-points and accents rather late, after Elias Levita, it is nonetheless true that they did not just make up the pronunciation.

David reproached Bickell for "torturing Hebrew and giving it a Syrian twist", and trying to modify the biblical text: "If theologians and philosophers start ripping out, each in his own way, the alleged weeds in the Bible, the text will be running [a] great danger. The slightest changes are important in a book to which so much knowledge, so much belief, so much system [*sic*] is attached." At that time, David was preparing a work on the Bible's versification and its song, and he was examining Hebrew poetry very closely: in 1886, he published in Berlin an edition of the *Tarshish* of Rabbi Moses ibn Ezra, a remarkable poet and philosopher of Grenada (c.1058–c.1138). Divided into ten chapters, each containing in order the twenty-two letters of the Hebrew alphabet, the collection obeyed the rules of the *tajnis*, the poet playing on the homonyms repeated in each stanza. A few years later, on the occasion of the scholarly jubilee of his colleague and friend Daniil Khvolson, David oversaw the publication of a collection of testimonials for which he wrote an article on "the first book printed in Hebrew".[30] In this article, he presents the life and work of two Jewish savants from southern Italy, Moses Benjamin Foa and Isaiah Carmi, about whom he says that they "had received as a heritage from their ancestors a taste for books and a passion for study" – an autobiographical remark disguised by the modest scholar.[31] In 1900, he founded in St Petersburg an Academy of Oriental Studies and Judaism, a private study centre conceived as a space of freedom for professors and students who had been driven out of the university. Throughout his scholarly activity, David faithfully carried out his father's wish expressed on the occasion of his twenty-sixth birthday: "Hold high Judaism's banner."[32]

22

L'Ornement hébreu

FOR DAVID, LANGUAGE was not the only cultural path. Quite the contrary: "It is time to be done with the legend that claims that the Israelites, incapable of any creative effort in the arts, were only following their natural impulse when they abandoned painting or sculpture in order to obey the Decalogue."[1] With these lines of protest, which remained unpublished, David was engaging in an original reflection on the place of Jews in the history of art:

> It is true that the religious character imprinted on the representations of the real or fantastic beings, which the imagination took pleasure in surrounding with a supernatural nimbus, frightened the legislators, elicited religious [condemnations] among exegetes and theologians, and in some places even caused artistic production to be prohibited altogether. We must nevertheless take care not to transform the reservations formulated by one group and the intransigence shown by the other into a senseless prohibition on everything that pleases the eye and speaks to the soul through the eyes, or to believe that the Jews' forced silence in the domain of the aesthetic was a consequence of their lack of aptitude correlated with their religious upbringing.[2]

By challenging the thesis that there is "a forced silence of the Jews in the domain of the aesthetic", David wants to show the vigour of their creative energy, notably in the medieval period: his cherished library provided him with raw material, thanks to the decorative elements, figurative or not, that ornamented the bindings and manuscripts. As an outcome of this reflection, in 1905 he published a magnificent art book, judiciously entitled *L'Ornement hébreu* (*Hebrew Ornament*).The product of a collaboration with the art critic Vladimir Stasov (1824–1906), printed in Berlin and written in French, this volume catalogues and reproduces numerous ornamental treasures contained in rare manuscripts. In his preface, David presents the work as an "atlas, lovingly composed from vestiges of another age and relics of a civilisation that has disappeared". He emphasises the originality of the approach:

> Our atlas has [...] a physiognomy that contrasts with what one usually sees, and in it the Hebrew style, recognised by Stasov, takes on a striking character of life and unity. Russian artists who have seen it are struck by the seal of originality that the obscure illuminators imprinted on their beautiful, singular works.[3]

To achieve such a result, David had patiently examined numerous manuscripts, drawing up an inventory of illustrations, illuminations and calligraphies from all over Europe that had never been studied as such, in order to identify the "aesthetic aspirations" of the Jewish people:[4]

> [This work] is not a museum of illuminations in Hebrew manuscripts, but rather a collection of what we consider to be the reflection of the aesthetic aspirations of a people which, even at the dawn of its history, saw the imprint of the divine seal on the forehead of artists, and, wandering in a terrible desert in search of a homeland, a nationality and a religion, occupied itself by embroidering precious hangings and chiselling vessels to meet the needs of a new kind of worship.[5]

Thirty years older than David, Vladimir Stasov was a charismatic St Petersburger: with his long, white beard and his kind eyes, he was a well-known, beloved and respected figure. His taste and expertise in the domain of the arts, both ancient and contemporary, made him an influential ally. Trained as an archivist, he began his career serving as librarian for the magnate and aesthete Anatoly Demidov at his estate of San Donato near Florence. Later he was appointed director of the arts department at the Imperial Library in St Petersburg. Familiar with both ancient and modern artists, combining culture, intelligence, sensitivity and generosity, this scholar supported new movements as soon as they appeared – the Wanderers in painting, Glinka and The Five [Russian composers] in music – of which he was, moreover, the theorist. Around him formed a society composed of scholars, intellectuals and artists who were bound together by the same spirit of curiosity, inventiveness and rigour. His connection with the Gunzburgs was long-standing and not founded solely on the fact that they were both friends of the Stasyulevich family: Demidov's brother Dmitry worked as a lawyer for the Gunzburg bank, and his sister-in-law Polina was a close friend of David's mother, Anna. Thanks to Stasov, Horace and Anna were in contact with many musicians and painters, such as Mussorgsky, Rimsky-Korsakov, Kramskoy, et al. At Horace's request, Stasov became a member of the Society for the Promotion of Culture among the Jews of Russia. The art critic willingly got involved in causes defended by the Gunzburgs, and their friendship was strengthened by his public statements in favour of Jews. Similarly, Horace actively supported the so-called "Bestuzhev" university-level courses for women that had been founded by Stasov's sister. In 1869, in response to Richard Wagner's anti-Semitic essay "Das Judentum in der Musik" ("Judaism in music"), Stasov published "Judaism in Europe, according to Richard Wagner": by highlighting "the most Europeanised Jews" who were "capable of revealing to the world original melodies, the most contemporary rhythms, and touching spiritual notes unlike any others", Stasov presented a plea for the recognition of the place of Jewish culture in the domain of the arts. As he saw it, there is "no art without national spirit": just as he identified the Slavic or Byzantine sources that could be of use to artists of his own time, he encouraged artists of Jewish origin to create in accord with their tradition.[6] In July 1879, on the occasion of the planned construction of the St Petersburg synagogue, Horace asked him to preside over a jury assigned to select the best project. Stasov urged the prize-winning architects Lev Bakhman and Ivan Shaposhnikov to choose a neo-Moorish style combined with a neo-Byzantine style, to give the building a character that was simultaneously traditional and exotic that would fit into the St Petersburg landscape in an unusual way.[7] Conducted alongside these different projects, the work on *L'Ornement hébreu* thus arose from the happy marriage of the art critic's innovative thinking and David's unique talent in Hebrew.[8]

The initiative for this work came from Stasov, who encouraged David to undertake for Jewish art what he himself was already doing for Slavic and Byzantine arts in *L'Ornement russe et oriental sur les manuscrits de l'Antiquité et du Moyen Age.*[9] The young orientalist threw himself into the project of *L'Ornement hébreu* in 1885 with all the energy and enthusiasm of a young man of twenty-eight. Justifying *a posteriori* the twenty long years devoted to this enterprise, he stressed the "research in every country of Europe, supplementary information, accumulation of new documents, important discussions on the fundamental idea of the book, various studies in libraries" and "personal difficulties" that delayed publication by ten years. In fact, the collapse of the family bank in 1892 turned the Gunzburgs' lives upside down, and forced David to devote himself primarily to his business affairs. His preparatory notes for *L'Ornement hébreu* have been preserved: they illuminate the methodology adopted by the two scholars. On the basis of David's descriptions, Stasov determined the originality of the works. In October 1885 David sent from Dresden twenty-one loose sheets of paper hastily scribbled on in French and Hebrew, accompanied by sketches.[10] Drawing on the young man's family and personal culture, these drafts offer an immersion in the knowledge of a learned Jew. In a fifteenth-century prayer book, an illustration sparks his interest:

> The hymn in honour of the law has given rise to a great composition in the form of a richly decorated gate. [...] The variegated colours probably represent precious stones that are one day to be used to rebuild Jerusalem, according to the assurances of the prophets.[11]

Remarks on Jewish customs enrich his descriptions:

> In the composition we see a woman in an accoutrement that does not differ from that of the men; her hair is covered by a white scarf – the sacrifice of her hair was not yet customary. [...] Some of the men wear a pointed white hat, others a red mitre with green stripes, others a Tatar bonnet with a fur brim, others a Louis XI bonnet. That is what makes me assign the manuscript to the fifteenth century. What a faithful résumé of the life and history of the Jewish people![12]

Also examined in Dresden was a "Bible on parchment dating from the fourteenth or fifteenth centuries, eastern Germany", with sixty pen-and-ink vignettes: the binding "was probably done by a Jewish artist; otherwise the book would no longer have been holy," David explains. Many of its illustrations "represent in some way tapestries of various designs, composed of straight lines, circles, segments, full arches, fragments of ellipses or parabolas." The realistic illustrations show artisans, weddings, peasants working in their fields, etc.:

> This description will suffice to show that even in barbarous times the artistic instinct had not disappeared among the Jews of eastern Germany, and that the recent war on painting did not last as long as people have wanted to assume. This holds [even] for the Rhine basin, an area of orthodoxy and even fanaticism up to the period of emancipation, a country irrigated over and over by the tears and the blood of Jews who were tested, persecuted and martyred by their compatriots![13]

Still in 1885, David continued his quest in Leipzig, Berlin, Paris and London, prolonging it in 1893 as far as Valladolid, where he examined a commentary on the Apocalypse on parchment, written in the eleventh century in the province of Santander, and noted resemblances to Coptic manuscripts and ancient Muslim books:[14]

Despite these numerous explorations abroad, *L'Ornement hébreu* ultimately relies almost exclusively on the manuscripts preserved in the Imperial Library in St Petersburg: twenty-two plates out of twenty-five issued from this source. Three outside examples were added for the sake of complementarity: a Provençal manuscript in the French National Library in Paris, a manuscript in the British Museum in London, and a Yemeni manuscript in David's personal collection. Even the history of the St Petersburg collection itself enriches *L'Ornement hébreu* by adding a cultural history perspective to the book's visual interest: in his preface, David points out that the manuscripts reproduced were bought by the Imperial Library in 1856, 1870 and 1876 from the Karaite collector Avraam Firkovich (1780–1874), to whom he devotes a fascinating micro-study. Still famous for having begun the excavation of the spectacular Jewish fortress of Chufut-Kale ("Jewish fortress") in Crimea, where he established his den, Firkovich was a *"hakham* [learned] adventurer", as David put it. "Pursued by the demon of bric-a-brac and haunted by the hope of an immense profit", he amassed one of the finest Hebrew libraries in the world by searching "the cellars and attics of the synagogues of the Orient" and thus began "the creation of Semitic palaeography". Out of respect for holy books, Jewish communities kept in secure "depositories" worn-out copies that could no longer be used for religious services:

> The *genizot* where they were discovered were put at his disposal, thanks to the authority he enjoyed among his brothers and the gift of persuasion that distinguished him [...]. He worked in Crimea, in the Caucasus, in Egypt, in Palestine, in Damascus, Aleppo and Hit in Babylonia at a time when no one was yet thinking about exploring incomplete archives of Rabbanite and Karaite books.[15]

Back from his travels and "established in Chufut-Kale among his immense collections, he began to dangle their beauties before the government and specialists": the scholars Khvolson and Garkavi catalogued them for the Imperial Library before David could plunge into them with delight. After the work of selection, the production of *L'Ornement hébreu* required special care:

> It was not easy to extract from manuscripts that were often falling apart the ornaments that we wanted to put in the Atlas, and to find a way to reproduce them exactly, with all the richness of the colours, without taking the originals out of the rooms where they are guarded piously and with jealous care.[16]

The authors were helped by three artists – Ilya Ginzburg (no relation), a young sculptor who was a pupil of Antokolsky and sponsored by Horace, who later acquired great fame, notably for Stasov's mausoleum; the illustrator Ivan Bogdanov; and a certain M. Nechayev, "who traced the drawings and noted down with perfection all their subtleties" – and the publishers Théodore Vinberg and M. Lentz, who "guided the craftsmen, supervising with consummate knowledge the use of colours and the spreading of pure gold dust in order to avoid any dubious chemical alloy." The initiator of the neo-Russian style, the architect Ivan Ropet, who had created the Russian pavilion at the Universal Exhibition of 1878, designed a spectacular frontispiece based on rinceaux and arabesques taken from the manuscripts. When it was published, the work was warmly received. From Vienna, Babita informed David that her father-in-law Gutmann wanted to obtain a copy: "Dear David, there is a rumour here that you have published a book that is very expensive [...]. The Jewish community of Vienna would like to own this book."[17] She also congratulated him on this work "interesting for those who understand nothing about it". But above all David had the satisfaction of inspiring the craftsmen and artists of St Petersburg. Even before the book had been published, the ornaments collected by David provided decorative elements for a silver plate given by the Jewish community to "Their Imperial Majesties on the occasion of their coronation in 1884", for a lamp placed in the synagogue in 1888 in commemoration of the accident at Borki,[18] for the embroidered curtain that covers the Holy Ark in the St Petersburg temple on solemn holy days, as well as for the "megillah given to the sculptor Antokolsky on the day of his demi-jubilee", 28 December 1896, a silver and enamel scroll with inscriptions in Russian and Yiddish made by the goldsmith Fabergé.[19] Not to mention the effect produced on Marc Chagall, who had, as we know, *L'Ornement hébreu* in his hands: better than anyone else, he was able to draw from tradition the inspiration for a new genre.[20]

23

Antokolsky, the "First Jewish Sculptor"

ANTOKOLSKY DIED IN Herzburg, near Frankfurt, during the night of 9 July [1902], 5 Tammuz of that year, before having reached the age of sixty and without having realised the full measure of his talent. He died in agony, aggravated by the incompetence of the physicians, and on his deathbed he showed, by citing Socrates and Spinoza, that he was imbued with their teachings. He was not only a great sculptor but also a profound and original thinker.[1]

In this homage, which has remained unpublished, David expresses a fitting admiration. Now on exhibit in the permanent collections of the Russian Museum in St Petersburg, and in the Tretyakov Gallery in Moscow, Mark Antokolsky's sculptures no longer need special pleading: in Russia their creator is considered an important nineteenth-century artist.[2] Asserting that he did not "realise the full measure of his talent" was, however, excessive, since Antokolsky produced a great deal of good work and obtained significant recognition during his lifetime, both in Russia and in France as well as in the rest of Europe.[3] But it is true that he worked in permanent adversity: within the St Petersburg Academy of Fine Arts, where from 1862 to 1869 he was the sole Jewish student, and even later, when the tsar in person commissioned work from him, he had no respite from criticism and scorn. Born in 1842, the seventh child of a modest family of innkeepers, he spent his childhood in Vilna, where the street on which he was born now bears his name. Antokolsky paid a high price for being a Jew, because he was proud of it, just as he was proud of being Russian, as he said himself, not without anger:

> What's wrong with the fact that I'm Jewish! Haven't my works proved that I love Russia a thousand times more than those who persecute me solely because I'm a Jew? Everything I've experienced and felt, all my joys and sufferings, everything I've expressed in my creations – doesn't that all come from Russia and for Russia? Weren't my rewards and prizes given me as a Russian?[4]

In describing him as the "first Jewish sculptor", David weighed his words: "For him, the goal was to grasp the essence of the Jewish spirit and to apply it to an activity unknown to those who have [that spirit]." Some of his works depict everyday Jewish life: *Jewish Porter, An Old Man's Evening Work, A Jewish Miser, A Talmudic Discussion*. In a biographical notice, David sensitively mentions the sculptor's sources of inspiration that were drawn from his childhood:

> At first, Mark Antokolsky lived in the suffocating atmosphere of a tavern in Vilna. The *cheder* where he studied left on him the impression of a place where children were often beaten; he found his father's house after school scarcely more attractive. [...] As a young child, he found warmth only in the sensitive, eminently kind, delicate heart of his mother. He had to take up an occupation: the boy was apprenticed to a braid-maker. This went against his nature, and it proved necessary to put him in other hands: an engraver took him on, and that was already better; driven by an irresistible force, the young adolescent began to shape wood, stone, anything to make figurines. [...] The tranquil charm of the Lithuanian landscape, the calm immensity of the pine forests, the absence of social and political life, the down-to-earth human labour in this Jewish anthill, the grandeur of the religious dream and the sincerity of Talmudic studies – all these disparate elements helped shape the mind and character of a man who would render with equal success the different types of Jewish life in the north, the internal intellectual battles, the solemn crushing of the idea by the Inquisition, the peaceful assurance of physical strength, the complex character of autocrats, the mythical gentleness of martyrs, the comforting beauty of moral duty, the overwhelming mystery of

illness and death, and all the healthy and elevated sentiments that women awaken in us.[5]

Between Jewish culture and the Russian melting-pot, Antokolsky fashioned a body of work of great originality, which Stasov quickly noticed, becoming his best friend and most ardent defender: "[Antokolsky] is the greatest sculptor of our time. In his personality he represents something truly different from what other sculptors consider classical and modern," the critic wrote in 1882.[6] The painter Kramskoy made a beautiful portrait of the man he also considered to be a friend and whose spectacular *Ivan the Terrible* he had exhibited in 1871, at the Wanderers' first salon: Alexander II bought the statue for 8,000 roubles to put in the Hermitage, and he came to visit the sculptor's studio. "I woke up poor," the sculptor wrote about that memorable day, "became rich, yesterday I was famous, today I'm fashionable."[7]

The Gunzburgs were the first and most important patrons of the arts in St Petersburg, to the point that Antokolsky's detractors presented his success as the result of the "group of Jewish bankers".[8] In 1862, a young student of art without money or relations, he had knocked at Joseph Evzel's door. Even his arrival in St Petersburg had been favoured by his extraordinary talent: in Vilna he had created a small *objet d'art* in wood that was religious in character, inspired by Van Dyck's *Christ and the Virgin*. Mme Nazimova, the wife of the governor-general, encouraged him to go to St Petersburg, giving him fifty roubles, food, and a letter for the Baron of Rhaden. The latter introduced him to Grand Duchess Helen, a patron of the arts, who put him in contact with Professor Nikolay Pimenov, who admitted him to his sculpture class at the Academy of Fine Arts as an unregistered student. The marvellous sequence of events in this year 1862 did not suffice to resolve the financial questions: "At first, finances naturally continued to be a problem; a nail and a bit of ivory were enough to let him render the features of my grandfather [Joseph Evzel] and allowed him to obtain a modest subsidy – the source of a lasting friendship that has never failed and that has passed from one generation to another without growing any weaker."[9] Today, this work has disappeared, but on that occasion Antokolsky received ten roubles a month from the banker; he spent six on rent, one on artistic materials. Starting in 1865, his *Miser* won him a silver medal and an imperial subsidy of twenty-five roubles a month, which gave him a certain independence. He travelled in Germany and Italy, and married a ravishing young lady from a good family in Vilna. Here David's notes can be supplemented by the memories of his brother Sasha:

> Passing through Paris on their way back from Rome, [the Antokolskys] dined on Rue de Tilsitt when Mama [Anna de Gunzburg] was still alive. It was the first time that I saw them. She was a pretty blonde, intelligent and good at languages. He was ugly but had expressive eyes and spoke no language. His speech was an extraordinary gibberish based on Yiddish, but for all that he was a poet, and what he said and what he wrote was always intelligent, giving, in words, the impression of a sketch made with broad brushstrokes. His health was rather precarious and his humour reflected that.[10]

Horace commissioned Antokolsky to create one artwork after another, at a steady rhythm, alternating between general patronage and family subjects: the bust of Peter the Great in 1863 was followed in 1877 by the posthumous bust of Anna, for which Antokolsky used photographs, a drawing by Kramskoy and Bonnat's oil portrait. Imbued with a sincere affection, his work shows that he had known Anna well. Antokolsky made a portrait both tender and realistic of a woman of thirty-eight whose slightly faded beauty was compensated by elegance, kindness and wit. He experienced her premature death as a personal ache, as he wrote to his friend Savva Mamontov:

> It's terrible! It's terrible! I found out by chance, through the newspaper account, and I couldn't believe it. I thought it was a mistake. From your letter I have understood that it was entirely true. Receiving this news, I was no longer myself and couldn't eat for the rest of the day. It's strange, but there are persons whom one cannot connect with the notion of death![11]

In homage to Baroness Gunzburg, Antokolsky named his eldest daughter Anna.[12] With the same affection, he created in 1878 the medallion in bas-relief for the late Marc, a young painter taken away from his art too soon. Afterwards, Horace entrusted him with his own portrait; this marble is imbued with the artist's respect for Horace, a true *mensch*.[13] In

Antokolsky's view, he was not only an influential banker but also a pillar of the community, the courageous defender of his fellow Jews: flat, strong surfaces set off his piercing eyes and his full lips pressed tightly together. However, the whole is conventional and a little bland: "At the time when he made the bust of our father, the latter was unwell and Antokolsky had great troubles of his own, and the bust, of which each of us was supposed to receive a copy, suffered from the general malaise that reigned over the sittings, and turned out to be plainly bad."[14] Antokolsky also made a bust of Joseph Evzel during the banker's lifetime, a work that has now disappeared.[15] Antokolsky was a noble-hearted man, and he introduced to the Gunzburgs his protégé, Ilya Ginzburg, who also received a subsidy from Horace and remained connected with the family, and Avraam Grilikhes, another fellowship student who was also originally from Vilna. Grilikhes won a medal, like his father; whereas in 1877 the father created a finely engraved medal of Joseph Evzel's profile, in 1889 his son sculpted Horace's face in rock crystal, a work for which he won a prize at the Universal Exhibition in Paris.

Since 1877 Antokolsky had been living in Paris, a member of the circle of Russian artists and even of the Institute, which delighted Horace: "Bravo, Mark Matveyevich [Antokolsky], the French rise in my esteem."[16] The Gunzburg children liked to visit the studio on Rue Bayen, in Les Batignolles, with their tutor M. Rohmann, as Sasha recounts:

> I no longer recall on what terms, but very frankly, the latter [Rohmann] asked him how it was that with the limited knowledge he had at his disposal, he produced works so characteristic, such as his Socrates, his Peter I or Ivan the Terrible? He replied: "It's like a pregnant woman: once I have an idea, it develops in spite of me, and one fine day I cannot help bringing it out into the daylight."[17]

A photograph of Antokolsky in his Parisian studio, taken by Adam Salomon, captures the powerful character of the master and his work. The slender silhouette of the artist blends harmoniously into the chaos of his works; holding his tools in his hand, he looks out of deep eyes; in the background, in the shadows, we can divine his famous statue of Spinoza. A large-scale work, the sculpture represents the philosopher sitting in a very natural pose, lost in his thoughts, his hands joined over his belly, with an open book on his lap and another at his feet. Antokolsky succeeded in creating a touching representation of the thinker, imbued with dignity and humility. For the generation of the *Haskalah*, Spinoza, a universal thinker excommunicated by his community, was a landmark figure, a source of comfort and stimulation. From 1873 on, Antokolsky began to steep himself in Spinoza's writings and to collect information on his life. In 1877, he refused to take part in the international competition organised in The Hague for the bicentennial of the philosopher's birthday, judging that he was not ready. Horace was then his sponsor: "Antokolsky is working on Spinoza for me," he wrote to Marc in November 1878.[18] It took four years and much expense. In October 1881, at the end of a second, crucial trip to Holland in Stasov's company, the Spinoza was finally finished.[19] On the occasion of the twenty-fifth anniversary of the liberation of the serfs in 1886, Horace then commissioned from him a statue of Alexander II. Intended for the Alexander room in the synagogue, this work ultimately became the property of Vladimir, Horace's son, in Kiev.

In 1894, Tsar Nicholas II commissioned his own effigy from Antokolsky, a work that aroused the Gunzburgs' interest: "He put a general's epaulettes on Emperor Nicholas II when he made his bust on the occasion of his marriage. But Nicholas II kept the rank of colonel that his father had conferred on him. No one in the entourage noticed that, but we, the children, discovered this inadvertent error, which he chose not to correct,"[20] Sasha recalled. Antokolsky subsequently proposed a project of statues for the future Alexandre III bridge in Paris, imagining that he would represent the tutelary figures of the Russian empire: Vladimir Monomakh (Grand Prince of Kiev, 1113–25), Peter the Great, Catherine II, Alexander II. But "his project was deemed too expensive". Although the decorative programme was finally entrusted to French sculptors, the cost was probably only a pretext to justify a refusal influenced by the desire not to hire a Jewish artist for a prestigious official project:

It is true to say that the conservative press – especially the *Novoe Vremya* – criticised him fiercely and relentlessly. Once at the home of Jacques Poliakov in Biarritz, Antokolsky met Suvorin, the famous director and owner of the *Novoye Vremya*. Suvorin told him he was happy to make the acquaintance of the famous sculptor who was one of our national glories. Antokolsky replied that he was touched by the compliment, but then he did not understand the unremitting campaign that Suvorin's paper was waging against him. "There is a great difference between our personal feelings and what the editorial board of the paper thinks it best to write."[21]

For Antokolsky, the persecutions of 1880 and 1890 were a terrible trial, even though two retrospective exhibitions of his work were organised in St Petersburg in 1881 and 1893. Between glory and denigration, he endured a painful period, about which Sasha's anecdote regarding his admirable *Christ Before the People* is particularly telling:

> The Emperor Alexander III, an anti-Semite par excellence, had a particular esteem for him. A curious fact: Antokolsky had made a statue of Christ before the people. He was represented with his hands tied and a skullcap on his head, the sculptor claiming that in the Orient no one could endure the sun bareheaded. When this statue was exhibited, the defenders of orthodoxy, with *Novoye Vremya* at their head, protested, and I do not believe I am far from the truth when I say that they demanded its destruction. The emperor saw the statue at the Academy, bought it, and had it put in his study in the Anichkov palace.[22]

This very striking statue can be seen in the photograph of his studio in Paris already mentioned: the profoundly human figure of *Christ Before the People* towers over the sculptor, who is finishing the full-length portrait of a young woman reading. To the left the eye is drawn by a statue of Mephistopheles; it was also commissioned by Horace. From Peter the Great to Spinoza, by way of Christ and the Devil, Antokolsky's work is marked by the theme of the struggle between good and evil. In February 1893, attending the inauguration of the exhibition devoted to his work at the Academy of Fine Arts, Antokolsky found the city of St Petersburg cold, damp and grey. But he was surrounded by affection: his friends Repin and Stasov personally supervised the installation of the exhibition; the catalogue was prepared with great care by F. I. Bulgakov, a journalist and photographer; in addition, the event attracted a large number of visitors. But at the party organised in his honour by the Society for the Promotion of Culture, the sculptor seemed sad and bitter. Although his friends Garkavi, Khvolson, Solovyov, Stasov and David de Gunzburg praised his work, in the press the anti-Semitic reactionaries launched a barrage of unjust criticism. While he was working on a statue of Yermak, the Russian hero of the conquest of Siberia, the Jews of Russia were suffering pogroms and vexations. "Where am I? What is happening to me? Who am I? Where is my homeland?" Antokolsky wondered.[23]

In 1897, Antokolsky took up residence in a pleasant villa near Lugano. A property that had formerly belonged to the anarchist Bakunin, it had been bought by Horace in the 1870s.

> [Bakunin] had left two daughters, and, since they needed money, Turgenev was able to persuade my father to buy for 40,000 francs this property that was located above Lugano and was named, by a curious coincidence, "La Baronata". Later on, my father made a gift of this property to Antokolsky. I say "gift" because Antokolsky had promised to give in exchange copies of his most important works, but except for one of them, he did not keep his promise.[24]

In this house that had been abandoned for nineteen years, Antokolsky spent marvellous days working and cultivating the soil. It was there that he wrote, in the form of a "Letter to Baron Horace de Gunzburg",[25] a curious essay on the condition of Jews. In the Gunzburgs, the sculptor found not only powerful protectors but also interlocutors with whom he could share his thoughts:

> I experienced great and numerous difficulties in my childhood, but not as many as now. I was young then, and life was before me and not behind me as it is today. At that time my ideal of youth was surrounded by a nimbus of holy light. This ideal warmed me and enlightened me, I believed in it and fought to reach it. We all believed then in a better future, in the victory of good, and we didn't doubt it for a minute. Hard work was demanded of us, but the soul of humanism had to win out over the beast in man. Now life has passed in working and struggling. Now my hair is grey and my ideals are a broken doll lying at my feet. The beast in man has won.[26]

The pogroms in Russia, the Dreyfus affair in France and the virulent expression of anti-Semitism in the French and Russian press sounded the death knell for the hopes born of the Haskalah. In 1902, Mark Antokolsky's funeral brought his faithful friends together in Vilna: the critic Vladimir Stasov, the painter Ilya Repin, the sculptor Ilya Ginzburg, the ballet impresario Serge Diaghilev and his patrons, the Mamontovs, the Varshavskys and, of course, the Gunzburgs. Six months later, a no less grandiose homage was paid in the Choral Synagogue of St Petersburg, every step of whose construction Antokolsky had followed passionately ever since Joseph Evzel had been authorised by the tsar in 1869 to construct a place of worship for the Jews of St Petersburg. All around the synagogue, the gates had been adorned with crowns of foliage decorated with "Hebrew ornaments". Thousands joined the funeral cortège, preceded by the synagogue's choir. In a letter to David written a few years later, Vladimir Stasov remembered their common friend: "Is it possible that a man as great as Antokolsky had to wade through a swamp for such a long time and perhaps forever, solely because he was a Jew?"[27]

24

Zionism: *pro et contra*

UNDER THE REIGN of Nicholas II (1894–1917), the policy of repressing revolutionary movements was aimed at Jewish students and intellectuals on the pretext that they belonged to the Zionist movement. To counter this unjust simplification, Horace entrusted David with writing a reply, based on arguments, to the question: "Does Zionism present a danger from the social and political point of view?"[1] In the margin of the manuscript, an annotation in David's hand adds: "Memoir composed by me in August 1901 and presented by my father to Zwolinski, the director of the police department, at the behest of the Minister of Public Instruction [Pyotr Vannovsky]." The document gives the Gunzburgs' "official" point of view at the dawn of the twentieth century, exactly twenty years after the first pogroms. David begins by defining Zionism, asserting that it is not a "party" but a "state of mind":

> Standing at a distance from this movement, which is merely the repetition of movements that have occurred in Israel at different times as a consequence of appalling persecution, I can state that it is not a spontaneous product of the Jewish religion and that it does not adequately represent the aspirations of our race. It is moreover rather difficult to define Zionism, which is not a sect, which does not form a party, and which contains within itself the most diverse elements; it is rather a very complex state of mind, if it is not simply a sonorous word devoid of meaning.[2]

Seeking to recall the importance of the Promised Land, he draws a distinction between "palestinophilia" and "Zionism":

> However, an abyss separates Zionism from Palestinophilia, which is merely a sentimental application of our religious ideal to agriculture, our old favourite occupation, for which Jews have once again definitively acquired a taste. A Jew naturally loves Palestine, even if he is not thinking of living there, or, at least, dying there, as those who have the faith have been accustomed to do. It is our cradle and the scene of our national history; and it is something else as well: the Promised Land of the Messianic times, but this concerns Providence.[3]

Modern Zionism was presented as a consequence of anti-Semitism and the degraded living conditions of the Jewish population. The *numerus clausus* adopted in secondary schools and universities was experienced as a blatant injustice: "thrown back into the ghetto" even though they had accomplished the task of emancipation, "Jewish young people" were taking refuge in the Zionist hope.

> Anti-Semitism, a product of militant clericalism at bay, swept into the world on the tide of an acute economic crisis, has been maintained by governments that think they have found in it a way of distracting attention from the sterile and pernicious agitation of politicians. It has literally terrified the peaceful Jewish populations of Europe. Suddenly exiled from society, Jewish young people, who had been preparing themselves for careers as lawyers and schoolteachers, for the usual manipulations [*sic*] of daily life in their homeland, have found themselves thrown back into the same ghetto where they were suffocating before and had nothing to do.

As *shtadlan* and philanthropists, the Gunzburgs were in the forefront of the battle against anti-Semitism. Since Horace's letter to Tsar Alexander III of 6 May 1890, the government had sent no encouraging signal. The new tsar, Nicholas II, stuck rigidly to his father's positions. And as David emphasises, the recrudescence of anti-Semitism was a European phenomenon. The Gunzburgs were thus explicitly named as a target by Edouard Drumont in his appalling essay *La France juive*, published in 1886:

In less than twenty years, if circumstances are favourable to him, the Jew reaches his full development; he is born at the end of a one-way street, he earns a few pennies in an initial operation, hurries off to Paris, has himself decorated through the mediation of some kind of Dreyfus, buys a baron's title, boldly presents himself in a large circle, takes on the airs of someone who has always been rich. In him the transformation is in some way instantaneous, he feels no astonishment, he knows no bashfulness of any kind. Take a Russian Jew at home, under his soiled, fleece-lined vest, with his sidelocks and his earrings, and, after a month of taking baths, he'll settle into a box at the opera with the aplomb of a Stern or a Gunzburg.[4]

Soon adapted by the Polish writer Calixte de Wolski in his book *La Russie juive*, the theme of a worldwide Jewish conspiracy fed articles and essays of all kinds. A genuine poison, anti-Semitism insinuated itself into every stratum of society. The conviction of Captain Albert Dreyfus on charges of treason in 1894 aroused strong international feeling: the Austro-Hungarian journalist Theodor Herzl, then living in France, concluded that only Zionism could resolve the "Jewish problem". In the Gunzburgs' circle, the ideal of "integration" had to be revised, as Heinrich Sliozberg, an eminent jurist and one of Horace's collaborators on the committee to help Jews suffering from pogroms, pointed out:

Yes, we are foreigners, not only here, but all over Europe, because it is not our homeland. Now I understand the word "anti-Semitism". It is the secret of our suffering in exile. Even in Alexandria, at the time of the Second Temple, and in all the countries of our diaspora, we have been foreigners, undesirable guests. [...] To be sure, we dream of becoming children of the nations of Europe, children with the same rights. Could we be more stupid?[5]

At that time, the Zionist idea excited people. The return to Zion made it possible to believe in the "salvation of the Jewish people" and the "guarantee of its eternal existence".[6] In 1897, an initial Zionist Congress held in Basle brought together representatives from all over Europe. Without supporting the movement, the Gunzburgs followed its creation – David's papers contain documents that resulted from this congress –

from its Russian genesis. In 1882, Lev Pinsker had published *Auto-Emancipation*. A physician, a member of the Society for the Promotion of Culture and supporter of integration, Pinsker revised his judgement in the tragic light of the pogroms. In his essay he analysed anti-Semitism as a permanent phenomenon transmitted from generation to generation and he put his ideas for salvation in a Promised Land, in Palestine or in America. *Hibat Tsiyon* (Love of Zion) was the name chosen in 1884 for the movement promoting the establishment of a homeland in Palestine: the *Hovevei Zion* (Lovers of Zion) defined Jews as a nation with a land – Israel – and a language – Hebrew (or, for some, Yiddish). This intellectual movement, already influential among the Jews of Russia, became a useful support to Herzl when he published *The Jewish State* in 1896.

In his note on Zionism, David distanced himself from the man who is today the most famous promoter of the "reconstitution of the Jewish state":

> We then witnessed this extraordinary fact: men who used to take pride in their indifference to matters of religion and who had rejected with horror any contact with their brothers [Herzl was not involved in any religious practice] became enthusiastic about Judaism's past and vowed to work to revive it. Naturally, they brought with them the methods used in the groups that formed around them, and being alien to our intellectual culture, or simply desirous of putting their diverse talents to work, they wanted to recover within Judaism, at least in imagination, what had been maliciously taken away from them elsewhere. Hence the chimerical idea of reconstituting the Jewish state with the Sultan's consent, the German emperor's support, and England's sympathy; hence the frequent meetings, lectures, regional and world-wide conferences; hence the foundation of a colonial bank and the plan for a general insurance company.

Even as they criticised Herzl's project, the Gunzburgs tried to show that it was not a democratic trend, and therefore it was revolutionary and threatening in the eyes of an autocratic regime, as the Russian administration assumed. In conclusion, David emphasised that "the danger resides not in Zionism itself; it begins to emerge in the situation that ill-advised statesmen have sought to prepare for all our young people, who are becoming Zionist under these sad auspices." Pointing out that the

Jewish people must be admired for its endurance and energy "wherever, as in Argentina and the Russian colonies, it is authorised to work the land," David denounced the numerous obstacles to its full blossoming in Russia:

> To restrict ourselves only to education, the ludicrous percentage of admissions to government schools (10 per cent here, 3 per cent there, 2 per cent in technical institutions, 0 in many schools: in Vilna, Jewish children have not been admitted to the city's secondary schools for two years, in Kovno for six years), the obstacles raised to opening school complexes in communities (especially in the report submitted by the trustee of Vilna), the prohibition on teaching Russian in the *cheders*, and the systematic weakening of religious education in our denominational schools, [...] all these things cause our young people to go astray and force them to travel abroad, if only for long enough to complete their studies. They will come back excited and upset, if these errors continue; then Zionism will be formidable, and nothing will be able to eliminate it. At the present moment, a little air and light would make it absolutely anodyne and inoffensive.[7]

In diagnosing a future radicalisation of Jewish youth, David proved clairvoyant. Like his father, he pinned all his hopes on the economic solution of the Jewish problem. His essay on Zionism refers on several occasions to Jews' attachment to "working the land". The Gunzburgs' commitment to agriculture led them to collaborate in the projects of Maurice de Hirsch, who founded the Jewish Colonisation Association (JCA) in London in 1891. A banker born in Bavaria, Hirsch decided to put his immense fortune at the service of his Russian co-religionists. The "Moses of the Americas" had certain things in common with Horace[8]: they belonged to the same generation, and were both members of Jewish high society. A family connection also bound them: Rosa Rosenberg, Horace's sister-in-law, had married Joseph de Hirsch, Maurice's first cousin. Ennobled around 1820, the "von Hirsch aus Gereuth" family also bore the title of baron. Like the Gunzburgs, the Hirsches had settled in France. In 1855 Maurice married Clara Bischoffsheim, with whom he moved to Paris in 1868 in order to take on the directorship of the Paris branch of his in-laws' bank in Brussels. Investments in the Russian and Ottoman railways (the Moscow–Ryazan and Constantinople–Sisak lines) gave Maurice de Hirsch a considerable fortune that allowed him, in particular, to support the educational work set up by the Alliance Israélite Universelle in the Ottoman provinces. The pogroms of 1881 drew Baron Hirsch's attention to Russia: in July 1881, as a result of a rumour that that the Alliance was promising to help Jews who wanted to emigrate, thousands of families spontaneously set out for Austria and ended up massed at Brody, a town in Galicia on the Austro-Russian border. Hirsch sent his colleague Emmanuel Veneziani there, equipped with "unlimited credit authorising him to provide, in his name, for the maintenance of the refugees". Six million francs were devoted to sending 8,000 migrants to the United States and to the upkeep of refugees in situ, who still numbered 12,000 in the summer of 1882.[9]

In the meantime, in St Petersburg, Horace found himself involved in a twofold power struggle with the Minister of the Interior, Nikolay Ignatyev, and young Jewish nationalists. Although he continued officially to defend integration, the inexhaustible *shtadlan* was nevertheless aware that emigration to the United States was an opportunity that had to be seized, believing that any hard-working emigrant who possessed technical or engineering skills would have no difficulty finding work or a career there.[10] But Horace occupied a position that was all the more delicate because he disapproved of the approach to the Russian administration adopted by Baron Hirsch's emissary, a certain Arnold White: in order to obtain the authorisation necessary for the Jewish Colonisation Association to function, White promised "to be able to free Russia of millions of undesirable Jews".[11] Horace's mistrust was justified. The correspondence between White and members of the Russian government subsequently showed that he was a convinced anti-Semite. But to keep Hirsch's project from perishing, Horace agreed to support it: aided by Samuel Polyakov (James de Hirsch's father-in-law, Maurice's brother), he managed to convince the generous philanthropist to devote to educational institutions part of the money intended for immigration, about fifty million francs. Unfortunately, the proposal for a foundation intended to spread professional primary education was rejected by the tsar. Following this failure, in 1888 Baron Hirsch created in Vienna the Baron Hirsch Stiftung, a foundation with a capital of twelve million francs; major sums were then transferred to the Society for the Promotion of Culture.

Aid for emigration, however, remained Baron de Hirsch's priority. In 1890 in New York he created the Baron de Hirsch Fund to ease immigrants' integration and fund their vocational training in the United

States. The following year he created the Jewish Colonisation Association in London with the aim of establishing agricultural colonies in South America, especially in Argentina. In September 1891 he addressed a letter "to his fellow Jews of Russia":[12] "You know that I am trying to make your lives easier. It seems to me indispensable to speak to you openly, in order to tell you what you must absolutely know." The letter announced the creation of committees on emigration and explained that only those who passed through these committees would have access to aid. He also asked his co-religionists to be patient: it would take time to prepare for this massive emigration, particularly with the Russian administration. The emigration's destination was yet to be defined: Hirsch shared the Gunzburgs' reservations with regard to Zionism. He envisaged emigration as an emergency measure to give the Jews of Russia a better life, and this excluded Palestine from the outset, since conditions there were not favourable: there was a shortage of land and a hostile Arab population, the colonists lacked agricultural skills, and it was difficult to obtain supplies of livestock, tools and seeds.[13] The general opinion was that early colonists were encountering trying difficulties: among the refugees in Brody, dozens of emigrants had succeeded in reaching Palestine. Most of them were students from the Bilu movement, which was founded in January 1882 and advocated returning to Israel to create a Jewish state there. Although he provided financial support for the initial colonists, Hirsch did not believe in the Palestinian project: in 1891, on the occasion of a meeting organised in Paris on the initiative of rabbis who had come from Russia to argue in favour of Zionism, the chief rabbi, Zadoc Kahn, tried to convince Barons Edmond de Rothschild and Maurice de Hirsch to combine forces in support of emigration to Palestine. Maurice de Hirsch proposed another destination: with its vast expanses of under-populated, fertile land and a government in favour of immigration, Argentina was better suited to receive numerous migrants. The Jewish Colonisation Association, which owned 112,000 hectares of land there, organised the settlement of 20,000 families in all, or 120,000 individuals: the attorney David Feinberg supervised the setting up of committees on emigration throughout the Pale of Settlement. In 1893, in St Petersburg, David assumed the direction of the JCA, whose meetings were held in the family offices at 4 Zamyatin Lane.[14] In 1893, 2,683 migrants were already living in the colonies of Mauricio (in the province of Buenos Aires) and of "Moses City" (in the province of Santa Fe), where the largest of the nineteen villages bore the name "Baron de Gunzburg".[15] In addition to clearing land and cultivating it, the colonists had to create everything: primary schools, *cheders*, clinics... David undertook to find Hebrew books for the schools and for the library in Mauricio.

In Russia, the JCA also offered a way of circumventing governmental prohibitions in the area of education by subsidising schools run by the Society for the Promotion of Culture: about fifty primary schools for boys and girls were opened. Shortly after Alexander III's death, the JCA also received permission to develop vocational and agricultural training for Jewish young people. In association with ORT, it helped existing vocational schools and created about twenty new schools in the Pale of Settlement, while at the same time offering scholarships for study abroad. Through the JCA, David also looked after the agricultural colonies on Russian soil, especially in Kherson and Ekaterinoslav. In the agricultural colonies, whether in Russia or in Argentina, Jews "acquired an admirable endurance and energy," as David wrote, because they were free to "put their aptitudes and their initiative to work",[16] without hindrances or privations of liberty.

25

The Ordeal of Bankruptcy

IN FEBRUARY 1893, David wrote his last will and testament for Mathilde. He was only thirty-six but had just lived through a trying year. He made his wife his sole heir in a will which he accompanied with a personal note:

> I want to tell you again here what I have already told you many times: all our household furnishings are already yours; my library of printed books and manuscripts became your property the day after the I. G. Gunzburg Bank collapsed;[1] the horses and tack were given to you from the outset by my father and in part by me; the art objects were, and naturally will be, acquired only for you. If I leave works that are finished or unfinished, they will belong to you and you will do with them whatever you think best. Alive or dead, I shall know no law but yours, for you are my only love and my only divinity, and I adore you on my knees, pressing my burning lips on your beloved, darling feet. Yours forever, David.

Without underestimating the emotional value of his act, the gift of the library seems to be part of a legal arrangement intended to avoid a judicial sale connected with "the collapse of the bank". Although David devoted as much of his time as he could to his linguistic work, he was above all his father's associate: thus in 1892 he was in the front line of the battle to cope with the difficulties that caused the bankruptcy of the establishment Joseph Evzel had created three decades earlier.

Among Horace's many children, David was at that point the one most involved in the family business. It had rapidly become clear that the eldest, Gabriel, who was a classic "bad lot", would never be his father's colleague. Even though he paid Gabriel's debts, Horace worried about his dissolute behaviour ("So long as it doesn't go beyond pecuniary affairs"[2]) and preferred geographical distance: Gabriel was sent to South America, where he remained for two years. Family memoirs report that "on the boat carrying migrants from southern Italy, there was a Catholic priest but no one who knew Latin. Gabriel, who had grown up in France, offered to assist the priest every day." At least he was helpful and a good Latinist. When he came back to Europe and continued his disorderly life, Horace again decided to put some distance between them: in 1885 or thereabouts, he sent him to the Far East, where he remained until 1904 without returning to Russia. Settled in Shanghai, he was close to the representatives of the Russian government there, who liked his honesty and discretion, and for whom he did a few favours.[3] In the spring of 1896 he was given the responsibility of taking to Beijing the terms of the agreement with China regarding the railway concession in Manchuria. In partnership with two regular visitors to the "Boulevard", the military men Alexandre Bezobrazov and Evgeny Alexeyev,[4] he was involved in the diabolical affairs along the Yalu, territories in the Korean peninsula whose possession was one of the issues in the Russo-Japanese War that broke out in 1904. Thus in the 1880s, when Mimi was pursuing his studies, Sasha was doing his military service and Vladimir, Berza and Pierre were still in secondary school, David was the first to work with his father. A continuing correspondence between the two men bears witness to their collaboration, which lasted until Horace's death in 1909 (closely followed by David's in 1910).

A letter of 29 July 1886 offers a detailed account of the bank's everyday operations. Most of the letter's ten points deal with business, but attention is also given to the situation of Jews in the region of Mogilno, in Podolia. The letter emphasises the diversity of the Gunzburgs' financial and entrepreneurial activities, as well as their networks in the international private sector and the Russian public sector. Without being a unique document (when Horace was abroad, he wrote to David every day), the coherence of the information transmitted makes it an interesting illustration of the way the family business functioned. And while the domestic Russian context was always delicate, nothing in it allows us to anticipate the difficulties to come.

Petersburg 29 VII 86

Dear Papa,

Your letter about the income tax arrived just in time. Today the commission's payment order taxing the bank at 7,080 roubles was delivered to us. Last year we paid less after a more favourable financial period. This year these gentlemen gathered no information and set an imaginary bill. We have one month to present our statements, and we await your decision on this subject.

This morning we saw your telegram regarding the loan taken out by the city of Hamburg, and we are awaiting further details from the Warburg bank regarding the contribution that you have reserved for social welfare.

We are going through a slow season.

[...] The gold mines seem to be working very well this year. In Aug.-Uf [in Lena, Siberia] a new lode of ore was found, the first that has not yet been explored or exploited. The value of this discovery has not yet been established. Aug.-Uf's mining engineer, Lenvitsky, is leaving today to travel around Sweden and Germany to study the procedures used in the "Bismarck" factories in Silesia, where sheet steel is manufactured for tinplating. Margrandt is proposing that we make this kind of sheet steel. They would promise to buy 1 million *pudi* [16,380,000 kg] of it from us, to be delivered within five years.[5]

[We are also talking about making] pipes for naphtha in view of the possibility of producing it in Baku. [...] [This will be] of capital importance if we decide to construct a pipeline to bring naphtha to Batum. The railway spikes could be manufactured in Serg[ievo] Uf[aleysky],[6] in the Urals, less expensively than Graskov at first supposed. [...] Find enclosed a letter from S. Levenson, the passage on the subject of salt in Chugar [Crimea] will especially interest you.

Mimi's work is with the censor. Mimi is getting ready to attend classes at the university as an unregistered student this winter; he has sent me the request to be presented to the rector. Kiss grandmother, my sisters, my little brothers, Henriette and Salomon for me, and give my best to Michel and Jacques. I am also sending you a tearful letter from a grandson of the late [Markus] Sukhostaver [Horace's Hebrew teacher in Kamenets-Podolsk]. Oh, the persecutions! In Mogilno people are rising up against the Jews with renewed vigour. The situation of Jellinek [the supervisor of the sugar refinery] is becoming very precarious. Aalson proposes the following means [of coping with this problem]: his brother-in-law Baron Alexander Alexandrovich Ikskov has been named governor of Pskov, where he has won the affection and the confidence of the population. In the south, he has never bothered Jews, far from it. A letter from you, supported perhaps by another from Aalson, would urge Ikskov to address himself confidentially to [Vasily] Glinka [governor of Podolia] (whom he surely knows) to ask him to put an end to persecutions that can only end up significantly prejudicing the Mogilno business in these difficult times or even suspending the refinery's operation, thereby striking a terrible blow against society, depriving the state of revenues of 170 million roubles a year, and casting into despair a large number of villages that live off the commerce and transportation required by the factory. [...] It might be a good means.[7]

The learned Hebrew scholar had mastered the language of business: financial speculation on the German markets, investments in industry (gold mines, the production of steel, sugar and salt), personnel management and lobbying representatives of the state held no secrets for David. This letter allows us to understand not only the management of private business affairs but also the importance of the family enterprises for the economic survival of hundreds of families in the Pale of Settlement: in Mogilno, "a large number of villages" depend on "the commerce and transportation" connected with the sugar refinery. The years went by with the usual mixture of successes and failures. In 1891, Russia went through a terrible crisis: after several years of bad harvests, a "dreadful" famine weakened the rural economy and led to a major public health problem.[8] For David, the year was marked above all by his grief over the death from tuberculosis of his son Marc, who was scarcely three years old. He thanked his father for "[his] repeated telegrams and [his] good, long letter", which "helped him endure with patience the trial that was inflicted on him": "It matters little that one is no longer a child; in suffering and adversity a man continues to seek refuge in his father's arms. At present, I am calm and envisage without bitterness the fate that has befallen me."[9] Back at the bank, he resumed running the business, which was performing well. The Gunzburgs' agricultural properties seemed not to have been affected by the disease carried by the Hessian fly: "We will have a year that will not be too bad, our fields are the most beautiful for 80 kilometres around."[10] The failure of the Raffalovich bank, an important establishment in Odessa, aroused neither his concern nor his compassion:

> Schultz has been named by the Minister as a member of the council overseeing the Raffalovich liquidation. At this time, the council consists of himself and the governor of the branch of the state bank. [...]
>
> In the meantime, the Raffalovichs have lost 140,000 francs as a result of Dall'orso's bankruptcy in Marseilles, a bankruptcy that will drag down the Dall'orso in Odessa as well. In general business is dead calm here.[11]

The persecution of Jews remains the principal object of concern:

> In Odessa, mass expulsions are expected; we are told that even those who own buildings there or were born in the city will not be left in peace. And then, Jews will not be allowed access to the better neighbourhoods, as in Kiev.[12]

The state of the international market, on the one hand, and the Russian economy on the other, had a direct impact on banking. In the events of 1892, bad investments, a negative economic situation and the unfavourable political context proved fatal to the J. E. Gunzburg establishment. In 1890, in Paris, Salomon speculated unsuccessfully in Argentine railway stocks at the very time when Argentina, deeply in debt, decided to suspend its payments, leading to large losses. In 1891–92, the worldwide economic crisis, combined with the Russian famine, also weakened the St Petersburg branch. In total, the bank lost between one and three million roubles. Moreover, the official devaluation of the rouble worked to the detriment of the bank on the international markets. At the same time the price of railway stocks, which the bank had largely supported, fell precipitously. In the spring of 1892 the bank's assets matched its debts: eight million roubles. For a businessman of Horace's level, this was not insurmountable. He turned to the finance minister, Ivan Vyshnegradsky: to resume payments, the bank needed a loan of 1.5 million roubles. The minister set as his condition that Horace guarantee him good relations with the Rothschild bank in Paris. Since Horace was unable to give such an assurance, his request for help was rejected. Clearly, the government no longer needed the Gunzburg bank: with the reintroduction of state credit institutions and the encouragement of the monopoly on banking, the importance of a private family bank had diminished.[13] In March 1892, a Swiss newspaper announced that: "The collapse of the Gunzburg bank is reported from St Petersburg. [...] St Petersburg is not much affected by this bankruptcy, but London and Paris are greatly affected."[14] Horace declared at the stock market the cessation of payments and the government named an administrative supervisor. But the bank's customers did not panic:

> The prefect of police, Gresser, had even believed that it was his duty to send an imposing detachment of officers to prevent the disorder that might be provoked by the crowd besieging the bank's counters. There were none. Not a single creditor, not a single customer of the Gunzburg bank panicked and hastened to withdraw the funds he had deposited there; Baron Horace enjoyed universal confidence, and people knew that no matter how difficult the situation of his bank, the money that had been entrusted to him was safe.[15]

Calm and determined, Horace did not change his schedule: the very day of the closing, he received as planned the vice-governor of Vilna to persuade him of the necessity of modifying his policy regarding the tax on kosher meat. Faithful to his habits, he spent the whole summer abroad, alternating spa cures, bathing at the seaside and stays with his children in Paris, Vienna, Karlsruhe, Boulogne-sur-Mer and Ashley Park. His mother Rosa having just died in Paris, he took advantage of the opportunity to settle her estate. In addition to the bank's collapse, there were also the numerous debts run up by Ury, Horace's brother and David's father-in-law, which potentially endangered the family's Russian possessions: "All of Ury's creditors have placed liens on his share of Grandmother's legacy," Horace explained, "and here the will gives him his share of the real estate alone – the house in Saint-Germain. The rest, of which Grandmother can dispose freely, she has bequeathed to her daughter Mathilde [...]. Finding nothing here, they will go for the assets in Russia."[16] To prevent the bankruptcy and French debts from leading to losses in Russia, Horace and Salomon acted: "S.[alomon] will again give some part of his assets in moveable goods and I will sell Chamb.[audoin]. And, if necessary, [I will give] my assurance that I will pay what is lacking, and perhaps my assurances that I will pay everything here by [selling] assets located in France without resorting to the million that appears on our balance sheet in St Petersburg."[17] The worst was soon avoided: "Everything has calmed down for the moment and I expect to receive the confirmation of the agreement [between the banks of issue] in Paris that is being voted on at this time. The bank of Dresden has sold its debt at 50 per cent, plus the buyer paid a commission of 2 to 3 per cent. [...] The [mine in] Lena is doing better [...] What you tell me about the harvest makes me think that we mustn't hasten to sell, except that if the cholera appears our business is done for. Sugar at 8 r[oubles] (that's too much), very beautiful beets. It's good to hear that."[18] With the farsightedness that distinguished him, Horace gave David his instructions. On 27 August he wrote: "Restrain yourself, yes, strangle yourself, no."[19] On 8 October: "Economy, economy, and no pointless reserve."[20] His correspondence for the year 1892 includes neither complaints nor reproaches. A single remark, made in passing, implies that at times of difficulty business relationships were not characterised by solidarity: "The only one who actually did something was L.[azar] Brodsky. Without neglecting his own interests, he acted, while the others talk and talk and forget their interests, to my detriment."[21] The Warburgs also behaved like loyal partners: creditors in the amount of 7 million marks, they gave the Gunzburgs the time needed to pay them back under the best possible conditions.[22]

In St Petersburg, "being placed under administration", equivalent to judicial liquidation in France, failed to prove a deficit that did not exist: the bank's assets were perfectly adequate to fulfil all the commitments it had made.[23] Russian government representatives made an attempt to seize the 50,000 hectares of land in Crimea that Joseph Evzel had bequeathed, the income from which partly covered Horace's charitable work, but the Minister of the Interior opposed including these lands among the assets of the bank in liquidation. Hard work ensured that no customer suffered: after four years of effort, the accounts were settled and the administrative supervision ended. But the ambient anti-Semitism no doubt influenced Horace's decision to close the bank definitively after the creditors had been completely reimbursed. On 31 January/12 February 1896, David dedicated to the Gunzburgs' "commercial rehabilitation" his work on Ibn Guzman, a twelfth-century poet from Cordoba:

To my father Baron Horace Gunzburg,
   Filial homage
   In memory of the sad days
   When he was able to manifest his firmness of mind, his great heart,
and his rare virtues.
   David de Gunzburg
   The day of our entire commercial rehabilitation.[24]

David found a job on the scientific committee of the Ministry of Education, and continued to manage the business in Mogilno, which consisted of agricultural lands and sugar refineries. On this estate, which was without charm but comfortable, he tried to live the life of a gentleman farmer, not without regrets: "I am concerned only with beets [...] in my case, white sugar has replaced the fire of inspiration."[25] But whereas the whole family spent the summer months there, he often remained alone in Petersburg, officially required by Horace. "It pleases me not at all that your father uses you for his business from morning to evening and does not leave you a moment of time," Mathilde complained. "You're not his secretary, nor his businessman."[26] The work was perhaps just a pretext for the distance between the two spouses, whose relations were less idyllic than the daily poems suggest. Mathilde found in the children's tutor, Mademoiselle Johanna de May, a dear friend with whom she could share everyday joys and concerns. The moving confession David slipped into the preface to *L'Ornement hébreu* here takes on its full meaning:

Public calamities, reversals of fortune, cruel periods of mourning and constant anxiety have dotted the path of my life with stumbling blocks; I have greatly suffered for myself and for others, that is the only excuse I can give for the silence that I have maintained despite the incessant entreaties of my old friend [Stasov].[27]

26

Baron Horace Osipovich's Seventieth Birthday

On 26 January 1903, family, friends and officials gathered in St Petersburg to celebrate Horace's seventieth birthday as well as his forty-year jubilee as head of the Society for the Promotion of Culture among the Jews of Russia. His daughter-in-law Rosa, Sasha's wife, described the private and public ceremonies:

> In the morning, there were congratulations from his closest friends followed by gifts from the families of the orphanage, the Jewish school, another school and numerous institutions. At 11 a.m., the finance minister came in person to award [to Horace] the Order of Saint Anna, first class. At 1:30 p.m. the reception of deputations began (there were 55 of them) in the conservatoire, which had been marvellously well set up. The choir sang at the beginning and end of the ceremony; there was only one really good speech and many mediocre, interminable ones. There were 800 people in the audience, all of them dignified, handsome and touching. After a family dinner, the friends were invited to a soirée where the scholarship students from the Conservatory performed a very nice concert.[1]

The presence at the "Boulevard" of Sergey Witte, head of the Council of Ministers, was significant: without being close, Witte and Horace were bound together by a mutual esteem. After the collapse of the J. E. Gunzburg Bank, Witte, who had succeeded Vyshnegradsky at the Ministry of Finance, had asked Horace (and the businessman Immanuel Nobel, a

241

member of the eminent Swedish family who had settled in Russia) to keep an eye on operations on the stock market.[2] By awarding to the former banker the prestigious decoration of the Order of Saint Anna, he was transmitting in his own voice the personal congratulations of Tsar Nicholas II. Horace saw in this chiefly a compensation for the emperor's recent rejection of his request that the hereditary title of "Barons of Gunzburg" be inscribed in the register of the Russian nobility. The Gunzburgs were in fact recognised for their membership in the nobility of the principality of Hesse. This rejection, in which anti-Semitism can be discerned, deeply wounded a man who felt himself to be above all a Russian patriot, and who regretted that he bore a foreign title.

Horace was especially celebrated by his fellow Jews. The St Petersburg community commissioned a gold medal bearing his image.[3] On his birthday a subscription was started to create the Baron Horace de Gunzburg Fund, intended to finance the retirement of elderly teachers in Jewish schools: more than 100,000 roubles were collected. The press saluted the presence in St Petersburg of delegations that came from many cities in Russia and abroad.[4] Horace received numerous letters from all over Europe. To the congratulations of Narcisse Leven, the president of the Alliance Israélite Universelle, and the Jewish Colonisation Association, and of Zadoc Khan, the chief rabbi of France, he replied in these terms: "Dear president and friend, you overwhelm me with praise! I am only following in the footsteps of my father, who so greatly succeeded in improving the condition of our brothers here."[5] The celebration continued a few days longer among the family, of which thirty-seven members had gathered for a joyous programme: on the next day the official ceremonies were followed by a breakfast at the "Boulevard", a piano and violin recital by the children, a "charming" ballet, a ride in a *troika* to Tsarskoye Selo, a dinner at Mimi (Alfred) and Sonia's house, and then a party at Mathilde and David's. The following day, everyone met for a dinner at the home of Sasha and Rosa, in their palace on Millionnaya Street. Horace had the immense satisfaction of seeing around him his children and grandchildren, who had come from St Petersburg, Vienna, Paris, London, Brăila, Kiev and Odessa.

The general context, however, was not joyful, quite the contrary. A few months after the celebrations of his jubilee, on 25 April 1903, Horace sent the Alliance Israélite Universelle the following telegram: "Disturbances, pillaging in Kishinev Sunday and Monday of Orthodox

David de Gunzburg, a distinguished orientalist, developed the family library into one of the richest collections of Judaica. In 1883, he married his cousin Mathilde (below), Ury's daughter, in Paris.

Henriette de Gunzburg, née Goldschmidt, Salomon's wife, with (from left to right) Jean, Daisy, and Robert. Paris, circa 1890.

Jean de Gunzburg as a young graduate of the Haute école d'études commerciales (HEC) and a promising banker, circa 1910.

Ury de Gunzburg and four of his daughters. From left to right: Thérèse, Mathilde, Olga, and Hélène. Paris, circa 1883

Rosa de Gunzburg (née Warburg) and four of her daughters. From left to right: Anna, Olga, Lia and Véra. St Petersburg, circa 1910.

Rosa and her husband Sasha modernised the town house at 13 Millionnaya Street, near the Winter Palace in St Petersburg.

Sasha de Gunzburg and his
uncle Jacques Rosenberg,
shortly before the pogrom
in Kiev on 17 October 1905.
They had just buried their
grandmother and mother,
Elka Rosenberg.

Vladimir and Clara de Gunzburg's house on Sadovaya Street in Kiev,
looted during the pogrom of 18 October 1905.

1914-1918   Jean de Gunzburg,
liaison officer (right).

Vladimir de Gunzburg, mobilised in
the Russian infantry in Kiev (below).

Robert de Gunzburg, of the Franco-Russian
mobile ambulance corps no. 1.

Alexis de Gunzburg, of the Royal Horse
Guards. He was killed at Zillebeke in
Flanders on 6 November 1914.

Easter, thousands of families ruined. Indescribable catastrophe, immediate aid indispensable. Please vote for the double credit requested for a local loan fund and have your directors make credit available to help distressed population." On 6/19 and 7/20 April Kishinev, capital of the governorate of Bessarabia, had suffered the most murderous pogrom in decades. With a population of more than 100,000 people, the city included about 45,000 Jews. Encouraged for a few years by the local newspaper *Bessarabets*, whose censor was the vice-governor of the region, anti-Semitism had been expressed with unprecedented violence as the Easter holidays approached. The press exploited the sordid murder of a young Christian, the investigation of which had already proven that the Jewish community was in no way involved in the killing; even the Orthodox religious hierarchy subscribed to the false reports about the Jews' alleged use of Christian blood to make unleavened bread. Having recruited henchmen, a group of individuals had provoked the massacre after distributing a forged manifesto allegedly emanating from the tsar, authorising violence against Jews on "the first two days of the Easter holiday". The usual stones thrown through the windows of shops kept by Jews escalated to physical abuse. Armed with iron bars, hammers and axes, the rioters spread terror in Jewish homes. Reports mentioned 60 dead, 86 seriously injured, 500 slightly injured; 200 women and girls were raped, 100 children orphaned, 800 houses sacked and shops looted, and 4,000 families were left without shelter.[6] The description Horace sent Narcisse Leven reveals his horrified reaction:

> In cruelty and destruction, what happened to this unfortunate city goes beyond all that has occurred in this line in the course of recent centuries...
>
> Encouraged by a few agitators, and having met no resistance from those whose mission it is to maintain order and guarantee public safety, people indulged in excesses that one would think impossible in a country and a city that are not inhabited by savages... Everything that vandalism can produce was produced during the henceforth unforgettable two days before Russian Easter, and it is with stupefaction that one reads the reports on everything that took place. Our poor co-religionists in Kishinev are, alas, only too convinced of the truth of the saying: "*Der schrecklichste aller Schrecken ist der Mensch in seinem Wahn*" [the most terrible of terrors is man in his madness].

Now this city looks as if a relentless war had just been waged there. More than 700 houses and shops have been devastated, there are many dead, crippled and, especially, disabled; the economic damage done by this catastrophe amounts to several million roubles. Committees have just been formed in Kishinev and elsewhere, almost everywhere there are Jews, [but] many non-Jews are hastening to show their sympathy by contributing to the subscription to help the victims. A great deal will certainly be collected, but everything that will be done in Russia will be only a drop in the ocean of misery. All generous men, without distinction of religion or nationality, must come to the aid of those who have suffered so much simply because of their beliefs.[7]

The Committee for the Organisation of Aid to Jews Suffering from the Pogroms was set up in the Gunzburgs' offices at 4 Zamyatin Lane. With David Feinberg as his main collaborator, Horace centralised the financing and organisation of aid: the delivery of food and clothing, the construction of housing for families without either a roof or income. A Ladies' Committee was concerned more specifically with orphans. Abroad, the Hilfsverein der deutschen Juden [Society for the Aid of German Jews], headed by Rabbi Paul Nathan, supervised the collection.[8]

In addition to emergency economic aid, Horace proposed to settle families from Kishinev on lands in Crimea in order to create an embryonic agricultural colony there that was intended to develop and offer a refuge for all those who were undergoing the same trials. Arguments fuelled by false information aimed to discredit the project: when he considered devoting some of the funds received from abroad to the purchase of land, Horace was suspected of seeking personal gain. A certain Cazès, sent by the Alliance Israélite, presented the project to Narcisse Leven in an unfavourable light:

You know that the Berlin assembly put 200,000 roubles at the disposal of the Kishinev committee for it to administer. But in the meantime the committee has received directly a more or less equivalent sum, so the funds approved in Berlin are available, and the committee here, wanting to use them in the interest of the people of Kishinev, is dreaming of a grandiose project, the purchase of a property of 7,000 desyatinas [7,649 hectares] that belongs to the Baron Gunzburg and is located not far from here. He wants to settle 500 families on it! I hope that, before implementing a project that is certainly very attractive but needs to be very carefully examined from all points of view, it will be submitted to the JCA.[9]

The available documents do not allow us to establish the facts with precision. To Leven, Horace expressed his "profound regret regarding the setback that [his] proposal to purchase the desyatinas of land near Odessa had suffered" and his complete incomprehension:

> My colleagues are all the more saddened because this acquisition would have been as advantageous as it is infinitely useful to the Jewish population in an area covering three provinces. We cannot understand this other than as a misunderstanding, because there is nothing, absolutely nothing, that can be said against this purchase.[10]

Feinberg also tried to clarify how much was at stake in such a project:

> Regarding the purchase of the property belonging to Baron Gunzburg, I would like to inform you that this matter is of great political importance, because if the government consented, a major breach in the laws of May would have been opened. This property contains 7,700 hectares of the best land and 500 families can be settled on it. The whole of Bessarabia is talking about this project and many people are asking us to put them down as future colonists. Mr Gunzburg is approaching the government and there is reason to hope that this transaction will be authorised. The Kishinev committee thinks that the 200 million r[oubles] allocated but not yet transferred to the Berlin Conference might, by prior consent, be used for this purpose.[11]

Whether because there was no consensus among the Russian officials and their foreign interlocutors, or because the Russian government opposed the project, it was never realised. Despite the energy he put into it, Horace had to endure a series of rejections. In a telegram addressed to the St Petersburg committee, Lord Rothschild reported a conversation he had had with Count Alexander Benkendorf, the Russian ambassador to the United Kingdom: "Benkendorf is supposed to have let Rothschild know that the Russian government looked with a jaundiced eye on the collections made to help victims of pogroms, and expressed the fear that the sums raised might be used to support the revolutionary cause."[12] This was a grave accusation, but Horace was not in St Petersburg, so his colleagues informed Witte, the head of the Council of Ministers, and, on the latter's recommendation, the Minister of the Interior. The two ministers let it be known publicly that they considered the ambassador's interference intolerable, that the imperial government was grateful to the foreign institutions that had come to the aid of victims, and that the central committee chaired by Baron Horace had the government's complete confidence.[13] At the same time, Horace found himself totally discredited by the Alliance Israélite Universelle, which accused him of a lack of effectiveness:

> We thought – and we still think – that the committee you head with such generous devotion and an energy that compels everyone's admiration should have no role other than that of a regulator. You are very distant from the scene of the disturbances. Necessarily, you know little about the small localities that have suffered the most, and, despite the zeal of the committee and the office employees, it is impossible for you to have a precise understanding of the urgent needs and future needs of the localities that have been most seriously affected.[14]

Lacking evidence, it is impossible to determine how well founded such a reproach might be. As is shown by the various misunderstandings mentioned, the activity carried out on site in Russia was difficult to understand from abroad. However, Horace continued his activity at the head of the central committee for aid to the victims and remained for the rest of his life an esteemed interlocutor of the Alliance Israélite. The climate of general crisis within the empire helped introduce confusion into dealings with the government, with foreign authorities, and with the various leaders of the Jewish community. As he had done during the pogroms of 1881–82, Horace tried to obtain from the government a condemnation of the massacres and the guilty parties. On 4 April 1904, he sent Narcisse Leven a report, in Hebrew, on a conversation between representatives of the Jewish community and the Minister of the Interior, Vyacheslav von Plehve.[15] Horace was not duped by the official position, which was still ambivalent. Plehve also accorded an interview to Theodor

Herzl, who saw in him a "friend of the Jews", an opinion shared by Lucien Wolf, the head of the Joint Commission for the Aid of Jews in Eastern Europe, who left St Petersburg convinced that the government would resolve "the Jewish problem" in the near future.[16] But no economic or social steps were taken to relieve the suffering of the Jews in the Pale of Settlement. While the autocratic government provoked numerous discontents, the state police department began to blame Jews for initiating all political fermentation, including unrest in the universities. The government's battle against the Jews entered a new phase: it shifted from the economic to the political. The pogrom in Kishinev was only the first of many. In a portrait painted by Eduard Veith in Baden, Horace is a pensive old man: he holds a Russian newspaper in his hand and his dark-ringed eyes are full of profound sadness. Age and fatigue were not the only causes of his torments.

Part V

The Dark Years

The tides of iniquity are rising to submerge us.
Far-right anarchists and the wretched press are
working together and crushing us. Without
counter-activity we will succumb.

Horace de Gunzburg to
Narcisse Leven, 24 January 1908[1]

27

1905 – A Tragic Year

IN 1905 THE autumn holidays were darkened by Salomon's unexpected death: on 14 September, Joseph Evzel's youngest son and Horace's youngest brother committed suicide at his home, upsetting his family and friends and the social elite of Paris. The French magazine *Gil Blas* published this account of his funeral:

> The funeral of Baron Salomon de Gunzburg took place yesterday morning. Military honours were not accorded and there were neither flowers nor garlands on the hearse. The cortège left the mortuary at 21 Avenue de l'Alma after the last prayers had been said by Rabbi Israel Lévy, and went to the Montparnasse cemetery.[1]

Condemned by the religious authorities, suicide required a discreet funeral. "Mourning was led by Barons Jean, Alexis and Robert de Gunzburg, the sons of the deceased; Baron Ury de Gunzburg, his brother, and Chevalier de Bauer, his son-in-law," the journalist added, before listing the other prominent people "recognised among those present": Paul Fould, Jules Ephrussi, Edouard Stern, Count de Camondo, Marquis de Ganay, Hubert Delamarre, Louis Cahen d'Anvers, and other representatives of the world of finance and high society. Neither Horace nor his sons made the trip from St Petersburg.

Salomon had just celebrated his fifty-fifth birthday, and was, so far as anyone knew, neither ill nor desperate. His sudden death gave rise to a few articles that provided many details regarding the circumstances of the tragedy, domestics and informers having spoken at length to the journalists:

> M. Salomon de Gunzburg had returned to Paris three days ago with his wife, née Goldschmidt, in whose company he had spent part of the summer in Lucerne. At that time, the financier seemed very satisfied with his holiday and appeared to be in good spirits, as usual. Yesterday, after lunch, he retired to his bedroom for a short rest. Suddenly, around 3.30, a gunshot was heard. Alarmed, the valet specially attached to the baron's service hastened to the part of the apartment from which the sound of the gunshot had come. Imagine his stupefaction when, upon opening the door of the bedroom, he saw his master lying fully dressed across his bed, his legs hanging over the carpet. On the floor lay a revolver with which M. Salomon had just shot himself in the heart. Death was immediate; the baron, who had sat down on the bed to kill himself, had simply fallen backwards, his head turned towards the wall.[2]

The deceased had left, "in his regular and very firm hand", a letter: "Life is a burden to me. And I'm killing myself." In light of the evidence, the inquest was soon closed, but the press wondered about the motivation for such an act. Pointing out that he was "one of the best-known financiers in Paris", the *Journal des débats* drew an unfounded parallel with the recent suicide of Ernest Cronier, the chairman of the great Say Sugar Refining Company, who was involved in the "sugar crash" of 1905.[3] The fall of the price of gold was also blamed, wrongly. One of Salomon's nephews, Jacques de Gunzburg, took care to make it known that his uncle had had no connection with his own banking establishments, the Bank of Commerce and Industry and the Bank of South Africa. According to a "close friend", recent business was not the cause, and Salomon's problems went back to the bank's liquidation in 1892: "He had been forced to sell his town house and adopt a much more modest way of life, and that had seriously wounded his self-respect."[4] The house on Avenue du Bois-de-Boulogne, where Salomon and Henriette had taken up residence in 1887 after selling the town house on Rue de Tilsitt, was known for its receptions.[5] In a similar analysis, the socialist newspaper *L'Humanité* offered an astonishingly respectful portrait of the former banker, who was, moreover, a Chevalier de la Légion d'Honneur and a member of the Russian Orders of Saint Vladimir and Saint Anna:[6]

> He was, we were told at the stock market by one of our colleagues, a
> man of great probity and an astute businessman. He was highly
> esteemed and even loved in Parisian society, and also in the groups to
> which he belonged: the Automobile Club, the Cercle du Bois de
> Boulogne, the Polo [Club], the Société hippique, the Union artistique,
> etc. Many examples of his loyalty could be cited. But it seems that his
> attitude towards his creditors in 1892 and the determination with
> which he worked, unaided by anyone, to pay back within a few years
> not only the sums he owed them, but also all the interest on those
> sums, provide adequate proof that he was not one of those men who
> fail to keep their word when difficulties arise.[7]

Although he had had to scale back his way of life, Salomon was still a rich
man: the account of the execution of his will shows that he remained in
possession of the dowry given by his parents (1 million francs in shares of
the Paris-Lyon-et-la-Méditerranée railway) along with numerous securities
and bonds; in addition, he had retained the Russian properties inherited
from Joseph Evzel;[8] and his wife Henriette had inherited part of the
fortune of her father, the banker Benedict Hayum Goldschmidt.[9]
Furthermore, the future of their four children seemed assured. In
November 1899, Robert was admitted to the Ecole des Mines as "the first
out of thirty in a series of foreigners, only eight of whom were admitted",
Salomon wrote proudly of his son in a rare letter in his handwriting that
has come down to us. "I was very afraid because it was his whole future."[10]
Jean had just graduated from the Ecole des Hautes Etudes Commerciales,
"17th out of 84", according to the official document dated 20 July 1905.
And in February Daisy – his daughter Marguerite – had married Robert
de Bauer, a Doctor of Laws and an authorised representative of the
Banque de Paris et des Pays-Bas, with whom she had settled in Brussels.
Only Alexis, who was still a minor, had not chosen his path in life. But
Daisy's departure had accentuated Salomon's loneliness:

> [It was] for all these reasons and other, more private ones of which all
> I can say is that he was a little lonely living in his apartment on Avenue
> de l'Alma, and also because he was suffering, that he put an end to his
> life. Yes, that is indeed the truth. He was bored and he was suffering.[11]

As a young man Salomon had loved the splendours of the Second Empire, his mistress Pepita Sanchez and the hunts at Chambaudoin in the company of Grand Duke Nicholas Nikolayevich. The belle époque was beautiful only in name: growing old in a nationalist France where anti-Semitism was openly expressed must have weighed on him. In addition, life may not have kept all its promises since his marriage to the ravishing Henriette. Nicknamed "Baroness Guigui"[12] by the young Marcel Proust, Henriette was known for her pronounced taste for society life and royal highnesses. There was a rumour that Alexis was the son of the Prince of Wales, the future King Edward VII.[13] After he died, the family memory relegated Salomon to the silence of things that are not mentioned. He is a figure all the more effaced because there remains no image of him, neither a photograph nor a painting. His portrait, which hung in his son Jean's bedroom until it was stolen by the Nazis during the Second World War, has never been found.[14] But given that he was a crack shot, it is likely that he appears in Dmitriev-Orenburgsky's famous hunting scene, previously mentioned, in which we can see him in the figure of an elegant gentleman.

A few days after Salomon's demise, another death, less tragic but just as upsetting, struck the Gunzburgs. On 6/18 October, Elka Rosenberg, Joseph Evzel's charismatic sister, died at the age of eighty-five. A pillar of the family and an authoritative figure in the Jewish community of Kiev, she had married her daughters to some of the best young men among the Jews of Europe. She was the grandmother of Gunzburgs, Warburgs and Ashkenasys. Many of her children and grandchildren, nephews and great-nephews attended her funeral in Kiev. "I came from Petersburg," Sasha recalls, "and David, accompanied by our cousin Jean [Salomon's son], came from the Mogilno sugar refinery, which I was supposed to visit after the funeral."[15] Jean was then meeting his "military obligations in Russia",[16] and took the opportunity to take stock of the assets inherited from his father. In Kiev, they were received by Vladimir, Horace's tenth child, married to Clara, the daughter of Lazar Brodsky, the famous "Sugar King". Elka's son, Jacques Rosenberg, came from Berlin and took advantage of the opportunity to cover the Russian revolutionary movement for the *Vossisches Zeitung,* a major liberal newspaper.[17] In that autumn of 1905, Kiev was in turmoil because of a more or less general strike "and the government had concentrated about thirty thousand troops there, including the garrison."[18] The funeral coincided exactly with the pogrom that raged in the city from 18/31 October to 20 October/2 November 1905. The Gunzburgs were not only witnesses but also one of the targets. In addition to Sasha's account there is a series of photographs of the material losses suffered by the family, probably intended for the insurers.[19] These unpublished documents cast a personal light on a particularly tragic episode.

During the passage of the funeral cortège through the city on 17 October, Sasha had already noticed gestures of ill will:

> With great ceremony we took the coffin to the city's Jewish cemetery, and a long line of open carriages belonging to the rich Jews of the city followed it. On entering the suburbs, I noticed people standing on their doorsteps, shaking their fists at us, but I attributed these gestures to the handsome horses and carriages of the bourgeoisie more than to their Jewish occupants.[20]

In the afternoon, Sasha and his cousin Jacques Rosenberg were the victims of a first attack as they attempted to take a telegram to the post office. They both suffered minor injuries:

> At a good distance from the post office, the street was occupied by a large group of excited and more or less drunk ruffians who threw stones at us. Jacques' ear was cut and my cheek was injured. The coachman did not think it prudent to gallop through this group and we were able to take refuge in the home of a Karaite tobacco merchant whose name I no longer remember, to my great regret. This Karaite locked the door and dressed our wounds as best he could. He gave us tea, and, in the evening, when the road was open again, we were able to return to Kreshchatik Boulevard [Kiev's main street].

The next day, 18 October, the pogrom proper broke out. The news spread that people were "looting the *podol*", the lower city where the Jewish artisans and shopkeepers were concentrated; some of them were beaten and killed; and a rumour circulated that "the pogrom might rise as far as the upper city", that is, to the neighbourhoods of the Jewish and Christian bourgeoisie:

Thus around 10 or 11 o'clock, Volodia, at whose home I was staying, left to join a deputation that was going to find the governor and beg him to put an end to the pogrom. As he went out, my brother showed me his revolver, which lay on his writing table. "Just in case," he told me.

Unfortunately General Kleygels, the governor-general, who was a friend of the Gunzburgs and an honourable man, had just been relieved of his duties. From the windows of the villa, Sasha "could see women and peasants carrying merchandise in their aprons or under their arms". The houses of the Brodskys, Zaitsevs and Gunzburgs were on Sadovaya Street, near the governor-general's palace and the state bank, two institutions that were being protected by troops. At Vladimir and Clara's home, the coachman (with the horses) and the servants sneaked away "one after the other, probably to avoid being obliged to take part in the potential brawl. There remained only an assistant chambermaid, Genya, a Polish girl scarcely twenty years old, and Clara's chambermaid, an Englishwoman by the name of Green." When the looters approached, Clara, her chambermaid, Jacques Rosenberg and Jean de Gunzburg went upstairs and locked themselves in a bedroom on the second floor. Sasha decided not to hide: "I remembered, for just an instant, that I had to set an example for my son [Fedia], and I went out to confront the assailants. I shouted at them: 'Aren't you afraid of Christ, then?' – thinking that the invocation of that name would make an impression on Christians." Armed with clubs, the looters dragged Sasha out of the house, according to the testimony of Genya, who was at his side. The description of the scene is shocking in its violence:

At this point, Gregory [Grisha] Alexandrovich Brodsky, who lived next door to his parents, across the way from Volodia's house on Sadovaya Street, came to our rescue. He was a good hunter and was armed with a rifle. He opened fire on the assailants. The two of us ran through the ground floor of the house and when we saw that there was no longer anyone there, Grisha went home. But it was not long before the house was attacked again. The battle resumed. I recall very well how a man picked up a heavy wooden chair and hit me on the head with it. One of his blows was so powerful that it drove my head into my body, so to speak. One of my teeth was broken and my collar-button popped off. I was dripping with blood, I collapsed and lost consciousness. I have to say that at that moment I felt a supreme sense of peace and well-being.

The rest of this account is devastating for certain representatives of the government and is worth quoting at length:

When I came to, I found myself on the threshold of the carriage entrance. Opening my eyes, I saw that the brigadier of the local police (*okolodnik*) was taking Grisha's rifle away from him. This was happening in front of the door to the house. A second later he [Grisha] was attacked and knocked down by hooligans, just as I had been. I got up and went to help him. A curious effect of a sense of proper behaviour: instinctively, I wrapped my collar covered with blood around my neck and held it there with my hand (it no longer had a button) as I crossed the street. In the doorway of the Brodsky house I got involved in another hand-to-hand fight near Grisha, who was lying on the ground. I've been told that at this point his younger brother opened the door of the house and fired a few shots with a revolver, but hit no one.

At the same time I spotted, coming from Institutskaya Street and led by an officer, about a dozen soldiers wearing black armbands (it was, I learned later, Kherson's regiment) and holding weapons in their hands. The hooligans scurried away, but I saw that the officer was aiming his gun at me, and I shouted: "Why are you shooting at me, there's what you should be shooting at," and I took cover behind a telegraph pole. The officer fired and I felt in my ankle a burning sensation that was intense but momentary. I said to myself: "The brute has broken my leg." I did not fall, and since the street had become free, I saw the *okolodnik* trying, with the help of the Brodskys' servants, to carry Grisha into his house. I returned home exhausted and continuing to bleed. I was received by the faithful Genya, who sat me on one of the wooden chairs in the vestibule. Across from me, on the floor, leaning against the wall, one of the looters hit by Brodsky's rifle shot was dying. He was a big young man with a blond beard, and I felt pity for him, reflecting that he was certainly not responsible for this skirmish.

Twice wounded, Sasha found the other members of the family safe and sound. The doctor Byshovsky, summoned by telephone and wearing his medical cap, was able to cross the cordons of troops to come and treat him. As for Vladimir, he was stuck on the other side. In the city, calm was far from being restored: they needed urgently to find shelter somewhere. All the occupants of the house were able to pass stealthily into the neighbouring garden, which belonged to the British consul, Mr Smith, who had prised two planks off his fence. Having run up the British flag, he had talked to an infantry sentry, and his house was spared – as were, moreover, all the houses belonging to Christians. Towards noon, the crowd, accompanied by the police, carrying icons and sacred banners and singing hymns, moved from the lower city towards Kreshchatik Boulevard by way of Alexandrovskaya Street, because Institutskaya Street was barred by troops defending access to the state bank.

> It was because of this step to restore order that the homes of Lazar Brodsky and one of the Zaitsevs were spared. In addition to these two houses, there was not a single one belonging to Jews that was not sacked. Later, from the consul's house, we went to visit Volodia's home. Not a single piece of furniture seemed to be intact, and debris of all kinds covered the floor. I no longer remember whether Volodia estimated the damage at 100 thousand or 200 thousand roubles.

Ten photographs of the looting of Vladimir's house have been preserved. The images convey clearly the rage of the mob that had been given leave to pillage. No room was spared: in the study there are crumpled papers, books opened and twisted, and the remains of furniture all over the floor, the windowsills and the armchairs. A backgammon table sits upended on a pile of chairs as if a strong gust of wind had thrown it there. In the drawing room, tapestries and hangings form a shapeless mass mixed with unidentifiable debris. The Louis XVI furniture lies strewn everywhere, more or less smashed. The walls are naked, stripped of their paintings. Bits of the ceiling have been torn away and hang down here and there. The winter garden is a chaos of broken glass and scattered papers. The rattan chaises longues have been overturned and the exotic plants behind the pretty bay window form a thicket that could be natural or not. In the music room, the grand piano, open, bears the marks of numerous blows, electrical wires have been pulled out on both sides of the mantel, and on the wall, only the bottom part of a painting hanging crookedly is visible: a portrait of a man who is difficult to identify. A second photo of the same room provides a wider view: in the foreground, emerging from a sea of debris, a photograph in a sculpted wooden frame shows a man with a long white beard: Lazar Brodsky, Vladimir's father-in-law, who had died the year before. A copper derby-handled cane, broken in two, lies balanced on an overturned armchair. In the dining room, the furniture is in the same disorder, with numerous fragments of a shattered bust on the floor. In a bedroom, closets and drawers have been opened and emptied, the floor is strewn with personal items and letters. In another bedroom, in the middle of a shapeless mass, is a man's hat, intact. A large hallway presents the same sad spectacle. In the pantry or kitchen, a large cabinet lies upside down and broken crockery litters the floor. In an eleventh photograph, two men stand side by side on a porch that looks out on the garden. The picture was taken on the first day of the violence: Sasha, elegant in a waistcoat and a long, dark redingote, stands very erect, his head in a bandage as immaculate as his shirt collar, contrasting with his thick, black beard and moustache; Jacques Rosenberg also has a bandaged head; his greying beard, long and fine, is very Tolstoyan. His hands are in his pockets, and he strikes a more nonchalant pose. "I no longer remember how many days our stay with Mr Smith lasted," Sasha said, continuing:

Nor do I remember how the family was separated. I only know that I remained alone at his home. When the surgeon allowed it, I gave up my visit to Mohilna [Mogilno] and set out for Semmering, where [Rosa] and the children had spent the winter and where Lilia was born. To take me to the railway station, the consul asked for an escort of dragoons, and it was with four horsemen surrounding our carriage that we arrived at the station, which produced a sensation, even though the station was still under military rule.

Grisha Brodsky, who was then completing his military service, was arrested on suspicion of murder and freed two weeks later, on the grounds that he had acted in legitimate self-defence. But under pressure from a nationalist and anti-Semitic organisation, the Union of the Russian People, the emperor overturned this initial judgment. After two months of secret detention Grisha appeared before the criminal court of Kiev, where he was once again acquitted, although Sasha, whom the defence had designated as the principal witness, was not called by the assistant prosecutor "on the pretext that he had not been able to find [Sasha's] address." When he had completed his service, the young Brodsky emigrated to England. Vladimir and his wife Clara left Russia, returning only for business or to spend the summer months. Sasha resumed his life as though nothing had happened.

28

The Union for Equal Rights: Horace's Last Battle

IN ST PETERSBURG, discontent and revolutionary agitation were threatening the established government. At the end of the Russo-Japanese War, the people, who had paid a heavy price for this absurd distant conflict, demanded political changes. In October 1905, a general strike paralysed the capital. Although Worker's Party militants sought to overthrow the tsar, most of the malcontents wanted a constitutional regime. Horace was not spared by the generalised criticism of political and economic elites: a satirical newspaper caricatured him sitting on a horse led by Minister Plehve while an old Jewish woman at her window dumps a chamber pot on Horace's head. The caption is "The Modern Mordecai", an allusion to the Jew at the court of the king of Persia who was able to foil a plan to massacre all his co-religionists. Faithful to his line of conduct, Horace continued to give priority to dialogue with the government. However, he remained a figure who was widely respected, "even by the hooligan who, when a pogrom in Petersburg was being planned in 1905, came to see Meyer, the steward of the 'Boulevard' (who had moreover arranged, as a precaution, for a policeman to watch over the house), and told him: 'Don't worry about the baron's house, it won't be attacked, because the baron does too much good for everyone, no matter who they are.'"[1] After what had happened in Kiev, the recognised influence of the Union of the Russian People (also known as the "Black Hundreds") did not bode well. If the Jews of St Petersburg were ultimately spared, all through the autumn many other cities in the empire were struck by pogroms of unprecedented brutality. As head of the committee for aid to victims of the pogroms, on 28 November Horace sent the Alliance Israélite a disturbing telegram: "Request you grant an immediate advance on our credits terrible misery statistics momentarily unavailable."[2] The same day he met at his home David Feinberg and Paul Nathan from Berlin and Carl Stettauer[3] from London. Together they drew up a list of the cities involved and set the amount of the aid.[4] They also arranged preliminary meetings with the lawyers present on site to help victims in their dealings with the courts.[5]

With the increased politicisation of life in St Petersburg, the *shtadlanut*'s informal way of operating was no longer adequate. Parties and pressure groups appeared. Created to defend minorities in the empire, the Union for Equal Rights was initiated by Ivan Tolstoy[6] and counted among its members influential members of the Jewish community, including Horace and David de Gunzburg, Heinrich Sliozberg, Mark Varshavsky, Mikhail Kulisher, and Maxim Vinaver. The latter, a lawyer, was a member of the Society for the Promotion of Culture and the founder of the Constitutional Democratic Party, commonly called the Cadet Party (KD). Without being actual members of this party or endorsing all of its demands, the Gunzburgs nonetheless had special bonds with it. Confronted by generalised discontent and the risk of a revolution, the tsar found himself obliged to grant concessions to the supporters of a constitutional regime. In his imperial manifesto of 30 October, he promised freedom of religion, speech, assembly and association, and announced the institution of a parliament, the Duma. Witte, who was president of the committee of ministers, became president of the Council of Ministers of the empire. This new political context led national minorities in general and Jews in particular to hope that their situation would improve: the Union for Equal Rights wanted especially to obtain the participation of all the emperor's subjects in the election scheduled to elect the Duma. On 28 October, Witte received Ivan Tolstoy, accompanied by Horace and David, to discuss this matter. The head of the government declared himself in favour of equal rights for Jews on the condition that they waited for the question to be put before the future Duma.[7] Thus he was endorsing the opinion of the Minister of the Interior, Alexander Bulygin, who had just proposed an electoral regulation in which Jews were to be excluded from the voting for as long as the laws concerning them were not amended. Despite this divergence in views, and since Bulygin was soon dismissed, Ivan Tolstoy agreed to enter the new government as education minister, an office he held from 31 October 1905 to 24 April 1906. A memorandum judiciously presented to the Council of Ministers emphasised the risk represented by a measure that would increase Jews' discontent and made it clear that, given the fixed tax quota for voting rights, many Jews would in any case not have the right to vote: as a "measure of equity and out of political prudence", it was therefore preferable to include Jews in the electoral process. The restriction was accordingly lifted, probably under the influence of Witte and Vladimir Kokovtsov, the finance minister, who had stressed that, given the country's poor financial situation, a large loan would have to be contracted abroad and for that purpose the support of Jewish bankers was indispensable.[8] However, Tolstoy, the Gunzburgs' best ally, was not to stay long in the government, where his views had proved controversial. He immediately informed David of his resignation:

> My dear Baron,
>
> Thank you for your kind and valued letter. I have today submitted my *doklad* [report] to the Emperor, who said not a word to me about my resignation; I thought it right not to ask questions. He shook my hand and bid me *do svidaniya* [farewell]. Witte and Durnovo say that I have a successor, but who? I don't know. My position is rather ridiculous.
>
> Sincerely yours,
>
> I. T.
>
> [Written in the margin]: May I propose this Monday as the day for the friendly dinner proposed by your father? Black tie, I assume? And what time?[9]

For the Russian government, the question of foreign loans remained as vital as ever. Since the pogrom in Kishinev in 1903, the Rothschild bank had refused to participate in loans to Russia. When he went to Paris to negotiate on 8 January 1906, Kokovtsov informed Witte that the prime minister, Maurice Rouvier, had spoken twice to James de Rothschild and that the latter had once again flatly refused. In January 1906, a new, murderous pogrom broke out in Homel. The inquest to evaluate the victims' needs was entrusted to Mark Varshavsky, David de Gunzburg and Heinrich Sliozberg.[10] Witte proposed organising a meeting between Nicholas II and the Jewish delegation. The representatives of the provincial committees for aid to Jews suffering from pogroms were then meeting in St Petersburg. Although some of them thought that a meeting with the tsar might relax tensions, most of them rejected the proposal because of the known close relations between the tsar and the Union of the Russian People, of which he was a member and whose insignia he wore. A delegation was sent, therefore, not to the tsar but to Witte: headed by David, it comprised Varshavsky, Kulisher, Sliozberg and Vinaver. Various testimonies allow us to reconstitute the interview: according to Witte, the delegation once again demanded his help in obtaining equal rights from the tsar. The head of the Council of Ministers reaffirmed that, personally, he saw no solution for the future other than "equal rights", but added that it was imperative that Jews distance themselves from the revolutionary movement and the battle for the "totality of rights". According to Sliozberg, Witte took advantage of the opportunity to make it known that, within the government, the principal actor in favour of the pogroms was General Dmitry Trepov. Witte himself had prepared a resolution to prevent pogroms, which he planned to submit to the Council of Ministers; and in fact there were no more until 1 June 1906. As was his habit, Witte distanced himself from the official anti-Semitic movement without, however, lending his unconditional support to the Jewish representatives' demands. Nonetheless, the hope of a satisfactory development spread among members of the Union for Equal Rights:

> All the committees [of aid to victims of pogroms] except the one in Petersburg have been dissolved. In all, they are supposed to have expended 6,500,000 roubles, including 2 million in funds collected in Russia. The orphans are included in that sum. The government ordered governors to take the most energetic steps to ensure that there will be no pogroms during the holidays. Our elections are going quite well. In all the large cities, it is the democratic party that has been elected. In the [Jewish] territory many Jews have been named as electors. The Duma will no longer be as bad as predicted.[11]

This improvement in the electoral situation paved the way for a new loan. In February 1906, Witte sent to Paris an agent, Arthur Raffalovich, to contact Rothschild, who was still not in favour of the Russian loan. In April, with the election of the Duma and the cessation of the pogroms, Witte finally obtained the signature in Paris of the largest loan by popular subscription that Russia had ever contracted. Raffalovich was charged with ensuring its success by financing laudatory articles in the French press. A few years later, the revelation of this widespread corruption led to a famous scandal. But for the Jews of Russia, the truce was short-lived.

Contrary to Witte's assurances, on 14, 15 and 16 June 1906 a new pogrom broke out in the little town of Byalistok: of the eighty-eight dead, eighty-two were Jews. Accompanied by Feinberg, David went to the site: what they saw there was "impossible to describe".[12] Once again, the authorities played an ambiguous role:

> But to be convinced from which side the signal came, it suffices to see and to speak with the families that have been its victims. The general impression can be summed up in a few words: the soldiers and the police received an order to massacre Jews. And in fact it is impossible to think otherwise, given that 99 per cent were massacred by the soldiers or by the police in the presence of their superiors and it was only a small number who were killed by the populace that the police had brought in from outside.[13]

Month after month, anti-Semitic violence increased, while the Union of the Russian People became more and more influential. No law seeking to alleviate the Jews' suffering was approved by the Duma, where the Jewish representatives, including Maxim Vinaver, were very much in the minority. Faced by the impossibility of reforming the autocracy, a feeling of powerlessness overcame the enlightened elites, as is noted by Ivan Tolstoy in his *Diary*:

> 4 May 1907. In the evening I went to tea at the home of Baron David Gunzburg, at the invitation of his wife. Present there were, among others, the former director of the police department, Lopukhin, declaring himself now to be a "cadet" [member of the KD party]. Regarding the current political situation, he has an original opinion; he is apparently not happy with the state Duma, accusing it of lacking decisiveness and energy. According to him, today there is a very great danger that political stagnation will emerge in the country, and that any hope of a change and improvement in the regime has been lost.[14]

Faced with this outbreak of physical, economic, political and verbal violence, Horace exclaimed in despair to the president of the Alliance Israélite Universelle: "The tides of iniquity are rising to submerge us. Far-right anarchists and the wretched press are working together and crushing us. Without counter-activity we will succumb."[15] In his reply, Narcisse Leven worries about the inexhaustible *shtadlan*'s health:

> You always think of others, but you tell me nothing about yourself: have you recovered your health? You haven't lost any of your ardour, but has your strength returned? You will need it for the battle, and, since you are battling, I like to think that you are not forgetting the concessions demanded by a health that has long been weakened.[16]

On 19 February 1909, Horace died in St Petersburg, at the age of seventy-six. For some time he had had difficulty walking because of the calcification of his hip, and he had used a wheelchair, as is shown by a photograph taken by his son Pierre.[17] His general health had declined during the year 1908. On 20 January 1909, David had written to a friend, Rabbi Simonsen: "My father is so ill that we fear for his life."[18] In accordance with Horace's wishes, his remains were taken to France. He wanted to be buried in the family mausoleum in the Montparnasse cemetery, alongside his wife, his parents, his brothers and his son Marc. After half a century of struggle, this "great son of Israel" received countless posthumous homages:

> Tens of thousands of Jews and Christians of all social levels followed the coffin to the Great Synagogue. Such a deviation from Jewish funeral rites is admissible only when the deceased is not merely a great man but the greatest son of Israel. Funeral orations were delivered in the synagogue and the crowd accompanied the remains to the special train carriage that was to take them to France.[19]

Many speeches recalled Horace's firmness of character, his pugnacity and his extreme generosity: "Find me a Jew who in a moment of distress and bitter suffering has not called upon the baron for help? He took action, made demands and requests, and never refused anything or anyone."[20] Maxim Vinaver praised with sensitivity the human qualities of a man who had fought "without ever bowing down before anyone":

Fight... The word is so unsuited to the kind, gentle face that is now motionless forever, to his appearance that was heavy but imprinted with a childlike goodness. What had been his means of fighting? For a sword he had his cordial smile, and for armour he had his loving heart, devoted to his people. He asked and persuaded, he went away and came back. Contemporaries reproached him for the steps that he took, countless steps that seemed to be empty. Those who blamed him did not imagine that it was easier to conquer in an open battle, and even to die in it as a hero, than to go knocking on doors every day, and to go away only to return the following day.[21]

Even Tsar Nicholas II told the Marchioness of Milford Haven, née Victoria of Hesse-Darmstadt, his sister-in-law: "This was a man whom no one ever disparaged."[22]

A few years later, the Horace de Gunzburg Museum in the St Petersburg synagogue displayed objects and homages given to Horace for his seventieth birthday and on the occasion of his death.

Naturally, David took over: his house on Vasilyevsky Island was open to Jews who had neither homes nor authorisation to reside in the capital. Every day brought its set of injustices. In October 1909, 120 delegates from forty-five Jewish communities met in Kovno to discuss the reforms to be made in the way the community functioned. A Permanent Commission of Jewish Affairs was named, composed of nine delegates from St Petersburg and twenty-four from the provinces. David was on it, as were Feinberg, Vinaver and the historian Simon Dubnov. The Jewish community pinned all its hopes on the sessions of the Duma being held:

> The bill proposing a law on the inviolability of the person that was presented by the right wing has been rejected by the Duma and a new bill will be presented a month from now. When that time comes, the left wing and a large part of the Octobrists [supporters of a constitutional monarchy] will demand the suppression of the "[Jewish] Territory".[23] If this attempt were to succeed, an enormous step forward will have been taken.[24]

Feinberg's use of the conditional was appropriate: once again, the suppression of the Pale of Settlement was not approved.

In the spring of 1910, Witte consulted David de Gunzburg regarding financial matters. He thought the time was propitious for taking up the question of equal rights again. Having easily obtained an interview, he asked Ivan Tolstoy to accompany him. The former education minister had no illusions: "I expressed serious doubt as to whether the conversation with that sly and conformist egotist could lead to any kind of practical result."[25] At this informal meeting on 23 April 1910, Witte presented a final view, both resigned and clear-sighted. According to Ivan Tolstoy, the head of the government delivered the following analysis: "The current reaction is a natural consequence of the liberation struggle of the years 1904–06; always and everywhere in history, after revolution comes reaction, and after reaction, a new liberal salvo." Witte thought that neither reaction, nor crude Russian nationalism, nor repression had said their last word: "The current situation is bad but it will get even worse." He criticised Stolypin's policy and even more the behaviour of minorities, starting with the Jews, who, according to him, "are playing a major role in this situation, since, instead of asking for themselves, at a certain point, 'equality of rights' with Russians, which they would have received, they demand 'all rights' [that is, the abolition of the autocratic regime]." Witte was being disingenuous: although the voice of the most extremist Jews made itself heard through the General Jewish Labour Bund (Union) of Russia, Poland and Lithuania or the RSDLP, the majority of the Jewish community waged its battle while respecting the empire's laws. Witte concluded the interview with a strikingly lucid prognosis regarding the political deadlock: "Today, the battle against obtuse Russian nationalism, which is threatening Russia with serious disturbances, is hopeless: the tsar himself is at the head of political and religious nationalism, and almost all the ministers subscribe to the same credo."[26]

On 22 December 1910, at the age of fifty-three, David died of cancer. He had survived his father by less than a year. Feinberg informed Bigard, secretary of the Alliance Universelle, in touching terms:

> Our good Baron David is no more, and this loss is even more painful than that of his father. With David we have lost an intellectual power, a great Jewish scholar, a great Hebraist, a distinguished Talmudist and one of the most ardent Jews. He is unfortunately the last Mohican in the Gunzburg family and in Russian Judaism. We will no longer have anyone who can equal him... In the Central Committee, in the

community, he will be replaced by M. Varshavsky and in part by M. Kamenka, but they will be very inferior to Gunzburg. Yes, we have had no luck, we are going through one of the most terrible political crises and we are losing our best fighters.[27]

Unlike Horace, David chose to be buried in the Jewish cemetery in St Petersburg for which Joseph Evzel had fought, and where even today he remains the only representative of the Gunzburg family. Shortly before he died, "the last Mohican" dedicated a poem to Mathilde entitled "A Voucher for a Boa. 1910 New Year's gift":

Finding it to her taste, a woman likes to press
To her bosom, to her throat, to complete her finery,
As a kind of boa, this beautiful fur.
You shall have it in two days, it's yours – smile!
Then the thick fog that veils my grey days
Will be dispelled by the brilliance of a smile
That radiates happiness and is better than an empire.[28]

29

In the Age of the Russian Ballet

AT THE DAWN of the twentieth century, life in St Petersburg appeared suspended. The empire's capital countered the difficulties of the time with all its artistic and celebratory energy. In his novel *Petersburg*, the writer Sholem Asch describes the opulent frivolity of the city where "the best wines came from the plains of Champagne," because the city "consumed more of it than the whole rest of the world", where young women transformed themselves into nymphs and bacchantes for extraordinary choreographed balls and where, late at night, sleighs sped across the frozen Neva at a brisk pace while the wind "sprinkled snow on the faces of travellers" wrapped in their sable overcoats.[1] In Asch's brilliant fresco of Jewish life in St Petersburg, fiction and reality are cleverly mixed. Petty courtiers dream of the glorious destiny of the Gunzburgs:

> In the Markovich household wealth was the great dream, opulence was adored. The lives of Russian millionaires were an open book to them. Every event that happened in the family of the Barons Gunzburg, in the home of the extravagantly rich Polyakovs, or in any other dynasty of the great financial magnates, was known to the Markovichs even before it had happened and became the subject of passionate discussions.[2]

According to the *Almanach of St Petersburg, Court, Society and City*,[3] four of Horace's children were residing in the capital of the tsars on the eve of the First World War: Gabriel occupied the "Boulevard" not far from Mimi, who lived at 61 Galernaya Street, while Berza and Sasha lived on Millionnaya Street, the former at number 26 and the latter at number 14, in an aristocratic residence that was particularly well located. Sasha was imposing in stature, and greatly resembled his father. Warm, rigorous almost to excess, he had also inherited Horace's frankness of character. At the J. E. Gunzburg Trading Agency, he supervised the management of family business, which was still flourishing despite the closure of the bank: timber and land, gold mines, the shipping company, insurance, etc. Since David's death, Sasha had naturally assumed the family's philanthropic and social responsibilities. He and his wife Rosa, née Warburg, formed a flawless couple. Raised in Hamburg, lively, organised and generous, Rosa had adapted well to Russia. In her portrait by Louise Abbema, she poses, elegant and svelte, wearing a silvery chinchilla toque, collar and muff, in front of St Isaac's Cathedral. In the background, the vastness of the snow, a few colourful sleighs and the gilt, neo-Byzantine dome create a charming and typical atmosphere.[4] From the main balcony of their luxurious home, which the young woman's dowry had allowed them to buy, Rosa and Sasha could see the Winter Palace, the residence of the imperial family. (The house has now been transformed into a school, and the former ballroom is used for school events.) Behind an eighteenth-century facade dating from the time of the Empress Elizabeth, stuccoed in ochre and with a pediment decorated with garlands of flowers, all modern comforts had been installed. At the rear, the main building had been extended by adding two wings and overlooked a second house that opened out onto the Moika canal. Commissioned by Rosa and Sasha to remodel the place, in 1913 the interior decorator Oskar Munts had published a collection of photographs of the interior, the sole remaining trace of what was to disappear in the revolutionary torment: in these photographs one can make out the colonnaded vestibule, the grand staircase and the stuccowork of the formal drawing room; chandeliers, woodwork in the Renaissance style, Chinese vases, comfortable office furniture in mahogany and even the family dog, drowsing peacefully on an oriental carpet – all of which suggests a conventional opulence.[5] It was in this deluxe cocoon that Sasha and Rosa raised their seven children: Anna, Fedia, Olga, Véra, Marc (who died in childhood), Lilia or Lia and Irène, all of them born between 1892 and 1910.

The high society of St Petersburg lived in a whirlwind of brilliant and extravagant social events: after leaving his office around ten in the evening,

Sasha usually joined his wife at a party, often followed by dinner in a restaurant, and then a ball that went on until four in the morning. The festivities sometimes continued "in the islands", that is, in one of the "gypsy" cabarets where people danced, drank and had their fortunes told. There was no shortage of amusements for the children, either: photographs have immortalised Anna, Fedia and Olga in traditional Russian costumes, all of them smiling and ravishing. With her round face and bright eyes, Olga seems to have emerged from a fairy tale: she inspired the illustrations in an anthology of popular poetry by T. G. Baerenstamm and was always well liked, as her father Sasha tells us. "The children went for walks with Mania in the streets of Tsarskoye Selo. As they passed near Grand Duke Vladimir's palace, they admired the little dogs that were playing in front of the carriage entrance. For his part, the guard admired Olga and offered her a poodle. This dog was named Lulu and stayed with us for a long time. It died of rabies, and the whole family had to be inoculated at the biological institute of the islands."[6] Many years later, the memory of this happy childhood in St Petersburg remained vivid: "In winter, the Neva was covered with ice so thick that a small tramway was set up on its surface and we crossed the big river that way."[7] Mania, their faithful nurse, transformed every walk into an exciting excursion, as Olga tells us: "In winter the Samoyeds, who had come from the North Pole, set up their picturesque wigwams around the city. [Mania] had us get into their sledges drawn by strange-looking reindeer."[8] Itinerant singers, bear-tamers, rides in a *troika* at Tsarskoye Selo, days in the country at Peterhof all provided marvellous entertainment. Anna, the eldest, who was particularly pretty, quickly became a much-courted young lady. She knew how to take advantage of a careless gilded youth, gently mocked by one of her sisters many years later on the occasion of her seventieth birthday:

Despite the instability of the years that preceded the First World War, Anna's sky was cloudless; she was heading for her high point. She arrived in Paris – dazzling –, in London – radiant –, everywhere, as in St Petersburg, surrounded by young people. At parties, balls, encounters while skating or learning to tango, roller coasters, bazaars and charity sales – she was seen everywhere, always surrounded by *pravovedy* [law students] and *litseisti* [secondary-school students] in dress uniforms. These fine days passed quickly, but they left an indelible memory. Today I still sometimes wonder who that ravishing

Mademoiselle Gunzburg was whom we saw in the world around 1914.[9]

Fedia was no less well liked: on the illuminated ice of the Neva, "it was [he] who skated best, knowing how to perform not only the *pas hollandais* but also the "waltz on the ice".[10] The fortunate owner of a *bouère* (sailing boat with runners) moored on the Gulf of Finland, he took long trips with his friends in the violent winter wind. Above all, he was an exceptional dancer, sought for his talents as a "director" who could lead a cotillion or a mazurka:

> The dancers had to be brought together, to have the steps explained to them, to enter into the spirit. Fedia was so accomplished at this that he was invited even by people whom he did not know well, to take advantage of his skill and his knowledge.[11]

Tall, slender, endowed with regular features and limpid blue eyes, he impressed people by the elegance of his bearing. A fashionable young man, he was "always up to date on the latest artistic movements, new trends, theatrical groups and the infatuations of "balletomanes".[12] In St Petersburg, ballet was very much the thing: from the *izvozchik* [coachman] to the tsar, everyone was excited about the ballerinas, the latest fashionable production, the composer of the moment. But in the limited circle of connoisseurs, Fedia could not compete with his uncle Dimitri, called Berza.

Like his brothers and sisters, Berza, Horace's eighth child, born in Ouchy in Switzerland during the war of 1870, had been brought up first in Paris and then in St Petersburg. His strange nickname came to him from his Breton nurse, and seems to be a deformation of *brazin*, or "baby" in Breton. In a photograph taken in 1907 he displays an impeccable bearing: tall and slim in his uniform, with a moustache trimmed to fine points and large, bright eyes. The same meticulous elegance emerges from the family photograph taken on the occasion of Mimi and Sonia's wedding. Having soon stopped wearing a beard, he was a dandy with the air of a perpetual young man. His style was legendary: in 1902, during a visit to his sister Aniouta in Odessa, he launched the fashion for unstarched shirts. Having just delivered his laundry for washing, he had received a last-minute invitation to the annual ball at the city hall. There was no time to prepare his clothes.

> The gilded youth of Odessa saw the famous dandy, Baron de Gunzburg, in an unstarched shirt and decided that it was a new fashion, and for two or three years everyone wore his dress shirt unstarched.[13]

Extravagant and luxury-loving, Berza was always in debt. In London, he had the same tailor as his brother-in-law Siegfried Ashkenasy: Cooling and Lawrence.

> One day he received an unexpected inheritance. [Siegfried] told him to pay his creditors, for example, his tailor. Berza said: "No, if I pay him, my whole inheritance will be used up." "Then pay him something." "No, that would be taken as a recognition of my debts and he would be after me."[14]

He lived carelessly, heedless of financial commitments, whether familial or occupational. Married in 1907 to Guétia Brodsky, Clara's sister, he fled his conjugal obligations after a few days, to his father's great disapproval. But Guétia did not hold it against him, always wearing around her neck the portrait of the man she continued to call "my husband". She justified this fiasco *a posteriori*: she claimed that Berza, an incorrigible womaniser, was interested not in a ballerina but in "the whole ballet troupe".[15] This devouring passion would soon have swallowed up the whole Brodsky fortune.

We can infer that Berza liked the male dancers even more than the females. In 1909, he became the associate and friend of Serge Diaghilev, the founder of the Ballets Russes company. A close bond linked the two men, who shared a similar imagination. Berza had just lost his father, a circumstance that gave him a new freedom, both financial and social. Diaghilev was at that time in the midst of financial difficulties to which he saw no solution: ahead of his second season in Paris, he sent Walter Nouvel and Berza to Paris to plead his case with the directors of the Opéra, André Messager and Leimistin Broussan. They had to be persuaded to accept the programming of a ballet without an opera, a necessary cost-cutting measure.[16] With performances like *Scheherazade* (music by Rimsky-Korsakov and sets by Léon Bakst) or *The Polovtsian Dances* (music by Alexander Borodin and sets by Nicholas Roerich), the company from Russia gave France an aesthetic shock that was to be renewed every year. "They immediately enchanted Paris, like fireworks," Jean Cocteau recalled.[17] In 1910, the Paris audience discovered Stravinsky and his *Firebird*, with choreography by Mikhail Fokin and costumes by Léon Bakst. The dancers Balanchine, Fokin, Nijinsky and Ida Rubinstein became international stars. Until the First World War, Berza not only solved Diaghilev's financial problems but also actively participated in the production of performances. The collaboration between the brilliant impresario and the gifted heir was marked by a perfect harmony.

Berza was a lover of art and antiquities: his friend, the ballet critic Valerian Svetlov, left a vivid and witty portrait of him.[18] In matters of lodging, Horace's son affirmed his *credo*: "An apartment is something so private that it should reflect its owner's personality, humours and tastes." After further remodelling, Berza invited Svetlov to visit him, no doubt on Millionnaya Street:

> I approached the panelling, which was very beautiful, and stretched out my hands to touch some oval silk medallions that were inset in the wood. [...]
> "Please, please don't touch those medallions, the silk is very delicate indeed," and, with a beam of triumph, "It is made from the dressing gown of Alexey Mikhailovich [tsar from 1645 to 1676]. There was just enough material for the four."
> I pulled up a chair, intending to sit down and smoke in comfort. [...]
> "Wait a moment. Are your trousers quite clean? That silk is very light and fragile. It is made from the waistcoat of Louis Philippe."
> "To the devil with all silk, bring me a kitchen chair. I refuse to stand all evening."
> He returned, bringing an uncomfortable wooden chair, with a low seat and a high narrow back.
> "This is the prie-dieu from the monastery described by J. K. Huysmans in *L'Oblat*."
> I sat down in some discomfort – at least there was nothing there I could damage – and pulled towards me a nondescript-looking jar. To be on the safe side, I asked, "Is it an ashtray?"

"Yes, but for God's sake don't use it for your ash or butts! It's very fragile. I paid 7,500 francs for it in Cairo. It is a tear bottle from Cheops's pyramid."

He went out and brought me a penny saucer.

"There is, I suppose, one thing I must be thankful for: not having to take my boots off before coming in."

Finally we adjourned to Cubat's for a meal, because his new dining room in the romantic style was not yet finished.[19]

The members of the Russian ballet company considered Berza the "director-administrator". He advanced money for current expenditure that was supposed to be reimbursed from the takings, and he had a voice in decisions regarding artistic questions. He was esteemed for his very reliable taste, his splendour and his humour. "Baron Gunzburg was a good man," Nijinsky wrote in his *Diary*.[20]

[In Paris] for all practical matters Diaghilev referred people to the Baron, but it was always difficult to find him. Usually he would lunch at Henri's, drive in the Bois [de Boulogne], have tea at the Ritz, dine at the Café de Paris, and arrive at the theatre in time to assist the artists in making up, which was his great specialty. He was an amateur artist and a costume designer of ability.[21]

From Egypt, where he had accompanied his sister Aniouta and her brother-in-law Siegfried, Berza brought back sketches that inspired the sets and costumes for Mikhail Fokin's ballet *Egyptian Nights*.[22] He shared with Diaghilev the art of improvisation: seeing in the display window of the Grande Maison de Blanc [a department store in Paris] furniture for a girl's room, he bought it to serve as a set for *The Spectre of the Rose* that very evening. He had his own sense of priorities, as is shown by this anecdote: a dressmaker refused to deliver a costume unless he was paid the same day.

Diaghilev was frantic. "Find the baron at once." He phoned every Paris restaurant, and finally ran him to ground.

"Come to the theatre at once."

"Let me finish my dinner first. It is a very good one. These partridges are excellent, and the wine is just the right temperature."

> The unfortunate baron raced through his dinner. The banks were closed, so he made the round of his Paris relations and the Rothschilds in search of the necessary money. The costumes were paid for a few moments before the curtain rose.[23]

After performances, he always went to the company's treasurer to reimburse his costs. "Shaking out the cuffs of his irreproachable tailcoat, he examined the pencilled figures. There were rarely any documents produced, and a lengthy argument always ensued. Most of the expenses were paid in cash. Sometimes Berza put the payments off from one day to the other, in a way that was incomprehensible to his collaborators. "I've been delayed, I'll take care of everything tomorrow," he explained. These voluntary delays were in reality the result of his business sense: a few additional days meant a little more interest in the bank. Another characteristic: he paid only for one step in the process, convinced that "one never knows what might happen between now and the next time." He shared with Diaghilev this philosophy of the present moment. In 1913, the year of Debussy's *L'Après-midi d'un faune*, the company was on tour in South America: right up until the last moment Diaghilev hesitated to leave. Finally, in Southampton, he abandoned the trip and entrusted the "baron" with the troupe. Nijinsky was under the special guard of Vasily, Diaghilev's valet. When the war broke out, most of the artists were forced to return to Russia. Svetlov recalled that when he was mobilised, Berza "went to the railway station to say goodbye, with a touching and characteristic farewell gift: an antique snuffbox, one of his favourite curios. I always have it with me," the critic concluded. Svetlov was made part of the cavalry of the Savage Division (*Dikaya diviziya*), an elite regiment composed in part of men from the Caucasus. In the middle of the war, Berza asked Svetlov if he could join his regiment. Svetlov remembered that in his "picturesque uniform", Berza made a sensation in Petersburg:

Gunzburg was sent to the Caucasus with important papers. No one knows exactly how he met his death. He was either treacherously killed by the mountain people or killed by the revolting Cossacks. It was a tragic end to a life that was a glorious light comedy. This is still another of those men who helped to make Diaghilev's dreams come true, asking nothing for himself but a share in the dreaming.[24]

The accounts left by "the baron" were so confused that, for a long time after his death, Diaghilev continued to pay the bills when he happened to be in Paris.

30

The Lena: From Gold to Massacre

IN 1912 THE small port of Bodaybo on the Vitim River, in eastern Siberia, was suddenly in the headlines. Founded in 1864 with the opening of the Stefano-Afanasyevsky mine in the Lena goldfields, the first of its kind in the region, the modest town had up to that point never been mentioned in the press. This part of the middle course of the Lena River, east of Lake Baikal, is a remote and wild area. What was to become a large-scale event began as a discreet news item. In *Birzhevye Vedomosti (Stock Market News)*, Baron Alfred Gunzburg, the director-general of the gold-mining company Lenzoto, announced that on the morning of 5 April he had received from Bodaybo a telegram sent the preceding night informing him that on 4 April, at 6 p.m., "the workers began to behave in a provocative way with the civil authorities [...]. On the road to Feodosievsk, they clashed with a regiment. The summons to stop and disperse having had no effect, the troops were forced to open fire." The same information presented in *Vechernoye Vremya (The Evening Times)*, a daily newspaper close to the Octobrist movement (constitutional monarchists) described the Lena miners' strike more precisely: after the strike's leaders were arrested on 4 April, a mob headed for Feodosievsk, where the mine's offices were located. The repression led to 150 killed and 250 wounded.[1] Mimi accused the strikers of being under the influence of political agitators: "Our workers have suitable schedules, do their work very well, and for many years there has been no misunderstanding. All that suddenly exploded."[2] Since the assassination of the prime minister, Stolypin, in Kiev in September 1911, the country had been caught between an escalation in revolutionary activity and its consequent repression, creating a poisonous atmosphere. The strikers at the gold mine included Bolsheviks and Mensheviks. The incident at Bodaybo provided material for a virulent polemic: a second article appeared in *The Evening Times* under the headline "In the Gunzburgs' Kingdom", asking "Who is responsible for this incredible catastrophe?" and then answering: "The bloody excesses [...] occur when dark forces interfere, daring to speculate in human blood in the interest of unbridled economic predation or political agitation." The expression "dark forces" caused a certain vagueness to hover over the identity of the presumed guilty parties. *Novoye Vremya* (*The New Times*) was more explicitly anti-Semitic: "The Jews who run the Lena Company are greedy for Russian gold but care little about the value of Russian blood." On 7 April, matters became more intense: *Russkoye Slovo* (*The Russian Word*) reported that the Duma had received a telegram mentioning 275 dead and 250 wounded. Between 150 and 275, the exact number of the victims of the repression of the strike on 4 April 1912 was never clearly established. But the massacre provoked an unprecedented strike movement throughout the country: 725,000 strikers were counted in 1912.[3] *Rech* (*Discourse*) blamed the government: criticising the troops' intervention, Pavel Milyukov, the leader of the KD (constitutional democrats) pointed out that the gold mines had nothing to do with state security. On 19 April 1912, in the Bolshevik newspaper *Zvezda* (*The Star*), a certain Stalin signed an article that marked a milestone:

> Everything has an end. The country's patience has an end. The shootings on the Lena have broken the law of silence and mobilised popular feeling. Precisely! Everything that was bad and harmful in our regime, everything that aggravated the pain of suffering Russia, all that has led to a fact: the events on the Lena.[4]

With the "events on the Lena", the newspaper's circulation rose to 60,000 copies. As a result, convinced that it was time to create a daily newspaper devoted to the Bolshevik cause, Lenin founded *Pravda*, whose first issue appeared on 22 April.[5] The income from sales was promised to the families of the victims in Bodaybo.

The Gunzburgs thus found themselves at the heart of a political and historiographic argument that would have an enduring future. For Soviet historians, the "massacre on the Lena" constitutes a crucial stage in the end of tsarism. The article in the *Great Soviet Encyclopaedia* devoted to the event is unambiguous on this point, as is shown by its conclusion: "In the context of the revolutionary effervescence of the years 1910–14, the events on the Lena served as an impulse to develop revolutionary feeling for a mass offensive against tsarism and capitalism."[6] A point of no return, these events marked the beginning of the communist process.[7] The union of capitalists and the autocratic government against the workers made the incident a textbook case for many years. Some people even said that Lenin found his pseudonym there, which in reality he had been using ever since 1901, long before the Lena massacre. Little information is available about how Horace's children experienced the event: no family document refers to it. So we must make do with the official correspondence and the contradictory versions that appeared in the press.

Before the tragedy in April 1912, the mines on the Lena were a model of gold-producing activity, a key component of the Russian economy. The Gunzburgs played an essential role in the development and modernisation of this sector. When he bought a merchant's debts in 1873, Joseph Evzel became the owner of Lenskoye Zolotoye Tovarishchestvo (the Company of the Gold Industry of the Lena), commonly known as Lenzoto. Since extraction of the gold was expensive, the mines were operating at a loss, but Joseph Evzel thought the investment promising. At his death, the Lena gold mines were constituted in "twenty parts for a value of 706,672.52 roubles" divided into half for Horace and a quarter each for Salomon and Ury.[8] Other mines were part of the legacy: Zabaikal, Innokenty, Amur, Amazar, Berezovsky, Aldan and Udevisk; taken together, they were valued at 344,566 roubles.[9] Horace continued the investments in technology and enlarged the zone of production: in 1882, he owned 680 of the 900 shares in the Lena company.[10] In 1892, because of the collapse of the family bank, Lenzoto experienced a shortage of operating funds; with the resulting delay in the payment of salaries, the mines were on the edge of revolt. In 1896, although Horace had reorganised the company with new shareholders,[11] Lenzoto was still not showing satisfactory profitability: each year it needed 4 million roubles to keep it running. In 1901–02 losses of more than 3 million roubles were recorded.[12] To prevent bankruptcy, the state bank granted the shareholders a short-term loan of 6–8 million roubles, accompanied by a long-term loan of 7 million roubles. Since the interest due to the state bank was high (7.5

to 8 per cent per annum), the shareholders sought new investors: on 11 June 1908, at the instigation of Sasha and Mimi, the Lena Goldfields Company was founded with Russian and British capital. The former Minister of Commerce and Industry, Vasily Timiryazev, served as president, while the British businessman Lord Harris was vice-president. Listed on the stock market since 1905, Lenzoto, which had become the Lena Goldfields Company, saw the price of its shares go up for the first time: from 750 roubles of nominal value they rose to 1850 roubles in 1909, and, under the impact of organised speculation, 6,075 roubles in 1910. The debt to the state bank was repaid and the activity finally showed a very satisfactory profitability. The Russo-Chinese Bank and the Russian Bank for Foreign Trade became shareholders. Prominent figures close to the government were involved in the business: Vasily Timiryazev, already mentioned, Alexey Putilov (a renowned financier and the president of the Russo-Chinese Bank), Alexander Vyshnegradsky (the son of the former finance minister), Sergey Witte and even the Empress Maria Fyodorovna, the tsar's mother. In 1908–09 the shareholders received 2,775,000 roubles in dividends and in 1909–10, 4,234,000 roubles. Although these profits were a fair reward on the investments made over the years, they were also increased by the low cost of labour. In the spring of 1912, the Gunzburgs no longer owned more than 30 per cent of the company, but they retained direct control of it, as is shown by the board's reappointment of Mimi as its director-general.

Alfred, Horace's sixth child, was put in charge of the gold mines when he was still quite young. Born in 1865 in Menton, brought up in France, he had received a solid classical, scientific and literary education. His ability to read works in ancient Greek was greatly admired by his friends and family: "Don't be impressed, it's a light novel, entertaining," he said modestly. In the photographs, he looks like a nice fellow, an impression increased by his thick moustache and his sempiternal *papirosa*, a rather crude Russian cigarette, which he holds in his hand. He died of lung cancer in 1936. In 1892, at the age of twenty-seven, he made his first long stay in the Lena area, attested by a letter to his brother David sent from Sukhoy Log on 21 November:

Dear David,

I'm a real swine for not having yet written to you since I left. [...] Thanks very much for the *Revue des Deux Mondes*, which in any case I receive fairly regularly, the mail currently behaving more strangely than one could ever imagine. [...] What is particularly delightful is that during the months of October and November, and in the month of May, this service does not operate at all. It has to be said that we are 400 km away from the post office and almost 900 km from the telegraph office. Newspapers in particular disappear with surprising ease. Sasha subscribed me to the *Vie Parisienne*, and from the first of July to 17 September, I received five issues of it. From which you may decide whether the service runs regularly or not. And what is particularly disagreeable is that letters take four to five days to cover the 140 km of road that separate us from the little river port of Bodaybo on the Vitim, where the steamboats coming from the Lena land. No, that's not all! They take three days to cross the 10 km that separate us from *Glavnaya stantsiya* [Main Station].

Fortunately, we have still greater annoyances in life that make it easier to put up with the little ones.

This profoundly philosophical reflection must not make you think that I have reason to complain about anything at all – everyone here has received me most warmly, both among [the management] and the subaltern employees. It is perhaps a bit early to say this, but I really believe that the prejudices – which I shared, moreover – were wrong. I still don't have a well-defined job. For the time being I am working in one of the forests of the *Sukhoy Log* to get my hand in. I have about thirty men under my command, plus an assistant. The workday is thirteen hours long, from 5 a.m. to 6 p.m., with one hour off for lunch. I expect to do this work for a month, after which it is likely that I will be entrusted with the whole [illegible] side. That will be far more interesting. As you see, we don't have much time for strolling around or even for sleeping. [...] Mimi.[13]

For a son from a good family, immersion in the most remote part of the taiga is totally disorienting. Although it is factual, this letter illuminates the extreme conditions under which gold was produced. To silence the malcontents of 1892 and to understand the nature of the dysfunction between management and the workers, Horace chose to send someone there whom he could trust. For Alfred, the experience served as an occupational initiation. Later on, he continued to devote several months a year to stays in eastern Siberia, covering incredible distances in a sledge or in a horse-drawn carriage supplied with the necessary provisions.[14] Completed in 1905, the Trans-Siberian Railway made his movements easier, making St Petersburg about six days away from Irkutsk; from there, one still had to travel 850 km to reach Sukhoy Log. Alfred became an expert on mines: in 1908, he published in Russian a juristic essay on gold-bearing property, in which he looked in particular at the examples of mines in the Transvaal and in Canada.[15]

Because of the remoteness and climate of this area, the work of extraction is complex. With temperatures below zero more than seven months of the year, and as low as thirty degrees below zero in the depth of winter, watercourses are frozen from November to May. In this almost desert-like region, gold mining led to major structural developments: the construction of roads, railways and ports, and the creation of a fleet of boats. A family photo album includes the picture of the *General Senelnikov*, one of the steamboats belonging to the Gunzburgs that was in service on the Lena.[16] The other boats were named *Baron Horace de Gunzburg* and *Alfred*. The mines at Bodaybo were among the most modern in the world: in 1882 hydraulic rinsing of gold-bearing sands had been introduced there; in 1896, the first hydroelectric station was installed in the Lena basin, making it possible to electrify the mines. Lenzoto became the largest gold-mining company in Russia; between 1908 and 1916, it extracted between eight and sixteen tons of gold a year, or between 43 and 60 per cent of Siberia's total production. Four hundred and thirty-one mines were scattered over 42,609 hectares of land. Today, the Sukhoy Log field still produces 28 per cent of Russian gold. The working conditions were hard: because of the permafrost, the ice had to be broken year round, and men were in the water up to their knees. Most of them were without a family, and in their daily life they had little comfort and few leisure activities. Alfred was attentive to profitability, but was he aware of the difficult situation of his 6,000 workers? In the letter of 1892 quoted above, he describes a long working day of thirteen hours without giving details of the men he was rubbing shoulders with. He adds that he has been received "most warmly". Twenty years later, in 1912, the situation had changed: the employees were no longer prisoners or deportees, but unemployed workers recruited in European Russia, where there was not enough work. In a letter to Belozorov, the local director, Alfred addresses precisely the sensitive question of recruitment:

> Now we are flooded by applications coming from various places, in particular from the Polish border and from Odessa [...]. Using the channels of the Minister of the Interior seems to us more desirable, and here is why: 1) the salary can be lower than it is today. To all these starving people, this reduced salary looks like an Eldorado. But in any case we have warned the police that the salary will be 30 per cent lower; 2) there is no risk involved in finding additional workers. With additional workers it will be easier for you to set more severe requirements for the work, and, moreover, this supply of additional workers in the taiga can help to reduce costs, that is, to achieve the goal of all these measures.[17]

The Lena Goldfields Company thus gave priority to cheap, dispensable labour. When it was listed on the stock market, the pressure to increase profitability grew. To Belozyorov, who was worried about possible rebellions, Alfred countered by saying that the police had promised to protect the mines: an agreement had clearly been made with the Ministry of the Interior regarding both the recruitment of labour and its surveillance. Upon signing their contract, the workers received 100 roubles as an advance on their salaries, and were guaranteed a monthly salary of 30 to 55 roubles, that is, twice what was paid in the factories of Petersburg or Moscow. They also had the option of increasing their income by up to 1,000 roubles a year by searching for nuggets on their own, outside their regular work hours. But shortly before the strike, that allowance had been cancelled.

The incidents in the spring of 1912 were triggered by an event that appears anodyne: on 29 February,[18] the sale of spoiled meat in a shop owned by the company provoked a general strike in the Andreyevsky mine. The strikers demanded an improvement in their living conditions, a 30 per cent increase in salary, and an eight-hour working day. Faced with the movement's hardening attitude, worried and aware of the problems, Alfred, who was then in St Petersburg, asked Sergey Timashev, the Minister of Commerce and Industry, to send a neutral observer to Bodaybo: when consulted, the governor of Irkutsk assured him that the strike was peaceful, rejected Alfred's proposal, and limited himself to reinforcing the military presence with a regiment of 340 men. With regard to the clash on 12 April, some witnesses said that the crowd was armed with sticks, stones and bricks, and that one soldier had been injured. Others said, on the contrary, that it was calm and peaceful. The reaction in the press and the spread of strikes across the whole empire forced the government to act: two investigative commissions were named, one led by Senator Sergey Manukhin, a former Minister of Justice, and the other by the Duma's deputy, the lawyer Alexander Kerensky, who was to play a leading role in 1917. Departing from St Petersburg on 19 May, they arrived in Irkutsk on 25 May. On 18 July, after two months of investigation, Manukhin ordered the prosecutor of the Irkutsk court to indict the "main person responsible": the police captain Treshchenko, who had given the order to fire, was demoted and assigned to the militia in St Petersburg. The strike continued until the end of August. Eighty per cent of the workers left the mines. In September, the whole board of directors resigned. On the stock market, speculation in the Lena company's stock led to fortunes being made and lost: the banker A. N. Trapeznikov, ruined, committed suicide. Showing 6 million roubles in losses, the Lena Goldfields Company's share of the ownership of the mines fell from 66 per cent to 17 per cent.[19] Mimi, his wife Sonia, and their daughter Anna (nicknamed Mamzelle) left Russia and took up residence on Avenue du Bois in Paris.[20] In the 1920s, until they were deemed definitively null and void, coupons on Lena Goldfields bonds still brought in modest sums for Joseph Evzel's heirs.[21]

31

Vladimir and the Ansky Expedition

AT THE TIME of the tragic events on the Lena but thousands of kilometres away from Bodaybo, Vladimir, Horace's youngest son, formed an exceptional friendship with the writer S. Ansky that led to the Baron Horace de Gunzburg Expedition, today better known as the Ansky Expedition. This extraordinary ethnographic undertaking collected, at the last moment before the chaos of the war and the revolution, many elements of the material and immaterial culture of the shtetls. In 1911, Ansky described to a friend the steps taken to finance his project:

> I succeeded in inspiring a certain number of millionaires in Moscow and Kiev, in particular in Kiev, Baron V. H. Gunzburg, Brodsky's son-in-law, to take an interest in the problem of Jewish ethnography and folklore. They promised me about 30,000 roubles for an expedition to collect these materials. I hope to begin this summer. It's a gigantic task, worthy of sacrificing the rest of my life to it.[1]

David would have been enthusiastic about such an enterprise. Ansky was following, in fact, the spirit of *L'Ornement hébreu*. And by a strange coincidence, Vladimir, the youngest of Horace's sons, who was then thirty-nine, was to be the main financial support for the Yiddish writer's project. A journalist and photographer, Ansky is celebrated today as a saviour of Yiddish culture. Of the various "millionaires" contacted, Vladimir was the only one who gave his aid. His correspondence with Ansky between 1912 and 1914 shows that Vladimir was convinced of the importance of the project and was able to lend it an essential energy in moments of discouragement. His interest in the life of the shtetls is not surprising: with his wife Clara, he had gone to live in Kiev, in the heart of the Pale of Settlement. Even though he had left Russia after the pogrom and the sacking of his home in 1905, he often returned there on business.

In addition to financial difficulties, Ansky had to cope with a certain indifference. The historian Simon Dubnov and the photographer Samuel Vermel, the only scholars Ansky considered familiar with traditional Jewish life, did not participate in the project. Even before the money had been collected, Vladimir persuaded Ansky to "put the machine in operation" without seeking an institutional framework: "Any scientific or financial limit imposed on the expedition would destroy it."[2] The steps taken failed one after the other: Mikhail Sheftel, a renowned lawyer and a member of the Duma, withdrew his support; Heinrich Sliozberg, although close to the Gunzburgs, fulfilled none of his promises, and demanded that Ansky himself be responsible for raising the necessary funds; when Ansky came to Moscow to see Vysotsky,[3] a very wealthy tea merchant, the latter objected that Moscow was much poorer than Kiev and St Petersburg, and that consequently he must not be counted on; at first enthusiastic, Maxim Vinaver "backed out" when "the financial question was raised." When Ansky was ready to give up, Vladimir, who had become the writer's confidant,[4] urged him, "Do your work. The support will come later." Ansky described his state of mind on the eve of his departure:

> I am very excited, as if something extraordinary might happen. How is this going to go? Will I be capable of winning the trust of these poor, illiterate people, among whom I grew up and from whom I have been so far away for all these years? At times I feel terribly afraid. I presently have the great and joyous feeling that the mad dream of my life is about to come true.[5]

On 24 and 25 March 1912, a lecture was organised in St Petersburg to launch the expedition. In it, the lawyer and amateur ethnographer Mikhail Kulisher compared Ansky's project with the work of Rabbi Yohanan ben Zakkai, who had been able to save a millennial culture by founding his Talmudic academy after the destruction of the temple of Jerusalem. In fact, the centuries-old culture of the Jews of eastern Europe was clearly threatened with extinction. Not having been able to travel from Odessa, the Yiddish writers Mendele Moykher Sforim and Simon Bialik sent their friendly congratulations. The expedition set out at the very same time that the Jewish community was once again the victim of a cruel injustice: in 1911, Menahem Beilis, a Jew who was the chief supervisor of the Zaitsev factories in Kiev, had been wrongly accused of having killed Andrey Yushinsky, a thirteen-year-old Christian boy. Before he could be put on trial, he endured two years of imprisonment in Kiev. The publicity surrounding the Beilis case gave the expedition a particular significance just when the Russian press, faithful to its habits, was spreading crude lies regarding Jewish folklore. In his inaugural speech, Ansky pointed out that it was necessary to "arm ourselves with popular artisanal products to counter anti-Semitic theories": the materials collected would serve to demonstrate the "spiritual character of the Jewish people, its attitudes, beliefs, hopes and occupations". Beilis's defence was organised in parallel with the expedition: "The Russian protest to the Russian public concerning the blood libel among Jews" was signed by about a hundred prominent figures. The best lawyers in St Petersburg and Kiev took responsibility for the case and made it possible for the accused to be acquitted.[6] The trial took place from 25 September to 28 October 1913 in Kiev, precisely where the expedition's headquarters were located. It was there that Ansky stored his collections and received the cables transferring Vladimir's financial aid.[7]

Three ethnographic campaigns were conducted between 1912 and 1915. The first expedition got under way during the summer of 1912: Ansky was accompanied by his young cousin, Shlomo Yudovin, a photographer and painter, Yury Engel, a composer from Moscow, Avraam Rechtman, an ethnographer and painter, Z. Kiselgof, an expert on Jewish popular music, and J. Pikangor and S. Shrier, students at the Jewish Academy of St Petersburg.[8] In the villages they all met with the population to collect tales, legends, proverbs, ancient objects, music and songs. They made an inventory of synagogues and prayer-houses, and described them. They looked for past and present traces of unrecognised Jewish artists and of local craftsmanship (the production of *tallits*, chandeliers, etc.) Many photographs annotated by Ansky were preserved: today, they constitute the most complete visual testimony concerning everyday life in the shtetls.[9] For the second season, in 1913, when once again the expected support was not forthcoming, Vladimir insisted on the expedition continuing "each time that the weather permits it". Attentive to money problems, he advised his friend "not to let himself be overwhelmed by financial conditions" or by the "indifference" of those around him, and "to keep his intellectual energy intact".[10] To arouse interest, 800 objects and manuscripts already collected were exhibited in St Petersburg in the offices of the Jewish Society for History and Ethnography.[11] The day of its inauguration, 19 April/2 May 1914, Ansky gave a lecture on "The results of the Baron H. O. Gunzburg Expedition, which studied more than sixty communes in the provinces of Volhynia and Podolia [and Kiev]." He presented it as an effort to reconcile traditional culture with the culture of the elites, the expression of the Jewish nation's "self-awareness". In June 1914, when Ansky was getting ready to draw on his personal resources to finance the third expedition, Vladimir added 2,000 roubles to the sum already allocated.

In parallel with the expedition, Ansky was continuing to write: in late 1913, he began composing *The Dybbuk*, a play that is now famous. Its subject was inspired by a scene he had observed as he was passing through the town of Yarmolinets in Podolia: a father was forcing his daughter to marry a neighbour. Ansky had been touched by the seventeen-year-old girl's suffering, as she was torn away from her love for a poor student at the Talmudic school. The writer chose Vladimir as the first reader of *The Dybbuk*. Vladimir sent him his impressions by return. His letter shows that he was able to appreciate the text's qualities:

> I thank you heartily for your letter of January 24/February 6 [new style] and for the manuscript that I received the other day.
>
> I found in it that which I sought – a bright, inspired picture of the spiritual life of the people, to the study of which you have dedicated so many years of your life. It positively captivated me, and I could not tear myself away until I had read to the last page. *The Dybbuk* represents for me the expression in artistic, poetic but realistic colours of all that has interested you and me so vividly over the past two or three years, set forth on a few pages. Thus it is unsurprising that I was in ecstasy. However, what I have said above relates to a general appraisal of your work. You demand something else of me, and expect a thorough analysis of the play both from an artistic point of view and

that of theatrical technique. In other words you want me to provide what is called a critical review of its literary-dramatic qualities. But I have neither the requisite experience, nor the knowledge, nor, moreover, the necessary impartiality. I am already too much inclined to find your work perfect, and I find myself too much under the general enchanted impression of the picture you have created.

Desiring nonetheless to fulfil your wishes and forcing myself to unearth failings in *The Dybbuk*, I will allow myself to say that the piece is designed more for a reader than for a viewer. For a theatrical piece, it is missing one serious element (for the most part in the first act) – it is missing movement. [...] I can also say that I do not believe in your tsadik. Your exposition does not leave any doubt that those surrounding him are filled with belief in his supernatural power, but nothing points to honesty, sincerity and belief. I see on his part the ability to utilise the condition of the minds of his flock and a desire to preserve his authority, to settle [the matter] in the interests of those with whom he happens to have dealings, a goal in pursuit of which he is prepared to do injustice to the victims, the dead. I do not see that he is filled with the greatness of his role, that he is to some degree a slave to his great calling. How would you have written it if you wanted to show us a sanctimonious charlatan, and not a sincere prophet?

Do you feel that I have already digressed too much?[12]

In his criticism of the character of the tsadik, Vladimir shows a great perspicacity that presupposes a certain interest in popular religion. His remarks are revelatory of the somewhat unnatural relationship that Ansky maintained with Hassidism.[13] But above all, the play "captivated" Vladimir, who saw in it the poetic result of the ethnographic work done over the previous few years. The first performance took place in 1917, in Vilna. Since then, *The Dybbuk* has been regularly performed throughout the world. The play has been adapted for film (in 1937 and 1998) and it inspired a ballet by Leonard Bernstein.

When war broke out on 1 August 1914, the Baron H. O. Gunzburg Expedition was in the middle of its third season. Because of their photographic equipment, Rechtman and Yudovin were arrested in Zhytomyr and accused of espionage. From St Petersburg, Ansky got them freed and their equipment returned to them. Working as an interpreter for the Jewish Committee for Aid to War Victims (EKOPO), Ansky continued his ethnographic work whenever he could: in the ruined towns and villages, among a persecuted population, he was still able to collect objects of everyday life. In 1917, for reasons of security, he entrusted the collection to the Russian Museum of St Petersburg.[14] Vladimir was mobilised and joined his regiment in Kiev. No one knows whether the two men ever met again. Europe and Russia had just fallen into a maelstrom that would leave no one unharmed.

32

Family Mobilisation

In June 1914 in St Petersburg – soon to be renamed Petrograd, the Russian version of the excessively Germanic *Sankt-Peterburg*, after the outbreak of war in August – Sasha was summoned by the head of the Council, Ivan Goremykin, to his country house on Krestovsky Island:

> Here is the reason I am summoning you. Yanushkevich [the Chief of Staff and a notorious anti-Semite] proposed to the Emperor the exclusion of Jews from the army, and he proposes to replace [military] service by a tax or in-kind labour. This idea troubles me considerably, and I would like you and your friends to make me a proposal that would allow me to present to the Council of Ministers a compensatory alternative to service.[1]

Since the victorious battle that Joseph Evzel had waged in 1872 to allow Jews to perform their military service, the subject had remained sensitive among the Gunzburgs. The eldest of the grandsons, Jacques, had been one of the first Jewish officers in the Imperial Army. With the exception of Pierre, who was considered "too narrow-shouldered", and Michel, who was also exempted,[2] all of Joseph Evzel's grandsons "fulfilled their military obligations" in Russia. A veteran of the lancers of Volhynia, Sasha did not wait twenty-four hours before expressing his feeling, in an unequivocal letter dated 10 June 1914:

> The question you asked me yesterday troubled me all night, and I see

now that I shall not be able to find anything that could replace military service for Jews. [...] You know, very esteemed Ivan Loginovich, that neither my father nor my grandfather, who had the honour of enjoying the favour of our Supreme Authority for three quarters of a century, and who considered it their holy duty to open the government's eyes to the situation of our people that is suffering so much, would not have differed from me on this point: our people is mentioned in the annals of Kiev, it has never betrayed Russia, and we consider ourselves citizens equal to other subjects of the Russian tsars, and that is why, despite the persecutions, we want to live as Russian citizens, we are worthy of enjoying the same rights as they do, and we endure without complaint all the burdens, including military service. For a thousand years, our people has been used to persecutions, but we never abandon the teachings of our ancestors, who command us to be loyal to the sovereigns that the Lord gives us, and we believe in the victory of justice.

And if there are among us lamentable individuals who avoid military service, an impartial judge who took the trouble to examine the conduct of the authorities with regard to these unfortunates throughout their lives, from the school classroom and during their presence in the army, such a judge would certainly be indulgent and comprehend the profound misunderstanding that forms the basis of this regrettable phenomenon.

If you find my words arrogant, I beg your pardon, but believe that they come from a wounded but loyal heart. With my sincere respect, I am your cordially devoted A. G.[3]

When, a month and a half later, on 31 July 1914, Russia mobilised its troops, more than 200,000 Jews were called up to fight in the Imperial Army.[4] Among them, two generations of Gunzburgs were represented; some also served under other flags. For this pan-European family, the war was an international experience to which an astonishing correspondence – preserved or not, depending on the circumstances – attests. These letters from soldiers, fathers, mothers, sisters and cousins allow us to retrace the everyday life of a privileged family facing the first great trial of the twentieth century.

The war took everyone by surprise on their summer holidays. Aniouta abruptly left Odessa with her children and fled to Switzerland, because her husband Siegfried feared a wave of pogroms. A few months later, once Odessa had calmed down, the young woman set out on a return journey worthy of an adventure novel: by sea from Marseilles to Salonica, by rail to Nish (the temporary capital of Serbia, Belgrade having been taken by the Germans), and then to Negotin; from there to Prahovo on the Danube, then by boat as far as Turnu Severin and by rail to Bucharest, and finally, thanks to a "great friend connected with the Russian railways", in a special car attached to the train, from Iaşi to Odessa.[5] The autumn was mild: the family ate delicious grapes all the way. At the same time, Ury, now seventy-four and ill, was in Baden-Baden, where he died on 21 September, leaving his wife Ida trapped in Germany: the order had been given "not to let any Russian lady leave Germany".[6] Rosa, Sasha's wife, who was also in Germany with their children, obtained authorisation to join her husband, who had not left Russia.[7] Born in 1863, Sasha, unlike his younger brothers Vladimir, Berza and Alfred, just missed the age of mobilisation for officers, set at fifty-five. Having resided in France since 1906, on 28 August 1914 Vladimir reported to the 433rd infantry company of Kiev.[8] Two photographs show him in his military uniform. In the first, hatless, his head shaved, eyes shadowed with dark rings, and wearing a thick moustache, he wears the ribbon of the Order of Saint Stanislas pinned to his chest; in the second he wears a long overcoat and a visored cap, with a second decoration, a ribbon of the Order of Saint Anna. Both decorations were awarded to him in 1916 when his regiment was fighting on the Eastern Front. As has already been mentioned, Berza enlisted in the Savage Division (*Dikaya diviziya*), a prestigious division of Caucasians commanded by Grand Duke Mikhail Alexandrovich. Mimi was assigned to a small town rather far from the front, where his wife and daughter came to join him.

For the youngest members of the family, mobilisation took on an international aspect. Born and residing in France but of Russian nationality, Salomon's three sons served in the French and British armies. On 26 August 1914, Jean enlisted as a volunteer in the Foreign Legion for the duration of the war; in November, he was made a military interpreter at the French Military Mission to the British army (19th squadron of the military supply train); he went to the front in March 1915 as an interpreter "attached to a field artillery group".[9] Robert served as a driver for the Russian mobile field hospital no. 1, put at the disposal of the French Fourth Army, under the command of General Langle de Cary;[10] Alexis, who had been educated at Eton, which he attended from 1901 to 1904, was assigned to the 11th Hussars, Prince Albert's Own, and then attached as an interpreter to the Royal Horse Guards. While serving in this capacity he was killed on 6 November 1914, at Zillebeke in Flanders.[11] There remains a moving photograph of this young second lieutenant: particularly elegant in his hussar's uniform, confident of his future, he has a sly smile. He was the family's first loss, and his death shocked everyone. Marcel Proust mentions it in a letter to Reynaldo Hahn: "P.S. Have you seen the death of Casadessus the cellist [...] and that of the young Gunzbourg [*sic*], who I suppose is the son of Baroness Guigui?"[12] From Geneva, Mathilde de Gunzburg, David's widow, informed her son Gino: "I don't know if you've been told that Alexis, Henriette's son, has been killed in a trench because he volunteered to replace an officer. He was an interpreter and had no need to put himself in the line of fire."[13] At the age of twenty, Gino was preparing to follow his father's path in oriental studies. But even though students could obtain a deferment, he volunteered for duty, arousing his mother's resigned pride:

> I understand perfectly and certainly do not want to keep you from going to do your duty. Just be careful and always keep your wits about you. You will first have to be trained, and so, I suppose, will Fedia [Sasha's son, a law student]. [...] In the newspapers they say that Jews will all be able to become officers, that it will give them more courage to fight. [...] Anyway, I wish you to be a good soldier and to feel that you have done something for your homeland.[14]

The young man's poor eyesight was a source of concern, however: "The only thing that worries me is that you will be in the cavalry, and you ride so badly and see even worse! You'll be in constant danger of breaking your neck."[15] Mathilde also asked him not to put "overly patriotic phrases" in the letters he sent to her in Switzerland, "because all that is cut out by the censors." In November 1914, she expressed her weariness with regard to the conflict, which was far from over:

> Everyone is tired of this war, we'd like to see its end! Try not to have headaches too often. If it's cold, cover your head at night. If the war

stops we'll come and visit Novgorod. I hope you continue to like your service. Your mother.[16]

The young soldier was admired. From Brăila, in Romania, his cousin Nadia Mendel, the daughter of Thérèse de Gunzburg, and thus Ury's granddaughter, warmly congratulated him:

Dear Gino, illustrious warrior! Thanks for your letter and your good wishes for my birthday. So now you are a great man! How proud you must be on horseback! Vladimir will soon begin his military service. Here we are doing nothing, we live in complete idleness. That is, we are working, I study as much as possible and give piano lessons [...]. Yesterday Mama received your letters via Switzerland [...]. Do you know where your uncles are? Although I shan't be unhappy to see you again, I shouldn't like you to come to visit us sword in hand. [...] From your cousin who loves you very much. Nadia[17]

For his part, Nadia's brother Vladimir Mendel wrote to Osip, Gino's brother, to tell him that he was about to finish his doctoral thesis (he does not say what the subject was) and begin his service. "In addition, I'm studying Romanian so that I can soon do my military service. When and how remains uncertain."[18] And to Gino he wrote:

A bit late, but better now than never: I congratulate you on your birthday with a little delay of three months. I have a pile of banknotes for you, but I don't dare put them in a simple letter. Your letters have just arrived via Geneva. The fact that you are doing well is no reason to believe the opposite of us, though we found ourselves on enemy territory. Wishing you success in the war, with best regards from your affectionate cousin. Vladi.[19]

Romania had adopted a wait-and-see neutrality before entering the war on the side of the Triple Entente in August 1916. In late November 1914, Vladimir Mendel began his studies at the military school in Bucharest. Gino, whose health was fragile, was given an easier assignment thanks to the family's intervention, to his mother's great satisfaction: "How kind it is on the part of Uncle Berzusha [Berza] to concern himself with you; I am going to write to him to thank him. So there you are, all the same, in a cavalry regiment, and you say that it also belongs to the Guard?"[20]

For those who were not fighting, the war was no less present, even in Switzerland, where many members of the family had taken refuge: Mathilde and her daughter, who were as much at ease in French as in Russian, German and English, made themselves useful at the Red Cross:

> Here we continue to lead a peaceful life and seek to be useful when we can. Sonia and I work in the offices that are trying to find prisoners and wounded men who have disappeared. [...] Thousands of letters arrive every day asking us to look for brothers, sons, husbands.[21]

In Petrograd, the question of the missing mobilised the officials of the Jewish community. In October 1914 Sasha helped found the EKOPO (Jewish Committee for the Assistance of War Victims):[22] expected to help combatants' families, "the committee had to double the effort it had proposed to make because of the devastation and ruin of the Jewish population in towns and localities in Poland and the expulsion, cruel in its forms and in its intensity, of the Jews in the area near the front."[23] In Poland and Lithuania, the war disturbed commercial activity and provoked a major economic crisis. The Jewish population was plunged into terrible poverty. Starting in the early weeks of the conflict, many Jews fled the combat zones and the persecutions encouraged by an anti-Semitic general staff.[24] On 25 January 1915, the military authorities ordered the expulsion of the whole Jewish population from more than forty localities in the Warsaw region.[25] As chairman of the EKOPO central committee, Sasha worked relentlessly on international correspondence for fund-raising, the implementation of aid, and the coordination of the 350 sub-committees and diverse organisations.[26] His nephew Osip, Gino's brother, having been discharged for reasons of health, worked alongside him. As a delegate of EKOPO, he went to the front to meet with General Yanushkevich's victims.

The Jewish Committee for Aid and Reconstruction tried to settle refugees far from the combat zones: in 1915, the Minister of the Interior, Shcherbatov, authorised them to reside outside the Pale of Settlement. Thus it took the exceptional circumstances of the war to open this first breach in imperial laws that had remained unchanged for many decades.

The refugees were settled in the provinces along the Volga. Sliozberg was charged by the committee with the setting up of a state-funded official special conference for aid to refugees, no matter what their nationality or religion. In close collaboration with the conference, the EKOPO made up the deficiencies in Russian financing, using large subsidies from abroad, notably from America, Great Britain and South Africa. A report written after the war, probably by Sasha, sets forth the scope of the difficulties:

> Until 1917, for more than two years, the central committee for aid was providing, on average, for 258,000 persons, including 46,000 children and almost 14,000 elderly people over the age of 60. Women who had numerous minor children and were unsuited to work made up 46 per cent of the total.[27]

The EKOPO coordinated its activities with those of the existing Jewish organisations: the Society for the Promotion of Culture (OPE), the Society for Agricultural and Artisanal Labour (ORT), and the Society for the Protection of the Health of the Jewish Population (OSE).[28]

> ORT established dozens of placement bureaus, thanks to which tens of thousands of Jewish refugees were able to find work. It also created workshop-schools to train artisans, special courses for refugee artisans, who were not numerous enough to satisfy the needs of the market in their new places of settlement, and provided organised groups of artisans with the tools they needed, especially sewing and knitting machines.[29]

The OPE set up schools and evening courses for refugee children; the OSE organised medical and public health branches in the areas where refugees settled to provide care, medicines and meals ("a drop of milk" and special diets).

The women were not idle: Rosa, Sasha's wife, was active in the committee of Grand Duchess Tatiana, under whose sponsorship she organised a collection to benefit Jews.[30] Anna and Olga, their eldest daughters, took the St George's Society nursing courses before working in the Red Cross hospitals in Petrograd. With the exception of contact with the wounded, life in the capital was hardly affected, however, as Olga recalls in a text written long afterwards: "The country was big and the repercussions of the fighting were not felt as quickly as they were in other countries. Large charity balls replaced high society parties."[31] For the girls, the war brought a breath of freedom. In the spring of 1915, when funds were being collected to benefit the anti-tuberculosis league, the beautiful Anna had a stand selling white flowers on the bank of the Neva. "Among the assiduous assistants we note Sioma Halperin," who came from Kiev. Soon the two young people were engaged. Under other circumstances, Sasha and Rosa would have wished their daughter to marry into a large European Jewish family. However, in a letter to a friend, Sasha expresses his satisfaction:

> The wedding is set for 10 August. Unfortunately, we will have no member of the family with us [...]. We are really very happy about our new connection. [The Halperins] are only too happy to have so much money; they must be going to earn 10,000 M[arks?] this year with their sugar. I hasten to praise the young Salomon [Sioma] (34 years old): he is very modest and behaves very courteously. In addition, he knows Hebrew well [...]; it seems to me that he is a good match for Anna.[32]

Again, when Leni von Gutmann, the daughter of Babita de Gunzburg, married Dr August Reyer in Vienna, no member of the family could attend the wedding. The war decidedly upset traditions, as Rosa stressed to her cousin Jacques Rosenberg:

> You were very kind to announce Leni's engagement to us. I am sorry that she is marrying a man so much older and so uninteresting, but, after all, if the mother is happy it's not for us to complain. In general, during a war people more easily accept any marriage at all. I beg you to congratulate the bride-to-be on our behalf.[33]

Dated late 1916, a letter from Sasha to his in-laws in Hamburg sums up well the atmosphere in the family after two years of war, when a couple of cousins had just died violently in Budapest:

> The news of the death of Isa and Armand is very shocking, and we are impatiently awaiting details of Isa's suicide. It is fortunate that Babita is close to the children and is always ready to help as much as she can.

[...] We recently had a collection for our Jewish societies that was a great success (112,500 roubles), but that makes too much work for my wife and I hope she will stop this kind of activity.

Olga is still [working] at the quarantine area, where she is very much appreciated. Véra is still in school. Lilia is very fond of her violin, but her English governess annoys her. Ira has just got over a bout of flu. Alfred [Mimi] is still in a small garrison in the rear. Volo [Vladimir] is going to the front with the infantry; Gino was here on leave, he is very enthusiastic about his service and full of optimism. Anna and her husband came to see us these past few weeks and will stay with us for six weeks. She is expecting a baby in July, I think.[34]

Coming all at once, the tribulations followed one another implacably: because she caught hepatitis, Anna gave birth prematurely, but fortunately the baby, named Horace, survived. The generous Babita died of pneumonia as she was bringing the little orphans back from Budapest with her. Succumbing at the age of fifty, already a widow, she left nine children behind her, the youngest of whom was sixteen years old:

> That was a terrible blow and I still cannot get used to the dreadful idea that our dear Babita is no longer with us. And how everything happened, how the poor soul got sick, whether she suffered, we do not know. It is so cold everywhere this winter, and Babita never thought enough about herself and she must have exposed herself to catch an inflammation of the lungs, she had such a good constitution.[35]

At the front, Vladimir contracted a serious illness, probably syphilis, and was put on leave. Since he had transformed his house in Kiev into a military hospital, he was taken in by his niece Anna during his long convalescence, and cared for by his sister Aniouta. With the revolutionary days of 23–27 February (8–13 March new style) 1917, the routine of war in the Russian empire was abruptly interrupted: within five days the monarchy would collapse, leading to Nicholas II's abdication and the fall of the Romanovs.

33

Revolutions, Departures and Deaths

ON 17 APRIL 1917, Sasha received a letter of congratulation from a rabbi in Copenhagen, David Simonsen, with whom he had been in contact through the Jewish Committee for Aid and Reconstruction. "I must personally congratulate you with all my heart on the liberation of Russia and especially the liberation of my fellow Jews from the yoke that weighed on the oppressed."[1] The provisional government had in fact just decreed, for all citizens of Russia, freedom of movement and residence, the right to hold property, to exercise all occupations, to be an entrepreneur, a government official, or an elector; the right to use their national language in schools or to draw up contracts; and the right to have academic institutions.[2] In his reply to Rabbi Simonsen, Sasha expressed in return his satisfaction that the civil equality so long awaited had been realised:

> Acknowledging reception of your letter of the 17th, I can hardly tell you how much your congratulations touched me. We finally see being realised, if I can put it that way, my whole family's dream over several generations, and I have no doubt that *our*[3] homeland, having become free, will find in its Jewish subjects true sons who are loyal and full of devotion.[4]

Addressing Jewish communities abroad, he launched, by telegram, an appeal for financial support of the new regime:

302

Have formed Jewish committee to promote Freedom loan stop supporting provisional government is not only a moral duty to our country but a vital question for liberation stop we ask you to support in any way find propitious Baron Pierre Gunzburg and Vladimir Friedlansky who in agreement with us are collecting contributions in France. For the committee Boris Kamenka, Baron Alexandre Gunzburg, Heinrich Sliozberg.[5]

All through the nineteenth century, the Gunzburgs had shown an unstinting loyalty to the tsar and the monarchy; confronted by official anti-Semitism and the last emperor's unkept promises, it was natural to subscribe to the regime change. Fedia, Sasha's only son, entered the service of the provisional government: a graduate of the St Petersburg school of law,[6] he was attached to the diplomatic mission of Boris Bakhmetev, the new Russian ambassador to the American government. After travelling for several months across the Russian Far East, China and Japan, the diplomatic mission was unfortunately not to assume its functions in Washington until after the Bolshevik coup d'état.

Wearing her nurse's uniform and representing the young people of Petrograd's Jewish community, Fedia's sister Olga was charged with delivering gifts to the soldiers in April 1917. The delegation consisted of Naftali Friedman (a Jewish deputy in the Duma), Abram Shternberg (director of the Institut contre la Tuberculose), Nadezhda Genrikhovna (Sliozberg's daughter and the representative of the Women's Committee of the Jewish community) and Varshaver, "a young, intelligent student and a handsome fellow to boot" who "helped iron out the trip's many complications." From Dvinsk, Olga sent a report that upset her mother:

Our journey has been extremely interesting, especially from the political point of view. Yesterday was a particular success. Shternberg, Varshaver and I, accompanied by the divisional commander, visited a regiment in the rear and another in the van, while Friedman and Nadezhda Genrikhovna went to see two others. In the camp in the rear, one of the officers gave an excellent speech about the Jews. Shternberg and Varshaver responded to him very appropriately. Musical instruments and razors were the most popular gifts. When the distribution was over, we went by car to the regiment's trenches. [...] After lunch, we were taken to another barrack where the gifts had been collected and where there were representatives of the army's companies. Thereupon Shternberg gave a speech, followed by another, delivered by a representative of the soldiers thanking us for the gifts. He spoke in a very touching way about Jews in general and Jewish women in particular. He complimented me personally as a representative of Jewish women and obviously expected me to reply. I was not prepared and moreover I was so moved that I was able to say only, on behalf of all Jewish women: "May God watch over you." After yet another speech, they cried "Hurrah" for the regiment, for the provisional government, for freedom and for us. Then the officers took us into the trenches. Recently the Germans have been behaving very decently, but despite that I was not advised to go into the forward trenches, because that very morning a telegraph man had been killed there. Moreover, the connecting paths are so muddy that it is impossible to use them. [...] Today I went out with Friedman and we watched a very stormy meeting of the regiment's committee. In general, the situation is very alarming. We don't trust the officers, though those whom we have met give the impression of being intelligent and equal to the challenge of the circumstances.[7]

Although the "hurrahs" for freedom revealed a general relief, the young woman lucidly realised that the "situation is very alarming." Bolshevik propaganda was then the rage in the army. At the same time, Gino thanked his cousins in Petrograd for their postcard "received in the line of fire, where the Germans treat us from time to time to shells with shrapnel and grenades, leaving deep craters in the porous and damp soil. But in general, the fire does no damage. On the other hand, we see our incomparable artillery score direct hits on their entrenchments. Planes visit us often and fire energetically on us."[8] The "citizen dragoon" described the life of the soldiers during the curious period of inertia in the summer of 1917, waiting to see what would happen and subject to various political pressures:

The weather is very fine. We seem to be in the countryside. During the day we sleep on the sand. Those who wish, walk about barefoot. We are gay and happy behind the lines. We play *gorodki* [ninepins] near our huts which decorate all the heights, not just in a line but on several levels, like the caves in which our ancestors the American

Indians lived. We read a lot of military newspapers and books, as well as all kinds of "communications" from military committees of soldiers and officers, social-democratic, social revolutionary, from Petro[grad], etc. We feel marvellous and hope you are feeling the same way. Don't expect me any time soon in Petro, because we still know nothing about the spring session of the officers' examinations. Discipline is being reborn, we are becoming increasingly aware of it. We will probably soon begin certain actions against the "militarist" enemy. I wish you a good and merry summer. Greetings and kisses to everyone on the second floor of 14 Millionnaya Street. I embrace you most heartily, your "extraordinary" and "invincibly courageous" citizen-dragoon, Gino.[9]

The climate of political struggle soon spread across the whole country: in Petrograd, the Jewish community and the organisations dependent on it were divided by opposing beliefs. Sasha, disagreeing with some of the decisions made within the EKOPO, resigned from it, not without having alerted his interlocutors abroad to the ideological excesses that were going on. The message he sent to the London committee is known only through the criticism of it formulated by Lucien Wolf, a British journalist engaged in the battle for Jews' rights and against tsarism: Sasha opposed the abandonment of the spiritual dimension of the aid given to the refugees. Helping rabbis, teaching religion in the schools and distributing *matzos* to the soldiers were originally part of the EKOPO's task. Wolf was scandalised by Sasha's belief that he was the only person on the committee who was concerned with religious questions:

> Is it imaginable that the Jewish committee of Petrograd, after Baron Gunzburg's resignation, would refuse to help Jews in distress because they are rabbis? There is no reason to think anything of the kind, and the only difference in this area may have to do with the efficacy of the methods employed.[10]

Wolf accused Sasha of defending a backward-looking Judaism: for example, during the Society for the Promotion of Culture's recent establishment of primary schools, Sasha had opposed the adoption of the curriculum in Yiddish, preferring Russian and Hebrew. He denounced the risk of "separatism", to which Wolf retorted:

But Baron de Gunzburg is the only man in Russia who calls this phenomenon separatist, even if he applies this terminology to Jews alone. [...] The Russian government has recognised the principle of granting a certain form of autonomous, national and centralised cultural administration for Jews all over Russia, and even *Novoye Vremya* has acknowledged that it is a good path to follow.

Unfortunately, the near future was to prove Sasha right: the Bolshevik coup d'état was to forbid any religious expression. In 1934, Birobidzhan, an autonomous Jewish territory in the Far East, on the border with China, was created, and living conditions there were hardly those of a "Promised Land".[11]

After the Bolsheviks seized power on 25 October (7 November new style), the tone of the family's letters changed radically: difficulties and fear definitively won out. On 2 November 1917, Gino, who was still mobilised, referred to money problems and the general chaos:

> The strangest thing about this situation is that I've survived. [...] And now our division has been sent towards Pskov (10 versts from the city). We will remain there and what will happen later cannot be foreseen. [...] Those of us who are in the neutral army are suffering from everything: hunger, the cold and internal quarrels weaken us as we face an enemy that is too big [for us].[12]

A letter from his brother Osip, written to their cousin Vladimir Mendel, takes stock of the situation on 1 January 1918. Posted but never sent, it has been preserved in the St Petersburg historical archives, and offers a realistic picture of the "new society" under construction:

> We are going through a very hard, even terrible time. We often wonder how we are still alive. Everyone is disgusted with what is going on, but we have arrived at a point where it is difficult to remedy the situation.
>
> Mama [Mathilde] and Sonia are in Theodosia [in Crimea], and up until now the rare news that we have had from them has been good; everything seemed quiet over there. But in today's newspaper I read

something worrying regarding what is going on right in their vicinity. [...]

Here we are already used to everything: to the shooting, the cannon fire, the shortage of food. At the moment this last question takes priority over all the rest. As a result of it, events may take a bad turn. We will see others of all kinds.

Gino has been discharged again, and is currently in Petrograd. He is trying to enter the university, or at least to enrol there, because it is not possible to work in the atmosphere that surrounds us.

We have suffered greatly from the cold this winter. There was a heavy snowfall and for most of last month the temperature remained around minus 15 degrees, sometimes even lower. In addition, many people have left the city and their apartments are hardly heated. So the other renters are freezing. And then, since the food problem is very acute and we lack most staples, we are much more susceptible to the cold. Given the lack of fuel, we have been deprived almost entirely of electricity and reduced to candles, and even those we use sparely because they are difficult to find.

I see almost no one, a few close friends. That's all. When we feel too depressed we go to the theatre to distract ourselves a little.

Since there is a strike in all the offices, I am momentarily without a job. I go off to read in the public libraries, and these moments of reading make me forget for a few hours the hard and horrible life that surrounds us.

What about you, how are you? It has been a long time since I've heard from you. I see that the war has also spread to your area.

Gino sends his greetings, and I cordially shake your hand. Your affectionate cousin, Osip.[13]

On Millionnaya Street, Sasha's family was adapting to the situation. "Everything's going very well," Sasha even wrote to his brother-in-law, while sketching a not very heartening picture:

My daughters are working. Olga gives lessons, and both of them supply sweet cakes (so to speak) to a café, where they earn good money. The same cannot be said for me. We have given our orphanage to the community: we can no longer receive funds from our usual donors and our capital has been placed under a not very agreeable guardianship. And in addition, our activities are monitored in an annoying way. Apart from that, everything is fine.[14]

Their house was searched, but the Red Army soldiers took only the wine in the cellars.[15] Rosa had linens and silver sent to Finland; they were returned many years later. To get food coupons, the adult girls had to work, one at the post office, the other in a bookstore, and then in Pavlovsk, where she was employed drawing up an inventory of the tsar's possessions. The smallest movement required a pass "from some committee".[16] Classified in categories (persons of private means, workers, unemployed) people received bread in proportion to their social usefulness. In another letter, Sasha announced the death of Nicholas II, without any special emotion:

> For a few days people have been talking a lot about the assassination of our former emperor. It is not yet confirmed, but does not astonish us; after [he] was imprisoned in Ekaterinburg, I was expecting news of that kind. The most convinced Bolsheviks are found beyond the Urals.[17]

Since "Baron de Gunzburg" and his family were automatically classified in the category of "counter-revolutionaries", they had to prepare to leave:

> I spent two hours, from 9 to 11 in the evening, with our neighbourhood work committee. As a representative of the class of the rich, I was supposed to be sent to the cemetery to care for the tombs of cholera victims. Because of my age, I was excused. Our friends Wawelberg, Schwartz and others were escorted to the cemetery under the surveillance of the Red Guard. Today we received from Anna [Halperin] a permit to travel to Kiev. [...] We will be accompanied by the Red Army as far as the border, we have an acquaintance who was killed on that road.[18]

Before the planned departure, restrictions were suddenly tightened: in early August 1918, Sasha was arrested as a former officer in the tsarist army.[19] His daughter Olga gave an account of this dreadful day:

> Men's footsteps in the hallway woke me at 8 a.m. A few minutes later

my mother entered my bedroom. She was very upset: "The soldiers are here and they're looking for Papa. I'm afraid they will arrest him. They're in Papa's office." In 5 mins I was up, at the same time as Papa. Our mother led the Red Army into the apartment. They didn't search anywhere, not even giving Papa's table a cursory examination. The soldiers authorised Papa to eat breakfast and we wrapped up a bit of bread and preserves in a basket for him. Who knows... The guards were attentive and not crude, didn't behave badly towards Papa. [...] I wanted to follow him, but that was impossible. I thought I would be able to understand the address that our father was going to say, and I ran after him. But I was wrong. After I had gone to all the different places where Papa might be, I came back home without success.[20]

Bolshevik repression had just struck on Millionnaya Street, and Rosa, aided by her daughters and her nephews, mobilised her relations and friends. At the delegation of the people's second neighbourhood council, she learned that Sasha had been interned at 2 Glinka Street. No one knew what was going to happen to him. The prisoners were rapidly transferred to the prison on Kronstadt Island, off St Petersburg. From the quay, Olga witnessed the prisoners' departure:

Papa's barge also quickly began to move. Papa stood up and waved with his hat until he was chased away. The barge looked empty. It slid silently over the water. It was frightening. I happened to think of the ship on the Loire in 1879. I stayed on the quay until the barge had disappeared. It was said that 8 boats of this type had left, and that in one night, 10,000 men had been arrested. Later I learned that at the Commission's headquarters they regretted not having sunk the barges. That would have been very simple – a hole in the hull – and it would all have been over.

At Kronstadt the Gunzburgs received the help of the rabbi and his family. By persisting, Olga obtained an interview with Comrade Egorov, the head of the Investigative Committee.

I told him that Papa was not an active officer and was not on duty. He asked me if Papa knew anyone among the Bolsheviks. I avoided giving a clear answer. He told me that if I could find someone to guarantee

Papa, he could free him. [...] The situation was very critical. By chance, this time we were able to persuade the people who were demanding the death of the officers to wait. The next time, it would be difficult to save them. The fear of being accused of being a "counter-revolutionary", which could result in a death sentence, was too great. The Jews of Kronstadt were convinced that we were all-powerful in Petersburg and did not understand why we couldn't obtain the required papers for Baron de Gunzburg.[21]

Obtaining a guarantee of loyalty from a member of the Bolshevik administration proved in fact to be a real headache. But they were able to establish direct contact with Sasha:

The window was open and we could talk. First in Russian, then in French, because Mama understood better. We could hear hardly anything, but I guessed a lot from the movements of their lips. Thus Mama learned a few things we didn't know – for example, where the money was. Papa was the only one who knew where the hiding place was.[22]

But it was the administrative steps that were urgent:

We learned that a certain Kuzmin had agreed to sign the paper. He was at Smolny [the seat of Lenin's government]. He was about to begin writing when another Bolshevik came in. "What are you writing there?" "A guarantee." "For whom?" "Baron de Gunzburg." "Do you know him?" "No, but I've heard of him." "You can guarantee him even though you don't know him personally?" "Yes, you're right." Our case was lost. We had advised Mama to write a letter to Uritsky [the head of the Cheka secret police in Petrograd]. She did so, and we took the letter to Uritsky's chancellery. It was located at 2 Gorokhovaya Street, a building that was very well known because it had been the site of the execution of death sentences. Monsieur Frumkin and Monsieur Smolzberg wrote a very flattering paper for Papa and it was up to us to obtain Krestinsky's signature. But the paper was still at Uritsky's chancellery, and we did not have it in our hands.[23]

In his five months in the job, Uritsky had already been responsible for the death of five thousand people. His assassination on 30 August 1918 was to mark the beginning of the Red Terror. At the same time, the Jewish community held a formal meeting. According to Rabbi Eisenstadt's account, "everyone, even those on the left who were great enemies of [Sasha], absolutely wanted to help [him]." Since the guarantee had not arrived, Olga and her mother decided to go back to Kronstadt:

> Only a few minutes remained before the boat's departure. And then Osip appeared. He had an envelope in his hand. It was the guarantee, signed by Commissar Grinberg.[24] The commissar recommended that Papa be freed. At the same time Osip brought me a permit to go to Kronstadt. Day by day, it was getting more difficult to get to Kronstadt, and I was afraid that I would not be allowed to pass.

Olga looked for Comrade Egorov, who had come out to inspect the prisons.

> The office where wives obtained information on the prisoners was due to close at 4 p.m. An immense line of women remained without a reply. Comrade Egorov's representative was a tall man with a shaved head, small, disagreeable eyes, and a drinker's voice. Mama called him "the dog" (*sobaka*). He chased the women away and threatened to shoot if they did not leave immediately. But no one was afraid anymore, and the sailors had to drive the women away with insults and blows; they continued so long as "the dog" was there. [...] An hour went by. In the distance we heard car horns – the committee was returning from the prisons. I knew that many people wanted to talk to Egorov. I tried to be in the front row. He was still in his car when I showed him the paper. "Is that the correct signature?" He quickly read the paper: "With this paper your father will be free tomorrow."

Sasha left his own account of the difficulty of obtaining this official guarantee. The only reliable contact the Gunzburgs had with the new government was Elena Stasova, the niece of the art critic Vladimir Stasov, a close friend of Horace and David:

> It was not easy, because the Party people had seldom frequented our bourgeois circles, and no one knew them. However that may be,

311

knowing the friendly relations that existed between Stasov and our family, they went to find Elena Dmitrievna (I think that must have been Ilya Ginzburg), but she refused to give her guarantee, saying that, knowing the Gunzburgs' ideas, she couldn't be sure that in time one of them might not act against the regime.[25]

After Sasha's miraculous liberation, it was time to leave Soviet Russia. During this period of civil war, the journey to freedom was fraught with danger. Thanks to the pass provided by Anna Halperin, and at risk of their lives, they were able to reach Kiev, which was still under German occupation. On 7 December 1918, they obtained seats in the train to Berlin chartered by the German Economic Organisation (*Wirtschafts-zentrale*), which was evacuating Ukraine.[26] The trip was made in a third-class carriage with broken windows and no heating. Olga was convalescing from Spanish flu, which had killed so many people that year. The packages of smoked meat prepared by Anna proved to be a useful precaution. Regularly deprived of its engine and having to give priority to military convoys, the train advanced very slowly through the war zones:

> After a few days we arrived in Basatin [*sic*] – the headquarters of Petlyura, who would become leader of the Directorate [provisional state committee of the Ukrainian People's Republic]. The leaders of our [economic] organisation were invited to see him. The rest of us were promised a warm meal in the railway station's restaurant. The first warm meal since our departure from Kiev. We were just about to get up when we heard a volley of rifle shots. We saw the bullets pass in front of our windows. None of us thought of taking shelter and that led to our being hailed as heroines for many years afterwards. When the shooting was over (they claimed to have been aiming at an aeroplane that we had neither heard nor seen), we were taken to the promised meal and I guarantee that our appetites were good. Petlyura, in high spirits, gave us an escort as far as Rovno (there begins the sector under the control of counter-revolutionary officers) and we had to give up our escort before leaving the communist zone.[27]

The convoy subsequently passed through Vinnitsa, where the Gunzburgs' train carriage caught fire, Zhmerynka, to avoid combat zones, and Kovel, where the tracks changed from broad gauge to narrow gauge. Forced to leave the Economic Organisation's train, they had to find a new means of transportation: because of the shortage of coal, the Gunzburgs boarded the last train to Brest-Litovsk which normally would have gone on to Berlin. But at Belostok (modern Białystok) the train stopped for lack of fuel. Once again, luck was involved. Véra tells what happened:

> Around 10 p.m., the D-Zug [the German Economic Organisation's train] entered the station. No question of getting on it. It was taken by storm by the soldiers with their knapsacks and rifles across their shoulders. I had a desperate idea: a valise in my hand, I ran alongside the train. Finally, I saw M. von Alvensleben [of the Economic Organisation] at the window. "Monsieur, at least let my mother and little sister get on the train!" Response: "Out of the question, I'm locked in." I hurried on to the next window – they were subaltern employees of the Economic Organisation. They showed some heart and took us in with all our baggage. They had plenty of room. Now we were all cramped. It was deliciously warm. A heated train, what a stroke of luck!

Twenty-four hours later, they were finally in Berlin. This was still not the end of the journey: while they were waiting for their visa for Switzerland, the Spartacist uprising broke out.

> Had we made such a difficult trip only to fall into the hands of German Bolsheviks? We obtained visas, but only for the Gunzburg family. Mania Kulakoff, our nanny, did not have the right [to accompany us]. A separate visa for her had to be requested.[28] Naturally, we weren't going to abandon her alone in Germany. While waiting, we moved on to Munich, closer to Switzerland. We had hardly arrived – Kapp uprising. What to do? We took refuge in Memmingen, a ravishing little town, almost on the Swiss border, where Uncle Marc Rosenberg lived with his wife Mathilde – my mother's sister.[29]

In Odessa, Aniouta and her family experienced the same fears. Identified as hostile to the Bolsheviks, Siegfried was being actively sought. Then eight years old, their daughter Gavrik later recalled these weeks of pursuit:

In fact, Germans and Austrians (in Odessa, the Austrians) saved our lives. Just after the invasion, the situation was very dangerous. My father and his best friend were very active in the resistance against the Bolsheviks, and we all had to go into hiding. Granny [Louise Ashkenasy, Anna de Gunzburg's sister] and Mimi [and his family] found refuge in the apartment of the bank's authorised representative, and we (Mama and the children) in the home of the inspector at [my brother] Ginks's secondary school. The inspector was a bachelor and had no servants, so no one could denounce us. He had an apartment in the school. My father slept in a different house every night.[30]

To obtain visas, Siegfried gave his mother's apartment to the Austrian commander-in-chief: they were all able to reach Switzerland safe and sound. Siegfried chose to remain for professional reasons. The Austrians having been replaced by the French, it was now a French general who was occupying the family home. At the time of the French naval mutiny [of April 1919], this general sent an aide-de-camp to Siegfried "to say that they were leaving the following day and that he had twenty-four hours to liquidate the bank. The only thing he was able to do was to collect all the foreign assets and take them with him." Anna and Salomon (Sioma) Halperin, the daughter and son-in-law of Sasha, with their little boy Horace, were also refugees at Siegfried's home at that time. Salomon had lost his brother, who had been killed in Baku. They all left Odessa on the same boat, which was transporting several hundred refugees:

> In Constantinople, the boat landed on the island of Khalki. The Turkish authorities refused to let anyone disembark, and tried to send the boat, with all its passengers, back to Odessa. It was just before Pesach, so Papa and others protested for religious reasons. All the passengers were given permission to disembark.[31]

Two members of the Gunzburg family died during the civil war. Reported missing in the Caucasus, where political battles were raging, Berza never returned from the Savage Division. Years later, the family learned from one of his friends exiled in Paris that the commander had asked for a volunteer to go to the northern Caucasus, emphasising that the chances of success were minimal. Berza had accepted the mission.

Four years after his death, since he had left debts, and after [his brother Pierre] had paid them, the great hotels in Paris, Vienna, Berlin and London sent immense trunks full of clothes from the beginning of the century that had been left as security for his debts.[32]

Having enlisted in the White Army, Gino, David's son, participated in its retreat towards the south. From Crimea he managed to reach Turkey; decorated with the Cross of St George, the "illustrious warrior" died at Gallipoli of typhus in 1921. During the war, he had had occasion to care for another soldier called Falkenhayn whose fate he shared at Gallipoli: it was the parents of this soldier who informed Mathilde of her son's death. With her daughter Sonia and not without difficulty, David's widow had succeeded in leaving Russian territory. A page had been definitively turned.

Part VI

From One Exile to Another

They were well dressed, some of them very handsome like my father, speaking with a Russian intonation and very loyal to Russia. They left a reputation for luxury, elegance and bearing.

Philippe de Gunzbourg, "Tout un ensemble"

34

Stateless Persons

IN PARIS, SAINT-GERMAIN-EN-LAYE, Basle, London, New York or Geneva, the family's papers contain old official documents that are worn, yellowed and folded in four: certificates of identity, birth and marriage; Russian passports, Nansen passports,[1] foreign identity cards and residence permits. Sometimes, stapled in a corner, a passport-size photograph catches the eye, a still and moving reflection, rarely faithful, of those who were abruptly dispossessed of their destiny. The official stamps recall the different paths into exile the Gunzburgs took: Russian consulates in France, Germany, Switzerland, Holland and Hungary. Some of them date from the 1920s, others from the 1930s and 1940s: every member of the family remained "Russian", that is, a subject of the old Russia, until their death. Robert, Salomon's son, died a Russian in New York in 1943; Sasha, Horace's son, died a Russian in Basle in 1948. On one of these papers we can read: "Paris, 31 May 1921. The Consulate General of Russia in Paris certifies that Mademoiselle Gabrielle Jacqueline Ashkenasy, a Russian citizen, residing at 14 Rue Lincoln in Paris VIIIᵉ, was born in Odessa on 13 December 1899." Signed by the Consul, Kondaurov, with a stamp from the French Minister of Foreign Affairs that "certifies as genuine M. Kondaurov's signature", this birth certificate is typical of that period of administrative uncertainty: such certificates were produced in large quantities by the consul on Rue de Grenelle "on presentation of the authentic document", however doubtful the latter might be. Having had to provide a birth certificate for the wedding of his daughter Olga in 1921, Sasha urgently advised his brothers and sisters to have papers prepared for their own children.

At first, the French government continued to recognise the old Russian diplomatic representation and its prerogatives as they had existed before the Bolshevik coup d'état in October 1917. The embassy and consulate of the old imperial Russia thus retained official status. The same consul certified on 15/28 June 1921 that "Mademoiselle Baroness Véra de Gunzburg, a Russian citizen, is continuing her residence abroad," a formula that well expresses the strangeness of the situation. In the photo, Sasha's third daughter, a brunette, has a serious air. The "certificate of identity" of her younger sister Lia [Hélène] is dated from The Hague, 10 June 1923: "Of Russian origin, not having acquired any other nationality". Lia has long, very dark hair and a sombre look; she followed her father into exile in Holland after his wife Rosa's death in Paris in 1922. On the basis of France's official recognition of the USSR in 1925, a Central Office for Russian Refugees[2] authenticated documents. Thus "The Office for Russian Refugees certifies by the present document that Baron Vladimir de Gunzburg, residing in Paris at 2 Rue de Lubeck, is the husband of Claire Brodsky. The marriage of the spouses was celebrated in Kiev, Russia, 9/18 October 1898."[3] Passports for the refugees were renewed each year until the appearance of Nansen passports in 1922. Ex-citizens of a country that no longer existed (the Russian empire), they lived without worrying too much about what nation they belonged to.

Some of them took steps to become French, however. The case of Jean, Salomon's second son, is unusual in this regard, as is shown by his thick naturalisation file preserved in the French National Archives. Long before the revolution, he first "repudiated" – to use the standard term – his French nationality. Born in France to a Russian father and a French mother (who, through marriage, had lost her French nationality in accordance with the law then in force), he was Russian by birth. But in 1906, according to a new law of nationality, he was considered automatically French. It was up to him to "decline the status of French [citizen]", which he did, giving the following justifications:

Jean Maurice de Gunzburg, secretary-general of the Westinghouse Company, Russian, born 26 November 1884 in Paris, residing in the same city at 21 Avenue de l'Alma, has declared that he wishes to decline the French status that was conferred on him by Art. 8399 of the Civil Code and claims Russian nationality. In support of his declaration M. Baron de Gunzburg has submitted: 1) his birth certificate 2) the marriage certificate of his father and mother 3) an attestation in due form proceeding from the country to which he claims to adhere and noting that he is considered as a citizen of that country 4) a certificate stating that he has satisfied the military obligation in force in the country he claims.[4]

The report drawn up by the magistrate for the 8th arrondissement warns the person concerned that his decision is irreversible: "Before closing we have pointed out to the declarer that in the event that he were later to apply for naturalisation, that favour would be denied him." His brothers Robert and Alexis went through the same formalities. But a few years after the revolution, Jean changed his mind. He was then able to base his request on his rights as a military veteran: the state had in fact promised French nationality to foreigners who had fought under the French flag. Thus on 26 November 1920, he sent the French Lord Chancellor a letter emphasising his military experience:

In the year that followed my majority I opted for my father's nationality. I met the requirements of the Russian military law.

On 26 August 1914, I enlisted in the Foreign Legion for the duration of the war, in Paris, under Supply Corps C, no. 6474.

I was assigned to the 20th section of the Staff Secretariat, then to the 22nd section C.O.A. and on 11 November 1914 I was assigned to the British Army (19th squadron of the military supply corps) as a military interpreter.

In March 1915 I was sent to the front, attached to a field artillery group, and remained in that post until the end of the war. I was demobilised on 10 February 1919.

During this period I was awarded the Order of the Brigade (French military mission to the British Army, Order of the Brigade, General Order no. 348 of 16 June 1918) and I received the Croix de Guerre; I also received the "Distinguished Conduct Medal" (G.H.Q. M.S./F.H./29 June 1918) and the "Military Medal" (War Office List, 20 June 1918).

I was promoted to *brigadier* [corporal] on 1 November 1915, *maréchal des logis* [sergeant] on 1 October 1916, and officer-interpreter 3rd class for English language, a temporary title for the duration of the war, by ministerial decision on 30 December 1918 (*Journal Officiel*, 8 January 1919).

As a banker residing at no 21 Rue Pierre-Ier-de-Serbie, Jean also satisfied all the requirements of the moral inquiry:

Does he enjoy public respect? Yes.
Does he have personal wealth? Yes.
Why is the applicant requesting naturalisation? Because he has always lived in France and has all his interests in France.
What is his political attitude? Correct.
Does he seem to have abandoned any intention to return to his country? Yes.

A letter from General de Laguiche, under whose command he served, sets forth the conditions under which the Croix de Guerre was awarded him: "During the night of 25–26 April 1918, near P... (Belgium), under a violent bombardment, he ventured as far as 400 metres beyond the front lines to reconnoitre battery positions. From 9 April to 4 May 1918, he intelligently provided the liaison between his brigade and various French batteries. During this whole period [he] showed courage and an absolute contempt for danger." The head of the staff personnel service stated that he was a "very valuable non-commissioned officer with perfect manners and an admirable knowledge of English. Intelligent, courageous, active, energetic, with very military spirit", who was certain to make "a very good officer-interpreter". The chief of police's opinion was equally favourable: after noting that "M. de Gunzburg, Jean, of Russian nationality, belongs to the well-known family of bankers," he concluded that "The information collected regarding his conduct and his attitude from national and political points of view being satisfactory, I would see no problem in granting his request." After having paid the sum of 500 francs and 50 centimes, Jean thus regained his "status as French by the decree of 4 November 1922".

His cousin Vladimir, Ansky's friend, took a similar step on 22 May 1925:[5] his letter, probably written by a lawyer, insists on the importance of France in the life of the Gunzburgs since Joseph Evzel:

The father and grandfather of Monsieur Vladimir Gunzburg came to Paris in 1857; they established a bank in Paris at 1 Rue Saint-Georges, and then at 25 Boulevard Haussmann. In 1869, Monsieur Vladimir Gunzburg's grandfather had a town house built in Paris, at 7 Rue de

Tilsitt, in which Monsieur Vladimir Gunzburg was born on 6 June 1873. After various sojourns in France and Russia, Monsieur Vladimir Gunzburg came to Paris in 1906 with his wife and children; he lived first at 15 Rue Lapérouse, and then, starting in 1907, at 8 Rue Alfred-Dehodencq, and finally, in December 1912, he purchased, according to a document recorded by Maître Huillier, a notary in Paris, a town house at 2 Rue de Lubeck, in which he still resides. The couple's children have received all their education in Paris [...]. And the second daughter lives with her parents and takes courses at the Sorbonne. Finally a son, aged 13 and a half, attends the Janson de Sailly lycée.

Vladimir is described as the "administrator of the Company of Mechanical Tools and Artillery Machining – head office at 146 Boulevard Victor Hugo St-Ouen", a position that he had occupied since his discharge in 1917. According to this declaration, his income was 50,000 francs per annum and he had assets totalling 1 million francs. Based on the prefect's favourable opinion, the Lord Chancellor approved the naturalisation of Vladimir and his family on 6 July 1925. In his file, Vladimir mentions his brothers and sisters, thus providing a family geography of exile: of Horace's eleven children, six were then still alive. Except for Sasha, who had settled in Holland, all of them lived in Paris, which had thus become the main family centre: Gabriel, seventy, lived at 9 Rue de Pomereu;[6] Alfred (Mimi), sixty, at 41 Avenue du Bois-de-Boulogne; Pierre, fifty-three, at 54 Avenue d'Iéna; Aniouta, "Ashkenasy spouse", forty-nine, at 86 Rue d'Assas.

With these few exceptions, most members of the family could be described as "stateless persons", a recently coined term. Although the practical problems inherent in this status were not yet obvious in the Europe of the 1920s, the sudden and involuntary change in situation led to many difficulties. Exile meant the loss not only of property, but also of an economic and social *raison d'être*. Sixty years after the Gunzburgs' first, flamboyant entry into Paris society, this "return" to France was bitter. It was not really a return: from Joseph Evzel's first day at the Hôtel des Trois-Empereurs, the family had never lost contact with France. Although the town house on Rue de Tilsitt had been sold, the house in Saint-Germain-en-Laye remained a family property held by Ury's descendants. Moreover, the exiles could count on the support of those who had put down roots in France and constituted a comfortable family network: of Alexandre's two sons, Michel lived on his private income and at a distance from his cousins, but Jacques held a prominent place in Parisian finance and willingly offered his support. Mathilde's descendants were well integrated into high society, Jewish or not: her daughter Louise, married to Emile Halphen, had two daughters. The elder, Germaine, married Edouard de Rothschild in 1905, and Alice married Maurice de Brémond d'Ars in 1914. Suzanne, who had married Raoul Gradis, a shrewd investor, had three children, Gaston, Jean and Marie-Louise, all brilliant and active; and finally, from the marriage of the youngest daughter, Marie, to Henry de Courcy was born Antoinette, who married Antoine de Gramont, Duke of Lesparre, in 1921,[7] and Aimery, who died in combat in 1916. Among Horace's children, in addition to Vladimir and Mimi, who came to Paris before the revolution for the reasons already mentioned (the pogrom in Kiev for the former, and the Lena affair for the latter), Pierre, the ninth child, had also permanently settled in the French capital. Thanks to the comfortable position that his in-laws provided for him, he was the most capable of helping his brothers and sisters, their spouses and their children during their exile in Paris.

Pierre had left Russia after his marriage: in 1902, he married Yvonne, the third daughter of Emile Deutsch de la Meurthe and Louise Halphen. The latter was also the sister-in-law of Louise Fould, Mathilde de Gunzburg's daughter. For the Deutsch de la Meurthe family, whose fortune was relatively recent, the Barons de Gunzburg were a very desirable connection. There were in fact two marriages, seven years apart, linking the Deutsch de la Meurthe family and the Gunzburgs: after Pierre and Yvonne, the latter's younger sister Lucie married Robert, Salomon's eldest son, in 1909. Originally from Lorraine, the Deutsch de la Meurthes (who during the First World War added "de la Meurthe" to their name to Gallicise it) were at the head of a flourishing industrial empire. Emile, the father-in-law, was a striking figure admired by his daughters, his grandchildren and his sons-in-law. He liked to gather all his family around him at Château de Boulains, a hunting estate of several thousand hectares. His fortune was based on refining. His father, Alexandre, had created a company that refined rapeseed oil for Carcel lamps, a system that revolutionised domestic lighting before the arrival of electricity, and, in the 1860s, he had been interested in petroleum derivatives. He was one of the first in France to import a barrel of petroleum from Pennsylvania.

His sons Henri and Emile also engaged in refining paraffin to produce petrol. From 1875, in association with the Rothschilds, they invested in refineries in Spain, and then in oilfields in the Caucasus. In 1883, the Deutsch firm was the largest French refining company, boosting the car industry, in which many investments were made, leading to the foundation of the Automobile Club de France. Emile developed the well-known five-litre cans of Luciline petrol, carried to the front by the famous red "taxis of the Marne". In 1922, with the collective name of "Les fils d'Alexandre", the firm became a limited company, "La Société des pétroles Jupiter", with capital of 50 million francs. Fifty per cent of the stock was then ceded to Royal Dutch Shell, an Anglo-Dutch petroleum company. To protect the family's interests, the industrial and financial contributions were brought together in a private bank, the Société de gestion d'intérêts privés (SOGIP). After the death of his brother Henri in 1919, Emile held sole control. Each of the two brothers had four daughters. As the historian Cyril Grange put it: "No transmission of responsibilities to the sons-in-law could take place: Gaston Gradis [who was Mathilde de Gunzburg-Fould's grandson] worked in Morocco alongside Marshal Lyautey. Arthur Weisweiller was a banker. Perhaps the foreign origin of the Gunzburg sons-in-law and of Joseph Esmond presented too many problems. The health of Henri Goldet, the most capable, was fragile (he had been gassed)."[8] More than their "foreign origin", their lack of interest in business explains Pierre's and Robert's disengagement. Even though Robert was an engineer with a diploma from the Ecole des Mines, both of them were content with their role as "prince-consorts", especially since at the time of their marriages they were wealthy in their own right. When Horace died, the Gunzburgs' property in Russia remained considerable, valued at 25 million gold roubles, or the equivalent of 275 million dollars in 2000.[9]

Pierre maintained cordial relations with his father-in-law, based on their common love of hunting. Amiable by nature, he led a comfortable and monotonous life in France, very different from his youth in St Petersburg, which had been rather hectic. Among his personal effects, only an old, carefully preserved album testifies to his attachment to Russia: it contains photos taken during his travels in Siberia and China when he was young. To cut short his affair with a divorced woman, his father had sent him away from St Petersburg; when he returned, he was put on a train to Paris, where a fiancée carefully chosen by Horace was waiting for him. In the Far East, Pierre photographed the Trans-Siberian Railway, which had just begun running, the steamers of the family fleet on the Lena, and Russian peasants transporting their houses on rafts. One photo shows him in Chinese clothing; another shows his brother Gabriel in the same outfit.[10] His last sojourn in Russia dated from 1902, when he took his young wife there. Yvonne was impressed by the long journey and the sable coat given to her by Horace, who was waiting for her at the Russian border.[11] Otherwise, she didn't much care for her stay in the homeland of the tsars, the Slavic soul perhaps not corresponding to her measured character. According to their eldest son Philippe, who in his memoirs sketched a vivid portrait of the Gunzburgs in the period between the wars, Pierre "never talked about Russia, that was a page that had been turned. But all these [Gunzburgs] had a certain idea that they were better than others: more elegant and better than other Judaics [*sic*] from the European countries they frequented."[12] But for all that Pierre never really got used to France. He did not request French nationality until 1938, and then only because his children insisted, worried about his statelessness in a threatening European context.[13] He rolled his "r"s when he spoke and found the manners of the Halphen and Deutsch families "bourgeois". He was "too kind, too gentle, too polite, too timid to express it, but in the end it was a fact",[14] his son explained, adding: "My father took no pleasure in assimilating himself to his in-laws, and except during events like those of 1918 and 1922, he no longer saw Russians. My father was turned towards Edward VII's England, and earlier, no doubt, towards that of Queen Victoria. He was fanatical about England and English elegance."[15] A product of this Franco-Russian union, Philippe, born in Paris in 1904, felt "squeezed between this Russian side, unreal, vague, generous, distant from things, and the French realities, bourgeois realities, whether of the upper bourgeoisie of the Halphen type, or of my grandfather [Deutsch]'s type of recent, still struggling bourgeoisie."[16]

A young man eager for experiences, Philippe felt an interest in his "uncles" who had come from that remote country. He showed empathy in describing their dull lives as rootless persons in whom he discerned a certain difficulty of being:

> I often served as a confidant for some of my aged uncles, my father's half-ruined elder brothers. Some of these people ended up living in Paris, more or less supported by my father, and they adored me. They

considered me one of theirs, I wasn't like the people in my French family; in their eyes, I was different, I was theirs: "You're different, you have nothing to do with them, you're like us." I heard that often. These people were seeing out their idle lives, speaking very little, playing solitaire in front of an open window, in summer.[17]

When the exiles arrived, Pierre in particular came to the aid of his sister Aniouta and her husband Siegfried, the Ashkenasy Bank having disappeared in the revolutionary turbulence. He was always there for Sasha and his family as well. Thus the Deutsch family entrusted Sasha with the management of the Westersche Bank in Holland. The old Emile Deutsch explained to his grandson Philippe that he was not doing this "to please his father" but in the interest of "his own business":

When I was a very young man, at the entrance to the Allée des Poteaux, a bridle path in the Bois de Boulogne, I was with my grandfather Deutsch, as I so often was, as I have said. We were warming up our horses, and he talked to me. He had just created a kind of financial institution in Amsterdam. Four or five years after the First World War, with Monsieur Prat, an accountant who wore silk shirts, he had settled, in a few nights, the business I have just mentioned. At that time he helped one of my Russian uncles, who was ten or twelve years older than my father, and who had just arrived from Russia. His family had first passed through Switzerland and at that point he was in Paris. This man, like most of the people in my Russian family, was pure, honest, unintelligent but scrupulous. [...] I can still see my grandfather turning around on his saddle and saying to me: "You know, I have appointed your uncle So-and-so in Holland. I didn't do it to please your father. I did it because he is the best. To handle a safe, to have the keys to the safe, you have to be absolutely honest and unintelligent. And that's the case."[18]

This anecdote is unfair to Sasha, but it nonetheless reveals the problems encountered by refugees who suddenly found themselves in a precarious situation. When they fled Russia, Sasha and Rosa abandoned their palace on Millionnaya Street and all their assets in the Gunzburg Trading Agency. For Rosa, exile was a sad trial: they moved into a furnished apartment with a very reduced domestic staff; they had their linen laundered by their sister-in-law Yvonne.[19] In 1921, at the time of their daughter Olga's marriage to the Spanish banker Ignacio Bauer, receptions were "given" by their friends and by the in-laws.[20] In a detailed letter, Rosa described for her brother Aby Warburg the series of festivities, which were very successful despite the circumstances: "The first dinner in honour of the young couple was given by Jacques de Gunzburg solely for the family. Twenty-three guests (even if a few nieces and nephews were not invited). This last week, 4 dinners and 2 breakfasts. The last two at the Russian and Spanish embassies. Dinner: Henriette [de Gunzburg] and her family, Emile Deutsch, old Cahen d'Anvers, with Robert de Rothschild and his wife, and with us at the Ritz: 18 guests were served, followed by dances and romantic readings in Russian. In the evening there were about eighty of us, only the family and Russian friends."[21] After the civil wedding, the in-laws gave a "truly nice and lively party" at the Ritz: "The cream of the Jewish society of Paris was there, along with a few Spanish aristocrats." For the religious wedding in the Rue de la Victoire synagogue, Rosa was glad to have "paid for a first-class ceremony [...] at bargain rates". The wedding dress from Worth and a lace veil three metres long were gifts from the fiancé. The bride "had a grand air", "the music was beautiful, the speech given by Rabbi Israel Levy very good, and the reception at Pierre's home was particularly elegant, with about 400 guests." Among their wedding presents, the happy couple found "many jewels from the Bauer family", "a snuffbox with a miniature portrait from Emile Deutsch, Meissen salt shakers from Jacques de Gunzburg, Chinese vases from Felix [Warburg], two eighteenth-century engravings from Henriette" and "the Rothschilds gave two groups of bronzes." The young couple spent their honeymoon first in Versailles, and then in Italy, before reaching the estate of Alameda in Spain. Olga's misfortunes seemed to be over. These happy days distracted Rosa and Sasha from their trials, which had recently been aggravated by illness. Rosa was suffering from a cancer that was to carry her off a few months later, on 17 February 1922, at the age of fifty-two, too soon to allow her to attend the wedding of her third daughter Véra to Paul Dreyfus, a banker in Basle. After this second marriage, which was as Parisian as Olga's, Sasha settled with his unmarried children in Holland, in charge of the Deutsch family's "safe". His son Fedia came to join him after the *de facto* interruption of the Bakhmetev mission, which the provisional government had sent in February 1917 to Washington, where he was "second secretary of the embassy". For this young man in his thirties, the victory of the Bolsheviks had sounded the death knell of a promising diplomatic career. In Amsterdam he married in January 1933 Wilhelmina Ptasznik, a serious young woman with an artless smile, who bore him two children, Dimitri and Macha. Sasha regretted having chosen exile: in a letter dated 1933, when his Warburg relatives in Germany were wondering whether they should leave, he wrote to his daughters, "My leaving Russia was Mama's [Rosa's] work [...]. And although it was successful in my case, that is not always the case for others. As I see it, if one can manage to remain, that is better than going to die of hunger outside."[22]

In Saint-Germain-en-Laye, David's widow and her daughters certainly had a roof over their heads, but few resources. By that point Mathilde had already understood that she could no longer draw any benefit from David's magnificent library, whose sale to the Jewish Theological Seminary she had negotiated in July 1914 for the price of 200,000 roubles.[23] Her son Osip was not in a position to help her: unlike his brother Gino, he had survived the revolution, but had settled in Japan after having passed through Romania. An orientalist like his father, specialising in the countries of the Far East, he had found employment in a bank. In a letter sent from Tokyo on 20 November 1921, he informed his mother of his new position. On reading this letter, it becomes clear that Osip had married a Russian nicknamed Lizette, whom he had met in Odessa, and who was already the mother of a little girl named Véroussia.

> Dear Mother, I hope these lines will reach you just in time to wish you a happy New Year. We have to hope that things will get better and that life will begin to smile on you again. [...] I go regularly to the bank, where I work from 9 a.m. to 4 or 4.30 p.m. [...] I've been authorised to sign for the bank and I think that in time I will be able to make a place for myself in this establishment, because I am the only one who knows the languages they need. Japanese has come back to me so well that I can read and write it again, and also talk with customers. That gives me an advantage over almost all the Europeans who live here.[24]

After a cataclysmic earthquake struck Japan, and especially Tokyo, on 1 September 1923, Osip and Lizette also took up residence in France. Was

Véroussia one of the many victims of the earthquake (the estimated death toll was 200,000)? Although we have no document confirming that hypothesis, the couple seem not to have been accompanied by a child when they moved to France.[25] Mathilde had to rely on help from the family: her cousin Pierre managed for her a few residual securities that provided a small income.[26] Vivacious and cultivated, her daughter Sonia was employed by her uncle Vladimir. She took responsibility for the education of Serge, the youngest of the family, and produced plays acted by the children, bringing together for the occasion cousins from the different branches of the family. In her *Souvenirs*, Monique, the daughter of Robert de Gunzburg and Lucie Deutsch de la Meurthe, recounts nostalgically her participation in a play – in the role of the maid in *Les Précieuses ridicules*. "There were other plays by Molière. The performances were a marvellous event for us."[27]

Among Joseph Evzel's many descendants who were in Paris in the 1920s, the refugees from Russia distinguished themselves by their greater loyalty to Jewish tradition, as was emphasised by their nephew Philippe: "My Russian family forced themselves, some very naturally, others by discipline, to be practising Jews – not totally, because the Jewish religion is a life, a life that is closed and complete, much more than mystical, but nonetheless they followed their religion in a rather precise way, and that obviously played a very great role."[28] None of Horace's children would have imagined not being involved, even secondarily, in the community's affairs: Mimi was close to the Alliance Israélite Universelle, a member of the Consistory of Paris and president of the "Ohel Jacob" association, which provided aid to Russian Jews, and was trying to help 120,000 Jews from Russia, Poland and Romania who had taken refuge in France. In particular, after-school courses offering religious instruction were set up: in them children were supervised until their parents got home.[29] With the help of his wife Yvonne, Pierre actively supported ORT (Organisation for Rehabilitation through Training, created in St Petersburg in the 1880s), whose French branch was established in 1921. Even the name of the dandy Gabriel is attached to a precious *tass* (an ornamental plaque for the Torah) given in memory of his father to the Victoire synagogue, which is now in the Musée d'Art et d'Histoire du Judaïsme in Paris.

35

Bankers

"Russian. Foreign banker residing in France, born 20 November 1853 in Kamenets-Podolsk, was promoted to Commandeur de la Légion d'Honneur by the decree of 21 February 1921 issued on the basis of the report of the Ministry of Foreign Affairs."[1] At the age of sixty-eight Jacques de Gunzburg was granted France's highest civilian award to a foreigner. He had been made a Chevalier in 1904 and an Officier in 1910. The "details of his extraordinary services" contained in his Légion file provide an overview of his professional qualifications and at the same time sum up the only available biographical information about Joseph Evzel's "favourite" grandson, who today has no descendants. A brilliant banker, as much at ease in complex financial arrangements as in promising industrial investments, Jacques was an excellent connoisseur of the stock market (in London as well as in Paris) and an efficacious intermediary between the world of business and that of politics, drawing on his international networks and his involvement in new sectors of the economy, such as electricity. Although Joseph Evzel had disinherited Alexandre, Jacques' father, he guaranteed the future of both Jacques and his brother Michel. Whereas Michel got by comfortably in Paris without any particular occupation, Jacques devoted himself passionately to business. Brought up in the town house on Rue de Tilsitt, he was initiated into the business world by his grandfather, whom he regularly accompanied on trips to Russia. As soon as he had been awarded a Bachelor of Science degree by the University of Poitiers, Jacques set out to complete his military service in the tsar's armies. Not having been able to join the prestigious guard regiment (because he was Jewish), the young man had entered, as a volunteer, the Narva lancers in Vilna, and then joined a regiment in St Petersburg, where his equestrian talents were noticed by Grand Duke Nicholas, as we have already seen. In the course of this service, on the occasion of the *razvod*, an annual military ceremony, the tsar personally congratulated this fine-looking officer cadet. Jacques later took part in the Turkish campaign of 1877–78, and was "decorated, for personal deeds in combat with the enemy, with the Order of Saint Stanislas with Sword".[2]

After almost a decade of military duty, Jacques returned to France and the Paris branch of the Gunzburg bank. He was nearly forty years old when the establishment founded by Joseph Evzel closed its doors in 1892. A hard worker, considered "a clever investor" by Hubert Bonin,[3] a specialist in economic history, Jacques then distinguished himself by re-establishing a bank under the name of Jacques de Gunzburg and Co. This was not a classic nineteenth-century bank, but a structure that allowed him to participate in transactions and financial and industrial arrangements in all domains. In the Parisian financial world in the first decade of the twentieth century, he belonged to "a cohort of banker-financiers of significant size and great talents who were prompt to seize the opportunities offered by foreign markets", men like Camondo, Hoskier, Erlanger, Neuflize and Kahn.[4] They acted as "certified stock market intermediaries", operating alongside investment banks and stockbrokers, all of which respected the regulation of the stock market dating from 1890.[5]

Obviously, the Russian market interested the Gunzburg heir. At the Paris stock market, he was initially a skilful intermediary facilitating access to Russian business, not without sometimes being a stakeholder in negotiations between European influence groups in Russia. He had as a partner – and competitor – the banker Jean-Emile Hoskier (and then his successor, Harald Hoskier), who was of Danish origin but had been living in St Petersburg since the 1880s.[6] Benefiting from efficient networks in the tsarist administration, they usually knew well in advance about plans for bond issues and the real state of health of borrowers or potential bond issuers.[7] From the 1890s, Jacques was very active in the London market, where he worked for the British bank Hirsch & Co.; he was particularly interested in the mining sector, "obtaining considerable orders for French industry".[8] The discovery of diamond and gold deposits in South Africa, in the Transvaal, revitalised a sector that the Gunzburgs knew well.[9] From

January 1895, many South African mines listed on the London stock market became available on the Paris stock market: Jacques was busy placing the securities recently issued by "Kimberley Central, Rand, De Beers, Gold Fields", the latter destined to be directly connected with the family's interests in the Lena.[10] In 1895, Jacques created, along with other investors, the Compagnie française des mines d'or de l'Afrique du Sud, also called Cofrador, and the Banque française de l'Afrique du Sud, which issued 400,000 stocks of a hundred francs, for a capital of about 2 million pounds sterling. This company was to play a decisive role in the gold mine stock market; in 1901, the fusion of the Banque de l'Afrique du Sud and the Banque Internationale de Paris (the ex-Banque d'Egypte) led to the foundation of the Banque française pour le commerce et l'industrie, of which Jacques became one of the administrators. This institution acquired an international outlook, notably Russian, and Hermann Raffalovich, the co-founder with Horace of the Rossiya insurance company, was one of its associates. His dynamic attitude to banking led him to invest in the new sector of electricity: Jacques had a share in the capital of the Société Générale d'Electricité, the Westinghouse Company (French branch) and the Société d'Energie Electrique; he raised the capital to found the Electro-Métallurgie de Dive company, which provided, notably, electrolytic tubes for the Ministry of the Navy; more unexpectedly, but in line with his partnerships with British investors, he also put together the Ritz Hotels Development Corporation, of which he was the financial director.[11] Thus it was not surprising that one of the receptions for his cousin Olga's wedding, for which Jacques also gave a dinner at his home, took place in the famous hotel on Place Vendôme.

Jacques' international expertise was not limited to Russia: he worked tirelessly on the economic rapprochement between France and two countries in full industrial development, Japan and Brazil: the Meiji era was then launching Japan into a particularly rapid phase of growth. After its military victories over China in 1895, and then over Russia in 1905, the flow of business coming from Japan was constantly increasing. Jacques' Légion d'Honneur file mentions that he "served as an intermediary between the French and Japanese governments" and that he "was the instigator of the first Japanese loan, in the amount of 300 million, issued in Paris in January 1906, and soon followed by a second issue, also in the amount of 300 million, issued in Paris in 1907".[12] With Brazil, "he contributed to the union of French and Brazilian interests in railway matters and credit enterprises." In the absence of documentation, it is impossible to say what Jacques' contacts were in Japan and Brazil, or in South Africa, where he completed numerous deals. But he definitely had "the connections and the density of relational capital of a fully international banker who could act as a facilitator and negotiator, ahead of the experts of the great establishments".[13]

Jacques was induced to put together in 1907 a group of investors to subscribe to the founding of Crédit Franco-Egyptien, which was supposed to guide Egypt's economic development; the other stakeholders included the Aghion and Crédit Mobilier groups. The Gunzburg group controlled 16,500 shares, of which 1,600 were in Jacques' name and 800 were in the name of his brother Michel. The other stakeholders were his usual clients.[14] Since the 1904 accords, which protected the country against its European rivals, economists had been optimistic about Egypt's development. But Crédit Franco-Egyptien had hardly been founded when, in the spring of 1907, there was a major economic crisis from which Egypt had still not recovered by the time of the First World War. Those are the risks of the trade and, to judge by his professional profile, it is clear that Jacques did not hesitate to take them.

No documents provide us with any additional information about Jacques' character, tastes or even physical appearance. All we know is that he was one of those rare "Russian uncles" who were regarded indulgently by Philippe, who was apt to make hasty judgements: "I don't think they were intelligent, except for one or two of them, including Jacques de Gunzburg."[15] Outside the world of business and banking, Jacques did not attract much attention: he had no famous collections nor did he give splendid receptions. He was a member of the Cercle de l'Union Interalliée and a founder of the Dieppe golf course. Clearly, work was the most important thing in his life. In 1902, at the age of almost fifty, he married the ravishing Quêta de Laska, the daughter of a Polish father and a Brazilian mother. Of all Joseph Evzel's male descendants of his generation, Jacques was the only one who married a non-Jewish wife. Moreover, the young woman was divorced from the jeweller Germain Bapst, with whom she had had a daughter, Audrey. In the family's view, the scandal was thus twofold. Jacques and Quêta had a son, Nicolas, called Nicky, born on 12 December 1904. The three of them lived at 10 Avenue Bugeaud, and then at 14 Avenue des Champs-Elysées. From time to time they made discreet appearances on the society pages. Thus on 24 August 1913, *Le Figaro* noted the "great activity yesterday at Dieppe, where the weather was marvellous. In the morning, on the beach, at the hour for bathing, we recognised His Excellency Sir Francis Bertie, the British ambassador, who is visiting the Baron and Baroness Jacques de Gunzburg at the Pré Saint-Nicolas." At that time the couple owned the spectacular villa Pré Saint-Nicolas, built by Gaston de Saint-Maurice, a great collector of Islamic art and a friend of Jacques. Jacques may have copied the style from the diplomat, who had built a residence combining mashrabiyas, Turkish baths and Gothic elements.[16] But Quêta soon divorced Jacques to marry Prince Basil Narichkin, who left her when she went mad. Jacques took care of her until her death in 1925, three years before his own demise.

The banker's generosity with regard to his family is corroborated by various facts: his involvement in Olga's marriage has already been mentioned; he also paid some of Gabriel's debts, as is shown by a "receipt" signed by the "Comtesse de Bryas": "Paris, 3 May 1907, received from Monsieur the Baron Jacques de Gunzburg, through the mediation of M. Castaignet, solicitor, paying in quittance and for the account of M. Gabriel de Gunzburg, the total sum of thirty thousand francs, as payment in full of all accounts between M. Gabriel de Gunzburg and me."[17] But above all, Jacques watched over the professional career of Jean, Salomon's son, who was thirty years younger than he. Their fathers were brothers – the eldest and the youngest of Joseph Evzel's children, respectively – and shared the Second Empire's taste for splendour. For more than twenty years, Jacques not only gave his cousin the benefit of his wise experience, in an almost paternal way, but also made him his closest collaborator.

At the tragic moment of Salomon's death in September 1905, and even if, as the newspapers reported, he had appeared within the hour to comfort his aunt Henriette, Jacques had also taken care to let it be known that his uncle had no involvement in his own banking activities. In the months that followed he sought to find a first job for Salomon's second son, who had just graduated from the Ecole des Hautes Etudes Commerciales and returned from his military service in Russia. At twenty-five, Jean worked first for Westinghouse, a company in which Jacques had invested, before joining, in 1911, the new Jacques de Gunzburg and Co. Bank, at 33 Rue Cambon. Through his mother, the young man also belonged to a family of bankers: his maternal grandfather was Salomon

Benedict Hayum Goldschmidt (1821–1888), an associate of the bank of Bischoffsheim, Goldschmidt and Co. Within the new Gunzburg bank, Jean participated in a series of international transactions: "Japanese treasury bonds at 5 per cent in 1913. Mexican treasury bonds at 6 per cent in 1913. Serbian loan at 5 per cent in 1913. French loan at 5 per cent in 1920. French loan at 6 per cent in 1920. City of Paris loan at 6 per cent in 1919 [...]. Loan of 50 million francs at 6 per cent for the Société Générale Coopérative de Reconstruction de Reims."[18] One of the Gunzburg bank's major exploits was its investment in "the great French business of TSF [*transmission sans fil*: wireless]" – the Compagnie Générale de TSF, Radio-France (the Sainte-Assise station) and Radio-Orient (the Beirut station).[19] At that point, the Gunzburgs had as their associate Henri Bousquet, an *agrégé de lettres* and a polyglot who acted on their behalf in many contracts signed in the period 1910–30: the Franco-Ethiopian railway, the Crédit Foncier Agricole of the province of Santa Fe in Argentina, Automobiles Brasier, Caoutchoucs de Padang and Plantations des Terres Rouges in Indochina, Electricity of Warsaw and the Société Industrielle d'Energie Electrique et Cables Télégraphiques (CFCT). In 1919, the CFCT participated in the foundation of the CSF (Compagnie Française de Télégraphie Sans Fil, the future Thomson). Bousquet became its president, Jacques and Jean were its directors. But Bousquet gradually became more independent: when the capital was increased in 1927, he bought more stock than the two Gunzburgs combined, and four times as much in 1929, when Jacques was already dead. The connections with Crédit Mobilier Français, the former Rouvier Bank of which Jacques was a friend, were also important: in 1913, the Gunzburgs thus found themselves on the board of Crédit Mobilier Français when the latter absorbed the Compagnie Française de Banques et de Mines, which specialised in the investment of the securities of South African mining companies.[20] When he died in Paris on 28 January 1929, at the age of seventy-six, Jacques had retired from business a few years earlier. Married on 4 March 1924 to Madeleine Hirsch, the daughter of the banker Louis Hirsch, Jean pursued his career in his father-in-law's bank, of which he became an associate in 1926, and subsequently succeeded Hirsch, sharing the bank's management with his brother-in-law André Louis-Hirsch. Although there was no longer any "Gunzburg bank", the family banking tradition remained very much alive.

36

Gunzburg Style

EDOUARD DUBUFE'S PORTRAIT of Joseph Evzel was made more than half a
century before the photographer Horst P. Horst's portrait of his great-
grandson Nicky. The same taste for luxurious parties connects the two
periods – the Second Empire and the "roaring Twenties" – and the two
men. From the ball at the Hôtel des Trois-Empereurs in 1857 to the
famous "Bal champêtre" in the Bois de Boulogne in 1931, the Gunzburgs
were part of the brilliance of Parisian life. For Horst, who was then a young
photographer working for the Paris edition of *Vogue*, Nicky was a choice
subject, simultaneously classic and exotic: in his striped tennis-style suit,
he radiated a distinctive charm that was probably related to his Russo-
Brazilian ancestry. In his particularly delicate hand, he holds a cigarette in
a pose that accentuates his woven leather watchband. This image, which
became a contemporary icon, made him a symbol of masculine elegance.
Later on, in the United States, where he was the artistic director of
Harper's Bazaar and then *Vogue*, he adopted a more casual style: a black
John Smedley shirt, tightly buttoned, and moccasins worn without socks,
a dress code so widespread today that it is difficult to imagine that he was
its inventor.[1]

Long before Nicky, his uncles Berza and Gabriel had already been
identified as dandies. The attraction of the spectacular Caucasian military
uniform had even led Berza to join the Savage Division during the First
World War. As for Gabriel, we already know that he launched the fashion
of unstarched shirts in Odessa. Their brother Pierre, sensibly married to
Yvonne Deutsch de la Meurthe, also possessed an uncommon elegance.

His son Philippe described his fanatical attention to his appearance, even on a tennis court:

> My father would have been wearing a panama hat from London, a shirt of the finest flannel made by his shirt-maker on Grafton Street, a slightly garish and daring silk cravat, white woollen stockings, very well cut, white flannel trousers from his tailor, Cooling and Lawrence on Maddox Street, and white shoes with red rubber soles, made to measure by Thomas, his London bootmaker. His trousers, which hung beautifully, were held up by a large silk scarf from his shirt-maker that was rolled as a belt and knotted.[2]

Countless black-and-white photos attest to this "extraordinarily refined, racy elegance", which was very British, no matter what the activity – smoking a pipe, reading a newspaper, playing golf, picnicking on a Scottish beach or hunting at the Deutsch family's Château de Boulains. Hats, caps, gaiters, ties and scarves always complemented perfectly cut suits in fine fabrics. Accompanied by his wife, less elegant but always smiling, and his four children, all of them magnificent, Pierre practised with rare talent the art of *farniente*. "Work is bad for the health," he said, deliberately contradicting the family motto, *Laboremus*. But for all that he was not a believer in Roman-style *otium*: he didn't much care for literature or art, theatre or opera, though he liked to play the violin, rather poorly, in memory of his years in St Petersburg. With no aspirations to be a prominent society figure either, he was content to be Baron de Gunzburg, a very handsome man, distinguished and well mannered. No one knows whether he had some mistress who inspired the care given to his appearance. The visible presence in the family album of a pretty niece, Nanny Habig, is intriguing: a dazzling beauty, with a perfect profile and masses of auburn hair, she signed her photograph "*Mille amitiés!*" Pierre's cousin Robert, who was also his brother-in-law by his marriage to Lucie Deutsch de la Meurthe, was not without charm, either. "Of middling height, he was elegant and good-looking," his daughter Monique wrote. Behind his solemn and often severe facade, he was very agreeable, could be charming, and liked pretty women.[3] He, too, showed a certain disdain for work. When Monique secretly took courses in shorthand and applied for a job as a secretary at Citroën, he berated her: "How dare you look for a job? Don't you know that you're taking the place of someone who needs it?"[4]

*

When it comes to matters of the heart, the family chronicle is full of out-of-the-ordinary stories. In a time of courtesans, having mistresses eased people's entry into high society: Joseph Evzel, Alexandre, Salomon and Ury had enjoyed the company of young actresses, providing them with horses and carriages, household staff, dresses and jewellery. Twenty years later, in St Petersburg, when the sons of prudent Horace mixed with "divorced women", he feared that they would make dangerous marriages: Gabriel was sent to Latin America and then to China, long enough for his passion and malicious gossip to die down. He was soon joined by his brother Pierre. In the following generation, Hans von Gutmann, Babita's son who had been brought up in Vienna, ended up marrying a certain Zita, an infamous *demi-mondaine*, who a few years later was accepted by the family, as Gavrik Ashkenasy tells us: "After the First World War, when Hans, his wife and my grandmother [Louise Ashkenasy] were in Nice at the same time, Granny invited them to dine at the Negresco. The maître d'hôtel thought that Granny didn't know who Zita was, and warned her that she could not sit next to such a woman."[5] Aniouta's son, Eugène Ashkenasy, also led a playboy's life: "exiled" from Odessa to Buenos Aires, he spent lavishly there before insisting on marrying Marie-Louise Bèche, his parents' maid; he had her sent from Russia to South America and enjoyed a long and blissful marriage with her. His father Siegfried, who had assembled the finest collection of erotic books in Russia, did not limit himself to the pleasure of reading. No doubt it was he who introduced his nephew Philippe to Gaby Berteau, "a *demi-mondaine*, one of the last", who was then in her forties.

A young man of twenty-two of highly attractive appearance, Philippe did not like being the son of a respected family. Gaby served as an escape route, and she educated him, not only in love. He described the circumstances of their meeting with his usual frankness:

> I became acquainted with her [...] through one of my Russian uncles, who did not have much money, but who wanted, in a somewhat excitable way, to make his young nephew known. It was very entertaining. He was a rather depraved man who did not hesitate to say about others: "*Grrrosse queue, ma chèrrre!* Has he fucked you? Did he hurt you?" He invited me to the country with her. And then, one night, in Montmartre, she danced with me and said: "I'm taking them home and then I'm taking you back to my place." Voilà![6]

Philippe moved in with his conquest; it is not hard to imagine the dismay of his parents, Pierre and Yvonne. But Gaby passionately loved her "Prince of the North"[7] and, through her, Philippe felt that he was discovering the "true France", as opposed to the artificial world of his parents: his father's British dream, his difficult-to-accept Russian roots, and especially the atmosphere of the family apartment on Avenue d'Iéna, which he found stifling:

> I was Colette's *Chéri* [...] On the pillow, in bed, she taught me about France, profoundly, gently... the peasantry (from which she had come), the land, the nobility, the products, the Catholic religion, the craftsmen, small-time commerce, the bailiff, the country doctor, the cattle merchant, the importance of village fairs, the little country notary, the social strata in Paris, the high and middle bourgeoisie...[8]

Gaby also told him how in 1910–11, in the bus operated by Maxim's, which she took four or five times a week, she met her customers, including the son of the Duke of Morny, who had himself courted Henriette, who had just married Salomon de Gunzburg... This life as a gigolo could not go on forever: after going off alone to Dakar, to get away from Gaby and his "status as a cherished lover and profiteer",[9] Philippe, who was incapable of breaking up with her, asked her to marry him. "She thought I was mad. She was frightened and opposed to this plan, but she felt that I was so distraught... she gave in." The civil wedding took place in Marrakech, quickly followed in Paris by a religious ceremony with a disparity in religion. "The lawyer advised my family," Philippe goes on, "not to cut me off but to support me only if I lived far from Paris, which suited me fine." Having taken up residence on a twenty-acre farm at Saint-Varent in the department of Deux-Sèvres, Philippe became acquainted with rural life and horse breeding. But after the sudden deaths that struck his family one after another, he ended up reconnecting with it: on 4 June 1925 his sister Béatrice died at Windsor Park in a riding accident, and on 20 January 1932 his brother Cyrille died in Briançon from the after-effects of pneumonia contracted when he was performing his military service as a "corporal in an Alpine skiing regiment (159th RIA)". The only member of his immediate family still alive was his young sister Aline, eleven years his junior, with whom he established a particularly affectionate bond from this painful period onwards. He changed his life. "After breaking up with Gaby, I saw Antoinette [Kahn] again when she came to play golf with my father and my cousin Diane [Esmond]... I was still married, but I had in fact left Gaby, to the delight of my poor parents, that goes without saying." "Extraordinarily beautiful, kind, sweet and ignorant", Antoinette rapidly accepted Philippe as her fiancé. "Everyone was happy," he concluded.[10]

By marrying Antoinette Kahn, a close friend of his late sister, Philippe rejoined his "milieu". He returned to the fold at 54 Avenue d'Iéna, a building owned by the Deutsch de la Meurthe family where Emile's daughters lived with their families. After the death of "Grandfather Deutsch" the first-floor apartment went to Pierre and Yvonne and their children; the Fould-Springers, descendants of Mathilde de Gunzburg and Paul Fould, took the second floor; the Esmonds (Valentine Esmond was a daughter of Emile Deutsch de la Meurthe and sister of Yvonne de Gunzbourg) occupied the third floor; and the top floor, under the roof, was occupied by the many servants. Each family had, in fact, its own staff: a chef, maître d'hôtel, nurse and under-nurse, a chambermaid for the mistress of the household, a chambermaid for the children, and two chauffeurs. Many years later, Aline recalled that "the automobiles were dark green with the family coat of arms painted on the side – the same went for the baby carriages!"[11] The maître d'hôtel wore the Gunzburg livery, which was also dark green, a survival from the time of Joseph Evzel and Rue de Tilsitt. Another tradition, this time the Deutsch family's: for fear of contagious illnesses, the children were taught at home. From the age of seven, the girls attended private lessons, but only twice a week. Under the surveillance of nurses and under-nurses, they played on Place des Etats-Unis with cousins and the children of neighbouring families – La Rochefoucauld, Yturbe and Koenigswarter. Mystery, and things unsaid, surrounded another family that had also settled on Place des Etats-Unis, the heirs of Joseph Evzel and his mistress, thought by some to be Mme Benardaki. Philippe later condemned this life detached from reality: as a child, he was incapable of asking the tramway conductor to tell him when they reached his stop, being ashamed to have to ask for something. He sometimes walked through the market on Avenue Victor-Hugo "as if in a dream": the vegetables, fish, meat... he saw nothing of this "raw" life in the home of his parents.

In their town house at 25 Avenue Bugeaud,[12] Robert and his family lived on an identical footing, described by Monique, who used it to illustrate the strict separation prevailing at that time between the world of adults and that of children:

> A grand staircase, with its blue carpet, led from the drawing room to my parents' floor: my mother's Louis XVI bedroom and her Chinese boudoir, and my father's quarters, furnished in mahogany. A narrower staircase ending with an iron grille led to the second floor, occupied by the children. My mother never went up there; she simply cried "good night" to us from below. My father sometimes came up to supervise our studies.[13]

Rather egocentric, Lucie was preoccupied chiefly with her Pekinese dogs, even if it was the chauffeur Aloïs who walked them, while their mistress took her daily walk at a rapid pace unsuited to little dogs. For receptions, "an enormous table seating twenty-four was set with a white damask tablecloth bearing the coat of arms surmounted by the Gunzburg crown, and silver engraved with the same crest and polished daily by Auguste [the major domo]." For their education, the three children – Monique, Guy and Yves – were entrusted to the care of the "marvellous Nana Baker, aided by her sister Molly". Every Thursday, they lunched at the home of their paternal grandmother, Henriette. She had left the house on Avenue de l'Alma and now lived in a garden apartment at 199 Boulevard Saint-Germain. Monique writes that:

> The weekly luncheons were a torture, and I dreaded those meals to the point that I wept every time before going there. She repeated over and over that we were ignorant, stupid and tongue-tied, that my mother (who had a complex about her mother-in-law) bought me terrible dresses. For these occasions my mother bought my clothes at "Marinda's", in particular a ravishing, cherry-red silk dress with countless pleats that I adored... No, we had to go to Lanvin and buy dresses for me in sea-green or mauve faille or moiré silk, with ruffles...[14]

Salomon's widow, whose elegance was praised year after year in the society pages, retained her remarkable reputation. She died in 1927, having bequeathed family portraits to the Louvre without her children's consent: her son Alexis painted by Salmson, her mother Mélanie Goldschmidt by Winterhalter, and herself as a child, by Ricard.[15]

Where to spend the summer holiday was determined by one essential criterion: golf, which the whole family played, even when they were still in St Petersburg! A regular at the Dieppe golf course, Jacques was one of its creators and directors in the years following 1910. From the age of thirteen onwards, the children were on the greens with their parents. Athletic activity thus bound the generations together. Monique remembers with nostalgia trips to the Basque coast, in a Plymouth, alone with her father. "During those journeys he talked to me about Russia, St Petersburg, the immense estate in Crimea that it took eight days to ride across, passing through Tatar villages, etc." Pierre and Yvonne took their passion for golf so far as to construct, in 1921, a house in Garches, on the Saint-Cloud golf course. "Owing to their anglophilia", it is an exact copy of a "stockbroker Tudor house" such as one sees in Surrey, a neo-medieval cottage in the "arts and crafts" mode, "dreadful", according to Philippe, who regretted the sale of the Château de Boulains and its 4,000 hectares of hunting grounds. Every summer, without exception, the whole family went to North Berwick in Scotland for the healthy holidays described by Aline: after "a good little Scottish breakfast – delicious porridge, eggs and bacon, kippers", they played golf and went swimming in a large rock pool that they found particularly icy, and thus "imperatively followed by a cup of Bovril (beef bouillon) and a Digestive biscuit".[16] The excellent lunch was followed by another round of golf and then tea, a tennis match, and possibly croquet – all usually in the rain. Trained by the best teachers, including George Duncan, Aline became an excellent golfer. In 1934 she won the French women's golf championship tournament: on the Mortfontaine course, a decisive fifteen-metre putt earned her the title and tributes in the press.[17] Tall and slim, she smiled happily in her impeccable pleated tweed skirt and English jumper.

In 1926, Robert and Lucie bought a magnificent estate a few kilometres from Biarritz, between La Négresse railway station, Arbonne, and Arcangues, with a view of La Rhune, a peak in the Pyrenees. An engineer and a good draughtsman, Robert devoted himself to the construction of the Villa Elhorria ("the bramble patch"). "He worked on it assiduously, did all the drawings and all the plans, and obtained, as a result, a genuine masterpiece. A house in the Spanish style with an interior patio, mosaic-lined pools and a tangle of tiled roofs. In the drawing room and dining room, panelling in polished oak that showed off the grain. The furniture was rustic in the Basque style, but of the highest quality, there was an enormous refectory table around which twenty people could easily be seated, and numerous bedrooms with numerous bathrooms (astonishing at the time) in multicoloured mosaics." The choice of furniture was entrusted to Jean-Michel Frank, advocate of a clean and uncluttered style.[18] At the time, the Basque coast was a meeting-place for gilded youth who vied with each other in elegance and insouciance, in an *art de vivre* that would disappear with the depression of the 1930s:

> It was the period between 1928 and 1932, the mad years between the wars: the balls, the galas, the Grand Dukes of Russia, Princess Nathalie Paley, Prince Dmitry, Grand Duke Boris; the couturiers Lucien Lelong, Poiret; rainbow-coloured beach pyjamas, the first sarongs designed by Jacques Heim, which replaced striped knitted swimsuits, the *concours d'élégance* for automobiles on the beach of La Chambre d'Amour, where the pretty passengers were elegantly dressed in a colour matching that of the automobile (even their poodles' leashes didn't clash); jazz, the Charleston, the Black Bottom, the dancing of Fred Astaire and Ginger Rogers, [...] women with short, platinum-blond hair with kiss-curls, flat-chested women; the Duke of Windsor (still the Prince of Wales) joined our group on the beach after his round of golf on the Chiberta course; the great tennis champions of the time, such as Jean Borotra, Cochet, Brugnon, Lacoste, Tilden and even Suzanne Lenglen, played on our tennis court (our fence separated us from the Borotras' farm). We danced the "fandango" with the ice-cream seller on the square in Saint-Jean-de-Luz.[19]

Monique does not mention her cousin Nicky, despite the fact that he was close to Lucien Lelong and Nathalie Paley, and was a magnificent dancer and a central figure in café society. Lelong is even supposed to have named his perfume "N" in homage to the famous "baron" rather than to the Russian princess Nathalie Paley, his wife by a marriage of convenience. A declared homosexual, Nicky may not have been *persona grata* at Villa Elhorria. But he was emblematic of those years of intense high society life, and also inspired one of the characters in Edouard Bourdet's play *La Fleur des pois*, which dramatised the homosexuals of fashionable Paris society.

When his father Jacques died in 1929, his legacy turned out to be smaller than expected.[20] The young man nonetheless lived in high style, notably organising two balls that were among the most remarkable Parisian events: the "Bal Champêtre" (Country Ball) and "Une Soirée à Schönbrunn" (A Party at Schönbrunn Palace). "I was grandiose at that time," Nicky explained. "I had a Rolls Royce, a little white dog and a Russian ex-colonel as my chauffeur."[21] Ephemeral, the balls were organised with the help of talented friends, painters, musicians and couturiers. Etienne de Beaumont had introduced themed parties in his town house: the guests were actors as much as they were spectators.[22] In 1927, at the "Proust Ball" held at the home of Jean-Louis and Baba de Faucigny-Lucinge, Nicky was the escort of the Countess of Brantes. He wore a curious outfit, that of a groom at Proust's Grand-Hôtel at Balbec; at the "Bal des Entrées de l'Opéra" he formed a romantic couple with Valentine Hugo; in 1929, he missed the Noailles' famous "Bal des Matières" because he was on a business trip to New York; but in 1931 he received, with Elsa Maxwell, guests for a "fête champêtre" (country party) in the little house (now demolished) that he rented from the City of Paris, near the Longchamp racetrack. The painter Christian Bérard, then Christian Dior's collaborator, oversaw its metamorphosis, draping the building in "blue satin" and transforming it "into an eighteenth-century baroque residence".[23] Hay wagons, heaps of vegetables and flowers, and life-size papier-mâché animals completed the decor.

> The guests were supposed to arrive on foot, on horseback or in a cart, an ordinary bicycle not being prohibited, Jean-Louis de Faucigny-Lucinge recalls. Cole Porter and his wife, Noël Coward, Elsa Maxwell, Princess Audrey Ilyinskaya (an American who was not badly off and had married the handsome Grand Duke Dmitry, Chanel's lover) and Robert de Rothschild made noteworthy entrances, perched on a hay wagon, dressed as a dairymaid, a harvester and a thresher.[24]

In 1934, Nicky threw himself into organising another festivity, along with his friends Jean-Louis and Baba Faucigny-Lucinge, on the island in the Bois de Boulogne, for the "Bal des Valses" (The Ball of the Waltzes), also called "Une Soirée à Schönbrunn":

> Baba, Nicky and I played "the family": I was Franz-Joseph; Baba was

Empress Elisabeth and wore a ravishing black dress studded with stars in diamonds, as in Winterhalter's picture; and Nicolas de Gunzburg played our son, a rather dark-skinned Archduke Rudolf.[25]

The costumes were designed by Christian Bérard and made by Karinska, the dressmaker at the Ballets Russes. Before the party the hosts and their guests were immortalised by Horst in the studios of *Vogue*: as an officer from an operetta Nicky was especially brilliant and sulphurous, with his shimmering decorations like so many jewels and his eyes outlined in kohl. He was then just beginning his career as an actor: he played the title role in Carl Theodor Dreyer's film *Vampyr: The Dream of Allan Gray*, which was released in 1934.

Nicky told journalists about the circumstances of this unique cinematographic experience:

> One night, Count Etienne de Beaumont gave a masked ball, whose theme was the opera. Valentine Hugo and I made an entrance dressed as Huguenots. Carl Dreyer was there... Like everyone else, I was dying to get into cinema. Through the mediation of mutual friends, Jean Hugo the painter and his wife Valentine, the interior decorator, who both knew Dreyer (Jean Hugo had worked with him on *The Passion of Joan of Arc*), I met Dreyer. The next day, he asked the Hugos if they thought I would agree to act in his next film, and I, of course, jumped at the opportunity.

Dreyer wanted to make a film in three versions, French, English and German, three languages that Nicky spoke. On screen, Baron Nicolas de Gunzburg chose to call himself Julian West to avoid being criticised by his family: "There was so much going on in my family when I decided to be an actor that I had to take a pseudonym," he explained. Dreyer wanted to make a film on the supernatural, and involved Nicky in its preparation. Together, they chose to adapt two stories by the Irish writer Sheridan Le Fanu, *Carmilla* and *The Room in the Dragon Inn*. The actor's involvement was also financial: "At first, I was not supposed to be the film's producer, but the project was not moving forward."[26] So he decided to finance it, remembering that "one of [his] father's cousins had been Diaghilev's backer, and that as a child he was taken to the Ballet Russe rather than to puppet shows." Nicky thus caused the Gunzburgs' name to be associated with one of the most original creators in the history of the cinema. In *Vampyr*, a film in which sound is more important than speech, Dreyer tried to do the opposite of what he had done in his earlier film, *The Passion of Joan of Arc*: "With *Vampyr*," Dreyer explained, "I tried to create on the screen a waking dream and show that the terrifying is found not in the things around us but in our own subconscious. If some event has provoked a state of over-excitement in us, there is no longer any limit to the inventions of our imagination or to the strange interpretations we give to the real things around us."[27] With his awkward, amateur actor's poses, Nicky magnificently fulfilled the director's sleepwalking intentions, naturally personifying a hesitant person shown in all the difficulty they feel in existing in the world.

The film took more than a year to make, from the spring of 1930 to the summer of 1931, each scene being repeated in the three languages, and thus three times, at the Château de Courtempierre near Montargis.: "I wasn't there all the time, however," Nicky recalled. This collaboration with Dreyer, a demanding man imbued with a minimalist aesthetic, put a lasting stamp on him: his pronounced taste for a grey palette cannot fail to remind us of Dreyer's unusual choice of grey tones in *Vampyr*. Considering taking up a career as an actor, Nicky, who had just turned thirty, decided to go to Hollywood. Before definitively leaving the Old World, he sold to his uncle Pierre the stocks in the Ritz that he had inherited from his father. Jean-Louis de Faucigny-Lucinge regretted that "we thereby lost, without any hope of return, several friends who were fascinated by the Yankee dream: Nathalie Paley, Nicky de Gunzburg." "I went to Hollywood to take a screen test for Fox, and over there I acted in a small theatre. When Fox became Twentieth Century, no one wanted an actor who was not under the same contract," Nicky said. Since the cinema had not met his expectations, he turned towards a promising career as the artistic director of *Harper's Bazaar* and then *Vogue*, a faithful colleague of the editor-in-chief, Diana Vreeland. Refined and cultivated, Nicky was an elegant soul, possessed of a dry sense of humour, "roaming around Condé-Nast's offices with his tall, slender figure and his strong, aristocratic jaw like Tutankhamun's."[28]

In this 1930s setting, a page turned for the whole younger generation of Gunzburgs. While Aline became engaged to André Strauss, an art-lover, Monique married, in June 1933, Raymond Leven, whom she had met at the Rothschilds' home: "The Edouard de Rothschilds had organised a dinner dance for forty young people, all but three of them Jewish, in the hope of finding 'suitors' for their daughter Bethsabée and her cousin Biba Springer. This big dinner with small tables was rather strange, because every one of us had the feeling that her neighbour was supposed one day to become her husband."[29] Little seemed to have changed since the 1880s, when balls were given to encourage favourable marriages. Monique immediately fell in love with a "sublime, tall, slim man of great distinction", with whom she danced several times. Although at first Robert doubted that a "Leven" was "good enough" for his only daughter,[30] he ended up looking favourably on this marriage. A family of jurists and stockbrokers, the Levens had long been connected with the Gunzburgs. Narcisse, Raymond's grandfather and the president of the Alliance Israélite Universelle from 1898 to 1915, had been one of Horace's regular interlocutors. The wedding took place in June 1933 at the Victoire synagogue. "The synagogue was packed with people and as full of flowers as one could wish. Below the dais, my relatives and the Levens' relatives witnessed the nuptial benediction, given by the Chief Rabbi of France, during which my mother never ceased weeping."[31] Then Monique, wearing a spectacular dress designed by Lucien Lelong, received the congratulations of relatives and friends at the town house on Avenue Bugeaud, "where wedding gifts had been piling up for weeks", before definitively leaving her family for a wedding night at the Ritz, followed by a honeymoon at the Danieli Hotel in Venice. "With my very handsome husband, whom I adored and of whom I was so proud, I led a great life."[32] Her father had taken care to order for Monique her "household linen whose monograms he designed himself".[33] But the threat coming from Germany soon disturbed this universe of "order and beauty, luxury, calm and pleasure".

37

At War

IN 1936 HITLER invaded the Saarland, with its coal mines and steelworks, violating the Treaty of Versailles, which more than twenty years earlier had put an end to the First World War. "In conformity with the accords signed, at that point France and Great Britain had to mobilise and move as quickly as possible towards the Rhine to dislodge and throw back the German army of re-occupation," Guy, Monique's brother, wrote in his unpublished study *Dunkerque oublié (Dunkirk Forgotten)*. He was then twenty-five years old and had recently been discharged from military service. "I was therefore recalled to Châlons-sur-Marne for a period of undetermined duration, where my regiment was preparing to leave for the East. Nothing happened, and thanks to the weakness and ineptitude of the French and British governments, the German army reoccupied the demilitarised zone, definitively and without hindrance. In 1936 Germany, which had not yet massively rearmed, could have been stopped."[1] A young graduate of the Ecole Libre des Sciences Politiques and the father of a young child (Jean-Louis, born in 1935), Guy had read *Mein Kampf* and had no illusions regarding the consequences of the Führer's policies. Opposed to the current attitude of wait-and-see, he decided to pursue his military preparation:

I knew that sooner or later we were going to have another war. I therefore decided to do what little I could to prepare myself for it. At that time, young people were being encouraged to take courses in paramilitary training at the Ecole Militaire des Invalides to improve their rank in the army. That is what I did for some time, one evening a week, in a course on radio and communication and a course in English, to learn military terms, since I already knew everyday English.[2]

Along with European tensions, anti-Semitism grew ever more prevalent: in France, the leading elites of the Central Consistory and the Alliance Israélite Universelle set up, in September 1936, the Centre de Documentation et de Vigilance (CDV), to "follow the development of anti-Semitism and take the steps necessary to combat it"; the Gunzburgs supported this initiative financially. For most young people, whose upbringing had generally placed little emphasis on religion, this strengthened their awareness of their Judaism. "It is certain that with the Hitler problem, from 1936 onwards I felt very Jewish again," Philippe noted. "I said to myself: 'I'm more Jewish than French! These Jews are suffering.' I was right, I wasn't thinking especially about a disastrous war but I felt very clearly that parties like the one supporting Doriot were gaining power."[3] Through philanthropic organisations such as OSE, known in France as Oeuvre de Secours aux Enfants (Organisation for Saving the Child), and ORT, help for refugees was being organised. Pierre and Yvonne bought properties throughout France in the 1930s to house young Jewish and non-Jewish refugees and orphans, in addition to donating sums to what became the French equivalent of the *Kindertransport*. They continued their support even after emigrating to America, where some of the children were also sent for.

The family soon witnessed the arrival in France of their Viennese cousins fleeing the Anschluss: Babita and Ludwig von Gutmann's eighth child, Lucia, known as Lutty, appeared with her husband Kurt Ippen and their two children, Ruth and Hans-Peter, fourteen and twelve years old respectively. They had left behind them an idyllic life: the Gutmann palace and its 2,000 square metres of floor space at 10 Schwarzenbergplatz (now the headquarters of the European Commission), and a company that made safes. Loyal employees sent on some of the family's furniture and the portrait of Horace that Veith had painted in Baden in 1908.[4] A devotion to horse-riding had brought this mixed couple together, Kurt being a Protestant (though probably of Jewish ancestry). The Amazon and the officer had met at the Spanish Riding School. Passionate riders, they both practised high-level dressage. They had shared the task of educating their children: their daughter was brought up Jewish and their son Protestant. But after 15 March 1938 both children were expelled from their schools. At Hans-Peter's Gymnasium, when the administration separated the Aryan and Jewish students in each class, he spontaneously joined the Jewish group.[5] Under the teacher's supervision, the Christian students then kicked out their Jewish classmates. Back at home and feeling happy about this unexpected holiday, Hans-Peter didn't understand why his mother seemed so upset. In May 1939, having obtained a visa, the Ippens went to live in Nice. They were not far from Cagnes-sur-Mer and its racetrack. Lutty re-established contact with some of her cousins, notably the Ashkenasys, who had been living for a few years in the Villa des Orangers at Cap d'Antibes. Everyone dissembled: people dressed elegantly to meet one another, as if nothing was wrong.

Summer 1939: most households started making arrangements, even before the invasion of Poland on 31 August. Pierre and Yvonne took up residence at the Villa Elisabeth in Deauville, where they were joined by Aline, already a widow, and her son Michel, aged three. The young woman remembered being on the famous *planches* (boardwalk) at Deauville when she heard that war had broken out.[6] Guy took his family, together with his baby daughter, Eliane, to Saint-Lunaire to join his parents, Robert and Lucie, who had also rented a house "just in case"; his sister Monique and her children, Solange and Hubert, were already there:

> We had decided to leave Paris in case the war began with a massive bombardment of the capital. So towards the middle of the month, with my then-wife Jacqueline, two babies and a nurse, we loaded our American Plymouth car with all our baggage and everything else we could pack into it, left our apartment at 3 Boulevard Emile-Augier and departed for Saint-Lunaire, near Dinard in Brittany.[7]

In this increasingly unsettled time, material advantages made life easier and led people to believe in a reassuring continuity: bridge and golf remained on the programme, while nannies still took care of the children. With her sister-in-law Jacqueline, Monique tried to set up a military hospital in Deauville, gathering equipment and recruiting staff: it was a fine organisation that was never to be used. A routine was established, and

Aline left Normandy to spend some time in Cannes, long enough to have a brief affair with the young "lieutenant" Aly Khan (the son of the Aga Khan, Rita Hayworth's future husband), to which a few tender epistolary exchanges testify: "It is only now that I realise how much I enjoyed my short stay in Cannes before my departure," he wrote. "My address is: Lieutenant Aly Khan, Etat Major, Postale 601. Do not forget it please. Love to you. A."[8] He regretted not being able to join her in Megève, was concerned about her health and the company she was keeping, reproached her for not writing at greater length, and ended by saying: "So many thoughts to you, darling."[9]

All able-bodied men of an age for military service were now mobilised: on 2 September Guy joined Laval's military centre in Mayenne as liaison officer and interpreter in a British regiment. His job was to serve as intermediary between the foreign troops and the local population: to find billeting for the troops, organise supplies, negotiate with local authorities – the municipal officials and gendarmes. During military action, he was in charge of liaison between his regiment and the French army, by transmitting directly, by radio or telephone or by writing in the appropriate language, orders and necessary information. His brother Alexis, who was doing his military service as a draughtsman, was sent to the Ardennes. Their cousin Philippe de Gunzbourg served at first as a nurse, then he too served as a liaison officer on the Maginot line.

Guy left interesting reminiscences of the Belgian campaign and the lightning retreat from Dunkirk. "By an extraordinary stroke of luck, I was among those who came out of it alive."[10] Before discussing the details of the catastrophic French collapse in 1940, he describes his experience of the "phony war" in the Douai region, not far from the border with Belgium, where, on 1 January 1940, he celebrated his twenty-ninth birthday: "On that occasion I received a magnificent gift from my mother: a large tin of excellent caviar. Since I had no intention of sharing it in the officers' mess, where I ate my meals, I had to eat my caviar for breakfast every morning, alone in my room."[11] The first weeks were devoted primarily to helping "His Majesty's soldiers" buy underwear, a regional specialty. When Belgium was invaded, the regiment was ordered to march on Brussels. But under massive assault by German panzers and the Luftwaffe, the offensive turned into a retreat. Passing near Ypres, Guy thought sadly of his uncle Alexis, who had been killed at precisely that place during the preceding world war, in November 1914. "He was also in the British army. It suddenly occurred to me that it would be a strange coincidence if I were killed there and buried alongside him."[12] He was spared that tragic fate. His regiment soon reached the beaches of Nord-Pas-de-Calais, where the Royal Navy organised the rescue of its soldiers by boat. Guy was at Bray-les-Dunes, "a poor little town completely emptied of its residents", "devastated, most of the houses damaged by bombardments". Hungry, weak and covered with dust, the soldiers tried to destroy the equipment that had to be left behind, so that it would not fall into German hands. "What a shame and what a waste!" the young man thought. He also had to think about his own survival:

> I climbed onto the dunes, which looked down on a vast beach extending for kilometres. The sight that lay before me was unimaginable: thousands of men scattered as far as the eye could see on this superb beach, some isolated, others gathered in groups of different sizes, but all looking lost and disorganised. [...] They were under constant attack by German Stukas, which came in waves, diving towards the beach and the sea in an attempt to prevent the troops from escaping. But despite their efforts, the evacuation was proceeding rather well.

Destroyers, along with passenger boats, a hospital ship and ferries requisitioned for the evacuation were subjected to sustained fire. A few Spitfires and Mosquitoes counter-attacked courageously and effectively. Unable to take part in the rescue by sea, Guy chose to head for Dunkirk, which he finally reached after an exhausting march over the sand: "At the end of our trek, we finally arrived at the edge of the canal leading out of the port of Dunkirk. Dark smoke rose over the city itself, and artillery shells were falling on the port, hitting several boats tied up along the jetties." Having found refuge aboard a destroyer, Guy was evacuated to Dover, where for several days his job was to receive troops landing from Dunkirk and direct them to the various trains that would take them to ports in the south of England so that they could return to France: "That is how Guy de Rothschild passed through my hands," he noted with amusement. His return to France proved more complicated than expected: after crossing the Channel towards Cherbourg "without mishap", the threat of a German attack forced him to immediately board a small, 2,000-tonne coaler, which sailed down the coast of France as the German advance proceeded: they passed Brest, then Lorient, Nantes, Saint-Nazaire and La Rochelle, before finally reaching the port of Bayonne, which was not occupied by the Germans. There Guy found himself on familiar terrain:

> I knew Bayonne, and my intention was naturally to rejoin my family, who had taken refuge in the villa that we owned near Biarritz. So I walked through the port, then crossed the bridge over the Adour and entered the streets of the city. Imagine my surprise when I found myself face-to-face with my father, who was running errands in town! I hadn't seen him since my departure from Paris the preceding year, and no one in my family knew where I was or what had become of me, because in that cataclysmic disorder it was impossible to send or receive news. So this was an extraordinary meeting on a street in Bayonne, and that was how, emaciated, dirty and bearded, I rejoined my family, parents, wife and children in the "Villa Elhorria" in Biarritz.

Although the joy of reunion was intense, Guy learned the sad news that his brother Alexis had been taken prisoner by the Germans. The youngest son, Yves, who had just celebrated his nineteenth birthday, was determined to go to England to join the Free French forces: the whole family accompanied him to Saint-Jean-de-Luz, where he fell in with a group of Polish soldiers who were ready to leave. The farewells were not without concern: when would the family next be together? Yves was never to see any of his friends and family again.[13] In Biarritz Robert and his family made themselves useful. Monique recounts:

> Every day, refugees fleeing before the German advance were arriving by the hundreds, by the thousands, from all parts of France. Elhorria filled up, we added beds, places at the table. Biarritz was crowded, as was Bayonne, and whole families were jammed up against the Pyrenees mountain range, seeking desperately to obtain passage to Spain and Portugal. [...] My parents and I organised a soup kitchen at the city hall in Biarritz, where we served a basic lentil soup and fed four hundred people a day.[14]

As the Basque country was being invaded in turn by the Germans, the whole family headed for the Côte d'Azur. The Villa Elhorria was transformed into the German headquarters and served as the residence of General von Rundstedt, who had been ordered by Hitler to oversee the defence of the Atlantic coast.[15]

For the French in general and for Jews in particular, the deterioration of the situation was a source of concern. During the French retreat Philippe noticed a new burst of anti-Semitism. "On the roads, one heard: 'It's the Jews,' 'It's Léon Blum,' 'We've been defeated by the Jews.'"[16] For the first time, the Jews of France wondered about their future in the country of the Enlightenment. With the establishment of the Vichy regime and the division of French territory into an occupied zone and a free zone, many Jews left for the south: "Despite the sun and the Mediterranean, in the late summer of 1940 the Côte d'Azur was lugubrious,"[17] Guy noted. The rationing of food and petrol was already beginning to disrupt everyday life. Everyone remembers the swedes and the "gazogène" cars that ran on fumes from burning wood or charcoal. On 3 October the French government promulgated the first Jewish law, prohibiting Jews from holding any public, commercial or industrial position. A year later, in July 1941, the law required Jewish businesses to be registered: the new legal framework threw into confusion the lives of hundreds of thousands of Jews who were dispossessed of their professions and jobs. Most members of the family were now involved in waging the legal battle against the Aryanisation of businesses, in the organisation of departures abroad between 1940 and 1943, or in the clandestine resistance.

In the autumn of 1940, after a short stay in the Basque country, Jean moved, with his wife Madeleine, their three children – Alain, François and Pierre – and his mother-in-law, Alice Hirsch, to Châtel-Guyon, not far from Vichy, the new political centre of France. They carefully locked up the family apartment building at 43 Avenue du Maréchal-Fayolle in Paris; the most valuable furniture and pictures were put in a vault at the Banque de France for safekeeping or entrusted to the neighbouring Argentine embassy. A Frenchman and the director of a reputable banking institution, Jean did not imagine that he was running any kind of risk. The children were sent to local schools and Alain even passed his baccalauréat. On 5 July 1941, Jean reacted promptly to the Aryanisation of his company by sending, in his own name and in that of his brother-in-law André Louis-Hirsch (who at the time was in a German prisoner-of-war camp, Oflag XVII), a letter addressed to the General Commissioner for Jewish Questions:

> [...] As statutory managers of the Louis Hirsch & Co. Bank, [we have] the honour to inform you
> – that the firm [that we manage], founded before 1799, has since that time remained in the same family, from father to son or son-in-law,
> – that this firm has always lent its full support to the French state and to its various Departments, as is attested in the attached appendix indicating the most prominent operations that it has dealt with to the benefit of public administrations,
> – that the Bank's staff amounted in 1939 to 55 employees, including 53 Aryans,
> – that since the war, its utility has borne principally on the subscription and investment of Treasury Bonds for considerable sums, approximately ½ billion per annum,
> – that in view of the military and civil services rendered to the French state, both by Monsieur André Louis-Hirsch and by his family for five generations, and by Monsieur Jean de Gunzburg, they request that the great benevolence of the government exempt both of them from the prohibition on exercising the profession of bankers.[18]

The better to defend his rights, Jean thought it wise to clarify his family history: he appended an autobiographical notice that mentioned concisely but clearly the services he and his ancestors had rendered to France, their adopted country. In particular he described Joseph Evzel as a "pioneer in the economic relations between France and Russia".[19] The documents preserved in the family archives show that from the middle of the 1930s, in reaction to the climate of growing anti-Semitism, Jean had begun drawing up a complete genealogy of the Gunzburgs. He made contact with his cousin Sasha, who arranged for David Maggid's work written in Hebrew in St Petersburg at the end of the nineteenth century to be translated into French.[20] The new context of the Vichy regime led Jean to complete the task; from Châtel-Guyon he wrote to various relatives to improve his knowledge of the family.[21] His correspondence has been preserved: typically of the period of the Occupation, the "war postcards" used were provided by the state and bore in red the following note: "Card exclusively reserved for family correspondence. It is permissible to write below a message of a family nature, seven lines long. [...] The message must be written very clearly to make it easy for the German authorities to read it." At the request of Jean, Bibka Merle d'Aubigné, Vladimir's daughter, went to check the funeral plaques in the mausoleum at the Montparnasse cemetery: "I went to the cemetery. The date of birth is not given. J.[oseph] de Gunzburg died on 12 January 1878 aged 65. That's all." She added: "I miss all my family members! You see how alone I am!" Then she concluded: "Dear Jean, how much I would like to receive more detailed news about you and your family."[22] Bibka refused to leave Paris and her apartment on Place Dauphine. Miraculously, she escaped arrest. In February 1942, from Saint-Germain-en-Laye, Robert Loewy, Ury's grandson, sent Jean "the result of a bit of research in which [he] had recently engaged":

> I had read in Sliozberg's book on H.[orace] de Gunzburg that during the war of 1870 J.[oseph] de Gunzburg had founded at his own cost a hospital for wounded soldiers. Thinking that this might be considered as an "exceptional service rendered to France", I looked for a document that would allow me to establish it with certainty.[23]

Robert, his mother Hélène and his aunt Mathilde flew a Swiss flag on Joseph Evzel's old house in Saint-Germain-en-Laye, the ground floor of which was occupied by a dressmaker's workshop.[24] Although they were registered as foreign Jews (Russians in the case of Hélène and Mathilde, and Swiss in that of Robert), they got through the war without serious damage.[25] Thanks to the research he had carried out, Jean thought he could justify his request for exemption from the prohibition on exercising the banker's trade.[26] The letter explains that "in an appendix are the origins and services of the two directors of the Louis Hirsch and Co. Bank and their families." Jean mentions his status as a Chevalier de la Légion d'Honneur and as a soldier decorated with the Croix de Guerre and the Croix du Combattant Volontaire in the First World War, adding that his "request is justified by the services [that he] was able to render to France, both as a soldier during the First World War and as a civilian during thirty-five years of professional activity, by the services rendered by my family resident in Paris since 1869, and by the Hirsch family, which took up residence in Paris before 1800, and with which I am linked by marriage.

Monsieur David Hirsch, awarded the medal of Saint Hélène, having been part of Napoleon's army at Waterloo."[27] But no argument could change the opinion of Marshal Pétain's regime, which had resolved to get rid of the Jews of France. They had to leave: in June 1942, Jean, his wife, his children and his mother-in-law arrived in New York with a permanent visa.

Stripped of their rights, Jews felt compelled to leave their French homeland. For the oldest of them, the dominant reaction was incomprehension, and the shock was immense. Aline writes simply: "For my parents, it was very unpleasant." In 1938 she had forced her father to request French citizenship. In June 1940, it was she who obliged her parents to leave Deauville and took them south, to Antibes and then to Cannes; when she passed through Paris, she filled several cars with useful things and stocked up on petrol at the "family" pump. She understood little about the general situation but she was certain of one thing: she was Jewish, and therefore in danger. It was not easy to obtain exit visas: in 1940, Aline went to Vichy twice to take the necessary steps. In the train, she met someone she knew, an eminent scientist. They talked about Vichy's Jewish statute. "It's not for people like you," he said, "but in general it is indispensable."[28] She absorbed the blow stoically, understanding that hostility against Jews was deeply ingrained. In Vichy she tried to persuade a secretary at the United States embassy to organise a meeting with the vice-consul in Nice. In December 1940 she again happened to be in Vichy on the day Pétain had Laval arrested. Having obtained the long-awaited papers, the family departed in haste: on 1 January 1941, Aline and her little boy left France alone for Spain and then Portugal, from where they sailed to New York. Three months later Aline's parents, Pierre and Yvonne, made the same journey. It was more prudent to travel separately. With his Nansen passport, Robert too went to New York, with Lucie, also via Spain and Portugal. Their daughter Monique managed to bid them farewell en route:

> From Montauban I set out in haste, by train, for Cerbère, on the Franco-Spanish border, to say farewell to them for this great departure: my father had also obtained papers to allow me to go with them, but I refused, not wanting to leave Raymond. I still see my poor mother kneeling down and kissing the soil of France before getting into the train.[29]

Robert, who had heart trouble, died a few months later, inconsolable about having left France and his children. Guy also took the necessary steps for himself, his wife Jacqueline and their two children, with the help of a specialist lawyer:

> Being Jewish, it was very difficult because it had to be done in Vichy. I waited six to eight months very anxiously. Thanks to my Franco-Brazilian company [founded before the war], I easily obtained a visa for Brazil. Finally I got my passport, which cost me very dearly. But that was not all. A rumour was circulating here and there that Brazil, despite the visa, was no longer willing to receive Jews. So I took the train to Marseilles several times, and by some discreet channel or another, I finally obtained a magnificent parchment certifying in Cyrillic characters, with a red ribbon and seals, that I was of the Russian Orthodox religion.[30]

In early May 1942, they left Europe from Barcelona and headed for Rio de Janeiro. Before the invasion of the Free Zone, the other members of the family managed to extricate themselves from danger: having first taken refuge at Cap d'Antibes, the Ashkenasys managed to travel to Switzerland, and so did Sasha, who had left Amsterdam in January 1940 for Antibes, Lavardac (in the department of Lot-et-Garonne) and then Orange, finally arriving in Basle in late 1941. On the other side of the border, the refugees were welcomed by Véra, Paul Dreyfus's wife. Throughout the war, this couple never ceased helping the numerous Gunzburgs in exile on neutral terrain. Having benefited from their aid, Fedia decided to take his family to the United States, a choice that displeased his father Sasha. "Life has to be begun anew," Fedia wrote to the latter. "Besides, I'm afraid I don't have a base on which to build. It will be a great adventure."[31] The assets left behind in Holland were blocked by the Americans to prevent them from falling into the hands of the invaders. As after the revolution of 1917, Sasha and Fedia found themselves deprived of any financial resources.

Those who chose to remain tried to live as discreetly as possible. In January 1941 Philippe purchased a small farm called "Le Barsalous" in Pont-du-Casse, in the Lot-et-Garonne. He bought five cows and a pair of oxen and installed "three toilets". To his sister Aline, who was living in New York, he described his new life in glowing terms: "I am perfectly happy and everything on my farm is going as planned, and I see many more changes to be made. [...] I rarely go into town and am getting set in my pleasure-loving ways, but that does mean I'm also very well-satisfied in the leg-over department."[32] With his young wife Antoinette he was enjoying a romantic idyll. Antoinette herself said much the same to Aline, who was an old friend of hers:

> We are very hot, but I love that. We take long naps and dine at 9.30. Everything about country life is wonderful and pleases me very much. Philippe is haying and we are eating only our own vegetables. I raise ducks and chicks. [...] Thanks for the rubber boots, which fit me very well. It reminded me of the good old days. It's changing our life. And thanks to you.[33]

Philippe tried to look like a wealthy Parisian who had taken refuge in the countryside. He liked working in the fields and the contact with the peasants. He was happy to be able to raise his sons – Patrice, born in 1936, and Jacques, born in 1939 – in an environment different from the one he had known as a child.[34] Le Barsalous welcomed friends and family members and became a rallying point during this period of general dispersal. Lia, Sasha's youngest daughter, stayed there at length with her husband and children, who were always to retain a happy memory of their wonderful uncle Philippe, with whom they toured the countryside on motorbikes. Contact with cousins living on the coast was frequent, as we see in a letter from Serge, Vladimir's son:

> Here we are all fine. I have just taken a little trip to Antibes with Xénia and Sylvie [his wife and his daughter]. We saw a great deal of the Ashkenasys, whom I really like very much, even the girls, now that I know them. Mourka will probably come to spend a few days here. Aniouta is still the same and reminds me so much of Papa! I saw Philippe, who is superb. His children too, especially little Jacques, who has become an enormous doll, likable, blond, friendly [...]. Philippe seems to be delighted with the country life that he is leading, and I think that's a very good thing.[35]

Philippe was also convinced that he had made a good choice: "I am grateful every day to be where I am and not where you are," he wrote to his sister.[36] "I'm still reading Gide, a little La Rochefoucauld, and books on our people lent to me by a very intelligent young rabbi. I often have long, useful conversations with him. In addition, I am vaguely involved in helping his protégés thanks to OSE and other groups."[37] Philippe was also called upon by the UGIF (Union Générale des Israélites de France), but he did not know that this organisation, which represented itself as a framework for help and financial aid, was used by the Vichy regime to identify Jews living in France.[38] He succeeded, however, in "warning a large number of people who might have been deported, because at the instigation of the Germans Vichy organised great roundups".[39]

From a distance, Philippe followed the despoliation going on in Paris and informed his sister about it: "[The profiteers] are rushing to seize our remaining property, even if they have been our guests; they can now be permanent owners of it,"[40] he wrote in December 1941, adding a few months later: "In Paris we have lost a great deal. Our private homes still belong to us, but we are moving towards a harder line."[41] The organised looting of Jewish property was just beginning under the auspices of Einsatzstab Reichsleiter Rosenberg (the ERR, Reichsleiter Alfred Rosenberg's action team). In Paris "Operation Furniture" ("Möbel Aktion") was entrusted to Kurt von Behr, appointed in March 1942 to head the Dienststelle Westen, a department of the Ministry of Occupied Territories of the East; the offices of this looting organisation were at nowhere other than 54 Avenue d'Iéna, the home of Pierre and Yvonne.[42] The goal was to empty the apartments of Jews who had left, been interned or been deported, and to transfer their furniture to Germany and to the occupied territories in the East. The town house next door to 2 Rue de Bassano, which belonged to the Cahen d'Anvers family, was used to store the most valuable goods seized, as was the apartment at 4 Place des Etats-Unis, which was owned by the Deutsch family.[43] Without knowing the sordid details of this whole operation, Philippe concluded: "It would be disagreeable if I were to be deprived of any of my property that I care about. And when one despoliation follows another, you end up undergoing one that is really painful for you."[44] More than material matters, it was the enforced separation from his family that he suffered from. "I miss many things about you, especially our laughter," he wrote to Aline, though he could not resist affectionately mocking her decision to live near her parents: "And then this mania to be on the same street, you're incorrigible." Aline would have liked to stay with her brother, but she did not want to deprive her parents of her comforting presence.

The threat of arrest hung over all the family members who were still in France. In 1942 two of Babita's daughters – who were, of course, Austrians – had taken up residence in Nice: Lutty Ippen and Anna Habig, called Nanny. Both were arrested in the roundup of 26 August 1942.[45] The Ippens had been living on the Côte d'Azur since the beginning of the war. They had been briefly interned in the camp at Gurs in 1940. In the Free Zone they felt safe: Kurt Ippen had served in the Czech army under a French commander. Their son Hans-Peter was enrolled in a Catholic secondary school, where he asked to be baptised on 12 September 1941, at the convent of the Clarisses de Cimiez. He possessed an ardent faith all his life, to the point of entering a Trappist monastery in 1979, under the name of Brother Jean-Pierre.[46] His sister Ruth took the same spiritual path. Convinced that they had nothing to fear, Lutty did not hesitate to register as a Jew. On the evening of 26 August 1942, when the BBC was reporting that there would be a large-scale roundup of Jewish refugees in the Free Zone, Lutty and her family went serenely to bed. At 2 a.m. they were arrested and taken to the community hall in Nice, where 610 foreign Jews were interned. Since the gendarmes had been ordered not to detain Jews under the age of sixteen, Hans-Peter was set free. He found himself alone, not knowing where the buses that were taking his parents and his sister away were going.[47] He turned first to the city's ecclesiastical authorities, without success. But soon Kurt and his daughter Ruth, to whom Hans-Peter had brought their papers, were freed. Lutty remained in detention at the Riquier barracks. The network of horse-racing aficionados proved useful. Kurt Ippen was close to a certain Vieil, a merchant who frequented racecourses and happened to be the president of the grocers' syndicate. Luckily, the person at the prefecture who was responsible for the roundups was his childhood friend: he obtained, not without difficulty, Lutty's release. Unfortunately, the young woman left behind her in the Auvare barracks her sister Nanny Habig. She was deported to Auschwitz in convoy no. 27, which left Drancy on 2 September 1942. She was fifty-two years old.

A year later, when the Germans had taken over the occupation of the Côte d'Azur from the Italians, Lutty was arrested again and temporarily interned in the Riviera Palace, where Kurt and Hans-Peter voluntarily joined her, while Ruth was hidden with a family in the countryside behind Nice. A train took the three of them to the Saint-Pierre prison in Marseilles, where men and women were separated. A fortnight later, after an exhausting thirty-hour journey, they arrived in Drancy in the suburbs northeast of Paris, from where convoys of deportees departed for Auschwitz. In the absence of Alois Brunner, the SS Hauptsturmführer of the internment camp, the Ippens were interrogated by his deputy, Weiszl, a Viennese. Kurt showed him an *Ariernachweis*, a certificate of supposed "Aryanness" obtained from the commune of Sadowa, where his father had been born, and which he had had prepared in order to leave Vienna in 1939. Kurt was freed, but refused to leave his wife: the three Ippens – the parents and their son – were then put in the "barbed-wire zone", between the Germans' office and the camp proper, where the "undeportables" were held.[48] For Lutty, née Gutmann in Vienna in 1901, the danger was great. Employed as an interpreter, Kurt enjoyed freedom of movement. His job put him in direct contact with Brunner, a confirmed murderer who without hesitation sent tens of thousands of Jews to their deaths, including many children. As a fellow Viennese, this SS notable offered to free Kurt's wife and son if Kurt could find a job and accommodation. Thanks to René Pélat, a trainer,[49] Kurt obtained a contract of convenience as the manager of a racehorse stable at Maisons-Laffitte. Once again, the horse world had played its part. Freed, the Ippens settled in Maisons-Laffitte, where they rented a house. In April 1944 they received a visit from an agent of the UGIF who announced the immediate arrival of Alois Brunner, who had been struck by a sudden desire to go riding.[50] Many years later, Hans-Peter recounted this nightmarish episode: Lutty, petrified, was forced to greet Brunner; the latter talked affably about his childhood in Hungary:

> He expounded the theories of the Nazi regime for my father's benefit. Jews are at the root of all the evil that exists in the world. Therefore humanity must be freed of them once and for all, using the most efficient methods, without succumbing to weakness [...]. When he returned from the stable, my father felt very shaken by what he had heard and experienced, but we were relieved that the danger was past and hoped we would never think about this "visit" again.[51]

In the family no one ever mentioned this episode. Having moved definitively to 11 Avenue Carnot in Maisons-Laffitte, the Ippens survived as exiles, dreaming of an impossible return to Vienna. After the war, Hans-Peter got his licence as a racehorse trainer, a passion that he left behind only when he entered the monastery thirty years later.[52]

38

Resistance Fighters

MONIQUE AND HER husband Raymond Leven thus remained in France with their children. In 1940 they first lived precariously at the Hôtel du Midi in Montauban, then also moved to a farm, as Monique tells us:

> At the end of those nine months, our hands and legs swollen with chilblains because of the cold and the lack of fatty foods, in danger of falling truly ill, we finally found, about fifteen kilometres from Montauban, hidden at the end of a long lane of magnificent parasol pines, a small, completely isolated farm four kilometres from the village of Lavilledieu.[1]

Cut off from everything, they acquired the habit of listening in secret to Claude Bouret's "Free France" news broadcast on the BBC:

> It was impossible to communicate, impossible to send or receive any news. We had learned indirectly that Yves had enlisted from London in the Foreign Legion. And then nothing more. Raymond was already quite active. He got in contact with my cousin Philippe de Gunzbourg, who directed the network in [the department of] Lot-et-Garonne.[2]

Their goal was to continue the fight alongside the Allies. Like them, many members of the family opposed Hitler's Germany, resisting "from the inside" (in clandestine networks) or "from the outside" (in Free France).

The story of their experiences reveals a shared capacity for resolute action that has its roots in a family tradition of combining a fight for justice with patriotism. After the war, they neither prided themselves on their resistance nor took advantage of it. Some of them left written accounts of this period, others never talked about it, even to those close to them.[3] As they saw it, they had taken on their natural responsibilities when faced with the barbarity of the time.

In 1942 Philippe was contacted by Maurice Pertschuk, known as "Eugène", on behalf of Winston Churchill's Special Operations Executive (SOE). SOE was looking for agents to organise the resistance in France. The young paterfamilias, who was both an anglophile and an anglophone, did not hesitate.[4] He carried messages and sought recruits. "Eugène" often visited Le Barsalous: he was under the spell of both the Yorkshire pudding made by Alice Joyce, the Gunzburgs' courageous nanny who chose to share their fate, and the beautiful Antoinette... Philippe was bothered less by this penchant than by "Eugène"'s lack of discretion: he took very few precautions. Unfortunately, Pertschuk was arrested on 12 April 1943 and deported to Buchenwald, where he was executed.[5] During this first year of resistance, Philippe's status as a Parisian who had taken refuge at Le Barsalous served as a cover for him. Antoinette and the nanny helped him pick up and hide British secret agents who had been parachuted in, as well as messages and weapons, sometimes in the baby's crib. "[Antoinette] occasionally also served as a liaison agent in town; she could meet SOE officers at a restaurant in Agen without attracting the attention of the local police. No one knew [that they] were Jews and, besides, it seems that at that time and in this region, no one cared."[6]

After Pertschuk's arrest, Philippe met George Starr, known as "Hilaire", the SOE's new agent. Far more professional, Starr found lodging in an inconspicuous railway worker's home in Agen. Philippe became the principal go-between in the Dordogne for a man he considered a "great leader". Starr took over the members of SOE's "Prunus" network who had escaped arrest. He was aided by Yvonne Cormeau, known as "Annette", who had been parachuted in to handle the radio connection with London. Philippe learned to assemble plastic explosive charges, organised sabotage missions on railway depots (at Eymet and Bergerac) and trained dozens of small groups of resistants to receive deliveries by parachute.[7] In the meantime he succeeded in getting Antoinette and their children into Switzerland. A member of the same network, Maurice Loupias, whose alias was "Bergeret", left an eloquent portrait of Philippe, who went by the name of "Philibert":

Philibert, who supervised the southern Dordogne and Lot-et-Garonne area, was a Frenchman, although he was often mistaken for an Englishman on account of his appearance. He had a property in Lot-et-Garonne that he had had to abandon, and that was how he had taken over the maquis in our region.

An ardent patriot, he had, I think, sense and a taste for adventure. On several occasions he showed extraordinary sangfroid.

One day, in Marmande, he was staying at the apartment of Christian, the head of that arrondissement. Three German police officers came in. They ran into Philibert on the stairs. They were not looking for him; they were looking for Christian. So they asked Philibert: "Are you M. Cambon [Christian]?" "No," Philibert replied. He walked calmly past the three policemen and went off to queue at the post office to buy some stamps. In him there was, mixed with a great deal of determination, a certain fatalism; he intended to buy stamps, and he was going to buy his stamps. He was right to do so.

The policemen searched the house, went into his bedroom, found the photo of his wife, whom they knew, and realised that they had made a mistake and let a big fish get away. They rushed out into the street to shoot him, and ran to the railway station. They did not find him and never for a moment thought that he was simply buying stamps at the post office.

Philibert played a leading role in the southern Dordogne. He not only obtained for us all the things parachuted in and approved our territories, but later on he also settled in the region and supervised the organisation of the Resistance down to the last detail. It was he, notably, who set up the sabotage of railway depots. He was the main architect of our victory.[8]

Philippe later explained his involvement in British operations as follows:

I was raised, especially on my father's side, in an atmosphere of immense admiration for Britain and its empire. I spoke the language almost as well as I spoke French. I knew the habits of the English and their customs, and above all I had – here I am not speaking of the

England of today, which I do not know – an absolute confidence in their word, their loyalty and their respect for the individual. On the other hand, it is certain that – like everyone, and like people like me in particular – I had been very shaken by the defeat, by the racist, anti-Jewish attitude and by people's rapid about-face, and in the end I was troubled by the notion of "collaboration".[9]

During the same period, Monique and Raymond Leven also received weapons parachuted in by the British, and concealed agents and refugees: "We hid in our house Jewish families who had fled Poland and other places," Monique wrote. "We took in Royal Air Force pilots who had been shot down and whom we accompanied back to Toulouse by rail."[10] Going to Toulouse was particularly perilous because of the presence of many German soldiers and the frequent checks made in the train: such missions, undertaken by one or other of them, always took place in an atmosphere of great fear. One day Monique received an alarming message from her aunt Daisy, Salomon's daughter, who was about sixty years old. Having fled Belgium alone, she had taken refuge in Rodez, in the Aveyron, and had been ordered to present herself at the Gurs camp in the department of Basses-Pyrénées within forty-eight hours. Monique saved her life:

Carrying false papers, I immediately boarded the train for Rodez. The journey took several hours. To avoid the German patrols that were going through the carriages, I had to spend the whole trip locked in the third-class toilet. Arriving in the evening, I rushed to the small hotel room where I found my poor aunt weeping, trembling with fear: she had become like a terrified child, incapable of controlling her actions, incapable of making any decision whatever. All night we shredded, cut up and burned linens, papers, etc. that bore her name or her initials. Then at dawn, while the night-watchman was still asleep, we left the hotel without any luggage. No one noticed us; and we got into the first train to Lyons, where, once again, we had to lock ourselves in the toilet during the whole trip.[11]

In the ladies' toilets at Lyons railway station, Monique hastily made a new identity card for her aunt, using false papers that she had taken care to bring with her, a stamp from police headquarters and a photo peeled off an old identity card. Then they took the train to Megève, but had to get off in the middle of the countryside to avoid a patrol with dogs. "By an incredible coincidence, my brother Alexis, who had escaped Germany, where he had been a prisoner, was trying to get into Switzerland. My aunt and he miraculously met in Megève and crossed the border together. I returned to Montauban, in the same comfort of the toilet, my mission accomplished."[12]

Shortly afterwards, when the small farm of Canteloube was providing shelter for more and more refugees (as many as eighteen people), a price was put on Raymond's and Monique's heads. To protect their children, in January 1943 they decided to move secretly to Annecy, in order to cross into Switzerland. Monique recounted this taxing adventure:

> Travelling through the countryside, avoiding roads, walking over ploughed fields covered with melting snow, mud into which the children's little shoes sank, slipping, stumbling on this clayey terrain of hills and woods. We had to avoid the roads at all costs because they were constantly watched and patrolled by German soldiers with their dogs, ready to shoot you at the slightest alert.[13]

After endless interrogations by the Swiss border guards, where the mere mention of the Deutsch de la Meurthe Cup (an international aeronautics contest) served as a guarantee, Monique and her children were interned in Les Charmilles, a military "triage" camp in Geneva. The day after she arrived, she received a message telling her that her father Robert had died the day she had entered Switzerland, 7 January 1943. In the end the pastor assigned to the camp, at the request of Monique's mother-in-law who was registered in Geneva as a Protestant, succeeded in obtaining the release of the children, swiftly followed by Monique's. "Immediately, all three of us moved into the Coupier pension in Geneva, where we were overjoyed to find Antoinette de Gunzburg and her sons Patrice and Jacques, accompanied by their English nanny [Philippe de Gunzburg was running the maquis in Lot-et-Garonne] and Liliane Rosenthal with her sons Jacky and Hubert [Jean Rosenthal was running the maquis in Haute-Savoie]." Raymond had also remained in France to continue the battle. Antoinette had crossed into Switzerland under identical conditions, but had not experienced the same internment. The British had automatically taken care of her, without Philippe "needing to point her out".[14] Before the war, in 1937, Robert had set up, with his habitual taste and in case it proved necessary, a house in Lausanne. Despite the tight restrictions on refugees, who were forbidden to leave Geneva, Monique moved into the Villa Fontvieille, where her Aunt Daisy joined her.[15] Although Monique and Antoinette resumed a normal life, communicating with their husbands in the Resistance was out of the question. Philippe was leading a particularly dangerous life. His daughter Hélène tells us:

> He never slept two nights in the same place, and roamed all over the Dordogne and Lot-et-Garonne on his bicycle. He had built up links with members of the Resistance everywhere in the zone, but he only trusted completely the few of whom he was certain: mostly women and a few men, among them André Ruff, a young fellow traveller and bodyguard whom I met later on. Secrecy was paramount and mobility of the essence. Philippe continued to handle the increasingly large parachute deliveries and the distribution of weapons to all the Resistance networks, along with the use of plastic explosives to blow up roads, railways and warehouses. He operated at night, very quickly and with few companions, and handled the most arduous and risky tasks himself, including the elimination of dangerous traitors. On several occasions he managed to elude the Gestapo, often by relying on his survival instinct, his knowledge of the terrain and his intuition.[16]

In the spring of 1944, agents of the SOE were coordinating the Resistance from Bergerac to Sarlat and from Toulouse to Auch. From 7 June onwards, well-trained networks were slowing the advance of the 2nd SS Panzer Division "Das Reich", which was moving up from the south towards Normandy. Reprisals were becoming increasingly savage, and reached a violent extreme on 10 June when one of the division's Waffen SS units sealed off the village of Oradour-sur-Glane and massacred 642 of its inhabitants. During this period of hard fighting, Philippe helplessly witnessed the death of some of his men. He remembered Loiseau, whose asparagus fields along the Dordogne had served as a hiding place for the Resistance fighters' weapons, and who was killed in July 1944: "Leading his group, he achieved a great deal, not least the nine German tanks he could take credit for. He died as he was on his way to meet me one evening, killed in a vineyard by the Germans."[17] "We didn't have military officers or stripes," Philippe finished by saying. "It was all done with terrible mistakes, mine were dreadful, but thanks to loyalty and friendship, in this region two thousand men delayed for some considerable time a

After the Bolshevik revolution, all the Gunzburgs living in Russia were forced to go into exile. Véra de Gunzburg's passport, delivered by the Russian consulate in Paris, 1918.

Pierre de Gunzbourg, his brother Vladimir (with a cane), and their wives, in Caux, above Montreux, in the 1920s.

Philippe de Gunzbourg and his grandfather Emile Deutsch de la Meurthe in the Bois de Boulogne, circa 1920.

Nicolas de Gunzburg, called Nicky,
a paragon of elegant living, in the 1930s.

Cyrille de Gunzbourg, in the Alpine
corps. He died of pneumonia during
his military service in Briançon in 1932.

Aline de Gunzbourg, golf champion of France in 1934.

The marriage of Hélène, called Lia, the daughter
of Sasha de Gunzburg, to Alexandre Berline,
in Amsterdam, 17 December 1936.

Aline de Gunzbourg and her brother Philippe in the French Free Zone, winter 1940. Philippe subsequently organised the resistance network in southern Dordogne and Lot-et-Garonne for the British SOE.

Sasha de Gunzburg and his daughter Anna Halpérin, Cannes, circa 1939. After fleeing the Bolsheviks in 1918, Sasha later experienced another exile, in Switzerland, to escape the Nazis.

Alain de Gunzburg at the Free France military academy (Bewdley, Worcestershire) in 1944. On his right, his friend Jean Géraud-Vinet (Société des cadets de la France libre).

Nanny Habig, née Gutmann, Horace de Gunzburg's granddaughter, was deported from Drancy on 2 September 1942, convoy no. 27. She was murdered at Auschwitz.

Four generations: Yvonne de Gunzbourg, her daughter Aline Berlin, her grandson Michel Strauss, and her great-grandson Andrew. Headington, Oxford, 1962.

German armoured division, which, exhausted and demoralised, arrived in Normandy six weeks late."[18]

Family members who had joined Free France then returned to French soil after several years of absence. Having left Saint-Jean-de-Luz in June 1940, Yves fought the whole African campaign in the Foreign Legion. His cousin Alain, Jean's son who had taken refuge in the United States and had enrolled at Harvard, soon followed his example: in New York, on his eighteenth birthday, 19 January 1943, he enlisted in the army created by General de Gaulle, as is shown by his declaration of support: "I, the undersigned Alain de Gunzburg, declare that I place myself at the disposal of the Free French forces in which I wish to serve in a military capacity. I further declare that I accept the rank and assignment that will be given to me and am ready to serve anywhere with honour, loyalty and discipline for the duration of the war currently being waged."[19] Having left New York on 13 August 1943, he arrived in Britain, at Bristol, on 28 August. On 13 September he was assigned to the Ecole des Cadets de la France Libre. This school had been established by de Gaulle to train for military service the hundreds of young men who had responded to his appeal of 18 June 1940. As the Saint-Cyr (that is, the elite military academy) of Free France, it mixed volunteers from all kinds of backgrounds, the children of fishermen alongside bankers' sons.[20] The volunteers were de Gaulle's pride and joy: he called them "my children". "Circumstances required that young people of very diverse origins, leanings and antecedents live together," wrote a teacher. "There were workers' sons, Catholics, Protestants, Jews and those with no religion at all; spoiled children, and others whose early years had been hard..."[21] At Ribbesford House in Worcestershire they were subject to strict discipline, both intellectual and physical. The instructors, André Baudoin (a teacher at the lycée in Kabul) and Louis de Cabrol (a cavalry officer), provided rigorous training. Rather than the clandestine action they had dreamed of when they signed up, the cadets found themselves taking courses and examinations: mathematics, history-geography, Morse code, mine-clearing, topography. Inside the school gates, everything was done at the double. The physical training was intensive: military obstacle courses, crossing rivers and marching 80 kilometres carrying equipment. In a film made on site, *Ils s'instruisent pour vaincre*, the future "class of 18 June", to which Alain belonged, is shown in all its activities. Discipline and high personal achievement are seen as second nature to a group of young people presented as "exemplary".[22] The future section leaders had to be "fighting animals" who "still bite when men no longer want to attack".[23] A photograph taken at this time shows a smiling Alain with his comrade Jean Géraud-Vinet, who had come directly from Madagascar, both wearing cadets' uniforms. In the class photograph, he is a young, myopic soldier wearing glasses, quite slight, confident of the future even if his poor eyesight made it impossible for him to be an airman, which had been his preference. He now knew that he was classed 49th out of 150. At the passing-out parade presided over by General Koenig, he chose his "arm" and unit: army, cavalry. His matriculation book gives the details of his service record: on 28 July 1944 he was appointed as a liaison officer, definitely a family speciality, to the technical military mission of the American Third Army. On 17 October 1944 he joined 2nd Armoured Division, where he served "in the reinforcement battalion, on the staff, and in the 12th regiment of cuirassiers". Thus he took part in the campaign to liberate France (the Royan operations) and then in the German campaign, notably the liberation of the Dachau camp. France awarded him the "médaille commemorative française de la guerre 1939–1945", with bars reading "Engagé volontaire", "Libération" and "Allemagne". The American government awarded him the Presidential Unit Citation. Described by his commander as "a young officer candidate who is intelligent, well brought up and well turned out", speaks "admirable English", "knows the American mentality very well", and was "rendering undeniable services" in his current position, even if he was not "a leader of men" and needed to improve his military knowledge."[24] Very discreet and keen to leave those testing years behind him, he hardly ever mentioned his Free France past.[25]

Alain's path did not cross that of his cousins who had also enlisted in the Gaullist forces. Serge, Vladimir's son, served with "extreme diligence" as a second lieutenant in the artillery and as a radio operator, and was awarded the Order of the Regiment, the citation for which listed his qualities: "On many occasions, he distinguished himself by his perfect knowledge of his duties, his calm and his clear thinking. Provided valuable help to his artillery lieutenant, allowing the battery to rapidly launch the shelling requested." No one had had any news of Yves since his departure for the Basque country. Monique decided to return to Paris to find her brother, whom the Red Cross had declared missing in action. "After endless searching, I learned indirectly that Yves was alive, that he had fought in the whole African campaign from Chad to Syria, Lebanon, the Egyptian border of Libya, the Battle of El-Alamein, the fierce fighting at Monte Cassino and finally to Alsace... He had fought the whole campaign as a simple soldier, refusing any advantage, carrying nothing more than his musette bag and a little monkey that was always with him." In a photograph from May 1944, Yves is a relaxed Legionnaire with a magnificent smile. Brother and sister agreed to meet in liberated Paris; Yves thought he could get leave to go there. In November 1944 Monique returned to France: "After so much worry and five years of absence, my capital was splendid. Alexis had escaped from Switzerland and reached Paris. All three of us were finally going to be together again: that seemed incredible."[26] But the war was not over: instead of resting, Yves' division went to the Vendée, where the fighting was intense. Then the Legion moved to Alsace, and near Colmar, in the forest of Elsenheim, just before Christmas, Yves was killed at the age of twenty-four. His posthumous citation with the Order of the Army appeared in the *Journal Officiel* for 24 June 1945:

> Gunzburg (Yves), 2nd Class, matriculation no. 353, of the Nth Brigade [*sic*] of the Foreign Legion: a model soldier. Escaped from France under difficult conditions, joined the Free French forces in 1941. Has since not stopped fighting, in Libya, Tunisia, Italy and France. Well known for his composure and courage under fire, surpassed himself in the hard fighting in the forest of Elsenheim, where he was admired by all for his bravery, his energy and his unfailing good humour. Voluntarily cut short a twenty-four-hour rest to take part in the operations in which he was killed on 30 January 1945. A fine figure of the "Free French" who, despite having an education and a culture that would have allowed him to become an officer, wished to serve in the inconspicuous role of an artillery Legionnaire, thereby setting an example of willing humility for the triumph of the great cause.[27]

Yves was buried in the Châtenais cemetery near Sélestat in the department of Bas-Rhin, along with five of his comrades from the First Division of the Foreign Legion who died in the same battle. In addition, his cousin Alain Prévost, the son of Bibka Merle d'Aubigné, who was in the Free French forces, was killed in the south in 1944, shortly after the landing in Normandy.

39

Spoils

ALTHOUGH LIFE SEEMED to be resuming its ordinary course, nothing would ever really be the same for the Gunzburgs. The loss of family members and friends was accompanied by many changes, both personal and financial. For those who survived, relief was at first the dominant emotion, as demonstrated by a letter from Philippe to his parents Pierre and Yvonne and to his sister Aline, dated 30 September 1944: "For you three, we met [with Antoinette] on 9 September. We are alive, in good health and happy, and have been at the Ritz for 48 hours. The children are in Switzerland and will remain there for a while, we will go to see them as soon as possible. We will also go to London, and come to see you before. Avenue d'Iéna is not available; it has been requisitioned again."[1] The Nazi administration had, in effect, been replaced by the Allies. Philippe's personal situation was uncomfortable: his involvement with the British SOE made the French Resistance suspicious of him. "I had become a foreign agent, paid, self-interested, sold," he recounts. But he was chosen to liquidate the networks in the southwest, "that is, charged with not only the recovery of weapons and documents after the war, but also with verifying the service of Resistance fighters." Disappointed and despondent, he thought about leaving, perhaps for England. After 1947, he also thought about becoming an Israeli citizen.[2] But he loved France too much, and ended up going to live in the Lot-et-Garonne, which he jokingly called "*le* Southwest", a region that he knew so well now and that had become dear to him. A baby daughter, Hélène, born in 1947, was followed by Alix in 1948. But his marriage to Antoinette was no longer so happy. He found Marguerite de Gramont, known as Margot, whom he had met in the

Resistance while in SOE, and married her in 1952.[3] Beautiful, courageous and elegant, Margot formed, with Philippe, a flamboyant couple. In 1953 they had a daughter, who died at the age of ten, several years after an accident in a park in Oxford that left her in a vegetative state; a loss that neither Margot nor Philippe ever got over.

Philippe's sister Aline, on the other hand, decided to settle permanently abroad. Remarried to the famous physicist Hans Halban[4] in 1946 in New York, she gave birth to a son, Peter, and then in 1950, in Oxford, where they had moved, to a second son, Philippe. Aline married again in 1956, to the charismatic philosopher Isaiah Berlin. Their mother Yvonne, who was widowed in 1948, decided to remain in the United States, returning every year for a long stay in Europe. New York had become a new home base for many members of the family. From time to time, the astonishing Nicky visited his aunt, always with pleasure. Yvonne had become very involved in the American branch of ORT, which was particularly active, and where her niece Gavrik Ashkenasy worked. Yvonne was also very close to Willy, the widow of Fedia, who had died prematurely of cancer in 1945, and to their children, Macha and Dimitri. They had fled Holland in 1940 and, after passing through southern France and Switzerland, had also settled in the United States. Lia, Fedia's little sister, and her husband Alexandre Berline, followed the same route of emigration from Holland to the United States, also with their two young children, Elisabeth and Michel, born in 1938 and 1941.

After the Liberation, two Frances confronted one another in an atmosphere of intense division. For those who came back from forced exile, their return was accompanied by the sad realisation that they had been dispossessed. It was no easy matter to recover property: for example, Robert and Lucie's town house at 25 Avenue Bugeaud had been bought, as a Jewish property, at a very low price by an industrialist from the north, a collaborator named Raoul Malard.[5] He was living there happily with his beautiful young mistress and refused to contemplate leaving. As he prepared to give a sumptuous New Year's Eve party there in 1944, Monique and Alexis put large posters with swastikas on the surrounding walls night after night: "House stolen by a German occupation profiteer."[6] They also tried to plead their case with various authorities: "Notaries, lawyers, the Minister of the Interior, the Ministry of War, the police chief, we told all of them, and Malard bribed all of them behind our backs." Malard finally offered to sell for 45 million francs, even though in 1940 he had paid a total of 1,200,000 francs since it was a Jewish property. The Gunzburgs categorically refused the offer and continued their campaign, supported by people in the neighbourhood; Malard was finally forced to leave.

> The shopkeepers and neighbours on Avenue Bugeaud rushed to witness this much-awaited departure. They came in their hundreds, gathered in front of our houses [*sic*], shouting and applauding, and their extraordinary enthusiasm exploded when the big garage door opened and six large cars emerged, including a Cord, a Packard, etc., followed by a large tanker full of petrol.[7]

There was a petrol shortage and everyone was getting around by bicycle. "The profound and sincere sympathy of all the residents of the neighbourhood moved Alexis and me indescribably." During this period, husband and wife were not always together. Monique spent the summer of 1945 in Biarritz, where the Villa Ehorria was one of those requisitioned for use by American officers. "Our duty as women was to organise the houses, to get them ready, to provide food and comfort for these heroes." She decided to go and see her mother in New York and took advantage of a Liberty ship that was sailing from Bordeaux. Mother and daughter had not seen each other since 1942. "At the Hotel Carlyle, my mother did not recognise me. She was bowled over, and so was I." But "the life there, suddenly so serene, so peaceful, seemed to me atrociously empty, hollow, goalless, with no *raison d'être*," Monique observed. Back in France, her reunion with Raymond did not go well. The couple divorced in 1947 and Monique went to live in the United States near her mother Lucie.

From New York, although his son Alain had not yet returned from his German campaign, Jean began, with his brother-in-law André Louis-Hirsch, to take steps for the so-called "recovery" of the numerous goods that had disappeared, despite the precautions taken in 1940. He put together a file entitled "Spoils", into which he put all correspondence with the authorities and the various inventories drawn up for the purpose. A perusal of these documents shows that the process begun in the spring of 1945 was to go on for a decade, with mixed results. The sub-file entitled "Recovered" proves that they won their claims for some of their property, but that the rest was still lost in the vast web of artworks sold off by the Nazis and their collaborators. Although they had not been known as great collectors, the Gunzburg and Hirsch families had nonetheless put together, over two generations, an exceptional group of artworks, as is attested by the lists drawn up at the time of the war. They had a taste for eighteenth-century – Regency, Louis XV and Louis XVI – furniture and art objects: chests of drawers, pedestal tables, roll-top desks, beds, armchairs, sometimes stamped (Leleu, Cressent, Boulle, etc.); they had a large number of ancient Chinese porcelain mounted on bronze bases, as well as sculptures and paintings by old masters, the latter being more definitively identified and consequently proving easier to "recover". These spoils represented a significant loss from a heritage point of view as well as financially and sentimentally, the effect of which is difficult to assess. Judged by the yardstick of loss of life, this page in the history of the Second World War may seem of minor importance. But "dispossession" was one more violent act suffered by Jews all over Europe, in addition to the other duresses they suffered.

A few weeks after the Liberation, and before the German army had even left French territory, General de Gaulle's provisional government embarked on a systematic search for works that had been stolen. The Commission de Récupération Artistique was set up in the Jeu de Paume museum, where hundreds of thousands of complaints were centralised: a *Répertoire des biens spoliés en France de 1939 à 1945* (Directory of Objects Despoiled in France from 1939 to 1945) was soon published, in which a few paintings or pieces of furniture that had belonged to the Gunzburg and Hirsch families are mentioned.[8] Published in French, English, German and Russian, this inventory was supposed to assist agents seeking to recover despoiled property from all over Europe. On 19 July 1945, André Louis-Hirsch sent a letter to the Office des Biens et Intérêts Privés, a department of the Ministry of Foreign Affairs:

> From the outset, I wish to mention that a certain number of art objects belonging to the widow of M. Louis Hirsch and to Baron Jean de Gunzburg, which were at the Banque de France, have been carried off by the Germans. These objects include, among others, several pastels by La Tour (*Portrait of the Marshal de Belle-Isle, Portrait of the Artist's Wife, Portrait of an Unknown Man*), a certain number of Guardis and several paintings by old masters, a list of which has been supplied to M. Karl Dreyfus, the curator of the Louvre Museum.

In addition, the objects that disappeared from Avenue du Maréchal-Fayolle, most of which are identifiable, were taken away by the Germans. For your information, [I mention that] this house was occupied during the war, first by Admiral Raeder, then by Admiral Doenitz, and became the headquarters of the *Kriegsmarine* [the term used to designate the German navy, 1935–45].[9]

In 1944 the German navy had been superseded in the family building by the Direction Générale des Etudes et Recherches (DGER), Free France's intelligence service. Steps were thus taken in parallel by André Louis-Hirsch so that the family could have use of their building again. As was legally required, testimonies describing the despoliation were enclosed with the letter. Thus Paul Chaignon, "Madame Louis Hirsch's authorised representative", recounted the conditions under which "room 104 at the Banque de France" had been pillaged: "On 12 March 1941, I was summoned by the D.S.K.[10] The room was opened in my presence and that of officers and delegates who took possession of crates, paintings, statuettes, bronzes, furniture, etc., without giving any receipt. [On the] order of the Paris headquarters, [these objects were] put at the disposal of Dr Rosenberg in the Louvre." The goods left on deposit at the Banque de France were inventoried: in addition to the clocks, carpets, china and objets d'art, twenty-four pictures (pastels, oils and drawings) are described, including "two views by Guardi", "three small landscapes painted on a cigar box by Hubert Robert" and "two portraits of Monsieur and Madame Boucher, by Roslin".[11]

In May 1946, André Louis-Hirsch sought advice from a member of the Commission de Récupération Artistique as to how best to proceed. "Forgive me for bothering you with this," he wrote, "but you will understand how much, after five years of captivity, including a year in a fortress, I would like to find this furniture of which I have been robbed." Taken prisoner by the Germans in Toul in June 1940, he had in fact just been freed by the British. He claimed that a "certain number of pieces of furniture [...] taken from [his home] on Avenue du Maréchal-Fayolle were stored in 1943 at the Hôtel de Lauzun [which belonged to the city] and in a building belonging to the City of Paris near the Arsenal. The watchman at the Hôtel de Lauzun states that much of this furniture must have been sold at auction."[12] In addition, two Sisleys (*Le Port de Moret* and *Soleil de printemps. Tournant du Loing*) and a Fragonard (*Fauchon la vielleuse*)[13] that were entrusted to the Argentine embassy, which in turn deposited them in a box at a Spanish bank in August 1940, were stolen as well. These three paintings constituted the key pieces in the family's collection. In July 1946, the stolen goods were evaluated at 2,541,391 francs in the case of Jean and 3,331,200 francs in the case of his mother-in-law. Some of them, however, were to be rapidly recovered: on 14 January 1947, the Service de Récupération Artistique restored to "Madame widow Louis Hirsch" sixteen paintings, including the two Guardis and the portraits of the Bouchers, husband and wife, by Roslin. "Furniture, pictures, and objets d'art belonging to Monsieur Jean de Gunzburg [...] stolen by the Germans, found in Germany" were also returned on the same day: Madrazo's portrait of Jean's mother Henriette was included in this lot. In 1954 and 1955, messages were again exchanged with the Ministry of Reconstruction and Urban Planning regarding the proposed compensation.[14] With Jean's death on 28 November 1959, at the age of seventy-five, in his apartment on Avenue du Maréchal-Fayolle, a part of the family memory disappeared. Along with his sister Daisy and his cousin Aniouta, he was one of the last of Joseph Evzel's grandchildren still alive. After his brother-in-law André Louis-Hirsch died in 1962, the "Spoils" file was closed for many years.

In 1979, when Madeleine, Jean's wife, died, Pierre, the youngest of their three sons, chanced to come across reproductions of the Sisleys in the family papers. Intrigued, he tried to find out what had happened to the paintings. In 1985, he discovered that *Soleil de printemps. Le Loing* had been exhibited in Tokyo, in a retrospective devoted to the famous impressionist. But it was not until 2004, after a long legal battle conducted by agents of the Office Central de Repression du Trafic des Biens Culturels, that the Japanese owner agreed to return the canvas. A systematic examination of the inventory of goods that disappeared from the apartment on Avenue du Maréchal-Fayolle leads one to think that many pieces of furniture and works of art are still "lost" today. Among the objects missing from the "master bedroom" two portraits are mentioned: *Portrait du baron Ury de Gunzburg,* signed by Meissonier, and *Portrait du baron Salomon de Gunzburg.* We can only hope that they will someday be restored to their rightful owners.

Epilogue

So ends our account of the destinies of Joseph Evzel and his very numerous descendants – "when I can't sleep I count Gunzburgs," one of them said. However, their history is not over. In his will the founder of the bank exhorted his children and grandchildren to accept their responsibilities both to their professions and to their communities, to their families and their countries. But the tragic course of events brutally severed their link with Russia. While geographically the family has never ceased to extend itself and is flourishing on all continents, a common spirit endures: a memory of their Russian past and loyalty to their Judaism. At the dawn of the 1950s, the generation that had experienced the war chose to live without wasting time: shortly after Sasha's death in Basle in 1948, Véra had the satisfaction of witnessing the marriage of her daughters Katia and Tania (the former to a Swiss banker, Hans Guth, and the latter to a French member of the Resistance and entrepreneur, Jean Blum). As an art historian and founder of the Jewish Museum of Basle, Katia has kept vigilant watch over the ad hoc collection of numerous family documents. Their cousin Alain married Minda Bronfman, a young Canadian whose father Samuel, a great philanthropist and early supporter of the state of Israel, founded the famous firm of Seagram, which specialises in the sale of alcoholic beverages. If the Free France cadet thus strengthened his ties with the American continent, faithful to the *art de vivre* inherited from his parents and grandparents, he nonetheless chose to settle in Paris, on Avenue Bugeaud. Married to Isaiah Berlin, the intrepid Aline recreated in her house in Oxford the brilliant universe of the former family homes and the gift of artistic friendships, sitting as a model for Lucian Freud. Her brother Philippe, who was passionate about the rural economy, succeeded in establishing himself professionally in the Lot-et-Garonne and successfully defended the production of the *prune d'Ente* (used to make the famous *pruneaux d'Agen*). Monique, remarried to Giorgio Uzielli and a worthy daughter of Robert, decorated with impeccable taste magnificent houses on Long Island and in Porto Santo Stefano. As the result of a journey to Cairo, where her aunt Clara von Gutmann lived, Ruth Ippen married Samy Harari there. They lived in Egypt until 1969, when they were forced to leave after the confiscation of their property and Samy's imprisonment. Ruth's brother Hans-Peter, having devotedly cared for his mother and bred Maisons-Laffitte's racehorses, finally entered the Trappist monastery at Soligny under the name of Brother Jean-Pierre, and established a major library of Hebrew theology there.

Although Joseph Evzel's descendants are scattered around the world, they all retain a portion of the family history: memories, letters, pictures, photographs, objets d'art, furniture, identity papers – so many scattered pieces that have enriched this book with valuable personal perspectives. Among the many personalities discussed, Anna, Horace's discreet wife, emerges as a central figure. Her sudden death in Paris in 1876 at the age of thirty-eight left her family inconsolable and no doubt slowed its ascent in Paris: she had been essential to her father-in-law Joseph Evzel's integration into French society, and, after her death, her husband chose to raise his family back in Russia. Her children, her brothers- and sisters-in-law, her nephews and nieces, all loved and admired her. She had watched over their upbringing with an exceptional devotion and had attracted distinguished friends to the town house on Rue de Tilsitt. In the St Petersburg Jewish community, her name was long honoured for the aid she gave to the most destitute, notably orphans. Many years after the death of the "marvellous Anna", her son Sasha, arriving in turn at the end of his life, mentioned her in his last wishes: "Addressing myself to all the children together, I give them no recommendation regarding their conduct, because to do so would be to lessen the certainty that I take with me to the grave that they are all equally worthy of Mama." Beyond borders and eras, the spirit of the family has remained intact.

Paris, November 2017

Notes

Part I

Dream World: Joseph Evzel in Paris

1. Alexandre de Gunzburg, Manuscript D, "Mémoires de jeunesse". Written in the 1930s, these memoirs refer to the period 1870–1917. Alexandre (designated in this book by the diminutive Sasha) should not be confused with his uncle Alexandre Sizkind, Joseph Evzel's eldest son.

1

The Hôtel des Trois-Empereurs

1. Official declarations made by some of Joseph Evzel's descendants confirm that the Gunzburgs took up residence in Paris in 1857. See AN, File no. 4213X13, "Demande de naturalisation de Michel de Gunzburg et de sa femme Thérèse née Hermann, 7 avril 1913", and File no. 5696X1925, "Demande de naturalisation de Vladimir Georges de Gunzburg, 22 mai 1925".
2. Alexandre de Gunzburg, Manuscript C, "Installation à Paris", and Manuscript D, "Mémoires de jeunesse": "During my childhood, the family ate 'kosher' and we never travelled without our 'shochet', M. Goldstein."
3. The Hôtel des Trois-Empereurs, which subsequently became the Grand Hôtel du Louvre, was located across the street from its current site on Place du Palais Royal.
4. *Le Monde illustré*, 8 May 1858.
5. This region, in the west-central part of present-day Ukraine, became a Russian imperial possession after the second partition of Poland in 1793. It then became the Podolia Governorate, whose administrative capital was the city of Kamenets-Podolsk (now Kamianets-Podilskyi).
6. Henri de Pène, *Le Figaro*, May 1858, rpt. in full in *Le Gaulois*, 24 August 1887. See also Alexandre de Gunzburg, Manuscript C, "Installation à Paris".
7. *Le Monde illustré*, 8 May 1858.
8. Oil on canvas, in the archive of Dimitri de Gunzburg. See also the engraving entitled "Portrait d'homme", in which we recognise Joseph Evzel, reproduced in Emmanuel Bréon, *Claude-Marie, Edouard et Guillaume Dubufe: Portraits d'un siècle d'élégance parisienne*, Paris, Délégation à l'action artistique de la ville de

Paris, 1988, p.173. To identify the portrait we can also refer to the mention of a "Portrait of I. E. Gunzburg par Dubufe" in the inventory of the lots constituted at the time of Horace de Gunzburg's death in 1909, RNB, f.183 ed. khr. 1653.

9. Theophile Gautier, *Les Beaux-Arts en Europe en 1855*, Paris, 1855.

10. Etienne-Jean Delécluze, *Les Beaux-Arts en 1855*, Paris, Charpentier, 1856, p. 277, quoted in Emmanuel Bréon, op. cit., p. 14.

11. In 1858 Edouard Dubufe painted the portraits of "Madame Callaghan, Monsieur Gunzbourg [*sic*, hence Joseph Evzel], Marquise d'Aramon, Mademoiselle Halephen [*sic*], Princess Youssoupov, Countess Andrassy, Monsieur Raimbaud, Madame Armand, Countess Tolstoy, Count Jaubert, Madame Amory's daughter, Princess Trubetskaya, Monsieur H.[orace] Gunzbourg [*sic*], the daughter of Countess Imécourt, Madame Douglas Baird, Monsieur and Madame Yussupov". Ibid., p. 161.

12. *Le Gaulois*, 15 January 1878: "Everyone knew his mansion in Rue de Presbourg, where he took pleasure in showing his friends and visitors a bed made of solid gold which he had had the singular idea of using to decorate his reception room."

13. Louise Halphen, "Récit de Louise Halphen, née Fould, écrit au Moulin Barry (Indre) en 1943", unpublished manuscript.

2

Mathilde's Marriage

1. Louise Halphen, loc. cit.

2. Following Berr Leon Fould, other young men belonging to Jewish families from eastern France succeeded in Paris: Salomon Halphen, Olry Worms de Romilly, Alexandre Deutsch de la Meurthe. On the Foulds, see the magisterial work by Frédéric Barbier, *Finance et politique. La dynastie des Fould XVIIIe–XXe siècle*, Paris, Armand Colin, 1991.

3. Ibid., pp. 182, 302. Cyril Grange, *Une élite parisienne. Les familles de la grande bourgeoisie juive (1870–1939)*, Paris, CNRS Editions, 2016.

4. Frédéric Barbier, op. cit., pp. 302–3.

5. Paul Fould left the Conseil d'Etat when it passed a law against congregations (decrees of 29 March 1880 signed by Charles de Freycinet, president of the Council, and Jules Ferry, the education minister, to expel the Jesuits and force other religious congregations to request authorisation within three months): "The conservative members resigned, and my father followed them." Louise Halphen, op. cit., p. 6.

6. Frédéric Barbier, op. cit., p. 171.

7. Ibid., p. 182.

8. AN, Minutier des notaires, MC/ET/LXXXVII/1635 (document signed on 9 March 1862, in the presence of Maître Delaporte), and MC/ET/VIII/1882 for the version bound in leather.

9. Paul Fould, *De jure dotum: "Du contrat de mariage"* thesis, University of Paris law school, 1859.

10. AN, Minutier des notaires, MC/ET/LXXXVII/1635.

11. Joseph Evzel endowed all his children comfortably: Alexandre, Horace and Ury

each received a portion of 500,000 roubles, or 1,200,000 francs, and Salomon received 2,300,000 francs. According to Cyril Grange, during the period between 1870 and 1939, the contributions made by future husbands were on average 8 per cent greater than those made by their wives. In Jewish families of the upper bourgeoisie, men and women taken together, the average contribution was 374,357 francs, which corresponds to 1.375 million euros at 2011 prices (Grange, op. cit.).

12. Ibid., p. 186.
13. AN, Minutier des notaires, MC/ET/LXXXVII/1635.
14. Ibid.
15. Elsa Warburg-Melchior, "That Dear Past: Random Memories", unpublished manuscript, 1949 (in collaboration with Ruth Melchior Fleck) (archive of Dimitri de Gunzburg / archive of Tania Blum).
16. Louise Halphen, op. cit., p. 1.
17. Ibid.
18. Ibid., p. 2.

3

7 Rue de Tilsitt

1. AN, Minutier des notaires, MC/ET/VIII/1748.
2. Philip Mansel, *Paris, capitale de l'Europe, 1814–1852*, Paris, Perrin, 2003, p. 471.
3. Théophile Gautier, *Paris et les Parisiens*, Paris, "Boîte à documents", 1996, p. 131 (1856).
4. With its recently restored roof and façades, the Gunzburg town house has retained its original appearance. It was classified as a historical monument in 1983. The first owner's monogram is still visible in certain rooms.
5. *Le Gaulois*, 24 January 1875.
6. Alexandre de Gunzburg, Manuscript D, "Mémoires de jeunesse".
7. Ibid.
8. *Le Gaulois*, 24 January 1875. In 1883, Ury de Gunzburg, Joseph Evzel's son, sold to the Paris auction house Druot "The Twelve Months of the Year and the five tapestries of the sequel to Don Quixote based on Coypel's paintings", the former for 62,500 francs and the latter for 99,600 francs (*Revue des arts décoratifs*, "La curiosité et les ventes. Courrier de l'hotel Drouot", Paris, 1883).
9. Alexandre de Gunzburg, Manuscript A, "Ricard".
10. Ibid.
11. Alexandre de Gunzburg, Manuscript D, "Mémoires de jeunesse".
12. Ibid.
13. Ibid.
14. Ibid. Sasha was remembering the winter of 1875, when sleighs were brought out in Paris. "Only Michel Ephrussi had a real Russian sleigh with a *polutroika* (a demi-troika), which aroused our patriotism and our pride." Astonishingly there is no trace of the Gunzburgs in the albums published by the Deltons, the "equestrian photographers" and faithful chroniclers of social events in the Bois de Boulogne. Published in 1876, *Les Equipages à Paris* shows Count Orlov's

Russian trotter, while the *Tour du Bois*, published in 1882, presents Mademoiselle Ephrussi and the counts of Camondo on horseback.

15. Alexandre de Gunzburg, Manuscript A, "Quelques souvenirs de la génération précédente".
16. Ibid.
17. Alexandre de Gunzburg, Manuscript D, "Mémoires de jeunesse".
18. Louise Halphen, op. cit., p. 4.
19. Alexandre de Gunzburg, Manuscript D, "Mémoires de jeunesse".
20. Ibid. En route from Switzerland to the Bohemian spas.
21. Ibid.
22. Joachim Ambert , "Le siège de Paris, 1870–1871", in *Gaulois et Germains: récits militaires*, Paris, Bloud et Barral, 1883–1885, p. 99.
23. Alexandre de Gunzburg, Manuscript D, "Mémoires de jeunesse".
24. Ludwig III, Grand Duke of Hesse and by Rhine, "Freiherr von Günzburg", 2 August 1874 [document of ennoblement] (archive of Gérard de Gunzburg). Regarding the ties between the House of Hesse and Horace de Gunzburg, Sasha wrote: "Prince Alexander of Hesse, the father of the reigning grand duke and of the empress [Alexandra], felt a very special friendship for my father and never failed to visit him when he came to Petersburg. These friendly relations continued with his children, the princes of Battenberg, and when Alexander of Battenberg was named Prince of Bulgaria, he asked my father to build him a railway and to set up a national bank. For several years we had visits from Bulgarian ministers and officials, but never managed to arrive at a final agreement." (Alexandre de Gunzburg, Manuscript A, "Ma chère Lilia").
25. Certificate of authorisation to use the title Baron by Salomon de Gunzburg (decision of the Russian Senate, 25 January 1882): "On the basis of the supreme order dated 27 May 1879, he is authorised to use the baronial title conferred on his family by his Royal Highness the Grand Duke of Hesse." Rights were granted on 15 February 1882 by *ukase* of his Imperial Majesty and in conformity with the Senate's decision; identical certificate issued for Jean Maurice, son of Baron Salomon (decision of the Russian Senate, 17 April 1889) (originals in Russian and French translation; archive of Jean de Gunzburg).

4

The J. E. Gunzburg Bank

1. The successive addresses of the bank: 3 Rue Drouot – 1 Rue Saint-Georges – 25 Boulevard Haussmann.
2. AMT Roubaix, fonds Rothschild, 132 AQ unlisted 76 (Gunzbourg J. E., Saint-Pétersbourg 1860–1869).
3. Nicolas Stoskopf, *Banquiers et financiers parisiens*, Paris, Picard/Cénomane, 2002. Ananich, Boris Vasilyevich, *Bankirskie doma, v Rossii. Ocherki istorii chastnogo predprinimatel'stva*, Leningrad, 1991. In Hebrew, Ilya Vovshin, *The Gintsburg Family and the Formation of the Jewish Plutocracy in the Russian Empire*, thesis directed by Professor Adam Teller, University of Haifa, September 2016.
4. Nicolas Stoskopf, ibid.

Notes

5. *Annuaire-Almanach du commerce, de l'industrie*, Paris, Didot-Bottin (annual publication).

6. Contract signed on 18 July 1876: partnership agreement between Joseph Evzel Gunzburg and his sons Horace and Salomon (J. E. Gunzburg Bank). In French. Archive of Jean de Gunzburg.

7. Ibid.

8. Ibid.

9. The exchange rate for the rouble given in the marriage contract for Salomon de Gunzburg and Henriette Goldschmidt (in 1877). AN, Minutier des notaires, MC/ET/LXIV/886.

10. Contract signed on 18 July 1876, op. cit.

11. Alexandre de Gunzburg, Manuscript A, "Mémoires de jeunesse".

12. Claude Dufresne, *Morny 1811–1865*, Paris, Perrin, 1983 (rpt. 2002).

13. La Grande Société des chemins de fer de Russie was, moreover, to encounter many difficulties in constructing the Warsaw–St Petersburg–Moscow and the Moscow–Nizhny Novgorod lines.

14. Nissim Camondo to Abraham Camondo, 12 March 1869, archives of the Nissim de Camondo museum. Quoted by Cyril Grange, op. cit., p. 20.

15. Nicolas Stoskopf, *Banquiers et financiers parisiens*, op. cit., p. 157. The Gunzburgs are not mentioned.

16. See Edmund de Waal, *The Hare with Amber Eyes: A Hidden Inheritance*, New York, Picador, 2011.

17. Alexandre de Gunzburg, Manuscript D, "Mémoires de jeunesse".

18. Ludwig von Stieglitz (1779–1843) had become the banker to the court of Alexander I and Nicholas I. Of Jewish heritage, he received the title of baron after his conversion to Christianity in 1826. His son Alexandre (1814–1884) became head of the bank until its voluntary liquidation in 1860. He was then named the head of the state bank from 1860 to 1866. He was one of the founders of the Russian Railway Company. A great philanthropist, he founded St Petersburg's Central Academy of Technical Drawing, which is known as the Stieglitz Academy of Art and Industry and has a museum of decorative arts. According to Sasha, Baron Stieglitz "liquidated his bank at the time when that of my grandfather was being founded [...]; [its] clientele passed over to us." Alexandre de Gunzburg, Manuscript C, "Les gens d'affaires".

19. 6/18 October 1861, AMT, fonds Rothschild, 132 AQ unlisted 76 (Gunzbourg J. E., Saint-Pétersbourg 1860–1869).

20. 14/26 December 1862, ibid.

21. 11/23 December 1862, ibid.

22. Rothschild Archives, London XI/118/8B, Sundry correspondence 9B, 1870.

23. AN, Minutier des notaires, MC/ET/VIII 1763, 20/12/1869. Cited by Jean-Yves Mollier, *Le Scandale de Panama*, Paris, Fayard, 1991, pp. 86–7. All the information concerning the Gunzburgs ("an influential St Petersburg banker") is presented in a somewhat confused manner, notably regarding the kinship relations between Joseph Evzel, Horace, Salomon and Jacques. The latter is confused with his grandfather concerning the Franco-Egyptian Bank.

24. AMT, fonds Fould, 115 AQ 006 (Avances Russie 1877–1878).

25. Hubert Bonin, *Histoire de la Société generale*, vol. I : *1864–1890. Naissance d'une banque*, Paris, Droz, 2006.

26. Letter from Joseph Evzel Gunzburg to A. and M. Heine, 3 May 1877. AMT, fonds Fould-Heine, 115 AQ 001, "Affaire Gunzburg. Affaire liquidée 1879."
27. In 1822 the Habers had settled in Paris, where Maurice de Haber (1798–1874) had become a partner of Félix Worms de Romilly. His brother Samuel (1813–1892) was also a banker in Paris.
28. A. or M. Heine to Joseph Evzel Gunzburg, 3 May 1877. AMT, fonds Fould-Heine, 115 AQ 001.
29. Joseph Evzel Gunzburg to A. or M. Heine, 4 May 1877. Ibid.
30. Jean-Yves Mollier, op. cit., p. 153.

5

High Society and the Demi-Monde

1. *Le Gaulois*, 24 January 1875. The ball was held on 22 January at the Gunzburgs' home.
2. In Sasha's memoirs: "It was also in 1872 that I saw at my mother's table the famous general [Nikolay] Muravyov-Amursky, who was already very old, and since we are talking about Siberia, I have not forgotten the old general [Nikolay] von Ditmar, who had been governor of Irkutsk. It seems to me that he had lost that post as a result of certain Athenian parties he had given in his palace, where in the groves of the garden there were naked statues in flesh and blood." Alexandre de Gunzburg, Manuscript A, "Ma chère Lilia".
3. Alexandre de Gunzburg, Manuscript D, "Mémoires de jeunesse".
4. Gustave Schlumberger, *Mes souvenirs, 1844–1928*, Paris, Plon, 1934, pp. 328–9.
5. Alexandre de Gunzburg, Manuscript D, "Mémoires de jeunesse".
6. Ibid.
7. Ibid.
8. *Le Gaulois*, 9 February 1875.
9. Ibid.
10. Ibid.
11. Archive of Christine de Gunzburg. The house in Saint-Germain-en-Laye is still in the family.
12. *La Cavalerie de la garde impériale à Saint-Germain-en-Laye 1854–1870*, Les amis du Vieux Saint-Germain, 16 January 1993.
13. Alexandre de Gunzburg, Manuscript D, "Mémoires de jeunesse".
14. *Le Gaulois*, 20 October 1875.
15. Sales contract for the estate, lands and chateau of Cambaudoin in Erceville deposited by Léon Urban François de Poilloüe, marquis of Saint-Mars, for the benefit of Baron Ury de Gunzburg 17 October 1879, Archives départementales du Loiret, AD45, 3 E 44283.
16. Nikolay Dmitriev-Orenburgsky, *Chasse donnée en l'honneur du grandduc Nikolaï Nikolaïevitch*, 1880, oil on canvas, Turgenev Museum, Bougival (France). To paint this picture, the artist had Ury's hunting outfit brought to him a few days after the event, in December 1879. In Paris, the Russian painter was called Dmitriev d'Orenbourg. The work is considered one of "his best pictures" by his colleague Ernst von Liphart, who enumerates thus the figures represented around the grand

duke: "The Gunzburg brothers, Turgenev, Colonel Popov, the organiser of the hunt and others." The picture seems to have been exhibited in the Romanov gallery of the Winter Palace. Ernst von Liphart (Lipgart), *Khudozhniki Salona vremen tret'ey respubliki. My Memoirs.*

17. In accordance with Russian custom, Joseph Evzel's sons went by their patronym Osipovich ("son of Osip", the Russian equivalent of "Joseph").

18. Alexey Bogolyubov to Horace de Gunzburg, 25 December/6 January 1880, in Russian. Archive of Aline Berlin (de Gunzbourg). According to Sasha: "It was probably thanks to Bogolyubov that Uncle Ury provided the hunt, on his Chambaudoin property, for the Grand Dukes Nicholas and Konstantin, who were spending a certain amount of time in France. After the Great Turkish War there had been frictions in St Petersburg between the high military authorities and Grand Duke Nicholas, who had not conducted the war the way those gentleman thought it should have been conducted. As for Grand Duke Konstantin, he was considered too liberal. They were thus urged to spend some time far from Russia." Alexandre de Gunzburg, Manuscript A, "Bogolyubov".

19. Ibid.

20. Ibid.

21. An illustrative list of portraits of members of the Gunzburg family whose existence is attested or simply mentioned in certain documents: Léon Bonnat (portraits of Anna, Henriette); Edouard Dubufe (Joseph Evzel, Horace, Anna); Marc de Gunzburg (Pierre as a child); Alexey Kharlamov (Horace, copy of the portrait by Kramskoy); Nikolay Kuznetsov (Anna Ashkenasy); Ivan Kramskoy (Horace, Louise and Rubinstein with Horace and Mathilde-Babita in public); Raimundo de Madrazo (Henriette); Hugues Merle (Louise Sassoon, Alfred-Mimi); Ernest Meissonier (Ury); Gustave Ricard (Rosa, Anna, Horace, Mathilde-Babita, sketch by Alexandre); Eduard Veith (Horace); Mihály Zichy (Vladimir as a child, Louise as a young girl).

22. Léon Bonnat to Anna de Gunzburg, 10 September 1874, archive of Aline Berlin (de Gunzbourg).

23. Ibid., undated [1874–1876], archive of Aline Berlin (de Gunzbourg).

24. Léon Bonnat to Horace de Gunzburg, undated [1877], archive of Aline Berlin (de Gunzbourg).

25. Ibid.

26. Léon Bonnat, *Portrait posthume d'Anna de Gunzburg*, oil on canvas, dimensions: 128 x 90 cm, signed "Ln. Bonnat" in the upper left corner, undated (as posthumous portraits often are). Fondation Comte Ciechanowiecki, London and Warsaw, deposited at the castle of Łańcut. A copy was made by the Russian painter Kharlamov, one of Bonnat's pupils, and is today at the Alliance Israélite Universelle. See Guy Saigne, *Léon Bonnat (1833–1922), portraitiste, catalogue raisonné des portraits peints, dessinés et gravés*, Thesis, Paris, Ecole doctorale histoire de l'art et archéologie, 2015.

27. Léon Bonnat to Horace de Gunzburg, 15 January 1878, archive of Aline Berlin (de Gunzbourg).

28. "Ricard painted portraits of my grandmother, my mother, my father, and my sister Gutmann that are in the Bonnat Museum of Bayonne, and made a sketch of me at the age of six." This sketch was in Sasha's house in St Petersburg, and was stolen after the revolution. "Merle painted portraits of my sister Sassoon and of my

brother Alfred." Alexandre de Gunzburg, Manuscript A, "Ricard".

29. Alexandre de Gunzburg, Manuscript B, "La Guerre".
30. Letter from Salomon de Gunzburg to David de Gunzburg, 18 November 1898, RNB, fonds 183 ed. khr. 424. "I wish to inform you that I would like to sell the portrait made by Meissonier because a few years ago you expressed the desire to have it, and perhaps now you would like to pay the 15,000 francs that I spent on it. As a painting it is very good. A single defect is that the costume is not Louis XV or Louis XVI, because then this portrait would find a buyer at 80,000 francs."
31. See chapter 39, "Spoils".
32. Alexandre de Gunzburg, Manuscript A, "Ricard".
33. Given by Vladimir de Gunzburg's descendants to the Serge Rachmaninoff Russian Conservatory in Paris, the portrait was sold by Christie's on 24 November 2014. Sasha mentions it in his memoirs: "Zichy had done a portrait of my brother Volodia. He was represented when he had just picked up his toys from the floor and his dress was hitched up, showing his behind. Maman had told the painter that the breeches were much too short and asked whether he could change something, given that flesh-coloured legs emerged from the white breeches, which were not coloured. No problem – seizing his charcoal, he lengthened the breeches with a shadow of six to ten centimetres, at a place that had no other shadow, and people did not notice this anomaly unless it was pointed out to them." Alexandre de Gunzburg, Manuscript A, "Zichy".
34. Alexandre de Gunzburg, Manuscript A, "Massenet".
35. Zichy and Horace de Gunzburg corresponded regularly. Archive of Aline Berlin (de Gunzbourg).
36. Alexandre de Gunzburg, Manuscript D, "Mémoires de jeunesse".
37. Alexandre de Gunzburg, Manuscript A, "Massenet".
38. Alexandre de Gunzburg, Manuscript D, "Mémoires de jeunesse".
39. Ibid.
40. Anne Martin-Fugier, *La Vié élégante ou la Formation du Tout-Paris (1815–1848)*, Paris, Fayard, 1990.
41. Lola Gonzalez-Quijano, "Le demi-monde: prostitution et réseaux sociaux dans le Paris du xixe siècle", online article (https://f.hypotheses.org/wp-content/blogs.dir/1429/files/2013/09/réseaux_demimonde_LGQ-1.pdf).
42. Ibid.
43. Ibid.
44. Gabrielle Houbre, *Le Livre des courtesans: archives secrètes de la police des moeurs (1861–1876)*, Paris, Tallandier, 2006, pp. 42–3.
45. APP, F 82. File with photo. 5 December 1871.
46. Ibid.
47. APP, BB7, Ernestine Blanche d'Antigny, quoted by Gabrielle Houbre, op. cit., p. 177.
48. Daria 306 September 1873. Quoted by Gabrielle Houbre, op. cit., p. 285.
49. APP, BB7 (40 individual files on loose women), DA389 Sylvia Asportas, known as Sylvie.
50. APP, BB7, Galinetti 684 (a photo in her file).
51. Chair of the central committee of the Alliance Israélite Universelle en 1881, Salomon Goldschmidt was the son of Benedict Hayum Salomon Goldschmidt

(1798–1873), who was himself the son of Hayum Salomon Goldschmidt.

52. AN, Minutier des notaires, MC/ET/LXIV/886.
53. *Le Gaulois*, 19 February 1885.

6

The Patriarch

1. Marc de Gunzburg to Horace de Gunzburg, 2 February 1874, RNB, f. 183 ed. khr. 1712.
2. Alexandre de Gunzburg, Manuscript D, "Mémoires de jeunesse".
3. Joseph Evzel Gunzburg to his grandson David, 6 September 1874, in Russian. RNB, f. 183 ed. khr. 398.
4. Russian will of Joseph Evzel, archive of Jean de Gunzburg.
5. A meeting point for these families from geographically different areas and different traditions, at that time Paris played a decisive role in the unification of the Jewish high society of Europe.
6. "In the family, we were very pious," Sasha wrote, "and [...] we said our prayers morning and evening, but at the same time Mama required us to greet the curés and nuns whom we met in the street." Alexandre de Gunzburg, Manuscript D, "Mémoires de jeunesse".
7. Ibid.
8. Ibid.
9. Ibid.
10. Miss Sheppard had already been the Rosenberg girls' governess in Kamenets-Podolsk in the 1830s. "She was of an exemplary severity and the word 'shocking' was constantly on her lips." Alexandre de Gunzburg, Manuscript D, "Mémoires de jeunesse".
11. Ibid.
12. Octave Mirbeau, "Tout-Paris", *Le Gaulois*, 17 September 1879.
13. Gavrik Ashkenasy and Elisabeth Lorin, *Gavrik's Memories As Told to Elisabeth*, unpublished manuscript, pp. 7–8.
14. Alexandre de Gunzburg, Manuscript D, "Mémoires de jeunesse".
15. Louise Halphen, op. cit.
16. Alexandre de Gunzburg, Manuscript D, "Mémoires de jeunesse".
17. Alexandre de Gunzburg, Manuscript D, "Mémoires de jeunesse", and Heinrich Sliozberg, op. cit., p. 34.
18. Alexandre de Gunzburg, Manuscript D, "Mémoires de jeunesse".
19. About the library Sasha writes: "What is interesting to note is that many of these documents were acquired, in agreement with his father [Joseph Evzel], by my Uncle Ury, who was one of the most lightweight and dissipated members of the family." Alexandre de Gunzburg Manuscript C, "Aperçu généalogique".
20. *Shire ha-Shirim Asher li-Shelomoh* (1868), poems by Ibn Gabirol edited, punctuated, and annotated by Sachs, published in Hebrew with the French title *Cantiques de Salomon Ibn Gabirole [Avicebron]*. Alexandre de Gunzburg, Manuscript C, "Collaborateurs de mon grand-père".
21. Alexandre de Gunzburg, Manuscript C, "Collaborateurs de mon grandpère".

22. Ibid.
23. David Patterson, *Abraham Mapu, the Creator of the Modern Hebrew Novel*, London, East and West Library, 1964.
24. Abraham Mapu to his brother, Kovno, 2/07/1859, Yivo, RG 223-2, Folder 39-1.
25. Alexandre de Gunzburg Manuscript C, "Collaborateurs de mon grandpère".
26. Alexandre de Gunzburg, Manuscript D, "Mémoires de jeunesse".
27. Ibid.
28. Ibid.
29. On 9 October 1805, near the city of Günzburg, Marshal Ney's armies defeated the Austrian troops commanded by General Mack.
30. Elsa Warburg-Melchior, "That Dear Past: Random Memories", unpublished manuscript, 1949 (in collaboration with Ruth Melchior Fleck) (archive of Dimitri de Gunzburg / archive of Tania Blum).
31. Alexandre de Gunzburg, Manuscript D, "Mémoires de jeunesse".
32. Anna de Gunzburg to Horace de Gunzburg, undated (1869), on a letter from David de Gunzburg to Horace de Gunzburg, RNB, f. 183 ed. khr. 1710.
33. Elsa Warburg-Melchior, op. cit.
34. Alexandre de Gunzburg, Manuscript D, "Mémoires de jeunesse".
35. *Notes of Olga Lachmann-Warburg*, archive of Katia Guth-Dreyfus.
36. Alexandre de Gunzburg, Manuscript D, "Mémoires de jeunesse".
37. Modest Mussorgsky to Vladimir Stasov, Tsarskoye Selo, 14–15 June 1877, quoted in *Moussorgski, Correspondence*, translated, presented and annotated by Francis Bayer and Nicolas Zourabichvili, preface by André Lischke, Fayard, 2001. *Josué Navine*, a composition for mezzo-soprano, mixed chorus and orchestra, is the version revised in 1874–75 of "Choeur des Libyens" extracted from the unfinished opera *Salammbô*.
38. Alexandre de Gunzburg, Manuscript D, "Mémoires de jeunesse".
39. Horace de Gunzburg to Marc de Gunzburg, 15 August 1877, Saint-Germain-en-Laye, RNB, f. 183 ed. khr. 1953.
40. Horace de Gunzburg to Marc de Gunzburg, 7 August 1877, Saint-Germain-en-Laye, RNB, f. 183 ed. khr. 1953.

Part II

The Time of Battles: In Tsarist Russia

1. Lazare Isidor, "Paroles prononcées sur la tombe du baron Joseph de Gunzburg," in *Oraisons funèbres prononcées sur la tombe du baron Joseph de Gunzburg le 15 janvier 1878*, Paris, D. Jouaust, 1878, p. 14.

Notes

7

Rabbis in Swabia and Lithuania

1. Lazare Isidor, ibid., p. 13.
2. Acronym of the Hebrew Morenou HaRav Loev, "our master Rabbi Loeb".
3. See Ada Ackerman, ed., *Golem. Avatars d'une légende d'argile*, Paris, Musée d'art et d'histoire du judaïsme, 2017.
4. Called the *editio princeps*, Bomberg's edition presents three texts side by side: in the centre, the Talmud (*Mishna* and *Gemara*), with Rashi's commentary in the inner margin and the commentary of Rashi's disciples in the outer margin. The *Mishna* is a collection of decisions and laws that issued from the tradition definitively established by Rabbi Juda Hanassi, in Israel, toward the end of the second century CE. The *Gemara* is the commentary. Two commentaries have come down to us: the *Gemara* of Jerusalem (the Jerusalem Talmud) and the *Gemara* of Babylon (the Babylonian Talmud). See Marc-Alain Ouaknin, *Invitation au Talmud*, Paris, Flammarion, "Champs essais", 2008, pp. 49–59.
5. He is also known as Rabbi Simon ben-Eliezer Gunzburg-Ulma.
6. David Maggid, *Sefer Toledoth Mischpechoth Ginzburg*, St Petersburg, 1894, and a partial French translation of the same, *Histoire de la famille Gunzburg* (unpublished manuscript in the archive of Katia Guth-Dreyfus). Maggid's work was expanded and corrected by Sigmar Ginsburg, *Die Geschichte unseres Zweiges der Familie Ginsburg*, Tel Aviv, 1946 (unpublished manuscript in The Center for Jewish History, New York). Notably, Sigmar Ginsburg corrects an error made by Maggid, who confused Simon ben Eliezer Gunzburg with Simon ben Abraham Gunzburg, whose grandfather Yehiel and father Abraham were natives of the city of Porto, on Lake Lugano, near Verona in Lombardy (and not in Portugal). The mistake was repeated by Heinrich Sliozberg in his biographical essay *Baron Horace O. de Gunzbourg, sa vie son oeuvre, publié à l'occasion du centenaire de sa naissance*, Paris, 1933. Sigmar Ginsburg based himself not only on Maggid but also on reference books and the following scholarly sources: Israel Tobiah Eisenstadt and Wiener Samuel, *Da'at Kedoshim, Materialen zur Geschichte der Familien welche ihre Abstammung von dem im Jahre 1659 im Litthauischen Städtchen Rushani in Folge einer Blutbeschuldigung als Märtyrer gefallenen herleiten*, Saint-Pétersbourg, 1897–1898; Leopold Löwenstein, "Günzburg und die schwäbischen Gemeinden", in *Blättern für jüdische Geschichte und Literatur*, Mosbach und Mainz, 1899–1902; "Memorbuch der Gemeinde Pfersee", in Dr Mosche Stern, *Memorbooks written during the 16th to the 19th Century in Suabian Jewish Communities*, Jerusalem, 1941, pp. 5–25.
7. Sigmar Ginsburg, op. cit., p. 3.
8. Marc-Alain Ouaknin, op. cit., p. 75.
9. The Jewish cemetery in Burgau was no longer used after 1634–35. It is supposed to have been located on the site of present-day Walter Ludwig Strasse.
10. David Maggid, op. cit.
11. Otto von Ausbourg, or Otto Truchsess von Waldburg-Trauchburg (1514–1573).
12. The scholar Chayim Josef David Azulai found the manuscript in 1754, among Simon's descendants in Pfersee. The current annotation in the library in Munich

explains: "This is the only manuscript in the world that contains, with the exception of two missing leaves, the complete text of the Babylonian Talmud, including non-canonical treatises: Derekh Eretz zuta, Pirkei Azzai, Kalla, Sôferîm and Gērîm. It also includes texts not directly related to the Talmud. Thanks to numerous entries of the owners' names, it is possible to follow the history of this manuscript, which was written in France in 1342. According to the entry of a manuscript of a bible now in the national and university library of Hamburg, this Talmud was in the possession of the Ulmas, a family of Jewish businessmen in Pfersee, near Augsburg, in 1772. Later it was sold to the Augustinian priory of Polling (in Upper Bavaria). After the dissolution of the monastery in 1803, the manuscript was transferred, along with other very valuable works, to the court library in Munich, today the Bavarian State Library."

13. According to David Gans, the author of the chronicle *Zémah David*, quoted by David Maggid, op. cit., p. 3.
14. Sigmar Ginsburg, op. cit., p. 9.
15. See especially Marc-Alain Ouaknin, op. cit., pp. 88–9. Regarding the *Shulkhan Arukh* and its additions, which are sometimes self-contradictory, Ouaknin writes: "When there is a discussion between Rabbi Yossef Karo and Rabbi Moshe Isserles, the *sefardi* (Jews who come from Spain and North Africa) follow the former's decisions, and the *ashkenazi* (Jews who come from Germany and eastern Europe) follow the latter's views."
16. David Maggid, op. cit., p. 3.
17. Sigmar Ginsburg, op. cit., p. 13.
18. *Kissenplate*, 1614. The child is Jacob, the son of Simon Ulmo-Gunzburg and his wife Breinel, the daughter of Simon's brother Abraham.
19. Katia Guth-Dreyfus, "Eine Süddeutsche Textilie aus dem frühen 17. Jahrhundert", in Rolf Kiessling and Sabine Ullmanna (eds), *Landjudentum im Deutschen Südwesten*, Akademie Verlag, pp. 220–25.
20. Sigmar Ginsburg, op. cit., p. 10.
21. Vilna is the former name of present-day Vilnius.
22. Jozef Finn Shmuel, *Kiryah Neemana* (a monograph on the rabbis of Vilna, "the faithful city", not translated).
23. Henri Minczeles, Yves Plasseraud, and Suzanne Pourchier, *Les Litvaks. L'Héritage universel d'un monde juif disparu*, Paris, La Découverte, 2008.
24. See Israël Halperin, *Pinkas vaad arba aratsot*, Jerusalem, Bialik Institute, 1945.
25. LVIA, f. 458, op. 1, d. 65-66 (1715), d. 98 (1728).
26. The *heder* was usually located in the home of the teacher (*Melamed*) and accepted boys from five to thirteen years of age.
27. David Maggid, op. cit., p. 8.
28. Unfortunately, the records of the supreme organ of Jewish autonomy in Poland have almost completely disappeared, with the exception of a few documents copied by the historian Simon Dubnov and preserved in the archives of the YIVO (Center for Jewish History, New York).
29. LVIA, F 11 Op. 1 D 1014.
30. David Maggid, op. cit., p. 24.
31. Notably for the years 1789 and 1790, LVIA, f. 620, op. 1 (Vilenskij evrejskij Kagal 1764-1921), d. 41.
32. David Maggid, op. cit., p. 24.

33. Ibid.
34. Samuel Joseph Fuenn, *Kiryah Neemana*, 1860, pp. 26–27, quoted by Jean Baumgarten, "Vilna, entre ultraorthodoxie et modernité (xviiie–xixe siècle)", *Revue germanique internationale*, 2010, no. 10, pp. 61–78.
35. YIVO, Simon Dubnov, Folder 979, Decisions of Lithuanian assessors in the trial of the Vilna *kahal* of 1867.
36. See Elie Wiesel, *Célébrations hassidiques. Portraits et légendes*, Paris, Le Seuil, 1976.
37. Alexandre de Gunzburg, Manuscript C, "Aperçu généalogique".
38. "Der Minister Naftali Herz Ginzburg von der Gemeinde Söhne Israel in der Stadt Wilna", 1803. A photograph of the holy ark is in the archive of Katia Guth-Dreyfus.
39. Henri Minczeles, Yves Plasseraud and Suzanne Pourchier, op. cit., p. 10.
40. The Talmud Torah was the religious school financed and administered by the Jewish community. At the beginning of the nineteeth century, Vilna still had three rabbis descended from the Gunzburg family and relatives of Joseph Evzel: Israel Gunzburg (or Ginzberg) (1784–1857), a judge and secretary of the rabbinate of Vilna, an expert in the domain of the licit and the illicit, and known as Rabbi Eliezer Zarecher, from the name of the neighbourhood where he lived. A man of great modesty, he asked that the answers he gave people who came from all over to consult him not be published. He advised his relatives and friends to be content to inscribe on his tomb only that he had taught in public, in Vilna, for forty-three years; Aryeh Leib Gunzburg (?–1850), very learned, head of the school in 1818, was also frequently consulted in the event of litigation. His younger brother, Eliah Samuel Gunzburg, who divided his time between writing and a not very flourishing commercial activity, ended his days in an old people's home in Vilna.

8

Gabriel Yakov, *kupets* (merchant)

1. Aelita Ambruleviciuté, *Vilniaus pirkliai žydai 1801–1861 metais (sąrašas)/Vilnius Jews Merchants 1801–1861 (list)*, Žydų kultūros ir informacijos centras, Vilnius, 2012.
2. Thus in 1824 the merchants of the Third Guild paid an annual tax of 438 roubles, those of the Second Guild paid 1,345 roubles, and those of the First Guild paid 3,212 roubles.
3. Account by Gavriil Dobrynin, quoted by Arkady Podlinsky, *Evrei v Vitebske*, Vitebskaya oblastnaya Tipografiya, 2004, p. 12.
4. Letter from Rabbi Chneer Zalman for the defence of Russia. See Saul M. Ginzburg, *Otechestvennaya voyna 1812 goda i russkie evrei*, St Petersburg, 1912.
5. Six major battles were waged nearby: the Battle of Ostrovno, the Battle of Klyastitsa, two battles in the region of Polotsk, the Battle of Czaśniki, in the northern part of Vitebsk province, at Verkhniadzvinsk, and at the fortified camp of Drissa, mentioned by Tolstoy in *War and Peace* – one of the Russian army's principal military fortifications and the headquarters of the Russian general Michel Barclay de Tolly.

6. David Maggid, op. cit, p. 36.
7. Alexandre de Gunzburg, Manuscript C, "Aperçu généalogique".
8. At that time there were 7,631 Jews in the government of Vitebsk.
9. Two letters from Joseph Evzel to Gabriel Yakov, 2 May and 6 June 1832, RNB, f. 183 ed. khr. 2262. Translated from the Hebrew by Professor Abraham L. Udovich.
10. David Maggid, op. cit., p. 37.
11. Ibid.
12. David Maggid, *Toledot Mishepot...*, op. cit., pp. 145–7.

9

Kamenets-Podolsk and the Gunzburg Trading Agency

1. A. Rosen, H. Sarig, and Y. Bernstein, eds., *Kaminits-Podolsk and its Environs: a memorial book of the Jewish communities in the cities of Kaminits-Podolsk, Balin, Dunivits, Zamekhov*, Bergenfield NJ, Avotaynu Foundation, 1999. Translated from the Hebrew by Bonnie Schooler Sohn.
2. In Podolia, 96 per cent of the merchants were Jews. See Alfred J. Richter, *Merchants and Entrepreneurs in Imperial Russia*, Chapel Hill, NC, 1982.
3. Aleksander Prusiewicz, *Kamieniec Podolski : Szkic historyczny*, Warsaw, 1915, p. 28.
4. Alexandre de Gunzburg Manuscript C, "Installation à Paris".
5. Ibid.
6. Philippe de Gunzbourg, "Tout un ensemble", unpublished manuscript, p. 5.
7. Heinrich Sliozberg, op. cit., p. 32.
8. Yuly Gessen, *Istoriya evreyev v Rossii*, St Petersburg, 1914, pp. 205–6.
9. Alexandre de Gunzburg, Manuscript D, "Mémoires de jeunesse".
10. The 16th day of Tebeth 5693, or 25 December 1832.
11. 6 September according to some documents, 11 September according to the inscription on his tomb in the Montparnasse Cemetery.
12. Or "Aktsiz" (paying a tax on trade in alcoholic beverages).
13. Ilya Vovshin, *The Gintsburg Family and the formation of the Jewish Plutocracy in the Russian Empire*, doctoral thesis directed by Professor Adam Teller and defended at the University of Haifa, in September 2015 (in Hebrew).
14. Ibid.
15. See for example Joseph Evzel's letter from Kamenets-Podolsk to F. L. Pereverzev, dated 1856, while the latter was director of the department of general land taxes and receipts: sending him his best wishes for the New Year, Joseph Evzel expresses "his purest gratitude with regard to Pereverzev", RNB f. 569, quoted in Ivanov Alexandre, ed., *Dokumenty po istorii i kul'ture evreyev v arkhivakh Sankt-Peterburga. Putevoditel'. Vedomstvennye arkhivy*, chast' I, Izdatel'skiy dom "Mir" St Petersburg, 2015, p. 209.
16. Alexandre de Gunzburg, Manuscript A, "Quelques souvenirs de la génération précédente".
17. Nikolay Leskov, *Evrei v Rossii: neskol'ko zamechaniy po evreyskomu voprosu*, St Petersburg, 1884, chap. 8. See Mikhail Gavlin, *Rol' vinnykh otkupov v formirovanii krupnykh kapitalov v Rossii XIX v.*, Ekonomicheskaya istoriya, 2002.

18. Avraam Yakov Paperna, in an article published in *Hamagid*, 1857, cited in V. Kel'ner, *Iz Nikolaevskoy epokhi. Rossiya v memuarakh. Evrei v Rossii. XIX vek*, Moscow, 2000, p. 116.

19. Ibid.

20. Alexandre de Gunzburg, Manuscript D, "Mémoires de jeunesse".

21. In *Le Livre de ma vie*, the historian Simon Dubnov describes his parents' destitution after the large family home burned down. All was lost and there was not enough money to rebuild. The Dubnovs were never to know security again. Simon Dubnov, *Le Livre de ma vie. Souvenirs et réflexions, matériaux pour l'histoire de mon temps*, translated from the Russian by Brigitte Bernheimer, Paris, Cerf, 2001.

22. Alexandre de Gunzburg, Manuscript C, "Pojmanniki".

23. Ibid.

24. Ibid.

25. Alexandre de Gunzburg, Manuscript A, "Quelques souvenirs de la génération précédente".

26. See Saul Ginzburg, "Die familye Baron von Gintzburg. Dray doyres shtadlones, tsoke un haskale", New York, Historisches verk, 1937, vol. 2, pp. 117–59. Translated from the Yiddish by Carrie Friedman-Cohen.

27. See "The Curriculum of the State Rabbinical Schools in Zhitomir and Vil'na" in Chaeran Y. Freeze and Jay M. Harris, eds, *Everyday Jewish Life in Imperial Russia, Selected Documents, 1792–1914*, Brandeis University Press, Waltham, Massachusetts, 2013, p. 415.

28. See Saul Ginzburg, "Die familye Baron von Gintzburg...", op. cit. The text refers to Benjamin (or Veniamin) Mandelstam's memories, Chazon la-Moed, II, Vienna, 1877. Veniamin Mandelstam was a journalist and the brother of Leo Mandelstam, hence the uncle of Iosif (the historian) and Max (a renowned ophthamologist), all of whom were involved in the battle for Jewish rights in the second half of the nineteenth century.

29. "Iz zapiski o položenie naroda evreyskogo v Rossii", 1850, YIVO, RG89 folders 754–64, pp. 63204–7.

30. Alexandre de Gunzburg, Manuscript A, "Petites scènes enfantines".

31. Konstantin Skalkovsky, *Vospominaniya molodosti: 1843–1869*, St Petersburg, 1906, p. 109.

32. Quoted by Alina Rebel, *Istoriya evreyev v Rossii*, Moscow, Eksmo, 2013, p. 131. This work also mentions the speech the finance minister gave praising Joseph Evzel Gunzburg: Pyotr F. Brok, "O Nagrazhdenii pochetnogo grazhdanina Gintsburga", 10 August 1856.

33. TsGIA, f. 560, op. 38, d. 143, l. 34.

10

Joseph Evzel, Head of the St Petersburg Jewish Community

1. "Iz vpechatleniy minuvshego veka. Vospominaniya srednego cheloveka", *Evreysakaya starina*, St Petersburg, 1914, vol. 7, vyp. 2, p. 430–31. Quoted in Mikhail Gavlin, *Rol' vinnykh otkupov v formirovanii krupnykh kapitalov v Rossii XIX v.*, Ekonomicheskaya istoriya, 2002.

2. Osip Mandelstam, "Le chaos judaïque", *Le Bruit du temps*, French translation by Edith Scherrer, Geneva, L'Age d'homme, 1990, pp. 33–4 (first edition 1925).
3. Ibid.
4. Horace succeeded him, and then Horace's son David, as did M. Varshavsky, and then Heinrich Sliozberg.
5. Alexander Halban, *A Window on Russia, A Window on the Jews. The Gintsburgs and the Problem of Jewish Integration in Late Imperial Russia*, BA history thesis, St John's College, University of Oxford, 2007.
6. Alexandre de Gunzburg, Manuscript C, "Aperçu généalogique".
7. In the register of St Petersburg merchants in 1867 Joseph Evzel is listed as living in "the Admiralty quarter, 2nd part, Shuvalov house", and in 1869 and the following years at 53 Galernaya Street, St Petersburg. Horace lived at 50 English Embankment and at 143 Fontanka in 1874, then at 62 Liteyny Avenue in 1876 and 1877, and at 20 Konnogvardeysky Boulevard from 1879 onwards.
8. Sasha mentions the "Shuvalov house on Bol'shaya Morskaya Street" as a place of residence in St Petersburg. Alexandre de Gunzburg, Manuscript D, "Mémoires de jeunesse".
9. Other shareholders mentioned were Edouard Meyer, Vineken, Tomson Bonar and Tvejer.
10. Heinrich Sliozberg, op. cit., pp. 28, 32.
11. Théophile married Siegmund Warburg (Hamburg), Rosa married Joseph von Hirsch Gereuth (Würtzburg), Rosalie married Siegmund Hertzfelder (Budapest) and Louise married Eugène Ashkenasy (Odessa).
12. Alexandre de Gunzburg, Manuscript C, "Les gens d'affaires". See chapter 4, note 18.
13. RNB, f. 183 ed khr. 1950, "Administration du comptoir des affaires des héritiers du baron I. E. Gunzburg". Letter of 11 December 1866, "chemin de fer Kiev-Balta". "M. Sobizszeransky has authorised us to pay you 63,000 roubles on his behalf. We promise to pay you in cash at the rate of 25 kopecks per sleeper, amounting, for the 22,000 sleepers to be cut in this forest (of Holaki), to the sum of 55,000 roubles. We hope that the 22,000 sleepers will be received [...] in the course of February."
14. Alexandre de Gunzburg, Manuscript A, "Ma chère Lilia".
15. At the time of the sale of lands to former serfs, Joseph Evzel owned the village of Valya Tsarepaduluy (today Tsarigrad) in the district of Soroksky in Bessarabia. TsGIA, f. 577 op. 2.
16. Ilya Vovshin, op. cit.
17. RGIA F. 1009 op. 2 d. 61. Letters from V. Lvov to Evzel (Osip) Gintsburg 1871–1875. Lvov received a salary of 1,800 roubles.
18. See Aaron David Gordon, *Our Tasks Ahead*, 1920. Aaron David Gordon (1856–1922) emigrated to Palestine in 1904. Influenced by Tolstoy's thought, he promoted agricultural labour there.
19. Alexandre de Gunzburg, Manuscript A, "Quelques souvenirs de la génération précédente".
20. Olga Lachmann-Warburg, op. cit.
21. Alexandre de Gunzburg, Manuscript C, "Les gens d'affaires".
22. In the property also known as the Laval house, built by the architect Jean-François Thomas de Thomon.

Notes

23. The E. M. Meyer & Co. Bank was not far away from the J. E. Gunzburg Bank (30 English Embankment/29 Galernaya Street).
24. Quoted by Aleksandr Lokshin, ed., *Evrei v Rossii, Neizvestnoye ob izvestnom*, Moscow, Dostoinstvo, 2012, p. 108.
25. Alexandre de Gunzburg, Manuscript A, "Le salon de Stassioulevitch" and Manuscript C, "Les gens d'affaires".
26. Mikhail Reutern, quoted in Alina Rebel, *Istoriya evreyev v Rossii*, Moscow, Eksmo, 2013, pp. 132–3.
27. *Diaries of Sir Moses Montefiore and Lady Montefiore comprising their life and works as recorded in their diaries from 1812 to 1883*, edited by L. Loewe, Chicago, Belford-Clarke Co. 1890, vol. II, p. 251.
28. Lev Levanda, *Ispoved' del'tsa*, St Petersburg, 1880. See Alexandre Lokshin, op. cit., p. 108.
29. M. Beyzer, *Evrei v Peterburge*, Jerusalem, 1990. In 1881, the registers listed 17,000. In the same year, Odessa's Jewish population was 150,000.
30. It was only in 1878 that the Gunzburgs obtained authorisation to purchase land on which to build a synagogue, on Ofitserkaya Street.
31. Alexandre de Gunzburg, Manuscript A, "Ma chère Lilia".
32. Alexandre de Gunzburg, Manuscript D, "Mémoires de jeunesse".
33. Mikhail Beyzer, *Evrei v Peterburge*, Jerusalem, 1990.
34. See "The Berman School for Jewish Children in St Petersburg (1865–84)", in Chaeran Y. Freeze and Jay M. Harris, eds, op. cit., p. 391–4.
35. Mikhail Beyzer, op. cit.
36. Zoya Kopel'man, "Gordon. Poet evreyskoy Gaskali", Otkrytiy universitet Izraila (http ://www-r.openu.ac.il).

11

The Struggle for Civil Equality: Military Service

1. Heinrich Sliozberg, op. cit., p. 87.
2. Simon Dubnov, op. cit., p. 242.
3. John D. Klier, "Krug Gintsburgov i politika shtadlanuta v imperatorskoy Rossii", Vestnik Evreyskogo Universiteta v Moskve, 1995, 3, 10. ("The Gintsburg Circle and the Politics of Shtadlanut in Imperial Russia".)
4. YIVO, Tcherikower Archive, Baron Gintsburg Collection, record group 89. These archives have been used notably by Saul Ginzburg, "Die familye Baron von Gintzburg. Dray doyres shtadlones, tsoke un haskale", New York, *Historisches Werk*, 1937, vol. 2, pp. 117–59. ("The Baron Gunzburg Family: Three Generations of Mediation, Charity and Enlightenments", translated from the Yiddish by Carrie Friedman-Cohen, unpublished.)
5. "Zapiska pochetnogo grazhdanina s-peterburgskogo pervoy gil'dii kuptsa Evzelya Gintsburga, Ob ogranichitelnikh uzakoneniyakh o evreyakh," August 1862, TsGIA f. 821, op. 9, d. 77, l.8-17.
6. In 1860 Joseph Evzel was asked to intervene in the case of the imprisonment of the cantonists Chlem Tkachev, Bentsion Nestrov, Yudel Kholyavsko and Abram Feyfer (for refusing to convert).

7. Joseph Evzel sent Brok a letter concerning recruits and the arrears of Jewish communities, January 1855, 4 p. YIVO, Elias Tcherikower Archives, RG 89, folders 754–64.

8. Ibid.

9. Ibid.

10. RNB, f. 183 d. 2263.

11. 15 May 1873.

12. *Statisticheskiye dannye ob otbyvanii evreyami voynskoy Povinnosti za desyatiletniy period 1875–1884*, St Petersburg, Tipografiya M.M. Stasyulevich, 1886.

13. Alexandre de Gunzburg, Manuscript C, "Aperçu généalogique".

14. Ibid.

15. Alexandre de Gunzburg, Manuscript A, "Bogolioubov".

16. Alexandre de Gunzburg, Manuscript C, "Aperçu généalogique".

17. AN, LH/1249/55.

18. Alexandre de Gunzburg, Manuscript C, "Aperçu généalogique".

12

Hevra Mefitsei Haskalah: Society for the Promotion of Culture

1. Alexandre de Gunzburg, Manuscript C, "Aperçu généalogique".

2. The Russian name of the organisation is commonly abridged as OPE: Obshchestvo dlya rasprostraneniya Prosveshcheniya mezhdu Evreyami v Rossii.

3. Note from Joseph Evzel Gunzburg to Prince Gagarin, 1863, quoted by Tcherikower, Elias M., *Istoriya obshchestva dlya rasprostraneniya prosveshcheniya mezhdu evreyami v Rossii. 1863–1913 gg.*, St Petersburg, 1913, vol. I.

4. Ibid., pp. 30–31.

5. Ibid.

6. Jewish secondary schools had been created at the initiative of Sergey Uvarov, Nicholas I's education minister, in 1836. Ibid., p. 33.

7. Written in Hebrew, the letter was addressed to the communities in Vilna, Vitebsk, Mogilev, Grodno, Poltava and Ekaterinoslav. Ibid.

8. YIVO, RG 89, folders 754–64.

9. "Otnoshenie kievskogo popechitelya ot 27 nov 1859", in Elias M. Tcherikower, op. cit., p. 37.

10. Ibid., p. 35.

11. YIVO, RG 89, folders 754–64. This document was signed, notably, by Gunzburg (honorary citizen of the First Guild of St Petersburg), Kershensky (merchant of the First Guild), L. Rosental, Abram Karasik (merchant of the First Guild of Vitebsk) (June 1861).

12. YIVO, RG 89, folders 754–64.

13. *Rassvet*, 1860, no. 27. Created by Osip Rabinovich and Joachim Tarnopol, *Rassvet* existed in Odessa from May 1860 to May 1861, and was continued in St Petersburg from September 1879 to February 1883 by Alexander Tsederbaum and Mikhail Kulisher.

14. *Rassvet*, 1860, no. 8, quoted by Elias M. Tcherikower, op. cit., p. 38.

15. *Rassvet*, 1860, no. 19.

16. Quoted by Elias M. Tcherikower, op. cit., p. 41.
17. Valuyev, 2 October 1863. Quoted by Elias M. Tcherikower, op. cit., p. 44.
18. In addition to Joseph Evzel and Horace de Gunzburg, the founders were I. M. Brodsky, M. D. Weinstein, M. B. Raykh', G. M. Rosenberg, L. M. Rozental, A. I. Gorvits, A. M. Varshavsky, I. German', C. M. Rozental, Ju. M. Rozental', A. Kupernik', V. V. Rozen', A. I. Zak', G. V. Bergenson, N. I. Gorvits', and I. V. Bertenson'.
19. Accounts for 1864 to 1880: of the total expenditure of 226,872 roubles for the Society for the Promotion of Culture, the Gunzburgs paid 63,560 roubles, or 28 per cent. Elias M. Tcherikower, op. cit., appendices.
20. In 1865, of the 10,248 roubles spent on operating costs, 5,819 were paid by Joseph Evzel.
21. Alexandre de Gunzburg, Manuscript C, "Fondateurs de la Société pour la propagation de l'instruction".
22. "Protokol pervogo obshchego sobraniya ot 17 dek. 1863." Quoted by Elias M. Tcherikower, op. cit., p. 61.
23. Elias M. Tcherikower, op. cit.
24. See the article "Ha-Melitz" on the Historical Jewish Press website. Chiefly published in Hebrew, the weekly also published a few articles in Yiddish.
25. J. E. Gunzburg to E. B. Levin, 23 February 1870. Elias M. Tcherikower, op. cit.
26. Plan for the "disarming of the press hostile to Jews", drawn up by Horace de Gunzburg in Paris on 31 August 1873 and sent to Levin. YIVO, RG 89, folders 754–64.
27. 11 January 1863: ukase on fellowships for Jewish students.
28. In 1864, the Society for the Promotion of Culture allocated 3,668 roubles for the encouragement of studies, to which must be added the 2,122 roubles given by Joseph Evzel for twenty individual scholarships. These sums were renewed from one year to the next, with modest variations. Elias M. Tcherikower, op. cit., p. 166 ff.
29. *Evreyskie bratstva mestnye i vsemirnye.*
30. Yakov Brafman, *Golos*, 1876, no. 216. Quoted by Elias M. Tcherikower, op. cit., p. 94.
31. The case of the murder in Saratov of two Christian boys, archives of the Council of State, 26 March 1860, YIVO, RG89 folders 754–64; Alexandre de Gunzburg, Manuscript C, "Aperçu généalogique".
32. The writers Isaac Baer Levinsohn (1788–1860) and Yakov Eichenbaum (1796–1861) inspired the *Haskala* in Russia. The former fought for his co-religionists' rights in the Russia of Nicholas I, defending notably the creation of agricultural colonies. His magnum opus *Bet Yehudah* seeks to explain Jewish spirituality. Letter quoted by Elias M. Tcherikower, op. cit, pp. 136–7.

13

Last Wishes

1. Horace de Gunzburg to David de Gunzburg, 4 September 1875, Paris, in French. RNB, f. 183 ed. khr. 394.
2. Lazare Isidor, op. cit., p. 12.
3. Ibid., pp. 8–9.
4. Alexandre de Gunzburg, Manuscript C, "Aperçu généalogique".
5. See the letter of the secretary of the Society for the Promotion of Culture, L. O. Gordon, sent to L. S. Varshavsky about the death of Baron J. E. Gunzburg and his merits with regard to young Jewish students and the necessity of organising a delegation of students from the university to attend his funeral. Alexander Ivanov, op. cit., vol. I, p. 215.
6. Alexandre de Gunzburg, Manuscript C, "Littérateurs et artistes".
7. *Le Gaulois*, 15 January 1878.
8. Russian will of Joseph Evzel Gunzburg, translated into French by Mathias Mapu, 20 July/1 August 1876, archive of Jean de Gunzburg. Sasha also mentions this testamentary intention of his grandfather's in his memoirs. Alexandre de Gunzburg, Manuscript C, "Aperçu généalogique".
9. Russian will of Joseph Evzel Gunzburg, op. cit.
10. "Pacte de famille", archive of Jean de Gunzburg.
11. 21 February 1878, Distribution of bequests by M. Alexandre (Siskind) Gunzburg to MM. Horace, Ury and Salomon Gunzburg, AN, MC/ET/VI/1284 (estate of Joseph de Gunzburg).
12. 24 February 1878, Transaction between M. and Mme Paul Fould and MM. Horace, Ury and Salomon de Günzburg, AN, MC/ET/VI/1284 (estate of Joseph de Gunzburg).
13. Russian will of Joseph Evzel Gunzburg, op. cit.

Part III

Horace: Banker, Patron of the Arts and Philanthropist

14

A New Head of the Family

1. Heinrich Sliozberg, op. cit., pp. 47–48.
2. Part of the family correspondence is preserved in the manuscript department of the Russian National Library (RNB) in St Petersburg (David de Gunzburg collection – David Gorasevich Gintsburg – f. 183).
3. Horace de Gunzburg to Marc de Gunzburg, 23 April 1876 [s.d], RNB, f. 183 ed. khr. 1953.

4. Horace de Gunzburg to Marc de Gunzburg (then in Paris), 25 February 1876, Nice, RNB, f. 183 ed. khr. 1953.
5. David de Gunzburg to Horace de Gunzburg, 21 February [1878], RNB, f. 183 ed. khr. 1708.
6. Horace de Gunzburg to Rosa, David and Louise de Gunzburg, Berlin, 4 May 1878 [on mourning stationery, with envelope: Mme la baronne de Gunzburg. M. David and Louise. Menton Alpes-Maritimes], RNB, f. 183 ed. khr. 394.
7. Horace de Gunzburg to Marc de Gunzburg, 1 March 1878, Berlin, RNB, f. 183 ed. khr. 1953.
8. Horace de Gunzburg to Marc de Gunzburg, 2/14 March 1878 (n. p.), RNB, f. 183 ed. khr. 1953.
9. Horace de Gunzburg to Marc de Gunzburg, telegram, 3 May 1878 (n. p.), RNB, f. 183 ed. khr. 1953.
10. Horace de Gunzburg to Marc de Gunzburg, St Petersburg, 8/20 March 1878, RNB, f. 183 ed. khr. 1953.
11. Horace de Gunzburg to Marc de Gunzburg, 17/29 March 1878 (n. p.), RNB, f. 183 ed. khr. 1953.
12. In Paris, Marc's teachers were Victor Chavet and Hugues Merle.
13. Horace de Gunzburg to Marc de Gunzburg, 12/24 March 1878 [on mourning stationery], RNB, f. 183 ed. khr. 1953.
14. Horace de Gunzburg to Marc de Gunzburg, 27 [March]/8 April 1878, St Petersburg, RNB, f. 183 d. 1953.
15. Horace de Gunzburg to Marc de Gunzburg, 29 July 1878 [Marc was in "Fontainebleau, villa Sainte-Marie, Seine-et-Marne"], RNB, f. 183 d. 1953.
16. *Catalogue de la section russe à l'Exposition universelle de Paris*, Paris, Imprimerie nationale, typographie Lahure, 1878.
17. Rosa de Gunzburg to Marc de Gunzburg, 19 August 1878, Kreuznach [mourning stationery; letter in French, probably written by Elodie Sternberg, Rosa's female companion], RNB, f. 183 ed. khr. 1956. The town of Kreuznach in the Rhineland was famous for its spa therapy and its chlorinated water.
18. Horace de Gunzburg to Marc de Gunzburg, n. p., [1878], RNB, f. 183 ed. khr. 1953.
19. Horace de Gunzburg to Marc de Gunzburg, 27 November 1878, Paris, RNB, f. 183 ed. khr. 1953.
20. Horace de Gunzburg to Marc de Gunzburg, 4 November 1878, from the steamer *American*, off Lisbon, RNB, f. 183 ed. khr. 1953.
21. Horace de Gunzburg to Marc de Gunzburg, 20 November 1878, Paris, RNB, f. 183 ed. khr. 1953.
22. Horace de Gunzburg to Marc de Gunzburg, 9 December 1878, Paris, RNB, f. 183 ed. khr. 1953.
23. Horace de Gunzburg to Marc de Gunzburg, 11 December 1878, Paris, RNB, f. 183 ed. khr. 1953.
24. Musya Glants, *Where Is My Home? The Art and Life of the Russian Jewish Sculptor Mark Antokolsky, 1842–1902*, Rowman and Littlefield Publishers, Lanham MD, Boulder CO, New York, Toronto, Plymouth UK, 2010, p. 299.
25. Alexandre de Gunzburg, Manuscript C, "Littérateurs et artistes".

15

Turgenev and the Society of Russian Artists in Paris

1. Le Comité de la Société de secours mutuel et d'aide aux artistes russes de Paris to Horace de Gunzburg, 26 December 1878, Paris, archive of Aline Berlin (de Gunzbourg).
2. RNB, f. 438 ed. khr. 28.
3. Le Comité de la Société de secours mutuel et d'aide aux artistes russes de Paris to Horace de Gunzburg, 18 June 1878, Paris, archive of Aline Berlin (de Gunzbourg).
4. According to Sasha, Ivan Turgenev and Horace de Gunzburg carried on an "extensive corrrespondence": "At one time I believed that it had remained in the hands of my Sassoon nephews, because their mother [Louise] collected autographs and Papa had given her quite a few of them. But since then I have learned that this packet of letters was at David's home [in Petrograd] and was scattered by the sailors who pillaged the house. A few of these letters have been rediscovered and published in a collection." Alexandre de Gunzburg, Manuscript A, "Tourgeniev".
5. Ivan Turgenev to Toporov, 2/14 June 1879, quoted by Irène De Vries-de Gunzburg, "Some letters of Ivan Turgenev to Baron Horace de Gunzburg, 1877–1883", *Oxford Slavonic Papers*, vol. IX, 1960, p. 80.
6. Horace de Gunzburg to Ivan Turgenev, 16/28 May 1880, St Petersburg (in Russian and in French), reproduced in Irène De Vries-de Gunzburg, op. cit., pp. 92–3.
7. Ibid.
8. Ivan Turgenev to Horace de Gunzburg, 22 January 1879, Paris, in Russian, reproduced in Irène De Vries-de Gunzburg, op. cit., p. 87.
9. Alexandre de Gunzburg, Manuscript C, "Littérateurs et artistes".
10. Alexandre de Gunzburg, Manuscript A, "Tourgueniev".
11. Ernst von Liphart (Lipgart), *Khudozhniki Salona vremen Tret'ey Respubliki. Mes Mémoires* (http://www.nasledie-rus.ru/podshivka/8314.php).
12. Ivan Turgenev to Horace de Gunzburg, 6/18 April 1879, Paris, reproduced in Irène De Vries-de Gunzburg, op. cit., p. 88.
13. Eugène Melchior de Vogüé, "L'exposition de Moscou et l'art russe", Paris, *La Revue des Deux Mondes*, November 1882.
14. Alexandre de Gunzburg, Manuscript A, "Bogolioubov".
15. Alexandre de Gunzburg, Manuscript C, "Littérateurs et artistes".
16. *Le Gaulois*, 23 February 1880.
17. Alexandre de Gunzburg, Manuscript A, "Ricard".
18. Initially there were 48 Russian signatures, and later 108. Léon Poliakov, *Histoire de l'antisémitisme*, vol. 2, op. cit., p. 311.
19. Quoted by Musya Glants, op. cit., p. 255.
20. Six days before he died, he signed in a trembling hand the agreement to sell his estate of Spasskoye-Lutovinovo to David de Gunzburg. 16/28 August 1883, in Russian, reproduced in Irène De Vries-de Gunzburg, op. cit., p. 100.
21. Horace de Gunzburg to David de Gunzburg, 4 September 1883, Dinard, RNB, f. 183 ed. khr. 394.

16

Confronting the Pogroms

1. Mathilde (Babita) de Gunzburg to David de Gunzburg, 3 November 1881, St Petersburg. "You probably know that the house where we live belongs to Papa and that Aniouta brought him *khleb sol.*" RNB, f. 183 ed. khr. 391.

2. Heinrich Sliozberg, *Baron G. O. Gintsburg, ego zhizn' i deyatel'nost' k stoletiyu so dnya ego rozhdeniya,* Paris, 1933, p. 70. Sasha reports that Meyer "was the right hand man of [Alexander] Bezak [who commanded the artillery] during the Crimean War, and it was because of his administrative talents that the Grand Master of the artillery recommended him to [Joseph Evzel] when his term of duty was over." Alexandre de Gunzburg, Manuscript C, "Aperçu généalogique". In 1865, after the Crimean War, Bezak was appointed governor-general of the regions of "Kiev, Volhynia and Podolia".

3. Alexandre de Gunzburg, Manuscript C, "Serviteurs".

4. Photographs of the interior of no. 17 Konnogvardeysky Boulevard in St Petersburg, made available to me by Marianna Mikheeva.

5. RNB, f. 183 d. 1653.

6. Heinrich Sliozberg, *Baron G. O. Gintsburg...,* op. cit., p. 53.

7. Ibid., p. 35.

8. Ibid., p. 59.

9. Ibid., p. 5.

10. Alexandre de Gunzburg, Manuscript A and Manuscript B, "Les gens d'affaires". In another passage of his memoirs, Sasha implies that the Gunzburgs were in France at the time of the tsar's assassination: "In 1881, when the news of Emperor Alexander II's assassination reached us, [Minsky] wanted to leave us, saying that he felt it his duty to go to Russia, where great things were going to happen." (See Alexandre de Gunzburg, Manuscript A, "Minsky, Nicolas Maximovitch Vilenkine".) But Horace's correspondence confirms their presence in the Russian capital.

11. RNB, f. 183 ed. khr. 1653. Description of Horace's possessions in 1909.

12. Having emerged from populist and anarchist movements, *Narodnaya Volya,* founded on 26 August 1879, had as its sole programme violent struggle inspired by the ideas of Sergey Nechayev. Its objective – assassinating Alexander II – was achieved on 1/13 March 1881, after five fruitless attempts.

13. Quoted by Jacqueline Proyart, "Le haut procureur du St-Synode Constantin Pobedonoscev et le 'coup d'Etat' du 29 avril 1881", *Cahiers du monde russe et soviétique,* 1962, vol. 3, pp. 408–58.

14. John Doyle Klier, *Russians, Jews and the Pogroms of 1881–1882,* Cambridge, Cambridge University Press, 2011.

15. "Komitet dlya okazaniya pomoshchi evreyam, postradavshim ot pogromov S. Pet".

16. Letter from the "Aid Committee for the ruined Jews of Kiev during the days of 26 and 27 April 1881". Kievskoye evreyskoye obshchestvo dlya vspomosh-chestvovaniya postradavshim ot besporyadkov na yuge Rossii 1881 g./AIU, URSS, IC1, 2nd file, Pogrom de Kiev.

17. By October 1881, the Committee had raised 218,482 roubles, of which 72,965 came from abroad (including 40,000 francs from the Alliance Israélite Universelle). By March 1882, Horace had contributed 82,000 roubles. *Rassvet*, 12 March 1882, quoted by John Doyle Klier, *Russians, Jews and the Pogroms of 1881–1882*, op. cit., p. 350.

18. "Kievskiy Komitet dlya vspomoshchestvovaniya postradavshim ot besporyadok 26 i 27 aprelya 1881", 3 signatories, including Dr. E. Mandelstamm and A. Kupernik.

19. Heinrich Sliozberg, *Dela minuvshikh dney: zapiski russkogo evreya*, Paris, 1933, vol. 1, p. 100.

20. Léo Errera, *Les Juifs russes, extermination ou émancipation*, with a letter-preface by Th. Mommsen, Brussels, Librairie européenne C. Muquardt, 1893.

21. According to the Austrian consul in St Petersburg, Kalnoky. See N. M. Gelber, "Di rusishe pogromen onheyb di 80-er yorn in shayn fun estraykhisher diplomatisher korespondents", *Historishe shriftn*, II, Vilna 1937, 469, quoted by John Doyle Klier, *Russians, Jews and the Pogroms of 1881–1882*, op. cit., p. 331.

22. Reported in *Golos*, 31. 13 May 1881.

23. Reported by the Austrian consul in St Petersburg, Kalnoky, quoted by John Doyle Klier, *Russians, Jews and the Pogroms of 1881–1882*, op. cit., p. 113.

24. For the various descriptions, see David Vital, *A People Apart: The Jews in Europe, 1789–1939*, Oxford, 1999, p. 293. Quoted by John Doyle Klier, *Russians, Jews and the Pogroms of 1881–1882*, op. cit., p. 332.

25. Ibid., p. 333.

26. Léo Errera, op. cit., p. 20. Shapiro quotes him, giving Sliozberg as his reference.

27. Mordecai ben Hillel Ha Kohen, Schlomo Zalman Luria, Schmuel Frugg. Quoted by John Doyle Klier, *Russians, Jews and the Pogroms of 1881–1882*, op. cit., pp. 328–9.

28. Ibid., p. 338.

29. See GARF f. 730, op. 1, d. 1622 (22/III/1882) and d. 1623 (IV/1882). Printed by V. L. Stepanov, ed., "Na shtyk mozhno operet'sya, na nego nel'zya sest", *Istochnik*, 3, 1993, pp. 54–69.

30. Zosa Szajkowski, "The Alliance Israélite Universelle and East-European Jewry in the 60s", *Jewish Social Studies*, 1942, 155, quoted by John Doyle Klier, *Russians, Jews and the Pogroms of 1881–1882*, op. cit., p. 350.

31. David Gordon, in *The Jewish Chronicle*, 682 (21/IV/82), quoted by John Doyle Klier, *Russians, Jews and the Pogroms of 1881–1882*, op. cit., p. 357.

32. *Vol'noye Slovo*, 38, 29 May 1882, quoted by John Doyle Klier, *Russians, Jews and the Pogroms of 1881–1882*, op. cit., p. 357.

33. Simon Dubnov, *Le Livre de ma vie. Souvenirs et réflexions, matériaux pour l'histoire de mon temps*, translated from the Russian by Brigitte Bernheimer, Paris, Ed. du Cerf, 2001, p. 210.

34. Ibid., p. 324. Having recourse to very numerous Russian sources, John Doyle Klier was able to prove that the pogroms of 1881–2 were as much a turning point for Jewish history as they were a moment of major crisis in the history of Russia. Giving priority to various levels of analysis, official or not, local or central, he was able to distinguish myths from reality, notably concerning the real role played by the "Gunzburg group" in defence of its co-religionists.

35. *Novoye Vremya*, 28 November 1881, an article translated into French for the Alliance Israélite Universelle, AIU, URSS IC 1, 1st file.

36. This memorandum was suggested by Count Baranov (a member of the Council of State) to the banker Abram Zak, another eminent member of the Gunzburg group. A few copies were printed and given to Baranov and a small number of high-ranking officials. A complete copy is held by the Jewish National Library in Jerusalem under the title "Evreyskiy vopros i anti-evreyskoye dvizhenie v Rossii v 1881 i 1882". John Doyle Klier, *Russians, Jews and the Pogroms of 1881–1882*, op. cit., p. 359.
37. Ibid., p. 390.
38. Quoted by John Doyle Klier, ibid., p. 250.
39. 11 February 1882, Rothschild Archives, London, XI-101-10. The letter is quoted by Herbert R. Lottman, *La Dynastie Rothschild*, Seuil, 1994, p. 83. See also Niall Ferguson, *The World's Banker. The History of the House of Rothschild*, London, Weidenfeld and Nicolson, 2000.
40. Ibid., pp. 83–4.
41. Letter of 4 October 1882, quoted by John Doyle Klier, *Russians, Jews and the Pogroms of 1881–1882*, op. cit., p. 251.

17

A Season at the Spas

1. Unsigned letter to David de Gunzburg, 7 July 1882, Marienbad (probably from Babita), RNB, f. 183 ed. khr. 1825.
2. Alexandre (Sasha) de Gunzburg to David de Gunzburg, 21 May/2 June 1882, Marienbad, RNB, f. 183 ed. khr. 1825.
3. Letter to David de Gunzburg, unsigned, probably from Louise de Gunzburg, 23 June 1882, Marienbad, RNB, f. 183 ed. khr. 1825.
4. Mathilde (Babita) de Gunzburg to David de Gunzburg, 16 June 1882, Marienbad, RNB, f. 183 ed. khr. 1825.
5. Horace de Gunzburg to David de Gunzburg, 13/25 July 1882, Franzensbad (written by Mathias Mapu), RNB, f. 183 ed. khr. 1825.
6. Alexandre (Sasha) de Gunzburg to David de Gunzburg, 21 May/2 June 1882, Marienbad, RNB, f. 183 ed. khr. 1825.
7. Alfred (Mimi) de Gunzburg to David de Gunzburg, undated [1882], in Hebrew and in French, RNB, f. 183 ed. khr. 1825.
8. Louise de Gunzburg to David de Gunzburg, 21 July 1882, Franzensbad, RNB, f. 183 ed. khr. 1825.
9. Mathilde (Babita) de Gunzburg to David de Gunzburg, 25 June/7 July1882, Marienbad, RNB, f. 183 ed. khr. 1825.
10. Mathilde (Babita) de Gunzburg to David de Gunzburg, Marienbad, 7 June 1882, RNB, f. 183 ed. khr. 1825.
11. Horace de Gunzburg to David de Gunzburg, 8/20 July 1882, Franzensbad, RNB, f. 183 ed. khr. 1825.
12. Horace de Gunzburg to David de Gunzburg, 13/25 July 1882, Franzensbad (written by Mathias Mapu), RNB, f. 183 ed. khr. 1825.
13. Horace de Gunzburg to David de Gunzburg, 18/30 July 1882, Franzensbad, RNB, f. 183 ed. khr. 1825.

14. Horace de Gunzburg to David de Gunzburg, 10/22 August 1882, Dinard, f. 183 ed. khr. 394.
15. Ibid.

18

Encouraging Crafts and Agricultural Work (ORT)

1. Horace de Gunzburg to David de Gunzburg, 10/22 August 1882, Dinard, f. 183 ed. khr. 394.
2. According to the 1897 census, the Russian Empire had 5,189,401 Jews, of whom 207,700 lived outside the Pale of Settlement.
3. Heinrich Sliozberg, *Baron Horace O. de Gunzbourg...*, op. cit.
4. Abram Zak (1829–1893) had worked for Joseph Evzel when he was an alcoholic beverages agent, then as an employee of the J. E. Gunzburg Bank, and finally as the director of the Discount Bank of St Petersburg in 1871.
5. Gregory Aronson, "The Genesis of ORT: pages from the history of Russian-Jewish intelligentsia", in Rachel Bracha, Adi Drori-Avraham, and Geoffrey Yantian, eds, *Educating for Life. New Chapters in the History of ORT*, London, World ORT, 2010, p. 45.
6. Leon Shapiro, *The History of ORT, a Jewish Movement for Social Change*, London, World ORT, 2010.
7. Quoted by Estraikh Gennady, "A Quest for Integration: Nikolai Bakst and 'his' ORT, 1880–1904", in Rachel Bracha, Adi Drori-Avraham, and Geoffrey Yantian, eds, *Educating for Life...*, op. cit., p. 32.
8. Remaining faithful to the spirit of its founders, the World ORT promotes the education of hundreds of thousands of children, adolescents and adults throughout the world. After Horace, many members of the Gunzburg family have been active in this organisation: in addition to his sons David and Sasha in Russia before the revolution of 1917, Alfred and Vladimir in Paris in the 1920s and 1930s, his grandchildren Daniel Halperin in Switzerland and Gavrik Ashkenasy in New York from the 1950s to the 1970s, and more recently Jean de Gunzburg (president of the World ORT from 2008 to 2014), Marc de Gunzburg and Vivien de Gunzburg.
9. "Allocations et dépenses du Comité provisoire. 4 November 1880–1er août 1882", in Leon Shapiro, op. cit., p. 368.
10. RNB, f. 183 ed. khr. 25.
11. Leon Shapiro, op. cit., pp. 46–7.
12. Heinrich Sliozberg, *Baron Horace O. de Gunzbourg*, op. cit., p. 99.
13. The son of a *melamed* (teacher in a *cheder*) from Poltava, Heinrich Sliozberg (1863–1937) studied at the secondary school in the same city before entering the University of St Petersburg's law school. He then completed his legal training in Heidelberg, Leipzig and Lyons. Because of the 1889 rules regarding the Jews, he could not serve as a judge, even though he had passed the relevant examinations in 1893. He became a legal assistant and was sworn in only in 1904. Starting in 1889, Sliozberg shared in Horace de Gunzburg's battle for Jews' rights. He contributed to publications on living conditions in the Jewish colonies

in the provinces of Kherson and Ekaterinoslav; he also participated in the work of a committee of the United States Congress assigned to study the causes of the emigration of Russian Jews, and he was active within the committee of the rabbis of all Russia in 1894 and in 1909 (Congress of Kovno). Starting with the pogrom in Kishinev (1903), he was Horace de Gunzburg's principal collaborator on the Aid Committee for Jews suffering from pogroms, and defended, as a lawyer, the rights of the victims. Along with Aronson Margolin, he founded the Committee for the Defence of Beilis. In the "courses on oriental studies" founded by David de Gunzburg he taught "The history of legal rulings regarding Jews in the Russian Empire". In 1907, he published an essay entitled *The Economic and Legal Situation of Jews in Russia*. After the Bolshevik revolution and a brief imprisonment, he succeeded in leaving Russia and went into exile in France, where he wrote his essay *Le Baron Horace O. de Gunzbourg, sa vie et son oeuvre*, in 1933. In 1934, in Berne, he testified in the suit brought by Swiss Jewish organisations against the publication by the local Nazi party of the *Protocols of the Elders of Zion*. The court ruled that the *Protocols* were a forgery and that their publication was indecent. Although he was a Freemason, he played a leading role in the community of Russian Jews who had emigrated to France.

14. Ibid., p. 102.
15. Sholem Aleikhem, "La grande panique des petits bonshommes", "Kasrilevke set out in haste", in Rachel Ertel, ed., *Royaumes juifs. Trésors de la littérature yiddish*, Paris, Robert Laffont, 2008, p. 355.
16. Heinrich Sliozberg, *Baron Horace O. de Gunzbourg*, op. cit., pp. 63–9.
17. See especially Vassili Schedrin, *Jewish Souls, Bureaucratic Minds: Jewish Bureaucracy and Policymaking in Late Imperial Russia, 1850–1917*, Wayne State University Press, 2016.
18. Heinrich Sliozberg, *Baron Horace O. de Gunzbourg*, op. cit., p. 94.
19. Ibid.
20. Ibid., p. 95.
21. Horace de Gunzburg to Tsar Alexander III, 6 March 1890, Papiers Alexandre III, GARF. Document reproduced and commented on by Olga Ederman, Vladimir Tol'ts and Yohanan Petrovsky-Shtern, "Zaochnyi dialog Goratsiya Gintsburga i imperatora Alexandra Tret'ego", 28 July 2007, Radio Svoboda (https://www.svoboda.org/a/404737.html).

19

Louise, a Charming Girl

1. Or more likely 1884, to judge by the correspondence between the painter and his model. See below.
2. The inventory made after Horace's death mentions the following works: *Portrait d'Anna de Gunzburg*, by Kramskoy (lot Mathilde [Babita] Gutmann), *Portrait d'Anna de Gunzburg sur son lit de mort*, by Kramskoy (lot David de Gunzburg), and, separate from any lot, *Portrait de femme* by Kramskoy (not evaluated).
3. Alexandre de Gunzburg, Manuscript A, "Petites scènes enfantines".
4. Louise de Gunzburg to David de Gunzburg, 21 July 1882, Franzensbad, RNB, f. 183 ed. khr. 1825.

5. Konstantin Kavelin to Lyubov Stasyulevich, 12 January 1880, in "M. M. Stasyulevich i ego sovremenniki v ikh perepiske", St Petersburg, 1912, p. 146, quoted by Heinrich Sliozberg, *Baron G. O. Gintsburg*, op. cit., pp. 62–3.
6. Ibid., p. 50.
7. Ibid.
8. Ivan Goncharov to Horace de Gunzburg, 26 January [year not given], St Petersburg, archive of Aline Berlin (de Gunzbourg).
9. Alexandre de Gunzburg, Manuscript A, "Petites scènes enfantines".
10. Ivan Goncharov to Horace de Gunzburg, undated, St Petersburg, in Russian, archive of Aline Berlin (de Gunzbourg).
11. Ivan Kramskoy to Horace de Gunzburg, 24 [month illegible] 1884, St Petersburg, in Russian, archive of Aline Berlin (de Gunzbourg).
12. Ivan Kramskoy to Louise de Gunzburg, St Petersburg, undated, in Russian, archive of Aline Berlin (de Gunzbourg).
13. Ivan Kramskoy to Louise de Gunzburg, 24 February 1883, St Petersburg, in Russian, archive of Aline Berlin (de Gunzbourg).
14. Ivan Kramskoy to Louise de Gunzburg, 1 May 1883, St Petersburg, in Russian, archive of Aline Berlin (de Gunzbourg).
15. Horace de Gunzburg to David de Gunzburg, 25/8 March 1880, St Petersburg, RNB, f. 183 ed. khr. 394.
16. Ibid.
17. Horace de Gunzburg to David de Gunzburg, 16 September 1883, St Petersburg, RNB, f. 183 ed. khr. 394.
18. Ibid.
19. Alexandre de Gunzburg, Manuscript C, "Les militaires".
20. Olga Karnovich married her second husband, Grand Duke Paul Alexandrovich, and received the title of "Princess Paley". Their daughter Nathalie Paley was the wife of the fashion designer Lucien Lelong. Alexandre de Gunzburg, Manuscript A, "Ma chère Lilia".
21. Alexandre de Gunzburg, Manuscript C, "Nos professeurs".
22. Alexandre de Gunzburg, Manuscript C, "Les militaires".
23. This Stradivarius is now known as "the Davidov".
24. Mathilde (Babita) de Gunzburg to David de Gunzburg, 3 November 1881, St Petersburg, RNB, f. 183 ed. khr. 391.
25. Alexandre de Gunzburg, Manuscript C, "Littérateurs et artistes".
26. Music was central to the family's preoccupations, as is shown by this letter from David de Gunzburg to Horace de Gunzburg, dated 17 October 1889: "Last year, I believe, I talked to you about a project that had sprouted in our heads: founding a Jewish *Gesangverein*. The man to do it is here now, and it's Goldenblum, the student you formerly sponsored. [...] He had the idea of connecting it with Rubinstein's jubilee, to prepare for that purpose a performance of his *Moses*, and to invite him to it *en famille*, so to speak, without noise or trumpets, or posters, and thus to make our idea popular with the children of Israel. Would you find anything objectionable in letting a Jewish chorus be heard – *in petto* – to celebrate the administration in our own way? If you do not object, send me a telegram saying 'consent' [or else] 'no'. [...] I would not want to undertake an affair that might displease you. I embrace you most heartily, your loving son, David." Then on 21 (October?) 1889: "We have completely abandoned the idea of celebrating

Rubinstein because of the difficulties inherent in the project. As for the choral meetings, we will begin them soon." RNB, f. 183 ed. khr. 1709.

27. Alexandre de Gunzburg, Manuscript C, "Littérateurs et artistes".
28. Mathilde de Gunzburg to David de Gunzburg, 9 May 1883, St Petersburg, RNB, f. 183 ed. khr. 405.
29. Mathilde de Gunzburg to David de Gunzburg, Monday 12 February, Paris, RNB, f. 183 ed. khr. 405.
30. Mathilde de Gunzburg to David de Gunzburg, 21 March 1883, Paris, RNB, f. 183 ed. khr. 405.
31. Mathilde de Gunzburg to David de Gunzburg, 27 April 1883, Paris, RNB, f. 183 ed. khr. 405.
32. Ibid.
33. Mathilde de Gunzburg to David de Gunzburg, undated, Paris, RNB, f. 183 ed. khr. 405.
34. Mathilde de Gunzburg to David de Gunzburg, undated (probably April 1883), Paris, RNB, f. 183 ed. khr. 405.
35. Mathilde de Gunzburg to David de Gunzburg, 18 April (probably 1883), Paris, RNB, f. 183 ed. khr. 405.
36. *Le Gaulois*, 11 November 1883. The connection with the Ephrussis promoted the Rothschilds' interest in the fate of Russian Jews.
37. *Le Gaulois*, 19 May 1883.
38. *Gil Blas*, 21 December 1883.
39. Ivan Kramskoy to Horace de Gunzburg, St Petersburg, 24 [month illegible] 1884, in Russian, archive of Aline Berlin (de Gunzbourg).
40. Ivan Goncharov to Louise de Gunzburg, 3 February (probably 1884), St Petersburg, in French, archive of Aline Berlin (de Gunzbourg).
41. Sasha de Gunzburg to Alfred (Mimi) de Gunzburg, 7/25 September 1885, Hamburg, RNB, f. 183 ed. khr. 1919.
42. Horace de Gunzburg to David de Gunzburg, 25/7 September 1887, Paris, RNB, f. 183 ed. khr. 394.
43. Elsa Warburg-Melchior, op. cit.
44. David de Gunzburg to Horace de Gunzburg, 21 [month illegible] 1889, St Petersburg, RNB, f. 183 ed. khr. 1708.
45. *Le Gaulois*, 5 July 1886: "The town house on 7 Rue de Tilsitt, which proceeded from the legacy of the Banker Gunzburg, was just bought for 2,200,000 [francs], after two unsuccessful attempts at adjudication, by one of our wealthiest entrepreneurs." See also the "contract for the sale of the town house at 7 Rue de Tilsitt, owned by Messieurs Gunzburg [Salomon, Ury and Horace], to M. Philippe Spiridion Vitali", 10 June 1886, AN MC/ET/XLII/1254.
46. Ida de Gunzburg to Mathilde de Gunzburg, Berlin 27 January (1888), RNB, f. 183 ed. khr. 399.
47. Ida de Gunzburg to Mathilde de Gunzburg, Berlin, 6 February (1888), RNB, f. 183 ed. khr. 399.
48. Ury de Gunzburg to Mathilde de Gunzburg, in French, RNB, f. 183 ed. khr. 1886.
49. Thérèse Mendel, née de Gunzburg, was buried in the Jewish cemetery in Braïla.
50. Ury de Gunzburg to Mathilde de Gunzburg, Pau, 29 April 1902, in French, RNB, f. 183 ed. khr. 1886.
51. Elsa Warburg-Melchior, op. cit., pp. 140–41.

52. Ibid.
53. *Le Gaulois*, 19 March 1896.
54. Ibid. See also Gavrik Ashkenasy and Elisabeth Lorin, op. cit.
55. Nikolay Kuznetsov, *A. H. Ashkenasy*, oil on canvas, V. Vereshchagin Museum, Mykolaiv (Ukraine). The painter's daughter, Maria Kuznetsova, a famous singer, married as her second husband Alfred Massenet, the nephew of the composer, with whom she worked. Like the Gunzburgs, the Kuznetsovs lived between Russia and France, where they were closely associated with the Society of Russian Artists in Paris.

20

The *Vestnik Evropy* Group

1. Students had protested the repression of the Polish liberation movement (1861).
2. Alexandre de Gunzburg, Manuscript A, "Le salon des Stassioulevitch".
3. Sasha also wrote that the Utin house belonged to his father Horace. Ibid.
4. Ibid.
5. Heinrich Sliozberg, *Le Baron Horace O. de Gunzbourg...*, op. cit., p. 54.
6. Ibid.
7. Ibid.
8. The items in the Botkin collection are now in the Otto Kahn collection.
9. Alexandre de Gunzburg, Manuscript A, "Vladimir Solovyov".

Part IV

Heralds of Jewish Culture

21

David, Bibliophile and Orientalist

1. His daughter Sophie suggests the figure of 52,000 volumes. Sophie Günzburg, "My Father, Baron David", in Lucy S. Davidowicz, *The Golden Tradition: Jewish Life and Thought in Eastern Europe*, New York, 1967, pp. 248–56.
2. David Gunzburg and Vladimir Stasov, *L'Ornement hébreu* (or *L'Ornement hébraïque*), Berlin, Calvary, 1908.
3. Elsa Warburg-Melchior, op. cit.
4. *Ma Mathilde*, 12 July 1898, RNB, f. 183 ed. khr. 50.
5. David Frischmann, quoted in Samuel Gol'denberg and Alina Lisitina, "Eto moya dusha, vse soderzhanie moey zhizni: o kollektsii Davida Gintsburga", *Lekhaim*, no. 263, March 2014.
6. "Baroness Mathilde de Gunzburg and the Jewish Theological Seminary of America, Agreement, July 21, 1914", archive of Christine de Gunzbourg.

7. According to Sasha, when the negotiations with the American seminary were interrupted by the war, a "Zionist group" had bought the library for 400,000 roubles, with the intention of offering it to the University of Jerusalem, and "it was transported to Moscow, to the home of Madame Persitz-Zlatopolsky, to await an opportunity to ship it to Palestine. The Bolshevik revolution broke out and the library was soon nationalised and transported to the cellars of the Rumyantsev Museum. The Zionists tried to buy it back from the Soviets, but were unable to raise the money to pay the exorbitant price put on it. The books and manuscripts have since been placed in a hall of the museum and the bookcases bear, it is said, the name of our family." Alexandre de Gunzburg, Manuscript C, "Aperçu généalogique".

8. In November 2017, the Russian National Library and the National Library of Israel announced a project to digitise 2,000 manuscripts from the "Gunzburg library".

9. Samuel Gol'denberg and Alina Lisitina, op. cit.

10. Sophie Gunzburg, op. cit., p. 254.

11. "The Gunzburg Haggadah: first printed edition of an illuminated manuscript from the USSR". Microfilm Collection in the New York University Library of Judaica and Hebraica.

12. David de Gunzburg to Horace de Gunzburg, in French [1869 or 1870, Saint-Valéry region of Normandy], RNB, f. 183 ed. khr. 1710.

13. Alexandre de Gunzburg, Manuscript C, "Nos professeurs".

14. The poem mentioned here seems not to be by Pushkin, but rather by Lermontov (*Parus*: "The Sail").

15. Is David confusing Alexander Sumarokov (1717–1777), a writer of fables, with Alexander Suvorov (1730–1800), a Russian generalissimo?

16. Horace de Gunzburg to David de Gunzburg, 4 September 1875, Paris, RNB, f. 183 ed. khr. 394.

17. Ibid.

18. Telegram from David de Gunzburg to Horace de Gunzburg, 11 May 1878, RNB, f. 183 ed. khr. 1710.

19. Horace de Gunzburg to David de Gunzburg, 24/5 January 1880, St Petersburg, RNB, f. 183 ed. khr. 394.

20. Horace de Gunzburg to David de Gunzburg, 25/8 March 1880, St Petersburg, RNB, f. 183 ed. khr. 394.

21. Horace de Gunzburg to David de Gunzburg, 18 July 1883, Marienbad, RNB, f. 183 ed. khr. 394.

22. Sophie Gunzburg, op. cit., p. 251.

23. Ibid.

24. Horace de Gunzburg to David de Gunzburg, 15/27 September 1892, Boulogne-sur-Mer, RNB, f. 183 ed. khr. 396.

25. Horace de Gunzburg to David de Gunzburg, 16/28 September 1892, Boulogne-sur-Mer, RNB, f. 183 ed. khr. 396.

26. 25 July 1890, Tsarskoye Selo, RNB, f. 183 ed. khr. 50.

27. 23 August/3 September 1891, Mogilno, RNB, f. 183 ed. khr. 50.

28. Gustav Bickell, *Metrices biblicae regulæ exemplis illustratae*, Innsbruck, 1879.

29. David de Gunzburg, *Monsieur Bickell et la métrique hébraïque*, Paris, Maisonneuve et Cie, 1881. (Reply to R. P. Bouvy of the Augustins de l'Assomption.)

30. David de Gunzburg, "Le premier livre imprimé en hébreu, *Recueil des travaux rédigés en mémoire du jubilé scientifique de M. Daniel Chwolson professeur émérite à l'université de St Pétersbourg (1846–1896)*, Berlin, S. Calvary and Co., 1899, pp. 57–121.
31. Quoted in David de Gunzburg, *Du rythme dans les vers, poésie arabe.* RNB, f. 183 ed. khr. 55.
32. Horace de Gunzburg to David de Gunzburg, 18 July 1883, Marienbad, RNB, f. 183 ed. khr. 394.

22

L'Ornement hébreu

1. David de Gunzburg, "Remarques sur l'art juif", unpublished (draft for the introduction to *L'Ornement hébraïque*), RNB, f. 183 ed. khr. 74.
2. Ibid.
3. David de Gunzburg and Vladimir Stasov, *L'Ornement hébreu*, op. cit., Preface.
4. A few copies of *L'Ornement hébreu* still exist, scattered around the world: in France at the Musée d'art et d'histoire du judaïsme, and in the United States, at Princeton and at Harvard.
5. David de Gunzburg and Vladimir Stasov, *L'Ornement hébreu*, op. cit., Preface.
6. Vladimir Stasov published a series of articles on this subject: "Le peuple juif dans ses rapports avec l'art européen" (*Evreyskaya Biblioteka*, vols. 3, 5, 6 ; 1873–1878), "Au sujet de la traduction de 'Nathan le sage'" (*Evreyskaya Biblioteka*, vol. 5, 1875), "Après l'Exposition universelle", on 82 items of Judaica from the thirteenth and seventeenth centuries in the collection of M. Strauss (*Evreyskaya Biblioteka*, vol. 7, 1879).
7. Vladimir Stasov, "Po povodu postroyki sinagogi v Sankt-Peterburge", 1872, "Otvet L. Gordonu. Pis'mo k redaktoru", *Rassvet*, 1879, no. 6.
8. David praised him for all this in David de Gunzburg, "Stasov i evreyskoye iskusstvo", *Sbornik vospominaniy o V. V. Stasove*, Prometey, 1907.
9. Vladimir Stasov, *Slavyanskiy i vostochnyi ornament po rukopisyam drevnego i novogo vremeni*, St Petersburg, 1887.
10. David de Gunzburg to Vladimir Stasov, four letters sent from Dresden, Berlin, and Valladolid, accompanied by handwritten notes describing the manuscripts, with marginal comments by Stasov, 1885–1893, RNB, f. 183 ed. khr. 118.
11. David de Gunzburg to Vladimir Stasov, 6 October 1885, Dresden, RNB, f. 183 ed. khr. 118.
12. Ibid.
13. Ibid.
14. David de Gunzburg to Vladimir Stasov, 8 May 1885, Valladolid, in French. RNB, f. 183 ed. khr. 118.
15. David de Gunzburg, Vladimir Stasov, *L'Ornement hébreu*, op. cit., Preface. The stupefying Geniza of the Ben Ezra synagogue in Cairo was opened later, in 1896, by Salomon Schechter.
16. Ibid.
17. Mathilde (Babita) de Gunzburg to David de Gunzburg, 20 December 1906/2 January 1907, Vienne, RNB, f. 183 ed. khr. 391.

18. The imperial train went off the rails on 17 October (29 October) 1888, near the station at Borki (Kharkov region): although the tsar and his family suffered only minor injuries, 21 people lost their lives in the accident.

19. *L'Ornement hébreu*, Preface.

20. In 1908–9, David de Gunzburg had repeated occasions to provide Marc Chagall with financial support, notably when the young painter had just arrived in St Petersburg. See the letters from Marc Chagall to David de Gunzburg, RNB, f. 183 ed. khr. 1251. It was thanks to the sculptor Ilya Ginzburg, Antokolsky's pupil, that the young painter from Vitebsk came into contact with the Gunzburgs: "[Ginzburg] enjoyed a great popularity – and I, I was nothing at all, without a residence permit, without even twenty roubles of monthly income. I don't know whether the sculptor Ginzburg would have found, or been able to find, a few merits in the works of my youth. In any case, as he was accustomed to do for all those who came to see him, he wrote a letter to introduce me to Baron Gunzburg. The latter, convinced that somebody like me existed, and seeing the possibility that another Antokolsky might emerge (how many broken dreams!), granted me a monthly subsidy of ten roubles for a short period of time... This cultivated baron, a friend of Stasov's, probably understood nothing about art. And yet, he had believed it was his duty, this time, to show me consideration. He chatted with me and recounted a moral fable concerning the prudence with which artists should act. For example, Antokolsky's wife was not a good spouse. She would not have let a poor man enter her home... you understand. Pay attention... a wife can be very important in an artist's life... Courteously, I thought about something else." Marc Chagall, *Mon univers. Autobiographie*, translated from the Yiddish by Chantal Ringuet and Pierre Anctil, Canada, Fides, 2017, pp. 80–81.

23

Antokolsky, the "First Jewish Sculptor"

1. David de Gunzburg, "Le premier sculpteur israélite", unpublished, in French, RNB, f. 183 ed. khr. 63.

2. See Musya Glants, *Where Is My Home ?...*, op. cit.

3. Antokolsky successfully exhibited his work at the Universal Exhibition in Paris (1869) and London (1872). In France, he was made a Chevalier (in 1878), then a Commandeur and Grand Cross of the Légion d'Honneur (in 1900). He also received the Great Gold Medal in Munich (1892), Berlin (1893) and Paris (1900). In Munich, the king gave a dinner in his honour.

4. Quoted by Musya Glants, op. cit., p. XIV.

5. Ibid.

6. Vladimir Stasov, "25 let russkogo iskusstva", *Vestnik Evropy*, 1882, quoted by Musya Glants, op. cit., p. XII.

7. Genrikh Agranovsky and Irina Guzenberg, *Vil'nius: po sledam Litovskogo Ierusalima Pamyatnye mesta evreyskoy istorii i kul'tury*, Vilnius, Vilnia, 2011, p. 81.

8. Notably in the work of the critic Alexandre Benois, the leader of the artistic trend

Mir iskusstva (The World of Art) and the journalists V. Burenin and A. Dyakov in Suvorin's newspaper, *Novoye vremya*. Musya Glants, op. cit. p. XIV.

9. David de Gunzburg, "Premier sculpteur israélite", op. cit.

10. Alexandre de Gunzburg, Manuscript A, "Antokolski".

11. Mark Antokolsky to Savva Mamontov, Rome, December 1876; Mark Antokolsky to Vladimir Stasov, Paris, 24 December 1877, quoted in Vladimir Stasov, *Mark Matveyevich Antokol'skii. Tvorenie, pisma i stat'i*, St Petersburg, 1905, pp. 344–5. See also Musya Glants, op. cit., p. 216.

12. Anna Antokolsky married Georges Montefiore, a nephew of the Cahen-d'Anvers.

13. An expression used by Ilya Ginzburg in his memoirs.

14. Alexandre de Gunzburg, Manuscript A, "Antokolski". Sasha adds: "Interesting to note that while I was writing these lines, we received from Petersburg offers to recover the busts of our parents, that is, to buy them back from the Soviets."

15. Marc Antokolsy to Vladimir Stasov, 16 January 1878, Paris, quoted in Vladimir Stasov, *Mark Matveyevich Antokol'skii*, op. cit., p. 355. Among the works executed by Antokolsky for the Gunzburgs, in addition to the busts of Joseph Evzel, Anna and Horace, Sasha mentions "Alexander II" and the "Mephisto". Alexandre de Gunzburg, Manuscript A, "Antokolski".

16. Horace de Gunzburg to Marc de Gunzburg, 5 August 1878, Franzensbad, RNB, f. 183 ed. khr. 1953.

17. Alexandre de Gunzburg, Manuscript A, "Antokolski".

18. Horace de Gunzburg to Marc de Gunzburg, 20 November 1878, Paris, RNB, f. 183 ed. khr. 1953.

19. The inventory made after Horace de Gunzburg's death mentions the following works: no. 531 statue by Antokolsky in marble; no. 532 bronze by Antokolsky; no. 553 bust of Artsimovich by Antokolsky; no. 534 terracotta by Antokolsky; no. 555 bust in bronze of Antokolsky by Ginzburg; bust of V. Solovyov by Ginzburg (the monetary value of these items is not given). Distribution of the lots: Vladimir de Gunzburg: Gunzburg bust in marble by Antokolsky. Dimitri de Gunzburg: bust of Anna de Gunzburg by Antokolsky and bust of Horace de Gunzburg by Antokolsky. RNB, f. 183 ed. khr. 1653.

20. Alexandre de Gunzburg, Manuscript A, "Antokolski".

21. Ibid.

22. Ibid.

23. Musya Glants, op. cit., p. 322.

24. Alexandre de Gunzburg, Manuscript C, "Littérateurs et artistes".

25. Marc Antokolsky, "Pis'mo baronu Goratsiyu Osipovichu Gintsburgu", RNB, f. 25, d. 11. A text dating from 1890–1900, manuscript: letter published by Musya Glants, in "Dual Existence of the Eternal Wanderer. M. Antokolsky's letter to Baron Horatsii Osipovich Gintsburg", *Arkhiv evreyskoy istorii* 1 (2004), pp. 195–239.

26. Musya Glants, op. cit., pp. 346–7.

27. Vladimir Stasov to David de Gunzburg, 8 June 1906, in Russian, RNB, f. 183 ed. khr. 1096, l. 35.

Notes

24

Zionism: *pro et contra*

1. David de Gunzburg, "Sur le sionisme", unpublished, in French, RNB, f. 183 ed. khr. 1654.
2. Ibid.
3. Ibid.
4. Edouard Drumont, *La France juive: essai d'histoire contemporaine*, Paris, Flammarion, 1886, vol. I.
5. Heinrich Sliozberg, *Dela minuvshikh dney: Zapiski russkogo evreya*, Paris, 1933, p. 129.
6. Heinrich Sliozberg, ibid.
7. David de Gunzburg, "Sur le sionisme", op. cit.
8. Dominique Frischer, *Le Moïse des Amériques. Vies et oeuvres du baron de Hirsch*, Paris, Grasset, 2002, pp. 163–4.
9. One franc was the equivalent of 20 francs in 2001, so that the 6 million francs expended was the equivalent of 120 million francs today, or more than 18 million euros.
10. Horace de Gunzburg to David de Gunzburg, 8/20 July 1882, Franzensbad, RNB, f. 183 ed. khr. 1825.
11. Dominique Frischer, op. cit.
12. Maurice de Hirsch, letter "A mes coreligionnaires russes", September 1891, Paris (in Russian), AIU, URSS VIII B (Riga).
13. See John Doyle Klier, *Russians, Jews and the Pogroms of 1881–1882*, op. cit., p. 313.
14. In 1901, David de Gunzburg became the chairman of the board of directors of "Jewish agricultural farms" in Minsk and the director of the school of agriculture in Novo-Poltavka.
15. At that time, the village of "Baron de Gunzburg" had 745 inhabitants, including 133 men, 188 women, 289 male minors and 185 female minors.
16. David de Gunzburg, "Sur le sionisme", op. cit.

25

The Ordeal of Bankruptcy

1. I.G. is an abbreviation of "Iosif Gavrilovich," in accord with Russian custom, even though the bank was registered under the name "J. E. Gunzburg".
2. The debts amounted to 16,500 francs. Horace de Gunzburg to David de Gunzburg, 16 [July] 1880, Paris, RNB, f. 183 ed. khr. 394.
3. Alexandre de Gunzburg, Manuscript A, "Les militaires".
4. Ibid.
5. An old unit of weight in imperial Russia, the *poud* is equivalent to 16.38 kg.
6. In David de Gunzburg's archive there is a series of photographs of factories in Sergeyevo-Ufaleysky in the Urals, dating from 1900 to 1903. RNB, f. 183 ed. khr. 2069.

7. David de Gunzburg to Horace de Gunzburg, 29 July 1886, St Petersburg, RNB, f. 183 ed. khr. 1709.

8. David de Gunzburg to Mathilde de Gunzburg, 8 November 1891, Mogilno, RNB, f. 183 ed. khr. 50.

9. David de Gunzburg to Horace de Gunzburg, 9 March 1891, Menton (on mourning stationery), RNB, f. 183 ed. khr. 1709.

10. David de Gunzburg to Horace de Gunzburg, 5 May 1891, Mogilno, RNB, f. 183 ed. khr. 1709.

11. David de Gunzburg to Horace de Gunzburg, 16 April 1891, Odessa, RNB, f. 183 ed. khr. 1709.

12. David de Gunzburg to Horace de Gunzburg, 5 May 1891, Mogilno, RNB, f. 183 ed. khr. 1709.

13. See Ilya Vovshin, op. cit.

14. *Feuilles d'avis de Neuchâtel,* Thursday 17 March 1892.

15. Heinrich Sliozberg, *Le Baron Horace O. de Gunzbourg...,* op. cit., p. 110.

16. Horace de Gunzburg to David de Gunzburg, 5/17 June 1892, Paris, RNB, f. 183 ed. khr. 396.

17. Ibid. Had the chateau of Chambaudoin, a property that belonged to Ury, been bought by Horace? Since the 1880s, Ury, probably in debt, seems to have been dependent on his brother. He sold his collections (including Jean-François Millet's *La Lessiveuse*) and tried to "get back on his feet" by taking part in various enterprises, without much success. On 21 September 1898, he applied for a patent:"Method of unfreezing and preserving skins" (with Joseph Chernyak).

18. Horace de Gunzburg to David de Gunzburg, 15/27 July 1892 (n.p.), RNB, f. 183 ed. khr. 395.

19. Horace de Gunzburg to David de Gunzburg, 27 August 1892, Boulogne-sur-Mer, RNB, f. 183 ed. khr. 395.

20. Horace de Gunzburg to David de Gunzburg, 8 October 1892, Boulogne-sur-Mer, RNB, f. 183 ed. khr. 395

21. Horace de Gunzburg to David de Gunzburg, 23 September/5 October 1892, Paris, RNB, f. 183 ed. khr. 395.

22. Ron Chernow, *The Warburgs, The Twentieth-Century Odyssey of a Remarkable Jewish Family,* First Vintage Books edition, 1994, p. 39.

23. *Otchet administratsii po delam torgovogo doma I. E. Gintsburg 1893,* St Petersburg, 1894; *Otchet administratsii po delam torgovogo doma I. E. Gintsburg 1894,* St Petersburg, 1895.

24. David de Gunzburg, *Le Divan d'Ibn Guzman. Texte, traduction, commentaire,* Berlin, Calvary, 1896.

25. David de Gunzburg to Mathilde de Gunzburg, 26 October 1898, RNB, f. 183 ed. khr. 50.

26. Mathilde de Gunzburg to David de Gunzburg, 19 October 1899, Mogilno, RNB, f. 183 ed. khr. 411.

27. David de Gunzburg and Vladimir Stasov, *L'Ornement hébreu,* op. cit., Preface.

Notes

26

Baron Horace Osipovich's Seventieth Birthday

1. Rosa de Gunzburg to Théophile Warburg, 28 January 1903, St Petersburg, in German, archive of Katia Guth-Dreyfus.
2. Alexandre de Gunzburg, Manuscript C, "Les gens d'affaires".
3. Archive of Elisabeth Lorin. Horace's profile is engraved on the obverse, and on the reverse, the dates 1832–1902. Horace was born on 25 December (1832) but his birthday seems usually to have been celebrated in January, thereby confusing people regarding his date of birth. The date 25 December 1832 comes from a document in Horace's hand that is mentioned by Sasha. Alexandre de Gunzburg to Jean de Gunzburg, 16 May 1935, Amsterdam, archive of Jean de Gunzburg.
4. *Voskhod*, 1903, no. 5.
5. Horace de Gunzburg to Narcisse Leven, president of the Alliance Israélite Universelle, in French. Letter received on 8 February 1903, AIU, URSS IV B (St Petersburg).
6. B.-A. Henry, *Les Massacres de Kichinev*, Publications du Siècle, Paris, 1903.
7. Horace de Gunzburg to Narcisse Leven, 7 May 1903, St Petersburg, in French, AIU, URSS IV B (St Petersburg).
8. Heinrich Sliozberg, *Le Baron Horace O. de Gunzbourg...*, op. cit., p. 122.
9. Cazès to Narcisse Leven, 14 July 1903, Kishinev, AIU, URSS III (Kishinev).
10. Horace de Gunzburg to Narcisse Leven, 11 May 1903, St Petersburg, AIU, URSS IV B (St Petersburg).
11. D. Feinberg to Narcisse Leven, 9 August 1903, Odessa, in French, AIU URSS IV B (Feinberg file 1867–1913 pogroms).
12. Heinrich Sliozberg, *Le Baron Horace O. de Gunzbourg...*, op. cit., p. 123.
13. Ibid.
14. Narcisse Leven to Horace de Gunzburg, 11 December [1904], draft, AIU URSS IV B (St Petersburg).
15. Horace de Gunzburg to Narcisse Leven, 4 April 1904, in Hebrew. AIU URSS IV B (St Petersburg).
16. Quoted by Edward H. Judge, *Easter in Kishinev, Anatomy of a Pogrom*, New York and London, New York University Press, 1992, pp. 104–5.

Part V

The Dark Years

1. Horace de Gunzburg to Narcisse Leven, 24 January 1908, AIU URSS IV B (St Petersburg).

27

1905 – A Tragic Year

1. *Gil Blas*, 19 September 1905.
2. *L'Humanité*, 16 September 1905, "Dans la Finance".
3. *Journal des débats*, 16 September 1905.
4. Ibid.
5. *Le Gaulois*, 26 June 1891. "A very elegant ball, evening before last, at the home of Baroness S. de Gunzburg, who opened for the first time the ground floor of her town house on Avenue du Bois-de-Boulogne." The prestigious guests were listed: the ambassadors of Spain and Turkey, ministers from the United States and Sweden, M. de Giers (the tsar's Minister of Foreign Affairs), Prince Orlov, the Duke and Duchess de Luynes, the Duchess de Gramont, Viscountess de La Rochefoucauld, the Marchioness d'Hervey de Saint-Denys, Baroness d'Estrella, Mme Porgès, Barons Gustave and Edmond de Rothschild and their wives, etc.
6. Autobiographical note, "Jean de Gunzburg", added as a postscript to the letter that André Louis-Hirsch and Jean de Gunzburg wrote to the General Commissioner for Jewish Questions on 5 July 1941. Archive of Jean de Gunzburg.
7. *L'Humanité*, op. cit.
8. "Compte de la succession testamentaire de Monsieur le baron Salomon de Gunzburg, présenté par Monsieur le baron Robert de Gunzburg et Monsieur Paul Augustin Huillier, notaire à Paris." Archive of Jean de Gunzburg.
9. AN MC/ET/VIII/1582. 21 June 1888, liquidation of the Goldschmidt inheritance. As her share, Henriette de Gunzburg received the equivalent of "1,409,444 francs and 70 centimes".
10. Salomon de Gunzburg to Mathilde de Gunzburg, 1 November 1899, Paris, RNB, f. 183 ed. khr. 424.
11. *Journal des débats*, op. cit.
12. Marcel Proust to Reynaldo Hahn, Thursday 26 October 1911: "The intellectual equivalence of extreme culture and extreme unculture among socialites is included in this twofold 'formula'. C[oun]tesse G. de L. Rd. 'But, but, do you know that Candide is a little masterpiece!' La Gun[zburg]. 'Vadig? What a strange name.'" And on 21 November 1914: "P.S. Have you seen the deaths of Casadessus the cellist (he was not Tolstoy's visitor, of course) and of the young Gunzbourg, the son, I suppose, of Baroness Guigui." (http://reynaldo-hahn.net/Html/ecritsdiversProust.htm.) (Marcel Proust, *Correspondance*, text established, presented and annotated by Philippe Kolb, Paris, Plon, 1978, 21 volumes.)
13. Monique de Gunzburg, *Souvenirs*, Paris, Jouve, 1996, p. 34.
14. The portrait of Ury de Gunzburg by Meissonier has also disappeared.
15. Alexandre de Gunzburg, Manuscript A, "Le pogrom".
16. "Jean de Gunzburg", autobiographical note, archive of Jean de Gunzburg.
17. Alexandre de Gunzburg, Manuscript A, "Le pogrom".
18. Ibid.
19. Ibid. Photographs of the pogrom in Kiev (1905), archive of Katia Guth-Dreyfus.

Notes

20. Alexandre de Gunzburg, Manuscript A, "Le pogrom". Subsequent quotations from Sasha's account cite the same source.

28

The Union for Equal Rights: Horace's Last Battle

1. Alexandre de Gunzburg, Manuscript C, "Aperçu généalogique", p. 10.
2. Horace de Gunzburg to Narcisse Leven, 28 November 1905, St Petersburg, AIU URSS IV B (St Petersburg).
3. A businessman with an excellent reputation and an influential member of the London Jewish community, Carl Stettauer was notably one of the founders of the synagogue in Hampstead (1892). In 1905, he travelled to Russia to observe the situation of Jews who had been victims of the pogroms. His observations, letters, photographs and newspaper clippings are preserved at the University of Southampton (MS 128 Papers of Carl Stettauer).
4. AIU, URSS IV B (St Petersburg).
5. Undated document received by the Alliance Israélite on 30 November 1905. Ten resolutions in German. AIU, URSS IV B (St Petersburg).
6. Ivan Tolstoy (1856–1916), a prominent archaeologist, numismatist and statesman, gave the Jewish community in Russia his constant support. As education minister, he proposed to the Council of Ministers the abolition of restriction on Jews with regard to their admission to institutions of higher education. With the historian Yuly Gessen, he published in 1907 the essay "Des faits et des pensées. La question juive en Russie".
7. A. B. Mindlin, "Politika S. Yu. Vitte po 'Evreyskomu voprosu'", *Voprosy istorii*, 2004, no. 4.
8. According to Sliozberg, the issue was in fact not resolved and was the subject, from 5 to 9 December, of a secret meeting in Peterhof, presided over by the tsar and attended by members of the Council of Ministers and other invitees: the main opponent of suffrage for Jews was General D. F. Trepov (governor-general of St Petersburg, assistant to the Minister of the Interior, and commander of the St Petersburg gendarmes). Only Witte dared to oppose his view. On behalf of the Union for Equal Rights, Sliozberg visited Witte, who stressed that it was essential that the finance minister Kokovtsov and the governor-general of Finland N. N. Guerard also be convinced of the injustice of prohibiting suffrage for Jews. Sliozberg went with Kulisher to see Kokovtsov, who promised that he would not oppose them. Guerard also accepted the idea of suffrage for Jews. Soon Kokovtsov announced that with the tsar's agreement, there would be no restriction for Jews. In the ukase of 11 December setting forth the modalities of the election law, Jews could vote. Heinrich Sliozberg, *Dela minuvshikh dney...*, op. cit.
9. Ivan Tolstoy to David de Gunzburg, 22 April 1906, St Petersburg, in French, RNB, f. 183 ed. khr. 1126.
10. Letter from David Feinberg to the Alliance Israélite Universelle, 31 January 1986: "The disaster in Homel was very great. The cause is the same as everywhere else. We have already sent help there [...]. [There is talk of holding an investigation.]

This matter will be entrusted to a commission composed of M. Warschawski, David Gunzburg and myself." AIU, IV B (Feinberg file 1867–1913, pogroms).

11. David Feinberg to the Alliance Israélite Universelle, 7 April 1906, Odessa, AIU, IV B (Feinberg file 1867–1913, pogroms).
12. David Feinberg to the Alliance Israélite Universelle, Bielostok, 30 June 1906, AIU, IV B (Feinberg file 1867–1913, pogroms).
13. Ibid.
14. Ivan Tolstoy, *Dnevnik 1906–1916*, St Petersburg, Izd. Evropeyskogo universiteta v Sankt-Peterburge, 1997.
15. Horace de Gunzburg to Narcisse Leven, 24 January 1908, AIU, URSS IV B (St Petersburg file).
16. Narcisse Leven to Horace de Gunzburg, 24 January 1908, AIU, URSS IV B (St Petersburg file).
17. Photograph album belonging to Pierre de Gunzbourg, archive of Aline Berlin (de Gunzbourg).
18. David de Gunzburg to Rabbi David Simonsen, 20 January 1909, in German, Royal Library of Denmark, The David Simonsen Archives (Digital Editions).
19. Heinrich Sliozberg, *Le Baron Horace O. de Gunzbourg...*, op. cit., pp. 124–5.
20. "Discours de W. J. Tiomkine", in Heinrich Sliozberg, *Le Baron Horace O. de Gunzbourg...*, op. cit., pp. 141–4.
21. "Discours de M. M. Vinaver," in Heinrich Sliozberg, *Le Baron Horace O. de Gunzbourg...*, op. cit., pp. 137–40.
22. Alexandre de Gunzburg, Manuscript C, "Aperçu généalogique".
23. The Jewish "Pale of Settlement".
24. David Feinberg to the Alliance Israélite Universelle, 8 October 1909, Vilna, AIU URSS IV B (Feinberg file 1867–1913, pogroms).
25. Ivan Tolstoy, *Dnevnik 1906–1916*, op. cit.
26. Ibid.
27. David Feinberg to Jacques Bigard, 27 January 1911 [n.p., probably St Petersburg], AIU, URSS IV B (Feinberg file 1867–1913, pogroms).
28. David de Gunzburg to Mathilde de Gunzburg, RNB, f. 183 ed. khr. 50.

29

In the Age of the Russian Ballet

1. Asch Schalom, *Pétersbourg*, translated from the German by Alexandre Vialatte, Paris, Mémoire du livre, 1999, p. 184.
2. Ibid., p. 242.
3. *Almanach de Saint-Pétersbourg cour, monde et ville, 1913/14*, Mellier et Cie, St-Petersburg and H. A. Ludwig Degener, Leipzig.
4. Louise Abbema, *Femme au manchon devant l'église Saint-Isaac, à Saint-Pétersbourg*, oil on canvas, Musée Carnavalet, Paris, Seligmann collection.
5. Album of photographs of the house at 13 Millionnaya Street. Archive of Macha Levinson (de Gunzburg).
6. Alexandre de Gunzburg, Manuscript A, "Le salon des Stassioulevitch".
7. Olga Bauer de Gunzburg, "Maria Andreevna Koulakova-Chepeliova, known as Mania (1879?–1962)". Archive of Katia Guth-Dreyfus.

8. Ibid.
9. Olga Bauer de Gunzburg, "Te rappelles-tu? 70 ans d'Anna Halpérin". Archive of Katia Guth-Dreyfus.
10. Olga Bauer de Gunzburg, "Souvenirs de Fedia (Theodore de Gunzburg)". Archive of Katia Guth-Dreyfus.
11. Ibid.
12. Ibid.
13. Gavrik Ashkenasy and Elisabeth Lorin, op. cit.
14. Ibid.
15. Ibid.
16. Arnold L. Haskell and Walter Nouvel, *Diaghileff, His Artistic and Private Life*, New York, Simon and Schuster, 1935. The materials concerning Dimitri de Gunzburg were provided by Valerian Svetlov, "doyen of ballet critics".
17. Roger Stéphane, *Portrait-souvenir de Jean Cocteau*, Paris, Tallandier, 1964.
18. Arnold L. Haskell and Walter Nouvel, op. cit.
19. Ibid., pp. 195–6.
20. *Journal de Nijinsky*, Paris, Gallimard, 1991.
21. Valerian Svetlov, quoted in Arnold L. Haskell and Walter Nouvel, op. cit., p. 197.
22. Gavrik Ashkenasy and Elisabeth Lorin, op. cit.
23. Arnold L. Haskell and Walter Nouvel, op. cit., p. 198.
24. Ibid., p. 199.

30

The Lena: From Gold to Massacre

1. *Vechernoye Vremya*, 5 April 1912. Quoted in Manfred Hagen, "Lenskiy rasstrel 1912 goda i rossiyskaya obshchestvennost', *Otechestvennaya istoriya: zhurnal*", 2002, no. 2.
2. Ibid.
3. Nicholas V. Riasanosvky, *A History of Russia*, 9th ed., Oxford, Oxford University Press, 2018; *Histoire de la Russie, des origines à 1996*, translated from the English by André Berelowitch, Paris, Robert Laffont, p. 464.
4. Manfred Hagen, op. cit.
5. 5 May new style.
6. "Lenskiy rasstrel", *Bolshaya sovetskaya entsiklopediya* (http://bse.sci-lib.com/article069626.html). The name Gunzburg is not mentioned among the stockholders, the publisher of the Encyclopedia retaining only Vyshnegradsky, Putilov, Witte and Empress Maria Fyodorovna. Moreover, the Gunzburgs are never mentioned in the *Great Soviet Encyclopaedia*.
7. Michael Melancon, *The Lena Goldfields Massacre and the Crisis of the Late Tsarist State*, College Station TX, Texas A. & M. University Press, 2006.
8. "Account for 1881 and liquidation of the inheritance of the late Baron Joseph de Gunzburg", archive of Jean de Gunzburg.
9. Ibid.
10. At that point, Horace's associates were Counts Pyotr and Pavel Shuvalov. The latter had commanded the Imperial Guard, and had then been Russia's

ambassador in Berlin before being named governor-general of Poland. He came to dine at the "Boulevard" but "set as a condition that he be served cheese at the end of the meal, and that tormented [the steward] Meyer because of the separate dairy dishes that had to be provided". Alexandre de Gunzburg, Manuscript A, "Ma chère Lilia".

11. In addition to the Gunzburgs, the other shareholders were M. Meyer, V. Vok, M. Varshaver and K. Vinberg.
12. Oleg N. Razumov, "Iz istorii vzaimootnosheniy rossiyskogo i inostrannogo aktsionernogo kapitala v sibirskoy zolotopromyshlennosti v nachale XX veka", in *Predprinimateli i predprinimatel'stvo v Sibiri v XVIII-nachale XX veka*, Barnaul, LGU, 1995, pp. 139–53.
13. Mimi (Alfred) de Gunzburg to David de Gunzburg, 21 November 1892, Sukhoy Log, RNB, f. 183 ed. khr. 388.
14. Gavrik Ashkenasy and Elisabeth Lorin, op. cit.
15. Alfred de Gunzburg, "On the question of the seizure of the gold industry. The order of the acquisition of mining properties for all the mining industries and the right of property in the law of foreign states" (in Russian).
16. "Album photographique de Pierre de Gunzbourg", archive of Aline Berlin (de Gunzbourg).
17. Letter from Alfred de Gunzburg to Innokenty Belozyorov, quoted by Manfred Hangen, op. cit.
18. 13 March new style.
19. On 7 June 1913, the report "Information d'Etat sur l'affaire de la grève du printemps 1912 dans les mines d'or de la Société de la Lena" was published. Manfred Hagen, op. cit.
20. Gavrik Ashkenasy and Elisabeth Lorin, op. cit. According to Gavrik Ashkenasy, Mamzelle married Jean-Alexandre David-Weill, the son of David David-Weill, a "very wealthy but violent" financier and collector, whom she divorced after five months. Her mother Sonia, who had arranged the marriage, was so upset by this that she committed suicide. Shortly afterwards Mamzelle married Charles Weil, an American, with whom she had a daughter.
21. Archive of Christine de Gunzbourg.

31

Vladimir and the Ansky Expedition

1. Ansky to Chaïm Jitlovsky, quoted in Gabriella Safran and Steven J. Zipperstein, eds, *The Worlds of S. An-sky A Russian Jewish Intellectual at the Turn of the Century*, Stanford CA, Stanford University Press, 2006, p. 5.
2. Vladimir de Gunzburg to Ansky, 22 April (12 May) 1912, Paris. The Vernardsky National Library in Kiev (Judaica section, department of manuscripts) preserves 22 letters and a postcard in Russian and one in Yiddish written by Ansky to Vladimir de Gunzburg between 1911 and 1913 (IR IFO NBUV, f. 339 ed. khr. 944–963), as well as 21 letters from Vladimir de Gunzburg to Ansky in Russian, written between 1910 and 1914 (IR IFO NBUV, f. 339 ed khr. 295–316). All the correspondence has been published: Irina Sergeeva (ed.), "Perepiska barona

Gintsburga i S. An-skogo po povodu etnograficheskikh ekspeditsii v cherte evreyskoy osedlosti", *Ab Imperio*, no. 4 (2003).

3. The Wissotzky Tea Company, founded in Moscow in 1849, still exists today in Israel.
4. Vladimir de Gunzburg to Ansky, 22 April (12 May) 1912, Paris. IR IFO NBUV, d. 339 ed. khr. 300, ll. 10–11.
5. Ansky to Chaïm Jitlovski, quoted in Gabriella Safran and Steven J. Zipperstein, eds, op. cit.
6. YIVO RG 348 Lucien Wolf and David Mowshowitch Papers, Folder 105, Mendel Beilis trial. The file contains two letters from Alexandre de Gunzburg to Lucien Wolf dated August 1913 that show the organisation of scientific reports by British scholars contradicting the prosecution's arguments.
7. Gabriella Safran and Steven J. Zipperstein, eds, op. cit., p. 97.
8. Yu. Engel, "Evreyskaya narodnaya pesnya. Etnograficheskaya poyezdka letom 1912", *Paralleli: Russko-evreyskii istoriko-literaturnyi almanakh*, nos. 4–5, Moscow, 2004, p. 287.
9. Alexander Ivanov, *Experiments of a "Young Man for Photographic Works": Solomon Yudovin and Russian Pictorialism of 1910s*, Petersburg Judaica, 2005.
10. Vladimir de Gunzburg, from Paris, to Ansky in St Petersburg, 29 May (11 June) 1913, IR IFO NBUV, d. 339 ed. khr. 306, l. 6. Quoted in Gabriella Safran and Steven J. Zipperstein, eds, op. cit., p. 93.
11. The exhibition took place on Vasilyevsky Island, 5th line, in the House of Charity belonging to the merchant Moses A. Ginsburg (no relation to the Barons de Gunzburg). It was visited by the writer Sholem Aleichem on 14 May (27 May) 1914.
12. Letter from Vladimir de Gunzburg to Ansky, sent from Cannes, 30 January (12 February) 1914, IR OFI NBUV, f. 339 ed. khr. 312, quoted in Gabriella Safran and Steven J. Zipperstein, eds, op. cit., pp. 362–3.
13. Ibid., p. 102.
14. 400 items in 1918.

32

Family Mobilisation

1. Alexandre de Gunzburg, Manuscript C, "Aperçu généalogique".
2. Gavrik Ashkenasy and Elisabeth Lorin, op. cit. See also AN, file no. 4213X13 (Michel de Gunzburg's request for naturalisation).
3. Alexandre de Gunzburg to I. L. Goremykin, 10 June 1914, St Petersburg. Translated from the Russian by Alexandre de Gunzburg. Alexandre de Gunzburg, Manuscript C, "Lettre à I. L. Goremykine".
4. *L'Univers israélite*, 12 February 1915, p. 351.
5. Gavrik Ashkenasy and Elisabeth Lorin, op. cit.
6. Mathilde de Gunzburg to Eugène (Gino) de Gunzburg, 14 December 1914, Geneva, RNB, f. 183 ed. khr. 1935.
7. "29 août 1914: autorisation de voyager de Francfort à Hambourg pour Anna, Olga, Véra et la gouvernante Wilhelmina Sanderson (née en 1881 à Melrose en Ecosse)". Archive of Katia Guth-Dreyfus.

8. "Livret militaire de réserviste, traduit du russe." AN, BB/11/4544, naturalisation file no. 5696 X1925, Vladimir Georges de Gunzburg.

9. AN, BB/11/4544, naturalisation file no. 7873X1906, Jean Maurice de Gunzburg.

10. Citation awarded by the Army (27 October 1915) to the mobile field hospital no. 1, commanded by Colonel Osnobishin, a Russian assistant military attaché. Archive of Gérard de Gunzburg.

11. Like the colonel of his regiment, Gordon Wilson, Alexis de Gunzburg was buried in the cemetery at Zillebeke. In 1924, his mother, Henriette de Gunzburg, gave the Zillebeke church two bells in memory of her son. See Jerry Murland, *Aristocrats go to war: Uncovering the Zillebeke Cemetery*, Pen and Sword, 2010, p. 20 (http://theyserved.wikia.com/wiki/Alexis_de_Gunzburg#cite_note-ari-4). The First World War memorial at Hoop Lane Cemetery in London mentions Alexis de Gunzburg.

12. Marcel Proust to Reynaldo Hahn, 21 November 1914, in Marcel Proust, *Correspondance*, op. cit.

13. Mathilde de Gunzburg to Eugène (Gino) de Gunzburg, 27 November 1914, Geneva, RNB, f. 183 ed. khr. 1935.

14. Mathilde de Gunzburg to Eugène (Gino) de Gunzburg, 16 September 1914, Geneva. Ibid.

15. Mathilde de Gunzburg to Eugène (Gino) de Gunzburg, 28 October 1914, Geneva. Ibid.

16. Mathilde de Gunzburg to Eugène (Gino) de Gunzburg, 27 November 1914, Geneva. Ibid.

17. Nadia Mendel to Eugène (Gino) de Gunzburg, 1 November 1914, Brăila, RNB, f. 183 ed. khr. 1948.

18. Vladimir Mendel to Osip and Eugène (Gino) de Gunzburg, 1 November 1914, Brăila, RNB, f. 183 ed. khr. 1965.

19. Ibid.

20. Mathilde de Gunzburg to Eugène (Gino) de Gunzburg, Geneva, 5 February 1915, RNB, f. 183 ed. khr. 1935.

21. Mathilde de Gunzburg to Eugène (Gino) de Gunzburg, Geneva, 28 October 1914, RNB, f. 183 ed. khr. 1935.

22. *Evreyskiy Komitet Pomoshchi Zhertvam Voyny.*

23. EKOPO report, in French, probably from 1917. YIVO, RG 348. Lucien Wolf and David Mowshowitch Papers, Folder 107, pp. 14537–41.

24. It was Grand Duke Nicholas Nikolayevich, whose bust Antokolsky had made in 1879, who decided to issue the ukase expelling Jews during the war.

25. "L'action du comité dans les régions voisines du front et dans les localités d'où furent [expulsés] les juifs (jusqu'à la fin de l'année 1917)", YIVO, RG 348. Lucien Wolf and David Mowshowitch Papers, Folder 107, pp. 14568–76.

26. *L'Univers israélite*, 2 June 1916, p. 5.

27. "L'action du comité dans les régions voisines du front et dans les localités d'où furent [expulsés] les juifs (jusqu'à la fin de l'année 1917)", YIVO, RG 348. Lucien Wolf and David Mowshowitch Papers, Folder 107, pp. 14568–76.

28. *Obshchetsvo Zdravookhraneniya Evreyev.*

29. "L'action du comité dans les régions voisines du front et dans les localités d'où furent [expulsés] les juifs (jusqu'à la fin de l'année 1917)", YIVO, RG 348. Lucien Wolf and David Mowshowitch Papers, Folder 107, pp. 14568–76.

30. Alexandre de Gunzburg to Aby Warburg, 15 June 1915, Petrograd, translated from the German, archive of Katia Guth-Dreyfus.
31. Olga Bauer de Gunzburg, "Te rappelles-tu? 70 ans d'Anna Halpérin", archive of Katia Guth-Dreyfus.
32. Alexandre de Gunzburg to Aby Warburg, 12/22 June 1915, Petrograd, translated from the German, archive of Katia Guth-Dreyfus.
33. Rosa de Gunzburg to Jacques Rosenberg, 30 June 1916, Petrograd, translated from the German, archive of Katia Guth-Dreyfus.
34. Alexandre de Gunzburg to M. Lamm, 16 (month illegible) 1916, Petrograd, translated from the German, archive of Katia Guth-Dreyfus.
35. Rosa de Gunzburg to Jacques Rosenberg, 15/28 February? 1917, Petrograd, mourning stationery bearing the censor's stamp. Archive of Katia Guth-Dreyfus.

33

Revolutions, Departures and Deaths

1. David Simonsen to Alexandre de Gunzburg, 17 April 1917, Copenhagen, Royal Library of Denmark, The David Simonsen Archives (Digital Editions).
2. Marc Ferro, "La politique des nationalités du gouvernement provisoire. Février–octobre 1917", *Cahiers du monde russe et soviétique*, 1961, vol. 2, pp. 131–65.
3. The stress is Sasha's.
4. Alexandre de Gunzburg to David Simonsen, 26 April/9 May 1917, Royal Library of Denmark, The David Simonsen Archives (Digital Editions).
5. Telegram in French from Boris Kamenka, Alexandre de Gunzburg and Heinrich Sliozberg to the Alliance Israélite Universelle, dated 8/5/1917. Kamenka was the director of the Azov-Don bank. Jacques Bigard, the secretary of the Alliance Israélite Universelle, replied that the AIU was doing everything it could to promote subscription to the Liberty loan. Alliance Israélite Universelle, URSS IC2 (Emigration file).
6. As a student Fedia had escaped mobilisation (he had been recruited as an assistant by the St Petersburg school of law and had written a dissertation on workers' insurance in England). Rosa de Gunzburg to M. Lamm, undated, Petrograd, archive of Katia Guth-Dreyfus.
7. Olga de Gunzburg to Rosa de Gunzburg, 13 April 1917, Dvinsk, translated from the Russian, archive of Katia Guth-Dreyfus.
8. Eugène (Gino) de Gunzburg to Véra de Gunzburg, 26 May 1917, translated from the Russian, archive of Katia Guth-Dreyfus.
9. Ibid.
10. "Baron de Gunzburg's letter on Jewish affairs in Russia", YIVO RG 348, Folder 115.
11. Very remote from the traditional centre of Jewish life in Russia, Birobidzhan was a poorly prepared project that was doomed to fail, though that did not much trouble the Soviet leadership. The first Jewish colonists lived there in squalor and isolation. Today, the Jewish population represents only 1 per cent of the population, or about 2,300 people.
12. Eugène (Gino) de Gunzburg to Osip de Gunzburg, 2 November 1917, translated from the Russian, RNB, f. 183 ed. khr. 1963.

13. Osip de Gunzburg to Vladimir Mendel, 13/26 January 1918, Petrograd, RGIA f. 1009 op. 2 ed. khr. 63.
14. Alexandre de Gunzburg to Aby Warburg, 3 July 1918, Petrograd, translated from the German, archive of Katia Guth-Dreyfus.
15. Elsa Warburg-Melchior, op. cit.
16. Alexandre de Gunzburg to Aby Warburg, 6 June 1918, Petrograd, archive of Katia Guth-Dreyfus.
17. Alexandre de Gunzburg to Aby Warburg, 20 June 1918, Petrograd, archive of Katia Guth-Dreyfus.
18. Alexandre de Gunzburg to Aby Warburg, 12 July 1918, Petrograd, archive of Katia Guth-Dreyfus.
19. Alexandre de Gunzburg to Anna and Theodore (Fedia) de Gunzburg, 10 August 1918, Petersbourg [*sic*]. "Arrestation et détention. Récit complet." Sasha explained that "in the course of Thursday night a new group of prisoners was brought, including Vladimir Trepov." Archive of Katia Guth-Dreyfus.
20. Olga Bauer de Gunzburg, "Es waren schritte...", translated from the German, archive of Katia Guth-Dreyfus.
21. Olga Bauer de Gunzburg, "Es waren schritte...", op. cit.
22. Ibid.
23. Ibid.
24. Isaak Grinberg (1897–1938) had been involved in the revolutionary youth movement.
25. Alexandre de Gunzburg, Manuscript A, "Le salon de Stassioulevitch".
26. Véra Dreyfus de Gunzburg, "Récit du voyage de la Russie en Allemagne en décembre 1918 écrit en 1971", archive of Katia Guth-Dreyfus.
27. Ibid.
28. Mania, who had entered the Gunzburgs' service in 1897, remained with Sasha and his children until her death in 1962. Thus she lived in France, Holland, Spain (after the Second World War) and Switzerland, finally bringing up Sasha's grandchildren. At the time of her death, she was living at the home of Irène, Sasha and Rosa's youngest daughter. Since she was a Russian Orthodox Christian, Irène asked an Orthodox priest to come and pray for the deceased. When Irène thanked him for having been willing to say the Panikhida in a Jewish house, he replied: "Maria Andreevna was a special soul, I am happy to have been able to carry out this supreme Christian act in your home, in a house of Jews, towards whom we have acted so culpably." Olga Bauer de Gunzburg, "Maria Andreevna Koulakova-Chepeliova, dite Mania (1879?–1962)". Archive of Katia Guth-Dreyfus.
29. Ibid.
30. Gavrik Ashkenasy and Elisabeth Lorin, op. cit.
31. Ibid.
32. Philippe de Gunzbourg, "Tout un ensemble", unpublished manuscript, p. 9.

Notes

Part VI

From One Exile to Another

34

Stateless Persons

1. The "Nansen passport" was established in 1922 by the League of Nations' High Commissariat for Russian Refugees.
2. The Central Office for Russian Refugees (OCRR) was established in May 1925 and functioned until the establishment of the French Office for the Protection of Refugees and Stateless Persons (OFPRA) in July 1952, with a pause between 1942 and 1945.
3. "Certificat de mariage de Vladimir de Gunzburg et Claire Brodsky", signed by Ailoff, director of the Office for Russian Refugees, 15 June 1925, archive of Cyrille de Gunzburg.
4. AN, BB/11/4544 file no. 7873X1906 De Gunzburg Jean Maurice.
5. AN, file no. 5696 X1925 Naturalisation Gunzburg Vladimir Georges. Before Jean and Vladimir, Michel de Gunzburg obtained French naturalisation in 1913: Alexandre's eldest son, he had at that point lived in Paris "for fifty-three years". In the file, we find the following handwritten annotation: "Request without interest. The applicant has no children. He is 63 years old. Although has paid all the fees for nationalisation and despite the prefect's favourable opinion, propose to reject, 15 May 1913." And in another hand: "The applicant pays 6,600 francs rent and thus has the greatest chance of never being a burden to us. The information collected on him is good. So then why reject this request? Granted 18 May 1913." AN, file no. 4213X13, Demande de naturalisation de Michel de Gunzburg et de sa femme Thérèse née Hermann, 7 April 1913.
6. Gabriel had retained habits formed during his long stay in the Far East. His niece Gavrik recalls the tea that he kept in large wooden boxes and rolls of Japanese white silk that was used to make his nieces' finest outfits. Gavrik Ashkenasy and Elisabeth Lorin, op. cit.
7. A few decades later, a second marriage was to unite the Gunzburgs and the Gramonts once again: Philippe de Gunzbourg married Marguérite de Gramont in 1952.
8. Cyril Grange, op. cit., p. 95.
9. https://web.archive.org/web/20110316114920/http://www.forbes.ru/article/19960-millionshchiki.
10. Photograph album belonging to Pierre de Gunzbourg, archive of Aline Berlin (de Gunzbourg).
11. Aline de Gunzbourg, Conversation with Andrew Strauss (1999), archive of Andrew Strauss.
12. Philippe de Gunzbourg, "Tout un ensemble", op. cit., p. 22.
13. He had himself registered with the spelling "Gunzbourg".
14. Ibid., p.22.

15. Ibid., p. 8.
16. Ibid., p. 23.
17. Ibid., p. 8.
18. Ibid., p. 165.
19. Elsa Warburg-Melchior, op. cit.
20. Olga thus became by marriage the sister-in-law of Gisel Ephrussi, who married Alfred Bauer in Vienna in 1924. See Edmund de Waal, *The Hare with Amber Eyes: A Hidden Inheritance*, London, Chatto & Windus, 2010.
21. Rosa de Gunzburg to Aby Warburg, 27 May 1921, Paris, translated from the German by Katia Guth-Dreyfus, archive of Katia Guth-Dreyfus.
22. Alexandre de Gunzburg to his daughters, 27 October 1933, Amsterdam, archive of Katia Guth-Dreyfus.
23. "Agreement, made and entered into this twenty-first day of July, 1914, between baroness Mathilde de Gunzburg, of St Petersburg, Russia, hereinafter called the Vendor, and the Jewish Theological Seminary of America, hereinafter called the Purchaser", archive of Christine de Gunzbourg.
24. Osip de Gunzburg to Mathilde de Gunzburg, Tokyo, 20 November 1921, archive of Christine de Gunzbourg.
25. Osip died in Berck-sur-Mer in 1930 and Lizette in Paris in 1935. Both of them were interred in the family mausoleum in the Montparnasse cemetery.
26. See the correspondence between Mathilde de Gunzburg and Pierre de Gunzbourg in the archive of Christine de Gunzbourg.
27. Monique de Gunzburg, op. cit., p. 36.
28. Ibid., p. 39.
29. "Dossier Alfred de Gunzburg", AIU, France IV 30 A, liasse 19-33 *bis*.

35

Bankers

1. AN, LH/1249/55, Jacques de Gunzburg.
2. Ibid.
3. Hubert Bonin, "Albert Kahn, financier et banquier" (www.hubertbonin.com).
4. Ibid.
5. Ibid.
6. In a letter to David de Gunzburg, dated Paris, 3 March 1898, Jacques mentions Hoskier anecdotally: "Hoskier paid me 1,000 f[rancs] a few days ago: I assume that this is the money I had advanced to Rivlin. Please confirm." RNB, f. 183 ed. khr. 428.
7. René Girault often refers to these brokers, but to date there is no in-depth study of their actual role. See René Girault, *Emprunts russes et investissements français en Russie, 1887–1914*, CHEFF, 1999.
8. AN, LH/1249/55, Jacques de Gunzburg.
9. See chapter 30, "The Lena: From Gold to Massacre".
10. Hubert Bonin, op. cit.
11. His title was "Director of the Ritz Hotels Development Corporation".
12. Hubert Bonin asserts, however, that "Rothschild directed the placement of the

French share of the Japanese loan of 1907 (almost 300 million francs) with subparticipants benefiting from a 'retrocession' of the share of the major banks that were the co-leaders: behind Rothschild, Crédit Lyonnais, Société Générale, Paribas, the CNEP, the CIC, as well as Hottinguer and Vernes." Referring to "Kahn, the pioneer of Euro-Japanese business", Bonin emphasises as well the existence of a delegation of businessmen in Japan in 1908–9 without saying whether Jacques de Gunzburg was or was not part of it.

13. Hubert Bonin, op. cit.
14. René Boucheron (the administrator of the Compagnie des Omnibus de Paris), the Compagnie Française des Mines d'Or de l'Afrique du Sud and the bankers or merchants Hubert Henrotte, Henry Hirsch, Raphaël-Georges Lévy, the Singer brothers, Benoît Tilche, Gaston Verdé-Delisle and Léonidas Zarifi.
15. Philippe de Gunzbourg, op. cit., p. 9.
16. From the years he spent in Cairo, Count de Saint-Maurice had brought back exceptional objects and decorative elements. With Jacques de Gunzburg, he was one of the founders of Dieppe golf course. The banker, who was already renting his villa, bought it upon the diplomat's death.
17. Archive of Cyrille de Gunzburg.
18. AN, LH/1249/55, Jacques de Gunzburg.
19. Autobiographical note, "Jean de Gunzburg", added as an appendix to the letter sent by André Louis-Hirsch and Jean de Gunzburg to the General Commissioner for Jewish Questions, 5 July 1941, archive of Jean de Gunzburg.
20. Cyril Grange, op. cit., pp. 100–101.

36

Gunzburg Style

1. Conversation with Ariel de Ravenel, Nicolas de Gunzburg's goddaughter.
2. Philippe de Gunzbourg, op. cit., p. 27.
3. Monique de Gunzburg, op. cit., p. 11.
4. Ibid., p. 46.
5. Gavrik Ashkenasy and Elisabeth Lorin, op. cit., p. 21.
6. Philippe de Gunzbourg, op. cit., p. 74.
7. Ibid., p. 41.
8. Ibid., p. 72. The reference is to the eponymous hero of Colette's novel *Chéri* (1920).
9. Ibid., p. 73.
10. Ibid., p. 77.
11. Aline de Gunzbourg, *Memories*, unpublished, p. 5. Archive of Aline Berlin (de Gunzbourg).
12. 25 Avenue Bugeaud remained in the family: from 1959 to 1980, Alain de Gunzburg (Jean's son) and his wife Minda (née Bronfman) lived there with their children Jean and Charles.
13. Monique de Gunzburg, op. cit., p. 29.
14. Ibid., pp. 34–5.
15. 9 April 1930, legacy of Madame Henriette Ernestine Goldschmidt, Baroness de Gunzburg, archives of the Musées Nationaux, 20 1447 90/87.

16. Aline de Gunzbourg, conversation with Andrew Strauss.
17. Archive of Aline Berlin (de Gunzbourg).
18. The house was subsequently bought by Karl Lagerfeld, who resold it to Alain Afflelou, the current owner.
19. Monique de Gunzburg, op. cit., p. 41.
20. Convinced that his father had hidden money in Switzerland, Nicky de Gunzburg hired a detective, who never found the hoped-for funds. However, Nicky inherited the Ritz-Carlton Company stocks his father had held.
21. Gretchen Weinberg and G. Hermann, "Entretiens avec le baron Nicolas de Gunzburg", translated by Dominique Villain, in Carl Th. Dreyer, *Réflexions sur mon métier*, Paris, *Cahiers du cinéma*, Editions de l'Etoile, 1983, p. 152.
22. Jean-Louis de Faucigny-Lucinge, *Un gentilhomme cosmopolite. Mémoires*, Paris, Perrin, 1990, p. 105.
23. Gretchen Weinberg and G. Hermann, op. cit., p. 152.
24. Jean-Louis de Faucigny-Lucinge, op. cit., pp. 113–14.
25. Ibid.
26. Gretchen Weinberg and G. Hermann, op. cit., pp. 182–8.
27. Carl Th. Dreyer, op. cit.
28. Jean-Louis de Faucigny-Lucinge, op. cit. The Faucigny-Lucinges' granddaughter, Ariel de Ravenel, recalls that Nicky spent every summer in their house Les Rocs at Cap d'Agde. When Ariel married, he gave her pretty Russian dishes in silver, which no doubt came from his father.
29. Monique Gunzburg, op. cit., p. 49.
30. Ibid., p. 50.
31. Ibid., p. 52.
32. Ibid., p. 53.
33. Ibid.

37

At War

1. Guy de Gunzburg, "Dunkerque oublié", p. 3. Archive of Eliane Beckman.
2. Ibid., p. 4.
3. Philippe de Gunzbourg, op. cit., p. 41.
4. Conversation with Guy Harari, son of Ruth Ippen-Harari.
5. Hans-Peter's account, reported by Dom Marie-Gérard Dubois, *Le Bonheur en Dieu. Souvenirs et réflexions du père abbé de La Trappe*, Paris, Robert Laffont, 1995, p. 256.
6. Aline de Gunzbourg, conversation in French. Archive of Aline Berlin (de Gunzbourg).
7. Guy de Gunzburg, op. cit., p. 4.
8. Aly Khan to Aline de Gunzbourg, 7 February 1940, in English, archive of Aline Berlin (de Gunzbourg).
9. Aly Khan to Aline de Gunzbourg, 5 April 1940, in English, archive of Aline Berlin (de Gunzbourg).
10. Guy de Gunzburg, op. cit., p. 4.

11. Ibid., p. 5.
12. Ibid., p. 7.
13. Yves de Gunzburg died in combat on 30 January 1945. See the following pages.
14. Monique de Gunzburg, op. cit., pp. 68–9.
15. Guy de Gunzburg, op. cit., p. 14.
16. Philippe de Gunzbourg, op. cit.
17. Guy de Gunzburg, op. cit., p. 14.
18. Jean de Gunzburg and André Louis-Hirsch to the General Commissioner for Jewish Questions, 5 July 1941, Chatel-Guyon. Archive of Jean de Gunzburg.
19. Autobiographical note, "Jean de Gunzburg", appended to the letter André Louis-Hirsch and Jean de Gunzburg sent to the General Commissioner for Jewish Questions, 5 July 1941, archive of Jean de Gunzburg.
20. David Maggid, *Histoire de la famille Gunzburg*, translated from the Hebrew, unpublished manuscript, archive of Katia Guth-Dreyfus.
21. His cousin by marriage, Pierre Hirsch, undertook the same task for the Hirsch family, as he wrote to Jean: "Your ideas and mine coincide, because I had already hired a genealogist to collect documents concerning our paternal ancestors, among others, those establishing that my great-grandfather David Hirsch, who fought at Waterloo, received the Saint Hélène medal. It was he who founded in 1830, on Rue Quincampoix, the gold and silver metals company." Pierre Hirsch to Jean de Gunzburg, "war postcard", date illegible, archive of Jean de Gunzburg.
22. Bibka (Anna) Merle d'Aubigné to Jean de Gunzburg, war postcard, date illegible, Paris, archive of Jean de Gunzburg.
23. Robert Loewy to Jean de Gunzburg, war postcard, February 1942, Saint-Germain-en-Laye, archive of Jean de Gunzburg. (A descendant of Ury's by his mother Hélène, Robert later had his name officially changed, giving up Loewy for Gunzbourg.)
24. Conversation with Christine de Gunzbourg.
25. AD, 300W78, Two lists of foreign Jews, undated (1941?), quoted in François Boulet, *Leçon d'histoire de France, Saint-Germain en Laye: des antiquités nationales à une ville internationale*, DISLAB, 2006, p. 349.
26. André Louis-Hirsch and Jean de Gunzburg to the General Commissioner for Jewish Questions, 5 July 1941, Chatelguyon, archive of Jean de Gunzburg.
27. Ibid.
28. Interview with Aline Berlin (de Gunzbourg) by Marie de Mouchy. Archive of Aline Berlin (de Gunzbourg).
29. Monique de Gunzburg, op. cit.
30. Guy de Gunzburg, op. cit., p. 15.
31. Letter from Fedia (Theodore) de Gunzburg to Sasha (Alexandre) de Gunzburg, 16 July 1940, archive of Macha Levinson (de Gunzburg).
32. Philippe de Gunzbourg to Aline de Gunzbourg, 16 May 1941, Le Barsalous, archive of Aline Berlin (de Gunzburg).
33. Antoinette de Gunzbourg to Aline de Gunzbourg, undated, Le Barsalous, archive of Hélène de Gunzbourg.
34. Hélène de Gunzbourg, biographical note, "Philippe de Gunzbourg". Archive of Hélène de Gunzbourg.
35. Serge de Gunzburg to Véra Valabrègue, 22 April 1941, archive of Nora Valabrègue.

36. Philippe de Gunzbourg to Aline de Gunzbourg, 10 July 1941, Le Barsalous, archive of Aline Berlin (de Gunzburg).
37. Philippe de Gunzbourg to Aline de Gunzbourg, 30 December 1941, Le Barsalous, archive of Aline Berlin (de Gunzbourg).
38. Philippe de Gunzbourg, op. cit., p. 42. See Michel Laffitte, "L'UGIF, collaboration ou résistance?", *Revue d'histoire de la Shoah*, Paris, 2006/2 (no. 185), pp. 45–64.
39. Ibid.
40. Philippe de Gunzbourg to Aline de Gunzbourg, Le Barsalous, 30 December 1941, archive of Aline Berlin (de Gunzbourg).
41. Philippe de Gunzbourg to Aline de Gunzbourg, 15 April 1942, archive of Aline Berlin (de Gunzbourg).
42. Hector Feliciano, *Le Musée disparu. Enquête sur le pillage des oeuvres d'art en France par les nazis*, translated from the Spanish by Svetlana Doubin, Paris, Gallimard, "Folio histoire," 2008.
43. Cyril Grange, op. cit., p. 335.
44. Philippe de Gunzbourg to Aline de Gunzbourg, 15 April 1942, archive of Aline Berlin (de Gunzbourg).
45. The family's efforts to help Nanny Habig leave France had failed: "Despite everyone's efforts, the countries of North, South and Central America have refused an entry visa to my father's cousin Nanny Habig, an Austrian Jew who had fled to Nice because of her two ravishing young daughters who were on the blacklist." Monique de Gunzburg, *Souvenirs*, op. cit., p. 73.
46. At the Trappist monastery of Soligny, he paradoxically reconnected with Jewish culture, as Father Paul recounts: "It was then that our brother rediscovered his Jewish roots. Head of the hostel, and then of the monastery's library, he became the "Jew with the Psalms", an indefatigable peddler of the Aggadah, whom many people know. The friend of numerous rabbis, he founded a study group, the "Beth Midrash Hallel", and then (in 2006) the Na'ir Association, which takes as its goal to adapt commentaries (ancient or contemporary) on the written or oral Torah to a French-speaking audience that is not familiar with rabbinical literature, to edit them and to disseminate them." Hans-Peter Ippen, having become the monk Jean-Pierre, had as his Hebrew teacher Georges Levitte (1918–1999), member of the Resistance, translator and writer.
47. Dom Marie-Gerard Dubois, op. cit., pp. 257–8.
48. On this subject, see Michel Laffitte and Annette Wieviorka, *A l'intérieur du camp de Drancy*, Paris, Perrin, 2012.
49. Conversation with Guy Harari.
50. Dom Marie-Gerard Dubois, op. cit., pp. 268–70.
51. Ibid., p. 270.
52. Conversation with Guy Harari.

Notes

38

Resistance Fighters

1. Monique de Gunzburg, op. cit., p. 77.
2. Ibid.
3. Philippe de Gunzbourg, "Tout un ensemble"; Monique de Gunzburg, *Souvenirs*; Hélène de Gunzbourg, "Philippe de Gunzbourg", biographical note.
4. Michael R. D. Foot, *SOE in France: An Account of the Work of the British Special Operations Executive in France, 1940–1944*, London, HMSO, History of the Second World War, 1966.
5. Max Hastings, *Das Reich. The March of the 2nd SS Panzer Division through France, June 1944*, London, Papermac, 1993, p. 81.
6. Hélène de Gunzbourg, op. cit.
7. Max Hastings, op. cit., p. 81.
8. Bergeret and Herman Grégoire, *Messages personnels*, Bordeaux, Edition Bière, 1945. The book opens with a photograph of "Philibert and Bergeret in the maquis" and bears a handwritten dedication from Bergeret: "To Philippe de Gunzbourg, who, better than I, is the author of this book and whose friendship, which he has shown me in the course of these adventures, is the best of my rewards." Archive of Jacques de Gunzbourg.
9. Philippe de Gunzbourg, op. cit., pp. 91–2.
10. Monique de Gunzburg, op. cit., p. 81.
11. Ibid., pp. 83–4.
12. Ibid., p. 84.
13. Ibid., p. 87.
14. Philippe de Gunzbourg, op. cit., p. 96
15. Monique de Gunzburg, op. cit., p. 101.
16. Hélène de Gunzbourg, op. cit.
17. Philippe de Gunzbourg, op. cit., p. 103.
18. Ibid.
19. "Déclaration d'engagement d'Alain de Gunzburg, Délégation du Comité national français aux Etats-Unis, Service des volontaires", SHDN, "De Gunzburg Lieutenant Alain François Jacques, Réserve arme blindée cavalerie", file no. 7013134.
20. Jean-Paul and Pierre Lavoix had crossed the Channel in a canoe, with three friends. René Marbot left from Beirut with a group of young men.
21. A. Baudoin quoted by André Casalis, *Cadets de la France libre. L'école militaire*, Paris, Lavauzelle, 1994.
22. Office français d'information cinématographique, *Ils s'instruisent pour vaincre*, 1944 (http://www.ina.fr/video/AFE00002108). See also Dominique Torrès, *Ils ont consolé la France*, a documentary film, 52 mn, 2010. Dominique Torrès is the daughter of Georges Torrès, known as Achard (a Free France cadet), married to Terezka Torrès, who was a Pole, the daughter of the sculptor Marel Schwarz, and an officer in Free France's corps of female volunteers.
23. Report by General Monclar, 6 January 1943, quoted by André Casalis, *Cadets de la France libre. L'école militaire*, Paris, Lavauzelle, 1994, p. 149.

24. Campaign note by Major Lannusse, unit commander of French 2nd Armoured Division (*2e Division Blindée*), 30 January 1945, SHDN, "De Gunzburg Lieutenant Alain François Jacques, Réserve arme blindée cavalerie", file no. 7013134.
25. He remained loyal to the spirit of the Cadets, keeping in touch with his former fellow students who had formed an association.
26. Monique de Gunzburg, op. cit., p. 105.
27. Ibid., p. 119.

39

Spoils

1. Philippe de Gunzbourg to Pierre, Yvonne et Aline, 30 September 1944, Paris, archive of Hélène de Gunzbourg.
2. Philippe de Gunzbourg, op. cit., p. 43.
3. Stephane Amélineau, "La comtesse Marguerite de Gramont dite Margot: une vie aventureuse dans les défilés pyrénéens", Itinerairesdememoire.com.
4. Hans Halban worked in Frédéric Joliot-Curie's team at the Collège de France (with Lew Kowarski and Francis Perrin), which discovered the emission of secondary neutrons, a phenomenon that triggers chain reactions and, in that way, the production of atomic energy. On 19 June 1940, Halban and Kowarski left France aboard a British ship onto which had been loaded the French stocks of heavy water, while the stocks of uranium oxide were shipped out through Morocco. In December 1940, Halban and Kowarski carried out, in Cambridge, the crucial experiment concerning the functioning of a heavy water atomic reactor. See Dominique Mongin, "Joliot et l'aventure de l'eau lourde française", *L'Histoire*, October 2017, no. 440, pp. 22–3.
5. He had bought the whole property: the town house with its garden, an adjoining house, the apartment building at 21 Avenue Bugeaud, and the garage at 19 Avenue Bugeaud.
6. Monique de Gunzburg, op. cit., pp. 109–10.
7. Ibid.
8. Hector Feliciano, op cit., p. 329.
9. André Louis-Hirsch to the Office des biens et intérêts privés, 19 July 1945, Paris, archive of Jean de Gunzburg.
10. *Devisenschutzkommando* (Foreign Exchange Protection Commando), a special looting unit established by the Nazis in 1940; it operated in France, Belgium and the Netherlands.
11. "Left at the Banque de France", archive of Jean de Gunzburg.
12. Ibid.
13. In the *Catalogue de l'Exposition des oeuvres de J. H. Fragonard*, 7 June to 10 July 1921 (by Georges Wildenstein), the painting *Fauchon la veilleuse* corresponds to no. 68, and was reproduced. It now belongs to M. Albert Lehman (Paris).
14. 15 January 1955, file no. 1378, Madame veuve Louis Hirsch, file no. 1377 Baron Jean de Gunzburg, archive of Jean de Gunzburg.

Sources

I. FAMILY ARCHIVES

Archive of Aline Berlin (de Gunzbourg) (London)

Letters from Léon Bonnat to Anna de Gunzburg and to Horace de Gunzburg.
Letters from Alexey Bogolyubov to Horace de Gunzburg.
Letter from Botkin to Horace de Gunzburg.
Letters from Louis Brassin to Horace de Gunzburg.
Letter from Carolus Duran to Anna de Gunzburg.
Letters from Ivan Goncharov to Horace and to Louise de Gunzburg.
Letters from Ivan Kramskoy to Horace and to Louise de Gunzburg.
Letters from Nikolay Orlov to Horace de Gunzburg.
Letters from Anton Rubinstein to Horace de Gunzburg.
Letters from Nikolay Rubinstein to Horace de Gunzburg.
Letters from Ivan Turgenev to Horace de Gunzburg.
Letters from Mihály Zichy to Horace de Gunzburg.
Letters from Philippe de Gunzbourg to Aline de Gunzbourg.
Letters from Aly Khan to Aline de Gunzbourg.
Manuscript score by Jules Massenet, *Sarabande espagnole*, dedicated to Marc de Gunzburg.
Photograph album belonging to Pierre de Gunzbourg (Russia, 1900).
Aline de Gunzbourg, "Memoires".
Interview with Aline Berlin (de Gunzbourg) by Marie de Mouchy.

Archive of Christine de Gunzbourg (Saint-Germain-en-Laye)

Civil status records of Ida de Gunzburg, Siegfried Ashkenasy, Louise Ashkenasy.
"Agreement, made and entered into this twenty-first day of July, 1914, between baroness Mathilde de Gunzburg, of St Petersburg, Russia, hereinafter called the Vendor, and the Jewish Theological Seminary of America, hereinafter called the Purchaser."
Share certificates of the Lena Goldfields Company.
Last will and testament of Anna (Aniouta) Ashkenasy de Gunzburg.
Crimea file.

The Gunzburgs

Letters from Pierre de Gunzbourg to Mathilde de Gunzburg.
Letters from Osip de Gunzburg to Mathilde de Gunzburg.

Archive of Hélène de Gunzbourg (Paris)

Letters from Antoinette de Gunzbourg to Aline de Gunzbourg.
Hélène de Gunzbourg, "Note biographique Philippe de Gunzbourg".
Photograph albums belonging to Pierre and Yvonne de Gunzbourg.

Archive of Cyrille de Gunzburg (Paris)

"Certificat de mariage de Vladimir de Gunzburg and Claire Brodsky", signed by Ailoff, director of the Office for Russian Refugees, 15 June 1925.

Archive of Gérard de Gunzburg (Naples, Florida)

Ludwig III, Grand Duke of Hesse and of the Rhineland, "Acte d'anoblissement 'Freiherr von Günzburg'", 2 August 1874.

Archive of Jean de Gunzburg (London)

Joseph Evzel's Russian last will and testament, in French.
Association agreement between Joseph Evzel Gunzburg and his sons Horace and Salomon (J. E. Gunzburg Bank), 18 July 1876.
Report for 1881 and fulfilment of the bequests of the late baron Joseph de Gunzburg.
Sharing agreement between Horace, Salomon and Ury de Gunzburg and a list of their properties held in common, 21 October 1881, Saint Petersburg.
Birth certificate, marriage certificate and *ketubah* of Salomon de Gunzburg.
Account of Baron Salomon de Gunzburg's testament presented by Baron Robert de Gunzburg and M. Paul Augustin Huillier, notary in Paris.
Legacy to the Louvre museum by Henriette de Gunzburg of two portraits.
Jean de Gunzburg's Légion d'Honneur file.
Letter from Alexandre de Gunzburg to Jean de Gunzburg, 16 May 1935.
Letter from André Louis-Hirsch and Jean de Gunzburg to the General Commissioner for Jewish Questions, 5 July 1941, Châtelguyon (request for exemption from the prohibition on exercising the trade of banker).
Autobiographical notice, "Jean de Gunzburg" appended to the letter from André Louis-Hirsch and Jean de Gunzburg to the General Commissioner for Jewish Questions, 5 July 1941.
Letter from Bibka Merle d'Aubigné to Jean de Gunzburg.
Letter from Robert Loewy to Jean de Gunzburg.
Letter from Pierre Hirsch to Jean de Gunzburg.
Letter from André Louis-Hirsch to the Office des Biens et Intérêts Privés, 19 July 1945.
"Laissé à la banque de France."
"Liste des meubles et objets disparus pendant l'occupation allemande de l'appartement de M. le baron Jean de Gunzburg, 43, avenue du Maréchal-Fayolle."

Sources

Archive of Katia Guth-Dreyfus (Basle)

Civil status records (Alexandre de Gunzburg and his children).
Last will and testament of Lazar Brodsky (1904).
Photographs of the pogrom of Kiev (1905).
"29 août 1914 : autorisation de voyager de Francfort à Hambourg pour Anna, Olga, Véra and la gouvernante Wilhelmina Sanderson (née en 1881 à Melrose en Ecosse)."
Letters from Alexandre de Gunzburg to Aby Warburg.
Letters from Rosa Warburg de Gunzburg to Jacques Rosenberg.
Letters from Alexandre de Gunzburg to M. Lamm.
Letters from Rosa Warburg de Gunzburg to M. Lamm.
Letter from Olga de Gunzburg to Rosa de Gunzburg.
Letter from Eugène-Gino de Gunzburg to Véra de Gunzburg.
Letters from Alexandre de Gunzburg to Anna and Theodore (Fedia) de Gunzburg, "Arrestation et détention. Récit complet", 10 August 1918, Petersburg.
Letters from Alexandre de Gunzburg to his children (1920, 1930, 1940).
Alexandre de Gunzburg, "A mes héritiers", 11 October 1947.
Bauer de Gunzburg, Olga, "Es waren Schritte..."
Bauer de Gunzburg, Olga, "Maria Andreevna Koulakova-Chepeliova, dite Mania (1879?–1962)".
Bauer de Gunzburg, Olga, "Te rappelles-tu? 70 ans d'Anna Halpérin"
Bauer de Gunzburg, Olga, "Souvenirs de Fedia (Theodore de Gunzburg)".
Dreyfus de Gunzburg, Véra, "Récit du voyage de la Russie en Allemagne en décembre 1918 écrit en 1971" (in French).

Archive of Macha Levinson (de Gunzburg) (Geneva)

Letters from Theodore (Fedia) de Gunzburg to Alexandre (Sasha) de Gunzburg.
Photograph album, 13 Millionnaya Street (St Petersburg).

Archive of Elizabeth Lorin (New York)
Personal papers of Gavrik (Gabrielle) Ashkenasy.

Archive of Andrew Strauss (Paris)
Aline de Gunzbourg, conversation with Andrew Strauss (1999).

Archive of Nora Valabrègue (Paris)
Letters from Serge de Gunzburg to Véra Valabrègue.

Unpublished (unless otherwise indicated) family memoirs
Ashkenasy, Gavrik, and Lorin, Elisabeth, "Gavrik's Memories as told to Elisabeth", c. 1980 (archive of Elizabeth Lorin).
Gunzbourg, Philippe de, "Tout un ensemble", 1978 (archive of Jacques and Hélène de Gunzbourg).
Gunzburg, Alexandre de:
— Manuscript A, undated [Ricard, Zichy, Turgenev, Minski, Bogolioubov, Soloviev, Antokolsky, Massenet, Petites scènes enfantines, Quelques souvenirs de la génération précédente, Le pogrom, Le salon de Stassioulevitch, Gontcharov, Coni, Vieux parchemin] (archive of Macha Levinson (de Gunzburg)).

— Manuscript B, 1939 [Aperçu généalogique, Littérateurs et artistes, Politiques, Militaires, Société pour la propagation de l'instruction, La guerre de 1870] (archive of Macha Levinson (de Gunzburg)).
— Manuscript C, "Mémoires du Baron Alexandre de Gunzburg", 1939 [Aperçu généalogique, Lettre à Gorémikyne, Livres mentionnés dans l'histoire de la famille, Pojmanniki, Collaborateurs de mon grand-père, Serviteurs, Gens d'affaires, Installation à Paris, Nos professeurs, Littérateurs and artistes, Politiques, Militaires, Fondateurs de la Société pour la propagation de l'instruction] (archive of Katia Guth-Dreyfus).
— Manuscript D, "Mémoires de jeunesse", 1932 (archive of Katia Guth-Dreyfus).
Gunzburg, Guy de, "Dunkerque oublié" (archive of Eliane Beckman de Gunzburg).
Gunzburg, Monique de, *Souvenirs*, Paris, Jouve, 1996.
Günzburg, Sophie, "My Father, Baron David", in Davidowicz, Lucy S., *The Golden Tradition: Jewish Life and Thought in Eastern Europe*, New York, 1967, pp. 248–256.
Halphen, Louise, "Récit de Louise Halphen née Fould, écrit au Moulin Barry (Indre) en 1943" (archive of Alexis de Bryas).
Lachmann-Warburg, Olga, Notes (in English) (archive of Katia Guth-Dreyfus).
Warburg-Melchior, Elsa, "That Dear Past: Random Memories", 1949 (in collaboration with Ruth Melchior Fleck) (archive of Dimitri de Gunzburg / archive of Tania Blum).
Raphel High, Monique, *The Four Winds of Heaven*, San Francisco, Penner Publishing, 2008.

II. Institutional Archives

Archives nationales de France / National archives (France)

• Dossiers de naturalisation / Naturalisation files

BB/11/4544 De Gunzburg, Jean Maurice.
BB/11/5652 De Gunzburg, Michel and his wife Thérèse, née Hermann.
BB/11/8709 Gunzburg, Vladimir Georges.

• Minutier des notaires de Paris / Notarial Register of Paris

MC/ET/VI/1274 (last will and testament of Joseph de Gunzburg, 1 August 1876).
MC/ET/VI/1284 (distribution of Joseph de Gunzburg's bequests).
AN MC/ET/VIII/1582 (Fould/Gunzburg, marriage contract of 9 March 1862).
MC/ET/VIII/1748 (purchase of 7 Rue de Tilsitt).
MC/ET/VIII/1763.
MC/ET/VIII/1834 (sale contract between Pierre Armand Donon and Eve Mathilde Gunzburg, épouse Fould, 19 August 1880–20 January 1881).
MC/ET/VIII/1882.
AN MC/ET/XLII/1254 (Gunzburg/Vitali, sale contract, 10 June 1886).
MC/ET/LXIV/886 (Salomon de Gunzburg/Henriette Goldschmidt, marriage contract 21 June 1877).
MC/ET/LXIV/943 (liquidation of the joint property and legacy of Salomon Benoît Hayem Goldschmidt).
MC/ET/LXXXVII/1635.

• Dossier de légion d'honneur / Register of the légion d'honneur
LH/1249/55, Jacques de Gunzburg.

Sources

Archives nationales du monde du travail / National Archive of Labour, Enterprise and Industry (Roubaix)

Fonds Fould-Heine, 115 AQ 001 (Gunzburg affair).
Fonds Fould-Heine, 115 AQ 006 (advances to Russia).
Fonds Fould-Heine, 115 AQ 030 ("Rossiya" company).
Fonds Fould-Heine, 115 AQ 036 (Syndicate studying the creation of a gas company in St Petersburg. Project abandoned, 1858–1960).
Fonds Rothschild 132 AQ unlisted 76 (Gunzbourg, J. E., Saint Petersburg 1860–1869).

Archives de la préfecture de police / Police Headquarters Archive (Bobigny)

BB1 F 82 (Pépita Sanchez).
BB1 F204 (Alice Regnault).
BB7. DA389 (Sylvia Asportas).

Alliance Israélite Universelle (Paris)

URSS, IC1, "Pogrom de Kiev".
URSS, IC2, "Emigration".
URSS IV B, "St Petersburg".
France IV 30 A, liasse 19–33 bis, "Dossier Alfred de Gunzburg".

Service historique de la Défense nationale / National Defence Records Office (Vincennes)

"De Gunzburg, Lieutenant Alain François Jacques, Réserve arme blindée cavalerie", file no. 7013134.

Rossiyskaya natsional'naya biblioteka / Russian National Library, Department of manuscripts (RNB) (St Petersburg)

• f. 25, Mark Matveyevich Antokolsky
ed. khr. 11 (letter to Baron Horace de Gunzburg, in Russian).
• f. 183, David Gorasevich Gunzburg
ed. khr. 3 (journey to the Caucasus, 5 October 1881, in Russian).
ed. khr. 10 (voting documents, state Duma, 1905–07, in Russian).
ed. khr. 13 (Society for the Promotion of Culture among the Jews of Russia, in Russian).
ed. khr. 25 (ORT, in Russian).
ed. khr. 26 (Society for apartments at reduced rents, 1906–09, in Russian).
ed. khr. 27 (Jewish Colonisation Association, 1907–10, in Russian).
ed. khr. 45 (accounts, financial documents,1881–1910, in Russian).
ed. khr. 48 (various commercial contracts 1905–10).
ed. khr. 50 (poems dedicated to Mathilde de Gunzburg).
ed. khr. 55 ("Du rythme dans les vers", 1893, in French).
ed. khr. 62 ("On the conscious and unconscious connections between Spinoza and Jewish thought", in Russian).
ed. khr. 63 ("Le premier sculpteur israélite", on Antokolsky, in French).

ed. khr. 65 ("Quelques remarques sur le texte des lamentations de Jérémie and des élégies", 1903, in French).

ed. khr. 66 ("L'ornement hébreu", in French).

ed. khr. 74 ("Sur l'art juif. Remarques", in French).

ed. khr. 79 ("La connaissance de la langue basque peut-elle être utile à l'hébreu?" in French).

ed. khr. 83 ("Discours pour le centenaire de naissance de S. D. Luzzato").

ed. khr. 91 (Materials for the publication of the Jewish Encyclopaedia, 1901–08).

ed. khr. 96 (notes on Jewish manuscripts in the Gunzburg library).

ed. khr. 118 (letters to V. V. Stasov, 1885–93).

ed. khr. 172 (letters from M. M. Antokolsky to David de Gunzburg, 1879–99).

ed. khr. 186 (letters from Leopold Auer, 1886–1903).

ed. khr. 187 (letters from Iosif Akhron, violinist, 1905–08).

ed. khr. 255 (letters from Alexey Bogolyubov, 1883–84).

ed. khr. 268 (letters from Zyoma Bratman, on his problems at the Mogilno refinery, 26 July 1904).

ed. khr. 297 (letter from Mark Varshavsky to David de Gunzburg, in French).

ed. khr. 386 (letter from Alfred-Mimi de Gunzburg to David de Gunzburg, in Hebrew).

ed. khr. 387 (letters from Alexandre de Gunzburg to David de Gunzburg, 1879–1907, in French).

ed. khr. 388 (letters from Alfred-Mimi de Gunzburg to David de Gunzburg, 1879–80, in French).

ed. khr. 389 (letters from Anna-Aniouta de Gunzburg to David de Gunzburg, 1880–87).

ed. khr. 391 (letters from Mathilde-Babita de Gunzburg to David de Gunzburg, Alfred-Mimi de Gunzburg, Mathilde de Gunzburg, 1879–1907).

ed. khr. 392 (letters from Vladimir de Gunzburg to David de Gunzburg, 1879–1903).

ed. khr. 394 (letters from Horace de Gunzburg to David de Gunzburg, 1875–87, in French).

ed. khr. 395 (letters from Horace de Gunzburg to David de Gunzburg, 1877–1905).

ed. khr. 396 (letters from Horace de Gunzburg to David de Gunzburg, 1890–1907).

ed. khr. 398 (letter from Joseph Evzel de Gunzburg to David de Gunzburg, 1874, in Russian).

ed. khr. 399 (letter from Ida de Gunzburg to David de Gunzburg, 1880–87, in French).

ed. khr. 400 (letters from Ilya Ginzburg, sculptor, to David de Gunzburg, in Russian).

ed. khr. 404 (letters from Marc de Gunzburg to David de Gunzburg, 1876–1904).

ed. khr. 405 (letters from Mathilde de Gunzburg to David de Gunzburg, 1883–84, in French).

ed. khr. 406 (letters from Mathilde de Gunzburg to David de Gunzburg, 1885, in French).

ed. khr. 407 (letters from Mathilde de Gunzburg to David de Gunzburg, 1888, in French).

ed. khr. 408 (letters from Mathilde de Gunzburg to David de Gunzburg, 1895, in French).

ed. khr. 409 (letters from Mathilde de Gunzburg to David de Gunzburg, 1896, in French).

ed. khr. 410 (letters from Mathilde de Gunzburg to David de Gunzburg, 1897–98, in French).

ed. khr. 411 (letters from Mathilde de Gunzburg to David de Gunzburg, 1899, in French).

ed. khr. 412 (letters from Mathilde de Gunzburg to David de Gunzburg, 1900, in French).

ed. khr. 414 (letters from Mathilde de Gunzburg to David de Gunzburg, 1904, in French).

ed. khr. 415 (letters from Mathilde de Gunzburg to David de Gunzburg, 1906, in French).

ed. khr. 416 (letters from Mathilde de Gunzburg to David de Gunzburg, 1907, in French).

ed. khr. 417 (letters from Mathilde de Gunzburg to David de Gunzburg, 1908, in French).

ed. khr. 418 (letters from Mathilde de Gunzburg to David de Gunzburg, 1910, in French).

ed. khr. 421 (letters from Osip de Gunzburg to David de Gunzburg, 1896–1908, in Russian).

ed. khr. 422 (letters from Pierre de Gunzbourg to David de Gunzburg, 1877 and 1881).

ed. khr. 423 (letters from Robert de Gunzburg to David de Gunzburg, 1907, in French).

ed. khr. 424 (letter from Salomon de Gunzburg to David de Gunzburg, 1898–99, in French).

ed. khr. 428 (letter from Gabriel de Gunzburg to David de Gunzburg, 1908).

ed. khr. 539 (letter from Simon Dubnov to David de Gunzburg, 1889–1908, in Russian).

ed. khr. 547 (letter from Markus Dynin to David de Gunzburg, 1902).

ed. khr. 796 (letters from David Maggid to David de Gunzburg, 1895–1909, in Hebrew).

ed. khr. 842 (letters from M. Meyer to David de Gunzburg, 1902–05, in French).

ed. khr. 1010 (letters from V. Rozen to David de Gunzburg, 1890–97, in Russian).

ed. khr. 1012 (letters from Elka Rosenberg to David de Gunzburg, 1881, in Yiddish).

ed. khr. 1095–96 (letters from Vladimir Stasov to David de Gunzburg, in Russian).

ed. khr. 1085 (letters from Vladimir Solovyov to David de Gunzburg, in Russian).

ed. khr. 1126 (letter from Ivan Tolstoy to David de Gunzburg, 1906, in French).

ed. khr. 1200 (letters from Semen Frug to David de Gunzburg, 1886–1901, in Russian).

ed. khr. 1251 (letters from Marc Chagall to David de Gunzburg, 1908, in Russian).

ed. khr. 1439 (letters from Harry Hirsch to David de Gunzburg – sale of manuscripts, 1899-1902, in German).

ed. khr. 1482 (letters from Isidor Loeb, 1886–1889, in French).

ed. khr. 1597 (Jewish community of Zvenigorodka, monument to Horace de Gunzburg, 1910, in Russian).

ed. khr. 1648 (Horace de Gunzburg, report for the minister of Education, 1892, in Russian).

ed. khr. 1649 (Horace de Gunzburg, terrain and construction of a house on the Admiralty Embankment, 1881–84, in Russian).

ed. khr. 1650 (Horace de Gunzburg, "Rossia", insurance company, 1891, in Russian).

ed. khr. 1653 (Horace de Gunzburg, property inventory, 1909, in Russian and French).

ed. khr. 1654 ("Sur le sionisme", 1901, in French).

ed. khr. 1659 (letter from Horace de Gunzburg to Alexander Dynin, in French).

ed. khr. 1668 (letter from Horace de Gunzburg to Marcos Sukhostaver).

ed. khr. 1681 (letters from Marc Antokolsky to Horace de Gunzburg, 1892–96).

ed. khr. 1707 (letters from David de Gunzburg to Horace de Gunzburg, 1871–74, in French).

ed. khr. 1708 (letters from David de Gunzburg to Horace de Gunzburg, 1874–80, in Russian).

ed. khr. 1709 (letters from David de Gunzburg to Horace de Gunzburg, 1886–97, in French).

ed. khr. 1710 (letters from David de Gunzburg to Horace de Gunzburg, undated).

ed. khr. 1712 (letters from Marc de Gunzburg to Horace de Gunzburg, 1869–74, in French).

ed. khr. 1742 (letter from Ivan Kramskoy to Horace de Gunzburg, undated, in Russian).

ed. khr. 1825 (letters from David and Horace de Gunzburg and to them, 1882).

ed. khr. 1860 (Mathilde de Gunzburg, accounts, 1895–1913).

ed. khr. 1873 (letters from Alexandre de Gunzburg to Mathilde de Gunzburg, 1887–89, in French).

ed. khr.1886 (letters from Ury de Gunzburg to Mathilde de Gunzburg, 1887–1902, in French).

ed. khr. 1900 (Banque russe de commerce and d'industrie, financial notice, 1917).

ed. khr. 1901 (letters from Louise Sassoon to Mathilde de Gunzburg, 1887–95, in French).

ed. khr. 1919 (letters from Alexandre de Gunzburg to Alfred-Mimi de Gunzburg, in French and in Russian).

ed. khr. 1920 (letter from Horace de Gunzburg to Alfred-Mimi de Gunzburg).

ed. khr. 1922 (letters from David de Gunzburg to Anna de Gunzburg, 1873–74, in Russian).

ed. khr. 1923 (letters from David de Gunzburg to Anna de Gunzburg, 1876, in Russian).

ed. khr. 1924 (letters from David de Gunzburg to Anna de Gunzburg, 1876, in Russian and French).

ed. khr. 1931 (letters from Alexandre de Gunzburg to Eugène-Gino de Gunzburg, 1905–15, in Russian).

ed. khr. 1935 (letters from Mathilde de Gunzburg to Eugène-Gino de Gunzburg, 1913–15, in French).

ed. khr. 1937 (letters from Osip de Gunzburg to Eugène-Gino de Gunzburg, 1914, in Russian).

ed. khr. 1948 (letter from Nadia Mendel to Eugène-Gino de Gunzburg, in French).

ed. khr. 1950 (administration of the trading agency of the heirs of Joseph Evzel de Gunzburg, 1866–97, in Russian, German, and French).

ed. khr. 1953 (letters and telegrams from Horace de Gunzburg to Marc de Gunzburg, 1872–78, in French).

ed. khr. 1956 (letter from Anna de Gunzburg to Marc de Gunzburg, in French).

ed. khr. 1963 (letters from Eugène-Gino de Gunzburg to Osip de Gunzburg, 1917, in Russian).

ed. khr. 1965 (letters from Vladimir Mendel to Osip de Gunzburg and Eugène-Gino de Gunzburg, in French)

ed. khr. 2001 (catalogue of the Gunzburgs' library, late 1890s).

ed. khr. 2262 and 2263 (letters from Joseph Evzel de Gunzburg to Gabriel Yakov Gunzburg, 1832, in Hebrew).

ed. khr. 2263 (letter from Joseph Evzel de Gunzburg to the representatives of Jewish communities in Russia, May–June 1873, in Hebrew).

ed.khr. 2069 (factory of Sergeyevo-Ufaley in the Urals, photographs).

Rossiyskiy Gosudarstvenny Istoricheskiy Arkhiv / Russian State Historical Archive (RGIA) (St Petersburg)

• f. 1009 op. 2.

ed. khr. 1 (personal material of David de Gunzburg).

ed. khr. 50 (letters in French).

Sources

ed. khr. 61 (letter from P. Lvov to Joseph Evzel de Gunzburg).
ed. kh. 63 (letters from Osip de Gunzburg to Vladimir Mendel).

Lietuvos Valstyb s Istorijos Archyvas / Lithuanian State Historical Archive (LVIA) (Vilnius)

f. 11, op. 1, d. 1038 (census of Karaites and Jews in the kingdom of Lithuania, 1765).
f. 11, op. 1, d. 1043 (account book of the tax office of the Vilna *kahal*).
f. 458, op. 1, d. 65–66 (1715), d. 98 (1728), d. 101 (1729) (inventory of houses in Vilna).
f. 620, op. 1, d. 41 (Jewish *kahal* of Vilna, 1764-1921, book registering revenues).

Rothschild Archives (London)

XI/118/8B Sundry correspondence 9B 1870.

YIVO (Institute for Jewish Research, New York)

Yivo Vilna Ethnographic Committee Records, Record Group 1-2, Folder 76, Minutes of the Jewish Ethnographic Expedition in the name of Baron Horace Guinzburg [*sic*], Folder 77 (Reports, budget, financial reports and plans of the Ansky Expedition).
Dubnov, Simon, Papers, Record Group 87, Folder 979 (Decisions of Lithuanian assessors in the trial of the Vilna *kahal* of 1767), Folder 986 (Minutes of the 3 meetings of the Pedagogic Council of the Baron Guenzburg [*sic*], Higher Courses in Oriental Studies).
Tcherikower Archive, Baron Gintsburg Collection, Record Group 89, Folders 754–759-764.
Mapu Letters, Record Group 223-2, Folder 39-1. Abraham Mapu to his brother, Kovno, 2/07/1859.
Lucien Wolf and David Mowshowitch (Papers), Record Group 348, Folder 105 (Mendel Beilis process), Folder 107 (EKOPO), Folder 115 (Baron de Gunzburg's letter on Jewish affairs in Russia).
Sutzkever Kaczerginski Collection, Part. II Record Group 223-2, Folder 39-1 (Letters from Abraham Mapu); Folder 184-10 (Pinkas of the Jewish Community of Vilna, 1770–94).

Royal Library of Denmark

The David Simonsen Archives (Digital Editions).
David Simonsen to Alexandre de Gunzburg, 17 April 1917, Copenhagen.
Alexandre de Gunzburg to David Simonsen, 26 April/9 May 1917, Petrograd.

III. Printed Sources

Encyclopaedias

Evreyskaya Entsiklopediya (16 vol.), St Petersburg, 1906–13.
Bolshaya Sovetskaya Entsiklopediya.

The Gunzburgs

Newspapers

Le Gaulois, 24 January 1875, 20 October 1875, 15 January 1878; 17 September 1879 (Octave Mirbeau, "Tout-Paris"); 23 February 1880; 19 May 1883, 11 November 1883; 20 April 1884; 6 January 1884; 24 August 1887 (republication in full of the article by Henri de Pène published in *Le Figaro* in May 1858); 26 June 1891; 19 March 1896; 30 May 1898; 4 June 1898; 4 July 1898; 4 March 1924.
Gil Blas, 21 December 1883; 19 September 1905.
Journal des débats, 16 September 1905.
L'Humanité, 16 September 1905.
Le Monde illustré, 8 May 1858.
L'Univers israélite, 2 June 1916.
Rassvet, 1860 no. 8, no. 19, no. 27.
Vechernoye Vremya, 5 April 1912.
Voskhod, 1903, no. 5.

Works

Almanach de St Petersburg cour, monde and ville, 1913/14, Mellier et Cie, St Petersburg and H. A. Ludwig Degener, Leipzig.
Ambert, Joachim (General), *Gaulois et Germains: récits militaires,* Paris, Bloud et Barral, 1883–85.
Annuaire de la finance, banque, bourse et professions qui s'y rattachent, Paris, 1893.
Annuaire-Almanach du commerce, de l'industrie, Paris, Didot-Bottin (published annually).
Asch, Sholem, *Petersburg,* translated by Siegfried Schmitz, Vienna, P. Zsolnay, 1929 (see also *Three Cities – A Trilogy: Petersburg, Moscow, Warsaw,* translated by Edwin and Willa Muir, New York, G. P. Putnam, 1943).
Bergeret and Herman, Grégoire, *Messages personnels,* Bordeaux, Edition Bière, 1945.
Catalogue de la section russe à l'Exposition universelle de Paris, Paris, Imprimerie nationale, Typographie Lahure, 1878.
Delécluze, E.-J., *Les Beaux-Arts en 1855,* Paris, Ed. Charpentier, 1856.
Delton, Louis-Jean, *Les Equipages à Paris,* 1876.
Delton, Louis-Jean, *Le Tour du Bois,* 1882.
Dubnov, Simon, *Le Livre de ma vie. Souvenirs et réflexions, matériaux pour l'histoire de mon temps,* translated from the Russian by Brigitte Bernheimer, Paris, Ed. du Cerf, 2001.
Dubois, Dom Marie-Gérard, *Le Bonheur en Dieu, Souvenirs and réflexions du père abbé de La Trappe,* Paris, Robert Laffont, 1995.
Drumont, Edouard, *La France juiv: essai d'histoire contemporaine,* Paris, Flammarion, 1886, vol. 1.
Errera, Léo, *Les Juifs russes, extermination ou émancipation,* with a preface by Th. Mommsen, Brussels, Librairie européenne C. Muquardt, 1893.
Faucigny-Lucinge, Jean-Louis de, *Un gentilhomme cosmopolite. Mémoires,* Paris, Perrin, 1990.
Finn, Shmuel Jozef, *Kiryah Neemana,* 1860.
Fould, Paul, *De jure dotum. "Du contrat de mariage",* Faculté de droit de Paris, 1859.
Gautier, Théophile, *Les Beaux-Arts en Europe en 1855,* Paris, 1855.
Gautier, Théophile, *Paris et les Parisiens,* Paris, "Boîte à documents", 1996.
Gessen, Yuly, *Istoriya evreyev v Rossii,* Petrograd, 1914.
Gessen, Yuly, *Istoriya evreyskogo naroda v Rossii,* Petrograd, 1916–1925, 2 vols (new edition Moscow–Jerusalem, Evreiskiy Universitet v Moskve/Gesharim, 1993).

Sources

Gunzburg, Saul M., *Otechestvennaya voyna 1812 goda i russkie evrei*, St Petersburg,1912.

Gunzburg, Alfred, *K voprosu o zolotopromyshlennykh zakhvatakh: Poryadok priobreteniya gornoy sobstvennosti dlya tseley zolotogo promysla i pravo vladeniya eyu v zakonodatel'stve inostrannykh gosudarstv*, St Petersburg, 1902, 2 vols.

Gunzburg, David de, *Monsieur Bickell et la métrique hébraïque*, Paris, Maisonneuve et Cie, 1881.

Gunzburg, David de, "Le premier livre imprimé en hébreu", *Recueil des travaux rédigés en mémoire du jubilé scientifique de M. Daniel Chwolson professeur émérite à l'université de St Pétersbourg (1846–1896)*, Berlin, S. Calvary, 1899, pp. 57–121.

Gunzburg, David de, "Stasov i evreyskoye iskusstvo", *Sbornik vospominaniy o V. V. Stasove*, Prometey, 1907.

Gunzburg, David de, and Stasov, Vladimir, *L'Ornement hébreu* (or *L'Ornement hébraïque*), Berlin, Calvary, 1908.

Haskell, Arnold L., and Nouvel, Walter, *Diaghileff, His Artistic and Private Life*, New York, Simon and Schuster, 1935.

Halperin, Israël, *Pinkas vaad arba aratsot*, Jerusalem, Bialik Institute, 1945.

Henry, B. A., *Les Massacres de Kichinev*, Paris, Publications du Siècle, 1903.

Isidor, Lazare, *Oraisons funèbres prononcées sur la tombe de Joseph de Gunzburg, le 15 janvier 1878*, Paris, D. Jouaust, 1878.

Journal de Nijinsky, Paris, Gallimard, 1991.

Leskov, Nikolay, *Evrei v Rossii: neskol'ko zamechaniy po evreyskomu voprosu*, St Petersburg, 1884.

Liphart (Lipgart), Ernst von, *Khudozhniki Salona vremen Tret'ey Respubliki. Mes Mémoires* (http://www.nasledie-rus.ru/podshivka/8314.php).

Mandelstam, Osip, "Le chaos judaïque," *Le Bruit du temps*, translated by Edith Scherrer, Geneva, L'Age d'Homme, 1990, pp. 33–34 (first edition 1925).

Mussorgsky, Modest, *Correspondence*, translated, presented and annotated by Francis Bayer and Nicolas Zourabichvili, preface by André Lischke, Paris, Fayard, 2001.

Otchet administratsii po delam torgovogo doma I. E. Gintsburg 1893, St Petersburg, 1894.

Otchet administratsii po delam torgovogo doma I. E. Gintsburg 1894, St Petersburg, 1895.

Prusiewicz, Aleksander, *Kamieniec, Podolski: Szkic historyczny*, Warsaw, 1915.

Revue des arts décoratifs, "La curiosité et les ventes. Courrier de l'hôtel Drouot", Paris, 1883.

Skal'kovsky, Konstantin, *Vospominaniya molodosti, 1843–1869*, St Petersburg, 1906.

Sliozberg, Heinrich B., *Dela minuvshikh dney: Zapiski russkovo evreya*, Paris, 1933.

Schlumberger, Gustave, *Mes souvenirs, 1844–1928*, Paris, Plon, 1934.

Stasov, Vladimir, *Mark Matveyevich Antokol'skiy. Ego zhizni, tvoreniya, pis'ma i stat'i*, St Petersburg, 1905.

Tcherikower, Elias M., *Istoriya obshchestva dlya rasprostraneniya prosveshcheniya mezhdu evreyami v Rossii. 1863–1913 gg.*, St Petersburg, 1913.

Tolstoy, Ivan, *Dnevnik 1906–1916*, St Petersburg, Izd. Evropeyskovo universiteta v Sankt-Peterburge, 1997.

Vogüé, Eugène Melchior de, "L'exposition de Moscou et l'art russe", *La Revue des Deux Mondes*, Paris, November 1882.

Film

Office français d'information cinématographique, *Ils s'instruisent pour vaincre*, 1944, 8 mn 10s.

Bibliography

Genealogies, essays and articles on the Gunzburg family

Berlin, Moisei, *Ein Wort über die Familie Günzburg*, St Petersburg, 1858.

De Vries-de Gunzburg, Irène, "Some letters from Ivan Turgenev to Baron Horace de Gunzburg, 1877-1883", *Oxford Slavonic Papers*, vol. IX, 1960, pp. 72–103.

Eisenstadt, Israel Tobiah, *Da'at Kedoshim, Materialen zur Geschichte der Familien welche ihre Abstammung von dem im Jahre 1659 im Litthauischen Städtchen Rushani in Folge einer Blutbeschuldigung als Märtyrer gefallenen herleiten*, St Petersburg, 1897–98.

Ederman, Olga, Petrovsky-Shtern, Yohanan, and Tol'ts, Vladimir, "Zaochnyi dialog Goratsiya Gintsburga i imperatora Alexandra Tret'ego", Radio Svoboda, 28 July 2007.

Ginsburg. Sigmar, "Die Geschichte unseres Zweiges der Familie Ginsburg", Tel Aviv, 1946 (unpublished manuscript, Center For Jewish History, New York).

Ginzburg, Saul, "Die familye Baron von Gintzburg. Dray doyres shtadlones, tsoke un haskale", New York, *Historisches verk*, 1937, vol. 2, pp. 117–159. ("The Family of Baron Gunzburg: Three Generations of Mediation, Charity and Enlightenment", translated from the Yiddish by Carrie Friedman-Cohen, unpublished.)

Gol'denberg, Samuel, and Lisitina, Alina, "'Eto moya dusha, vse soderzhanie moey zhizni: o kollektsiy Davida Gintsburga'", *Lekhaim*, no. 263, March 2014.

Halban, Alexander, *A Window on Russia, A Window on The Jews. The Gintsburgs and the Problem of Jewish Integration in Late Imperial Russia*, BA history thesis, St John's College, University of Oxford, 2007.

Klier, John D., *Krug Gintsburgov i politika shtadlanuta v imperatorskoy Rossii*, Vestnik Evreiskovo Universiteta v Moskve, 1995, 3, 10.

Lawford, Valentine, *Horst: His Work and His World*, New York, Alfred A. Knopf, 1984.

Lokshin, Aleksandr (ed.), *Evrei v Rossii, Neizvestnoe ob izvestnom*, Moscow, Dostoinstvo, 2012.

Löwenstein, Leopold, "Günzburg und die schwäbischen Gemeinden", in *Blättern für jüdische Geschichte und Literatur*, Mosbach und Mainz, 1899–1902.

Maggid, David, *Sefer Toledoth Mischpechoth Ginzburg*, St Petersburg, 1894 [history of the Gunzburg family, partial translation into French, unpublished manuscript (archive of Katia Guth-Dreyfus)].

Sergeyeva, Irina (ed.), "Perepiska barona Gintsburga i S. An-skogo po povodu etnograficheskikh ekspeditsiy v cherte evreyskoye osedlosti", *Ab Imperio*, no. 4 (2003).

Sliozberg, Heinrich, *Baron Horace O. de Gunzbourg, sa vie son oeuvre, publié à l'occasion du centenaire de sa naissance*, translated from the Russian by Vladimir Bariatinsky, Paris, 1933.

Stanislawski, Michael, "An Unperformed Contract: The Sale of Baron Gunzburg's Library to the Jewish Theological Seminary of America", in *Transition and Change in Modern Jewish History: Essays Presented in Honor of Shmuel Ettinger*, Jerusalem, Merkaz Shazar, 1987, and in Dicker, Herman, *Of Learning and Libraries: the Seminary Library at One Hundred*, Jewish Theological Seminary of America, 1988.

Stern, Mosche, "Memorbuch der Gemeinde Pfersee", *Memory books written during the 16th to 19th Century in Swabian Jewish Communities*, Jerusalem, 1941, pp. 5–25.

Vovshin, Ilya, *The Gintsburg Family and the Formation of the Jewish Plutocracy in the Russian Empire*, thesis written under the direction of Adam Teller, University of Haifa, September 2016 (in Hebrew).

Weinberg, Gretchen, and Hermann, G., "Entretiens avec le baron Nicolas de Gunzburg", translated by Dominique Villain, in Dreyer, Carl Th., *Réflexions sur mon métier*, Paris, Cahiers du Cinéma, Editions de l'Etoile, 1983.

Works and articles cited

Agranovsky, Genrikh, and Guzenberg, Irina, *Vil'nius: po sledam Litovskogo Ierusalima Pamyatnye mesta evreyskoy istorii i kul'tury*, Vilnius, 2011.

Ambruleviciuté, Aelita, *Vilniaus pirkliai zhydai 1801–1861 metais (sa.rashas)/Vilnius Jewish Merchants 1801–1861 (list)*, Zhydu. kultūros ir informatsiyos tsentras, Vilnius, 2012.

Ananich, Boris Vasilyevich, *Bankirskie doma, v Rossii 1860–1914 gg. Ocherki istorii chastnogo predprinimatel'stva*, Leningrad, 1991.

Archives juives, *Dossier: La grande bourgeoisie juive parisienne (1850–1940)*, Paris, no. 42/1, 1st semester 2009.

Barbier, Frédéric, *Finance et Politique. La dynastie des Fould, XVIIIe–XXe siècle*, Paris, Armand Colin, 1991.

Baumgarten, Jean, "Vilna, entre ultraorthodoxie et modernité (XVIIIe–XIXe siècle)", *Revue germanique internationale*, 2010, no. 10, pp. 61–78.

Beyzer, Mikhail, *The Jews of St Petersburg: Excursions through a noble past*, translated from the Russian by Michael Sherbourne, Philadelphia, Martin Gilbert, 1989 (in Russian *Evrei v Peterburge*, Jerusalem, 1990).

Bibliography

Bergeron, Louis, *Les Rothschild et les autres... La gloire des banquiers*, Paris, Perrin, 1991.

Bonin, Hubert, "Albert Kahn, financier et banquier" (www.hubertbonin.com).

Bonin, Hubert, *Histoire de la Société générale*, vol. I: *1864–1890, Naissance d'une banque*, Paris, Droz, 2006.

Boulet, François, *Leçon d'histoire de France, Saint-Germain-en-Laye: des antiquités nationales à une ville internationale*, DISLAB, 2006.

Bracha, Rachel, Drori-Avraham, Adi, Yantian, Geoffrey (eds.), *Educating for Life. New Chapters in the History of ORT*, London, World ORT, 2010.

Bréon, Emmanuel, Edouard, Claude-Marie, and Dubufe, Guillaume, *Portraits d'un siècle d'élégance parisienne*, Paris, Délégation à l'action artistique de la ville de Paris, 1988.

Budnitsky, Oleg, *Russian Jews between the Reds and the Whites, 1917–1920*, translated from the Russian by Timothy J. Portice, Philadelphia, University of Pennsylvania Press, 2011.

Casalis, André, *Cadets de la France libre. L'école militaire*, Paris, Lavauzelle, 1994.

Chernow, Ron, *The Warburgs, The Twentieth-Century Odyssey of a Remarkable Jewish Family*, New York, Vintage, 1994.

Dubnov, Simon, *History of the Jews in Russia and Poland*, translated from the Russian by I. Frielaender, Philadelphia, Jewish Publication Society of America, 1916–1920.

Dufresne, Claude, *Morny 1811–1865*, Paris, Perrin, 1983 (and 2002).

Engel, Yu., "Evreyskaya narodnaya pesnya. Etnograficheskaya poyezdka letom 1912", *Paralleli: Russko-evreyskiy istoriko-literaturnyi almanakh*, no. 4–5, Moscow, 2004.

Ertel, Rachel (ed.), *Royaumes juifs. Trésors de la littérature yiddish*, Paris, Robert Laffont, "Bouquins", 2008.

Ferguson, Niall, *The World's Banker. The history of the house of Rothschild*, London, Weidenfeld and Nicolson, 2000.

Ferro, Marc, "La politique des nationalités du gouvernement provisoire. Février–octobre 1917", *Cahiers du monde russe et soviétique*, 1961, vol. 2, pp. 131–165.

Foot, M. R. D., *SOE in France: an account of the work of the British Special Operations Executive in France, 1940–1944*, London, HMSO, 1966.

Frankel, Jonathan, *Prophecy and Politics: Socialism, nationalism and the Russian Jews, 1862–1917*, Cambridge, 1981.

Freeze, Chaeran Y., and Harris, Jay M. (eds.), *Everyday Jewish Life in Imperial Russia, Select Documents, 1792–1914*, Waltham, Massachusetts, Brandeis University Press, 2013.

Frischer, Dominique, *Le Moïse des Amériques. Vies and oeuvres du baron de Hirsch*, Paris, Grasset, 2002.

Gavlin, Mikhail, *Rol' vinnykh otkupov v formirovanii krupnykh kapitalov v Rossii XIX v.*, Ekonomicheskaya istoriya, 2002.

Ginzburg, E., *Otechestvennaya voyna 1812 goda*, St Petersburg, 1912.

Girault, René, *Emprunts russes et investissements français en Russie, 1887–1914*, CHEFF, 1999.

Gonzalez-Quijano, Lola, "Le demi-monde: prostitution et réseaux sociaux

dans le Paris du XIXe siècle", article on line. https://f.hypotheses.org/
wpcontent/blogs.dir/1429/files/2013/09/réseaux_demimonde_LGQ-
1.pdf.

Glants, Musya, *Where is my home? The art and life of the Russian Jewish sculptor
Mark Antokolsky, 1842–1902*, Rowman and Littlefield, Lanham, Boulder,
New York, Toronto, Plymouth, UK, 2010.

Glants, Musya, "Dual Existence of the Eternal Wanderer. M. Antokolsky's
Letter to Baron Horatsii Osipovich Gintsburg", *Arkhiv evreyskoy istorii* 1,
2004, pp. 195–239.

Grange, Cyril, *Une élite parisienne. Les familles de la grande bourgeoisie juive
(1870–1939)*, Paris, CNRS Editions, 2016.

Greenberg, Louis, *The Jews in Russia: The struggle for emancipation*, New
Haven, CT, 1944–1951, 2 vols.

Guth-Dreyfus, Katia, "Eine Süddeutsche Textilie aus dem frühen 17.
Jahrhundert", in Kiessling, Rolf, and Ullmanna, Sabine (eds.),
Landjudentum im Deutschen Südwesten, Akademie Verlag, pp. 220–225.

Hagen, Manfred, "Lenskiy rasstrel 1912 goda i rossiyskaya obshchevennost",
Otechestvennaya istoriya: zhurnal, 2002, no. 2.

Hastings, Max, *Das Reich. The march of the 2nd SS Panzer Division through
France, June 1944*, London, Papermac, 1993.

Houbre, Gabrielle, *Le Livre des courtisanes: archives secrètes de la police des
moeurs (1861–1876)*, Paris, Tallandier, 2006.

Ivanov, Alexander, *Dokumenty po istorii i kul'ture evreyev v arkhivakh Sankt-
Peterburga. Putevoditel'. Vedomstvennye arkhivy*, chast' I, Izdatel'skiy dom
"Mir", St Petersburg, 2015.

Ivanov, Alexander, *Experiments of a "Young Man for Photographic Works".
Solomon Yudovin and Russian Pictorialism of the 1910s*, Petersburg Judaica,
2005.

Judge, Edward H., *Easter in Kishinev, Anatomy of a Pogrom*, New York and
London, New York University Press, 1992.

Kel'ner, Viktor, *Iz Nikolayevskoy epokhi. Rossiya v memuarakh. Evrei v Rossii.
XIX vek*, Moscow, 2000.

Kel'ner, Viktor, *Missioner istorii. Zhizn' i Trudy Semena Markovicha Dubnova*,
Mir, Moscow, 2008.

Klier, John Doyle, *Imperial Russia's Jewish Question 1855–1881*, Cambridge
University Press, 1995.

Klier, John Doyle, *Russians, Jews and the Pogroms of 1881–1882*, Cambridge
University Press, 2011.

Kopel'man, Zoya, "Gordon. Poet evreyskoy Gaskali", Otkrytyi universitet
Izraila, http://www-r.openu.ac.il.

Laffitte, Michel, "L'UGIF, collaboration ou résistance?", *Revue d'histoire de la
Shoah*, Paris, 2006/2 (no. 185), pp. 45–64.

Laffitte, Michel, and Wieviorka, Annette, *A l'intérieur du camp de Drancy*,
Paris, Perrin, 2012.

Lawford, Valentine, *Horst: His Work and His World*, New York, Alfred A.
Knopf, 1984.

Lokshin, Aleksandr (ed.), *Evrei v Rossii, Neizvestnoye ob izvestnom*, Moscow,
Dostoinstvo, 2012.

Lottman, Herbert R., *La Dynastie Rothschild*, Paris, Seuil, 1994.

Mansel, Philip, *Paris, capitale de l'Europe, 1814–1852*, Paris, Perrin, 2003.

Mark Matveyevich Antokol'skii (album by unnamed author), Moscow, 1959.

Martin-Fugier, Anne, *La Vie élégante ou la Formation du Tout-Paris (1815–1848)*, Paris, Fayard, 1990.

Melancon, Michael, *The Lena Goldfields Massacre and the Crisis of the Late Tsarist State*, College Station TX, Texas A. & M. University Press, 2006.

Mindlin, A. B., "Politika S. Yu. Vitte po 'Evreyskomu voprosu'", *Voprosy istorii*, 2004, no. 4.

Minczeles, Henri, Plasseraud, Yves, and Pourchier, Suzanne, *Les Litvaks. L'Héritage universel d'un monde juif disparu*, Paris, La Découverte, 2008.

Mollier, Jean-Yves, *Le Scandale de Panama*, Paris, Fayard, 1991.

Murland, Jerry, *Aristocrats go to War: Uncovering the Zillebeke Cemetery*, Barnsley (UK), Pen and Sword, 2010.

Nathans, Benjamin, *Beyond the Pale: The Jewish Encounter in Imperial Russia*, Berkeley, 2002.

Ouaknin, Marc-Alain, *Invitation au Talmud*, Paris, Flammarion, "Champs essais", 2008.

Patterson, David, *Abraham Mapu, the Creator of the Modern Hebrew Novel*, London, East and West Library, 1964.

Podlinsky, Arkady, *Evrei v Vitebske*, Vitebskaya oblastnaya Tipografiya, 2004.

Poliakov, Léon, *Histoire de l'antisémitisme, vol. I: L'Age de la foi; vol. II: L'Age de la science*, Paris, Calmann-Lévy, "Points Histoire", 1981 (first edition 1955).

Proyart, Jacqueline, "Le haut procureur du saint-synode Constantin Pobedonoscev et le 'coup d'état' du 29 avril 1881," *Cahiers du monde russe et soviétique*, 1962, vol. 3, pp. 408–458.

Razumov, Oleg N., "Iz istorii vzaimootnosheniy rossiyskogo i inostrannogo aktsionernogo kapitala v sibirskoy zolotopromyshlenosti v nachale XX veka", in *Predprinimateli i predprinimatel'stvo v Sibiri v XVIII nachale XX veka*, Barnaul, LGU, 1995, pp. 139–153.

Rebel', Alina, *Istoriya evreyev v Rossii*, Moscow, Eksmo, 2013.

Rieber, Alfred J., *Merchants and Entrepreneurs in Imperial Russia*, Chapel Hill NC, University of North Carolina Press, 1982.

Rosen, Abraham (ed.), *Kaminits-Podolsk and its Environs*, Randolph NJ, Avotaynu Foundation, Bergenfield, 1999.

Rosenstein, Neil, *The Unbroken Chain. Biographical sketches and genealogy of illustrious Jewish families from the 15th to the 20th Century*, 2 vols., 1990.

Safran, Gabriella, and Zipperstein, Steven J. (eds.), *The Worlds of S. An-sky: A Russian Jewish intellectual at the turn of the century*, Stanford CA, Stanford University Press, 2006.

Saigne, Guy, *Léon Bonnat le portraitiste de la IIIe République, catalogue raisonné des portraits*, Marc & Martin, 2017.

Schama, Simon, *Two Rothschilds and the Land of Israel*, London, Collins, 1978.

Schedrin, Vassili, *Jewish Souls, Bureaucratic Minds: Jewish bureaucracy and policymaking in late imperial Russia, 1850–1917*, Detroit, Wayne State University Press, 2016.

Shapiro, Leon, *The History of ORT, a Jewish Movement for Social Change*, London, World ORT, 2010.

Solzhenitsyn, Alexander, *Deux siècles ensemble*, translated from the Russian by A. Kichilov, G. Filippenko and N. Struve, Paris, Fayard, 2002 (see also *Dvesti Let Vmeste*, Moscow, Vagrius, 2008, 2 vols).

Stoskopf, Nicolas, *Banquiers and financiers parisiens*, Paris, Picard/Cénomane, 2002.

Strauss, Michel, *Pictures, Passions and Eye. A life at Sotheby's*, London, Halban Publishers, 2011.

Vital, David, *A People Apart: A Political History of the Jews in Europe, 1789–1939*, Oxford University Press, 1999.

Waal, Edmund de, *The Hare with Amber Eyes: A Hidden Inheritance*, London, Chatto and Windus 2011, New York, Farrar, Straus and Giroux, 2012.

Genealogical tables

These genealogical tables do not show all the ancestors and descendants of Joseph Evzel de Gunzburg. Their goal is to facilitate the reading of this book. Some dates are also missing.

I

Eliezer (1477–1544 Günzburg); Simon Günzburg (1506–1585 Burgau); Asher Aaron Ulmo-Günzburg (1535–c. 1605 Burgau); Jacob Ulmo-Günzburg (?–1616 Burgau); Simon (Schatles) Günzburg (?–1633 Frankfurt); Isaac Eitsik Günzburg (c. 1600–c. 1650 Pfersee-Wirmiser); Aaron "representative of Vilna" (active c. 1660–1670 Vilna); Asher Günzburg (? Vilna); Isaac Eitsik Günzburg (? Vilna); Kalonimos Kalman (c. 1690–c. 1758 Pinsk); Asher Kalmanowicz Klaczko (c. 1710–1791 Vilna); Leib Günzburg (?–1808 Vilna); Naftali Herz Günzburg (?–1797 Vilna)

Gabriel Yakov Günzburg (1793 Vilna–1853 Simferopol) m. Léa Rashkes (?–1848 Kamenets-Podolsk)

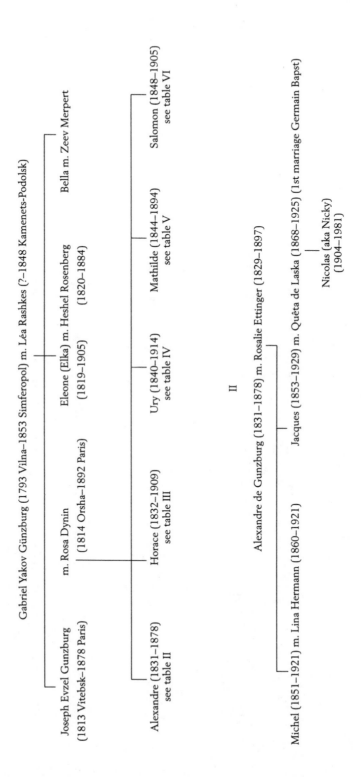

Joseph Evzel Gunzburg
(1813 Vitebsk–1878 Paris)

m. Rosa Dynin
(1814 Orsha–1892 Paris)

Eleone (Elka) m. Heshel Rosenberg
(1819–1905)   (1820–1884)

Bella m. Zeev Merpert

Horace (1832–1909)
see table III

Alexandre (1831–1878)
see table II

Ury (1840–1914)
see table IV

Mathilde (1844–1894)
see table V

Salomon (1848–1905)
see table VI

II

Alexandre de Gunzburg (1831–1878) m. Rosalie Ettinger (1829–1897)

Michel (1851–1921) m. Lina Hermann (1860–1921)

Jacques (1853–1929) m. Quêta de Laska (1868–1925) (1st marriage Germain Bapst)

Nicolas (aka Nicky)
(1904–1981)

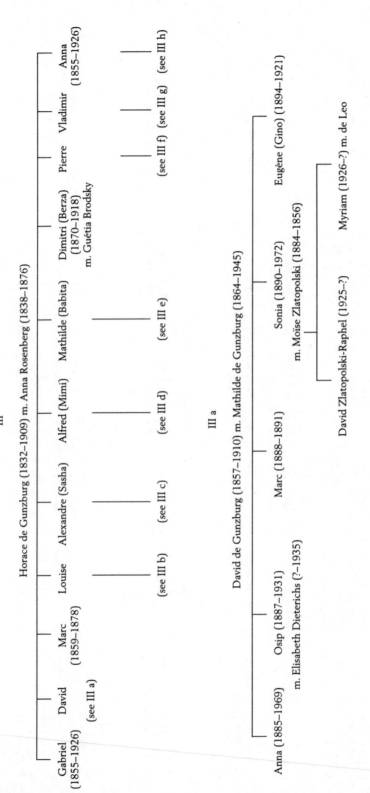

III

Horace de Gunzburg (1832–1909) m. Anna Rosenberg (1838–1876)

Gabriel (1855–1926)   David   Marc (1859–1878)   Louise   Alexandre (Sasha)   Alfred (Mimi)   Mathilde (Babita)   Dimitri (Berza) (1870–1918) m. Guétia Brodsky   Pierre   Vladimir   Anna (1855–1926)

(see III a)   (see III b)   (see III c)   (see III d)   (see III e)   (see III f)   (see III g)   (see III h)

III a

David de Gunzburg (1857–1910) m. Mathilde de Gunzburg (1864–1945)

Anna (1885–1969)   Osip (1887–1931) m. Elisabeth Dieterichs (?–1935)   Marc (1888–1891)   Sonia (1890–1972) m. Moïse Zlatopolski (1884–1856)   Eugène (Gino) (1894–1921)

David Zlatopolski-Raphel (1925–?)   Myriam (1926–?) m. de Leo

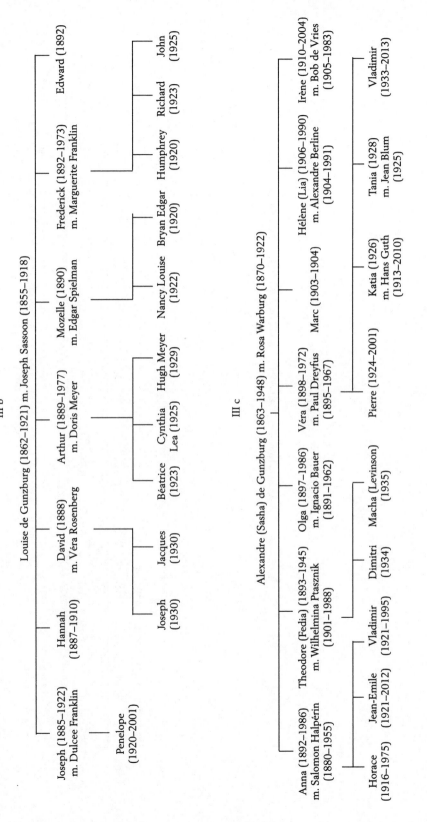

III b

Louise de Gunzburg (1862–1921) m. Joseph Sassoon (1855–1918)

Joseph (1885–1922)
m. Dulcee Franklin

Hannah
(1887–1910)

David (1888)
m. Véra Rosenberg

Arthur (1889–1977)
m. Doris Meyer

Mozelle (1890)
m. Edgar Spielman

Frederick (1892–1973)
m. Marguerite Franklin

Edward (1892)

Penelope
(1920–2001)

Joseph
(1930)

Jacques
(1930)

Béatrice
(1923)

Cynthia
Lea (1925)

Hugh Meyer
(1929)

Nancy Louise
(1922)

Bryan Edgar
(1920)

Humphrey
(1920)

Richard
(1923)

John
(1925)

III c

Alexandre (Sasha) de Gunzburg (1863–1948) m. Rosa Warburg (1870–1922)

Anna (1892–1986)
m. Salomon Halpérin
(1880–1955)

Theodore (Fedia) (1893–1945)
m. Wilhelmina Ptasznik
(1901–1988)

Olga (1897–1986)
m. Ignacio Bauer
(1891–1962)

Véra (1898–1972)
m. Paul Dreyfus
(1895–1967)

Marc (1903–1904)

Hélène (Lia) (1906–1990)
m. Alexandre Berline
(1904–1991)

Irène (1910–2004)
m. Bob de Vries
(1905–1983)

Horace
(1916–1975)

Jean-Emile
(1921–2012)

Vladimir
(1921–1995)

Dimitri
(1934)

Macha (Levinson)
(1935)

Pierre (1924–2001)

Katia (1926)
m. Hans Guth
(1913–2010)

Tania (1928)
m. Jean Blum
(1925)

Vladimir
(1933–2013)

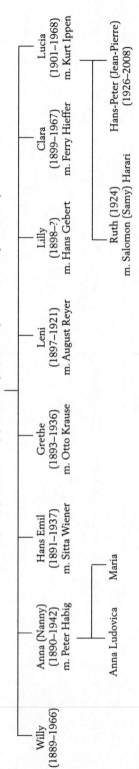

III d

Alfred (Mimi) de Gunzburg (1865–1936) m. Sonia Ashkenasy (1875–1929)

Anne (Mamzelle) (1901–?) m. 1. Jean David-Weill. 2. Charles-Emile Weil

Sonia (1931–2010) m. Michel Périer

III e

Mathilde (Babita) de Gunzburg (1866–1917) m. Ludwig von Gutmann (1860–1900)

Willy
(1889–1966)

Anna (Nanny)
(1890–1942)
m. Peter Habig

Hans Emil
(1891–1937)
m. Sitta Wiener

Grethe
(1893–1936)
m. Otto Krause

Leni
(1897–1921)
m. August Reyer

Lilly
(1898–?)
m. Hans Gebert

Clara
(1899–1967)
m. Ferry Hieffer

Lucia
(1901–1968)
m. Kurt Ippen

Anna Ludovica

Maria

Ruth (1924)
m. Salomon (Samy) Harari

Hans-Peter (Jean-Pierre)
(1926–2008)

III f

Pierre de Gunzbourg (1872–1948) m. Yvonne Deutsch de la Meurthe (1882–1962)

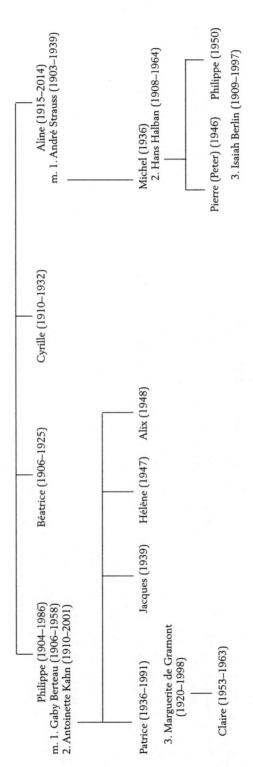

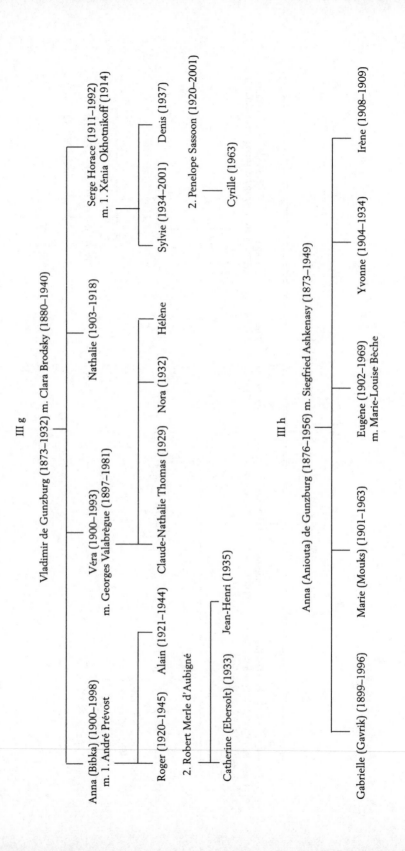

III g

Vladimir de Gunzburg (1873–1932) m. Clara Brodsky (1880–1940)

Anna (Bibka) (1900–1998)
m. 1. André Prévost

Véra (1900–1993)
m. Georges Valabrègue (1897–1981)

Nathalie (1903–1918)

Serge Horace (1911–1992)
m. 1. Xénia Okhotnikoff (1914)

Roger (1920–1945)   Alain (1921–1944)

2. Robert Merle d'Aubigné

Claude-Nathalie Thomas (1929)   Nora (1932)   Hélène

Sylvie (1934–2001)   Denis (1937)

2. Penelope Sassoon (1920–2001)

Catherine (Ebersolt) (1933)   Jean-Henri (1935)

Cyrille (1963)

III h

Anna (Aniouta) de Gunzburg (1876–1956) m. Siegfried Ashkenasy (1873–1949)

Gabrielle (Gavrik) (1899–1996)

Marie (Mouks) (1901–1963)

Eugène (1902–1969)
m. Marie-Louise Bèche

Yvonne (1904–1934)

Irène (1908–1909)

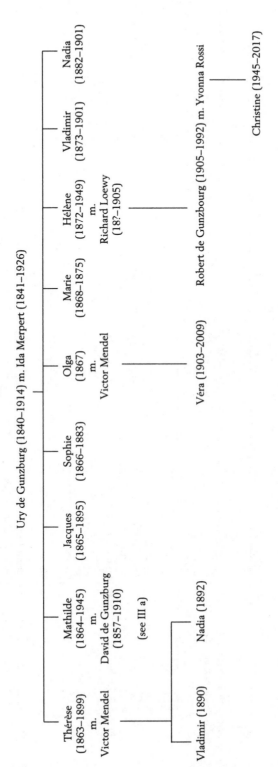

IV

Ury de Gunzburg (1840–1914) m. Ida Merpert (1841–1926)

Thérèse (1863–1899) m. Victor Mendel

Mathilde (1864–1945) m. David de Gunzburg (1857–1910) (see III a)

Jacques (1865–1895)

Sophie (1866–1883)

Olga (1867) m. Victor Mendel

Marie (1868–1875)

Hélène (1872–1949) m. Richard Loewy (18?–1905)

Vladimir (1873–1901)

Nadia (1882–1901)

Vladimir (1890)

Nadia (1892)

Véra (1903–2009)

Robert de Gunzbourg (1905–1992) m. Yvonna Rossi

Christine (1945–2017)

V

Mathilde de Gunzburg (1844–1894) m. Paul Fould (1837–1917)

Louise (1862–1945)
m. Emile Halphen (1857–1913)

Suzanne (1867–1901)
m. Raoul Gradis (1861–1943)

Marie (1870–1931)
m. Henry de Courcy

Germaine (1884–1975)
m.
Edouard de Rothschild

Alice (1887–1968)
m.
Maurice de Brémond d'Ars

Gaston (1889–1968)

Jean (1900–1975)

Marie-Louise (1894–1979)

Antoinette (1899–1939)
m.
Antoine de Gramont

Aimery (1893–1916)

Alphonse (1906–1911)

Guy (1909–2007)

Jacqueline (1911–2012)

Bethsabée (1914–1999)

Pierre (1914–2012)

Eliette (1916–2003)

Catherine (1918–2000)

Hervé (1925–?)

Arnaud (1928–1982)

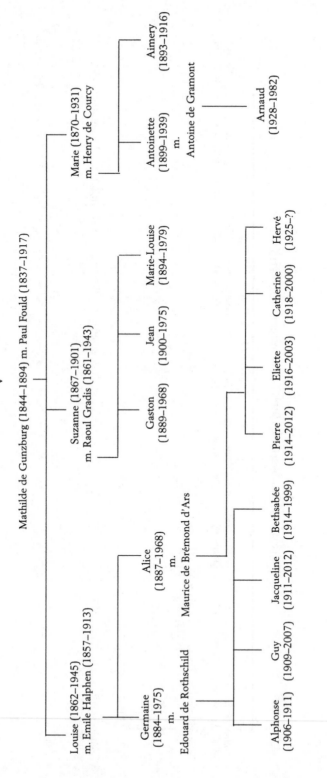

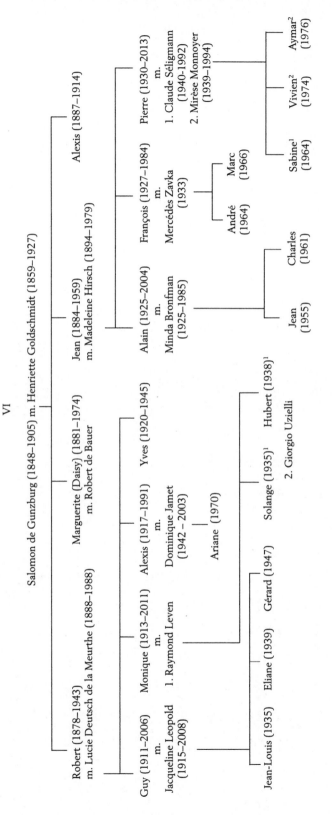

VI

Salomon de Gunzburg (1848–1905) m. Henriette Goldschmidt (1859–1927)

Robert (1878–1943)
m. Lucie Deutsch de la Meurthe (1888–1988)

Marguerite (Daisy) (1881–1974)
m. Robert de Bauer

Jean (1884–1959)
m. Madeleine Hirsch (1894–1979)

Alexis (1887–1914)

Guy (1911–2006)
m.
Jacqueline Leopold
(1915–2008)

Monique (1913–2011)
m.
1. Raymond Leven

Alexis (1917–1991)
m.
Dominique Jamet
(1942–2003)

Yves (1920–1945)

Alain (1925–2004)
m.
Minda Bronfman
(1925–1985)

François (1927–1984)
m.
Mercédès Zavka
(1933)

Pierre (1930–2013)
m.
1. Claude Séligmann
(1940–1992)
2. Mirèse Monnoyer
(1939–1994)

Jean-Louis (1935)

Eliane (1939)

Gérard (1947)

Solange (1935)[1]

Hubert (1938)[1]
2. Giorgio Uzielli

Ariane (1970)

Jean
(1955)

Charles
(1961)

André
(1964)

Marc
(1966)

Sabine[1]
(1964)

Vivien[2]
(1974)

Aymar[2]
(1976)

Chronology

1543–85	Simon Gunzburg is representative of the Jewish population of Swabia to the kingdom of Bavaria.
1670	Aaron Gunzburg settles in Vilna, capital of the Grand Duchy of Lithuania, where he is a delegate to the Council of the Four Provinces.
c. 1750	Asher Gunzburg marries Yuta Klaczko in Vilna.
c. 1760	In Vilna the Gunzburgs oppose the influence of Rabbi Shlomo ben Avigdor.
1772	First partition of Poland between Austria, Prussia, and Russia.
1783	Annexation of Crimea by Russia.
1791	Creation of the Pale of Settlement which defines the western territories of the Russian Empire in which the Jewish population is allowed to live.
1793 & 1795	Second and third partitions of Poland. Vilna is in one of the areas annexed by Russia.
1811	Jews are permitted to hold concessions for trade in alcoholic beverages in the Pale of Settlement.
1812	Gabriel Yakov Gunzburg marries Léa Rashkes in Vitebsk. 12 June: Napoleon's Grand Army enters Russia and occupies Vitebsk 7 October: Napoleon leaves Moscow; the retreat begins.
1813	4 January: birth of Joseph Evzel Gunzburg in Vitebsk.
1825	1 December: death of Alexander I. 14 December: Decembrist uprising in St Petersburg.
1827	Jewish communities are obliged to provide "cantonists" (child conscripts) for the Russian army.
1830	State Jewish schools open. Joseph Evzel Gunzburg marries Rosa Dynin in Orsha.
1831	Birth of Alexander Gunzburg in Orsha.
1832	Birth of Horace Gunzburg in Zvenigorodka.
1833	Joseph Evzel Gunzburg becomes a merchant of the First Guild.
1835	Regulation of the Jews.
1839	Joseph Evzel is an alcoholic beverages concessionaire for Khotin.
1840	Birth of Ury Gunzburg in Khotin.
1844	Birth of Mathilde Gunzburg in Kamenets-Podolsk.

467

1846	Moses Montefiore's first visit to St Petersburg.
1848	Birth of Salomon Gunzburg in Kamenets-Podolsk.
1849	Gabriel Yakov Gunzburg becomes a merchant of the First Guild and an honorary citizen.
	Joseph Evzel becomes an honorary citizen.
1853–56	Crimean War. Joseph Evzel Gunzburg is alcoholic beverages concessionaire in the combat zone.
1853	Death of Gabriel Yakov Gunzburg in Simferopol.
1856	July: Joseph Evzel Gunzburg petitions the tsar to authorise certain categories of Jews to live outside the Pale of Settlement (petition signed by 18 merchants).
1857	Joseph Evzel Gunzburg and his family move to Paris; Senior Sachs enters the Gunzburgs' service as a librarian.
1858	May: The Gunzburgs give a ball at the Hôtel des Trois-Empereurs in Paris.
1859	15 March: Tsar Alexander II gives Jewish merchants of the First Guild the right to live outside the Pale of Settlement. The Gunzburgs take up residence in St Petersburg.
	15 November: Foundation of the J. E. Gunzburg Bank in St Petersburg.
1860	In France the Alliance Israélite Universelle is founded.
1861	Tsar Alexander II abolishes serfdom.
	Joseph Evzel Gunzburg buys 55,000 hectares of land in Bessarabia (region of Bender).
1862	Joseph Evzel Gunzburg submits to the Russian administration a memorandum on the development of agricultural work among Jews and requests the right for Jewish artisans to live outside the Pale of Settlement.
1863	Establishment of Jewish community authorities in St Petersburg, presided over by Joseph Evzel Gunzburg
	Foundation of the Society for the Promotion of Culture among the Jews of Russia.
1864	Judiciary reform, educational reform, the creation of *zemstva*.
	The Jewish sculptor Mark Antokolsky enters the St Petersburg Academy of Fine Arts.
1865	Jewish artisans obtain the right to live outside the Pale of Settlement.
1867–69	Construction of the Gunzburg town house at 7 Rue de Tilsitt in Paris.
1867	October: opening of the J. E. Gunzburg Bank's Paris branch.
1868	The Gunzburgs help found the Kiev Private Commercial Bank and the Discount and Lending Bank of St Petersburg.
1869	The tsar authorises the building of a synagogue in St Petersburg. Start of a lengthy construction project.
1870	During the Franco-Prussian War the Gunzburg town house at 7 Rue de Tilsitt serves as a military hospital.
1871	The Gunzburgs help found the "Russian Bank of Foreign Commerce".
	Joseph Evzel Gunzburg purchases the headquarters of the Imperial Guard in Saint-Germain-en-Laye.
	The Gunzburgs take part in the foundation of the Siberian Bank of Commerce.

	Joseph Evzel Gunzburg buys a perpetual burial plot in the Montparnasse cemetery.
1873	Joseph Evzel Gunzburg buys the gold-mining company of the Lena. 15 May: letter from Joseph Evzel Gunzburg to the heads of Jewish communities in Russia promoting Jews' participation in military service.
1874	The prince of Hesse grants the title of baron to Joseph Evzel and his descendants. Joseph Evzel receives the title of "commercial counsellor". The law establishing compulsory military service in Russia does not exempt Jews.
1875	David de Gunzburg is a student at the Faculty of Oriental Languages in St Petersburg. 9 December: death in Paris of Anna de Gunzburg, Horace's wife.
1877	The J. E. Gunzburg Bank participates in a loan granted by the syndicate of Paris bankers; marriage of Salomon de Gunzburg to Henriette Goldschmidt in Paris. Mark Antokolsky sculpts a posthumous bust of Anna deGunzburg. 10 December: Foundation of the Society of Russian Artists in Paris.
1878	12 January: death of Joseph Evzel Gunzburg in Paris. 3 March: Russian victory over Turkey; peace of San Stefano. June–July: Berlin congress. Posthumous portrait of Anna de Gunzburg by Léon Bonnat.
1879	The Gunzburgs help found the Discount Bank of Odessa. Alexandre II authorises the Gunzburgs to use the title of baron in Russia. Ury de Gunzburg purchases the Château de Chambaudoin; he organizes a hunt there in honour of Grand Duke Nicholas Nikolayevich.
1880	Lev Levanda publishes in Russian the novel *Confession of a Businessman*, inspired by the Gunzburgs. 30 September: foundation of the "Craftsmanship Fund", the future ORT (Obshchestvo Remeslennovo i zemledelcheskovo Truda, Society for Artisanal and Agricultural Work).
1881	Horace de Gunzburg takes up residence in St Petersburg in the palace at 17 Konnogvardeysky Boulevard 1 March: assassination of Alexander II. 5 April (27 April new style): pogrom in Elisavetgrad, the first of a long series. 11 May: Alexander III receives a Jewish delegation that includes Horace de Gunzburg.
1882	May: Ignatyev's "anti-Jewish laws" Léon Bonnat's portrait of Henriette de Gunzburg.
1883–85	Pahlen Commission on the Jewish Question. Abrogation of the law of 1865 authorising Jewish artisans to live outside the Pale of Settlement.
1883	18 December: David de Gunzburg marries his cousin Mathilde de Gunzburg in Paris.
1884	Creation of the Russian Hibat Tsiyon society for the promotion of a Jewish homeland in Palestine.
c. 1884	Ivan Kramskoy paints Louise de Gunzburg's portrait.

1886	Appearance of Edouard Drumont's anti-Semitic essay *La France juive*.
1887	Sale of the Gunzburg town house at 7 Rue de Tilsitt in Paris.
1890	16 May: letter from Horace de Gunzburg to Alexander III about the rights of Jews.
1891–92	Economic crisis and famine in Russia.
1891	In London Baron Hirsch creates the Jewish Colonisation Association (JCA).
1892	As a Jew Horace loses the right to sit on the St Petersburg municipal council.
	March: bankruptcy of the J. E. Gunzburg Bank in St Petersburg and its branch in Paris.
1893	December: inauguration of the St Petersburg synagogue.
	Exhibit devoted to the works of Mark Antokolsky at the St Petersburg Academy of Fine Arts.
1894	In France Captain Alfred Dreyfus is arrested on a charge of treason.
1896	Herzl publishes *L'Etat juif*.
1897	Russia adopts the gold standard.
	First Zionist congress in Basle.
1898	Foundation of the Russian Social-Democratic Party.
	David de Gunzburg moves his library to Vasilyevsky Island, line 1, no. 4.
1902	Marriage of Pierre de Gunzbourg to Yvonne Deutsch de la Meurthe in Paris.
1904–05	Russo-Japanese War
1904	Pogrom in Kishinev.
1905	9 January: Red Sunday in St Petersburg.
	14 September: Salomon de Gunzburg commits suicide in Paris.
	18–20 October (31 October–2 November new style): pogrom in Kiev.
	17 October: imperial manifesto promising a constitution.
1906	7 April–8 July: first Duma.
1907	20 February–2 June: second Duma.
	1 November–9 June 1912: third Duma.
1908–09	David de Gunzburg provides financial support for Marc Chagall in St Petersburg.
1908	Vladimir Stasov and David de Gunzburg publish *L'Ornement hébreu*.
1909	19 February: death of Horace de Gunzburg in St Petersburg.
	Dimitri (Berza) de Gunzburg becomes Serge Diaghilev's associate.
1910	22 December: death of David de Gunzburg in St Petersburg.
1911	Creation of the Jacques de Gunzburg & Cie Bank in Paris.
1912–15	Ansky organises the Baron Horace de Gunzburg ethnographic expedition.
1912	April: repression of the strike at the Lena gold mines.
	23 April: appearance of the first issue of *Pravda*.
1913	Sasha and Rosa de Gunzburg move into 13 Millionnaya Street in St Petersburg.
	23 September–28 October: Beilis trial in Kiev. A Jew accused of a ritual murder, Beilis is acquitted by the jury.
1914	10 June: letter from Sasha de Gunzburg to Ivan Goremykin, Chairman of the Council, about military service.
	19 and 24 July (1 and 6 August new style): Germany, then Austria-Hungary declare war on Russia. St Petersburg becomes Petrograd.

	October: Foundation of the Jewish Committee for Aid Reconstruction (EKOPO) in Petrograd.
1917	23–27 February (8–12 March new style): revolution in Petrograd.
	2 March: formation of the provisional government. Theodore (Fedia) de Gunzburg a member of the Russian diplomatic mission sent to the United States.
	3 March: abdication of Nicholas II. Abolition of the Pale of Settlement.
	18 June: beginning of the Kerensky offensive on the front.
	25 October (7 November new style): Armed insurrection of Bolsheviks in Petrograd.
	25–27 October: Second Soviet pan-Russian conference. Decree regarding peace, land and formation of a Soviet government.
1918	Dimitri (Berza) de Gunzburg, an officer in the Savage Division, disappears in the Caucasus.
	1 August: Sasha de Gunzburg is arrested in Petrograd, freed a few weeks later.
	December: Sasha de Gunzburg and his family leave Russia.
1921	Gino de Gunzburg, an officer in the White Army, dies at Gallipoli from typhus.
1922	Creation of Nansen passports for refugees.
1925	France recognises the USSR.
1931	Nicky de Gunzburg gives a "bal champêtre" in the Bois de Boulogne.
1934	Aline de Gunzbourg wins the French women's golf championship. Nicky de Gunzburg acts in *Vampyr, or the Strange Adventure of Allan Gray* by Carl Theodor Dreyer.
1939	May: the Ippens, descendants of Horace de Gunzburg, leave Austria to take up residence in Nice.
1941	2 June: in France the second Jewish statute comes into force, notably prohibiting Jews from exercising the profession of bankers.
1942	"Operation Furniture" ("Möbel Aktion") by Reichsleiter Rosenberg's Einsatzstab (ERR) installs its offices in the home of Pierre and Yvonne de Gunzbourg at 54 Avenue d'Iéna.
	Many members of the Gunzburg family flee Vichy France to live in the United States or in Switzerland.
	Philippe de Gunzbourg organises the Resistance network in the southern Dordogne and Lot-et-Garonne for the British SOE (Special Operations Executive).
	26 August: Lucia Ippen is arrested in Nice and interned in the camp at Drancy.
	Nanny Habig is arrested in Nice, interned at Drancy and deported to Auschwitz where she is murdered.
1943	19 January: in New York Alain de Gunzburg signs up to fight for Free France.
	7 February: Monique de Gunzburg enters Switzerland with her two children.
1944	June: Alain de Gunzburg, having completed his training in the class of 18 June at the Ecole des Cadets de la France libre, is assigned to 2nd Armoured Division as a liaison officer.
1945	30 January: Yves de Gunzburg, fighting for Free France, dies in combat at Elsenheim in Alsace.

Acknowledgements

This book could not have been written without the support of very many people, to whom I wish to express my deepest gratitude.

My thanks go first to the descendants of Joseph Evzel de Gunzburg: to Jean de Gunzburg, without whom this book would not exist; to Alexis de Bryas, who was the first to awaken my interest in this subject; to Peter and Martine Halban, who have been marvellous interlocutors at every stage, and above all for their help in the publication of the English edition; to Katia Guth-Dreyfus for her memory and unfailing support; and to Tania Blum, Macha Levinson (de Gunzburg), Dimitri de Gunzburg, Hélène de Gunzbourg, Jacques de Gunzbourg, Elisabeth Lorin, Jean-Louis de Gunzburg, Gérard de Gunzburg, Eliane and Johan Beckman, Hubert Leven, Guy Harari, Claude-Nathalie Thomas, Nora Valabrègue, Michel Strauss, Andrew Strauss, Cyrille de Gunzburg, Ruxandra Bordeianu, Vivien de Gunzburg, Charles de Gunzburg, Chloé Szulzinger, Alexander Halban, Nadia Guth-Biasani, Alexis Blum, Béatrice Halpérin, and Daniel Halpérin. They have all shared memories and documents with generosity, trust and enthusiasm. I am particularly thankful to Christine de Gunzbourg, who took great joy in this book and whom we miss especially now that it is finished.

Thanks to World ORT – Vladimir Dribinskiy, Steve West, Lee Bush, Rachel Bracha – for having made it possible for my research to take place under the best possible conditions.

Thanks to those who have given me their scholarly help: Aelita Ambruleviciuté, Alexandre Ivanov, Jean-Claude Kuperminc, Guy Saigne, Melanie Aspey, Gunnar Berg, Olya Vovshin, Sophie Harendt, Jean-Jacques Wahl and Marianna Mikheeva.

For their translations, I thank Abraham L. Udovich, Olga Maslova-Walther, Carmit Shaltiel, Svetlana McMillin and Carrie Friedman-Cohen.

Thanks to Haïm Korsia, the Chief Rabbi of France, for his informed and careful reading of the text.

Thanks too to Pierre-André Maus, Alix de Beistegui, Philippe and Aude Charquet, Jean-Marc Choblet, Nicolas Kaenzig, Hugues Lavoix, René Marbot, Roger Lebon, Diane Cassigneul, Guilhem Touratier, René Aridon, Frédéric Mitterrand, Ariel de Ravenel, Kara Casanova, Olivier Patey, Sébastien de Ganay and Laurent Theis.

My gratitude to Steven Rendall for his translation into English, and to Julian Evans for his excellent editing.

And finally I thank Daniel and Noëlle Rondeau, most invaluable supporters, and Antoine de Meaux, unerring advisor.

Index

Index

Index

Index

Index